ANDERSON'S
Law School Publications

Administrative Law Anthology
Thomas O. Sargentich

Administrative Law: Cases and Materials
Daniel J. Gifford

An Admiralty Law Anthology
Robert M. Jarvis

Alternative Dispute Resolution: Strategies for Law and Business
E. Wendy Trachte-Huber and Stephen K. Huber

The American Constitutional Order: History, Cases, and Philosophy
Douglas W. Kmiec and Stephen B. Presser

American Legal Systems: A Resource and Reference Guide
Toni M. Fine

Analytic Jurisprudence Anthology
Anthony D'Amato

An Antitrust Anthology
Andrew I. Gavil

Appellate Advocacy: Principles and Practice, *Third Edition*
Ursula Bentele and Eve Cary

Arbitration: Cases and Materials
Stephen K. Huber and E. Wendy Trachte-Huber

Basic Accounting Principles for Lawyers: With Present Value and Expected Value
C. Steven Bradford and Gary A. Ames

A Capital Punishment Anthology (and Electronic Caselaw Appendix)
Victor L. Streib

Cases and Materials on Corporations
Thomas R. Hurst and William A. Gregory

Cases and Problems in California Criminal Law
Myron Moskovitz

Cases and Problems in Criminal Law, *Fourth Edition*
Myron Moskovitz

The Citation Workbook: How to Beat the Citation Blues, *Second Edition*
Maria L. Ciampi, Rivka Widerman, and Vicki Lutz

Civil Procedure Anthology
David I. Levine, Donald L. Doernberg, and Melissa L. Nelken

Civil Procedure: Cases, Materials, and Questions, *Second Edition*
Richard D. Freer and Wendy Collins Perdue

Clinical Anthology: Readings for Live-Client Clinics
Alex J. Hurder, Frank S. Bloch, Susan L. Brooks, and Susan L. Kay

Commercial Transactions Series: Problems and Materials
Louis F. Del Duca, Egon Guttman, Alphonse M. Squillante, Fred H. Miller,
Linda Rusch, and Peter Winship
Vol. 1: Secured Transactions Under the UCC
Vol. 2: Sales Under the UCC and the CISG
Vol. 3: Negotiable Instruments Under the UCC and the CIBN

Communications Law: Media, Entertainment, and Regulation
Donald E. Lively, Allen S. Hammond, Blake D. Morant, and Russell L. Weaver

A Conflict-of-Laws Anthology
Gene R. Shreve

Constitutional Conflicts
Derrick A. Bell, Jr.

A Constitutional Law Anthology, *Second Edition*
Michael J. Glennon, Donald E. Lively, Phoebe A. Haddon, Dorothy E. Roberts,
and Russell L. Weaver

Constitutional Law: Cases, History, and Dialogues, *Second Edition*
Donald E. Lively, Phoebe A. Haddon, Dorothy E. Roberts, Russell L. Weaver,
and William D. Araiza

The Constitutional Law of the European Union
James D. Dinnage and John F. Murphy

The Constitutional Law of the European Union: Documentary Supplement
James D. Dinnage and John F. Murphy

Constitutional Torts
Sheldon H. Nahmod, Michael L. Wells, and Thomas A. Eaton

A Contracts Anthology, *Second Edition*
Peter Linzer

Contract Law and Practice
Gerald E. Berendt, Michael L. Closen, Doris Estelle Long, Marie A. Monahan,
Robert J. Nye, and John H. Scheid

Contracts: Contemporary Cases, Comments, and Problems
Michael L. Closen, Richard M. Perlmutter, and Jeffrey D. Wittenberg

A Copyright Anthology: The Technology Frontier
Richard H. Chused

Corporate Law Anthology
Franklin A. Gevurtz

Corporate and White Collar Crime: An Anthology
Leonard Orland

A Criminal Law Anthology
Arnold H. Loewy

Criminal Law: Cases and Materials
Arnold H. Loewy

A Criminal Procedure Anthology
Silas J. Wasserstrom and Christie L. Snyder

Criminal Procedure: Arrest and Investigation
Arnold H. Loewy and Arthur B. LaFrance

Federal Wealth Transfer Tax Anthology
Paul L. Caron, Grayson M.P. McCouch, Karen C. Burke

First Amendment Anthology
Donald E. Lively, Dorothy E. Roberts, and Russell L. Weaver

The History, Philosophy, and Structure of the American Constitution
Douglas W. Kmiec and Stephen B. Presser

Individual Rights and the American Constitution
Douglas W. Kmiec and Stephen B. Presser

International Environmental Law Anthology
Anthony D'Amato and Kirsten Engel

International Human Rights: Law, Policy, and Process, *Second Edition*
Frank C. Newman and David Weissbrodt

Selected International Human Rights Instruments and
  Bibliography for Research on International Human Rights Law, *Second Edition*
Frank C. Newman and David Weissbrodt

International Intellectual Property Anthology
Anthony D'Amato and Doris Estelle Long

International Law Anthology
Anthony D'Amato

International Law Coursebook
Anthony D'Amato

International Taxation: Cases, Materials, and Problems
Philip F. Postlewaite

Introduction to the Study of Law: Cases and Materials
John Makdisi

Judicial Externships: The Clinic Inside the Courthouse, *Second Edition*
Rebecca A. Cochran

A Land Use Anthology
Jon W. Bruce

Law and Economics Anthology
Kenneth G. Dau-Schmidt and Thomas S. Ulen

The Law of Disability Discrimination, *Second Edition*
Ruth Colker and Bonnie Poitras Tucker

The Law of Disability Discrimination Handbook: Statutes and Regulatory Guidance
  Second Edition
Ruth Colker and Bonnie Poitras Tucker

Lawyers and Fundamental Moral Responsibility
Daniel R. Coquillette

Mediation and Negotiation: Reaching Agreement in Law and Business
E. Wendy Trachte-Huber and Stephen K. Huber

Microeconomic Predicates to Law and Economics
Mark Seidenfeld

Natural Resources: Cases and Materials
Barlow Burke

FORTHCOMING PUBLICATIONS

Basic Themes in Law and Jurisprudence
Charles W. Collier

Cases and Materials on the Law Governing Lawyers
James E. Moliterno

First Amendment Law: Cases, Comparative Perspectives, and Dialogues
Donald E. Lively, Phoebe A. Haddon, John C. Knechtle, and Dorothy E. Roberts

Introduction to the Study of Law: Cases and Materials, *Second Edition*
John Makdisi

The Question Presented: Model Appellate Briefs
Maria L. Ciampi and William H. Manz

Secured Transactions Under the Uniform Commercial Code and International Commerce
Louis F. Del Duca, Egon Guttman, William H. Henning, Fred H. Miller, and Peter Winship

Principles of Evidence, *Fourth Edition*
Irving Younger, Michael Goldsmith, and David A. Sonenshein

ENVIRONMENTAL DECISIONMAKING

THIRD EDITION

ENVIRONMENTAL DECISIONMAKING

THIRD EDITION

ROBERT L. FISCHMAN

Professor of Law
Indiana University School of Law—Bloomington

MARK S. SQUILLACE

Distinguished Professor of Law
University of Wyoming College of Law

Based on ENVIRONMENTAL DECISIONMAKING: NEPA AND THE ENDANGERED SPECIES ACT, *Second Edition*, by Jackson B. Battle, Robert Fischman, and Mark S. Squillace

ANDERSON PUBLISHING CO.
CINCINNATI, OHIO

ENVIRONMENTAL LAW SERIES

ENVIRONMENTAL DECISIONMAKING

WATER POLLUTION

AIR POLLUTION

HAZARDOUS WASTE

ENVIRONMENTAL DECISIONMAKING, THIRD EDITION
ROBERT L. FISCHMAN AND MARK S. SQUILLACE

© 2000 by Anderson Publishing Co.

Anderson Publishing Co.
2035 Reading Road / Cincinnati, Ohio 45202
800-582-7295 / e-mail andpubco@aol.com / Fax 513-562-5430
World Wide Web http://www.andersonpublishing.com

ISBN: 0-87084-308-7

TABLE OF CONTENTS

PREFACE

Publication of this casebook completes the third generation of the Anderson Environmental Law series. These four volumes provide comprehensive, up-to-date coverage of the field in a flexible, economical format. This volume contains background material for an introductory environmental law class and more detailed material for a study of the National Environmental Policy Act (NEPA) and the Endangered Species Act (ESA). This volume may be combined with one (or more) of the other volumes for a three (or more) credit introductory environmental law class. Or, it may be used alone to provide reading for a two credit class or seminar on environmental decisionmaking.

This new edition incorporates the material included in the 1997 supplement and updates the information as of June, 1999.

It builds on the integration of ESA materials into the study of assessment-based decisionmaking, begun in the second edition. In the four-and-a-half years since we published the second edition, the ESA has become a more mature field of law that allows for instructive comparative analysis with NEPA. Both NEPA and ESA claims continue to be combined in litigation even as agencies search for new ways to meld procedures under the two laws. Since both statutes are so important for natural resources management, chapters four through seven of this volume, containing the core NEPA and ESA material, may be especially appropriate for a course in natural resources law. This new edition also incorporates material on the National Historic Preservation Act.

This volume retains the series of problems scattered throughout the chapters. The problems both explore new issues raised in the chapter at hand and synthesize previous material for practical application. Each problem can be used as the framework for an entire class discussion. Alternatively, students may use a problem on their own to test their skills and review material.

We continue to strive for a balance between providing a reasonable amount of reading for students and retaining the unedited flavor of the primary material. In general, in this volume, we have tended to reprint longer excerpts from judicial opinions than in other casebooks in order to better focus student attention on the multifarious considerations and rich texture of environmental decisionmaking.

Close scrutiny of the text of the applicable statutes and regulations, of course, is indispensable to the study of environmental law, and we have included with this book, as a separately bound supplement, the texts of NEPA, the ESA, and many of their most important implementing regulations. The STATUTES AND REGULATIONS APPENDIX now contains more interpretive information, such as the widely used "Forty-Questions" CEQ guidance on NEPA. The statutes and regulations are also available on-line at *http://www.law.indiana.edu/envdec/envdec.html*. The web version of the STATUTES AND REGULATIONS APPENDIX contains hyper-text links to help students work through problems. Questions about or problems with accessing these materials should be directed to webmaster@polecat.law.indiana.edu.

The Council on Environmental Quality now maintains an informative web site dealing with NEPA at *http://ceq.eh.doe.gov/nepa/nepanet.htm*. Official information on the ESA can be found at *http://www.fws.gov/~r9endspp/endspp.html*.

Our thanks go to Sean Caldwell at Anderson Publishing for his patient nurturing of the environmental law series. An Indiana University School of Law Summer Faculty Fellowship and a University of Wyoming College of Law George Hopper Research Fund grant supported work for this edition of ENVIRONMENTAL DECISIONMAKING.

Robert Fischman, Bloomington, Indiana   June, 1999
Mark Squillace, Laramie, Wyoming

ACKNOWLEDGMENTS

We gratefully acknowledge the following authors and publishers who have graciously allowed us to reproduce portions of their work.

Terry L. Anderson & Donald R. Leal, *Free Market Versus Political Environmentalism*, 15 HARV. J.L. & PUB. POL'Y 297 (1992).

Wendell Berry, *Solving for Pattern*, in THE GIFT OF THE GOOD LAND: FURTHER ESSAYS CULTURAL AND AGRICULTURAL. Copyright © 1981 by Wendell Berry. Reprinted by permission of North Point Press, a division of Farrar, Straus and Giroux, LLC.

Barry Commoner, *Failure of the Environmental Effort*, 18 Envtl. L. Rep. (Envtl. L. Inst.) 10195 (1988).

Timothy Dyk, *The Supreme Court's Role in Shaping Administrative Law*, 17 ADMIN. L. NEWS 1 (1991).

Garrett Hardin, *The Tragedy of the Commons*, 162 SCIENCE 1243 (1968).

Aldo Leopold, *The Land Ethic, in* A SAND COUNTY ALMANAC (1949, 1977).

Joseph Mendelson III and Andrew Kimbrell, *The Legislative Environmental Impact Statement: An Analysis of* Public Citizen v. Office of the U.S. Trade Representative, 23 Envtl. L. Rep. (Envtl. L. Inst.) 10653 (1993).

Robert B. Reich, *The Miasma of Regulation, in* TALES OF A NEW AMERICA (1987).

DANIEL J. ROHLF, THE ENDANGERED SPECIES ACT: A GUIDE TO ITS PROTECTIONS AND IMPLEMENTATION (1989).

Joseph L. Sax, *The Search for Environmental Rights*, 6 J. LAND USE & ENVTL. L. 93 (1990).

Karin P. Sheldon, *Habitat Conservation Planning: Addressing the Achilles Heel of the Endangered Species Act*, 6 N.Y.U. ENVTL. L.J. 279 (1998).

Lynn White, Jr., *The Future of Compassion*, 30 ECUMENICAL REVIEW 99 (1978).

TABLE OF CASES

Principal cases and their page references are in italic type.

1 PERSPECTIVES

In the complex world of environmental law, it is easy to lose perspective in the narrow technicalities of statutes and regulations. This chapter samples some of the important philosophical and political views that continue to shape environmental law. Students should consider not only the proper goals of environmental law but also how closely existing law achieves such aims.

The following excerpt from Aldo Leopold's posthumously published collection of essays is probably the most influential statement of ethics in the American environmental movement. In addition to his pioneering work at the U.S. Forest Service to preserve wild tracts of land and at the University of Wisconsin to establish the field of wildlife management, Leopold also helped found The Wilderness Society in 1935.

THE LAND ETHIC
ALDO LEOPOLD
A SAND COUNTY ALMANAC (1949, 1977)[*]

When God-like Odysseus returned from the wars in Troy, he hanged all on one rope a dozen slave-girls of his household whom he suspected of misbehavior during his absence.

This hanging involved no question of propriety. The girls were property. The disposal of property was then, as now, a matter of expediency, not of right and wrong.

Concepts of right and wrong were not lacking from Odysseus' Greece: witness the fidelity of his wife through the long years before at last his black-prowed galleys clove the wine-dark seas for home. The ethical structure of that day covered wives, but had not yet been extended to human chattels. During the three thousand years which have since elapsed, ethical criteria have been extended to many fields of conduct, with corresponding shrinkages in those judged by expediency only.

The Ethical Sequence

This extension of ethics, so far studied only by philosophers, is actually a process in ecological evolution. Its sequences may be described in ecological as well as in philosophical terms. An ethic, ecologically, is a limitation on freedom of action in the struggle for existence. An ethic, philosophically, is a differentiation of social from anti-social conduct. These are two definitions of one thing. The thing has its origin in the tendency of interdependent individuals or groups to evolve modes of co-operation. The ecologist calls these symbioses. Politics and economics are advanced symbioses in which the original free-for-all competition has been replaced, in part, by co-operative mechanisms with an ethical content.

The complexity of co-operative mechanisms has increased with population density, and with the efficiency of tools. It was simpler, for example, to define the anti-social uses of sticks and stones in the days of the mastodons than of bullets and billboards in the age of motors.

The first ethics dealt with the relation between individuals; the Mosaic Decalogue is an example. Later accretions dealt with the relation between the individual and society. The golden rule tries to integrate the individual to society; democracy to integrate social organization to the individual.

There is as yet no ethic dealing with man's relation to land and to the animals and plants which grow upon it. Land, like Odysseus' slave-girls, is still property. The land-relation is still strictly economic, entailing privileges but not obligations.

The extension of ethics to this third element in human environment is, if I read the evidence correctly, an evolutionary possibility and an ecological necessity. It is the third step in a sequence. The first two have already been taken. Individual thinkers since the days of Ezekiel and Isaiah have asserted that the despoliation of land is not only inexpedient but wrong. Society, however, has not yet affirmed their belief. I regard the present conservation movement as the embryo of such an affirmation.

An ethic may be regarded as a mode of guidance for meeting ecological situations so new or intricate, or involving such deferred reactions, that the path of social expediency is not discernible to the average individual. Animal instincts are modes of guidance for the individual in meeting such situations. Ethics are possibly a kind of community instinct in-the-making.

The Community Concept

All ethics so far evolved rest upon a single premise; that the individual is a member of a community of interdependent parts. His instincts prompt him to compete for his place in the community, but his ethics prompt him also to co-operate (perhaps in order that there may be a place to compete for).

The land ethic simply enlarges the boundaries of the community to include soils, waters, plants, and animals, or collectively: the land.

This sounds simple: do we not already sing our love for and obligation to the land of the free and the home of the brave? Yes, but just what and whom do we love? Certainly not the soil, which we are sending helter-skelter downriver. Certainly not the waters, which we assume have no function except to turn turbines, float barges, and carry off sewage. Certainly not the plants, of which we exterminate whole communities without batting an eye. Certainly not the animals, of which we have already extirpated many of the largest and most beautiful species. A land ethic of course cannot prevent the alteration, management, and use of the "resources," but it does affirm their right to continued existence, and, at least in spots, their continued existence in a natural state.

In short, a land ethic changes the role of *Homo sapiens* from conqueror of the land-community to plain member and citizen of it. It implies respect for his fellow-members, and also respect for the community as such.

In human history, we have learned (I hope) that the conqueror role is eventually self-defeating. Why? Because it is implicit in such a role that the conqueror knows, *ex cathedra*, just what makes the community clock tick, and just what and who is valuable, and what and who is worthless, in community life. It always turns out that he knows neither, and this is why his conquests eventually defeat themselves.

In the biotic community, a parallel situation exists. Abraham knew exactly what the land was for: it was to drip milk and honey into Abraham's mouth. At the present moment, the assurance with which we regard this assumption is inverse to the degree of our education.

* * *

To sum up: a system of conservation based solely on economic self-interest is hopelessly lopsided. It tends to ignore, and thus eventually to eliminate, many elements in the land community that lack commercial value, but that are (so far as we know) essential to its healthy functioning. It assumes, falsely, I think, that the economic parts of the biotic clock will function without the uneconomic parts. It tends to relegate to government many functions eventually too large, too complex, or too widely dispersed to be performed by government.

An ethical obligation on the part of the private owner is the only visible remedy for these situations.

The Land Pyramid

An ethic to supplement and guide the economic relation to land presupposes the existence of some mental image of land as a biotic mechanism. We can be ethical only in relation to something we can see, feel, understand, love, or otherwise have faith in.

The image commonly employed in conservation education is "the balance of nature." For reasons too lengthy to detail here, this figure of speech fails to describe accurately what little we know about the land mechanism. A much truer image is the one employed in ecology: the biotic pyramid. I shall first sketch the pyramid as a symbol of land, and later develop some of its implications in terms of land-use.

Plants absorb energy from the sun. This energy flows through a circuit called the biota, which may be represented by a pyramid consisting of layers. The bottom layer is the soil. A plant layer rests on the soil, an insect layer on the plants, a bird and rodent layer on the insects, and so on up through various animal groups to the apex layer, which consists of the larger carnivores.

The species of a layer are alike not in where they came from, or in what they look like, but rather in what they eat. Each successive layer depends on those below it for food and often for other services, and each in turn furnishes food and services to those above. Proceeding upward, each successive layer decreases in numerical abundance. Thus, for every carnivore there are hundreds of his prey, thousands of their prey, millions of insects, uncountable plants. The pyramidal form of the system reflects this numerical progression from apex to base. Man shares an intermediate layer with the bears, raccoons, and squirrels which eat both meat and vegetables.

* * *

Land, then, is not merely soil; it is a fountain of energy flowing through a circuit of soils, plants, and animals. Food chains are the living channels which conduct energy upward; death and decay return it to the soil. The circuit is not closed; some energy is dissipated in decay, some is added by absorption from the air, some is stored in soils, peats, and long-lived forests; but it is a sustained circuit, like a slowly augmented revolving fund of life. There is always a net loss by downhill wash, but this is normally small and offset by the decay of rocks. It is deposited in the ocean and, in the course of geological time, raised to form new lands and new pyramids.

* * *

The process of altering the pyramid for human occupation releases stored energy, and this often gives rise, during the pioneering period, to a deceptive exuberance of plant and animal life, both wild and tame. These releases of biotic capital tend to becloud or postpone the penalties of violence.

* * *

The Outlook

It is inconceivable to me that an ethical relation to land can exist without love, respect, and admiration for land, and a high regard for its value. By value, I of course mean something far broader than mere economic value; I mean value in the philosophical sense.

Perhaps the most serious obstacle impeding the evolution of a land ethic is the fact that our educational and economic system is headed away from, rather than toward, an intense consciousness of land. Your true modern is separated from the land by many middlemen, and by innumerable physical gadgets. He has no vital relation to it; to him it is the space between cities on which crops grow. Turn him loose for a day on the land, and if the spot does not happen to be a golf links or a "scenic" area, he is bored stiff. If crops could be raised by hydroponics instead of farming, it would suit him very well. Synthetic substitutes for wood, leather, wool, and other natural land products suit him better than the originals. In short, land is something he has "outgrown."

Almost equally serious as an obstacle to a land ethic is the attitude of the farmer for whom the land is still an adversary, or a taskmaster that keeps him in slavery. Theoretically, the mechanization of farming ought to cut the farmer's chains, but whether it really does is debatable.

* * *

The case for a land ethic would appear hopeless but for the minority which is in obvious revolt against these "modern" trends.

The "key-log" which must be moved to release the evolutionary process for an ethic is simply this: quit thinking about decent land-use as solely an economic problem. Examine each question in terms of what is ethically and esthetically right, as well as what is economically expedient. A thing is right when it tends to preserve the integrity, stability, and beauty of the biotic community. It is wrong when it tends otherwise.

* * *

The mechanism of operation is the same for any ethic: social approbation for right actions: social disapproval for wrong actions.

By and large, our present problem is one of attitudes and implements. We are remodeling the Alhambra with a steam-shovel, and we are proud of our yardage. We shall hardly relinquish the shovel, which after all has many good points, but we are in need of gentler and more objective criteria for its successful use.

* * *

NOTES

1. What is Leopold's "land ethic"? Does it reflect a realistic goal for modern societies? Can Leopold's "land ethic" be modified to achieve his basic goals, while recognizing the inevitability of some loss to the "integrity, stability and beauty of the biotic community"?

2. Professor Charles Wilkinson suggests that we need to develop an "ethic of place," a recognition that the environment and its people are equals and are both sacred. Wilkinson sees an ethic of place as a shared community value, resulting in respect for animals, vegetation, water, and air, as well as for the people of the land. *See* Charles Wilkinson, *Law and the American West: The Search for an Ethic of Place,* 59 U. COLO. L. REV. 401, 405 (1988); CHARLES WILKINSON, THE EAGLE BIRD: MAPPING A NEW WEST (1992). Does an ethic of place that accommodates extractive use of natural resources compromise the land ethic? CHARLES WILKINSON, CROSSING THE NEXT MERIDIAN 17 (1992).

3.   Does Leopold's ethic ultimately ignore the fact that the human species is a part of the biotic community? If the human species is a part of the biotic community, can all of its supposed transgressions against nature be simply attributed to the natural evolution of the human species? If so, is it even possible that human actions can be "wrong" in a biological sense? In this context, consider the views of Herbert Spencer, the renowned nineteenth century philosopher, on the evolution of the human species:

> The ultimate development of the ideal man is logically certain—as certain as any conclusion in which we place the most implicit faith; for instance that all men will die. * * * Progress, therefore, is not an accident, but a necessity. Instead of civilization being artificial, it is part of nature; all of a piece with the development of the embryo or the unfolding of a flower.

Herbert Spencer, Social Statics 79-80 (1850), *quoted in* Richard Hofstadter, Social Darwinism in American Thought 40 (Revised Ed. 1955).

4.   Roderick Nash, an influential historian of the American environmental movement, argues that:

> environmental ethics [is] a logical extrapolation of powerful liberal traditions as old as the republic. The American past contains a highly visible liberation movement with interesting similarities to contemporary environmentalism. If the abolition of slavery marked the limits of American liberalism in the mid-nineteenth century, perhaps biocentrism and environmental ethics are at the cutting edge of liberal thought in the late twentieth.

Roderick Nash, The Rights of Nature 200 (1989). How apt is the liberation analogy for a movement concerned less with the sanctity of individual parts of an ecosystem than with the healthy functioning of the whole? *See* Mark Sagoff's essay, *Can Environmentalists Be Liberals?*, in Mark Sagoff, The Economy of the Earth 146 (1988). Is hunting compatible with the land ethic?

5.   Leopold asserts that instincts prompt us to compete but that ethics prompt us to cooperate within a community. For an explanation of how cooperation may arise solely from individual self-interest, see Robert Axelrod, The Evolution of Cooperation (1984).

Lynn White Jr. was a historian whose controversial views on the environment were first articulated in a 1967 essay entitled *The Historical Roots of Our Ecological Crisis,* 155 Science 1203 (1967). Although White approaches his subject from a Christian perspective, he also suggests the basic dichotomy between anthropocentrism and biocentrism which marks the secular debate over environmental ethics.

THE FUTURE OF COMPASSION
Lynn White, Jr.
30 ECUMENICAL REVIEW 99 (1978)[*]

* * *

Compassion is showing reverence actively to another human being. Preaching to an ethnocentric Israel, Jesus included Samaritans and, by implication, gentiles, within the scope of compassion. As the Church expanded among Greeks, Romans and barbarians, the entire human race became potentially objects of compassion. * * * St. Francis went further; he looked upon all the creatures, both organic and inorganic as brothers of men, joining as we do in the perpetual praise of God. This novel attitude, however, was not understood by even some of his closest followers, and it had no later influence in the Church.

Scripture warrants any of three human attitudes towards nature external to man.

The one that has been overwhelmingly dominant in western Christian thinking is the assumption of man's absolute rule over the rest of nature. This is based on Genesis 1:26-28, confirmed by God's words to Noah's family in Genesis 9:2-3. It is assumed that all things are created for mankind's use or edification and for no other purpose.

The second possible Scriptural view is that man is a trustee responsible to God for the decent care of his fellow creatures. This is based on the second of the two stories of creation, in Genesis 2:15, where Adam is placed as a gardener in Eden "to dress it and to keep it".

The third possible attitude was that adopted by St Francis: that man is a comrade of the other creatures in God's praise. It is based on several parts of the Psalms, for example 96:11-13 * * * . Its supreme expression, however, is found in the so-called "Song of the Three Children of Israel in the Fiery Furnace", found in Daniel 3:57-90. Here the entire creation—angels; sun, moon and stars; rain, dew, wind and fires; frost, ice and snow; nights and days; lightnings and clouds; mountains and hills; green things, seas and rivers; sea creatures, birds, beasts; the children of men; Israel, the priests of God, the souls of the righteous, men of humble heart, and, lastly, the three in the furnace—all are enjoined to praise and magnify God forever. * * *

* * *

Fifteen years ago, almost no theologian knew what the word *ecology* meant. Having discovered it, and the dire problems implied in it, religious thinkers have been precipitously abandoning the doctrine of Man's Dominion over Nature for Man's Trusteeship of Nature. This is rational, because no other visible creature seems to be capable of analysing complex situations and calculating the options as is *homo sapiens*. Yet it is precisely for this reason that this choice will only deepen disaster; it overlooks the fact of sin, which is compounded of inertia, of a nice talent for discovering moral reasons for committing evil deeds, and for self-love, both individual and for our species over other creatures. Mankind cannot be trusted to be trustee for the rest of Nature. When we must decide whether to benefit lilies or sparrows or ourselves, we will recall that while our Heavenly Father is mindful of both lilies and sparrows, he cares evens more deeply for us; so, in obedience to the divine preference, we shall opt for us.

I have myself concluded that Christian compassion must be based on an ascetic and self-restraining conviction of man's comradeship with other creatures. * * *

* * *

Some conservationists, in reaction against the old axiom of Man's Dominion, talk as though man has no rights as against the whooping crane or the whale. But man too is a creature

---

with rights that must be balanced—but not merely on an anthropocentric pivot—with those of his companion creatures. Ecology, as it is now developing, provides us with new religious understandings of our own being, of other beings, and of being.

The core of spiritual comity is courtesy, that is not impinging on the ability of our companions to satisfy their needs. A man has a right to build a house, and a right to kill living things—vegetable or animal—to eat, just as a coyote has a right to dig a den and to kill to eat. But men must not crowd coyotes, or coyotes men. When locusts breed so prolifically that they swarm by the millions, devastating not only the farmers' planted fields but also green areas essential to other kinds of being, people have a right to kill locusts, but not to try to exterminate locusts. The locusts have been discourteous and must be taught cosmic manners.

Today, partly because of the probably temporary burst of material productivity achieved by scientific engineering, but chiefly because of the related sophisticated medicine and medical technology that historically has found so much of its motivation in Christian compassion, it is we, *homo sapiens*, that are swarming and turning the green earth into desert by our ravening. The escalating shortages of food, energy and materials cannot be blamed solely on runaway population growth, but until that growth is not merely stemmed but sharply reversed, none of the related problems can be solved.

* * *

The two new, and essential, elements in Christian ethics, then, as I see it, must be man's self-denying comradeship with the other creatures, and the abandonment of prudential considerations. How can this ethics be implemented?

First, Christians must recognize the point where religious thinking in the past has done the greatest damage with the best of intentions: human reproduction. Christians must assist a drastic global rollback in population, including their own. This goes beyond birth control. We cannot evade reappraisal of abortion, especially since it is now beyond debate that the success of modern medicine in postponing the deaths of those carrying defective gene until after they reproduce is swiftly burdening mankind with an insupportable overload of genetic troubles. The once shocking question "Shall we tamper with human genetics?" is obsolete. We are already tampering with human genetics on an immense scale, but blindly, bumblingly, cruelly. How may we do it compassionately?

Second, from Christian compassion we must defend the continued existence of our fellow animal, plant, insect and marine species, as well as the integrity of landscapes, seascapes and airscapes that are periled by human activity, whether or not these in any way affect human existence. We must do this because of our belief that they are all creatures of God, and not from expediency. We must extend compassion to rattlesnakes and not just to koala bears.

This will involve a religious rethinking of the ecological concept of territoriality. Western Christians, who for so long have considered man's total dominion over nature to be axiomatic, will find this difficult. What is the rightful territory of *homo sapiens*? Must courtesy to other creatures require us to with draw from some of their rightful territories that we have overrun? If so, who pays the bill? How forcefully may we defend our own rightful territory, including our own bodies? Recently the smallpox virus was totally eradicated. Its sole territory was the human anatomy, which it devoured with dreadful results from the human point of view. Mankind has exterminated many species in the past, usually by inadvertence or over-enthusiasm in the hunt. This is the first time we have altogether eliminated a fellow creature by deliberate planning. From our standpoint the advisability of the action is beyond debate. *Variola* [the smallpox virus] could not be consulted because of a communication gap. What the God who created both *homo sapiens* and *Variola* thinks about all this, we do not yet know.

Third, from compassion we must encourage and support scientists and engineers to find and develop new ways of using replaceable materials and more careful ways of using irreplaceable materials; to discover methods of recycling, and ways of preventing pollution so that we and other creatures may flourish together.

Fourth, from compassion we must engage ourselves in a vast and rapid simplification of the forms of culture in industrialized societies to reduce waste, duplication of effort, and redundant production. We must increase emphasis on the relatively nonconsumptive activities of education, the arts, contemplation and worship. We must help less industrialized societies to avoid the imbalance between life-styles and resources that is so rapidly becoming evident in the industrialized societies, and encourage them to develop feasible new life-styles, based on their own cultural suppositions, that will provide dignity and freedom for their people.

* * *

NOTES

1.   In a 1973 essay, White suggested that human ethical obligations extend even beyond living creatures to inanimate objects:

> Do people have ethical obligations toward rocks? * * * To almost all Americans still saturated with ideas historically dominant in Christianity * * * the question makes no sense at all. If the time comes when to any considerable group of us such a question is no longer ridiculous, we may be on the verge of a change of value structures that will make possible measures to cope with the growing ecological crisis. One hopes that there is enough time left.

Lynn White, Jr., *Continuing the Debate, in* WESTERN MAN AND ENVIRONMENTAL ETHICS 63 (Ian Barbour ed., 1973). Justice Douglas grapples with the legal standing of non-human objects in his dissent in the Mineral King case, *Sierra Club v. Morton,* 405 U.S. 727 (1972), Chapter 3, *infra.*

2.   Yi-Fu Tuan observes that a wide gap exists between an expressed attitude toward the environment and actual practice. He suggests that a dominant religious ethic that regards nature with the kind of compassion and respect White advocates may not significantly improve the treatment of the environment. Yi-Fu Tuan, *Our Treatment of the Environment in Ideal and Actuality*, 58 AM. SCIENTIST 244 (1970).

3.   An early advocate of animal rights, Peter Singer, takes the seemingly more moderate view that humans have ethical obligations only toward sentient creatures.

> The capacity for suffering and enjoyment is *a prerequisite for having interests at all*, a condition that must be satisfied before we can speak of interests in a meaningful way. It would be nonsense to say that it is not in the interests of a stone to be kicked along the road by a schoolboy. A stone does not have interests because it cannot suffer. Nothing that we can do to it could possibly make a difference to its welfare. A mouse, on the other hand, does have an interest in not being kicked along the road, because it will suffer.

PETER SINGER, ANIMAL LIBERATION 9 (1975). Singer argues that all sentient creatures should receive "equal consideration," although he admits that this does not necessarily require equal treatment. Does Singer's ethic require humans to intercede on behalf of sentient creatures that are made to suffer by other sentient creatures, as for example, when a wolf attacks and kills the mouse for food? Is sentience an appropriate basis upon which to limit "equal consideration"? Should the ancient forests of the Pacific Northwest receive "equal consideration" before they are logged? Should the geothermal features of Yellowstone National Park be given "equal consideration" before humans are permitted to damage those resources?

4.   In light of his comments regarding the smallpox virus, *Variola*, how might Lynn White view the AIDS virus? According to White, is the eradication of such a virus necessarily a desirable goal for society? Why not? A pseudonymous "Miss Ann Thropy" welcomed the AIDS epidemic as "a necessary solution" to the "population problem." *Population and AIDS*, EARTH FIRST!, May 1, 1987 at 32, *quoted in* Murray Bookchin, *Where I Stand Now, in* DEFENDING THE EARTH 123 (David Levine ed., 1991). Extermination of the smallpox virus presents serious problems in the ethics of science as well. *See* Lawrence K. Altman, *Stocks of Smallpox Virus Edge Nearer to Extinction*, N.Y. TIMES, Jan. 25, 1996, at A1, A5; Charles Siebert, *Smallpox Is Dead: Long Live Smallpox*, N.Y. TIMES MAGAZINE, Aug. 21, 1994, at 32.

THE TRAGEDY OF THE COMMONS
Garrett Hardin
162 SCIENCE 1243 (1968)[*]

The tragedy of the commons develops in this way. Picture a pasture open to all. It is to be expected that each herdsman will try to keep as many cattle as possible on the commons. Such an arrangement may work reasonably satisfactorily for centuries because tribal wars, poaching, and disease keep the numbers of both man and beast well below the carrying capacity of the land. Finally, however, comes the day of reckoning, that is, the day when the long-desired goal of social stability becomes a reality. At this point, the inherent logic of the commons remorselessly generates tragedy.

As a rational being, each herdsman seeks to maximize his gain. Explicitly or implicitly, more or less consciously, he asks. "What is the utility to me of adding one more animal to my herd?" This utility has one negative and one positive component.

1) The positive component is a function of the increment of one animal. Since the herdsman receives all the proceeds from the sale of the additional animal, the positive utility is nearly +1.

2) The negative component is a function of the additional overgrazing, created by one more animal. Since, however, the effects of overgrazing are shared by all the herdsmen, the negative utility for any particular decisionmaking herdsman is only a fraction of -1.

---

*   Excerpted with permission from *Tragedy of the Commons*, Garrett Hardin, 162 SCIENCE 1243 (1968). Copyright © 1968, American Association for the Advancement of Science.

Adding together the component partial utilities, the rational herdsman concludes that the only sensible course for him to pursue is to add another animal to his herd. And another: and another. . . . But this is the conclusion reached by each and every rational herdsman sharing a commons. Therein is the tragedy. Each man is locked into a system that compels him to increase his herd without limit—in a world that is limited. Ruin is the destination toward which all men rush, each pursing his own best interest in a society that believes in the freedom of the commons. Freedom in a commons brings ruin to all.

Some would say that this is a platitude. Would that it were! In a sense, it was learned thousands of years ago, but natural selection favors the forces of psychological denial. The individual benefits as an individual from his ability to deny the truth even though society as a whole, of which he is a part, suffers. Education can counteract the natural tendency to do the wrong thing, but the inexorable succession of generations requires that the basis for this knowledge be constantly refreshed.

* * *

Pollution

In a reverse way, the tragedy of the commons reappears in problems of pollution. Here it is not a question of taking something out of the commons, but of putting something in—sewage, or radioactive chemicals, and heat wastes into water; noxious and dangerous fumes into the air; and distracting and unpleasant advertising signs into the line of sight. The calculations of utility are much the same as before. The rational man finds that his share of the cost of the wastes he discharges into the commons is less than the cost of purifying his wastes before releasing them. Since this is true for everyone, we are locked into a system of "fouling our own nest," so long as we behave only as independent, rational, free-enterprisers.

The tragedy of the commons as a food basket is averted by private property, or something formally like it. But the air and waters surrounding us cannot readily be fenced, and so the tragedy of the commons as a cesspool must be prevented by different means, by coercive laws or taxing devices that make it cheaper for the polluter to treat his pollutants than to discharge them untreated. We have not progressed as far with the solution of this problem as we have with the first. Indeed, our particular concept of private property, which deters us from exhausting the positive resources of the earth, favors pollution. The owner of a factory on the bank of a stream—whose property extends to the middle of the stream—often has difficulty seeing why it is not his natural right to muddy the waters flowing past his door. The law, always behind the times, requires elaborate stitching and fitting to adapt it to this newly perceived aspect of the commons.

* * *

Mutual Coercion Mutually Agreed Upon

The social arrangements that produce responsibility are arrangements that create coercion of some sort. Consider bank-robbing. The man who takes money from a bank acts as if the bank were a commons. How do we prevent such action? Certainly not by trying to control his behavior solely by a verbal appeal to his sense of responsibility. Rather than rely on propaganda we * * * insist that a bank is not a commons: we seek the definite social arrangements that will keep it from becoming a commons. That we thereby infringe on the freedom of would-be robbers we neither deny nor regret.

The morality of bank-robbing is particularly easy to understand because we accept complete prohibition of this activity. We are willing to say "Thou shalt not rob banks," without providing for exceptions. But temperance also can be created by coercion. Taxing is a good coercive device. To keep downtown shoppers temperate in their use of parking space we introduce parking meters for short periods, and traffic fines for longer ones. We need not actually forbid a citizen to park as long as he wants to: we need merely make it increasingly expensive for him to do so. Not prohibition, but carefully biased options are what we offer him. A Madison Avenue man might call this persuasion; I prefer the greater candor of the word coercion.

Coercion is a dirty word to most liberals now, but it need not forever be so. As with the four-letter words, its dirtiness can be cleansed away by exposure to the light, by saying it over and over without apology or embarrassment. To many, the word coercion implies arbitrary decisions of distant and irresponsible bureaucrats; but this is not a necessary part of its meaning. The only kind of coercion I recommend is mutual coercion, mutually agreed upon by the majority of the people affected.

To say that we mutually agree to coercion is not to say that we are required to enjoy it, or even to pretend we enjoy it. Who enjoys taxes? We all grumble about them. But we accept compulsory taxes because we recognize that voluntary taxes would favor the conscienceless. We institute and (grumblingly) support taxes and other coercive devices to escape the horror or the commons.

An alternative to the commons need not be perfect just to be preferable. With real estate and other material goods, the alternative we have chosen is the institution of private property coupled with legal inheritance. Is this system perfectly just? As a genetically trained biologist I deny that it is. It seems to me that, if there are to be differences in individual inheritance, legal possession should be perfectly correlated with biological inheritance—that those who are biologically more fit to be the custodians of property and power should legally inherit more. But genetic recombination continually makes a mockery of the doctrine of "like father, like son" implicit in our laws of legal inheritance. An idiot can inherit millions, and a trust fund can keep his estate intact. We must admit that our legal system of private property plus inheritance is unjust—but we put up with it because we are not convinced, at the moment, that anyone has invented a better system. The alternative of the commons is too horrifying to contemplate. Injustice is preferable to total ruin.

* * *

NOTES

1.   How does Hardin distinguish between prohibition and coercion? Does Hardin explain how to choose between them in responding to an environmental problem? Is pollution more like bank robbery or illegal parking? What systems of "mutual concern" might be used to control pollution?

2.   How do people "mutually agree" upon coercion? Is unanimity required?

3.   The tragedy of the commons leads Hardin to suggest that the alternative of private property may be preferable even if it is unjust. How might a system of private property be established to control pollution? Is such a system preferable to direct regulation? Can it be made just? *See* Terry Anderson & Donald Leal, *Free Market Versus Political Environmentalism*, 15 HARV. J. L. & PUB. POL'Y 297 (1992); Carlisle Ford Runge, *The Fallacy of "Privatization"*, J. CONTEMPORARY STUDIES, Spr. 1984, at 8.

One of the key issues facing regulators is whether the risk posed by an environmental problem is sufficiently serious to warrant government intervention. Risk assessment and cost-benefit analysis are two related techniques that are designed to assist agencies in making good choices about when to regulate private conduct. They have become increasingly popular as government officials seek ways to control regulatory costs and promote efficient economic results. The following Executive Order issued by President Clinton is intended to help agencies understand the costs and benefits of proposed rulemaking actions before they become final.

REGULATORY PLANNING AND REVIEW
EXECUTIVE ORDER 12866
58 Fed. Reg. 51735 (1993)

The American people deserve a regulatory system that works for them, not against them: a regulatory system that protects and improves their health, safety, environment, and well-being and improves the performance of the economy without imposing unacceptable or unreasonable costs on society; regulatory policies that recognize that the private sector and private markets are the best engine for economic growth; regulatory approaches that respect the role of State, local, and tribal governments; and regulations that are effective, consistent, sensible, and understandable. We do not have such a regulatory system today.

With this Executive order, the Federal Government begins a program to reform and make more efficient the regulatory process. The objectives of this Executive order are to enhance planning and coordination with respect to both new and existing regulations; to reaffirm the primacy of Federal agencies in the regulatory decision-making process; to restore the integrity and legitimacy of regulatory review and oversight; and to make the process more accessible and open to the public. In pursuing these objectives, the regulatory process shall be conducted so as to meet applicable statutory requirements and with due regard to the discretion that has been entrusted to the Federal agencies.

Accordingly, by the authority vested in me as President by the Constitution and the laws of the United States of America, it is hereby ordered as follows:

Section 1. Statement of Regulatory Philosophy and Principles.

(a) The Regulatory Philosophy. Federal agencies should promulgate only such regulations as are required by law, are necessary to interpret the law, or are made necessary by compelling public need, such as material failures of private markets to protect or improve the health and safety of the public, the environment, or the well-being of the American people. In deciding whether and how to regulate, agencies should assess all costs and benefits of available regulatory alternatives, including the alternative of not regulating. Costs and benefits shall be understood to include both quantifiable measures (to the fullest extent that these can be usefully estimated) and qualitative measures of costs and benefits that are difficult to quantify, but nevertheless essential to consider. Further, in choosing among alternative regulatory approaches, agencies should select those approaches that maximize net benefits (including potential economic, environmental, public health and safety, and other advantages; distributive impacts; and equity), unless a statute requires another regulatory approach.

(b) The Principles of Regulation. To ensure that the agencies' regulatory programs are consistent with the philosophy set forth above, agencies should adhere to the following principles, to the extent permitted by law and where applicable:

(1) Each agency shall identify the problem that it intends to address (including, where applicable, the failures of private markets or public institutions that warrant new agency action) as well as assess the significance of that problem.

(2) Each agency shall examine whether existing regulations (or other law) have created, or contributed to, the problem that a new regulation is intended to correct and whether those regulations (or other law) should be modified to achieve the intended goal of regulation more effectively.

(3) Each agency shall identify and assess available alternatives to direct regulation, including providing economic incentives to encourage the desired behavior, such as user fees or marketable permits, or providing information upon which choices can be made by the public.

(4) In setting regulatory priorities, each agency shall consider, to the extent reasonable, the degree and nature of the risks posed by various substances or activities within its jurisdiction.

(5) When an agency determines that a regulation is the best available method of achieving the regulatory objective, it shall design its regulations in the most cost-effective manner to achieve the regulatory objective. In doing so, each agency shall consider incentives for innovation, consistency, predictability, the costs of enforcement and compliance (to the government, regulated entities, and the public), flexibility, distributive impacts, and equity.

(6) Each agency shall assess both the costs and the benefits of the intended regulation and, recognizing that some costs and benefits are difficult to quantify, propose or adopt a regulation only upon a reasoned determination that the benefits of the intended regulation justify its costs.

(7) Each agency shall base its decisions on the best reasonably obtainable scientific, technical, economic, and other information concerning the need for, and consequences of, the intended regulation.

(8) Each agency shall identify and assess alternative forms of regulation and shall, to the extent feasible, specify performance objectives, rather than specifying the behavior or manner of compliance that regulated entities must adopt.

(9) Wherever feasible, agencies shall seek views of appropriate State, local, and tribal officials before imposing regulatory requirements that might significantly or uniquely affect those governmental entities. Each agency shall assess the effects of Federal regulations on State, local, and tribal governments, including specifically the availability of resources to carry out those mandates, and seek to minimize those burdens that uniquely or significantly affect such governmental entities, consistent with achieving regulatory objectives. In addition, as appropriate, agencies shall seek to harmonize Federal regulatory actions with related State, local, and tribal regulatory and other governmental functions.

(10) Each agency shall avoid regulations that are inconsistent, incompatible, or duplicative with its other regulations or those of other Federal agencies.

(11) Each agency shall tailor its regulations to impose the least burden on society, including individuals, businesses of differing sizes, and other entities (including small communities and governmental entities), consistent with obtaining the regulatory objectives, taking into account, among other things, and to the extent practicable, the costs of cumulative regulations.

(12) Each agency shall draft its regulations to be simple and easy to understand, with the goal of minimizing the potential for uncertainty and litigation arising from such uncertainty.

* * *

Section 5. Existing Regulations. In order to reduce the regulatory burden on the American people, their families, their communities, their State, local, and tribal governments, and their industries; to determine whether regulations promulgated by the executive branch of the Federal Government have become unjustified or unnecessary as a result of changed circumstances; to confirm that regulations are both compatible with each other and not duplicative or inappropriately burdensome in the aggregate; to ensure that all regulations are consistent with the President's priorities and the principles set forth in this Executive order, within applicable law; and to otherwise improve the effectiveness of existing regulations:

(a) Within 90 days of the date of this Executive order, each agency shall submit to OIRA a program, consistent with its resources and regulatory priorities, under which the agency will periodically review its existing significant regulations to determine whether any such regulations should be modified or eliminated so as to make the agency's regulatory program more effective in achieving the regulatory objectives, less burdensome, or in greater alignment with the President's priorities and the principles set forth in this Executive order. Any significant regulations selected for review shall be included in the agency's annual Plan. The agency shall also identify any legislative mandates that require the agency to promulgate or continue to impose regulations that the agency believes are unnecessary or outdated by reason of changed circumstances.

* * *

Section 10. Judicial Review. Nothing in this Executive order shall affect any otherwise available judicial review of agency action. This Executive order is intended only to improve the internal management of the Federal Government and does not create any right or benefit, substantive or procedural, enforceable at law or equity by a party against the United States, its agencies or instrumentalities, its officers or employees, or any other person.

* * *

WILLIAM CLINTON
THE WHITE HOUSE,
September 30, 1993

NOTES

1.   Do you see any possible problems with taking an approach toward regulation which "maximizes net benefits"? How confident are you about accuracy of the scientific and economic data used to determine net benefits?

2.   Risk assessment is an important part of analyzing benefits and costs. Risk assessment involves four steps:

Hazard identification: The determination of whether a particular chemical is or is not causally linked to particular health effects.

Dose-response assessment: The determination of the relation between the magnitude of exposure and the probability of occurrence of the health effects in question.

Exposure assessment: The determination of the relation between the magnitude of exposure before or after application of regulatory controls.

Risk characterization: The description of the nature and often the magnitude of human risk, including attendant uncertainty.

NATIONAL RESEARCH COUNCIL, RISK ASSESSMENT IN THE FEDERAL GOVERNMENT: MANAGING THE PROCESS 3 (1983).

3.   Risk assessment has become increasingly popular because it "helps provide a foundation for the effort to focus on high-priority risks and compare benefits and costs of new regulations." This trend responds to critics like Justice Breyer who have used risk assessment in an attempt to demonstrate misplaced government priorities. STEPHEN BREYER, BREAKING THE VICIOUS CIRCLE: TOWARD EFFECTIVE RISK REGULATION (1993). He notes for example, that the risk of dying from exposure to asbestos in schools is trivial when compared with many other risks that we face in our daily lives, yet billions of dollars are being spent to remove asbestos from schools, often at a risk to workers that is far greater than the risk to students attending these schools. *Id.* at 12-14. Nonetheless, risk assessment remains controversial. As one commentator has noted:

> Much of the current debate over risk regulation is a product of sharply different visions concerning the rationality of public perceptions of environmental risk. Those who focus largely on quantitative risk assessments argue that regulatory priorities are misplaced because the public is too concerned about some risks that are statistically smaller than others. * * * Yet risk regulation choices implicate a far richer mix of values than simple comparisons of statistical lives saved. These include the voluntariness of exposure to risks, fairness in the distribution of risks, uncertainty, the potentially catastrophic nature of certain risks, environmental damage, and non-fatal health risks.
>
> What is striking about this debate is that economists, whose discipline traditionally has not questioned the rationality of consumer preferences, have been among the harshest critics of the public's regulatory priorities. Rather than viewing harmony between current regulatory priorities and public preferences as a sign of a functioning, pluralistic democracy, these critics decry it as a misallocation of societal resources because the public seemingly places a higher risk on controlling certain risks than cost-benefit analyses do.

Robert V. Percival, *Responding to Environmental Risk: A Pluralistic Perspective,* 14 PACE ENVTL. L. REV. 513, 521-22 (1997). Another problem is the high level of uncertainty that frequently pervades risk assessment conclusions. As the National Research Council has noted:

> The dominant analytic difficulty [with risk assessment] is pervasive uncertainty. Risk assessment draws extensively on science, and a strong scientific basis has developed for linking exposure to chemicals to chronic health effects. However, data may be incomplete, and there is often great uncertainty in estimates of the types, probability and magnitude of health effects associated with a chemical agent, of the economic effects of a proposed regulatory action, and of the extent of possible future human exposures.

NATIONAL RESEARCH COUNCIL, RISK ASSESSMENT IN THE FEDERAL GOVERNMENT: MANAGING THE PROCESS 11 (1983). One commentator has put it more bluntly: "The hard fact is that quantitative risk assessment generates numbers that are meaningless." Mark E. Shere, *The Myth of Meaningful Environmental Risk Assessment,* 19 HARV. ENVT'L L. REV. 409, 414 (1995).

4.   The uncertainties surrounding risk assessment are so significant that any conclusion that, for example, an individual faces a risk of contracting cancer of one in ten thousand, may be wrong by many orders of magnitude. Nonetheless, because the conclusion is often expressed as a single number, the conclusion tends to have greater influence on agency decisions than perhaps it should. For example, in a recent article, Cass Sunstein reproduced a table that states precisely the "Cost per Premature Death Averted" (in millions of dollars). The table plainly suggests that   EPA's "trihalomethane drinking water standards," which are projected to cost $200,000 per premature death saved, should be given priority over hazardous air pollution standards for copper and arsenic, which are projected to cost $23 million per premature death saved. Cass Sunstein, *Congress, Constitutional Moments, and the Cost Benefit State,* 48 STAN. L. REV. 247, 259 (1996). But from the information provided we know nothing about the uncertainties associated with these two numbers. How should government decisionmakers address this problem? Lisa Heinzerling recently has argued that many of these commonly cited risk values are inaccurate. *Regulatory Costs of Myth Perspectives,* 107 YALE L.J. 1981 (1998).

5.   Traditional risk assessment techniques express health risks as single numerical values. So, for example, a particular risk assessment might suggest that an individual would have a one in one thousand chance of contracting cancer from exposure to a certain chemical, at a certain level, and over a certain period of time. Unfortunately, as suggested above, this technique can be misleading since it does not provide information about the uncertainty or variability surrounding the estimate. To overcome these problems, some statisticians and government agencies have begun to employ a more complex technique known as Monte Carlo simulation. The EPA describes Monte Carlo simulation as follows:

> Monte Carlo simulation is a statistical technique by which a quantity is calculated repeatedly, using randomly selected "what if" scenarios for each calculation. Though the simulation process is internally complex, commercial computer software performs the calculations as a single operation, presenting results in simple graphs and tables. These results approximate the full range of possible outcomes and the likelihood of each.

Http://www.epa.gov/reg3hwmd/risk/guide1.htm. The chief advantage of Monte Carlo simulation over "single point" estimates is that the decisionmaker can see the probability distributions of a particular exposure level. Thus, with Monte Carlo simulation a graph can display both an estimate of risk associated with particular exposure levels, and the level of uncertainty or variability associated with each risk estimate. In this way, the decisionmaker can choose the level of risk deemed appropriate given the degree of uncertainty and variability, and set the exposure level on the basis of the graph produced through Monte Carlo simulation. *See* Susan R. Poulter, *Monte Carlo Simulation in Environmental Risk Assessment—Science, Policy, and Legal Issues,* 9 RISK: HEALTH SAFETY & ENV'T 7 (1998).

6.   Risk assessment is typically performed to assist an agency in preparing a cost-benefit analysis. As the CEQ Report suggests, Executive Order 12866 is designed to insure that agencies engage in cost-benefit analysis whenever they make regulatory decisions. Moreover, Section 1 of the order expressly provides that "in choosing among alternative regulatory approaches, agencies should select those approaches that maximize net benefits * * * unless a statute requires another regulatory approach." Federal legislation has been proposed that would go even further by requiring agencies to maximize net benefits regardless of other statutory mandates. *See, e.g., The Risk Assessment and Cost Benefit Act of 1995,* H.R. 1022, 104th Cong. (1995). In light of the uncertainties surrounding risk assessment, is H.R. 1022 good policy? Although critical of H.R. 1022 as "sloppy, confusing, and filled with provisions that had not been thought through," Professor Cass Sunstein is generally supportive of the idea that government decisionmaking should make better use of cost-benefit analysis. Cass Sunstein, *Congress, Constitutional Moments, and the Cost Benefit State,* 48 STAN. L. REV. 247 (1996). His approach, however, would emphasize the importance of qualitative, as well as quantitative, values, including: (1) whether the risk is catastrophic in nature; (2) whether the risk is uncontrollable; (3) whether the risk involves irretrievable or permanent losses; (4) whether the risk is voluntarily incurred; (5) whether the risk is equitably distributed or concentrated on identifiable, innocent, or traditionally disadvantaged victims; (6) whether the risk is well understood; (7) whether the risk would be faced by future generations; and (8) whether the risk is familiar. *Id.* at 293. How should a government decisionmaker display these qualitative values, and how should they be integrated with quantitative values in making a decision?

Professor Thomas McGarity takes issue with Sunstein's view that a consensus has emerged to support the use of cost-benefit analysis in decisionmaking. Thomas O. McGarity, *A Cost-Benefit State,* 50 ADMIN. L. REV. 7 (1998). He is also skeptical that Sunstein's more humanistic approach to cost-benefit analysis will emerge from the political forces that currently support this approach.

7.   Another idea for promoting efficient regulation is integrated pollution control, which emphasizes pollution prevention, and regulation and enforcement across different environmental media and statutory mandates. *See Integrated Pollution Control: A Symposium,* 22 ENVTL. L. 1 (1992). A similar concept for managing natural resources is an "ecosystem" or "biodiversity" approach, which blends natural science principles and social goals to coordinate currently disparate efforts aimed at human health and nature conservation. *See* Robert Fischman, *Biodiversity and Environmental Protection: Authorities to Reduce Risk,* 22 ENVTL. L. 435 (1992).

8.   Vice President Al Gore believes that environmental protection can enhance economic performance. In this view, there is no trade-off between environmental protection and prosperity. Vice President Gore illustrated his view in his widely read book, EARTH IN THE BALANCE (1992):

> Public concerns can prod even the largest corporations to take action, and some companies have found that in the process of addressing their environmental problems they have been able to improve productivity and profitability at the same time. For example, 3M, in its Pollution Prevention Pays program, has reported significant profit improvements as a direct result of its increased attention to shutting off all the causes of pollution it could find. What some of our best

companies have come to realize is that as their way of thinking about the environmental consequences of the industrial process changes, their way of thinking about other consequences of the process changes too. An effective quality control program that reduces the number of defects, for examples, requires a level of attention to detail and to the interaction of all facets of the production process, and this is precisely the approach required to identify the best ways to eliminate pollution. That is yet another reason why some companies have begun to feel that an emphasis on environmental responsibility makes good business sense. Some, like du Pont, have even begun to calculate executive compensation and bonus partly on the basis of performance in environmental stewardship.

Some companies that have not changed their approach are beginning to face stockholder challenges from institutional investors. In fact, a large, highly organized program—the Coalition for Environmental Responsible Economics— now works full time to focus the attention of investors and corporate boards on the environmental performance of corporations with publicly traded stock, and an increasing number of large pension funds, universities, and churches are basing their investment decisions on the Valdez Principles, which embody criteria for assessing the environmental performance of corporations.

Id. at 342. For criticism of the Vice President's economics, see Robert Hahn, *Toward a New Environmental Paradigm*, 102 YALE L.J. 1719 (1993) (reviewing EARTH IN THE BALANCE). *Can Regulation Help the Economy?*, ENVTL. F., Mar/Apr. 1994, at 6, reviews the economic studies on both sides of the dispute over whether environmental regulations encourages innovation, efficiency, and prosperity.

9.   The National Environmental Policy Act (NEPA) established the Council on Environmental Quality (CEQ). The CEQ reports annually to the President on the state of the environment. These reports often contain a wealth of data about current trends and issues relating to the environment. *See, e.g.*, THE 25TH ANNIVERSARY REPORT OF THE COUNCIL ON ENVIRONMENTAL QUALITY (1997). The CEQ also documents, defines and analyzes changes in the environment and reviews and recommends federal programs and policies concerning the nation's environmental quality. *See* 42 U.S.C. §§ 4342-47.

10.   The principal tool used by government agencies to guide decisions that may impact the environment is the environmental impact statement (EIS), or its simpler cousin, the environmental assessment (EA). This document is intended to provide information about the environmental and other impacts of the proposed action, and other reasonable alternatives to that action, so that the decision maker has a reasonable basis for making a decision. GIS and risk assessment techniques are generally employed within the broader framework of an EIS or EA.

THE MIASMA OF REGULATION
ROBERT REICH
TALES OF A NEW AMERICA 212-21 (1987)[*]

Ask any business executive about government regulations, and he will tell you a horror story of bureaucratic excess. This is his version of the Rot at the Top. But the executive will not, most likely, object to the goal of regulation. Most executives agree that the public deserves protection from toxic wastes, nuclear accidents, air and water pollutants, unsafe products, fraudulent claims, and monopoly. Even in eras like the present, when business is ascendant and government suspect, the public supports these broad objectives. The complaints of American business center not on the purposes of regulations, but on the ways they are designed and implemented: Statutes are overly complicated; the rules devised to fulfill them are excruciatingly detailed, comprising voluminous rulings and interpretations, interpretations of interpretations, opinions and dissenting opinions of interpretations of interpretations. Even the simplest public goal spawns an imposing herd of rules requiring exhaustive filings, reports, nitpicking inspections, and picayune compliance with every jot and tittle for the law. And they are subject to constant alteration, elaboration, and ever more detailed explication. Under the spell of congressional committees, regulatory agency officials, hearing examiners, administrative law judges, appellate judges, and scores of zealous government lawyers, inspectors, and bureaucrats, regulations grow more complicated by the hour. They multiply in the *Federal Register*; they engorge the *Code of Federal Regulations*; they inundate companies with their petty requirements.

Tales of bureaucratic atrocities abound. The chairman of one large pharmaceutical firm complains that his company spends more hours filling out government forms and reports than it does on research for cancer and heart disease combined. Others tell of trivial, often silly requirements, like giving loan applicants pages of detailed information that nobody ever reads, or putting a toilet within one hundred yards of each employee. The laws are impenetrable: The Employee Retirement Income Security Act, which regulates private pension plans, runs to more than two hundred pages. It has been estimated that federal agencies each year require American businesses to fill out 4,400 different forms, together consuming 143 million hours of executive and clerical time, and costing 25 billion dollars.

Nitpicking regulation has been blamed for slowing America's productivity and impairing the nation's competitiveness. Yet other advanced industrial nations require that their companies achieve similar regulatory goals. Environmental, health, and safety requirements in Japan and most of Western Europe are no less stringent than in the United States.

There is one significant difference, however. Although the results of regulation are about the same among all advanced nations, the means of regulating are quite distinct. In these other nations, regulations are far less detailed than they are in the United States. Their regulations involve fewer rules and interpretations, impose less paperwork, entail only informal inspections and reports, and generate significantly lower compliance costs. If American business is conspicuously burdened by government regulation, it is not due to the ends that regulation seeks, but to the means employed. Among advanced industrial nations, the regulation of American business is uniquely picayune. Why should this be so?

2

Many who speak from or for American business attribute the trouble to the attitudes and values of the people who inhabit government regulatory agencies: These people must want to be nettlesome. In this story, the Rot at the Top is traceable to a "new class" of college-educated social planners and public policy professionals who disdain economic growth and abhor private enterprise. In the words of Irving Kristol, a principal exponent of such views, regulators and their fellow travelers "find it convenient to believe the worst about business because they have certain adverse intentions toward the business community to begin with." They seek "the power to shape our civilization—a power which, in the capitalist system, is supposed to reside in the free market." Their ambition is "to see much of this power redistributed to the government, where *they* will have a major say in how it is exercised [emphasis in the original]."

In this story, many denizens of the new class populate the staffs of regulatory agencies—surviving administration after administration. These individuals relish any chance to harass American business with endless, trivial commands, to clog the channels of commerce with their piddling requirements and endless forms. They take delight in transforming commonsensical regulatory goals into reams of irritating detail. According to Kristol and others who share his views, the new class is waging a war of attrition against capitalism.

> The New Regulation [to protect the environment, safety, and health] is the social policy of the new class. . . . They have merely transferred power from those who produce material goods to those who produce ideological ones—to the intellectuals, policy professionals, journalists, and "reformers," who are arguably much less representative of the American people as a whole than those whose influence has been curtailed. . . . With each passing year it becomes clearer that the real animus of the new class is not so much against business or technology as against the liberal values served by corporate capitalism and the benefits these institutions provide to the broad mass of the American people.

This conspiracy has proven to be an oddly comforting phantom for American businessmen. First, it provides a ready explanation for why business has felt so besieged. It is not any serious failings or erosion of legitimacy on the part of industry, but rather the machinations of a group bent on undermining free enterprise. It is an enemy within, an ally of the Mob at the Gates that seeks to substitute centralized planning for free markets. Second, the story suggests a plan of action. All we need do is to expel from government these ideological traitors and put in their place teams of levelheaded and unbiased civil servants. (Hunting out the miscreants should be no problem; they leave a trail of red tape wherever they wander.) Finally, the story promises a happy ending. Once these saboteurs have been ejected, the present regulatory miasma will be transformed into simple, sensible rules. The public will continue to be protected—as it should be—from the irresponsible acts of a few misguided managers. The rest of American business will be freed of the nitpicks, technicalities, and meticulous excesses of the present system.

Unfortunately for those who find the story satisfying, it wilts in the face of the facts. To begin with, the "new class" of interventionist zealots who are supposedly responsible for the picayune character of so much modern regulation have been far harder to track down than expected. Both the Carter and Reagan administrations were committed to reducing the burden of government regulation. The latter, indeed, installed its own counterzealots at the controlling levels of government agencies to track down the guilty parties. The Reagan administration did succeed in abandoning some regulatory efforts. But—and here is the important point—it did nothing to change the way in which the remaining regulations were administered. Notwithstanding its concerted efforts, the Code of Federal Regulations continued to swell with detail, the

Federal Register bulged with new interpretations and elaborations, and American business continued to writhe under the burden of pettifogging directives from Washington. The underlying problem had nothing to do with nefarious forces hidden within regulatory agencies; it was inherent in the American regulatory process itself. A probusiness administration might succeed in rescinding particular regulations, but not in reducing the amount of niggling minutiae surrounding any regulatory goal that survived.

In addition, it turned out that the vast majority of regulatory agency lawyers and middle-level managers aspire not to undermine America capitalism but to live off it. After gaining experience in government, they move on to the private sector. They gain jobs in law firms, representing companies before regulatory agencies. They join consulting firms, accounting firms, research institutes, and public relations firms. They move into government affairs offices of large corporations, and into trade associations. Some have even been known to join university faculties, from where they sell extracurricular insights to corporations. Their experience in government makes them valuable to the private sector, and they are not reluctant to trade upon that value. Far from comprising a "new class" of intellectuals animated by an antibusiness bias, these former civil servants prove themselves adept at making money off what they have to sell—their inside knowledge of how regulations are made. They bring as much zealousness to their newfound corporate jobs as they did to their former ones.

3

Let us return to our inventor friend, Henry, and his turbo-charged automatic vacuum cleaner. (You remember: Just leave the vacuum on a shelf for five minutes and—presto!—the room is spanking clean.) Imagine, as before, that the product proves enormously popular. But this time imagine that it suffers from a small flaw: It emits a roar something like a jet engine at full throttle, but louder. Every time the machine is switched on, the noise loosens tooth fillings and induces deep neurosis in dogs within a radius of two hundred yards. This flaw does not deter consumers from using the vacuum; following operating instructions, they simply set the timer, sedate the dog, and go off to the movies while the machine cuts loose. Soon in neighborhoods all over America the vacuum's roar issues from empty houses, causing flocks of passing birds to fall stunned from the sky and neighbors at table to drop plates and fling drinks into the air. Henry would like to make a quieter version of the product, but so far has had no luck; adding an adequate muffler would triple the cost of the vacuum.

Now suppose that several years before all this Congress had instructed the Environmental Protection Agency to take steps to "ensure no household appliance emits excessive noise." That was all the legislation said. Congress decided to leave it to the EPA to devise and enforce regulations concerning neighborhood noise pollution. Since then, the agency has issued only one broad rule: "No consumer product shall generate noise in excess of 110 decibels." That's it— nothing more specific than this, no reporting requirements, no interpretations, no elaborations. The EPA publishes the rule and considers the problem settled.

Henry has hired a Washington lawyer named Seymour, who informs him of the EPA's regulation. Worried about the threat to his company, Henry asks Seymour if he can think of some legal way to continue selling the turbo-charged vacuum cleaner. Seymour is a smart lawyer who specializes in federal regulations. "Not to worry," Seymour assures Henry. "I can think of two hundred ways to dodge this regulation." Henry rests easier.

Two months later, the EPA inquires about the vacuum. It seems they have been getting complaints about its noise. Seymour meets with the EPA's attorney. "The regulation doesn't apply to the turbo-charged automatic vacuum," says Seymour, matter-of-factly. "It says no consumer product should emit a sound in excess of 110 decibels, but this isn't a consumer product. It's designed for industrial applications, although consumers happen to use it. And it's not even a product, but a service, since under our unique payment plan it is leased rather than purchased outright." The EPA attorneys silently take off their hats to Seymour and go back to their law books and word processors.

Two months after that, the EPA announces a more detained set of rulings, which define "consumer product" as "any product or service sold or leased to industrial or consumer users." They then return to Seymour's office. "Still doesn't apply," says Seymour calmly. "The regulation prohibits sounds in excess of 110 decibels. But our automatic vacuum records only 95 decibels when we've tested it outside in the middle of a field during a hailstorm. Here's the proof." He hands the EPA attorneys computerized results of the experiment. They take off their hats again, solemnly shake his hand, and drag back to the office.

Two months later, the EPA announces precise specifications for how such products are to be tested to determine decibel levels—the kind of sound chamber in which testing is to occur, the type of testing equipment, scientific definitions for "decibel," and detailed requirements for when the testing must be done and under whose auspices. The agency also announces that hereafter all manufacturers of a new product "designed for or adaptable to household use" must file a report with the agency indicating its decibel level according to the prescribed test. All over America, developers of new cat beds, corn poppers, and sock matchers fume as they pay for the premarketing decibel tests Washington demands.

Over the next several years Seymour meets with the EPA attorneys innumerable times. Each time, he claims that the burgeoning regulations, rules, and interpretations still do not apply. Each time thereafter, they become more detailed. Seymour also disputes their applicability before administrative law judges and he appeals their rulings to the federal courts. He argues, as the occasion warrants and the spirit moves him, that the EPA has exceeded its mandate from Congress, or that the agency has acted arbitrarily in singling out the turbo-charged automatic vacuum, or that the company's constitutional rights have been violated. The administrative judges and appellate courts issue opinions that further elaborate upon the EPA's regulations and interpretations, and its authority to regulate in this area. Meanwhile, the original statute has been amended by Congress to avoid the loopholes and ambiguities that Seymour (and others like him) have discovered. The new law is far more detailed and complex, spelling out in excruciating specificity what is required.

Five years later, Henry meets with Seymour. "I'm afraid," says Seymour, "we've reached the end of the line." Seymour points to a bookshelf sagging under the weight of statutes, EPA regulations, rulings, advisory opinions, interpretations, court opinions, and appellate decisions, all concerning noise pollution. "But at least I got you more than five years of delay." Henry is downcast nonetheless. "Does this mean we have to stop selling the turbo-charged automatic vacuum, or else install the muffler?" he asks. "Either that," Seymour warns, "or you'll have to pay the fine every year you violate the regulation." "How much?" Henry asks, trembling. "A full twenty-five hundred American dollars," Seymour says as he grins and takes off his hat to himself. Henry jubilantly goes back to his company, where he asks his secretary to organize a bake sale to cover the fine.

This example exaggerates, but not much, the typical fate of a regulatory effort. It describes a familiar dynamic between American business and government. American corporations are not reluctant to test the limits of the law. They pay lawyers handsome sums to discover loopholes, technicalities, and elegant circumventions. In many instances the investment is worth it to the corporation. It buys the firm at least temporary relief from a regulation, enabling the company to profitably continue doing what it was doing before. Nor do American lawyers recoil from the challenge. They relish it. They cultivate reputations for their elegant pirouettes around statutes. The art of Washington practice is to stake out an area of government regulation and then become expert at outwitting those who administer it. Talented people have been known to spend entire careers circumventing a single, arcane area of regulation for the benefit of a few corporations.

This ploy may be rational from the standpoint of the lawyer and his client, but it is often irrational for American business as a whole. Each such maneuver generates a countermaneuver from within the regulatory bureaucracy and Congress; every feint and dodge, a more complicated prophylactic for the next encounter. The result, over time, is a profusion of legislative and regulatory detail that confounds American business. The underlying dynamic is analogous to the commercial gridlock examined earlier, and the crippling dilemma of irresponsibility in social programs, which was also explored. American business finds itself strangled by the red tape that government uses to seal the loopholes through which American business repeatedly tries to sneak.

The profession of discovering and exploiting loopholes is both intellectually and financially rewarding. It is also eminently respectable. Some of the nation's most erudite and honorable people do it. Those who play the game on the other side—the lawyers and middle-level bureaucrats within regulatory agencies and pertinent congressional committees—are simply trying to realize a simple and often sensible congressional mandate. Honor and financial reward will come to them later on, moreover, it they have gained a reputation for expertise and adroitness. The best law firms and largest corporations will hire them out of government, paying them many times their government salaries, to outwit their successors.

Washington lawyers who advise American business have a certain stake in the profusion of regulatory detail. When an area of regulation, like noise pollution, is compounded by such maneuver and countermaneuver into volumes of detailed statutory language, rules, interpretations, and opinions, it becomes accessible only to those, like Seymour and his tenacious opponents inside the agency, who have spent long hours refining it. The very complexity of the area generates new business and further elaboration. Soon every major corporation whose activities touch upon the area of law must have tactical advice about it. Seymour and his younger partners (who have once enforced EPA regulations on noise pollution) are sought out. Their practice mushrooms.

Unlike the story of the "new class," there are no plotting villains to this tale, which makes it far less satisfying. Seymour and other lawyers like him have no intention of confounding American capitalism. Seymour does his job as he understands it, and is good at what he does. Henry and other chief executives are no revolutionaries either. Henry also is trying to do his job, protecting his company's interests. Indeed, Henry has a responsibility to his shareholders to do whatever he can, within the limits of the law, to maximize the firm's profits. If he did not hire good lawyers to maneuver around statutes and regulations that were open to such circumnavigation, Henry might be found liable for breach of fiduciary duty to his shareholders, or he might be taken over by someone with fewer scruples about exploiting every possible route to higher profits. Every actor in this sad and silly tale is simply carrying out the responsibilities assigned him within a set of rules that we all have accepted.

The story, exasperatingly, suggests no obvious plan of action. For any fundamental improvement to occur would require a broader definition of responsibility by which businesses would not simply yield to the letter of the law but endorse its spirit, or else openly challenge the goals underlying the laws. And the story promises no happy ending, because such a change in attitude and practice will be difficult to achieve. Business executives, like Henry, lawyers like Seymour, shareholders and regulatory officials alike, act on the expectation that American business will try to outmaneuver government. As thrust meets parry, the miasma of regulation thickens.

NOTES

1.   Whether or not you agree with Reich, it is hard to deny one of his central points—that lawyers acting on behalf of business clients have greatly increased the complexity of government regulatory programs. Note also that the very possibility of a legal challenge may lead government lawyers and policy makers to increase the level of detailing their policy instruments such as regulations. What, if anything, can be done to reverse this trend toward ever increasing complexity?

2.   A related problem, suggested by Reich, is the tendency of both agency officials and legislators to build on existing laws or rules rather than rewriting the existing rule for clarity. A good example is the vacuum cleaner rule that applied to "consumer products." Instead of revising the original rule to apply to "any product or service," the agency chose to keep the old rule but add a new definition of "consumer product" that includes "services." Unfortunately, the new definition does violence to the ordinary dictionary meaning of the term "product."

SOLVING FOR PATTERN
WENDELL BERRY
THE GIFT OF GOOD LAND (1980)[*]

Our dilemma in agriculture now is that the industrial methods that have so spectacularly solved some of the problems of food production have been accompanied by "side effects" so damaging as to threaten the survival of farming. Perhaps the best clue to the nature and the gravity of this dilemma is that it is not limited to agriculture. My immediate concern here is with the irony of agricultural methods that destroy, first, the health of the soil and, finally, the health of human communities. But I could just as easily be talking about sanitation systems that pollute, school systems that graduate illiterate students, medical cures that cause disease, or nuclear armaments that explode in the midst of people they are meant to protect. This is a kind of surprise that is characteristic of our time: the cure proves incurable; security results in the evacuation of a neighborhood or a town. It is only when it is understood that our agricultural dilemma is characteristic not of our agriculture but of our time that we can begin to understand why these surprises happen, and to work out standards of judgment that may prevent them.

To the problems of farming, then, as to other problems of our time, there appear to be three kinds of solutions:

> There is, first the solution that causes a ramifying series of new problems, the only limiting criterion being, apparently, that the new problems should arise beyond the purview of the expertise that produced the solution—as, in agriculture, industrial solutions to the problem of production have invariably caused problems of maintenance, conservation, economics, community health, etc., etc.
>
> If, for example, beef cattle are fed in large feed lots, within the boundaries of the feeding operation itself a certain factory-like order and efficiency can be achieved.

---

*   Copyright © 1980. Reprinted with permission.

But even within those boundaries that mechanical order immediately produces biological disorder, for we know that health problems and dependence on drugs will be greater among cattle so confined than among cattle on pasture.

* * *

The second kind of solution is that which immediately worsens the problem it is intended to solve, causing a hellish symbiosis in which problem and solution reciprocally enlarge one another in a sequence that, so far as its own logic is concerned, is limitless—as when the problem of soil compaction is "solved" by a bigger tractor, which further compacts the soil, which makes a need for a still bigger tractor, and so on and on. There is an identical symbiosis between coal-fired power plants and air conditioners. It is characteristic of such solutions that no one prospers by them but the suppliers of fuel and equipment.

These two kinds of solutions are obviously bad. They always serve one good at the expense of another or of several others, and I believe that if all their effects were ever to be accounted for they would be seen to involve, too frequently if not invariably, a net loss to nature, agriculture, and the human commonwealth.

Such solutions always involve a definition of the problem that is either false or so narrow as to be virtually false. To define an agricultural problem as if it were solely a problem of agriculture—or solely a problem of production or technology or economics—is simply to misunderstand the problem, either inadvertently or deliberately, either for profit or because of a prevalent fashion of thought. The whole problem must be solved, not just some handily identifiable and simplifiable aspect of it.

Both kinds of bad solutions leave their problems unsolved. Bigger tractors do not solve the problem of soil compaction any more than air conditions solve the problem of air pollution. Nor does the large confinement feeding operation solve the problem of food production; it is, rather, a way calculated to allow large-scale ambition and greed to profit from food production. The real problem of food production occurs within a complex, mutually influential relationship of soil, plants, animals, and people. A real solution to that problem will therefore be ecologically, agriculturally, and culturally healthful.

Perhaps it is not until health is set down as the aim that we come in sight of the third kind of solution: that which causes a ramifying series of solutions—as when meat animals are fed on the farm where the feed is raised, and where the feed is raised to be fed to the animals that are on the farm. Even so rudimentary a description implies a concern for pattern, for quality, which necessarily complicates the concern for production. The farmer has put plants and animals into a relationship of mutual dependence, and must perforce be concerned for balance or symmetry, a reciprocating connection in the pattern of the farm that is biological, not industrial, and that involves solutions to problems of fertility, soil husbandry, economics, sanitation—the whole complex of problems whose proper solutions add to health: the health of the soil, of plants and animals, of farm and farmer, of farm family and farm community, all involved in the same internested, interlocking pattern—or pattern of patterns.

A bad solution is bad, then, because it acts destructively upon the larger patterns in which is contained. It acts destructively upon those patterns, most likely, because it is formed in ignorance or disregard of them. A bad solution solves for a single purpose or goal, such as increased production. And it is typical of such solutions that they achieve stupendous increases in production at exorbitant biological and social costs.

A good solution is good because it is in harmony with those larger patterns—this harmony will, I think, be found to have the nature of analogy. A bad solution acts within the larger pattern the way a disease or addiction acts within the body. A good solution acts within the larger pattern the way a healthy organ acts within the body. But it must at once be understood that a healthy organ does not—as the mechanistic or industrial mind would like to say—"give" health, but is a part of its health. The health of organ and organism is the same, just as the health of organism and ecosystem is the same.

NOTES

1.   What does Wendell Berry's essay tell us about finding solutions to environmental problems? Consider, for example, the following problems, whose solution could adversely impact the environment:

(a) increased energy demand;
(b) increased traffic congestion;
(c) unhealthy air quality that comes from a combination of motor vehicle use and a myriad of stationary sources of air pollution; and
(d) sediment and pesticide residues from agricultural lands contaminating streams making them unfit for fishing and other forms of recreation.

How might you solve these problems using the approach suggested by Wendell Berry? What kinds of "solutions" to these problems would not find favor with Berry?

2.   As we shall see, the National Environmental Policy Act requires federal agencies to prepare an environmental impact statement (EIS) for proposed major federal actions that may significantly affect the environment. How might the EIS process be used to support the approach to decisionmaking suggested by Wendell Berry? Should it be used in this way?

FAILURE OF THE ENVIRONMENTAL EFFORT
Barry Commoner
18 ENVTL. L. REP. 10195 (1988)[*]

The enactment of the National Environmental Protection Act (NEPA), and the creation of the Environmental Protection Agency (EPA) to administer it in 1970 marked a turning point in the recent environmental history of the United States. Beginning in 1950, new forms of environmental pollution appeared and rapidly intensified: smog, acid rain, excess nitrate and phosphate in water supplies, pesticides and toxic chemicals in the food chain and our bodies, and dangerous accumulations of radioactive waste. Then, in 1970, pressed by a newly aroused public, Congress began a massive effort to undo the damage. Now, nearly 20 years later, the time has come to ask an important and perhaps embarrassing question: How far have we progressed toward the goal of restoring the quality of the environment?

The answer is in fact embarrassing. Apart from a few notable exceptions, environmental quality has improved only slightly, and in some cases has become worse. Since 1975, when most

---

of the consistent environmental measurements began, overall improvement amounts to only about 15 percent. And at least in the case of air emissions (other than lead), since 1981—the advent of the current Administration—the annual rate of improvement has dropped from 1.52 percent per year to only 1.16 percent per year.

Although the massive national effort that began in 1970 has failed to restore the quality of the environment—or to even come close to that goal—the record shows that success is possible. In a few scattered instances, pollution levels have been significantly reduced, by 70 percent or more: lead in the air; DDT and PCBs in wildlife and people; mercury pollution in the Great Lakes; strontium 90 in the food chain; and in some local rivers, phosphate pollution. These few successes explain the far more common failures. Each of these pollutants has been effectively controlled not by high-tech devices, but by simply stopping its production or use. Air emissions of lead have declined by 86 percent because much less lead is now added to gasoline and therefore there is that much less in the environment. The environmental levels of DDT and PCBs have dropped sharply because their production and use have been banned. Mercury is much less prevalent in the environment because it is no longer used in manufacturing chlorine. Strontium 90 has decayed to low levels because we and the Soviet Union have had the simple wisdom to stop the atmospheric nuclear bomb tests that produce it.

* * *

The lesson of both the few successes and the far more numerous failures is the same: environmental pollution is a nearly incurable disease, but it can be prevented.

Environmental degradation is built into the technical design of the modern instruments of production. A high-compression car engine is not only high-powered, but a smog generator. A farm that uses chemical fertilizers and pesticides is not only highly productive, but also an uncontrollable source of water pollution. A trash-burning incinerator not only produces energy, but dioxin as well.

The environmental hazard is just as much an outcome of the facility's technological design as is its productive benefit. High compression is the cause of both the auto engine's power and its production of nitrogen oxide, which triggers smog. The extensive use of fertilizers and pesticides accounts for productivity of the modern farm—and for the pollution of rivers and groundwater as well. The same combustion process that extracts energy from trash also releases the chemical precursors that then combine to produce dioxin.

* * *

Most of our environmental problems are the inevitable result of the sweeping changes in the technology of production that transformed the U.S. economic system after World War II: the new large, high-powered, smog-generating cars; the shift from fuel-efficient railroads to gas-guzzling trucks and cars; the substitution of undegradable and hazardous petrochemical products for biodegradable and less toxic natural products; the substitution of fertilizers for manure and crop rotation and of toxic synthetic pesticides for ladybugs and birds.

By 1970 it was clear that these changes in the technology of production are the root cause.

Unfortunately, the legislative base of the U.S. environmental program was created without reference to the origin of the crisis that it was supposed to solve. Our environmental laws do not discuss the origin of environmental pollutants—why we have been afflicted with the pollutants that the laws were designed to control. Not that theories weren't offered to the legislators. Some ecologists told them the country and the world are polluted because there are too many people using more of the planet's resources than it can safely provide. A different point of view was heard from as well, but with a good deal of skepticism. I well remember the incredulity in Senator Muskie's voice during NEPA hearings when he asked me whether I was really testifying that the technology that generated post-World War II economic progress was also the cause of pollution. I was.

Because environmental legislation ignored the origin of the assault on environmental quality, it has dealt only with its subsequent effects. And, having defined the disease as a collection of symptoms, the legislation mandates only palliative measures. The notion of preventing pollution—the only measure that really works—appears but fitfully in the environmental laws and has never been given any administrative force.

This fundamental fault in our environmental laws has had a major impact on the operation of the agency that is chiefly responsible for administering and enforcing them—EPA.

The failed effort to deal with the automobile's most notorious environmental impact—photochemical smog—is an instructive example. That failure was recently commemorated on December 31, 1987, when dozens of urban areas were once again allowed to miss the deadline for meeting ambient air standards for carbon monoxide and ozone. Why has the effort to rid the environment of its automotive nemesis, which has generated a mass of environmental analyses, emission standards, administrative rulings, and litigation, nevertheless only ended in failure?

For more than 20 years we have understood the origin of photochemical smog: the high-compression engines introduced after World War II to drive the suddenly enlarged American cars necessarily run hot; they therefore convert oxygen and nitrogen in the cylinder air to nitrogen oxides. Once out the exhaust, nitrogen oxides are activated by sunlight and react with airborne fuel and other hydrocarbons—many of them otherwise relatively benign—to produce ozone and the other noxious components of photochemical smog.

EPA has tried to deal with the smog problem by aiming at everything except the crucial target: the engine's production of nitrogen oxides. The effort is largely designed to reduce emissions of the bewildering array of hydrocarbon sources. It has clearly failed; nitrogen oxide emissions have increased in the last decade, not only perpetuating smog but becoming a major source of acid rain as well.

Suppose, now, that guided by the few environmental successes, we seek to control automotive smog at its origin, the production of nitrogen oxides. The goal would be zero production of nitrogen oxides by cars and the complete elimination of this dominant source of smog. It is worth noting that this approach accords well with a corresponding approach to health: prevention of disease rather than curing or simply tolerating it. The preventive approach to disease is the source of some of the major advances in public health. The classical example is smallpox; widespread use of a preventive measure—vaccination—has now completely eradicated the disease. A zero incidence has actually been attained world-wide. Like smallpox, the great majority of the assaults on the environment are, in fact, preventable. After all, nearly all of them—the major exception is natural radiation—have been created, chiefly since 1950, by introducing inherently polluting forms of production technology. They are not the result of natural processes but of human action, and human action can once again change the technologies and undo their harm.

Is this approach to the automotive smog problem really practical? Can smogless engines that do not produce nitrogen oxides be built? They can. Indeed, they have been. Every pre-World War II car was driven by such an engine; that's why the country was then free of smog. In fact, nitrogen oxide production can be prevented without giving up the American car's precious over-powered engine (which is, nevertheless, a good idea). The so-called "stratified charge" engine can do just that. According to a 1974 National Science Foundation (NSF) study, prototypes were then already operating in Detroit, and tests showed that the engines would meet the 90 percent reduction in nitrogen oxide emissions required by the Clean Air Act Amendments. But, according to the NSF report, the engine would need to be considerably redesigned, requiring new fuel injector, fuel pump, ignition spark-plug system, cylinder head, piston, intake, and exhaust manifolds. Unlike the addition of a catalytic converter to the exhaust system of the existing engine, this would mean extensive retooling in the manufacturing plants. According to the report, had the auto industry decided in 1975 to take this course, the stratified charge engine could now be driving most U.S. cars—and automotive nitrogen oxide emissions would have been sharply reduced instead of increasing.

In sum, the goal established by the 1970 Clean Air Act Amendments could have been met—but only if EPA had confronted the auto industry with a demand for fundamental changes in engine design. EPA was unwilling to take on this task. EPA's reluctance to tell the automobile industry what kind of engine it should build has helped to undermine the goal of the Clean Air Act.

Of course, all this is easier said than done. I am fully aware that what I am proposing is no small thing, easily accomplished by bureaucratic fiat. It means that sweeping changes in the major systems of production—agriculture, industry, power production, and transportation— would be undertaken for a social purpose: environmental improvement. As I have pointed out in explicit detail elsewhere, this represents social (as contrasted with private) governance of the means of production—an idea that is so foreign to what passes for our national ideology that even to mention it violates a deep-seated taboo.

* * *

The present, largely unsuccessful regulatory effort is based on a now well-established process. First, EPA must estimate the degree of harm represented by different levels of the numerous environmental pollutants. Next, some "acceptable" level of harm is chosen (for example, a cancer risk of one in a million) and emission and/or ambient concentration standards that can presumably achieve that risk level are established. Polluters are then expected to respond by introducing control measures (such as automobile exhaust catalysts or power plant stack scrubbers) that will bring emissions or ambient concentrations to the required levels. If the regulation survives the inevitable challenges from industry (and in recent years from the Administration itself), the polluters will invest in the appropriate control systems. Catalysts are appended to the cars, and scrubbers to the power plants and trash-burning incinerators. If all goes well—as it frequently does not—at least some areas of the country and some production facilities are then in compliance with the regulation.

The net result is that the "acceptable" pollution level is frozen in place. The industries, having heavily invested in equipment designed to just reach the required level, are unlikely to invest more in further improvements. The public, having been told that the accompanying hazard to health is "acceptable," is likely to be equally satisfied. Some optimistically inclined people will look upon exposure at the acceptable level as a kind of guarantee of health. Others, perhaps aware of the linear relation between pollution level and the risk to health, will conclude that we are doing as much as we can and will, in most cases, accept the remaining risk fatalistically.

Clearly this process is the inverse of the preventive, public health approach. It strikes not for the continuous improvement of environmental health, but for the social acceptance of some, hopefully low, risk to health. In a way this is a return to the medieval approach to disease, when illness—and death itself—was regarded as a debit on life that must be incurred in payment for original sin. Now we have recast this philosophy into a more modern form: some level of pollution and some risk to health is the unavoidable price that must be paid for the material benefits of modern technology.

The preventive approach aims at progressively reducing the risk to health; it does not mandate some socially convenient stopping point. The medical professions, after all, did not decide that the smallpox prevention program could quit when the risk reached one in a million. In contrast, the present regulatory approach, by setting a standard of "acceptable" exposure to the pollutant, erects an administrative barrier that blocks further improvement in environmental quality. This is, I believe, a major cost of our failure to confront the environmental crisis at its source.

* * *

FREE MARKET VERSUS POLITICAL ENVIRONMENTALISM
Terry L. Anderson & Donald R. Leal
15 HARV. J.L. & PUB. POL'Y 297 (1992)[*]

* * *

II. FREE MARKET ENVIRONMENTALISM

Free market environmentalism considers the potential for market solutions and the problems with political ones. Anthony Fisher summarizes the change in emphasis:

> We have already abandoned the assumption of a complete set of competitive markets. ... But if we now similarly abandon the notion of a perfect planner, it is not clear, in my judgement, that the government will do any better. Apart from the question of the planner's motivation to behave in the way assumed in our models, to allocate resource [sic] efficiently, there is the question of his ability to do so.[21]

Free market environmentalism challenges both the government planner's motivation and his ability. The approach recognizes two facts. First, *incentives affect all human behavior*. Professional managers, no matter how well-intended, respond to the incentives they face. This holds as true for bureaucrats as it does for profit-maximizing owners of firms. We readily accept the argument that business operators would dump wastes into the airways if they did not have to pay for the costs of their action. We often fail, however, to recognize the same elements at work in the political sector. If a politician is not personally accountable for allowing oil development on federal lands or for permitting an agency to dump hazardous wastes into the environment, then we can expect too much development and too much dumping. Moreover, when the beneficiaries of these activities do not have to pay the full costs, they will demand more of each from their political representatives.

Second, *information costs are positive*. In a world of scarcity, private and public decisionmakers must obtain information on the relative values of resource uses. When one use competes with another, tradeoffs are inevitable. Unfortunately, these tradeoffs are complicated when decisionmakers lack valuable information. In the absence of markets, a resource manager must rely on his own personal valuation of the tradeoffs or on information provided by special interest groups. In either case, there is little reason to believe that these values will necessarily reflect the social good.

With markets for commodities and amenities, prices provide the necessary information for making tradeoffs. Consider the influence a market for recreational and environmental amenities has had on International Paper (IP), one of the nation's largest private timber landowners. When leasing recreational opportunities on its land, IP has systematically improved wildlife habitats. IP's fee hunting and fee recreation programs yield approximately twenty-five percent of the

---

[21]   ANTHONY C. FISHER, RESOURCE AND ENVIRONMENTAL ECONOMICS 54 (1981).

operating profits in the mid-South region, with timber making up the rest. Populations of white-tailed deer, turkeys, rabbits, bobwhite quail, and mourning dove benefit from controlled burns that stimulate forage and from protected riparian zones that preserve cover and food. According to IP's wildlife managers, profits from these programs induced company executives to listen to proposals for improving habitats at the expense of timber production. In contrast, political managers in the Forest Service, who "give away" recreational activities on federal lands, lack this price information and have less incentive to react to changing values.

Free market environmentalism stresses the importance of well-specified property rights as the proper mechanism to provide the incentive for entrepreneurs acting on specific time and space information. Before a landowner can sell access to those interested in recreation or an easement to a land trust, there must be clearly defined and enforceable property rights to the resources. With such rights, imaginative entrepreneurs can capture the value of environmental amenities. For example, a stream owner who can devise ways of charging fishermen can internalize the benefits and costs of improving fishing quality. Similarly, a subdivider who puts covenants on deeds to preserve open space, improve views, and harmonize development with the environment, establishes property rights to these values and captures value in higher asset-prices.

III. FROM THE IMAGINABLE TO THE IMAGINATIVE

Skeptics are quick to point out that harmonizing wildlife needs with timber harvesting or livestock grazing is an easy solution and that free market environmentalism fails to provide solutions to the tougher problems. For example, although wildlife migrate across boundaries, landowners can at least benefit by improved management; in the open ocean, however, there are no boundaries and no ways to fence in fish. The result is over-fishing like that which occurs in the North Sea.

The free market environmentalist approach to this problem would establish property rights through individual transferable quotas (ITQs). ITQs give each fisherman a right to a proportion of the catch, thereby eliminating the incentive to over-fish the resource. The market establishes a price for the quota and more efficient fishermen buy quotas from those who are less efficient. The ITQ system has been successfully applied in Australia and New Zealand. Six months after ITQs were applied to Australia's bluefin tuna fishery, fleet capacity dropped by sixty percent, the value of quotas doubled, and the average size of the catch rose as operators with access to larger fish bought out operators with access to smaller fish. Similarly, two years after ITQs were applied to New Zealand's abalone fishery, the value of quotas increased nearly six-fold and abalone numbers increased with the aid of a new breeding program which fishermen financed.

Free market environmentalism can also solve pollution problems through common law tort remedies if property rights are established and polluters can be identified. In England, an association of anglers and clubs has monitored pollution since the 1960s. Angler's Cooperative Association officials point out that the organization was protecting the environment twenty years before the general public became concerned and pressured the government to act:

> The A.C.A. has had an extraordinary record of success. It has fought hundreds of pollution cases (not all of which have gone to court) and only lost one minor one on a legal technicality. The damages it has secured on behalf of members, and member clubs, runs [sic] into hundreds of thousands of pounds.[26]

---

[26]   Esmond Drury, *John Eastwood and the A.C.A.*, ANGLERS' COOPERATIVE ASSN. REV. 12-13 (Summer 1984).

The British experience suggests that pollution could be reduced if private fishing rights were established in the United States. Liability rules would evolve so that owners of fishing rights could bring against an upstream polluter whose effluent damaged their fishing resource.[27]

The challenge to the property rights approach occurs when the polluter cannot be identified and damages cannot be assessed. For example, with acid rain, it is clear that sulfur dioxide is the cause, but the actual damage caused by a specific polluter will vary with air currents, moisture, and other climatic conditions. A free market environmentalist solution would require "branding" the pollutants so it would be clear who is causing what damage.

New technology offers the potential for such branding by introducing tracers into the smoke stacks of suspected polluters. This technology was applied in the Winter Haze Intensive Tracer Experiment in Canyonlands National Park, Utah. The park commonly experiences a haze-causing pollutant that some suspected originated from a coal-fired generating plant several hundred miles away. To identify the source, chemical tracers that mimicked the pollutant were introduced into the stack of the plant and a battery of air monitoring stations was set up around the park. The experiment concluded that the plant was contributing to the haze.

The possibility of using tracers has enormous potential for tracking a variety of effluents and media. Tracers can identify users of pesticides and fertilizers, growing contributors to non-point sources of pollution. Tracers can also brand chemicals that contaminate groundwater basins. Just as the government requires registration and monitoring of pets to minimize nuisances, the government can require the branding and monitoring of emissions.

Technology has played a key in the evolution of free market environmentalism solutions. Technology provided the means to change dramatically the face of the American West. In the 1870s, homesteaders and ranchers began using barbed wire to define property rights to their land. Previously, the lack of trees and other materials made it very costly to establish property rights. Barbed wire, however, lowered the cost of fencing the western range dramatically.[30]

IV. FROM THEORY TO PRACTICE: ENDANGERED SPECIES

* * *

The first dispute involves the Northern Spotted Owl, which was declared a threatened species under the Endangered Species Act of 1973 in June of 1990. The controversy concerns the amount of federal timberland that would be removed from timber harvesting because of the Act. A government-sponsored plan to increase breeding owl pairs from 739 to 1,180 in the long term would remove from logging perhaps three million acres of timberland. If the plan were implemented, it is estimated that 25,000 to 40,000 timber-related jobs would be lost.

The second controversy surrounds the potential declaration of the sockeye salmon (and possibly other salmon species on the Columbia River) as endangered. Eight federal mainstem dams are located along the Columbia and Snake Rivers, where over ninety percent of the juvenile salmon are killed trying to migrate from their spawning grounds to the ocean. Salmon

---

[27]   *See, e.g.*, A. Mitchell Polinsky, AN INTRODUCTION TO LAW AND ECONOMICS 89-94 (1983). With well-specified rights, owners have an incentive to discover innovative ways to detect and monitor pollution. In Britain, the water company for Bournemouth has enlisted the services of twenty West African elephant fish, *Gnathonemus petersii*, to monitor water pollution. The four-inch creature emits an easily tracked electrical discharge, the rate of which depends on the pollution level of the water. A contented fish puts out 300 to 500 pulses a minute, but if it becomes distressed by the presence of pollutants, the rate shoots up to more than 1,000 pulses a minute. Sensors in the water supply pick up the pulse rate and pass them on to a computer. If more than half of the fish suddenly increase their pulse rate, an alarm is sounded and scientists step in to assay the water. *See A Fishy Kind of Pollution Detector*, 249 SCIENCE 983 (1990).

[30]   *See* WALTER PRESCOTT WEBB, THE GREAT PLAINS 309 (1931).

die when they are shredded or shocked as they are sucked into the giant turbines. They also fall victim to predators, high temperatures, and disease when they are trapped in the slack water behind the dams. According to salmon proponents, the solution is to increase river flows for several months during the spring, the period when juvenile salmon migrate to the sea.

Use of the Endangered Species Act to force a solution has sparked controversy. If sockeye and other salmon are declared endangered, their safety would be given highest priority relative to other uses of the Columbia Basin, such as hydroelectric power generation, shipping, and irrigation. Both hydroelectric power generation and shipping would be severely limited if water is released from the dams to increase river flows. Furthermore, these flows would not be available to fill reservoirs for later power production and irrigation. The Bonneville Power Administration also estimates that rates for Northwestern power could rise by thirty percent or more. Columbia River barge operators predict the possible demise of their industry, and irrigators say farming in Washington and southern Idaho will be devastated if water for irrigation is confiscated.

Why are the Northern Spotted Owl and Columbia River salmon in trouble? The answer is simple: No one owns them or their habitat; thus, no one has the incentive to protect them. In both cases, the federal government controls most of their habitats. The Forest Service and the Bureau of Land Management control the forests that the spotted owl inhabits, and the Bureau of Reclamation and the Army Corps of Engineers control the dams that kill the salmon.

The two cases do differ, however, in the extent of the subsidized destruction of the respective habitats. While federal timber programs run million-dollar deficits or more on many national forests, forests in the Pacific Northwest are money-makers. The thirteen national forests in Oregon and Washington affected by the spotted owl decision net more than $500 million in timber revenues each year. The government will lose $150 million in revenues in these forests alone, where forest planners project a thirty percent harvest reduction.[37]

The economics of water development in the Columbia River basin are quite different. Here the rule of subsidized development applies to the 6.5 million acre-feet of water used annually for irrigation. The costs of development allocated to irrigation are $745 million. Of this amount, irrigators pay $136 million, while hydroelectric power consumers pay the rest. In addition to the power subsidy, irrigators receive an implicit interest subsidy: They have a ten-year grace period during which they do not have to pay their reclamation loans and they are not charged interest during the forty-year repayment period; this amounts to an interest subsidy of seventy-nine percent. Water supplied for irrigation has made the "desert bloom like a rose," but only at a tremendous cost.

Free market environmentalism can correct these problems. Short of privatizing the national forests, timber leases could be put up for competitive bid with no requirement that timber be harvested; environmentalists could then bid with timber companies. Environmental groups could lease the most critical owl habitat and allow no logging there. On other tracts, they might allow some logging, thus partially offsetting lease costs, but require that logging be done with minimal impact on the owls. Because it owns its timberlands, International Paper has successfully minimized impacts on endangered species such as the red-cockaded woodpecker, and the Audubon Society has demonstrated that oil development can occur on its private preserves without significant damage to bird habitat.

Similarly, efforts to save the sockeye and other species of salmon in the Columbia River basin can be enhanced through water marketing. Environmentalists have embraced water

---

[37]   When all affected federal forests in Washington, Oregon, and California are taken into account, the loss could be as high as $625 million per year.

marketing because it raises water prices and reduces water consumption. As the Ruby River example indicates, water leasing for instream purposes offers an innovative way of increasing stream flows to help migrating salmon. If environmental groups, commercial and sports fishermen, and the U.S. Fish and Wildlife Service could negotiate with power producers and irrigators for increased water flows, cooperation would replace conflict. This has happened elsewhere. On the Gunnison River in Colorado, the Nature Conservancy has obtained the rights to 20,000 acre-feet of water to maintain flows for the hump-backed chub, an endangered species with no commercial or sport value. If those who care about the fate of the salmon could lease water for instream flows, they could directly invest their dollars where the salmon are threatened instead of spending time and money on costly lobbying efforts or litigation.

V. CONCLUSION

Critics of free market environmentalism contend that it does not offer a solution to all environmental problems. They contend that although free market environmentalism may work for some recreational and environmental amenities produced from land, it is inconceivable that property rights can be used to solve problems such as ozone depletion or global warming.[41]

If free market environmentalism stimulates environmentalists to apply free market solutions to the easier problems, it can free political resources to work on the tougher problems that, at the moment, seem to be the domain of government. If free market environmentalist solutions spark the imagination of environmental entrepreneurs, technological progress toward fencing the atmosphere may be accelerated. The "free" in free market environmentalism refers to the individual liberty that only markets can provide; and without that human freedom, environmental quality will be of little consequence.

NOTES

1. For differing views on the free market approach to environmentalism, *see* Symposium, *Free Market Environmentalism*, 15 HARV. J.L. & PUB. POL'Y 297 (1992).

2. Which approach, Commoner's prohibitions or Anderson & Leal's markets, best responds to the tragedy of the commons? Which best expresses Leopold's land ethic? Professor Krier points out that Commoner and Anderson & Leal agree that government regulation has predictably failed due to design flaws. James E. Krier, *The Tragedy of the Commons, Part Two*, 15 HARV. J.L. & PUB. POL'Y 325, 329 (1992). Moreover, both commentaries promote transferring control of environmental issues "to the people." *Id.* How do the two approaches differ in the mechanisms to achieve popular control? Do Commoner and free market environmentalists differ in their respective views on the root cause of environmental problems?

3. Commoner raises the example of the eradication of smallpox in support of his approach. Was eradication of smallpox worthwhile at any cost? Does a policymaker need

---

[41]   *But see* ROBERT STAVINS ET AL., PROJECT 88: HARNESSING MARKET FORCES TO PROTECT OUR ENVIRONMENT 10-23 (1988) (recommending a tradeable permit system for phasing out potential ozone depleters, international emissions trading in greenhouse gases, and prevention of deforestation through debt-forest swaps).

to quantify the value of a life to decide whether to spend money on smallpox eradication or a competing public health program?

4. How would free market environmentalists initially assign property interests in the environment? Can markets capture the value of environmental amenities currently enjoyed by thousands or millions of people?

5. Free market environmentalism places a great deal of reliance on common law liability to protect environmental property interests. What problems might court enforcement present for plaintiffs seeking to prevent an environmental harm?

6. Does free market environmentalism work for amenities that yield no revenues? Consider, for example, the goals of promoting ecosystem protection and biodiversity. Can the value of these resources fairly be determined solely on the basis of what some group of people is willing to pay for them? If no one is willing to pay anything, does that mean that these resources lack value? Does a remote ecosystem that is essentially unknown to civilization lack substantial value?

7. Some economists and ecologists have begun estimating the value of ecological services, such as pollinating crops, assimilating wastes, and buffering hydrologic extremes. NATURE'S SERVICES (Gretchen Daily ed., 1997); Robert Costanza et al., *The Value of the World's Ecosystem Services and Natural Capital*, 387 NATURE 253 (1997). What opportunities for environmental law reform does improved valuation of ecosystem services raise? *See* James Salzman, *Valuing Ecosystem Services*, 24 ECOL. L.Q. 887 (1997).

THE SEARCH FOR ENVIRONMENTAL RIGHTS
Joseph L. Sax
6 J. LAND USE & ENVTL. L. 93 (1990)[*]

For nearly two decades, efforts have been made to formulate an environmental right. Among the most prominent examples are the Stockholm Declaration of 1972 and, more recently, the statement of principles for environmental protection and sustainable development of the United Nation's World Commission on Environment and Development. Parallel endeavors also have been made in the domestic context. Proposals have been made periodically in the United States for amendments to the federal Constitution, and a number of states have adopted broad-ranging environmental provisions in their constitutions.

Putting aside the specific issue of judicial supremacy that arises with the recognition of a constitutional right, there remains a pervasive problem that vexes every effort to state principles of environmental protection in the form of legal rights: what is the source of the claim that there is a fundamental environmental right, and how is one to determine its content? Specific rights usually grow out of some core social value. If environmental claims are to be taken as more than rhetorical flourishes or broad aspirational statements and are to be set in the context of rights, it is necessary to ask how they fit into the values underlying other basic rights.

I propose here to sketch out a preliminary framework suggesting that while asserted environmental rights at first seem alien to most accepted conceptions of fundamental rights, there is an important link between certain environmental claims of right and baseline democratic values.

I. FINDING A BASIS FOR ASSERTING FUNDAMENTAL RIGHTS

Where do we begin? There is no legal tradition in our system that recognizes rights to nature preservation, so we cannot turn to precedent for guidance. Moreover, by contrast with the most basic human rights like freedom of speech or of conscience, there is no historical experience on which to draw to give content to an asserted ecological right. Indeed, as often observed, our experience deals more with the conquest and exploitation of nature than with its protection.

If we seek guidance from the established tradition of human rights, we find profound differences between any proposed environmental rights and other recognized fundamental rights. Most human rights are designed to protect individual integrity where the essential goal is being left alone by government. That is the root of freedoms like speech, press, religion and association, freedom from coercion for criminal defendants, the rights to move freely, to emigrate, etc. However difficult the determination of such rights may be in particular cases, at least the central idea is clear: individuals are to be left free of state coercion, secure in person and property, and at liberty to follow their own consciences.

Environmental issues are not at all parallel. They arise primarily out of the management of the economy, where government abstention is certainly not the goal. Indeed, positive government involvement is essential in dealing with externalities like pollution. There is no evident environmental principle analogous to the "hands off" principle that underlies basic human rights.

Surely there can be no precept to leave nature untouched, so that no tree should be cut down and no river dammed. Nor, unless we are prepared to demand completely closed-cycle industrial processes, could it be set down as principle that conduct should never increase the risk of health damage to any worker or neighbor. An urban and industrial society inevitably will disrupt pristine natural systems more than a rural and agricultural society, and such a society is, in turn, more disruptive than a hunting and gathering culture. It seems implausible that every movement away from this latter form of social organization should be branded as a transgression of fundamental human rights. If the questions of environmental regulation are matters of adjustment in the process of economic development, of more and less, they seem ill-fitted to the sort of ethical imperatives usually associated with fundamental rights.

The right to vote, notions of equality, and even such positive rights as universal free education seem to be another species of basic rights undergirded by a conception of the structural preconditions for a democratic society. Environmental issues seem not to provide a parallel to this sort of right either. Environmental claims, whether they focus on matters like health or on species diversity, seem to import certain substantive values, rather than being concerned with protection of the structure of democracy.

The closest analogy would seem to be found among the precepts of a modern welfare state. The effort to guarantee each individual a basic right to decent housing, health care, nutrition, safe working conditions, and cultural opportunity seems most closely fitted to the effort of articulating basic environmental rights. Terms like "decent environment," "environment adequate for their health and well-being" or "environment of quality" suggest that a significant driving idea behind efforts to establish environmental rights is a version of welfare-state ideology. If so, the goal would not be government abstention, but rather a call for affirmative action by the state—a demand that it assure, as a right of each individual, some level of freedom from environmental hazards or some degree of access to environmental benefits.

As I shall suggest, this is precisely one of the directions that the search for fundamental environmental rights should take. However, it must be recognized that there presently is no existing standard by which to measure an appropriate welfare standard of environmental well-being nearly as clear-cut as the concepts of a right to basic education or even basic medical care. It needs to be recognized as well that at least in some countries, the United States for one, welfare entitlements do not, or do not yet, have constitutional status as human rights. In this respect, recognition of a basic right to a healthy environment would be a novel step. So the question of why such claims should be granted fundamental rights status still needs to be addressed. I try to respond to that question later in this paper.

* * *

II. BASELINE DEMOCRATIC VALUES

Where shall we seek guidance? I believe a starting point for articulating environmental rights and responsibilities can be derived from three values that are already widely recognized as essential to modern societies. The first two are entirely familiar, though their application to environmental issues needs to be explicated; the third, though only episodically has it attained the status of public duty, describes a value that is quite generally, and increasingly, becoming a part of our core values and an element of public responsibility. The three value commitments to which I refer are these: (1) an open process of decision making; (2) recognition of the intrinsic value of each individual; and (3) patrimonial responsibility as a public duty.

A. An Open Process of Decision Making

It is a common error to believe that an environmentally sound society is a place without significant risk or hazard. This is to miss a primary point about the premises of a democratic society which is founded on self-government. In a self-governing society, risk is acceptable so long as it is knowingly assumed. Willingness to sacrifice in a cause thought worthwhile, even to sacrifice one's life, is neither wrong nor unworthy. However, this is only true if the risk is knowingly and willingly borne. The most tragic images of environmental harm are those involving hapless victims, those who without sufficient knowledge or involvement and without choice have had risk and damage imposed upon them.

* * *

We cannot demand unanimity, but we can insist that decisions be made under conditions of sufficient knowledge and consideration so as to reflect a true choice fully appreciative of the consequences. The first environmental right, then, is the right to choose, and that is a right that has often been denied. The repeated efforts to portray environmentally risky activity as entirely benevolent has not only been a tactical error on the part of both government and private enterprise, but also has denied to the public a primary right in a democratic society—the right to determine its own destiny.

* * *

The first step is information, because without detailed knowledge of effects there is no way to make an informed decision. The specific mechanism for such information is the environmental assessment. Impact assessment is not just desirable; it is a crucial element in legitimating risky environmental decisions. But the assessment is not the only element in the informational category. Funds must be available to assure that assessments are adequate in scope and content, and a mechanism must be available to assure its fulfillment. An initial assessment does not suffice either. Knowledge of environmental impacts requires baseline data, which translates into extensive and ongoing monitoring.

A second step is the public release of information. The public will be the consumers of whatever environmental harm comes from permitted activity, and the public is entitled to know, inquire, and respond to the fullest information which can be provided. Whatever is withheld for fear of public reaction undermines the legitimacy of decisions made thereafter because self-determination by those affected is the central principle.

Finally, there is the question of public participation. How will the information gathered and then publicly disseminated be utilized so as to set the stage for an informed decision? Unless there is some effective means for the affected public to convey its responses to decision makers, and for those responses to be conscientiously considered, the requirement that the process of consent be adequately representative—so it can legitimately serve as the consent of the public—cannot be met.

There has been much debate and controversy over so-called NEPA litigation. But this process is one of the very few means by which the obligation to gather adequate information and then to subject it to careful and detailed consideration can be enforced. There are other institutions besides courts that can be organized to serve similar goals. One example is the jeopardy opinion process under the Endangered Species Act. The specific device can vary, but it is essential that some "triggering mechanism" foment a search for necessary information followed by a careful analysis done by a disinterested party.

Assume that procedures are instituted which assure full information and an adequate process for consideration and decision. Is that sufficient? Is "process" enough? Where an adequately informed public is genuinely willing to submit itself to a known risk for a known benefit, the first requirement of a fundamental right—the right to take charge of one's own destiny—is fulfilled. But there are at least two additional hurdles that must be overcome. The first arises from situations where risk, though democratically chosen as described above, is thrust upon some small segment of the population. The second is where the decision forecloses future opportunities. The following two sections of my paper take up these questions respectively.

B.   Recognition of the Intrinsic Value of Each Individual

What of risks that fall particularly heavily on certain groups or individuals: the workers in a uranium mine, neighbors of a nuclear power plant, or fishermen in a bay plied by oil tankers? Where there is an element of discrimination or invidiousness in the selection of those who are to bear special burdens, ordinary precepts of equal protection of the law can be invoked. A more common and more difficult problem is presented where no element of discrimination exists and the risks of an otherwise appropriate activity falls heavily upon relatively few individuals or groups.

The siting of potentially hazardous facilities like waste dumps or power plants presents this problem in its most familiar form. It is true that if modern industrial life is to continue, someone must be the neighbor of a hazardous waste site or power plant. The society as a whole may want the activity, but no one—understandably enough—wants to be the special target of its hazards. That is why we see such frantic maneuvering on the part of virtually every community to avoid being the chosen site for undesired facilities. Local community tactics have been widely observed, and even given an acronymic name—the NIMBY (not in my back yard) syndrome. The phenomenon is familiar enough. The question is what appropriate claims underlie the resistance of people to avoid being chosen as an area of sacrifice to the irreducible, or at least unreduced, minimum of hazard of the desired facility.

The question is whether the majority can be said to owe to each individual a basic right not to be left to fall below some minimal level of substantive protection against hazard. The question is not free from doubt, but I believe a fundamental right to a substantive entitlement which designates minimum norms should be recognized.

This is only a problem that affects some individuals more than others. Where the norm itself is lowered for everyone, *i.e.*, acceptance of a pervasive risk, it can hardly be said that any individual's right has been violated. And, as indicated above, assuming genuinely free choice, the public can, in democratic theory, accept even substantial risk if it does so with full knowledge and consent.

The source of such a claimed right may be found in the growing commitment of modern societies to provide to each individual, as an entitlement, basic means essential to make it possible to flourish as a human being. It is in response to recognition of the importance of such means, as opportunity, that states commit themselves to provide the basics of food, shelter and medical care as a public welfare responsibility, if not yet as an individual right.

It is in this setting that a claimed right of protection from environmental hazard may be considered. It seems a small step from the proposition that each individual should be entitled to needed medical care to the proposition that each individual should be entitled to living and working conditions free from unwarranted health hazards. What is the appropriate level of protection that measures whether a hazard is "unwarranted"? There is no objectively correct answer. But just as a standard is set in various countries for other affirmative elements of opportunity, *i.e.*, basic education or a decent minimum standard of housing, a standard of maximum permissible exposure to environmental hazards could be articulated in terms of a minimal standard of permissible exposure to mortal hazard. This would be no easy task; indeed it would be formidable. But, as with the problem of genuine consent, discussed above, the issue of exposure invokes fundamental value questions. Just how much can individuals be required to submit to risk as a "conscript" in the struggle to achieve the benefits of a modern society? The cognate issue of how much sacrifice of our natural resources can be hazarded is taken up in section C, below.

Two additional matters should be noted at this point. First, nothing said here suggests that there is, or should be, a particular standard that each society or nation should adopt. Affirmative rights to a level of freedom from risk would be designed to create a basic norm of opportunity so that the least advantaged individual is insulated against imposition of risk below some minimal threshold within his or her own society. Second, nothing said here suggests that an individual on a genuinely voluntary basis may not opt for a lower standard than the social norm. The determination of true voluntarism is itself a profoundly difficult subject that will not be sounded here, and one can assume that the most desperate persons are not likely to make genuinely voluntary choices, *i.e.*, toxic contamination versus unemployment and hunger But it is, nonetheless, important to emphasize that true voluntarism deserves respect in a democratic society. The test pilot who is prepared to take extraordinary risks, or the skilled worker who is willing to trade extra hazard for extra pay, are legitimate exceptions to the rule. One could imagine a rule of thumb that treated choices made by those already at the society's median or above, and opting for greater risk at higher pay, as setting a minimal standard of voluntarism.

So far I have spoken only of an individual's opportunity to flourish, but individuals are also members of communities that are central to their well-being. Where those communities are fully integrated in the dominant culture, no special problems are presented. But where one is a member of a distinctive community that has its own distinctive values, such as the native peoples in North America, a respect for the right of the individual to thrive must, of necessity, command respect for the opportunity to maintain the essential elements of that culture. This is a claim that previously only had sporadic and inconsistent recognition as a matter of right in the United

States, yet has garnered important recognition in our statutory law. Perhaps the most significant example is the legislative recognition of the right of native peoples in Alaska to maintain subsistence activities.

One important aspect of respect for distinctive communities is a demand to insulate them, at least in the absence of some compelling conflicting need, from imposed pressures of modernization and development that foment destruction of their cultural life. This is not to say that modernization should be prevented if it is desired, for self-determination is itself a central value. Rather, the goal is to assure that modernization is not imposed in ways that inevitably eradicate ways of life that such communities seek to preserve. In offering such protection, we are likely to enhance a variety of other important values: established sustaining economies may be protected from developmental forces that would uproot them; the pace of transformation of the remaining relatively pristine areas of the earth, such as tropical forests and the Alaskan tundra, may be moderated; and human and cultural diversity will be promoted, thus enriching our heritage.

C. Patrimonial Responsibility as a Public Duty

Choice is central to any idea of control over one's own destiny. Choice can be constrained by reducing the objective possibilities for choosing. By burning books considered bad, future generations are deprived the possibility of deciding for themselves what is good and bad. One of the most powerful intuitions about rights in the environmental realm appropriately grows from this sort of concern. The sense that the world is being impoverished permeates a wide range of environmental concerns, most notably in the effort to halt the decline of species. Other concerns include loss of wetlands, monocultural agricultural practices, and destruction of wilderness and ancient forests.

The notion that the deprivation of choice impairs a fundamental interest has been elegantly put forward by C.S. Lewis:

> Each generation exercises power over its successors: and each, in so far as it modifies the environment bequeathed to it and rebels against tradition, resists and limits the power of its predecessors. This modifies the picture which is sometimes painted of a progressive emancipation from tradition and a progressive control of natural processes resulting in a continual increase of human power. In reality, of course, if any one age really attains, by eugenics and scientific education, the power to make its descendants what it pleases, all men who live after it are the patients of that power. They are weaker, not stronger: for though we may have put wonderful machines in their hands we have pre-ordained how they are to use them. . . . The last men, far from being the heirs of power, will be of all men most subject to the dead hand of the great planners and conditioners and will themselves exercise least power upon the future.[20]

As the Lewis quotation should make clear, the issue is not simply leaving the earth as it is—for if that were the case, only remaining as cave dwellers would have been acceptable—but refraining from those acts that impoverish by leaving less opportunity for freedom of action and thought by those who follow us. Though all change necessarily modifies primordial nature, some changes enhance choice and opportunity. The increase of knowledge, the creation of great urban centers, and the proliferation of art also contribute to the enrichment of the world. At the same time, those practices that are heedless of biological and cultural diversity, whether in

---

[20]   C. LEWIS, THE ABOLITION OF MAN 36-37 (1947). * * *

agriculture, forestry or urbanization, reduce choice through impoverishment and thereby make those who follow the "patients of our power."

To be sure, there is no ordinary legal precept that speaks of a duty not to impoverish the world, nor is there formal recognition of social capital or patrimonial property. I suppose that in a purely technical sense we could leave an empty world to those who follow us, destroying all evidence of the accumulated knowledge of the ages, a sterile earth, with all our cities reduced to rubble. One of the more bizarre notions of Anglo-American property law is the asserted right of an owner to destroy what he owns, even if in doing so he deprives the world of something valuable and unique, such as a great work of art. * * *

There are longstanding traditions of preserving and maintaining a collective inheritance. From the ancient oral traditions passing myths and legends from one generation to the next to modern libraries and museums, canons of science, and botanical and zoological parks, the notion of safeguarding and passing on cultural capital reveals itself in many forms. Increasingly in modern times that intuition has been institutionalized and reflected in the positive law. Statutes requiring designation and preservation of historic monuments and laws safeguarding national art treasures are familiar examples, as are laws setting aside nature reserves, preserving green areas within cities, and protecting wildlife and its habitat. The public trust doctrine in American law imposes a duty upon the state to protect navigable waters and the lands beneath them for the permanent use of the public, not only for navigation and fishery but, according to more recent developments, for ecosystem protection as well.

What is all this but a recognition of a patrimonial duty—a commitment to enrich choice and opportunity not only by maintaining the variety we have received, but by also adding value to it. Perhaps the point is clearest with knowledge. It would be unthinkable to destroy that which is learned in each generation and leave our children to start anew. What is true of knowledge is no less true of the products of human labor—the pioneer farmer who aspires to leave a cultivated estate to his children or the builders of cities who aim to leave to those who follow a great metropolis. After all, the United States Constitution, it is said, was made to endure for the ages.

A general sense of a duty to maintain our capital endowment without diminution or impoverishment suggests a number of prescriptions appropriate to the endowment of the earth, the natural world. Most of these propositions are by now familiar enough, for they have been often stated, but it may be useful to restate them, this time not as a newly discovered earth ethic, but as the logical extension of a precept grounded in the preconditions of a world of genuine opportunity and choice.

The programmatic implications of a commitment not to impoverish the world might look something like the following:

> The genetic stock should be maintained essentially undiminished. The practical application is to make habitat and species preservation a primary programmatic obligation of environmental law.

> Biological diversity, with adequate representatives of various ecosystem types, should be protected. The application is establishment and maintenance of nature reserves, whether in the form of parks or refuges or biosphere reserves, as primary embodiments of our heritage.

> The stock of resources that constitutes our primary natural endowment should be conserved. The application here is a policy of sustaining yield in the management of resources, whether privately or publicly held, with the goal of undiminished productive capacity. For non-renewable resources, the now well-established notion of a heritage trust fund, consisting of income earned from mining the resource, and

committed to programs for sustaining development, provides a practical means to implement our obligation to the future.

Private rights in the natural endowment of water, soil and air can never be more than usufructuary. No one may acquire a property right to destroy or to impair the productivity of our endowment, and any rights acquired should be considered subordinate to the public trust obligation to commit these resources to the foregoing purposes.

An obligation to sustained productivity mandates that irreversible contamination of soil, water and air be avoided and where damage has occurred, a concerted effort to repair the damage inflicted in the past should be undertaken so as to restore diminished capital.

Lest the foregoing precepts be unintentionally violated, institutionalized caution is the appropriate response to perceived risk where there is incomplete knowledge.

III. CONCLUSION

Three basic precepts may thus be elicited from the central values of the modern world and adapted as the source of basic environmental rights: (1) fully informed open decision making based upon free choice, (2) protection of all at a baseline reflecting respect for every member of the society, and (3) a commitment not to impoverish the earth and narrow the possibilities of the future.

NOTES

1.   In the late 1980s, the question of whether the U.S. Constitution ought to protect environmental rights reemerged. *See* Lynton Caldwell, *NEPA Revisited: A Call for a Constitutional Amendment*, THE ENVIRONMENTAL FORUM, Nov./Dec. 1989, at 18; J. William Futrell, *Environmental Rights and the Constitution, in* BLESSINGS OF LIBERTY: THE CONSTITUTION AND THE PRACTICE OF LAW (ALI-ABA Comm. on Continuing Professional Education ed., 1988); James Krier, *The Environment, the Constitution, and the Coupling Fallacy*, LAW QUADRANGLE NOTES, Spr. 1988, at 35.

2.   As Professor Sax notes, international agreements may also be a source of environmental rights. *See* Dinah Shelton, *Human Rights, Environmental Rights, and the Right to Environment*, 28 STAN. J. INT'L L. 103 (1991). *See, e.g.,* Principle 1, RIO DECLARATION ON ENVIRONMENT AND DEVELOPMENT, U.N. Doc. A/CONF.151 (June 13, 1993) ("Human beings * * * are entitled to a healthy and productive life in harmony with nature.").

3.   Professor Sax argues that all individuals have a right to some minimum level of protection from environmental hazards. What is the baseline against which an individual would be protected? Should it depend on known or potential risks? If the latter, what level of certainty should be required? How should scientific disagreements about the level of risk be resolved? Suppose that a court finds a particular risk to fall within permissible limits. Should a party be allowed to reopen a case where new information suggests that the risks are higher than were believed at the time the case was heard?

4.   What legal tools exist to account for intergenerational equity? How do the public trust doctrine and preservation statutes work? What about the doctrine of waste in property law? Do future generations have interests that can be protected? Should future costs or benefits of environmental policies be discounted in the same way that businesses and individuals discount the value of liabilities or payments scheduled to occur in the future? The existence and content of a patrimonial obligation is hotly debated in legal, economic, and philosophical literature. *See, e.g.,* John Baden & Richard Stroup, *Transgenerational Equity and Natural Resources, in* BUREAUCRACY VS. ENVIRONMENT 203 (John Baden and Richard Stroup eds., 1981); MARK SAGOFF, THE ECONOMY OF THE EARTH 60-65 (1988); R.I. SIKORA & BRIAN BARRY (eds.), OBLIGATIONS TO FUTURE GENERATIONS (1978); EDITH BROWN WEISS, IN FAIRNESS TO FUTURE GENERATIONS: INTERNATIONAL LAW, COMMON PATRIMONY & INTERGENERATIONAL EQUITY (1989).

5.   A 1987 study issued by the United Church of Christ's Commission for Racial Injustice focused attention on the disproportionate burden minority communities bear in the siting of waste facilities and other environmental hazards. Professors Bunyan Bryant and Paul Mohai have analyzed the results of this and other studies and have found that race is "more strongly related to the incidence of pollution than income." Bunyan Bryant & Paul Mohai, *Environmental Injustice: Weighing Race and Class as Factors in the Distribution of Environmental Hazards*, 63 U. COLO. L. REV. 921, 927 (1992) (relying partly on COMMISSION FOR RACIAL INJUSTICE, TOXIC WASTES AND RACE IN THE UNITED STATES: A NATIONAL REPORT ON THE RACIAL AND SOCIO-ECONOMIC CHARACTERISTICS OF COMMUNITIES WITH HAZARDOUS WASTE SITES (1987)). Other studies dispute the conclusions of Bryant and Mohai. *See Two Reports Dispute Claims That Siting of Commercial Facilities Discriminatory*, Env't Rep. (BNA) 2100 (Apr. 15, 1994). See Richard L. Lazarus, *Pursuing "Environmental Justice": The Distributional Effects of Environmental Protection,* 87 NW. U. L. REV. 787 (1993), for an excellent overview of the categories of environmental inequity and proposals to cure these defects in environmental law.

Professor Gerald Torres and other legal scholars have termed the policies and decisionmaking processes that disproportionately burden minorities with the nation's pollution disposal problem "environmental racism." Gerald Torres, *Introduction: Understanding Environmental Racism*, 63 U. COLO. L. REV. 839 (1992) (arguing that such policies are racist in their impact and contribute to the subordination of minorities even though they may not have been implemented with racist intent). While many legal scholars use the term "environmental racism," they support different remedies for the problem. Some argue that the use of existing civil rights laws—such as the Equal Protection Clause of the Fourteenth Amendment, U.S. CONST. amend. XIV, § 1, and section 1983 of the Civil Rights Act of 1866, 42 U.S.C. § 1983 (1988)—will not remedy environmental racism because they require persons seeking relief to prove discriminatory intent. Rachel D. Godsil, Note, *Remedying Environmental Racism*, 90 MICH. L. REV. 394, 397 (1991). Recent cases show that discriminatory intent is difficult to prove in landfill siting cases. *Id.* at 410 (*East Bibb Twiggs Neighborhood Ass'n v. Macon-Bibb County*, 706 F. Supp. 880 (M.D. Ga. 1989), *aff'd*, 896 F.2d 1264 (11th Cir. 1989), and *Bean v. Southwestern Waste Management Corp.*, 482 F. Supp. 673 (S.D. Tex. 1979)). Godsil proposes new federal legislation that would allow a remedy based upon a showing of disparate impact only, without a showing of discriminatory intent. *Id.* at 421. Other authors believe that the best way to challenge environmental racism is by empowering the minority community with more authority to make siting decisions. *See* Luke W. Cole, *Remedies for Environmental Racism: A View from the Field*, 90 MICH. L. REV. 1991 (1992) (arguing that grassroots activism is a better remedy for environmental racism than new legislation because existing civil rights legislation has done a poor job of remedying other types of racism). *See also* Kevin Gover & Jana Walker, *Escaping Environmental Paternalism: One Tribe's Approach to Developing a Commercial Waste Disposal Project in Indian Country*, 63 U. COLO. L. REV. 933 (1992) (arguing that because of the economic benefits that can accompany the siting of a landfill, there are times when it makes sense for an economically depressed minority community to site a landfill in its area and that efforts by environmentalists to prevent the implementation of such a siting decision represent nothing more than arrogant, racist paternalism).

In 1994, President Clinton signed an executive order requiring federal agencies to integrate environmental justice as part of their missions, to the extent practicable and permitted by law. To implement this goal, the executive order creates an interagency working group on environmental justice to work with individual agencies to develop strategies that identify and address disproportionately high and adverse human health or environmental effects of agency programs on minority and low-income populations. Executive Order 12,898, 59 Fed. Reg. 7629 (1994). Under the terms of the Executive Order, its requirements are not enforceable in court. Nonetheless, in *In re Chemical Waste Management of Indiana*, RCRA Appeal No. 95-2, 95-3, IND 078 911 146, 25 Envtl. L. Rep. 40392 (1995), EPA's Environmental Appeals Board held that the environmental justice Executive Order could be enforced by the agency.

6. Journalist Mark Dowie argues that the diversity and inclusiveness of the environmental justice movement may save environmentalism from sliding into irrelevance. LOSING GROUND: AMERICAN ENVIRONMENTALISM AT THE CLOSE OF THE TWENTIETH CENTURY (1995). Dowie describes three waves of environmental history: the first is the conservation movement that began in the late nineteenth century; the second is the era of environmental lawmaking that began in the mid-1960s and lasted until the Reagan Administration took office in 1981; the third is the current era of "relatively fruitless" attempts at reconciliation between conservative environmentalists and corporate polluters. *Id.* at 8. Dowie hopes the fourth wave will be the heart of a new movement that broadens its constituency to include "people of color and working people" who currently feel that the establishment environmentalists threaten their security. *Id.*

2 CONSTITUTIONAL ISSUES

HODEL V. VIRGINIA SURFACE MINING & RECLAMATION ASSOCIATION

452 U.S. 264 (1981)

Justice MARSHALL delivered the opinion of the Court.

These cases arise out of a pre-enforcement challenge to the constitutionality of the Surface Mining Control and Reclamation Act of 1977 (Surface Mining Act or Act). The United States District Court for the Western District of Virginia declared several central provisions of the Act unconstitutional and permanently enjoined their enforcement. In these appeals, we consider whether Congress, in adopting the Act, exceeded its powers under the Commerce Clause of the Constitution, or transgressed affirmative limitations on the exercise of that power contained in the Fifth and Tenth Amendments. We conclude that in the context of a facial challenge, the Surface Mining Act does not suffer from any of these alleged constitutional defects, and we uphold the Act as constitutional.

I

A

The Surface Mining Act is a comprehensive statute designed to "establish a nationwide program to protect society and the environment from the adverse effects of surface coal mining operations." § 102(a). Title II of the Act creates the Office of Surface Mining Reclamation and Enforcement (OSM), within the Department of the Interior, and the Secretary of the Interior (Secretary) acting through OSM, is charged with primary responsibility for administering and implementing the Act by promulgating regulations and enforcing its provisions. The principal regulatory and enforcement provisions are contained in Title V of the Act. Section 501 establishes a two-stage program for the regulation of surface coal mining: an initial, or interim regulatory phase, and a subsequent, permanent phase. The interim program mandates immediate promulgation and federal enforcement of some of the Act's environmental protection performance standards, complemented by continuing state regulation. Under the permanent phase, a regulatory program is to be adopted for each State, mandating compliance with the full panoply of federal performance standards, with enforcement responsibility lying with either the State or Federal Government.

* * *

Under § 503, any State wishing to assume permanent regulatory authority over the surface coal mining operations on "non-Federal lands" within its borders must submit a proposed permanent program to the Secretary for his approval. The proposed program must demonstrate that the state legislature has enacted laws implementing the environmental protection standards established by the Act and accompanying regulations, and that the State has the administrative and technical ability to enforce these standards. The Secretary must approve or disapprove each such proposed program in accordance with time schedules and procedures established by §§ 503(b), (c). In addition, the Secretary must develop and implement a federal permanent program for each State that fails to submit or enforce a satisfactory state program. In such situations, the

Secretary constitutes the regulatory authority administering the Act within that State and continues as such unless and until a "state program" is approved. No later than eight months after adoption of either a state-run or federally administered permanent regulatory program for a State, all surface coal mining and reclamation operations on "non-Federal lands" within that State must obtain a new permit issued in accordance with the applicable regulatory program.

B

On October 23, 1978, the Virginia Surface Mining and Reclamation Association, Inc., an association of coal producers engaged in surface coal mining operations in Virginia, 63 of its member coal companies, and 4 individual landowners filed suit in Federal District Court seeking declaratory and injunctive relief against various provisions of the Act. The Commonwealth of Virginia and the town of Wise, Va., intervened as plaintiffs. Plaintiffs' challenge was primarily directed at Title V's performance standards. Because the permanent regulatory program was not scheduled to become effective until June 3, 1980, plaintiffs' challenge was directed at the sections of the Act establishing the interim regulatory program. Plaintiffs alleged that these provisions violate the Commerce Clause, the equal protection and due process guarantees of the Due Process Clause of the Fifth Amendment, the Tenth Amendment, and the Just Compensation Clause of the Fifth Amendment.

The District Court held a 13-day trial on plaintiffs' request for a permanent injunction. The court subsequently issued an order and opinion declaring several central provisions of the Act unconstitutional. The court rejected plaintiffs' Commerce Clause, equal protection, and substantive due process challenges to the Act. The court held, however, that the Act "operates to 'displace the States' freedom to structure integral operations in areas of traditional functions,' . . . and, therefore, is in contravention of the Tenth Amendment." [483 F. Supp. 425, 435 (1980)] quoting *National League of Cities v. Usery*, 426 U.S. 833, 852 (1976). The court also ruled that various provisions of the Act effect an uncompensated taking of private property in violation of the Just Compensation Clause of the Fifth Amendment. Finally, the court agreed with plaintiffs' due process challenges to some of the Act's enforcement provisions. The court permanently enjoined the Secretary from enforcing various provisions of the Act.

* * *

II

On cross-appeal, appellees argue that the District Court erred in rejecting their challenge to the Act as beyond the scope of congressional power under the Commerce Clause. They insist that the Act's principal goal is regulating the use of private lands within the borders of the States and not, as the District Court found, regulating the interstate commerce effects of surface coal mining. Consequently, appellees contend that the ultimate issue presented is "whether land *as such* is subject to regulation under the Commerce Clause, *i.e.*, whether land can be regarded as 'in commerce.'" In urging us to answer "no" to this question, appellees emphasize that the Court has recognized that land-use regulation is within the inherent police powers of the States and their political subdivisions, and argue that Congress may regulate land use only insofar as the Property Clause[18] grants it control over federal lands.

We do not accept either appellees' framing of the question or the answer they would have us supply. The task of a court that is asked to determine whether a particular exercise of congressional power is valid under the Commerce Clause is relatively narrow. The court must

---

[18]   The Property Clause provides: "The Congress shall have Power to dispose of and make all needful Rules and Regulations respecting the Territory or other Property belonging to the United States." U.S. Const., Art. IV, § 3, cl. 2.

defer to a congressional finding that a regulated activity affects interstate commerce, if there is any rational basis for such a finding. *Heart of Atlanta Motel, Inc. v. United States,* 379 U.S. 241, 258 (1964); *Katzenbach v. McClung,* 379 U.S. 294, 303-04 (1964). This established, the only remaining question for judicial inquiry is whether "the means chosen by [Congress] must be reasonably adapted to the end permitted by the Constitution." *Heart of Atlanta Motel, Inc. v. United States, supra,* at 262. * * *

Judicial review in this area is influenced above all by the fact that the Commerce Clause is a grant of plenary authority to Congress. This power is "complete in itself, may be exercised to its utmost extent, and acknowledges no limitations other than are prescribed in the constitution." *Gibbons v. Ogden,* 9 Wheat. 1, 196 (1824). Moreover, this Court has made clear that the commerce power extends not only to "the use of channels of interstate or foreign commerce" and to "protection of the instrumentalities of interstate commerce . . . or persons or things in commerce," but also to "activities affecting commerce." *Perez v. United States,* 402 U.S. 146, 150 (1971). As we explained in *Fry v. United States,* 421 U.S. 542, 547 (1975), "[e]ven activity that is purely intrastate in character may be regulated by Congress, where the activity, combined with like conduct by others similarly situated, affects commerce among the States or with foreign nations."

Thus, when Congress has determined that an activity affects interstate commerce, the courts need inquire only whether the finding is rational. * * * Section 101(c) recites the congressional finding that

> many surface mining operations result in disturbances of surface areas that burden and adversely affect commerce and the public welfare by destroying or diminishing the utility of land for commercial, industrial, residential, recreational, agricultural, and forestry purposes, by causing erosion and landslides, by contributing to floods, by polluting the water, by destroying fish and wildlife habitats, by impairing natural beauty, by damaging the property of citizens, by creating hazards dangerous to life and property by degrading the quality of life in local communities, and by counteracting governmental programs and efforts to conserve soil, water, and other natural resources.

The legislative record provides ample support for these statutory findings. * * *

* * *

The Committees also explained that inadequacies in existing state laws and the need for uniform minimum nationwide standards made federal regulations imperative. In light of the evidence available to Congress and the detailed consideration that the legislation received, we cannot say that Congress did not have a rational basis for concluding that surface coal mining has substantial effects on interstate commerce.

Appellees do not, in general, dispute the validity of the congressional findings. Rather, appellees' contention is that the "rational basis" test should not apply in this case because the Act regulates land use, a local activity not affecting interstate commerce. But even assuming that appellees correctly characterize the land use regulated by the Act as a "local" activity, their argument is unpersuasive.

The denomination of an activity as a "local" or "intrastate" activity does not resolve the question whether Congress may regulate it under the Commerce Clause. * * * Appellees do not dispute that coal is a commodity that moves in interstate commerce. Here, Congress rationally determined that regulation of surface coal mining is necessary to protect interstate commerce from adverse effects that may result from that activity. This congressional finding is sufficient to sustain the Act as a valid exercise of Congress' power under the Commerce Clause.

Moreover, the Act responds to a congressional finding that nationwide "surface mining and reclamation standards are essential in order to insure that competition in interstate commerce among sellers of coal produced in different States will not be used to undermine the ability of the several States to improve and maintain adequate standards on coal mining operations within their borders." 30 U.S.C. § 1201(g). The prevention of this sort of destructive interstate competition is a traditional role for congressional action under the Commerce Clause. In *United States v. Darby*, [312 U.S. 100 (1941)] the Court used a similar rationale to sustain the imposition of federal minimum wage and maximum hour regulations on a manufacturer of goods shipped in interstate commerce. * * *

Finally, we agree with the lower federal courts that have uniformly found the power conferred by the Commerce Clause broad enough to permit congressional regulation of activities causing air or water pollution, or other environmental hazards that may have effects in more than one State. * * *

* * *

In sum, we conclude that the District Court properly rejected appellees' Commerce Clause challenge to the Act. We therefore turn to the court's ruling that the Act contravenes affirmative constitutional limitations on congressional exercise of the commerce power.

III

The District Court invalidated §§ 515(d) and (e) of the Act, which prescribe performance standards for surface coal mining on "steep slopes," on the ground that they violate a constitutional limitation on the commerce power imposed by the Tenth Amendment. These provisions require "steep-slope" operators: (i) to reclaim the mined area by completely covering the highwall and returning the site to its "approximate original contour"; (ii) to refrain from dumping spoil material on the downslope below the bench or mining cut; and (iii) to refrain from disturbing land above the highwall unless permitted to do so by the regulatory authority. § 515(d). Under § 515(e), a "steep-slope" operator may obtain a variance from the approximate-original-contour requirement by showing that it will allow a post-reclamation use that is "deemed to constitute an equal or better economic or public use" than would otherwise be possible.

The District Court's ruling relied heavily on our decision in *National League of Cities v. Usery*, 426 U.S. 833 (1976). The District Court viewed the central issue as whether the Act governs the activities of private individuals, or whether it instead regulates the governmental decisions of the States. And although the court acknowledged that the Act "ultimately affects the coal mine operator," 483 F. Supp. at 432, it concluded that the Act contravenes the Tenth Amendment because it interferes with the States' "traditional governmental function" of regulating land use. The court held that, as applied to Virginia, the Act's steep-slope provisions impermissibly constrict the State's ability to make "essential decisions." The court found the Act accomplishes this result "through forced relinquishment of state control of land use planning; through loss of state control of its economy; and through economic harm, from expenditure of state funds to implement the act and from destruction of the taxing power of certain counties, cities, and towns." *Id.* at 435. The court therefore permanently enjoined enforcement of §§ 515(d) and (e).

The District Court's reliance on *National League of Cities* requires a careful review of the actual basis and import of our decision in that case. There, we considered a constitutional challenge to the 1974 amendments to the Fair Labor Standards Act which had extended federal minimum wage and maximum hour regulations to most state and local government employees. Because it was conceded that the challenged regulations were "undoubtedly within the scope of the Commerce Clause," 426 U.S. at 841, the only question presented was whether that particular exercise of the commerce power "encounter[ed] a . . . constitutional barrier because [the regulations] applied directly to the States and subdivisions of States as employers." *Ibid.* We began by drawing a sharp distinction between congressional regulation of private persons and businesses "necessarily subject to the dual sovereignty of the government of the Nation and of the State in which they reside," *Id.* at 845, and federal regulation "directed, not to private citizens, but to the States as States." *Ibid.*

    * * * [The Court] indicated that when Congress attempts to directly regulate the States as States the Tenth Amendment requires recognition that "there are attributes of sovereignty attaching to every state government which may not be impaired by Congress, not because Congress may lack an affirmative grant of legislative authority to reach the matter, but because the Constitution prohibits it from exercising the authority in that manner." *Id.* at 845. The Court held that the power to set the wages and work hours of state employees was "an undoubted attribute of state sovereignty." *Ibid.* And because it further found that the challenged regulations would "displace the States' freedom to structure integral operations in areas of traditional governmental functions," *Id.* at 852, the Court concluded that Congress could not, consistently with the Tenth Amendment, "abrogate the States' otherwise plenary authority to make [these decisions]." *Id.* at 846.

    It should be apparent from this discussion that in order to succeed, a claim that congressional commerce power legislation is invalid under the reasoning of *National League of Cities* must satisfy each of three requirements. First, there must be a showing that the challenged statute regulates the "States as States." *Id.* at 854. Second, the federal regulation must address matters that are indisputably "attribute[s] of state sovereignty." *Id.* at 845. And, third, it must be apparent that the States' compliance with the federal law would directly impair their ability "to structure integral operations in areas of traditional governmental functions." *Id.* at 852. When the Surface Mining Act is examined in light of these principles, it is clear that appellees' Tenth Amendment challenge must fail because the first of the three requirements is not satisfied. The District Court's holding to the contrary rests on an unwarranted extension of the decision in *National League of Cities*.

    As the District Court itself acknowledged, the steep-slope provisions of the Surface Mining Act govern only the activities of coal mine operators who are private individuals and businesses. Moreover, the States are not compelled to enforce the steep-slope standards, to expend any state funds, or to participate in the federal regulatory program in any manner whatsoever. If a State does not wish to submit a proposed permanent program that complies with the Act and implementing regulations, the full regulatory burden will be borne by the Federal Government. Thus, there can be no suggestion that the Act commandeers the legislative processes of the States by directly compelling them to enact and enforce a federal regulatory program. The most that can be said is that the Surface Mining Act establishes a program of cooperative federalism that allows the States, within limits established by federal minimum standards, to enact and administer their own regulatory programs, structured to meet their own particular needs. In this respect, the Act resembles a number of other federal statutes that have survived Tenth Amendment challenges in the lower federal courts.[30]

    Appellees argue, however, that the threat of federal usurpation of their regulatory roles coerces the States into enforcing the Surface Mining Act. Appellees also contend that the Act directly regulates the States as States because it establishes mandatory minimum federal standards. In essence, appellees urge us to join the District Court in looking beyond the activities

---

    [30]   See, e. g., *Friends of the Earth, Inc. v. Carey,* 552 F.2d 25, 36-39 (2d Cir.) (upholding the Clean Air Act), *cert. denied,* 434 U.S. 902 (1977); *Sierra Club v. EPA,* 540 F.2d 1114, 1140 (1976) (upholding the Clean Water Act), *cert. denied,* 430 U.S. 959 (1977).

actually regulated by the Act to its conceivable effects on the States' freedom to make decisions in areas of "integral governmental functions." And appellees emphasize, as did the court below, that the Act interferes with the States' ability to exercise their police powers by regulating land use.

Appellees' claims accurately characterize the Act insofar as it prescribes federal minimum standards governing surface coal mining, which a State may either implement itself or else yield to a federally administered regulatory program. To object to this scheme, however, appellees must assume that the Tenth Amendment limits congressional power to pre-empt or displace state regulation of private activities affecting interstate commerce. This assumption is incorrect.

A wealth of precedent attests to congressional authority to displace or pre-empt state laws regulating private activity affecting interstate commerce when these laws conflict with federal law. Moreover, it is clear that the Commerce Clause empowers Congress to prohibit all—and not just inconsistent—state regulation of such activities. Although such congressional enactments obviously curtail or prohibit the States' prerogatives to make legislative choices respecting subjects the States may consider important, the Supremacy Clause permits no other result.

* * *

Thus, Congress could constitutionally have enacted a statute prohibiting any state regulation of surface coal mining. We fail to see why the Surface Mining Act should become constitutionally suspect simply because Congress chose to allow the States a regulatory role.

* * *

This conclusion applies regardless of whether the federal legislation displaces laws enacted under the States' "police powers." The Court long ago rejected the suggestion that Congress invades areas reserved to the States by the Tenth Amendment simply because it exercises its authority under the Commerce Clause in a manner that displaces the States' exercise of their police powers. * * *

* * *

IV

The District Court held that two of the Act's provisions violate the Just Compensation Clause of the Fifth Amendment. First, the court found that the steep-slope provisions discussed above effect an uncompensated taking of private property by requiring operators to perform the "economically and physically impossible" task of restoring steep-slope surface mines to their approximate original contour. The court further held that, even if steep-slope surface mines could be restored to their approximate original contour, the value of the mined land after such restoration would have "been diminished to practically nothing." Second, the court found that § 522 of the Act effects an unconstitutional taking because it expressly prohibits mining in certain locations and "clearly prevent[s] a person from mining his own land or having it mined."[36] Relying on this Court's decision in *Pennsylvania Coal Co. v. Mahon*, 260 U.S. 393

---

[36]   With certain specified exceptions, and subject to "valid existing rights," § 522(e) prohibits surface mining operations in national parks and forests, or where they will adversely affect publicly owned parks or places that are included in the National Register of Historic Sites. It also prohibits surface mining within 100 feet of a cemetery or the right-of-way of a public road, and within 300 feet of an occupied dwelling, public building, school, church, community or institutional building, or public park. §§ 522(e)(4) and (5).

Sections 522(a), (c), and (d), which become applicable during the permanent phase of the regulatory program, require the establishment of procedures for designating particular lands as unsuitable for some or all surface mining. * * *

(1922), the District Court held that both of these provisions are unconstitutional because they "depriv[e] [coal mine operators] of any use of [their] land, not only the most profitable . . .."

We conclude that the District Court's ruling on the "taking" issue suffers from a fatal deficiency: neither appellees nor the court identified any property in which appellees have an interest that has allegedly been taken by operation of the Act. By proceeding in this fashion, the court below ignored this Court's oft-repeated admonition that the constitutionality of statutes ought not be decided except in an actual factual setting that makes such a decision necessary. Adherence to this rule is particularly important in cases raising allegations of an unconstitutional taking of private property. Just last Term, we reaffirmed that

> "this Court has generally 'been unable to develop any "set formula" for determining when "justice and fairness" require that economic injuries caused by public action be compensated by the government, rather than remain disproportionately concentrated on a few persons.' Rather, it has examined the 'taking' question by engaging in essentially ad hoc, factual inquiries that have identified several factors—such as the economic impact of the regulation, its interference with reasonable investment backed expectations, and the character of the government action—that have particular significance."

Kaiser Aetna v. United States, 444 U.S. 164 (1979) (citations omitted).

These "ad hoc, factual inquiries" must be conducted with respect to specific property, and the particular estimates of economic impact and ultimate valuation relevant in the unique circumstances.

Because appellees' taking claim arose in the context of a facial challenge, it presented no concrete controversy concerning either application of the Act to particular surface mining operations or its effect on specific parcels of land. Thus, the only issue properly before the District Court and, in turn, this Court, is whether the "mere enactment" of the Surface Mining Act constitutes a taking. The test to be applied in considering this facial challenge is fairly straightforward. A statute regulating the uses that can be made of property effects a taking if it "denies an owner economically viable use of his land . . .." *Agins v. Tiburon,* 447 U.S. 255, 260 (1980). The Surface Mining Act easily survives scrutiny under this test.

First, the Act does not, on its face, prevent beneficial use of coal-bearing lands. Except for the proscription of mining near certain locations by § 522(e), the Act does not categorically prohibit surface coal mining; it merely regulates the conditions under which such operations may be conducted.[37] The Act does not purport to regulate alternative uses to which coal-bearing lands may be put. Thus, in the posture in which these cases come before us, there is no reason to suppose that "mere enactment" of the Surface Mining Act has deprived appellees of economically viable use of their property.

Moreover, appellees cannot at this juncture legitimately raise complaints in this Court about the manner in which the challenged provisions of the Act have been or will be applied in specific circumstances, or about their effect on particular coal mining operations. There is no indication in the record that appellees have availed themselves of the opportunities provided by the Act to obtain administrative relief by requesting either a variance from the approximate-original-contour requirement of § 515(d) or a waiver from the surface mining restrictions in

---

[37]   Although § 522(e) prohibits any surface coal mining in certain areas, appellees' "taking" challenge to this provision is premature. First, appellees made no showing in the District Court that they own tracts of land that are affected by this provision. Second, § 522(e) does not, on its face, deprive owners of land within its reach of economically viable use of their land since it does not proscribe nonmining uses of such land. Third, § 522(e)'s restrictions are expressly made subject to "valid existing rights." * * *

§ 522(e). If appellees were to seek administrative relief under these procedures, a mutually acceptable solution might well be reached with regard to individual properties, thereby obviating any need to address the constitutional questions. The potential for such administrative solutions confirms the conclusion that the taking issue decided by the District Court simply is not ripe for judicial resolution.

V
A

The District Court next ruled that the Act contravenes the Fifth Amendment because a number of its enforcement provisions offend the Amendment's Due Process Clause. One such provision is § 521(a)(2), which instructs the Secretary immediately to order total or partial cessation of a surface mining operation whenever he determines, on the basis of a federal inspection, that the operation is in violation of the Act or a permit condition required by the Act and that the operation "creates an immediate danger to the health or safety of the public, or is causing, or can reasonably be expected to cause significant, imminent environmental harm to land, air, or water resources . . .." A mine operator aggrieved by an immediate cessation order issued under § 521(a)(2) or by a cessation order issued after a notice of violation and expiration of an abatement period under § 521(a)(3) may immediately request temporary relief from the Secretary, and the Secretary must respond to the request within five days of its receipt. Section 526(c) of the Act authorizes judicial review of a decision by the Secretary denying temporary relief. In addition, cessation orders are subject to informal administrative review under § 521(a)(5), and formal administrative review, including an adjudicatory hearing, under § 525(b). The Secretary's decision in the formal review proceeding is subject to judicial review pursuant to § 526(a)(2).

* * *

Our cases have indicated that due process ordinarily requires an opportunity for "some kind of hearing" prior to the deprivation of a significant property interest. The Court has often acknowledged, however, that summary administrative action may be justified in emergency situations. The question then, is whether the issuance of immediate cessation orders under § 521(a) falls under this emergency situation exception to the normal rule that due process requires a hearing prior to deprivation of a property right. We believe that it does.

The immediate cessation order provisions reflect Congress' concern about the devastating damage that may result from mining disasters. They represent an attempt to reach an accommodation between the legitimate desire of mining companies to be heard before submitting to administrative regulation and the governmental interest in protecting the public health and safety and the environment from imminent danger. Protection of the health and safety of the public is a paramount governmental interest which justifies summary administrative action. Indeed, deprivation of property to protect the public health and safety is "[o]ne of the oldest examples" of permissible summary action. Moreover, the administrative action provided through immediate cessation orders responds to situations in which swift action is necessary to protect the public health and safety. This is precisely the type of emergency situation in which this Court has found summary administrative action justified.

Rather than taking issue with any of these principles, the District Court held that the Act does not establish sufficiently objective criteria governing the issuance of summary cessation orders. We disagree. In our judgment, the criteria established by the Act and the Secretary's implementing regulations are specific enough to control governmental action and reduce the risk of erroneous deprivation. Section 701(8) of the Act defines the threat of "imminent danger to the health and safety of the public" as the existence of a condition or practice which could "[r]easonably be expected to cause substantial physical harm to persons outside the permit area before such condition, practice, or violation can be abated. A reasonable expectation of death or serious injury before abatement exists if a rational person, subjected to the same conditions or practices giving rise to the peril, would not expose himself or herself to the danger during the time necessary for abatement."[45] If anything, these standards are more specific than the criteria in other statutes authorizing summary administrative action that have been upheld against due process challenges. * * *

* * * Here, mine operators are afforded prompt and adequate post-deprivation administrative hearings and an opportunity for judicial review. We are satisfied that the Act's immediate cessation order provisions comport with the requirements of due process.

* * *

VI

Our examination of appellees' constitutional challenges to the Surface Mining Act persuades us that the Act is not vulnerable to their pre-enforcement challenge. Accordingly, we affirm the judgment of the District Court upholding the Act against appellees' Commerce Clause attack, and we reverse the judgment below insofar as it held various provisions of the Act unconstitutional. The cases are remanded to the District Court with instructions to dissolve the injunction issued against the Secretary, and for further proceedings consistent with this opinion.

So ordered.

* * *

Justice POWELL, concurring.

The Surface Mining Act mandates an extraordinarily intrusive program of federal regulation and control of land use and land reclamation, activities normally left to state and local governments. But the decisions of this Court over many years make clear that, under the Commerce Clause, Congress has the power to enact this legislation.

The Act could affect seriously the owners and lessees of the land and coal in the seven westernmost counties of Virginia. The Federal Government is required by the Fifth Amendment to pay just compensation for any "taking" of private property for public use. But whether there has been such a "taking" and, if so, the amount of just compensation, are questions to be decided in specific cases. I agree with the Court, therefore, that it is premature to consider in these cases questions under the Compensation Clause. * * *

I add a word about the area of Virginia that will be affected by this Act, as its location, topography, and geology are highly relevant to an understanding of the "taking" question. Bituminous coal, Virginia's most valuable natural resource, is found in a region marked by steep

---

[45]   The Secretary's regulations define "a significant, imminent environmental harm" in the following terms:

(a)   An environmental harm is any adverse impact on land, air, or water resources, which resources include, but are not limited to, plant and animal life.

(b)   An environmental harm is imminent, if a condition, practice, or violation exists which—(1) Is causing such harm, or, (2) May reasonably be expected to cause such harm at any time before the end of the reasonable abatement time that would be set under Section 521(a)(3) of the Act.

(c)   An environmental harm is significant if that harm is appreciable and not immediately reparable.

30 CFR §§ 700.5 and 701.5 (1980).

mountain slopes, sharp ridges, massive outcrops of rock, and narrow valleys—conditions that severely limit alternative uses of the land. Because of thin soil and rugged terrain, the land in its natural state is not suited for agricultural use or the growing of merchantable timber. Its value lies, in most instances, solely in its coal. Mining the coal is a major industrial activity in an otherwise impoverished area of Virginia.

A number of the Act's provisions appear to have been written with little comprehension of its potential effect on this rugged area. For example, the requirement in § 515(d) that steep-slope areas be restored approximately to their original contours seems particularly unrealistic. As the District Court found, 95% of the strippable coal lands in Virginia are located on slopes in excess of 20 degrees. The cost of restoration in some situations could exceed substantially the value of the coal. In any event restoring steep mountain slopes often would diminish rather than increase the land's worth.

In sum, if the Act is implemented broadly in accordance with its terms, the consequences to individual lessees and owners, and to the area as a whole, could be far-reaching. But adjudication of claims arising from such implementation is for the future. I agree with the Court that we cannot say that the Act is facially invalid, and I therefore join its opinion.

Justice REHNQUIST, concurring in the judgment.

It is illuminating for purposes of reflection, if not for argument, to note that one of the greatest "fictions" of our federal system is that the Congress exercises only those powers delegated to it, while the remainder are reserved to the States or to the people. The manner in which this Court has construed the Commerce Clause amply illustrates the extent of this fiction. Although it is clear that the people, through the States, delegated authority to Congress to "regulate Commerce . . . among the several States," U.S. Const., Art. I, § 8, cl. 3, one could easily get the sense from this Court's opinions that the federal system exists only at the sufferance of Congress.

As interpreted by the Court, Congress' power under the Commerce Clause is broad indeed. The power has evolved through the years to include not simply the regulation of interstate commerce itself, as in *Gibbons v. Ogden,* 9 Wheat. 1 (1824), but also the power "to *exclude* from the commerce articles whose use in the states for which they are destined it may conceive to be injurious to the public health, morals or welfare, even though the state has not sought to regulate their use." *United States v. Darby,* 312 U.S. 100, 114 (1941). * * * And in *Wickard v. Filburn,* 317 U.S. 111 (1942), the Court expanded the scope of the Commerce Clause to include the regulation of acts which taken alone might not have a substantial economic effect on interstate commerce, such as a wheat farmer's own production, but which might reasonably be deemed nationally significant in their cumulative effect, such as altering the supply-and-demand relationships in the interstate commodity market. As summarized by one commentator: "In recent years, Congress has relied upon the 'cumulative effect' principle as its constitutional justification for civil rights legislation, certain criminal statutes, regulatory measures affecting the sale of foods and additives, and a registration law for drug producers. In each case, congressional fact-findings stressed that the regulation of local incidents of an activity was necessary to abate a cumulative evil affecting national commerce." L. TRIBE, AMERICAN CONSTITUTIONAL LAW 237 (1978).

Despite the holdings of these cases, and the broad dicta often contained therein, there *are* constitutional limits on the power of Congress to regulate pursuant to the Commerce Clause. * * *

* * *

Thus it would be a mistake to conclude that Congress' power to regulate pursuant to the Commerce Clause is unlimited. Some activities may be so private or local in nature that they simply may not be *in* commerce. Nor is it sufficient that the person or activity reached have *some* nexus with interstate commerce. Our cases have consistently held that the regulated activity must have a *substantial* effect on interstate commerce. Moreover, simply because Congress may conclude that a particular activity substantially affects interstate commerce does not necessarily make it so. Congress' findings must be supported by a "rational basis" and are reviewable by the courts. In short, unlike the reserved police powers of the States, which are plenary unless challenged as violating some specific provision of the Constitution, the connection with interstate commerce is itself a jurisdictional prerequisite for any substantive legislation by Congress under the Commerce Clause.

* * * Though there can be no doubt that Congress in regulating surface mining has stretched its authority to the "nth degree," our prior precedents compel me to agree with the Court's conclusion. I therefore concur in the judgments of the Court.

There is, however, a troublesome difference between what the Court does and what it says. In both cases, the Court asserts that regulation will be upheld if Congress had a rational basis for finding that the regulated activity affects interstate commerce. The Court takes this statement of the proper "test" from *Heart of Atlanta Motel, Inc. v. United States,* 379 U.S. 241 (1964). In my view, the Court misstates the test. As noted above, it has long been established that the commerce power does not reach activity which merely "affects" interstate commerce. There must instead be a showing that regulated activity has a *substantial effect* on that commerce. * * *

In sum, my difficulty with some of the recent Commerce Clause jurisprudence is that the Court often seems to forget that legislation enacted by Congress is subject to two different kinds of challenge, while that enacted by the States is subject to only one kind of challenge. Neither Congress nor the States may act in a manner prohibited by any provision of the Constitution. Congress must show that the activity it seeks to regulate has a substantial effect on interstate commerce. It is my uncertainty as to whether the Court intends to broaden, by some of its language, this test that leads me to concur only in the judgments.

NOTES

1. *Wickard v. Filburn,* 317 U.S. 111 (1942), contains one of the broadest statements of the Commerce Clause authority. That case involved a challenge to the Agricultural Adjustment Act, which, among other things, allowed the Secretary of Agriculture to set quotas for wheat sold interstate and intrastate, as well as for the amount of wheat that could be consumed on a farm. Filburn, a farmer, claimed that his growing wheat for use on his farm was a "local activity" and therefore was beyond federal control. The Court, however, held that the cumulative effect of home consumption of wheat could affect the wheat market, which was a concern reasonably related to protecting interstate commerce. How is *Wickard* relevant to the study of environmental law? Can any form of federal regulation of the environment escape the broad reach of the Commerce Clause as construed by the Supreme Court?

2. Did then-Justice Rehnquist support the majority's interpretation of the Commerce Clause in *Virginia Surface Mining & Reclamation Ass'n*? Why does he concur?

In 1995, Chief Justice Rehnquist wrote the 5-4 majority opinion in *United States v. Lopez*, 514 U.S. 549, which found, for the first time since the New Deal, that Congress had exceeded its Commerce Clause authority. *Lopez* ruled unconstitutional the Gun-Free School Zones Act, which criminalized the possession of a firearm in school zones in an effort to quell violence and improve educational achievement in schools. *Lopez* stressed, consistent with the Rehnquist concurrence in *Virginia Surface Mining*, that a regulated activity must *substantially* affect interstate commerce, unless it is itself a channel or instrumentality of interstate commerce. The majority stated that the Act

> is a criminal statute that by its terms has nothing to do with "commerce" or any sort of economic enterprise, however broadly one might define those terms. [It] is not an essential part of a larger regulation of economic activity, in which the regulatory scheme could be undercut unless the intrastate activity were regulated. It cannot, therefore, be sustained under our cases upholding regulations of activities that arise out of or are connected with a commercial transaction, which viewed in the aggregate, substantially affects interstate commerce.

514 U.S. at 561.

In his dissent, Justice Breyer criticized this distinction between commercial and noncommercial activities as overly formulaic and indeterminate. How might the *Lopez* decision affect Congress' authority to enact environmental protection legislation?

3. How does filling in a wetland, which is subject to regulation under the Clean Water Act, 33 U.S.C. §§ 1311a & 1344a, "affect" commerce? *See United States v. Riverside Bayview Homes, Inc.*, 474 U.S. 121 (1985) (upholding application of the Act to nonnavigable wetlands adjacent to navigable waters); *United States v. Holland*, 373 F. Supp. 665 (M.D. Fla. 1974) (discussing Congress' Commerce Clause authority to regulate water pollution). Although subsequently vacated, Judge Manion's opinion in *Hoffman Homes, Inc. v. United States Environmental Protection Agency*, 961 F.2d 1310 (7th Cir. 1992), *vacated*, 975 F.2d 1554 (7th Cir. 1992) (en banc), *rehearing decided*, 999 F.2d 256 (7th Cir. 1993), offers a more skeptical view of the relationship between filling wetlands and interstate commerce. *See generally*, Stephen M. Johnson, *Federal Regulation of Isolated Wetlands,* 23 ENVTL. L. 1 (1993). Should it matter whether the wetland destruction occurred in the course of a traditional commercial activity, such as logging, or occurred as an indirect effect of construction of an addition to a single-family residential home? *See* 60 Fed. Reg. 38662 (1995) (Nationwide General Permit for Single-Family Residential Housing Activities).

4. The Commerce Clause is the most common constitutional basis for federal environmental regulation because the Court construes the commerce power so broadly. However, Congress has other sources of authority to legislate in the environmental area. Congress can use the Treaty Clause, U.S. CONST. art. II, § 2, cl. 2, as a basis for enacting laws under the Necessary and Proper Clause, U.S. CONST. art. I, § 8, cl. 18. *See, e.g.,* Migratory Bird Treaty Act, 16 U.S.C. §§ 703-12; Endangered Species Act, 16 U.S.C. §§ 1531-43. Other legislation relies on the Property Clause, U.S. CONST. art. IV, § 3, cl. 2. *See, e.g.,* the National Forest Management Act, 16 U.S.C. §§ 1600-04, and the Federal Land Policy and Management Act, 43 U.S.C. §§ 1701-82.

5.   The Tenth Amendment to the United States Constitution has spawned a surprising amount of controversy in recent years. The amendment simply states that "[t]he powers not delegated to the United States by the Constitution, nor prohibited by it to the States, are reserved to the States respectively, or to the people." For many years, the Amendment was treated by the Court as a "truism" simply stating "that all is retained which has not been surrendered." *United States v. Darby*, 312 U.S. 100, 124 (1941). In *National League of Cities v. Usery*, 426 U.S. 833 (1976), however, the Supreme Court by a 5-4 majority struck down certain provisions of the Fair Labor Standards Act which applied minimum wage and maximum hour provisions to state and local government employees, as an unwarranted interference on state sovereignty, which was prohibited by the Tenth Amendment. The unanimous decision in *Hodel* signaled that the Court was not inclined to extend *National League of Cities* beyond the narrow confines of that case; and indeed, *National League of Cities* was itself overturned in another 5-4 decision, *Garcia v. San Antonio Metro. Transit Auth.*, 469 U.S. 528 (1985).

Subsequently however, in *New York v. United States*, 505 U.S. 144 (1992), the Court made clear that the Tenth Amendment would continue to wield influence with respect to issues of federalism, which often arise in federal environmental legislation. *New York* involved a challenge to certain provisions of the Low-Level Radioactive Waste Policy Amendments Act of 1985, 42 U.S.C. §§ 2021b *et seq.*, that encouraged states to address the disposal of low level radioactive wastes generated within their borders. Three particular provisions were at issue. The first allowed states with disposal sites to impose a surcharge on wastes generated in other states. The second allowed states to deny other states access to their disposal sites, if those states failed to meet certain deadlines imposed under the Act. Finally, states which failed to address the disposal of domestic low-level wastes as required by the law would be required after January 1, 1996 to take title of those wastes upon the request of the generator and be held liable for all damages resulting from the state's failure to take timely possession of the wastes. The Court had no trouble upholding the first two provisions under a traditional Commerce Clause analysis. However, it found the "take title" provisions unconstitutional because they had "commandee[red] the legislative processes of the States by directly compelling them to enact and enforce a federal regulatory program." 505 U.S. at 161 (quoting *Hodel*, 452 U.S. at 288). According to Justice O'Connor, this provision "crossed the line distinguishing encouragement from coercion." *Id.* at 175. How does the "take title" provision at issue in the *New York* case differ from the "steep slope" provisions in the *Hodel* case that were sustained by the Court against a Tenth Amendment challenge?

Relying on *New York*, an appeals court found unconstitutional provisions of the Forest Resources Conservation and Shortage Relief Act, 16 U.S.C. §§ 620-620j, which restrict exports of unprocessed timber harvested from western federal and state public lands. *Board of Natural Resources v. Brown*, 992 F.2d 937 (9th Cir. 1993). The court held that sections of the Act requiring states to issue regulations implementing the export ban violated the Tenth Amendment. In *ACORN v. Edwards*, 81 F.3d 1387 (5th Cir. 1996), the court found a violation of the Tenth Amendment in a provision of the Federal Lead Contamination Control Act that required states to test for and remove lead contamination in public school drinking water.

6.   The *New York* opinion made clear that Congress can always exercise its authority under the Supremacy Clause, U.S. CONST. art VI, cl. 2, to preempt state regulation of waste or any other area subject to the Commerce Clause. 505 U.S. at 167. Because Congress seldom explicitly preempts state law, most preemption cases turn on implicit intent. The Court will find implicit federal preemption where: (1) a scheme of federal regulation is so pervasive as to leave little room for states to supplement it; (2) the federal interest is so dominant that the federal system precludes enforcement of state laws on the same subject; or (3) a federal statute's goals or obligations imposed reveal a purpose to preclude state authority. *Wisconsin Pub. Intervenor v. Mortier*, 501 U.S. 597, 603-04 (1991) (upholding local regulation of pesticides more restrictive than required by the Federal Insecticide, Fungicide, and Rodenticide Act, 7 U.S.C. §§ 136-136y). Although states enjoy a presumption that their police powers are not preempted unless the clear and manifest purpose of Congress is to the contrary, preemption may occur in the absence of Congressional intent where a state law actually conflicts with a federal law. 501 U.S. at 605.

Gade v. National Solid Wastes Management Ass'n, 505 U.S. 88 (1992), held that the Occupational Safety and Health Act, 29 U.S.C. §§ 651 *et seq.*, which authorizes the Secretary of Labor to promulgate standards for employees engaged in hazardous waste operations, preempted aspects of Illinois laws providing for training, testing, and licensing of hazardous waste site workers. A plurality of the Court looked to the effect of the state regulation, rather than to its purpose, to find implicit preemption.

7.   Agencies generally act by rule and by order. Because rules apply broadly to all affected persons, the promulgation of rules does not generally give rise to any right to be heard. *See Vermont Yankee Nuclear Power Corp. v. Natural Resources Defense Council*, 435 U.S. 519 (1978); *Bi-Metallic Investment Co. v. State Board of Equalization*, 239 U.S. 441 (1915). By contrast, when an agency acts by order in individual cases, due process requirements frequently apply, *Londoner v. Denver*, 210 U.S. 373 (1908), although as the *Hodel* case suggests, the amount of process that is due may well depend on the circumstances.

8.   In an omitted portion of the *Hodel* opinion, the Court vacated the district court's ruling that § 518(c) of the Surface Mining Act was unconstitutional. That provision requires a mine operator who is cited for a violation of the law to deposit the amount of any proposed civil penalty into an escrow account as a condition for obtaining a hearing on the charges. Since no plaintiff alleged that any such penalties had been assessed against them, the Court found that the claim was not ripe for review. Subsequently, several Courts of Appeal have upheld § 518(c) even in the case where the mine operator alleged that it lacked the resources to pay the proposed fine. *See Graham v. Office of Surface Mining*, 722 F.2d 1106, 1111 (3d Cir. 1983); *Blackhawk Mining Co. v. Andrus*, 711 F.2d 753 (6th Cir. 1983); *B & M Coal Corp. v. Office of Surface Mining*, 699 F.2d 381 (7th Cir. 1983). In each case, the court emphasized that certain procedures to contest the violation and the penalty amount were available to the operator before payment of the proposed penalty was required.

Even though the Commerce Clause is now construed to grant almost limitless power to Congress, bear in mind that, in its "dormant" state, it may impose very real limits on state environmental regulation which interferes with interstate commerce.

CHEMICAL WASTE MANAGEMENT, INC. V. HUNT
504 U.S. 334 (1992)

Justice WHITE delivered the opinion of the Court.

Alabama imposes a hazardous waste disposal fee on hazardous wastes generated outside the State and disposed of at a commercial facility in Alabama. The fee does not apply to such waste having a source in Alabama. The Alabama Supreme Court held that this differential treatment does not violate the Commerce Clause. We reverse.

I

Petitioner, Chemical Waste Management, Inc., a Delaware corporation with its principal place of business in Oak Brook, Illinois, owns and operates one of the Nation's oldest commercial hazardous waste land disposal facilities, located in Emelle, Alabama. Opened in 1977 and acquired by petitioner in 1978, the Emelle facility is a hazardous waste treatment, storage, and disposal facility operating pursuant to permits issued by the Environmental Protection Agency (EPA) under the Resource Conservation and Recovery Act of 1976 (RCRA), 42 U.S.C. § 6901 *et seq.*, and the Toxic Substances Control Act, 15 U.S.C. § 2601 *et seq.* (1988 ed. and Supp. II), and by the State of Alabama under Ala. Code § 22-30-12(i) (1990). Alabama is 1 of only 16 States that have commercial hazardous waste landfills, and the Emelle facility is the largest of the 21 landfills of this kind located in these 16 States.

The parties do not dispute that the wastes and substances being landfilled at the Emelle facility "include substances that are inherently dangerous to human health and safety and to the environment. Such waste consists of ignitable, corrosive, toxic and reactive wastes which contain poisonous and cancer causing chemicals and which can cause birth defects, genetic damage, blindness, crippling and death." 584 So.2d 1367, 1373 (1991). Increasing amounts of out-of-state hazardous wastes are shipped to the Emelle facility for permanent storage each year. From 1985 through 1989, the tonnage of hazardous waste received per year has more than doubled, increasing from 341,000 tons in 1985 to 788,000 tons by 1989. Of this, up to 90% of the tonnage permanently buried each year is shipped in from other States.

Against this backdrop Alabama enacted Act No. 90-326 (the Act). Ala. Code §§ 22-30B-1 to 22-30B-18 (1990 and Supp.1991). Among other provisions, the Act includes a "cap" that generally limits the amount of hazardous wastes or substances that may be disposed of in any 1-year period, and the amount of hazardous waste disposed of during the first year under the Act's new fees becomes the permanent ceiling in subsequent years. Ala. Code § 22-30B-2.3 (1990). The cap applies to commercial facilities that dispose of over 100,000 tons of hazardous wastes or substances per year, but only the Emelle facility, as the only commercial facility operating within Alabama, meets this description. The Act also imposes a "base fee" of $25.60 per ton on all hazardous wastes and substances disposed of at commercial facilities, to be paid by the operator of the facility. Ala. Code § 22-30B-2(a) (Supp.1991). Finally, the Act imposes the "additional fee" at issue here, which states in full: "For waste and substances which are generated outside of Alabama and disposed of at a commercial site for the disposal of hazardous waste or hazardous substances in Alabama, an additional fee shall be levied at the rate of $72.00 per ton." § 22-30B-2(b).

* * *

II

No State may attempt to isolate itself from a problem common to the several States by raising barriers to the free flow of interstate trade. Today, in *Fort Gratiot Sanitary Landfill, Inc. v. Michigan Dept. of Natural Resources*, 112 S. Ct. 2019 (1992), we have also considered a Commerce Clause challenge to a Michigan law prohibiting private landfill operators from accepting solid waste originating outside the county in which their facilities operate. In striking down that law, we adhered to our decision in *Philadelphia v. New Jersey*, 437 U.S. 617 (1978), where we found New Jersey's prohibition of solid waste from outside that State to amount to economic protectionism barred by the Commerce Clause:

> [T]he evil of protectionism can reside in legislative means as well as legislative ends. Thus, it does not matter whether the ultimate aim of ch. 363 is to reduce the waste disposal costs of New Jersey residents or to save remaining open lands from pollution, for we assume New Jersey has every right to protect its residents' pocketbooks as well as their environment. And it may be assumed as well that New Jersey may pursue those ends by slowing the flow of all waste into the State's remaining landfills, even though interstate commerce may incidentally be affected. But whatever New Jersey's ultimate purpose, it may not be accompanied by discriminating against articles of commerce coming from outside the State unless there is some reason, apart from their origin, to treat them differently. Both on its face and in its plain effect, ch. 363 violates this principle of nondiscrimination." The Court has consistently found parochial legislation of this kind to be constitutionally invalid, whether the ultimate aim of the legislation was to assure a steady supply of milk by erecting barriers to allegedly ruinous outside competition or to create jobs by keeping industry within the State; or to preserve the State's financial resources from depletion by fencing out indigent immigrants.

Fort Gratiot Sanitary Landfill, 112 S. Ct. at 2024 (quoting *Philadelphia v. New Jersey*, 437 U.S. at 626-27). To this list may be added cases striking down a tax discriminating against interstate commerce, even where such tax was designed to encourage the use of ethanol and thereby reduce harmful exhaust emissions, *New Energy Co. of Ind. v. Limbach*, 486 U.S. 269, 279 (1988), or to support inspection of foreign cement to ensure structural integrity, *Hale v. Bimco Trading, Inc.*, 306 U.S. 375, 379-80 (1939). For in all of these cases, "a presumably legitimate goal was sought to be achieved by the illegitimate means of isolating the State from the national economy." *Philadelphia v. New Jersey*, 437 U.S. at 627.

The Act's additional fee facially discriminates against hazardous waste generated in States other than Alabama, and the Act overall has plainly discouraged the full operation of petitioner's Emelle facility. Such burdensome taxes imposed on interstate commerce alone are generally forbidden: "[A] State may not tax a transaction or incident more heavily when it crosses state lines than when it occurs entirely within the State." *Armco Inc. v. Hardesty*, 467 U.S. 638, 642, (1984). Once a state tax is found to discriminate against out-of-state commerce, it is typically struck down without further inquiry.

The State, however, argues that the additional fee imposed on out-of-state hazardous waste serves legitimate local purposes related to its citizens' health and safety. Because the additional fee discriminates both on its face and in practical effect, the burden falls on the State "to justify it both in terms of the local benefits flowing from the statute and the unavailability of nondiscriminatory alternatives adequate to preserve the local interests at stake." *Hunt v. Washington Apple Advertising Comm'n*, 432 U.S. 333, 353 (1977). "At a minimum such facial discrimination invokes the strictest scrutiny of any purported legitimate local purpose and of the absence of nondiscriminatory alternatives." *Hughes v. Oklahoma*, 441 U.S. 322, 337 (1979).

The State's argument here does not significantly differ from the Alabama Supreme Court's conclusions on the legitimate local purposes of the additional fee imposed, which were:

> "The Additional Fee serves these legitimate local purposes that cannot be adequately served by reasonable nondiscriminatory alternatives: (1) protection of the health and safety of the citizens of Alabama from toxic substances; (2) conservation of the environment and the state's natural resources; (3) provision for compensatory revenue for the costs and burdens that out-of-state waste generators impose by dumping their hazardous waste in Alabama; (4) reduction of the overall flow of wastes traveling on the state's highways, which flow creates a great risk to the health and safety of the state's citizens." 584 So.2d at 1389.

These may all be legitimate local interests, and petitioner has not attacked them. But only rhetoric, and not explanation, emerges as to why Alabama targets only interstate hazardous waste to meet these goals. As found by the Trial Court, "[a]lthough the Legislature imposed an additional fee of $72.00 per ton on waste generated outside Alabama, there is absolutely no evidence before this Court that waste generated outside Alabama is more dangerous than waste generated in Alabama. The Court finds under the facts of this case that the only basis for the additional fee is the origin of the waste." In the face of such findings, invalidity under the Commerce Clause necessarily follows, for "whatever [Alabama's] ultimate purpose, it may not be accomplished by discriminating against articles of commerce coming from outside the State unless there is some reason, apart from their origin, to treat them differently." *Philadelphia v. New Jersey*, 437 U.S. at 626-27; *see New Energy Co.*, 486 U.S. at 279-80. The burden is on the State to show that "the discrimination is demonstrably justified by a valid factor unrelated to economic protectionism," *Wyoming v. Oklahoma*, 112 S. Ct. 789, 801 (1992), and it has not carried this burden.

Ultimately, the State's concern focuses on the volume of the waste entering the Emelle facility. Less discriminatory alternatives, however, are available to alleviate this concern, not the least of which are a generally applicable per-ton additional fee on all hazardous waste disposed of within Alabama, *cf. Commonwealth Edison Co. v. Montana*, 453 U.S. 609, 619 (1981), or a per-mile tax on all vehicles transporting hazardous waste across Alabama roads, *cf. American Trucking Assns., Inc. v. Scheiner*, 483 U.S. 266, 286 (1987), or an evenhanded cap on the total tonnage landfilled at Emelle, *see Philadelphia v. New Jersey*, 437 U.S. at 626, which would curtail volume from all sources. To the extent Alabama's concern touches environmental conservation and the health and safety of its citizens, such concern does not vary with the point of origin of the waste, and it remains within the State's power to monitor and regulate more closely the transportation and disposal of all hazardous waste within its borders. Even with the possible future financial and environmental risks to be borne by Alabama, such risks likewise do not vary with the waste's State of origin in a way allowing foreign, but not local, waste to be burdened. In sum, we find the additional fee to be "an obvious effort to saddle those outside the State" with most of the burden of slowing the flow of waste into the Emelle facility. *Philadelphia v. New Jersey*, 437 U.S. at 629. "That legislative effort is clearly impermissible under the Commerce Clause of the Constitution." *Ibid.*

* * *

III

The decision of the Alabama Supreme Court is reversed, and the cause remanded for proceedings not inconsistent with this opinion, including consideration of the appropriate relief to petitioner.

So ordered.

Chief Justice REHNQUIST, dissenting.

I have already had occasion to set out my view that States need not ban all waste disposal as a precondition to protecting themselves from hazardous or noxious materials brought across the State's borders. *See Philadelphia v. New Jersey*, 437 U.S. 617, 629 (1978) (REHNQUIST, J., dissenting). In a case also decided today, I express my further view that States may take actions legitimately directed at the preservation of the State's natural resources, even if those actions incidentally work to disadvantage some out-of-state waste generators. *See Fort Gratiot Sanitary Landfill, Inc. v. Michigan Dept. of Natural Resources*, 112 S. Ct. 2019 (1992) (REHNQUIST, C.J., dissenting). I dissent today, largely for the reasons I have set out in those two cases. Several additional comments that pertain specifically to this case, though, are in order.

Taxes are a recognized and effective means for discouraging the consumption of scarce commodities—in this case the safe environment that attends appropriate disposal of hazardous wastes. *Cf.* 26 U.S.C.A. §§ 4681, 4682 (Supp.1992) (tax on ozone-depleting chemicals); 26 U.S.C. § 4064 (gas guzzler excise tax). I therefore see nothing unconstitutional in Alabama's use of a tax to discourage the export of this commodity to other States, when the commodity is a public good that Alabama has helped to produce. *Cf. Fort Gratiot*, 112 S. Ct. at 2029 (REHNQUIST, C.J., dissenting). Nor do I see any significance in the fact that Alabama has chosen to adopt a differential tax rather than an outright ban. Nothing in the Commerce Clause requires Alabama to adopt an "all or nothing" regulatory approach to noxious materials coming from without the State. *See Mintz v. Baldwin*, 289 U.S. 346 (1933) (upholding State's partial ban on cattle importation).

In short, the Court continues to err by its failure to recognize that waste—in this case admittedly hazardous waste—presents risks to the public health and environment that a State may legitimately wish to avoid, and that the State may pursue such an objective by means less Draconian than an outright ban. Under force of this Court's precedent, though, it increasingly appears that the only avenue by which a State may avoid the importation of hazardous wastes is to ban such waste disposal altogether, regardless of the waste's source of origin. I see little logic in creating, and nothing in the Commerce Clause that requires us to create, such perverse regulatory incentives. The Court errs in substantial measure because it refuses to acknowledge that a safe and attractive environment is the commodity really at issue in cases such as this, *see Fort Gratiot*, 112 S. Ct. at 2029-30 (REHNQUIST, C.J., dissenting). The result is that the Court today gets it exactly backward when it suggests that Alabama is attempting to "isolate itself from a problem common to the several States," *ante*, at 2012. To the contrary, it is the 34 States that have no hazardous waste facility whatsoever, not to mention the remaining 15 States with facilities all smaller than Emelle, that have isolated themselves.

NOTES

1.   In a companion case decided on the same day as *Chemical Waste Management*, the Court struck down a Michigan law which prohibited private landfill operators from accepting solid waste that originates outside the county in which the facilities are located, without first obtaining the approval of the state and certain local authorities within the affected county. *Fort Gratiot Sanitary Landfill, Inc. v. Michigan Dep't of Natural Resources*, 504 U.S. 353 (1992). As with the Alabama law, the Court found that the Michigan statute discriminated on its face against out-of-state wastes, and that less discriminatory means were available to the state to achieve the health and safety objectives allegedly sought under the legislation. The Court rejected the argument that the law did not discriminate based on state of origin because in-state generators of solid wastes from outside the county of disposal would suffer as much as out-of-state generators. A state "may not avoid the strictures of Commerce Clause by curtailing the movement of articles of commerce through subdivisions of the State, rather than through the State itself." 504 U.S. at 361.

2.   Despite *Lopez*, the Commerce Clause still grants Congress almost boundless legislative power to regulate polluting activities; but the *Chemical Waste Management* decision reminds us that in its "dormant" state, the Commerce Clause may impose significant limits on a state's authority to protect the environment. In *Maine v. Taylor*, 477 U.S. 131, 138 (1986), the Court explained the essence of the two-pronged, dormant commerce clause analysis:

> In determining whether a State regulation has overstepped its role in regulating interstate commerce, this Court has distinguished between state statutes that burden interstate transactions only incidentally, and those that affirmatively discriminate against such transactions. While statutes in the first group violate the Commerce Clause only if the burdens they impose are "clearly excessive in relation to the putative local benefits" * * * statutes in the second group are subject to more demanding scrutiny. * * * [O]nce a state law is shown to discriminate against interstate commerce * * * the burden falls on the state to demonstrate both that the statute "serves a legitimate local purpose" and that this purpose could not be served as well by available nondiscriminatory means.

Maine involved state legislation which banned the import of live bait fish into the state of Maine. Although the statute discriminated on its face against out-of-state bait fish (and was thus subject to strict scrutiny), the Maine law survived a dormant commerce clause challenge because at least one of Maine's purposes in enacting the ban was to prevent the possible introduction of parasites into Maine's wild fish population. Since no adequate testing methods for parasites existed, Maine had no less discriminatory means available to protect its native fish populations. *See also Sporhase v. Nebraska*, 458 U.S. 941 (1982) (invalidating Nebraska's restrictions on water transfers across state boundaries).

3.   State health and environmental legislation which does not discriminate against foreign commerce has a much higher survival rate. Although it might burden interstate commerce, it does not facially discriminate and is, therefore, merely subjected to a "balancing" test. *See, e.g., Huron Portland Cement Co. v. Detroit*, 362 U.S. 440 (1960) (Detroit's regulation of smoke pollution from ships upheld); *Minnesota v. Clover Leaf Creamery Co.*, 449 U.S. 456 (1981) (Minnesota statute banning the sale of milk in plastic, nonreturnable, nonrefillable containers upheld despite "incidental" burden on interstate commerce); *Aseptic Packaging Council v. State*, 637 A.2d 457 (Me. 1994) (Maine ban on the sale of aseptic beverage containers upheld).

Although the distinction between the strict scrutiny applied to state legislation that discriminates against interstate commerce and the lenient balancing test applied to neutral burdens is easily stated, in actual practice the lines separating the standards are occasionally blurred. The Supreme Court itself has recognized that "there is no clear line separating the category of state regulation that is virtually per se invalid under the Commerce Clause and the category subject to the balancing approach." *Brown-Forman Distillers v. New York State Liquor Authority*, 476 U.S. 573, 579 (1986).

4.   Low disposal costs, proximity to the Northeast, and good transportation lines make Indiana "an economically favorable disposal site for municipal waste from other regions of the United States." *Government Suppliers Consolidating Services, Inc. v. Bayh*, 975 F.2d 1267, 1272 (7th Cir. 1992), *cert. denied*, 113 S. Ct. 977 (1993). In 1990, Indiana enacted a discriminatory fee for out-of-state waste aimed at reducing the volume of imported trash. After this discriminatory fee schedule was invalidated by a federal district court in 1990, *Government Suppliers Consolidating Services, Inc. v. Bayh*, 753 F. Supp. 739 (S.D. Ind. 1990), the state enacted new provisions to restrict the influx of municipal solid waste. The provisions included a partial ban on "backhauling," a common practice for truckers that carry goods from the Midwest to New York, New Jersey, or Pennsylvania. Instead of returning to the Midwest with empty vehicles, truckers "backhaul" trash to deposit in Indiana landfills. 975 F.2d at 1272. Municipalities in Indiana typically ship their wastes in dedicated garbage trucks. *Id.* at 1273. Indiana argued that the "backhauling" ban did not discriminate and served the legitimate state interests in public health and commercial reputation. The Court of Appeals rejected Indiana's argument in declaring the new law unconstitutional as both discriminatory and unnecessary in light of alternatives. *Id.* at 1280. Are there any legal options for states seeking to restrict importation of waste?

5.   Can state-, county-, or municipally-owned landfills discriminate against interstate commerce in selecting their customers? In *Fort Gratiot, supra* Note 1, the Court emphasized that the case did not "raise any question concerning policies that municipalities or other governmental agencies may pursue in the management of publicly owned facilities."

An exemption from the restrictions of the dormant commerce clause, known as the "market participant" exemption, has been developed by the Supreme Court. *See Reeves, Inc. v. Stake*, 447 U.S. 429 (1980); *Hughes v. Alexandria Scrap Corp.*, 426 U.S. 794 (1976). This applies when a state or local government acts *solely* as a market participant, as opposed to a market regulator. The line between market participant and market regulator may not always be bright and clear. *See South-Central Timber Development, Inc. v. Wunnicke*, 467 U.S. 82 (1984). However, if a state, county, or municipality owns a landfill and does not simultaneously regulate the landfill services market, recent lower court decisions indicate that the state or local government may restrict their waste processing and disposal to waste originating within their geographic boundaries, without violating the Commerce Clause. *See Lefrancois v. Rhode Island*, 669 F. Supp. 1204 (D.R.I. 1987); *Evergreen Waste Sys. v. Metropolitan Serv. Dist.*, 643 F. Supp. 127 (D. Or. 1986), *aff'd*, 820 F.2d 1482 (9th Cir. 1987); *Shayne Bros. v. District of Columbia*, 592 F. Supp. 1128 (D.D.C. 1984); *Swin Resource Systems, Inc. v. Lycoming County*, 883 F.2d 245 (3d Cir. 1989), *cert. denied*, 493 U.S. 1077 (1990); *County Comm'rs of Charles County v. Stevens*, 299 Md. 203, 473 A.2d 12 (1984).

According to EPA, approximately 80% of the landfills receiving municipal solid waste nationwide are owned by state or local governments. Should this fact be relevant to the application of the market participant exemption to bans on the disposal of out-of-state waste? If so, which way should it cut? Local governments that own solid waste incinerators often seek to assure themselves a steady stream of fuel to remain economical. The New York town of Babylon succeeded in surmounting the dormant Commerce Clause problems with waste "flow control" by establishing a commercial waste hauling district and contracting with a single hauler to serve as its agent by collecting waste from each commercial generator and disposing the waste at the town incinerator. *USA Recycling v. Town of Babylon*, 66 F.3d 1272 (2d Cir. 1995), *cert. denied,* 517 U.S. 1150 (1996).

6. Many states are now seeking to limit their importation of solid waste through congressional enactment. For instance, Senate Bill 2877, the Interstate Transportation of Municipal Waste Act of 1992, would have granted governors limited authority to ban out-of-state solid waste. Although it passed the Senate by a vote of 89 to 2, the session closed before the legislation reached the floor of the House. This proposed legislation and others like it are based on the established constitutional doctrine that congressional permission to states to freely regulate an aspect of interstate commerce renders any state action within the scope of that authorization invulnerable to a Commerce Clause challenge; and this is the case whether or not the state regulation might be classified as discriminatory. *Western & Southern Life Ins. Co. v. State Board of Equalization*, 451 U.S. 648 (1981). This principle may be especially significant for state environmental legislation and administrative rules which have been approved by a federal agency under statutory directives like those found in the Resource Conservation and Recovery Act, the Surface Mining Control and Reclamation Act, the Clean Water Act, and the Clean Air Act.

LUCAS V. SOUTH CAROLINA COASTAL COUNCIL
505 U.S. 1003 (1992)

Justice SCALIA delivered the opinion of the Court.

In 1986, petitioner David H. Lucas paid $975,000 for two residential lots on the Isle of Palms in Charleston County, South Carolina, on which he intended to build single family homes. In 1988, however, the South Carolina Legislature enacted the Beachfront Management Act, S.C. Code § 48-39-250 *et seq.* (Supp. 1990) (Act), which had the direct effect of barring petitioner from erecting any permanent habitable structures on his two parcels. A state trial court found that this prohibition rendered Lucas's parcels "valueless." This case requires us to decide whether the Act's dramatic effect on the economic value of Lucas's lots accomplished a taking of private property under the Fifth and Fourteenth Amendments requiring the payment of "just compensation."

I

A

South Carolina's expressed interest in intensively managing development activities in the so-called "coastal zone" dates from 1977 when, in the aftermath of Congress's passage of the federal Coastal Zone Management Act of 1972, * * * the legislature enacted a Coastal Zone

Management Act of its own. *See* S.C. Code § 48-39-10 *et seq.* (1987). In its original form, the South Carolina Act required owners of coastal zone land that qualified as a "critical area" (defined in the legislation to include beaches and immediately adjacent sand dunes, § 48-39-10(J)) to obtain a permit from the newly created South Carolina Coastal Council (respondent here) prior to committing the land to a "use other than the use the critical area was devoted to on [September 28, 1977]." § 48-39-130(A).

In the late 1970s, Lucas and others began extensive residential development of the Isle of Palms, a barrier island situated eastward of the City of Charleston. Toward the close of the development cycle for one residential subdivision known as "Beachwood East," Lucas in 1986 purchased the two lots at issue in this litigation for his own account. No portion of the lots, which were located approximately 300 feet from the beach, qualified as a "critical area" under the 1977 Act; accordingly, at the time Lucas acquired these parcels, he was not legally obliged to obtain a permit from the Council in advance of any development activity. His intention with respect to the lots was to do what the owners of the immediately adjacent parcels had already done: erect single-family residences. He commissioned architectural drawings for this purpose.

The Beachfront Management Act brought Lucas's plans to an abrupt end. Under that 1988 legislation, the Council was directed to establish a "baseline" connecting the landward-most "point[s] of erosion . . . during the past forty years" in the region of the Isle of Palms that includes Lucas's lots. § 48-39-280(A)(2) (Supp. 1988). In action not challenged here, the Council fixed this baseline landward of Lucas's parcels. That was significant, for under the Act construction of occupiable improvements was flatly prohibited seaward of a line drawn 20 feet landward of, and parallel to, the baseline, § 48-39-290(A) (Supp. 1988). The Act provided no exceptions.

B

Lucas promptly filed suit in the South Carolina Court of Common Pleas, contending that the Beachfront Management Act's construction bar effected a taking of his property without just compensation. Lucas did not take issue with the validity of the Act as a lawful exercise of South Carolina's police power, but contended that the Act's complete extinguishment of his property's value entitled him to compensation regardless of whether the legislature had acted in furtherance of legitimate police power objectives. Following a bench trial, the court agreed. Among its factual determinations was the finding that "at the time Lucas purchased the two lots, both were zoned for single-family residential construction and . . . there were no restrictions imposed upon such use of the property by either the State of South Carolina, the County of Charleston, or the Town of the Isle of Palms." * * * ˙

* * *

III

A

Prior to Justice Holmes' exposition in *Pennsylvania Coal Co. v. Mahon,* 260 U.S. 393 (1922), it was generally thought that the Takings Clause reached only a "direct appropriation" of property, *Legal Tender Cases,* 79 U.S. (12 Wall.) 457, 551 (1871), or the functional equivalent of a "practical ouster of [the owner's] possession." *Transportation Co. v. Chicago,* 99 U.S. 635, 642 (1879). Justice Holmes recognized in *Mahon,* however, that if the protection against physical appropriations of private property was to be meaningfully enforced, the government's power to redefine the range of interests included in the ownership of property was necessarily constrained by constitutional limits. 260 U.S. at 414-15. If, instead, the uses of private property were subject to unbridled, uncompensated qualification under the police power, "the natural tendency of human nature [would be] to extend the qualification more and more until at last private property disappear[ed]." *Id.* at 415. These considerations gave birth in that case to the oft-cited maxim that, "while property may be regulated to a certain extent, if regulation goes too far it will be recognized as a taking." *Ibid.*

Nevertheless, our decision in *Mahon* offered little insight into when, and under what circumstances, a given regulation would be seen as going "too far" for purposes of the Fifth Amendment. In 70-odd years of succeeding "regulatory takings" jurisprudence, we have generally eschewed any "set formula" for determining how far is too far, preferring to "engag[e] in . . . essentially ad hoc, factual inquiries," *Penn Central Transportation Co. v. New York City,* 438 U.S. 104, 124 (1978) (quoting *Goldblatt v. Hempstead,* 369 U.S. 590, 594 (1962)). *See* Epstein, *Takings: Descent and Resurrection,* 1987 SUP. CT. REV. 1, 4. We have, however, described at least two discrete categories of regulatory action as compensable without case-specific inquiry into the public interest advanced in support of the restraint. The first encompasses regulations that compel the property owner to suffer a physical "invasion" of his property. In general (at least with regard to permanent invasions), no matter how minute the intrusion, and no matter how weighty the public purpose behind it, we have required compensation. For example, in *Loretto v. Teleprompter Manhattan CATV Corp.,* 458 U.S. 419 (1982), we determined that New York's law requiring landlords to allow television cable companies to emplace cable facilities in their apartment buildings constituted a taking, *id.* at 435-40, even though the facilities occupied at most only 1½ cubic feet of the landlords' property, *see id.* at 438 n.16. *See also United States v. Causby,* 328 U.S. 256, 265, and n.10 (1946) (physical invasions of airspace); *cf. Kaiser Aetna v. United States,* 444 U.S. 164 (1979) (imposition of navigational servitude upon private marina).

The second situation in which we have found categorical treatment appropriate is where regulation denies all economically beneficial or productive use of land. *See Agins v Tiburon,* 447 U.S. 255, 260; *see also Nollan v. California Coastal Comm'n,* 483 U.S. 825, 834 (1987); *Keystone Bituminous Coal Assn. v. DeBenedictis,* 480 U.S. 470, 495 (1987); *Hodel v. Virginia Surface Mining & Reclamation Assn., Inc.,* 452 U.S. 264, 295-96 (1981). As we have said on numerous occasions, the Fifth Amendment is violated when land-use regulation "does not substantially advance legitimate state interests *or denies an owner economically viable use of his land.*" *Agins, supra,* at 260 (citations omitted) (emphasis added).[7]

We have never set forth the justification for this rule. Perhaps it is simply, as Justice Brennan suggested, that total deprivation of beneficial use is, from the landowner's point of view, the equivalent of a physical appropriation. *See San Diego Gas & Electric Co. v. San*

---

[7]   Regrettably, the rhetorical force of our "deprivation of all economically feasible use" rule is greater than its precision, since the rule does not make clear the "property interest" against which the loss of value is to be measured. When, for example, a regulation requires a developer to leave 90% of a rural tract in its natural state, it is unclear whether we would analyze the situation as one in which the owner has been deprived of all economically beneficial use of the burdened portion of the tract, or as one in which the owner has suffered a mere diminution in value of the tract as a whole. (For an extreme—and, we think, unsupportable—view of the relevant calculus, *see Penn Central Transportation Co. v. New York City,* 366 N.E.2d 1271, 1276-77 (1977), *aff'd,* 438 U.S. 104 (1978), where the state court examined the diminution in a particular parcel's value produced by a municipal ordinance in light of total value of the taking claimant's other holdings in the vicinity.) Unsurprisingly, this uncertainty regarding the composition of the denominator in our "deprivation" fraction has produced inconsistent pronouncements by the Court. The answer to this difficult question may lie in how the owner's reasonable expectations have been shaped by the State's law of property—*i.e.,* whether and to what degree the State's law has accorded legal recognition and protection to the particular interest in land with respect to which the takings claimant alleges a diminution in (or elimination of) value. In any event, we avoid this difficulty in the present case, since the "interest in land" that Lucas has pleaded (a fee simple interest) is an estate with a rich tradition of protection at common law, and since the South Carolina Court of Common Pleas found that the Beachfront Management Act left each of Lucas's beachfront lots without economic value.

Diego, 450 U.S., at 652 (Brennan, J., dissenting). "[F]or what is the land but the profits thereof[?]" 1 E. COKE, INSTITUTES § 1 (1st Am. ed. 1812). Surely, at least, in the extraordinary circumstance when no productive or economically beneficial use of land is permitted, it is less realistic to indulge our usual assumption that the legislature is simply "adjusting the benefits and burdens of economic life," *Penn Central Transportation Co.,* 438 U.S. at 124, in a manner that secures an "average reciprocity of advantage" to everyone concerned. *Pennsylvania Coal Co. v. Mahon,* 260 U.S. at 415. And the functional basis for permitting the government, by regulation, to affect property values without compensation—that "Government hardly could go on if to some extent values incident to property could not be diminished without paying for every such change in the general law," *Id.* at 413—does not apply to the relatively rare situations where the government has deprived a landowner of all economically beneficial uses.

On the other side of the balance, affirmatively supporting a compensation requirement, is the fact that regulations that leave the owner of land without economically beneficial or productive options for its use—typically, as here, by requiring land to be left substantially in its natural state—carry with them a heightened risk that private property is being pressed into some form of public service under the guise of mitigating serious public harm. As Justice Brennan explained: "From the government's point of view, the benefits flowing to the public from preservation of open space through regulation may be equally great as from creating a wildlife refuge through formal condemnation or increasing electricity production through a dam project that floods private property." *San Diego Gas & Elec. Co.* 450 U.S. at 652 (Brennan, J., dissenting). The many statutes on the books, both state and federal, that provide for the use of eminent domain to impose servitudes on private scenic lands preventing developmental uses, or to acquire such lands altogether, suggest the practical equivalence in this setting of negative regulation and appropriation.

We think, in short, that there are good reasons for our frequently expressed belief that when the owner of real property has been called upon to sacrifice all economically beneficial uses in the name of the common good, that is, to leave his property economically idle, he has suffered a taking.[8]

B

The trial court found Lucas's two beachfront lots to have been rendered valueless by respondent's enforcement of the coastal-zone construction ban. Under Lucas's theory of the case, which rested upon our "no economically viable use" statements, that finding entitled him to compensation. Lucas believed it unnecessary to take issue with either the purposes behind the Beachfront Management Act, or the means chosen by the South Carolina Legislature to effectuate those purposes. The South Carolina Supreme Court, however, thought otherwise. In

---

[8]   Justice STEVENS criticizes the "deprivation of all economically beneficial use" rule as "wholly arbitrary," in that "[the] landowner whose property is diminished in value 95% recovers nothing," while the landowner who suffers a complete elimination of value "recovers the land's full value." This analysis errs in its assumption that the landowner who deprivation is one step short of complete is not entitled to compensation. Such an owner might not be able to claim the benefit of our categorical formulation, but, as we have acknowledged time and again, "[t]he economic impact of the regulation on the claimant and . . . the extent to which the regulation has interfered with distinct investment-backed expectations" are keenly relevant to takings analysis generally. *Penn Central Transportation Co. v. New York City,* 438 U.S. 104, 124 (1978). It is true that in at least some cases the landowner with 95% loss will get nothing, while the landowner with total loss will recover in full. But that occasional result is no more strange than the gross disparity between the landowner whose premises are taken for a highway (who recovers in full) and the landowner whose property is reduced to 5% of its former value by the highway (who recovers nothing). Takings law is full of these "all-or-nothing" situations. * * *

its view, the Beachfront Management Act was no ordinary enactment, but involved an exercise of South Carolina's "police powers" to mitigate the harm to the public interest that petitioner's use of his land might occasion. 404 S.E.2d at 899. By neglecting to dispute the findings enumerated in the Act[10] or otherwise to challenge the legislature's purposes, petitioner "concede[d] that the beach/dune area of South Carolina's shores is an extremely valuable public resource; that the erection of new construction, *inter alia*, contributes to the erosion and destruction of this public resource; and that discouraging new construction in close proximity to the beach/dune area is necessary to prevent a great public harm." *Id.* at 898. In the court's view, these concessions brought petitioner's challenge within a long line of this Court's cases sustaining against Due Process and Takings Clause challenges the State's use of its "police powers" to enjoin a property owner from activities akin to public nuisances. *See Mugler v. Kansas,* 123 U.S. 623 (1887) (law prohibiting manufacture of alcoholic beverages); *Hadacheck v. Sebastian,* 239 U.S. 394 (1915) (law barring operation of brick mill in residential area); *Miller v. Schoene,* 276 U.S. 272 (1928) (order to destroy diseased cedar trees to prevent infection of nearby orchards); *Goldblatt v. Hempstead,* 369 U.S. 590 (1962) (law effectively preventing continued operation of quarry in residential area).

It is correct that many of our prior opinions have suggested that "harmful or noxious uses" of property may be proscribed by government regulation without the requirement of compensation. For a number of reasons, however, we think the South Carolina Supreme Court was too quick to conclude that that principle decides the present case. The "harmful or noxious

---

[10]   The legislature's express findings include the following:

The General Assembly finds that: (1) The beach/dune system along the coast of South Carolina is extremely important to the people of this State and serves the following functions: (a) protects life and property by serving as a storm barrier which dissipates wave energy and contributes to shoreline stability in an economical and effective manner; (b) provides the basis for a tourism industry that generates approximately two-thirds of South Carolina's annual tourism industry revenue which constitutes a significant portion of the state's economy. The tourists who come to the South Carolina coast to enjoy the ocean and dry sand beach contribute significantly to state and local tax revenues; (c) provides habitat for numerous species of plants and animals, several of which are threatened or endangered. Waters adjacent to the beach/dune system also provide habitat for many other marine species; (d) provides a natural health environment for the citizens of South Carolina to spend leisure time which serves their physical and mental well-being. (2) Beach/dune system vegetation is unique and extremely important to the vitality and preservation of the system. (3) Many miles of South Carolina's beaches have been identified as critically eroding. (4) * * * [D]evelopment unwisely has been sited too close to the [beach/dune] system. This type of development has jeopardized the stability of the beach/dune system, accelerated erosion, and endangered adjacent property. It is in both the public and private interests to protect the system from this unwise development. (5) The use of armoring in the form of hard erosion control devices such as seawalls, bulkheads, and rip-rap to protect erosion-threatened structures adjacent to the beach has not proven effective. These armoring devices have given a false sense of security to beachfront property owners. In reality, these hard structures, in many instances, have increased the vulnerability of beachfront property to damage from wind and waves while contributing to the deterioration and loss of the dry sand beach which is so important to the tourism industry. (6) Erosion is a natural process which becomes a significant problem for man only when structures are erected in close proximity to the beach/dune system. It is in both the public and private interests to afford the beach/dune system space to accrete and erode in its natural cycle. This space can be provided only by discouraging new construction in close proximity to the beach/dune system and encouraging those who have erected structures too close to the system to retreat from it. * * * (8) It is in the state's best interest to protect and to promote increased public access to South Carolina's beaches for out-of-state tourists and South Carolina residents alike.

S.C. Code § 48-39-250 (Supp. 1991).

uses" principle was the Court's early attempt to describe in theoretical terms why government may, consistent with the Takings Clause, affect property values by regulation without incurring an obligation to compensate—a reality we nowadays acknowledge explicitly with respect to the full scope of the State's police power. *See, e.g., Penn Central Transportation Co.,* 438 U.S. at 125 (where State "reasonably conclude[s] that 'the health, safety, morals, or general welfare' would be promoted by prohibiting particular contemplated uses of land," compensation need not accompany prohibition). * * *

The transition from our early focus on control of "noxious" uses to our contemporary understanding of the broad realm within which government may regulate without compensation was an easy one, since the distinction between "harm-preventing" and "benefit-conferring" regulation is often in the eye of the beholder. It is quite possible, for example, to describe in either fashion the ecological, economic, and aesthetic concerns that inspired the South Carolina legislature in the present case. One could say that imposing a servitude on Lucas's land is necessary in order to prevent his use of it from "harming" South Carolina's ecological resources; or, instead, in order to achieve the "benefits" of an ecological preserve. * * * A given restraint will be seen as mitigating "harm" to the adjacent parcels or securing a "benefit" for them, depending upon the observer's evaluation of the relative importance of the use that the restraint favors. *See* Sax, *Takings and the Police Power,* 74 YALE L.J. 36, 49 (1964) ("[T]he problem [in this area] is not one of noxiousness or harm-creating activity at all; rather it is a problem of inconsistency between perfectly innocent and independently desirable uses"). Whether Lucas's construction of single-family residences on his parcels should be described as bringing "harm" to South Carolina's adjacent ecological resources thus depends principally upon whether the describer believes that the State's use interest in nurturing those resources is so important that any competing adjacent use must yield.

When it is understood that "prevention of harmful use" was merely our early formulation of the police power justification necessary to sustain (without compensation) any regulatory diminution in value; and that the distinction between regulation that "prevents harmful use" and that which "confers benefits" is difficult, if not impossible, to discern on an objective, value-free basis; it becomes self-evident that noxious-use logic cannot serve as a touchstone to distinguish regulatory "takings"—which require compensation—from regulatory deprivations that do not require compensation. *A fortiori* the legislature's recitation of a noxious-use justification cannot be the basis for departing from our categorical rule that total regulatory takings must be compensated. If it were, departure would virtually always be allowed. The South Carolina Supreme Court's approach would essentially nullify *Mahon's* affirmation of limits to the noncompensable exercise of the police power. Our cases provide no support for this: None of them that employed the logic of "harmful use" prevention to sustain a regulation involved an allegation that the regulation wholly eliminated the value of the claimant's land. *See Keystone Bituminous Coal Assn.,* 480 U.S. at 513-14 (REHNQUIST, C.J., dissenting).

Where the State seeks to sustain regulation that deprives land of all economically beneficial use, we think it may resist compensation only if the logically antecedent inquiry into the nature of the owner's estate shows that the proscribed use interests were not part of his title to begin with. This accords, we think, with our "takings" jurisprudence, which has traditionally been guided by the understandings of our citizens regarding the content of, and the State's power over, the "bundle of rights" that they acquire when they obtain title to property. It seems to us that the property owner necessarily expects the uses of his property to be restricted, from time to time, by various measures newly enacted by the State in legitimate exercise of its police powers; "[a]s long recognized, some values are enjoyed under an implied limitation and must yield to the police power." *Pennsylvania Coal Co. v. Mahon,* 260 U.S. at 413. And in the case of personal property, by reason of the State's traditionally high degree of control over commercial dealings, he ought to be aware of the possibility that new regulation might even render his property economically worthless (at least if the property's only economically productive use is sale or manufacture for sale), *see Andrus v. Allard,* 444 U.S. 51, 66-67 (1979) (prohibition on sale of eagle feathers). In the case of land, however, we think the notion pressed by the Council that title is somehow held subject to the "implied limitation" that the State may subsequently eliminate all economically valuable use is inconsistent with the historical compact recorded in the Takings Clause that has become part of our constitutional culture.

Where "permanent physical occupation" of land is concerned, we have refused to allow the government to decree it anew (without compensation), no matter how weighty the asserted "public interests" involved, *Loretto v. Teleprompter Manhattan CATV Corp.,* 458 U.S. at 426— though we assuredly *would* permit the government to assert a permanent easement that was a pre-existing limitation upon the landowner's title. We believe similar treatment must be accorded confiscatory regulations, *i.e.,* regulations that prohibit all economically beneficial use of land: Any limitation so severe cannot be newly legislated or decreed (without compensation), but must inhere in the title itself, in the restrictions that background principles of the State's law of property and nuisance already place upon land ownership. A law or decree with such an effect must, in other words, do no more than duplicate the result that could have been achieved in the courts—by adjacent landowners (or other uniquely affected persons) under the State's law of private nuisance, or by the State under its complementary power to abate nuisances that affect the public generally, or otherwise.

On this analysis, the owner of a lake bed, for example, would not be entitled to compensation when he is denied the requisite permit to engage in a landfilling operation that would have the effect of flooding others' land. Nor the corporate owner of a nuclear generating plant, when it is directed to remove all improvements from its land upon discovery that the plant sits astride an earthquake fault. Such regulatory action may well have the effect of eliminating the land's only economically productive use, but it does not proscribe a productive use that was previously permissible under relevant property and nuisance principles. The use of these properties for what are now expressly prohibited purposes was always unlawful, and (subject to other constitutional limitations) it was open to the State at any point to make the implication of those background principles of nuisance and property law explicit. * * * [T]hat the Takings Clause does not require compensation when an owner is barred from putting land to a use that is proscribed by those "existing rules or understandings" is surely unexceptional. When, however, a regulation that declares "off-limits" all economically productive or beneficial uses of land goes beyond what the relevant background principles would dictate, compensation must be paid to sustain it.

The "total taking" inquiry we require today will ordinarily entail (as the application of state nuisance law ordinarily entails) analysis of, among other things, the degree of harm to public lands and resources, or adjacent private property, posed by the claimant's proposed activities, *see, e.g.,* RESTATEMENT (SECOND) OF TORTS §§ 826, 827, the social value of the claimant's activities and their suitability to the locality in question, *see, e.g., id.* §§ 828(a) and (b), 831, and the relative ease with which the alleged harm can be avoided through measures taken by the claimant and the government (or adjacent private landowners) alike, *see, e.g., id.* §§ 827(e), 828(c), 830. The fact that a particular use has long been engaged in by similarly situated owners ordinarily imports a lack of any common-law prohibition (though changed circumstances or new knowledge may make what was previously permissible no longer so, *see* RESTATEMENT (SECOND) OF TORTS, *supra,* § 827, comment g). So also does the fact that other landowners, similarly situated, are permitted to continue the use denied to the claimant.

It seems unlikely that common-law principles would have prevented the erection of any habitable or productive improvements on petitioner's land; they rarely support prohibition of the "essential use" of land, *Curtin v. Benson,* 222 U.S. 78, 86 (1911). The question, however, is one of state law to be dealt with on remand. We emphasize that to win its case South Carolina must do more than proffer the legislature's declaration that the uses Lucas desires are inconsistent with the public interest, or the conclusory assertion that they violate a common-law maxim such as *sic utere tuo ut alienum non laedas.* As we have said, a "State, by *ipse dixit,* may not transform private property into public property without compensation . . .." *Webb's Fabulous Pharmacies, Inc. v. Beckwith,* 449 U.S. 155, 164 (1980). Instead, as it would be required to do if it sought to restrain Lucas in a common-law action for public nuisance, South Carolina must identify background principles of nuisance and property law that prohibit the uses he now intends in the circumstances in which the property is presently found. Only on this showing can the State fairly claim that, in proscribing all such beneficial uses, the Beachfront Management Act is taking nothing.[18]

* * *

The judgment is reversed and the cause remanded for proceedings not inconsistent with this opinion.

So ordered.

* * *

Justice BLACKMUN, dissenting.

Today the Court launches a missile to kill a mouse.

The State of South Carolina prohibited petitioner Lucas from building a permanent structure on his property from 1988 to 1990. Relying on an unreviewed (and implausible) state trial court finding that this restriction left Lucas' property valueless, this Court granted review to determine whether compensation must be paid in cases where the State prohibits all economic use of real estate. According to the Court, such an occasion never has arisen in any of our prior cases, and the Court imagines that it will arise "relatively rarely" or only in "extraordinary circumstances." Almost certainly it did not happen in this case.

Nonetheless, the Court presses on to decide the issue, and as it does, it ignores its jurisdictional limits, remakes its traditional rules of review, and creates simultaneously a new categorical rule and an exception (neither of which is rooted in our prior case law, common law, or common sense). I protest not only the Court's decision, but each step taken to reach it. More fundamentally, I question the Court's wisdom in issuing sweeping new rules to decide such a narrow case. * * *

My fear is that the Court's new policies will spread beyond the narrow confines of the present case. For that reason, I, like the Court, will give far greater attention to this case than its narrow scope suggests—not because I can intercept the Court's missile, or save the targeted mouse, but because I hope perhaps to limit the collateral damage.

---

[18]   Justice BLACKMUN decries our reliance on background nuisance principles at least in part because he believes those principles to be as manipulable as we find the "harm prevention"/"benefit conferral" dichotomy. There is no doubt some leeway in a court's interpretation of what existing state law permits—but not remotely as much, we think, as in a legislative crafting of the reasons for its confiscatory regulation. We stress that an affirmative decree eliminating all economically beneficial uses may be defended only if an objectively reasonable application of relevant precedents would exclude those beneficial uses in the circumstances in which the land is presently found.

I

In 1972 Congress passed the Coastal Zone Management Act. * * * In the 1980 Amendments to the Act, Congress directed the States to enhance their coastal programs by "[p]reventing or significantly reducing threats to life and the destruction of property by eliminating development and redevelopment in high-hazard areas."[1] 16 U.S.C. § b(a)(2).

* * *

B

Petitioner Lucas is a contractor, manager, and part owner of the Wild Dune development on the Isle of Palms. He has lived there since 1978. In December 1986, he purchased two of the last four pieces of vacant property in the development. The area is notoriously unstable. In roughly half of the last 40 years, all or part of petitioner's property was part of the beach or flooded twice daily by the ebb and flow of the tide. Between 1957 and 1963, petitioner's property was under water. Between 1963 and 1973 the shoreline was 100 to 150 feet onto petitioner's property. In 1973 the first line of stable vegetation was about halfway through the property. Between 1981 and 1983, the Isle of Palms issued 12 emergency orders for sandbagging to protect property in the Wild Dune development. Determining that local habitable structures were in imminent danger of collapse, the Council issued permits for two rock revetments to protect condominium developments near petitioner's property from erosion; one of the revetments extends more than halfway onto one of his lots.

* * *

IV

The Court does not reject the South Carolina Supreme Court's decision simply on the basis of its disbelief and distrust of the legislature's findings. It also takes the opportunity to create a new scheme for regulations that eliminate all economic value. From now on, there is a categorical rule finding these regulations to be a taking unless the use they prohibit is a background common-law nuisance or property principle.

A

I first question the Court's rationale in creating a category that obviates a "case-specific inquiry into the public interest advanced," if all economic value has been lost. If one fact about the Court's taking jurisprudence can be stated without contradiction, it is that "the particular circumstances of each case" determine whether a specific restriction will be rendered invalid by the government's failure to pay compensation. This is so because although we have articulated certain factors to be considered, including the economic impact on the property owner, the ultimate conclusion "necessarily requires a weighing of private and public interests." *Agins*, 447 U.S. at 261. When the government regulation prevents the owner from any economically valuable use of his property, the private interest is unquestionably substantial, but we have never before held that no public interest can outweigh it. Instead the Court's prior decisions "uniformly reject the proposition that diminution in property value, standing alone, can establish a 'taking.'" *Penn Central Transp. Co. v. New York City,* 438 U.S. 104, 131 (1978).

This Court repeatedly has recognized the ability of government, in certain circumstances, to regulate property without compensation no matter how adverse the financial effect on the

---

[1]   The country has come to recognize that uncontrolled beachfront development can cause serious damage to life and property. * * * Hurricane Hugo's September 1989 attack upon South Carolina's coast, for example, caused 29 deaths and approximately $6 billion in property damage, much of it the result of uncontrolled beachfront development. * * * The beachfront buildings are not only themselves destroyed in such a storm, "but they are often driven like battering rams into adjacent inland homes." Moreover, the development often destroys the natural sand dune barriers that provide storm breaks.

owner may be. More than a century ago, the Court explicitly upheld the right of States to prohibit uses of property injurious to public health, safety, or welfare without paying compensation: "A prohibition simply upon the use of property for purposes that are declared, by valid legislation, to be injurious to the health, morals, or safety of the community, cannot, in any just sense, be deemed a taking or an appropriation of property." *Mugler v. Kansas,* 123 U.S. 623, 668-69 (1887). On this basis, the Court upheld an ordinance effectively prohibiting operation of a previously lawful brewery, although the "establishments will become of no value as property." *Id.* at 664; *see also, id.* at 668.

Mugler was only the beginning in a long line of cases. In *Powell v. Pennsylvania,* 127 U.S. 678 (1888), the Court upheld legislation prohibiting the manufacture of oleomargarine, despite the owner's allegation that "if prevented from continuing it, the value of his property employed therein would be entirely lost and he be deprived of the means of livelihood." *Id.* at 682. In *Hadacheck v. Sebastian,* 239 U.S. 394 (1915), the Court upheld an ordinance prohibiting a brickyard, although the owner had made excavations on the land that prevented it from being utilized for any purpose but a brickyard. *Id.* at 405. In *Miller v. Schoene,* 276 U.S. 272 (1928), the Court held that the Fifth Amendment did not require Virginia to pay compensation to the owner of cedar trees ordered destroyed to prevent a disease from spreading to nearby apple orchards. * * *

More recently, in *Goldblatt,* the Court upheld a town regulation that barred continued operation of an existing sand and gravel operation in order to protect public safety. 369 U.S. at 596. "Although a comparison of values before and after is relevant," the Court stated, "it is by no means conclusive." *Id.* at 594. In 1978, the Court declared that "in instances in which a state tribunal reasonably concluded that 'the health, safety, morals, or general welfare' would be promoted by prohibiting particular contemplated uses of land, this Court has upheld land-use regulation that destroyed . . . recognized real property interests." *Penn Central Transp. Co.,* 438 U.S. at 125. In *First Lutheran Church v. Los Angeles County,* 482 U.S. 304 (1987), the owner alleged that a floodplain ordinance had deprived it of "all use" of the property. *Id.* at 312. The Court remanded the case for consideration whether, even if the ordinance denied the owner all use, it could be justified as a safety measure.[2] *Id.* at 313. And in *Keystone Bituminous Coal,* the Court summarized over 100 years of precedent: "the Court has repeatedly upheld regulations that destroy or adversely affect real property interests." 480 U.S. at 489, n.18.

The Court recognizes that "our prior opinions have suggested that 'harmful or noxious uses' of property may be proscribed by government regulation without the requirement of compensation," but seeks to reconcile them with its categorical rule by claiming that the Court never has upheld a regulation when the owner alleged the loss of all economic value. Even if the Court's factual premise were correct, its understanding of the Court's cases is distorted. In none of the cases did the Court suggest that the right of a State to prohibit certain activities without paying compensation turned on the availability of some residual valuable use. Instead, the cases depended on whether the government interest was sufficient to prohibit the activity, given the significant private cost.

These cases rest on the principle that the State has full power to prohibit an owner's use of property if it is harmful to the public. "[S]ince no individual has a right to use his property so as to create a nuisance or otherwise harm others, the State has not 'taken' anything when it asserts its power to enjoin the nuisance-like activity." *Keystone Bituminous Coal,* 480 U.S. at 491, n.20. It would make no sense under this theory to suggest that an owner has a

---

[19]   On remand, the California court found no taking in part because the zoning regulation "involves this highest of public interests—the prevention of death and injury." *First Lutheran Church v. Los Angeles,* 258 Cal. Rptr. 893, 904 (1989), *cert. denied,* 493 U.S. 1056 (1990).

constitutionally protected right to harm others, if only he makes the proper showing of economic loss.

B

Ultimately even the Court cannot embrace the full implications of its *per se* rule: it eventually agrees that there cannot be a categorical rule for a taking based on economic value that wholly disregards the public need asserted. Instead, the Court decides that it will permit a State to regulate all economic value only if the State prohibits uses that would not be permitted under "background principles of nuisance and property law." *Ante,* at 19.

Until today, the Court explicitly had rejected the contention that the government's power to act without paying compensation turns on whether the prohibited activity is a common-law nuisance. The brewery closed in *Mugler* itself was not a common-law nuisance, and the Court specifically stated that it was the role of the legislature to determine what measures would be appropriate for the protection of public health and safety. *See* 123 U.S. at 661. In upholding the state action in *Miller,* the Court found it unnecessary to "weigh with nicety the question whether the infected cedars constitute a nuisance according to common law; or whether they may be so declared by statute." Instead the Court has relied in the past, as the South Carolina Court has done here, on legislative judgments of what constitutes a harm.

* * *

The threshold inquiry for imposition of the Court's new rule, "deprivation of all economically valuable use," itself cannot be determined objectively. As the Court admits, whether the owner has been deprived of all economic value of his property will depend on how "property" is defined. The "composition of the denominator in our 'deprivation' fraction," is the dispositive inquiry. Yet there is no "objective" way to define what that denominator should be. "We have long understood that any land-use regulation can be characterized as the 'total' deprivation of an aptly defined entitlement. . . . Alternatively, the same regulation can always be characterized as a mere 'partial' withdrawal from full, unencumbered ownership of the landholding affected by the regulation. . . ." Michelman, *Takings, 1987*, 88 COLUM. L. REV. 1600, 1614 (1988).

The Court's decision in *Keystone Bituminous Coal* illustrates this principle perfectly. In *Keystone,* the Court determined that the "support estate" was "merely a part of the entire bundle of rights possessed by the owner." 480 U.S. at 501. Thus, the Court concluded that the support estate's destruction merely eliminated one segment of the total property. *Ibid.* The dissent, however, characterized the support estate as a distinct property interest that was wholly destroyed. *Id.* at 519. The Court could agree on no "value-free basis" to resolve this dispute.

Even more perplexing, however, is the Court's reliance on common-law principles of nuisance in its quest for a value-free taking jurisprudence. In determining what is a nuisance at common law, state courts make exactly the decision that the Court finds so troubling when made by the South Carolina General Assembly today: they determine whether the use is harmful. Common-law public and private nuisance law is simply a determination whether a particular use causes harm. *See* Prosser, *Private Action for Public Nuisance,* 52 VA. L. REV. 997, 997 (1966) ("*Nuisance* is a French word which means nothing more than harm"). There is nothing magical in the reasoning of judges long dead. They determined a harm in the same way as state judges and legislatures do today. If judges in the 18th and 19th centuries can distinguish a harm from a benefit, why not judges in the 20th century, and if judges can, why not legislators? There simply is no reason to believe that new interpretations of the hoary common law nuisance doctrine will be particularly "objective" or "value-free." Once one abandons the level of generality of *sic utere tuo ut alienum non laedas,* one searches in vain, I think, for anything resembling a principle in the common law of nuisance.

* * *

V

* * *

I dissent.

NOTES

1.   On remand, the South Carolina Supreme Court ruled that Lucas suffered a temporary taking. 424 S.E.2d 484 (S.C. 1992).

2.   Richard Epstein, William Fisher, Richard Lazarus, and Joseph Sax have published excellent analyses of *Lucas* in a symposium published at 45 STAN. L. REV. 1369 (1993).

3.   Does the majority change takings jurisprudence as substantially as Justice Blackmun suggests? How has the law changed as a result of this decision? How does the application of nuisance law principles differ from the noxious use theory it replaces? Can a state legislature modify nuisance law to address current environmental concerns or do courts have to make the change? Since the explosion of statutory environmental law in the early 1970s, people have come to rely far less on common law causes of action to resolve environmental disputes. Does this trend mean that the common law has not kept pace with changes in expectations about use of property?

4.   In an unusual "Statement" issued with the *Lucas* opinions, Justice Souter explained that he would have dismissed the writ of certiorari as having been granted improvidently because the Court's assumption that the South Carolina regulation deprived Lucas of his entire economic interest is questionable and could not be reviewed. 505 U.S. at 1076. What do you think Lucas should have to show to prove that his property has no remaining economic use?

5.   A key unanswered question in *Lucas* is suggested by Justice Scalia at footnote seven. Can a property owner segment property rights such that she can show that one stick in the bundle of rights has been "totally taken"? Suppose, for example, that a regulation prohibits filling of wetlands which comprise 60% of your land. Does such a restriction constitute a total taking if the 60% is without an economically viable use? Previous case law suggests not (*see, e.g., Keystone Bituminous Coal Ass'n v. DeBenedictis*, 480 U.S. 470 (1987), *Penn Central Transp. Co. v. New York City*, 438 U.S. 104 (1978)), but Justice Scalia suggests that this remains an open question. This segmentation issue is playing a particularly important role in Tucker Act compensation cases involving wetlands regulation. *See, e.g., Tabb Lakes, Ltd. v. United States*, 10 F.3d 796 (Fed. Cir. 1993) (dictum supporting the view that the entire subdivision, not individual lots, should be the area considered for determining economically viable use of property); *cf. Loveladies Harbor, Inc. v. United States*, 28 F.3d 1171 (Fed. Cir. 1994) (finding a compensable taking for denial of a permit to fill a wetland representing approximately 5% of the original development tract; rejecting a "bright-line" rule for resolving segmentation issues; and adopting a "flexible approach" to account for factual nuances).

6.   If the court finds a "total taking," is compensation automatically warranted?

7. In *Nollan v. California Coastal Comm'n*, 483 U.S. 825 (1987), the State of California conditioned an oceanfront home construction permit on the requirement that the landowner allow an easement for public access along the beach. California argued that the regulation served the purpose of protecting visual and physical access to the beach. Although the Supreme Court found the State's interest to be legitimate, it held that the regulation did not substantially advance the State's purpose, and effectively amounted to "extortion" of the landowner. *See also Dolan v. City of Tigard*, 512 U.S. 374 (1994).

8. One of the more extreme results in a takings case is *Whitney Benefits, Inc. v. United States*, 926 F.2d 1169 (Fed. Cir. 1991), *cert. denied*, 502 U.S. 952 (1991). The Surface Mining Control and Reclamation Act (SMCRA) prohibits approval of a mining permit if the operation would interrupt, discontinue, or preclude farming on alluvial valley floors. Whitney Benefits, a company owning coal reserves in an alluvial valley floor in Wyoming, claimed that as a result of SMCRA it was precluded from developing its coal reserves. The Court of Appeals affirmed the holding of the Claims Court which concluded that a compensable taking had occurred, and awarded $140 million to Whitney Benefits. *See* Claire E. Sollars, Note, *To Take or Not to Take—Was That Question Really Worth 140 Million Dollars?*, 27 LAND & WATER L. REV. 403 (1992). As described earlier in this chapter, *Hodel v. Virginia Surface Mining & Reclamation Ass'n*, 452 U.S. 264 (1981), and its companion case, *Hodel v. Indiana*, 452 U.S. 314 (1981), upheld SMCRA against a number of constitutional challenges, including claims that the act violated the Fifth Amendment. How do you reconcile *Whitney Benefits* with these Supreme Court cases?

9. Professor Richard Lazarus, who represented the South Carolina Coastal Council in *Lucas*, writes:

> The majority's current zeal to repel the perceived environmentalist assault on private property rests on serious misperceptions regarding the nature of land. The Court does not appreciate the now-settled ecological notion that land "is not merely soil; it is a fountain of energy flowing though a circuit of soils, plants, and animals." [ALDO LEOPOLD, A SAND COUNTY ALMANAC.] Land is not a discrete, severable resource that respects the surveyor's binary-based boundaries. It is part of a complex, interdependent ecological system. Nor does the Court appreciate that over the past century our relationship to the land has fundamentally changed. Land is now a highly regulated commodity, and its ownership is no longer the touchstone of human autonomy or the source of individual freedom.

Richard J. Lazarus, *Putting the Correct "Spin" on* Lucas, 45 STAN. L. REV. 1411, 1421 (1993). How relevant are scientific (ecological) developments to constitutional interpretation? What is the relationship between the takings clause and individual freedom?

10. In 1988, President Reagan issued Executive Order 12630 which requires federal agencies to prepare a "takings impact analysis" (TIA) in conjunction with major regulatory actions. The TIA is intended to insure that the agency considers the potential impact of the rule on private property. The likely cost of any possible takings must also be assessed. The possibility of a taking is not intended to preclude the agency from issuing the rule, but rather to make the agency more aware of the impacts of the proposed rule on private property so that such impacts can be better taken into account. Margaret N. Strand, *Federal Wetlands Law: Part II*, 23 Envtl. L. Rep. (Envtl. L. Inst.) 10284, 10313 (1993). The TIA was modeled after an earlier Reagan executive order (Exec. Order No. 12291, 46 Fed. Reg. 13193 (1981), *revoked by* Exec. Order No. 12866, 58 Fed. Reg. 51735 (1993)) that required agencies to prepare a regulatory impact analysis (RIA) for every major rule. A Reagan Administration official described the purpose of the takings executive order as both to minimize the impact of government policies on private property and to budget for those regulatory takings that will inevitably occur. Roger J. Marzulla, *The New "Takings" Executive Order and Environmental Regulation—Collision or Cooperation?*, 18 Envtl. L. Rep. (Envtl. L. Inst.) 10254, 10255 (1988). Critics charge that the takings executive order has the unstated goal of "chilling" agency regulation through delay and needless bureaucratic meddling. Jerry Jackson & Lyle D. Albaugh, *A Critique of the Takings Executive Order in the Context of Environmental Regulation,* 18 Envtl. L. Rep. (Envtl. L. Inst.) 10463, 10464 (1988) (arguing that the executive order describes an analysis that finds a much wider range of regulation to be a taking than courts have, and requires consideration of factors in making regulatory decisions that go beyond many agencies' statutory authorities).

11. Although not required by the Constitution, legislatures may offer compensation to owners whose property value declines by a certain percentage as a result of government regulation. Recent sessions of Congress have considered but rejected a number of bills containing property compensation requirements. Should new governmental restrictions on pollution that reduce the competitive advantage of "dirty" businesses trigger compensation to these businesses for the reduction in property value? Should the government compensate other businesses, such as canoe liveries, if their property declines as a result of less stringent pollution regulation that lowers water quality?

Since 1991, all fifty state legislatures have considered some kind of takings or compensation bill. By the end of 1996, twenty-six states had enacted property rights laws. The most prevalent version of these statutes requires some form of takings impact analysis by state agencies (and in some states, local governments as well). Known as assessment or planning laws, they mandate explicit evaluation criteria and procedures for determining the extent to which a proposed governmental action could pose a risk of being ruled a regulatory taking in court. Another, less common, version of these state property rights laws focus on compensation. They place statutory limits on the extent to which regulatory action can reduce the economic value of private property—establishing, for example, a threshold of a 50 percent reduction in property value which would automatically require compensation. Kirk Emerson and Charles R. Wise, *Statutory Approaches to Regulatory Takings: State Property Rights Legislation Issues and Implications for Public Administration*, 57 PUB. ADMIN. REV. 411 (1997). *See also* John Martinez, *Statutes Enacting Takings Law: Flying in the Face of Uncertainty*, 26 URB. L. 327 (1994). Who should decide where to draw the line between protected property rights and the extent of regulation: the courts or the legislatures? What are the implications for implementation of environmental law?

3 THE ADMINISTRATIVE PROCESS

A. Standing, Ripeness, and Other Defenses

SIERRA CLUB V. MORTON
405 U.S. 727 (1972)

Mr. Justice STEWART delivered the opinion of the Court.

I

The Mineral King Valley is an area of great natural beauty nestled in the Sierra Nevada Mountains in Tulare County, California, adjacent to Sequoia National Park. It has been part of the Sequoia National Forest since 1926, and is designated as a national game refuge by special Act of Congress. Though once the site of extensive mining activity, Mineral King is now used almost exclusively for recreational purposes. Its relative inaccessibility and lack of development have limited the number of visitors each year, and at the same time have preserved the valley's quality as a quasi-wilderness area largely uncluttered by the products of civilization.

The United States Forest Service, which is entrusted with the maintenance and administration of national forests, began in the late 1940's to give consideration to Mineral King as a potential site for recreational development. Prodded by a rapidly increasing demand for skiing facilities, the Forest Service published a prospectus in 1965, inviting bids from private developers for the construction and operation of a ski resort that would also serve as a summer recreation area. The proposal of Walt Disney Enterprises, Inc., was chosen from those of six bidders, and Disney received a three-year permit to conduct surveys and explorations in the valley in connection with its preparation of a complete master plan for the resort.

The final Disney plan, approved by the Forest Service in January 1969, outlines a $35 million complex of motels, restaurants, swimming pools, parking lots, and other structures designed to accommodate 14,000 visitors daily. This complex is to be constructed on 80 acres of the valley floor under a 30-year use permit from the Forest Service. Other facilities, including ski lifts, ski trails, a cog-assisted railway, and utility installations, are to be constructed on the mountain slopes and in other parts of the valley under a revocable special-use permit. To provide access to the resort, the State of California proposes to construct a highway 20 miles in length. A section of this road would traverse Sequoia National Park, as would a proposed high voltage power line needed to provide electricity for the resort. Both the highway and the power line require the approval of the Department of the Interior, which is entrusted with the preservation and maintenance of the national parks.

Representatives of the Sierra Club, who favor maintaining Mineral King largely in its present state, followed the progress of recreational planning for the valley with close attention and increasing dismay. They unsuccessfully sought a public hearing on the proposed development in 1965, and in subsequent correspondence with officials of the Forest Service and the Department of the Interior, they expressed the Club's objections to Disney's plan as a whole and to particular features included in it. In June 1969 the Club filed the present suit in the United States District Court for the Northern District of California, seeking a declaratory judgment that various aspects of the proposed development contravene federal laws and regulations governing the preservation of national parks, forests, and game refuges,[2] and also seeking preliminary and permanent injunctions restraining the federal officials involved from granting their approval or issuing permits in connection with the Mineral King project. The petitioner Sierra Club sued as a membership corporation with "a special interest in the conservation and the sound maintenance of the national parks, game refuges and forests of the country," and invoked the judicial-review provisions of the Administrative Procedure Act, 5 U.S.C. § 701 *et seq.*

After two days of hearings, the District Court granted the requested preliminary injunction. It rejected the respondents' challenge to the Sierra Club's standing to sue, and determined that the hearing had raised questions "concerning possible excess of statutory authority, sufficiently substantial and serious to justify a preliminary injunction . . .." The respondents appealed, and the Court of Appeals for the Ninth Circuit reversed. 433 F.2d 24. With respect to the petitioner's standing, the court noted that there was "no allegation in the complaint that members of the Sierra Club would be affected by the actions of (the respondents) other than the fact that the actions are personally displeasing or distasteful to them" * * *.

II

The first question presented is whether the Sierra Club has alleged facts that entitle it to obtain judicial review of the challenged action. Whether a party has a sufficient stake in an otherwise justiciable controversy to obtain judicial resolution of that controversy is what has traditionally been referred to as the question of standing to sue. Where the party does not rely on any specific statute authorizing invocation of the judicial process, the question of standing depends upon whether the party has alleged such a "personal stake in the outcome of the controversy," *Baker v. Carr*, 369 U.S. 186, 204, as to ensure that "the dispute sought to be adjudicated will be presented in an adversary context and in a form historically viewed as capable of judicial resolution." *Flast v. Cohen*, 392 U.S. 83, 101. Where, however, Congress has authorized public officials to perform certain functions according to law, and has provided by statute for judicial review of those actions under certain circumstances, the inquiry as to standing must begin with a determination of whether the statute in question authorizes review at the behest of the plaintiff.[3]

The Sierra Club relies upon § 10 of the Administrative Procedure Act (APA), 5 U.S.C. § 702, which provides: "A person suffering legal wrong because of agency action, or adversely affected or aggrieved by agency action within the meaning of a relevant statute, is entitled to

---

[2]   As analyzed by the District Court, the complaint alleged violations of law falling into four categories. First, it claimed that the special-use permit for construction of the resort exceeded the maximum-acreage limitation placed upon such permits by 16 U.S.C. § 497, and that issuance of a "revocable" use permit was beyond the authority of the Forest Service. Second, it challenged the proposed permit for the highway through Sequoia National Park on the grounds that the highway would not serve any of the purposes of the park, in alleged violation of 16 U.S.C. § 1, and that it would destroy timber and other natural resources protected by 16 U.S.C. §§ 41 and 43. Third, it claimed that the Forest Service and the Department of the Interior had violated their own regulations by failing to hold adequate public hearings on the proposed project. Finally, the complaint asserted that 16 U.S.C. § 45c required specific congressional authorization of a permit for construction of a power transmission line within the limits of a national park.

[3]   Congress may not confer jurisdiction on Art. III federal courts to render advisory opinions, *Muskrat v. United States*, 219 U.S. 346, or to entertain "friendly" suits, *United States v. Johnson*, 319 U.S. 302, or to resolve "political questions," *Luther v. Borden*, 7 How. 1, because suits of this character are inconsistent with the judicial function under Art. III. But where a dispute is otherwise justiciable, the question whether the litigant is a "proper party to request an adjudication of a particular issue," *Flast v. Cohen*, 392 U.S. 83, 100, is one within the power of Congress to determine.

judicial review thereof." Early decisions under this statute interpreted the language as adopting the various formulations of "legal interest" and "legal wrong" then prevailing as constitutional requirements of standing. But, in *Data Processing Service v. Camp*, 397 U.S. 150, and *Barlow v. Collins*, 397 U.S. 159, decided the same day, we held more broadly that persons had standing to obtain judicial review of federal agency action under § 10 of the APA where they had alleged that the challenged action had caused them "injury in fact," and where the alleged injury was to an interest "arguably within the zone of interests to be protected or regulated" by the statutes that the agencies were claimed to have violated.

In *Data Processing*, the injury claimed by the petitioners consisted of harm to their competitive position in the computer-servicing market through a ruling by the Comptroller of the Currency that national banks might perform data-processing services for their customers. In *Barlow*, the petitioners were tenant farmers who claimed that certain regulations of the Secretary of Agriculture adversely affected their economic position vis-a-vis their landlords. These palpable economic injuries have long been recognized as sufficient to lay the basis for standing, with or without a specific statutory provision for judicial review. Thus, neither *Data Processing* nor *Barlow* addressed itself to the question, which has arisen with increasing frequency in federal courts in recent years, as to what must be alleged by persons who claim injury of a noneconomic nature to interests that are widely shared. That question is presented in this case.

III

The injury alleged by the Sierra Club will be incurred entirely by reason of the change in the uses to which Mineral King will be put, and the attendant change in the aesthetics and ecology of the area. Thus, in referring to the road to be built through Sequoia National Park, the complaint alleged that the development "would destroy or otherwise adversely affect the scenery, natural and historic objects and wildlife of the park and would impair the enjoyment of the park for future generations." We do not question that this type of harm may amount to an "injury in fact" sufficient to lay the basis for standing under § 10 of the APA. Aesthetic and environmental well-being, like economic well-being, are important ingredients of the quality of life in our society, and the fact that particular environmental interests are shared by the many rather than the few does not make them less deserving of legal protection through the judicial process. But the "injury in fact" test requires more than an injury to a cognizable interest. It requires that the party seeking review be himself among the injured.

The impact of the proposed changes in the environment of Mineral King will not fall indiscriminately upon every citizen. The alleged injury will be felt directly only by those who use Mineral King and Sequoia National Park, and for whom the aesthetic and recreational values of the area will be lessened by the highway and ski resort. The Sierra Club failed to allege that it or its members would be affected in any of their activities or pastimes by the Disney development. Nowhere in the pleadings or affidavits did the Club state that its members use Mineral King for any purpose, much less that they use it in any way that would be significantly affected by the proposed actions of the respondents.[8]

---

[8]   The only reference in the pleadings to the Sierra Club's interest in the dispute is contained in paragraph 3 of the complaint, which reads in its entirety as follows:

> Plaintiff Sierra Club is a non-profit corporation organized and operating under the laws of the State of California, with its principal place of business in San Francisco, California since 1892. Membership of the club is approximately 78,000 nationally, with approximately 27,000 members residing in the San Francisco Bay Area. For many years the Sierra Club by its activities and conduct has exhibited a special interest in the conservation and the sound maintenance of the national parks, game refuges and forests of the country, regularly serving as a responsible representative of persons

The Club apparently regarded any allegations of individualized injury as superfluous, on the theory that this was a "public" action involving questions as to the use of natural resources, and that the Club's longstanding concern with and expertise in such matters were sufficient to give it standing as a "representative of the public." This theory reflects a misunderstanding of our cases involving so-called "public actions" in the area of administrative law.

* * *

The trend of cases arising under the APA and other statutes authorizing judicial review of federal agency action has been toward recognizing that injuries other than economic harm are sufficient to bring a person within the meaning of the statutory language, and toward discarding the notion that an injury that is widely shared is ipso facto not an injury sufficient to provide the basis for judicial review. We noted this development with approval in *Data Processing*, 397 U.S. at 154, in saying that the interest alleged to have been injured "may reflect 'aesthetic, conservational, and recreational' as well as economic values." But broadening the categories of injury that may be alleged in support of standing is a different matter from abandoning the requirement that the party seeking review must himself have suffered an injury.

Some courts have indicated a willingness to take this latter step by conferring standing upon organizations that have demonstrated "an organizational interest in the problem" of environmental or consumer protection. *Environmental Defense Fund v. Hardin*, 428 F.2d 1093, 1097. It is clear that an organization whose members are injured may represent those members in a proceeding for judicial review. *See, e.g., NAACP v. Button*, 371 U.S. 415, 428. But a mere "interest in a problem," no matter how longstanding the interest and no matter how qualified the organization is in evaluating the problem, is not sufficient by itself to render the organization "adversely affected" or "aggrieved" within the meaning of the APA. The Sierra Club is a large and long-established organization, with a historic commitment to the cause of protecting our Nation's natural heritage from man's depredations. But if a "special interest" in this subject were enough to entitle the Sierra Club to commence this litigation, there would appear to be no objective basis upon which to disallow a suit by any other bona fide "special interest" organization, however small or short-lived. And if any group with a bona fide "special interest" could initiate such litigation, it is difficult to perceive why any individual citizen with the same bona fide special interest would not also be entitled to do so.

The requirement that a party seeking review must allege facts showing that he is himself adversely affected does not insulate executive action from judicial review, nor does it prevent any public interests from being protected through the judicial process. It does serve as at least a rough attempt to put the decision as to whether review will be sought in the hands of those who have a direct stake in the outcome. That goal would be undermined were we to construe the APA to authorize judicial review at the behest of organizations or individuals who seek to do

---

similarly interested. One of the principal purposes of the Sierra Club is to protect and conserve the national resources of the Sierra Nevada Mountains. Its interests would be vitally affected by the acts hereinafter described and would be aggrieved by those acts of the defendants as hereinafter more fully appears.

In an *amici curiae* brief filed in this Court by the Wilderness Society and others, it is asserted that the Sierra Club has conducted regular camping trips into the Mineral King area, and that various members of the Club have used and continue to use the area for recreational purposes. These allegations were not contained in the pleadings, nor were they brought to the attention of the Court of Appeals. Moreover, the Sierra Club in its reply brief specifically declines to rely on its individualized interest, as a basis for standing. Our decision does not, of course, bar the Sierra Club from seeking in the District Court to amend its complaint by a motion under Rule 15, Federal Rules of Civil Procedure.

no more than vindicate their own value preferences through the judicial process. The principle that the Sierra Club would have us establish in this case would do just that.

As we conclude that the Court of Appeals was correct in its holding that the Sierra Club lacked standing to maintain this action, we do not reach any other questions presented in the petition, and we intimate no view on the merits of the complaint. The judgment is Affirmed.

Mr. Justice DOUGLAS, dissenting.

I share the views of my Brother BLACKMUN and would reverse the judgment below.

The critical question of "standing" would be simplified and also put neatly in focus if we fashioned a federal rule that allowed environmental issues to be litigated before federal agencies or federal courts in the name of the inanimate object about to be despoiled, defaced, or invaded by roads and bulldozers and where injury is the subject of public outrage. Contemporary public concern for protecting nature's ecological equilibrium should lead to the conferral of standing upon environmental objects to sue for their own preservation. *See* Stone, *Should Trees Have Standing?—Toward Legal Rights for Natural Objects*, 45 S. CAL. L. REV. 450 (1972). This suit would therefore be more properly labeled as *Mineral King v. Morton.*

Inanimate objects are sometimes parties in litigation. A ship has a legal personality, a fiction found useful for maritime purposes. The corporation sole—a creature of ecclesiastical law—is an acceptable adversary and large fortunes ride on its cases. The ordinary corporation is a "person" for purposes of the adjudicatory processes, whether it represents proprietary, spiritual, aesthetic, or charitable causes.

So it should be as respects valleys, alpine meadows, rivers, lakes, estuaries, beaches, ridges, groves of trees, swampland, or even air that feels the destructive pressures of modern technology and modern life. The river, for example, is the living symbol of all the life it sustains or nourishes—fish, aquatic insects, water ouzels, otter, fisher, deer, elk, bear, and all other animals, including man, who are dependent on it or who enjoy it for its sight, its sound, or its life. The river, as plaintiff, speaks for the ecological unit of life that is part of it. Those people who have a meaningful relation to that body of water—whether it be a fisherman, a canoeist, a zoologist, or a logger—must be able to speak for the values which the river represents and which are threatened with destruction.

* * *

Mineral King is doubtless like other wonders of the Sierra Nevada such as Tuolumne Meadows and the John Muir Trail. Those who hike it, fish it, hunt it, camp in it, frequent it, or visit it merely to sit in solitude and wonderment are legitimate spokesmen for it, whether they may be few or many. Those who have that intimate relation with the inanimate object about to be injured, polluted, or otherwise despoiled are its legitimate spokesmen.

The Solicitor General, whose views on this subject are in the Appendix to this opinion, takes a wholly different approach. He considers the problem in terms of "government by the Judiciary." With all respect, the problem is to make certain that the inanimate objects, which are the very core of America's beauty, have spokesmen before they are destroyed. It is, of course, true that most of them are under the control of a federal or state agency. The standards given those agencies are usually expressed in terms of the "public interest." Yet "public interest" has so many differing shades of meaning as to be quite meaningless on the environmental front. Congress accordingly has adopted ecological standards in the National Environmental Policy Act of 1969, 42 U.S.C. § 4321 *et seq.*, and guidelines for agency action have been provided by the Council on Environmental Quality of which Russell E. Train is Chairman. *See* 36 Fed. Reg. 7724.

Yet the pressures on agencies for favorable action one way or the other are enormous. The suggestion that Congress can stop action which is undesirable is true in theory; yet even Congress is too remote to give meaningful direction and its machinery is too ponderous to use very often. The federal agencies of which I speak are not venal or corrupt. But they are notoriously under the control of powerful interests who manipulate them through advisory committees, or friendly working relations, or who have that natural affinity with the agency which in time develops between the regulator and the regulated. * * *

* * *

The Forest Service—one of the federal agencies behind the scheme to despoil Mineral King—has been notorious for its alignment with lumber companies, although its mandate from Congress directs it to consider the various aspects of multiple use in its supervision of the national forests.

The voice of the inanimate object, therefore, should not be stilled. That does not mean that the judiciary takes over the managerial functions from the federal agency. It merely means that before these priceless bits of Americana (such as a valley, an alpine meadow, a river, or a lake) are forever lost or are so transformed as to be reduced to the eventual rubble of our urban environment, the voice of the existing beneficiaries of these environmental wonders should be heard.

Perhaps they will not win. Perhaps the bulldozers of "progress" will plow under all the aesthetic wonders of this beautiful land. That is not the present question. The sole question is, who has standing to be heard?

Those who hike the Appalachian Trail into Sunfish Pond, New Jersey, and camp or sleep there, or run the Allagash in Maine, or climb the Guadalupes in West Texas, or who canoe and portage the Quetico Superior in Minnesota, certainly should have standing to defend those natural wonders before courts or agencies, though they live 3,000 miles away. Those who merely are caught up in environmental news or propaganda and flock to defend these waters or areas may be treated differently. That is why these environmental issues should be tendered by the inanimate object itself. Then there will be assurances that all of the forms of life which it represents will stand before the court—the pileated woodpecker as well as the coyote and bear, the lemmings as well as the trout in the streams. Those inarticulate members of the ecological group cannot speak. But those people who have so frequented the place as to know its values and wonders will be able to speak for the entire ecological community.

* * *

That, as I see it, is the issue of "standing" in the present case and controversy.

NOTES

1.   What is the test for standing established by the Supreme Court in *Sierra Club*? Why does Justice Douglas dissent from the majority opinion? Justice Douglas suggests in his dissent that the Court should confer standing on "environmental objects to sue for their own preservation." What practical problems attend this approach? Are these problems outweighed by the advantages? *See* Christopher Stone, *Should Trees Have Standing?—Toward Legal Rights for Natural Trees*, 45 S. CAL. L. REV. 450 (1972); Laurence H. Tribe, *Ways Not to Think About Plastic Trees: New Foundations for Environmental Law*, 83 YALE L.J. 1315 (1974).

2. A plaintiff whose claim is dismissed for lack of standing may refile or be permitted to amend the pleadings without being barred by *res judicata*. The Sierra Club was subsequently allowed to amend its complaint to comply with the Supreme Court's requirements. 348 F. Supp. 219 (N.D. Cal. 1972). In its amendment, the Sierra Club alleged that its members used the Mineral King valley and added as co-plaintiffs a group of nearby property owners and nine members who regularly visited the area.

3. In its amended complaint following the remand, the Sierra Club also added a new claim—that the Forest Service was required by the National Environmental Policy Act (NEPA) to prepare an environmental impact statement (EIS) for the proposed Mineral King project. By the time the Forest Service released its draft EIS in 1975, the Mineral King issue had gained national attention. Subsequently, the final EIS, released in 1976, recommended a significantly smaller development project due to severe environmental impacts from the proposed project. In 1977, Sierra Club's lawsuit was dismissed without prejudice. The ski resort was never built, and Mineral King became part of the Sequoia National Park in 1978. *See* TOM TURNER, WILD BY LAW: THE SIERRA CLUB LEGAL DEFENSE FUND AND THE PLACES IT HAS SAVED 21-23 (1990).

4. In *Sierra Club*, the Supreme Court reiterated its holding in *NAACP v. Button* that an organization may represent its injured members in litigation. Subsequently, in *Hunt v. Washington Apple Advertising Committee*, 432 U.S. 333, 343 (1977), the Court established a three-part test for "organizational" or "representational" standing: (1) the organization's members would otherwise have standing in their own right; (2) the interests which the organization seeks to protect are germane to the organization's purpose; and (3) neither the claim asserted nor relief requested requires participation of individual members in the lawsuit. Considering that the constitutional basis for standing is Article III's "case" or "controversy" requirement, why does the Court make standing more difficult for an organization than for an individual? Do the requirements promote excessive litigation to determine standing? Are the case and controversy requirements of the Constitution well served by granting standing to an individual who occasionally uses a natural resource such as Mineral King, but denying standing to an organization whose longstanding mission is to preserve areas like Mineral King? Note the Court's reasoning in *Sierra Club*: "[I]f a 'special interest' in this subject were enough * * * there would appear to be no objective basis upon which to disallow a suit by any other bona fide 'special interest' organization however small or short-lived." *Sierra Club*, 405 U.S. at 739.

5. The Supreme Court's most generous holding for standing in environmental cases is *United States v. Students Challenging Regulatory Agency Procedures* (*SCRAP*), 412 U.S. 669 (1973), in which standing was granted to a group of law students challenging Interstate Commerce Commission (ICC) freight rate increases. The students alleged that their members "use[d] the forests, rivers, streams, mountains and other natural resources in the Washington metropolitan area * * * for camping, hiking, fishing, [and] sightseeing * * *." *Id.* at 678. The higher freight rate, they claimed, would decrease the use of recyclable goods and increase the use of raw materials, resulting in additional litter and air pollution, increased resource extraction, and higher taxes. The Court accepted the allegations as sufficient to establish injury-in-fact. Although the injury to the plaintiffs seemed insignificant, the Court held that "an identifiable trifle is enough for standing." *Id.* at 689 n.14. How does the alleged injury-in-fact in *SCRAP* differ from that in *Sierra Club*?

6.   Economists have responded to the problem of incorporating preservation concerns into their methods by devising "existence values" that they quantify in cost-benefit analyses. A preserved environment has "existence value" for people who do not experience the environment directly but who reserve the option to encounter it in the future or who derive satisfaction just from knowing it is there. For instance:

> Individuals and households which may never visit the Grand Canyon may still value visibility there simply because they wish to preserve a national treasure. Individuals also may wish to know that the Grand Canyon retains relatively pristine air quality even on days when they are not visiting the park. Concern about preserving air quality at the Grand Canyon may be just as intense in New York or in Chicago as in nearby states and communities.

William Schulze et al., *The Economic Benefits of Preserving Visibility in the National Parklands of the Southwest*, 23 NAT. RESOURCES J. 149, 154 (1983). Should courts respond to preservation concerns in a similar manner? Does a New Yorker suffer "injury in fact" from or have a personal stake in Grand Canyon visibility problems? See Richard Zerbe, *Comment: Does Benefit Cost Analysis Stand Alone? Rights and Standing*, 10 J. POL'Y ANALYSIS & MGMT. 96 (1991), for a discussion of the standing issues economists face when determining whose interests should be considered in cost-benefit analysis.

7.   As the following two cases suggest, in recent years the Court has taken a less generous approach toward standing.

LUJAN V. DEFENDERS OF WILDLIFE
504 U.S. 555 (1992)

Justice SCALIA delivered the opinion of the Court with respect to Parts I, II, III-A, and IV, and an opinion with respect to Part III-B in which the Chief Justice, Justice WHITE, and Justice THOMAS join.

This case involves a challenge to a rule promulgated by the Secretary of the Interior interpreting § 7 of the Endangered Species Act of 1973 (ESA), 16 U.S.C. § 1536, in such fashion as to render it applicable only to actions within the United States or on the high seas. The preliminary issue, and the only one we reach, is whether the respondents here, plaintiffs below, have standing to seek judicial review of the rule.

I

The ESA, 16 U.S.C. § 1531 *et seq.*, seeks to protect species of animals against threats to their continuing existence caused by man. The ESA instructs the Secretary of the Interior to promulgate by regulation a list of those species which are either endangered or threatened under enumerated criteria, and to define the critical habitat of these species. Section 7(a)(2) of the Act then provides, in pertinent part: "Each Federal agency shall, in consultation with and with the assistance of the Secretary [of the Interior], insure that any action authorized, funded, or carried out by such agency . . . is not likely to jeopardize the continued existence of any endangered species or threatened species or result in the destruction or adverse modification of habitat of such species which is determined by the Secretary, after consultation as appropriate with affected States, to be critical." 16 U.S.C. § 1536(a)(2).

In 1978, the Fish and Wildlife Service (FWS) and the National Marine Fisheries Service (NMFS), on behalf of the Secretary of the Interior and the Secretary of Commerce respectively, promulgated a joint regulation stating that the obligations imposed by § 7(a)(2) extend to actions taken in foreign nations. 43 Fed. Reg. 874 (1978). The next year, however, the Interior Department began to reexamine its position. A revised joint regulation, reinterpreting § 7(a)(2) to require consultation only for actions taken in the United States or on the high seas, was proposed in 1983, and promulgated in 1986, 50 C.F.R. 402.01 (1991).

Shortly thereafter, respondents, organizations dedicated to wildlife conservation and other environmental causes, filed this action against the Secretary of the Interior, seeking a declaratory judgment that the new regulation is in error as to the geographic scope of § 7(a)(2), and an injunction requiring the Secretary to promulgate a new regulation restoring the initial interpretation. The District Court granted the Secretary's motion to dismiss for lack of standing. *Defenders of Wildlife v. Hodel*, 658 F. Supp. 43, 47-48 (Minn. 1987). The Court of Appeals for the Eighth Circuit reversed by a divided vote. *Defenders of Wildlife v. Hodel*, 851 F.2d 1035 (1988). On remand, the Secretary moved for summary judgment on the standing issue, and respondents moved for summary judgment on the merits. The District Court denied the Secretary's motion, on the ground that the Eighth Circuit had already determined the standing question in this case; it granted respondents' merits motion, and ordered the Secretary to publish a revised regulation. *Defenders of Wildlife v. Hodel*, 707 F. Supp. 1082 (Minn. 1989). The Eighth Circuit affirmed. 911 F.2d 117 (1990). We granted certiorari.

II

While the Constitution of the United States divides all power conferred upon the Federal Government into "legislative Powers," Art. I, § 1, "[t]he executive Power," Art. II, § 1, and "[t]he judicial Power," Art. III, § 1, it does not attempt to define those terms. To be sure, it limits the jurisdiction of federal courts to "Cases" and "Controversies," but an executive inquiry can bear the name "case" (the Hoffa case) and a legislative dispute can bear the name "controversy" (the Smoot-Hawley controversy). Obviously, then, the Constitution's central mechanism of separation of powers depends largely upon common understanding of what activities are appropriate to legislatures, to executives, and to courts. In The Federalist No. 48, Madison expressed the view that "[i]t is not infrequently a question of real nicety in legislative bodies whether the operation of a particular measure will, or will not, extend beyond the legislative sphere," whereas "the executive power [is] restrained within a narrower compass and . . . more simple in its nature," and "the judiciary [is] described by landmarks still less uncertain." The Federalist No. 48, p. 256 (Carey and McClellan eds. 1990). One of those landmarks, setting apart the "Cases" and "Controversies" that are of the justiciable sort referred to in Article III—"serv[ing] to identify those disputes which are appropriately resolved through the judicial process," *Whitmore v. Arkansas*, 495 U.S. 149, 155 (1990)—is the doctrine of standing. Though some of its elements express merely prudential considerations that are part of judicial self-government, the core component of standing is an essential and unchanging part of the case-or-controversy requirement of Article III. *See, e.g., Allen v. Wright*, 468 U.S. 737, 751 (1984).

Over the years, our cases have established that the irreducible constitutional minimum of standing contains three elements: First, the plaintiff must have suffered an "injury in fact"—an invasion of a legally-protected interest which is (a) concrete and particularized; and (b) "actual or imminent, not 'conjectural' or 'hypothetical.'" Second, there must be a causal connection between the injury and the conduct complained of—the injury has to be "fairly . . . trace[able] to the challenged action of the defendant, and not . . . th[e] result [of] the independent action of some third party not before the court." *Simon v. Eastern Kentucky Welfare Rights Org.*, 426

U.S. 26, 41-42 (1976). Third, it must be "likely," as opposed to merely "speculative," that the injury will be "redressed by a favorable decision." *Id.* at 38, 43.

The party invoking federal jurisdiction bears the burden of establishing these elements. Since they are not mere pleading requirements but rather an indispensable part of the plaintiff's case, each element must be supported in the same way as any other matter on which the plaintiff bears the burden of proof, *i.e.*, with the manner and degree of evidence required at the successive stages of the litigation. At the pleading stage, general factual allegations of injury resulting from the defendant's conduct may suffice, for on a motion to dismiss we "presum[e] that general allegations embrace those specific facts that are necessary to support the claim," *National Wildlife Federation, supra,* 497 U.S. at 889. In response to a summary judgment motion, however, the plaintiff can no longer rest on such "mere allegations," but must "set forth" by affidavit or other evidence "specific facts," Fed. Rule Civ. Proc. 56(e), which for purposes of the summary judgment motion will be taken to be true. And at the final stage, those facts (if controverted) must be "supported adequately by the evidence adduced at trial."

When the suit is one challenging the legality of government action or inaction, the nature and extent of facts that must be averred (at the summary judgment stage) or proved (at the trial stage) in order to establish standing depends considerably upon whether the plaintiff is himself an object of the action (or forgone action) at issue. If he is, there is ordinarily little question that the action or inaction has caused him injury, and that a judgment preventing or requiring the action will redress it. When, however, as in this case, a plaintiff's asserted injury arises from the government's allegedly unlawful regulation (or lack of regulation) of someone else, much more is needed. In that circumstance, causation and redressability ordinarily hinge on the response of the regulated (or regulable) third party to the government action or inaction—and perhaps on the response of others as well. The existence of one or more of the essential elements of standing "depends on the unfettered choices made by independent actors not before the courts and whose exercise of broad and legitimate discretion the courts cannot presume either to control or to predict;" and it becomes the burden of the plaintiff to adduce facts showing that those choices have been or will be made in such manner as to produce causation and permit redressability of injury. *E.g., Warth, supra,* 422 U.S. at 505. Thus, when the plaintiff is not himself the object of the government action or inaction he challenges, standing is not precluded, but it is ordinarily "substantially more difficult" to establish.

III

* * *

A

Respondents' claim to injury is that the lack of consultation with respect to certain funded activities abroad "increas[es] the rate of extinction of endangered and threatened species." Of course, the desire to use or observe an animal species, even for purely aesthetic purposes, is undeniably a cognizable interest for purpose of standing. *See, e.g., Sierra Club v. Morton,* 405 U.S. at 734. "But the 'injury in fact' test requires more than an injury to a cognizable interest. It requires that the party seeking review be himself among the injured." *Id.* at 734-35. To survive the Secretary's summary judgment motion, respondents had to submit affidavits or other evidence showing, through specific facts, not only that listed species were in fact being threatened by funded activities abroad, but also that one or more of respondents' members would thereby be "directly" affected apart from their "'special interest' in th[e] subject." *Id.* at 735, 739.

With respect to this aspect of the case, the Court of Appeals focused on the affidavits of two Defenders' members—Joyce Kelly and Amy Skilbred. Ms. Kelly stated that she traveled to Egypt in 1986 and "observed the traditional habitat of the endangered Nile crocodile there and intend[s] to do so again, and hope[s] to observe the crocodile directly," and that she "will suffer harm in fact as a result of [the] American . . . role . . . in overseeing the rehabilitation of the Aswan High Dam on the Nile . . . and [in] develop[ing] . . . Egypt's . . . Master Water Plan." Ms. Skilbred averred that she traveled to Sri Lanka in 1981 and "observed th[e] habitat" of "endangered species such as the Asian elephant and the leopard" at what is now the site of the Mahaweli Project funded by the Agency for International Development (AID), although she "was unable to see any of the endangered species;" "this development project," she continued, "will seriously reduce endangered, threatened, and endemic species habitat including areas that I visited . . . [which] may severely shorten the future of these species;" that threat, she concluded, harmed her because she "intend[s] to return to Sri Lanka in the future and hope[s] to be more fortunate in spotting at least the endangered elephant and leopard." When Ms. Skilbred was asked at a subsequent deposition if and when she had any plans to return to Sri Lanka, she reiterated that "I intend to go back to Sri Lanka," but confessed that she had no current plans: "I don't know [when]. There is a civil war going on right now. I don't know. Not next year, I will say. In the future."

We shall assume for the sake of argument that these affidavits contain facts showing that certain agency-funded projects threaten listed species—though that is questionable. They plainly contain no facts, however, showing how damage to the species will produce "imminent" injury to Mss. Kelly and Skilbred. That the women "had visited" the areas of the projects before the projects commenced proves nothing. As we have said in a related context, "'[p]ast exposure to illegal conduct does not in itself show a present case or controversy regarding injunctive relief . . . if unaccompanied by any continuing, present adverse effects.'" And the affiants' profession of an "inten[t]" to return to the places they had visited before—where they will presumably, this time, be deprived of the opportunity to observe animals of the endangered species—is simply not enough. Such "some day" intentions—without any description of concrete plans, or indeed even any specification of when the some day will be—do not support a finding of the "actual or imminent" injury that our cases require.

Besides relying upon the Kelly and Skilbred affidavits, respondents propose a series of novel standing theories. The first, inelegantly styled "ecosystem nexus," proposes that any person who uses any part of a "contiguous ecosystem" adversely affected by a funded activity has standing even if the activity is located a great distance away. This approach, as the Court of Appeals correctly observed, is inconsistent with our opinion in *National Wildlife Federation,* which held that a plaintiff claiming injury from environmental damage must use the area affected by the challenged activity and not an area roughly "in the vicinity" of it. 497 U.S. at 887-89; *see also Sierra Club,* 405 U.S. at 735. It makes no difference that the general-purpose section of the ESA states that the Act was intended in part "to provide a means whereby the ecosystems upon which endangered species and threatened species depend may be conserved," 16 U.S.C. § 1531(b). To say that the Act protects ecosystems is not to say that the Act creates (if it were possible) rights of action in persons who have not been injured in fact, that is, persons who use portions of an ecosystem not perceptibly affected by the unlawful action in question.

Respondents' other theories are called, alas, the "animal nexus" approach, whereby anyone who has an interest in studying or seeing the endangered animals anywhere on the globe has standing; and the "vocational nexus" approach, under which anyone with a professional interest in such animals can sue. Under these theories, anyone who goes to see Asian elephants in the Bronx Zoo, and anyone who is a keeper of Asian elephants in the Bronx Zoo, has standing to sue because the Director of AID did not consult with the Secretary regarding the AID-funded project in Sri Lanka. This is beyond all reason. Standing is not "an ingenious academic exercise in the conceivable," *United States v. Students Challenging Regulatory Agency Procedures*

(SCRAP), 412 U.S. 669, 688 (1973), but as we have said requires, at the summary judgment stage, a factual showing of perceptible harm. It is clear that the person who observes or works with a particular animal threatened by a federal decision is facing perceptible harm, since the very subject of his interest will no longer exist. It is even plausible—though it goes to the outermost limit of plausibility—to think that a person who observes or works with animals of a particular species in the very area of the world where that species is threatened by a federal decision is facing such harm, since some animals that might have been the subject of his interest will no longer exist, *see Japan Whaling Assn. v. American Cetacean Soc.,* 478 U.S. 221, 231, n.4 (1986). It goes beyond the limit, however, and into pure speculation and fantasy, to say that anyone who observes or works with an endangered species, anywhere in the world, is appreciably harmed by a single project affecting some portion of that species with which he has no more specific connection.

B

Besides failing to show injury, respondents failed to demonstrate redressability. Instead of attacking the separate decisions to fund particular projects allegedly causing them harm, the respondents chose to challenge a more generalized level of government action (rules regarding consultation), the invalidation of which would affect all overseas projects. This programmatic approach has obvious practical advantages, but also obvious difficulties insofar as proof of causation or redressability is concerned. As we have said in another context, "suits challenging, not specifically identifiable Government violations of law, but the particular programs agencies establish to carry out their legal obligations . . . [are], even when premised on allegations of several instances of violations of law, . . . rarely if ever appropriate for federal-court adjudication." *Allen,* 468 U.S. at 759-60.

The most obvious problem in the present case is redressability. Since the agencies funding the projects were not parties to the case, the District Court could accord relief only against the Secretary: He could be ordered to revise his regulation to require consultation for foreign projects. But this would not remedy respondents' alleged injury unless the funding agencies were bound by the Secretary's regulation, which is very much an open question. * * * When the Secretary promulgated the regulation at issue here, he thought it was binding on the agencies, *see* 51 Fed. Reg. at 19928 (1986). The Solicitor General, however, has repudiated that position here, and the agencies themselves apparently deny the Secretary's authority. * * *

Respondents assert that this legal uncertainty did not affect redressability (and hence standing) because the District Court itself could resolve the issue of the Secretary's authority as a necessary part of its standing inquiry. Assuming that it is appropriate to resolve an issue of law such as this in connection with a threshold standing inquiry, resolution by the District Court would not have remedied respondents' alleged injury anyway, because it would not have been binding upon the agencies. They were not parties to the suit, and there is no reason they should be obliged to honor an incidental legal determination the suit produced. The Court of Appeals tried to finesse this problem by simply proclaiming that "[w]e are satisfied that an injunction requiring the Secretary to publish [respondents' desired] regulatio[n] . . . would result in consultation." *Defenders of Wildlife,* 851 F.2d at 1042, 1043-44. We do not know what would justify that confidence, particularly when the Justice Department (presumably after consultation with the agencies) has taken the position that the regulation is not binding. The short of the matter is that redress of the only injury-in-fact respondents complain of requires action (termination of funding until consultation) by the individual funding agencies; and any relief the District Court could have provided in this suit against the Secretary was not likely to produce that action.

A further impediment to redressability is the fact that the agencies generally supply only a fraction of the funding for a foreign project. AID, for example, has provided less than 10% of the funding for the Mahaweli Project. Respondents have produced nothing to indicate that the projects they have named will either be suspended, or do less harm to listed species, if that fraction is eliminated. * * * [I]t is entirely conjectural whether the nonagency activity that affects respondents will be altered or affected by the agency activity they seek to achieve. There is no standing.

IV

The Court of Appeals found that respondents had standing for an additional reason: because they had suffered a "procedural injury." The so-called "citizen-suit" provision of the ESA provides, in pertinent part, that "any person may commence a civil suit on his own behalf (A) to enjoin any person, including the United States and any other governmental instrumentality or agency . . . who is alleged to be in violation of any provision of this chapter." 16 U.S.C. § 1540(g). The court held that, because § 7(a)(2) requires interagency consultation, the citizen-suit provision creates a "procedural righ[t]" to consultation in all "persons"—so that anyone can file suit in federal court to challenge the Secretary's (or presumably any other official's) failure to follow the assertedly correct consultative procedure, notwithstanding their inability to allege any discrete injury flowing from that failure. 911 F.2d at 121-22. To understand the remarkable nature of this holding one must be clear about what it does not rest upon: This is not a case where plaintiffs are seeking to enforce a procedural requirement the disregard of which could impair a separate concrete interest of theirs (*e.g.*, the procedural requirement for a hearing prior to denial of their license application, or the procedural requirement for an environmental impact statement before a federal facility is constructed next door to them).[7] Nor is it simply a case where concrete injury has been suffered by many persons, as in mass fraud or mass tort situations. Nor, finally, is it the unusual case in which Congress has created a concrete private interest in the outcome of a suit against a private party for the government's benefit, by providing a cash bounty for the victorious plaintiff. Rather, the court held that the injury-in-fact requirement had been satisfied by congressional conferral upon all persons of an abstract, self-contained, noninstrumental "right" to have the Executive observe the procedures required by law. We reject this view.[8]

---

[7]   There is this much truth to the assertion that "procedural rights" are special: The person who has been accorded a procedural right to protect his concrete interests can assert that right without meeting all the normal standards for redressability and immediacy. Thus, under our case-law, one living adjacent to the site for proposed construction of a federally licensed dam has standing to challenge the licensing agency's failure to prepare an Environmental Impact Statement, even though he cannot establish with any certainty that the Statement will cause the license to be withheld or altered, and even though the dam will not be completed for many years. (That is why we do not rely, in the present case, upon the Government's argument that, even if the other agencies were obliged to consult with the Secretary, they might not have followed his advice.) What respondents' "procedural rights" argument seeks, however, is quite different from this: standing for persons who have no concrete interests affected—persons who live (and propose to live) at the other end of the country from the dam.

[8]   The dissent's discussion of this aspect of the case distorts our opinion. We do not hold that an individual cannot enforce procedural rights; he assuredly can, so long as the procedures in question are designed to protect some threatened concrete interest of his that is the ultimate basis of his standing. The dissent, however, asserts that there exist "classes of procedural duties . . . so enmeshed with the prevention of a substantive, concrete harm that an individual plaintiff may be able to demonstrate a sufficient likelihood of injury just through the breach of that procedural duty." If we understand this correctly, it means that the government's violation of a certain (undescribed) class of procedural duty satisfies the concrete injury requirement by itself,

We have consistently held that a plaintiff raising only a generally available grievance about government—claiming only harm to his and every citizen's interest in proper application of the Constitution and laws, and seeking relief that no more directly and tangibly benefits him than it does the public at large—does not state an Article III case or controversy. * * *

* * *

To be sure, our generalized-grievance cases have typically involved Government violation of procedures assertedly ordained by the Constitution rather than the Congress. But there is absolutely no basis for making the Article III inquiry turn on the source of the asserted right. Whether the courts were to act on their own, or at the invitation of Congress, in ignoring the concrete injury requirement described in our cases, they would be discarding a principle fundamental to the separate and distinct constitutional role of the Third Branch—one of the essential elements that identifies those "Cases" and "Controversies" that are the business of the courts rather than of the political branches. "The province of the court," as Chief Justice Marshall said in *Marbury v. Madison,* 5 U.S. (1 Cranch) 137, 170 (1803), "is, solely, to decide on the rights of individuals." Vindicating the public interest (including the public interest in government observance of the Constitution and laws) is the function of Congress and the Chief Executive. * * * To permit Congress to convert the undifferentiated public interest in executive officers' compliance with the law into an "individual right" vindicable in the courts is to permit Congress to transfer from the President to the courts the Chief Executive's most important constitutional duty, to "take Care that the Laws be faithfully executed," Art. II, § 3. * * *

* * *

We hold that respondents lack standing to bring this action and that the Court of Appeals erred in denying the summary judgment motion filed by the United States. The opinion of the Court of Appeals is hereby reversed, and the cause remanded for proceedings consistent with this opinion.

It is so ordered.

Justice KENNEDY, with whom Justice SOUTER joins, concurring in part and concurring in the judgment.

Although I agree with the essential parts of the Court's analysis, I write separately to make several observations.

I agree with the Court's conclusion in Part III-A that, on the record before us, respondents have failed to demonstrate that they themselves are "among the injured." *Sierra Club v. Morton,* 405 U.S. 727, 735 (1972). This component of the standing inquiry is not satisfied unless "[p]laintiffs . . . demonstrate a 'personal stake in the outcome.' . . . Abstract injury is not enough." * * *

---

without any showing that the procedural violation endangers a concrete interest of the plaintiff (apart from his interest in having the procedure observed). We cannot agree. The dissent is unable to cite a single case in which we actually found standing solely on the basis of a "procedural right" unconnected to the plaintiff's own concrete harm. Its suggestion that we did so in *Japan Whaling Association, supra,* and *Robertson v. Methow Valley Citizens Council,* 490 U.S. 332 (1989), is not supported by the facts. In the former case, we found that the environmental organizations had standing because the "whale watching and studying of their members w[ould] be adversely affected by continued whale harvesting," *see* 478 U.S. at 230-31, n.4; and in the latter we did not so much as mention standing, for the very good reason that the plaintiff was a citizens' council for the area in which the challenged construction was to occur, so that its members would obviously be concretely affected, *see Methow Valley Citizens Council v. Regional Forester,* 833 F.2d 810, 812-13 (9th Cir. 1987).

While it may seem trivial to require that Mss. Kelly and Skilbred acquire airline tickets to the project sites or announce a date certain upon which they will return, this is not a case where it is reasonable to assume that the affiants will be using the sites on a regular basis, *see Sierra Club v. Morton, supra,* 405 U.S. at 735, n.8, nor do the affiants claim to have visited the sites since the projects commenced. With respect to the Court's discussion of respondents' "ecosystem nexus," "animal nexus," and "vocational nexus" theories, I agree that on this record respondents' showing is insufficient to establish standing on any of these bases. I am not willing to foreclose the possibility, however, that in different circumstances a nexus theory similar to those proffered here might support a claim to standing. *See Japan Whaling Assn. v. American Cetacean Soc.,* 478 U.S. 221, 231, n.4 (1986) ("respondents . . . undoubtedly have alleged a sufficient 'injury in fact' in that the whale watching and studying of their members will be adversely affected by continued whale harvesting").

In light of the conclusion that respondents have not demonstrated a concrete injury here sufficient to support standing under our precedents, I would not reach the issue of redressability that is discussed by the plurality in Part III-B.

I also join Part IV of the Court's opinion with the following observations. As government programs and policies become more complex and far-reaching, we must be sensitive to the articulation of new rights of action that do not have clear analogs in our common-law tradition. * * * In my view, Congress has the power to define injuries and articulate chains of causation that will give rise to a case or controversy where none existed before, and I do not read the Court's opinion to suggest a contrary view. *See Warth v. Seldin,* 422 U.S. 490, 500 (1975). In exercising this power, however, Congress must at the very least identify the injury it seeks to vindicate and relate the injury to the class of persons entitled to bring suit. The citizen-suit provision of the Endangered Species Act does not meet these minimal requirements, because while the statute purports to confer a right on "any person . . . to enjoin . . . the United States and any other governmental instrumentality or agency . . . who is alleged to be in violation of any provision of this chapter," it does not of its own force establish that there is an injury in "any person" by virtue of any "violation." 16 U.S.C. § 1540(g)(1)(A).

The Court's holding that there is an outer limit to the power of Congress to confer rights of action is a direct and necessary consequence of the case and controversy limitations found in Article III. I agree that it would exceed those limitations if, at the behest of Congress and in the absence of any showing of concrete injury, we were to entertain citizen-suits to vindicate the public's nonconcrete interest in the proper administration of the laws. While it does not matter how many persons have been injured by the challenged action, the party bringing suit must show that the action injures him in a concrete and personal way. This requirement is not just an empty formality. It preserves the vitality of the adversarial process by assuring both that the parties before the court have an actual, as opposed to professed, stake in the outcome, and that "the legal questions presented . . . will be resolved, not in the rarefied atmosphere of a debating society, but in a concrete factual context conducive to a realistic appreciation of the consequences of judicial action." *Valley Forge Christian College v. Americans United for Separation of Church and State, Inc.,* 454 U.S. 464, 472 (1982). In addition, the requirement of concrete injury confines the Judicial Branch to its proper, limited role in the constitutional framework of government.

* * *

Justice STEVENS, concurring in the judgment.

Because I am not persuaded that Congress intended the consultation requirement in § 7(a)(2) of the Endangered Species Act of 1973 (ESA), 16 U.S.C. § 1536(a)(2), to apply to activities in foreign countries, I concur in the judgment of reversal. I do not, however, agree with the Court's conclusion that respondents lack standing because the threatened injury to their interest in protecting the environment and studying endangered species is not "imminent." Nor do I agree with the plurality's additional conclusion that respondents' injury is not "redressable" in this litigation.

I

In my opinion a person who has visited the critical habitat of an endangered species, has a professional interest in preserving the species and its habitat, and intends to revisit them in the future has standing to challenge agency action that threatens their destruction. Congress has found that a wide variety of endangered species of fish, wildlife, and plants are of "aesthetic, ecological, educational, historical, recreational, and scientific value to the Nation and its people." 16 U.S.C. § 1531(a)(3). Given that finding, we have no license to demean the importance of the interest that particular individuals may have in observing any species or its habitat, whether those individuals are motivated by aesthetic enjoyment, an interest in professional research, or an economic interest in preservation of the species. * * *

The Court nevertheless concludes that respondents have not suffered "injury in fact" because they have not shown that the harm to the endangered species will produce "imminent" injury to them. I disagree. An injury to an individual's interest in studying or enjoying a species and its natural habitat occurs when someone (whether it be the government or a private party) takes action that harms that species and habitat. In my judgment, therefore, the "imminence" of such an injury should be measured by the timing and likelihood of the threatened environmental harm, rather than—as the Court seems to suggest—by the time that might elapse between the present and the time when the individuals would visit the area if no such injury should occur.

* * *

* * * In my view, Joyce Kelly and Amy Skilbred have introduced sufficient evidence to negate petitioner's contention that their claims of injury are "speculative" or "conjectural." As Justice BLACKMUN explains, a reasonable finder of fact could conclude, from their past visits, their professional backgrounds, and their affidavits and deposition testimony, that Ms. Kelly and Ms. Skilbred will return to the project sites and, consequently, will be injured by the destruction of the endangered species and critical habitat.

* * *

Justice BLACKMUN, with whom Justice O'CONNOR joins, dissenting.

I part company with the Court in this case in two respects. First, I believe that respondents have raised genuine issues of fact—sufficient to survive summary judgment—both as to injury and as to redressability. Second, I question the Court's breadth of language in rejecting standing for "procedural" injuries. I fear the Court seeks to impose fresh limitations on the constitutional authority of Congress to allow citizen-suits in the federal courts for injuries deemed "procedural" in nature. I dissent.

I

Article III of the Constitution confines the federal courts to adjudication of actual "cases" and "controversies." To ensure the presence of a "case" or "controversy," this Court has held that Article III requires, as an irreducible minimum, that a plaintiff allege (1) an injury that is (2) "fairly traceable to the defendant's allegedly unlawful conduct" and that is (3) "likely to be redressed by the requested relief." *Allen v. Wright,* 468 U.S. 737, 751 (1984).

A

To survive petitioner's motion for summary judgment on standing, respondents need not prove that they are actually or imminently harmed. They need show only a "genuine issue" of material fact as to standing. Fed. Rule Civ. Proc. 56(c). This is not a heavy burden. A "genuine issue" exists so long as "the evidence is such that a reasonable jury could return a verdict for the nonmoving party [respondents]." *Anderson v. Liberty Lobby, Inc.,* 477 U.S. 242, 248 (1986). This Court's "function is not [it]self to weigh the evidence and determine the truth of the matter but to determine whether there is a genuine issue for trial." *Id.* at 249.

The Court never mentions the "genuine issue" standard. Rather, the Court refers to the type of evidence it feels respondents failed to produce, namely, "affidavits or other evidence showing, through specific facts" the existence of injury. The Court thereby confuses respondents' evidentiary burden (*i.e.*, affidavits asserting "specific facts") in withstanding a summary judgment motion under Rule 56(e) with the standard of proof (*i.e.*, the existence of a "genuine issue" of "material fact") under Rule 56(c).

1

Were the Court to apply the proper standard for summary judgment, I believe it would conclude that the sworn affidavits and deposition testimony of Joyce Kelly and Amy Skilbred advance sufficient facts to create a genuine issue for trial concerning whether one or both would be imminently harmed by the Aswan and Mahaweli projects. In the first instance, as the Court itself concedes, the affidavits contained facts making it at least "questionable" (and therefore within the province of the factfinder) that certain agency-funded projects threaten listed species. The only remaining issue, then, is whether Kelly and Skilbred have shown that they personally would suffer imminent harm.

I think a reasonable finder of fact could conclude from the information in the affidavits and deposition testimony that either Kelly or Skilbred will soon return to the project sites, thereby satisfying the "actual or imminent" injury standard. The Court dismisses Kelly's and Skilbred's general statements that they intended to revisit the project sites as "simply not enough." But those statements did not stand alone. A reasonable finder of fact could conclude, based not only upon their statements of intent to return, but upon their past visits to the project sites, as well as their professional backgrounds, that it was likely that Kelly and Skilbred would make a return trip to the project areas. Contrary to the Court's contention that Kelly's and Skilbred's past visits "proves nothing," the fact of their past visits could demonstrate to a reasonable factfinder that Kelly and Skilbred have the requisite resources and personal interest in the preservation of the species endangered by the Aswan and Mahaweli projects to make good on their intention to return again. Similarly, Kelly's and Skilbred's professional backgrounds in wildlife preservation, also make it likely—at least far more likely than for the average citizen—that they would choose to visit these areas of the world where species are vanishing.

By requiring a "description of concrete plans" or "specification of when the some day [for a return visit] will be," the Court, in my view, demands what is likely an empty formality. No substantial barriers prevent Kelly or Skilbred from simply purchasing plane tickets to return to the Aswan and Mahaweli projects. * * *

I fear the Court's demand for detailed descriptions of future conduct will do little to weed out those who are genuinely harmed from those who are not. More likely, it will resurrect a code-pleading formalism in federal court summary judgment practice, as federal courts, newly doubting their jurisdiction, will demand more and more particularized showings of future harm. * * *

2

The Court also concludes that injury is lacking, because respondents' allegations of "ecosystem nexus" failed to demonstrate sufficient proximity to the site of the environmental harm. To support that conclusion, the Court mischaracterizes our decision in *Lujan v. National Wildlife Federation,* 497 U.S. 871 (1990), as establishing a general rule that "a plaintiff claiming injury from environmental damage must use the area affected by the challenged activity." In *National Wildlife Federation,* the Court required specific geographical proximity because of the particular type of harm alleged in that case: harm to the plaintiff's visual enjoyment of nature from mining activities. One cannot suffer from the sight of a ruined landscape without being close enough to see the sites actually being mined. Many environmental injuries, however, cause harm distant from the area immediately affected by the challenged action. Environmental destruction may affect animals traveling over vast geographical ranges. It cannot seriously be contended that a litigant's failure to use the precise or exact site where animals are slaughtered or where toxic waste is dumped into a river means he or she cannot show injury.

The Court also rejects respondents' claim of vocational or professional injury. The Court says that it is "beyond all reason" that a zoo "keeper" of Asian elephants would have standing to contest his government's participation in the eradication of all the Asian elephants in another part of the world. I am unable to see how the distant location of the destruction necessarily (for purposes of ruling at summary judgment) mitigates the harm to the elephant keeper. If there is no more access to a future supply of the animal that sustains a keeper's livelihood, surely there is harm.

I have difficulty imagining this Court applying its rigid principles of geographic formalism anywhere outside the context of environmental claims. As I understand it, environmental plaintiffs are under no special constitutional standing disabilities. Like other plaintiffs, they need show only that the action they challenge has injured them, without necessarily showing they happened to be physically near the location of the alleged wrong. * * *

B

A plurality of the Court suggests that respondents have not demonstrated redressability: a likelihood that a court ruling in their favor would remedy their injury. *Duke Power Co. v. Carolina Environmental Study Group, Inc.,* 438 U.S. 59, 74-75, and n.20 (1978) (plaintiff must show "substantial likelihood" that relief requested will redress the injury). The plurality identifies two obstacles. The first is that the "action agencies" (*e.g.*, the Agency for International Development) cannot be required to undertake consultation with petitioner Secretary, because they are not directly bound as parties to the suit and are otherwise not indirectly bound by being subject to petitioner Secretary's regulation. Petitioner, however, officially and publicly has taken the position that his regulations regarding consultation under § 7 of the Act are binding on action agencies. 50 C.F.R. § 402.14(a) (1991). And he has previously taken the same position in this very litigation, having stated in his answer to the complaint that petitioner "admits the Fish and Wildlife Service (FWS) was designated the lead agency for the formulation of regulations concerning section 7 of the ESA." I cannot agree with the plurality that the Secretary (or the Solicitor General) is now free, for the convenience of this appeal, to disavow his prior public and litigation positions. * * *

Emphasizing that none of the action agencies are parties to this suit (and having rejected the possibility of their being indirectly bound by petitioner's regulation), the plurality concludes that "there is no reason they should be obliged to honor an incidental legal determination the suit produced." I am not as willing as the plurality is to assume that agencies at least will not try to follow the law. Moreover, I wonder if the plurality has not overlooked the extensive involvement from the inception of this litigation by the Department of State and the Agency for International Development. Under principles of collateral estoppel, these agencies are precluded from subsequently relitigating the issues decided in this suit. * * * In *Montana v. United States*, 440 U.S. 147 (1979), this Court held that the Government was estopped from relitigating in federal court the constitutionality of Montana's gross receipts tax, because that issue previously had been litigated in state court by an individual contractor whose litigation had been financed and controlled by the Federal Government. "Thus, although not a party, the United States plainly had a sufficient 'laboring oar' in the conduct of the state-court litigation to actuate principles of estoppel." *Id.* at 155. * * * As a result, I believe respondents' injury would likely be redressed by a favorable decision.

The second redressability obstacle relied on by the plurality is that "the [action] agencies generally supply only a fraction of the funding for a foreign project." What this Court might "generally" take to be true does not eliminate the existence of a genuine issue of fact to withstand summary judgment. Even if the action agencies supply only a fraction of the funding for a particular foreign project, it remains at least a question for the finder of fact whether threatened withdrawal of that fraction would affect foreign government conduct sufficiently to avoid harm to listed species.

The plurality states that "AID, for example, has provided less than 10% of the funding for the Mahaweli project." The plurality neglects to mention that this "fraction" amounts to $170 million, not so paltry a sum for a country of only 16 million people with a gross national product of less than $6 billion in 1986 when respondents filed the complaint in this action.

The plurality flatly states: "Respondents have produced nothing to indicate that the projects they have named will . . . do less harm to listed species, if that fraction is eliminated." As an initial matter, the relevant inquiry is not, as the plurality suggests, what will happen if AID or other agencies stop funding projects, but what will happen if AID or other agencies comply with the consultation requirement for projects abroad. Respondents filed suit to require consultation, not a termination of funding. Respondents have raised at least a genuine issue of fact that the projects harm endangered species and that the actions of AID and other U.S. agencies can mitigate that harm.

* * *

As for the Aswan project, the record again rebuts the plurality's assumption that donor agencies are without any authority to protect listed species. Kelly asserted in her affidavit—and it has not been disputed—that the Bureau of Reclamation was "overseeing" the rehabilitation of the Aswan project.

* * *

II

The Court concludes that any "procedural injury" suffered by respondents is insufficient to confer standing. It rejects the view that the "injury-in-fact requirement . . . [is] satisfied by congressional conferral upon all persons of an abstract, self-contained, noninstrumental 'right' to have the Executive observe the procedures required by law." Whatever the Court might mean with that very broad language, it cannot be saying that "procedural injuries" as a class are necessarily insufficient for purposes of Article III standing.

Most governmental conduct can be classified as "procedural." Many injuries caused by governmental conduct, therefore, are categorizable at some level of generality as "procedural" injuries. Yet, these injuries are not categorically beyond the pale of redress by the federal courts. When the Government, for example, "procedurally" issues a pollution permit, those affected by the permittee's pollutants are not without standing to sue. Only later cases will tell just what the

Court means by its intimation that "procedural" injuries are not constitutionally cognizable injuries. In the meantime, I have the greatest of sympathy for the courts across the country that will struggle to understand the Court's standardless exposition of this concept today.

The Court expresses concern that allowing judicial enforcement of "agencies' observance of a particular, statutorily prescribed procedure" would "transfer from the President to the courts the Chief Executive's most important constitutional duty, to 'take Care that the Laws be faithfully executed,' Art. II, sec. 3." In fact, the principal effect of foreclosing judicial enforcement of such procedures is to transfer power into the hands of the Executive at the expense—not of the courts—but of Congress, from which that power originates and emanates.

Under the Court's anachronistically formal view of the separation of powers, Congress legislates pure, substantive mandates and has no business structuring the procedural manner in which the Executive implements these mandates. To be sure, in the ordinary course, Congress does legislate in black-and-white terms of affirmative commands or negative prohibitions on the conduct of officers of the Executive Branch. In complex regulatory areas, however, Congress often legislates, as it were, in procedural shades of gray. That is, it sets forth substantive policy goals and provides for their attainment by requiring Executive Branch officials to follow certain procedures, for example, in the form of reporting, consultation, and certification requirements.

* * *

To prevent Congress from conferring standing for "procedural injuries" is another way of saying that Congress may not delegate to the courts authority deemed "executive" in nature. Here Congress seeks not to delegate "executive" power but only to strengthen the procedures it has legislatively mandated. "We have long recognized that the nondelegation doctrine does not prevent Congress from seeking assistance, within proper limits, from its coordinate Branches." *Touby v. United States,* 111 S. Ct. 1752, 1756, (1991). "Congress does not violate the Constitution merely because it legislates in broad terms, leaving a certain degree of discretion to executive or *judicial actors*" (emphasis added). *Ibid.*

Ironically, this Court has previously justified a relaxed review of congressional delegation to the Executive on grounds that Congress, in turn, has subjected the exercise of that power to judicial review. The Court's intimation today that procedural injuries are not constitutionally cognizable threatens this understanding upon which Congress has undoubtedly relied. In no sense is the Court's suggestion compelled by our "common understanding of what activities are appropriate to legislatures, to executives, and to courts." In my view, it reflects an unseemly solicitude for an expansion of power of the Executive Branch.

It is to be hoped that over time the Court will acknowledge that some classes of procedural duties are so enmeshed with the prevention of a substantive, concrete harm that an individual plaintiff may be able to demonstrate a sufficient likelihood of injury just through the breach of that procedural duty. For example, in the context of the NEPA requirement of environmental impact statements, this Court has acknowledged "it is now well settled that NEPA itself does not mandate particular results [and] simply prescribes the necessary process," but *"these procedures are almost certain to affect the agency's substantive decision." Robertson v. Methow Valley Citizens Council,* 490 U.S. 332, 350 (1989) (emphasis added). This acknowledgement of an inextricable link between procedural and substantive harm does not reflect improper appellate factfinding. It reflects nothing more than the proper deference owed to the judgment of a coordinate branch—Congress—that certain procedures are directly tied to protection against a substantive harm.

* * *

III

In conclusion, I cannot join the Court on what amounts to a slash-and-burn expedition through the law of environmental standing. In my view, "[t]he very essence of civil liberty certainly consists in the right of every individual to claim the protection of the laws, whenever he receives an injury." *Marbury v. Madison,* 1 Cranch 137, 163 (1803).

I dissent.

NOTES

1. The plaintiffs produced two affidavits of its members who had travelled to Egypt and Sri Lanka to observe endangered species and their habitats. Both members averred an intent to return to the countries in the future for the same purpose. Why does the Court consider these affidavits inadequate for demonstrating injury? How does the Court change the plaintiff's burden for demonstrating injury? If the plaintiff can refile or amend the complaint with the necessary allegations, does the Court's decision create a logical restriction or does it merely create a formalistic barrier to standing, as suggested by Justice Blackmun's dissent? How does such a barrier affect judicial economy?

2. What are the constitutional requisites of standing as described by Justice Scalia in *Defenders of Wildlife*? Could Congress enact a law which allows lawyers from public interest organizations to serve as private attorneys general in cases germane to their organization's purposes, without any further showing of individual injury? To overcome the uncertain constitutionality of citizen suits after *Defenders*, Professor Sunstein proposes that Congress enact bounties for citizens who petition courts to enforce statutes against the executive branch or private defendants. Cass Sunstein, *What's Standing After* Lujan? *Of Citizen Suits, "Injuries," and Article III,* 91 MICH. L. REV. 163 (1992). In another approach suggested by Professor Sunstein, Congress would create a new property right, "a tenancy in common," in an environmental asset such as clean air or the continued existence of endangered species. *Id.* at 234. Are these modifications to environmental law advisable?

3. Justice Scalia's plurality opinion was joined by three other members of the Court (White, Rehnquist and Thomas). Justice White no longer sits on the Court. Three other Justices (Stevens, Blackmun and O'Connor) would have granted the plaintiff standing. Two Justices (Souter and Kennedy) agreed that standing should be denied on the facts of this case, but appear to be much more inclined to recognize Congress' authority to afford greater access to the courts. Thus, while the *Defenders of Wildlife* case certainly breaks new ground, it is not yet clear how well it will endure. Justice Scalia's approach to standing has been widely analyzed and criticized. *See, e.g.,* Karin Sheldon, Lujan v. Defenders of Wildlife: *The Supreme Court's Slash and Burn Approach to Environmental Standing,* 23 Envtl. L. Rep. (Envtl. L. Inst.) 10031 (1993); Cass Sunstein, *What's Standing After* Lujan? *Of Citizen Suits, "Injuries," and Article III,* 91 MICH. L. REV. 163 (1992).

4. Note the Court's statement in *Defenders of Wildlife* that "we have consistently held that a plaintiff raising only a generally available grievance about government * * * does not state an Article III case or controversy." Recall the *Sierra Club v. Morton* and *SCRAP* decisions, *supra,* which both addressed generalized grievances. Is the Court's analysis of generalized grievances in this case consistent with its precedents in *Sierra Club* and *SCRAP*?

5.   Standing requires a personal, redressable injury-in-fact, economic or otherwise, which can fairly be traced to the defendant's conduct. The Supreme Court's application of these principles has, at times, seemed inconsistent.

In *Warth v. Seldin*, 422 U.S. 490 (1975), plaintiffs challenged zoning laws which they claimed had the purpose and effect of preventing persons of low and moderate income from living in the town of Penfield, NY. The zoning ordinance allocated 98% of vacant land to single-family detached housing. The Court denied standing both to individuals who wanted housing in the town and to builders who had attempted to build moderate income housing there. According to the Court, the plaintiffs failed to allege specific facts showing (1) that housing could have been built and obtained but for the zoning laws and (2) a substantial probability of redressability. The Court was not assured that judicial relief would remove the plaintiffs' alleged injuries, because the injuries could have been due to economics rather than to the zoning laws.

In *Simon v. Eastern Kentucky Welfare Rights Organization*, 426 U.S. 26 (1976), the plaintiffs challenged an IRS rule granting tax exempt "charitable" status to hospitals without requiring treatment of indigents. The plaintiffs, indigents and organizations for indigents, claimed that the rule encouraged hospitals not to treat them. The Court denied standing, stating that "[i]t is purely speculative whether the denials of [hospital treatment] can be traced to [the rule] or instead result from decisions made by the hospitals without regard to the tax implications." *Id.* at 42-43. Redressability was also speculative, since the hospitals could choose to forfeit tax exempt status and continue to deny treatment to indigents if the rule were changed.

By contrast, the Court granted standing to the plaintiffs in *Duke Power Co. v. Carolina Environmental Study Group*, 438 U.S. 59 (1978). There, citizen groups challenged the Price-Anderson Act, which limits liability of nuclear energy licensees for damages resulting from a nuclear accident. The plaintiffs lived near the proposed site of two nuclear power plants, and aimed to prevent development of the plants by having the liability limitation of the act declared unconstitutional. The Court based its decision on the theory that the power companies would not participate in nuclear energy development "but for the enactment and implementation of the Price-Anderson Act," and therefore a substantial likelihood of redressability existed. *Id.* at 78.

6.   Recall the discussion of *United States v. SCRAP*, *supra*. Did the plaintiffs in *SCRAP* and *Duke Power* demonstrate the elements of standing more strongly than in *Warth* and *Eastern Kentucky*? Or did the Court construe the requirements more narrowly in *Warth* and *Eastern Kentucky*? Is the probability of redress more substantial in *SCRAP* and *Duke Power*? Professor Davis, among others, has criticized the Court's standing jurisprudence for its lack of consistency. In particular, he classifies *Warth* and *Eastern Kentucky* as exceptional cases in which standing should have been granted, and *SCRAP* and *Duke Power* as exceptional cases in which standing should have been denied. Additionally, Professor Davis criticizes *Warth* for advancing ten propositions which are contrary to other recent Supreme Court law. *See* 4 KENNETH DAVIS, ADMINISTRATIVE LAW TREATISE §§ 24.27-34 (2d ed. 1978); *see also* Jonathan D. Varat, *Variable Justiciability and the* Duke Power *Case*, 58 TEX. L. REV. 273 (1980).

7.   Justice Scalia suggests that the alleged injury to the plaintiff may not have been redressable since two of the federal agencies involved in the projects had denied the applicability of relevant U.S. Fish and Wildlife Service regulations to their actions. How did the Court of Appeals for the Eighth Circuit overcome this apparent obstacle? On what grounds does Justice Scalia reject the lower court's approach?

In *Bennett v. Spear*, 520 U.S. 154 (1997), Justice Scalia, writing for a unanimous Court, granted standing to ranchers to challenge an opinion of the Fish & Wildlife Service finding that a water project of the Bureau of Reclamation would illegally jeopardize the continued existence of endangered fishes. The ranchers claimed that they would suffer economic harm if the Bureau reduced water deliveries to avoid jeopardy to the fishes. The Court found the ranchers' imminent injury to be both fairly traceable to the Fish & Wildlife Service opinion as well as redressable by that agency despite the fact that the Bureau retained ultimate responsibility for determining how the water project should be administered. Although the Fish & Wildlife Service opinion serves an advisory function, the court found that, "in reality it has a powerful coercive effect on the action agency." *Id.* at 169. Is this holding consistent with *Defenders of Wildlife*?

8.   The plurality opinion and Justice Blackmun's dissent differ on the issue of procedural standing. However, in footnote seven, the Court clearly recognizes the denial of procedural rights as the basis for standing, and dismisses the requirement that a plaintiff show redressability when alleging a procedural injury. Without this concession, NEPA might have been rendered unenforceable, since the statute grants primarily procedural rights. Suppose, for example, that a citizens' group challenged an agency decision not to prepare an EIS on a proposed coal lease. Under the *Warth* and *Eastern Kentucky* analyses of standing, the group would be required to make the impossible showing that preparation of the EIS would result in a decision by the agency not to lease the coal. Under *Defenders of Wildlife*, however, standing could be granted despite the plaintiffs' inability to show with certainty what would happen if an EIS were prepared.

9.   If the plurality and the dissent both recognize the right of procedural standing, how do they reach opposite conclusions in this case? What is the basis each uses in determining if Defenders of Wildlife has standing? Is the plurality willing to grant a general right of standing for procedural injuries? Is the dissent?

10.   Perhaps the most common kind of procedural injury occurs when an agency denies people information which they are entitled to receive by law. The concept of "informational standing" originated with a footnote in an early but important NEPA case. *Scientists' Institute for Public Information v. Atomic Energy Commission*, 481 F.2d 1079, 1087, n.29 (D.C. Cir. 1973), *infra*, Chapter 6. In *Federal Election Commission v. Akins*, 524 U.S. 11 (1998), the Supreme Court granted standing to plaintiffs who claimed that the Federal Election Commission (FEC) denied them information required to be provided under the Federal Election Campaign Act. In particular, the plaintiffs alleged that the FEC had failed to require an organization to register with the FEC as a "political committee." Registration would have forced the organization to file reports with the FEC that included lists of donors giving in excess of $200 per year. The plaintiffs claimed that the FEC's failure denied them information that would help them evaluate candidates for public office. The FEC claimed that the plaintiffs lacked standing because, among other things, they held only a generalized grievance that was shared by other voters. Justice Breyer, writing for six members of the

Court, however, found that the plaintiffs' injury was sufficiently concrete and specific to support standing, even if it was an injury that was widely shared. In a dissent, Justice Scalia argued that standing should be denied because the plaintiffs' injury could not be differentiated from that of other members of the public.

How should the language in footnote 7 of the *Lujan v. Defenders of Wildlife* case be applied in the context of an informational standing claim? The Court of Appeals for the District of Columbia Circuit has suggested that a plaintiff relying on informational standing must allege "a sufficient geographical nexus to the site of the challenged project that he may be expected to suffer whatever environmental consequences the project may have." *City of Los Angeles v. NHSTA*, 912 F.2d 478, 492 (D.C. Cir. 1990). *See also Competitive Enterprise Institute v. NHTSA*, 901 F.2d 107, 122-23 (D.C. Cir. 1990); *National Wildlife Federation v. Hodel*, 839 F.2d 694, 712 (D.C. Cir. 1988); *Sierra Club v. Andrus*, 581 F.2d 895, 900 n.16 (D.C. Cir. 1978), *rev'd on other grounds*, 442 U.S. 347 (1979); *City of Davis v. Coleman*, 521 F.2d 661, 671 (9th Cir. 1975). Is the result in *City of Los Angeles* affected in any way by the Court's decision in *Akins*?

11. Compare the result in *Akins* with the decision in *Florida Audubon Soc'y v. Bentsen*, 94 F.3d 658 (D.C. Cir. 1996) (en banc). In that case, the court rejected a relaxed standing requirement for procedural injury in an environmentalist challenge to the failure of the Treasury Department to prepare an environmental impact statement before implementing a "clarification" to the tax code. *Florida Audubon Soc'y v. Bentsen*, 94 F.3d 658 (D.C. Cir. 1996) (en banc). The "clarification" authorized a tax credit for the use of a fuel additive derived from ethanol. The Florida Audubon Society claimed that the Treasury Department's decision would stimulate production of corn, sugar cane, and sugar beets, which are used to make ethanol. This increased agricultural production, the plaintiffs claimed, would create environmental problems in wildlife areas enjoyed by Audubon members. In interpreting footnote seven of *Defenders of Wildlife*, the court held that plaintiffs must show that their interests are more than general interests common to all members of the public by showing that "the government act performed without the procedure in question will cause a distinct risk to a particularized interest of the plaintiff." *Id.* at 664. Furthermore, the plaintiff must "show not only that the defendant's acts omitted some procedural requirement, but also that it is substantially probable that the procedural breach will cause the essential injury to the plaintiff's own interest." *Id.* The court found, first, that appellants failed to show any particularized environmental interest that will suffer demonstrably increased risk. The court held that claimed interests demand more exacting scrutiny when the challenged government action, such as a tax interpretation, is not one located at a particular site. *Id.* at 667. Second, the court determined that the plaintiffs did not demonstrate the substantial probability required by the standing analysis that the alleged environmental harms were fairly traceable to the tax credit. Does the *Florida Audubon Soc'y* holding survive *Akins*?

12. Suppose that a person is unlawfully denied one or more documents under the Freedom of Information Act. Is that person's interest sufficiently "concrete" to confer standing if the person wants the information to prepare a research paper for school? To write a newspaper article on a project to which the documents relate? To draft comments for an EIS on behalf of an organization with no members living near the project and no other direct ties to the project?

LUJAN V. NATIONAL WILDLIFE FEDERATION
497 U.S. 871 (1990)

Justice SCALIA delivered the opinion of the Court.

In this case we must decide whether respondent, the National Wildlife Federation (hereinafter respondent), is a proper party to challenge actions of the Federal Government relating to certain public lands.

I

Respondent filed this action in 1985 in the United States District Court for the District of Columbia against petitioners the United States Department of the Interior, the Secretary of the Interior, and the Director of the Bureau of Land Management (BLM), an agency within the Department. In its amended complaint, respondent alleged that petitioners had violated the Federal Land Policy and Management Act of 1976 (FLPMA), 43 U.S.C. § 1701 *et seq.* (1982 ed.), the National Environmental Policy Act of 1969 (NEPA), 42 U.S.C. § 4321 *et seq.,* and § 10(e) of the Administrative Procedure Act (APA), 5 U.S.C. § 706, in the course of administering what the complaint called the "land withdrawal review program" of the BLM. Some background information concerning that program is necessary to an understanding of this dispute.

* * *

In 1976, Congress passed the FLPMA, which repealed many of the miscellaneous laws governing disposal of public land, 43 U.S.C. § 1701 *et seq.*, and established a policy in favor of retaining public lands for multiple use management. It directed the Secretary to "prepare and maintain on a continuing basis an inventory of all public lands and their resource and other values," 43 U.S.C. § 1711(a), required land use planning for public lands, and established criteria to be used for that purpose, § 1712. It provided that existing classifications of public lands were subject to review in the land use planning process, and that the Secretary could "modify or terminate any such classification consistent with such land use plans." § 1712(d). It also authorized the Secretary to "make, modify, extend or revoke" withdrawals. § 1714(a). Finally it directed the Secretary, within 15 years, to review withdrawals in existence in 1976 in 11 western States, § 1714(l)(1), and to "determine whether, and for how long, the continuation of the existing withdrawal of the lands would be, in his judgment, consistent with the statutory objectives of the programs for which the lands were dedicated and of the other relevant programs," § 1714(l)(2). The activities undertaken by the BLM to comply with these various provisions constitute what respondent's amended complaint styles the BLM's "land withdrawal review program," which is the subject of the current litigation.

Pursuant to the directives of the FLPMA, the petitioners engage in a number of different types of administrative action with respect to the various tracts of public land within the United States. First, the BLM conducts the review and recommends the determinations required by 43 U.S.C. § 1714(l) with respect to withdrawals in 11 western States. * * *

Second, the Secretary revokes some withdrawals under § 204(a) of the Act, which the Office of the Solicitor has interpreted to give the Secretary the power to process proposals for revocation of withdrawals made during the "ordinary course of business." * * *

Third, the Secretary engages in the ongoing process of classifying public lands, either for multiple-use management, 43 C.F.R. Part 2420 (1988), for disposal, 43 C.F.R. Part 2430 (1988), or for other uses. * * *

II

In its complaint, respondent averred generally that the reclassification of some withdrawn lands and the return of others to the public domain would open the lands up to mining activities, thereby destroying their natural beauty. Respondent alleged that petitioners, in the course of administering the Nation's public lands, had violated the FLPMA by failing to "develop, maintain, and, when appropriate, revise land use plans which provide by tracts or areas for the use of the public lands," 43 U.S.C. § 1712(a); failing to submit recommendations as to withdrawals in the 11 western States to the President, § 1714(l); failing to consider multiple uses for the disputed lands, 1732(a), focusing inordinately on such uses as mineral exploitation and development; and failing to provide public notice of decisions, §§ 1701(a)(5), 1712(c)(9), 1712(f), and 1739(e). Respondent also claimed that petitioners had violated NEPA, which requires federal agencies to "include in every recommendation or report on . . . major Federal actions significantly affecting the quality of the human environment, a detailed statement by the responsible official on . . . the environmental impact of the proposed action." 42 U.S.C. § 4332(2)(C). Finally, respondent alleged that all of the above actions were "arbitrary, capricious, an abuse of discretion, or otherwise not in accordance with law," and should therefore be set aside pursuant to § 10(e) of the APA, 5 U.S.C. § 706. Appended to the amended complaint was a schedule of specific land status determinations, which the complaint stated had been "taken by defendants since January 1, 1981"; each was identified by a listing in the Federal Register.

In December 1985, the District Court granted respondent's motion for a preliminary injunction prohibiting petitioners from "[m]odifying, terminating or altering any withdrawal, classification, or other designation governing the protection of lands in the public domain that was in effect on January 1, 1981," and from "[t]aking any action inconsistent" with any such withdrawal, classification, or designation. In a subsequent order, the court denied petitioners' motion under Rule 12(b) of the Federal Rules of Civil Procedure to dismiss the complaint for failure to demonstrate standing to challenge petitioners' actions under the APA, 5 U.S.C. § 702. The Court of Appeals affirmed both orders. *National Wildlife Federation v. Burford,* 835 F.2d 305 (1987). As to the motion to dismiss, the Court of Appeals found sufficient to survive the motion the general allegation in the amended complaint that respondent's members used environmental resources that would be damaged by petitioners' actions. It held that this allegation, fairly read along with the balance of the complaint, both identified particular land-status actions that respondent sought to challenge—since at least some of the actions complained of were listed in the complaint's appendix of Federal Register references—and asserted harm to respondent's members attributable to those particular actions. To support the latter point, the Court of Appeals pointed to the affidavits of two of respondent's members, Peggy Kay Peterson and Richard Erman, which claimed use of land "in the vicinity" of the land covered by two of the listed actions. Thus, the Court of Appeals concluded, there was "concrete indication that [respondent's] members use specific lands covered by the agency's Program and will be adversely affected by the agency's actions," and the complaint was "sufficiently specific for purposes of a motion to dismiss." *Ibid.* On petitions for rehearing, the Court of Appeals * * * stood by its denial of the motion to dismiss and directed the parties and the District Court "to proceed with this litigation with dispatch." *National Wildlife Federation v. Burford,* 844 F.2d 889, 890 (1988).

Back before the District Court, petitioners again claimed, this time by means of a motion for summary judgment under Rule 56 of the Federal Rules of Civil Procedure (which motion had been outstanding during the proceedings before the Court of Appeals), that respondent had no standing to seek judicial review of petitioners' actions under the APA. After argument on this motion, and in purported response to the court's postargument request for additional briefing, respondent submitted four additional member affidavits pertaining to the issue of standing. The District Court rejected them as untimely, vacated the injunction and granted the Rule 56 motion to dismiss. It noted that neither its earlier decision nor the Court of Appeals' affirmance controlled the question, since both pertained to a motion under Rule 12(b). It found the Peterson and Erman affidavits insufficient to withstand the Rule 56 motion, even as to judicial review of the particular classification decisions to which they pertained. And even if they had been adequate for that limited purpose, the court said, they could not support respondent's attempted APA challenge to "each of the 1250 or so individual classification terminations and withdrawal revocations" effected under the land withdrawal review program. *National Wildlife Federation v. Burford,* 699 F. Supp. 327, 332 (D.C. 1988).

This time the Court of Appeals reversed. *National Wildlife Federation v. Burford,* 878 F.2d 422 (1989). It both found the Peterson and Erman affidavits sufficient in themselves, and held that it was an abuse of discretion not to consider the four additional affidavits as well. The Court of Appeals also concluded that standing to challenge individual classification and withdrawal decisions conferred standing to challenge all such decisions under the land withdrawal review program. We granted certiorari. 493 U.S. 1041, 1042 (1990).

III

A

We first address respondent's claim that the Peterson and Erman affidavits alone suffice to establish respondent's right to judicial review of petitioners' actions. Respondent does not contend that either the FLPMA or NEPA provides a private right of action for violations of its provisions. Rather, respondent claims a right to judicial review under § 10(a) of the APA, which provides: "A person suffering legal wrong because of agency action, or adversely affected or aggrieved by agency action within the meaning of a relevant statute, is entitled to judicial review thereof." 5 U.S.C. § 702. This provision contains two separate requirements. First, the person claiming a right to sue must identify some "agency action" that affects him in the specified fashion; it is judicial review "thereof" to which he is entitled. The meaning of "agency action" for purposes of § 702 is set forth in 5 U.S.C. § 551(13), see 5 U.S.C. § 701(b)(2) ("For the purpose of this chapter . . . 'agency action' ha[s] the meanin[g] given . . . by section 551 of this title"), which defines the term as "the whole or a part of an agency rule, order, license, sanction, relief, or the equivalent or denial thereof, or failure to act," 5 U.S.C. § 551(13). When, as here, review is sought not pursuant to specific authorization in the substantive statute, but only under the general review provisions of the APA, the "agency action" in question must be "final agency action." *See* 5 U.S.C. § 704 ("Agency action made reviewable by statute and *final* agency action for which there is no other adequate remedy in a court are subject to judicial review" (emphasis added).)

Second, the party seeking review under § 702 must show that he has "suffer[ed] legal wrong" because of the challenged agency action, or is "adversely affected or aggrieved" by that action "within the meaning of a relevant statute." Respondent does not assert that it has suffered "legal wrong," so we need only discuss the meaning of "adversely affected or aggrieved . . . within the meaning of a relevant statute." As an original matter, it might be thought that one cannot be "adversely affected or aggrieved within the meaning" of a statute unless the statute in question uses those terms (or terms like them)—as some pre-APA statutes in fact did when conferring rights of judicial review. We have long since rejected that interpretation, however, which would have made the judicial review provision of the APA no more than a restatement of pre-existing law. Rather, we have said that to be "adversely affected or aggrieved . . . within the meaning" of a statute, the plaintiff must establish that the injury he complains of (his aggrievement, or the adverse effect upon him) falls within the "zone of interests" sought to be

protected by the statutory provision whose violation forms the legal basis for his complaint.
* * *

B

Because this case comes to us on petitioners' motion for summary judgment, we must assess the record under the standard set forth in Rule 56 of the Federal Rules of Civil Procedure. Rule 56(c) states that a party is entitled to summary judgment in his favor "if the pleadings, depositions, answers to interrogatories, and admissions on file, together with the affidavits, if any, show that there is no genuine issue as to any material fact and that the moving party is entitled to a judgment as a matter of law." Rule 56(e) further provides:

> "When a motion for summary judgment is made and supported as provided in this rule, an adverse party may not rest upon the mere allegations or denials of the adverse party's pleading, but the adverse party's response, by affidavits or as otherwise provided in this rule, must set forth specific facts showing that there is a genuine issue for trial. If the adverse party does not so respond, summary judgment, if appropriate, shall be entered against the adverse party."

* * *

These standards are fully applicable when a defendant moves for summary judgment, in a suit brought under § 702, on the ground that the plaintiff has failed to show that he is "adversely affected or aggrieved by agency action within the meaning of a relevant statute." The burden is on the party seeking review under § 702 to set forth specific facts (even though they may be controverted by the Government) showing that he has satisfied its terms. *Sierra Club v. Morton,* 405 U.S. 727, 740 (1972). * * *

C

We turn, then, to whether the specific facts alleged in the two affidavits considered by the District Court raised a genuine issue of fact as to whether an "agency action" taken by petitioners caused respondent to be "adversely affected or aggrieved . . . within the meaning of a relevant statute." We assume, since it has been uncontested, that the allegedly affected interests set forth in the affidavits—"recreational use and aesthetic enjoyment"—are sufficiently related to the purposes of respondent association that respondent meets the requirements of § 702 if any of its members do. *Hunt v. Washington State Apple Advertising Comm'n,* 432 U.S. 333 (1977).

* * *

The Peterson affidavit averred:

> "My recreational use and aesthetic enjoyment of federal lands, particularly those in the vicinity of South Pass-Green Mountain, Wyoming have been and continue to be adversely affected in fact by the unlawful actions of the Bureau and the Department. In particular, the South Pass-Green Mountain area of Wyoming has been opened to the staking of mining claims and oil and gas leasing, an action which threatens the aesthetic beauty and wildlife habitat potential of these lands." App. to Pet. for Cert. 191a.

Erman's affidavit was substantially the same as Peterson's, with respect to all except the area involved; he claimed use of land "in the vicinity of Grand Canyon National Park, the Arizona Strip (Kanab Plateau), and the Kaibab National Forest."

The District Court found the Peterson affidavit inadequate for the following reasons:

"Peterson . . . claims that she uses federal lands *in the vicinity* of the South Pass-Green Mountain area of Wyoming for recreational purposes and for aesthetic enjoyment and that her recreational and aesthetic enjoyment has been and continues to be adversely affected as a result of the decision of BLM to open it to the staking of mining claims and oil and gas leasing. . . . This decision [W-6228] opened up to mining approximately 4500 acres within a two million acre area, the balance of which, with the exception of 2000 acres, has always been open to mineral leasing and mining. . . . There is no showing that Peterson's recreational use and enjoyment extends to the particular 4500 acres covered by the decision to terminate classification to the remainder of the two million acres affected by the termination. All she claims is that she uses lands 'in the vicinity.' The affidavit on its face contains only a bare allegation of injury, and fails to show specific facts supporting the affiant's allegation." 699 F. Supp. at 331 (emphasis in original).

The District Court found the Erman affidavit "similarly flawed."

"The magnitude of Erman's claimed injury stretches the imagination. . . . [T]he Arizona Strip consists of all lands in Arizona north and west of the Colorado River on approximately 5.5 million acres, an area one-eighth the size of the State of Arizona. Furthermore, virtually the entire Strip is and for many years has been open to uranium and other metalliferous mining. The revocation of withdrawal [in Public Land Order 6156] concerned only non-metalliferous mining in the western one-third of the Arizona Strip, an area possessing no potential for non-metalliferous mining." *Id.* at 332.

The Court of Appeals disagreed with the District Court's assessment as to the Peterson affidavit (and thus found it unnecessary to consider the Erman affidavit) for the following reason:

"If Peterson was not referring to lands in this 4500-acre affected area, her allegation of impairment to her use and enjoyment would be meaningless, or perjurious. . . . [T]he trial court overlooks the fact that unless Peterson's language is read to refer to the lands affected by the Program, the affidavit is, at best, a meaningless document.

At a minimum, Peterson's affidavit is ambiguous regarding whether the adversely affected lands are the ones she uses. When presented with ambiguity on a motion for summary judgment, a District Court must resolve any factual issues of controversy in favor of the non-moving party. . . . This means that the District Court was obliged to resolve any factual ambiguity in favor of NWF, and would have had to assume, for the purposes of summary judgment, that Peterson used the 4500 affected acres." 878 F.2d at 431.

That is not the law. In ruling upon a Rule 56 motion, "a District Court must resolve any factual issues of controversy in favor of the non-moving party" only in the sense that, where the facts specifically averred by that party contradict facts specifically averred by the movant, the motion must be denied. That is a world apart from "assuming" that general averments embrace the "specific facts" needed to sustain the complaint. As set forth above, Rule 56(e) provides that judgment "shall be entered" against the nonmoving party unless affidavits or other evidence "set forth specific facts showing that there is a genuine issue for trial." The object of this provision is not to replace conclusory allegations of the complaint or answer with conclusory allegations of an affidavit. *Cf. Anderson v. Liberty Lobby, Inc.,* 477 U.S. 242, 249 (1986) ("[T]he plaintiff could not rest on his allegations of a conspiracy to get to a jury without 'any significant probative evidence tending to support the complaint'"), quoting *First National Bank of Arizona v. Cities Service Co.*, 391 U.S. 253, 290 (1968). Rather, the purpose of Rule 56 is to enable a party who believes there is no genuine dispute as to a specific fact essential to the other side's case to demand at least one sworn averment of that fact before the lengthy process of litigation continues.

At the margins there is some room for debate as to how "specific" must be the "specific facts" that Rule 56(e) requires in a particular case. But where the fact in question is the one put in issue by the § 702 challenge here—whether one of respondent's members has been, or is threatened to be, "adversely affected or aggrieved" by Government action—Rule 56(e) is assuredly not satisfied by averments which state only that one of respondent's members uses unspecified portions of an immense tract of territory, on some portions of which mining activity has occurred or probably will occur by virtue of the governmental action. * * *

Respondent places great reliance, as did the Court of Appeals, upon our decision in *United States v. Students Challenging Regulatory Agency Procedures (SCRAP)*, 412 U.S. 669 (1973). The *SCRAP* opinion, whose expansive expression of what would suffice for § 702 review under its particular facts has never since been emulated by this Court, is of no relevance here, since it involved not a Rule 56 motion for summary judgment but a Rule 12(b) motion to dismiss on the pleadings. The latter, unlike the former, presumes that general allegations embrace those specific facts that are necessary to support the claim. *Conley v. Gibson*, 355 U.S. 41, 45-46 (1957).

IV

We turn next to the Court of Appeals' alternative holding that the four additional member affidavits proffered by respondent in response to the District Court's briefing order established its right to § 702 review of agency action.

A

It is impossible that the affidavits would suffice, as the Court of Appeals held, to enable respondent to challenge the entirety of petitioners' so-called "land withdrawal review program." That is not an "agency action" within the meaning of § 702, much less a "final agency action" within the meaning of § 704. The term "land withdrawal review program" (which as far as we know is not derived from any authoritative text) does not refer to a single BLM order or regulation, or even to a completed universe of particular BLM orders and regulations. It is simply the name by which petitioners have occasionally referred to the continuing (and thus constantly changing) operations of the BLM in reviewing withdrawal revocation applications and the classifications of public lands and developing land use plans as required by the FLPMA. It is no more an identifiable "agency action"—much less a "final agency action"—than a "weapons procurement program" of the Department of Defense or a "drug interdiction program" of the Drug Enforcement Administration. As the District Court explained, the "land withdrawal review program" extends to, currently at least, "1250 or so individual classification terminations and withdrawal revocations." 699 F. Supp. at 332.[2]

---

[2]   Contrary to the apparent understanding of the dissent, we do not contend that no "land withdrawal review program" exists, any more than we would contend that no weapons procurement program exists. We merely assert that it is not an identifiable "final agency action" for purposes of the APA. If there is in fact some specific order or regulation, applying some particular measure across-the-board to all individual classification terminations and withdrawal revocations, and if that order or regulation is final, and has become ripe for review in the manner we discuss subsequently in text, it can of course be challenged under the APA by a person

Respondent alleges that violation of the law is rampant within this program—failure to revise land use plans in proper fashion, failure to submit certain recommendations to Congress, failure to consider multiple use, inordinate focus upon mineral exploitation, failure to provide required public notice, failure to provide adequate environmental impact statements. Perhaps so. But respondent cannot seek wholesale improvement of this program by court decree, rather than in the offices of the Department or the halls of Congress, where programmatic improvements are normally made. Under the terms of the APA, respondent must direct its attack against some particular "agency action" that causes it harm. Some statutes permit broad regulations to serve as the "agency action," and thus to be the object of judicial review directly, even before the concrete effects normally required for APA review are felt. Absent such a provision, however, a regulation is not ordinarily considered the type of agency action "ripe" for judicial review under the APA until the scope of the controversy has been reduced to more manageable proportions, and its factual components fleshed out, by some concrete action applying the regulation to the claimant's situation in a fashion that harms or threatens to harm him. (The major exception, of course, is a substantive rule which as a practical matter requires the plaintiff to adjust his conduct immediately. Such agency action is "ripe" for review at once, whether or not explicit statutory review apart from the APA is provided. *See Abbott Laboratories v. Gardner,* 387 U.S. 136, 152-54 (1967); *Gardner v. Toilet Goods Assn., Inc.,* 387 U.S. 167, 171-73 (1967). *Cf. Toilet Goods Assn., Inc. v. Gardner,* 387 U.S. 158, 164-66 (1967).)

In the present case, the individual actions of the BLM identified in the six affidavits can be regarded as rules of general applicability (a "rule" is defined in the APA as agency action of "general or particular applicability *and future effect,*" 5 U.S.C. § 551(4) (emphasis added)) announcing, with respect to vast expanses of territory that they cover, the agency's intent to grant requisite permission for certain activities, to decline to interfere with other activities, and to take other particular action if requested. It may well be, then, that even those individual actions will not be ripe for challenge until some further agency action or inaction more immediately harming the plaintiff occurs. But it is at least entirely certain that the flaws in the entire "program"—consisting principally of the many individual actions referenced in the complaint, and presumably actions yet to be taken as well—cannot be laid before the courts for wholesale correction under the APA, simply because one of them that is ripe for review adversely affects one of respondent's members.

The case-by-case approach that this requires is understandably frustrating to an organization such as respondent, which has as its objective across-the-board protection of our Nation's wildlife and the streams and forests that support it. But this is the traditional, and remains the normal, mode of operation of the courts. * * *

* * *

For the foregoing reasons, the judgment of the Court of Appeals is reversed. It is so ordered.

---

adversely affected—and the entire "land withdrawal review program," insofar as the content of that particular action is concerned, would thereby be affected. But that is quite different from permitting a generic challenge to all aspects of the "land withdrawal review program," as though that itself constituted a final agency action.

Justice BLACKMUN, with whom Justice BRENNAN, Justice MARSHALL, and Justice STEVENS join, dissenting.

In my view, the affidavits of Peggy Kay Peterson and Richard Loren Erman, in conjunction with other record evidence before the District Court on the motions for summary judgment, were sufficient to establish the standing of the National Wildlife Federation (Federation or NWF) to bring this suit. I also conclude that the District Court abused its discretion by refusing to consider supplemental affidavits filed after the hearing on the parties' cross-motions for summary judgment. I therefore would affirm the judgment of the Court of Appeals.

I

The Federation's asserted injury in this case rested upon its claim that the Government actions challenged here would lead to increased mining on public lands; that the mining would result in damage to the environment; and that the recreational opportunities of NWF's members would consequently be diminished. Abundant record evidence supported the Federation's assertion that on lands newly opened for mining, mining in fact would occur.[3] Similarly, the record furnishes ample support for NWF's contention that mining activities can be expected to cause severe environmental damage to the affected lands.[4] The District Court held, however, that the Federation had not adequately identified particular members who were harmed by the consequences of the Government's actions. Although two of NWF's members expressly averred that their recreational activities had been impaired, the District Court concluded that these affiants had not identified with sufficient precision the particular sites on which their injuries occurred. The majority, like the District Court, holds that the averments of Peterson and Erman were insufficiently specific to withstand a motion for summary judgment. Although these affidavits were not models of precision, I believe that they were adequate at least to create a genuine issue of fact as to the organization's injury.

* * *

* * * These affidavits, as the majority acknowledges, were at least sufficiently precise to enable Bureau of Land Management (BLM) officials to identify the particular termination orders to which the affiants referred. And the affiants averred that their "recreational use and aesthetic enjoyment of federal lands . . . have been and continue to be adversely affected in fact by the unlawful actions of the Bureau and the Department." The question, it should be emphasized, is not whether the NWF has proved that it has standing to bring this action, but simply whether the materials before the District Court established "that there is a genuine issue for trial," *see* Rule 56(e), concerning the Federation's standing. In light of the principle that "[o]n summary judgment the inferences to be drawn from the underlying facts contained in [evidentiary]

---

[3]   Prior to the District Court's entry of the preliminary injunction, 406 mining claims had been staked in the South Pass-Green Mountain area alone. App. 119. An exhibit filed by the Government indicated that over 7200 claims had been filed in 12 Western States. Affidavit of Joseph Martyak (April 11, 1986) Exh. 1.

[4]   A Bureau of Land Management draft of a Resource Management Plan/Environmental Impact Statement for the Lander, Wyo., Resource Area stated: "[I]n the Green Mountain Management Unit . . . significant long-term impacts to elk and mule deer herds could occur from habitat losses caused by oil and gas activities over the next 60 years. . . . In the South Pass Management Unit, significant acreages of lodgepole pine forest and aspen conifer woodland habitat types could be disturbed, which would cause significant long-term impacts to moose and elk. . . . If gold mining activities continue to erode these high-value habitats, trout fisheries, the Lander moose herd, the beaver pond ecosystems, and the populations of many other wildlife species would suffer significant negative effects." Draft RMP/EIS 226-228 * * *.

* * *

materials must be viewed in the light most favorable to the party opposing the motion," *United States v. Diebold, Inc.,* 369 U.S. 654, 655 (1962), I believe that the evidence before the District Court raised a genuine factual issue as to NWF's standing to sue.

No contrary conclusion is compelled by the fact that Peterson alleged that she uses federal lands "in the vicinity of South Pass-Green Mountain, Wyoming," rather than averring that she uses the precise tract that was recently opened to mining. The agency itself has repeatedly referred to the "South Pass-Green Mountain area" in describing the region newly opened to mining. Peterson's assertion that her use and enjoyment of federal lands have been adversely affected by the agency's decision to permit more extensive mining is, as the Court of Appeals stated, *National Wildlife Federation v. Burford,* 878 F.2d 422, 431 (1989), "meaningless, or perjurious" if the lands she uses do not include those harmed by mining undertaken pursuant to termination order W-6228. To read particular assertions within the affidavit in light of the document as a whole is, as the majority might put it, "a world apart" from "presuming" facts that are neither stated nor implied simply because without them the plaintiff would lack standing. The Peterson and Erman affidavits doubtless could have been more artfully drafted, but they definitely were sufficient to withstand the Government's summary judgment motion.

* * *

IV

Since I conclude that the Peterson and Erman affidavits provided sufficient evidence of NWF's standing to withstand a motion for summary judgment, and that the District Court abused its discretion by refusing to consider the Federation's supplemental affidavits, I would affirm the judgment of the Court of Appeals. I respectfully dissent.

NOTES

1. Did *Lujan v. National Wildlife Federation* change the requirements for standing? How is it likely to change the way in which plaintiffs construct their complaints and supporting documentation? *See* Karin Sheldon, Lujan v. NWF, *Justice Scalia Restricts Environmental Standing to Constrain the Courts,* 20 Envtl. L. Rep. (Envtl. L. Inst.) 10557 (1990).

2. The *Lujan* decision involved a motion for summary judgment under Rule 56 of the Federal Rules of Civil Procedure. How does the standard for deciding a motion for summary judgment differ from the standard for a motion to dismiss under Rule 12(b)? Why is the standard different?

3. Many environmental statutes expressly provide for judicial review of actions taken under the statute, and many of these include provisions for citizen suits. These citizen suit provisions generally authorize interested members of the public to act as "private attorneys general" to vindicate the public interest. Prevailing parties can usually recover their legal costs, including attorneys' fees. *See, e.g.,* Endangered Species Act, § 11; 16 U.S.C. § 1540; Clean Air Act, §§ 304, 307; 42 U.S.C. §§ 7604, 7607; Clean Water Act, §§ 505, 509; 33 U.S.C. §§ 1365, 1369. Other laws, however, such as NEPA, the Federal Land Policy and Management Act (FLPMA), and the National Forest Management Act (NFMA) contain no judicial review provisions. Under these circumstances plaintiffs are relegated to § 10 of the APA. How does this affect their standing to sue?

4. The "zone of interests" test was first articulated by Justice Douglas in *Association of Data Processing Service Organizations v. Camp*, 397 U.S. 150 (1970), and has been used by the Court as a prudential (as opposed to constitutional) limit on standing in cases brought under § 10 of the Administrative Procedure Act, 5 U.S.C. § 702. The test determines:

> whether the interest sought to be protected by the complainant is arguably within the zone of interests to be protected or regulated by the statute or constitutional guarantee in question. Thus the Administrative Procedure Act grants standing to a person "aggrieved by agency action within the meaning of a relevant statute." 5 U.S.C. § 702.

397 U.S. at 153. In *Clarke v. Securities Industry Association*, 479 U.S. 388, 399-400 (1987), the Court explained that "[t]he test is not meant to be especially demanding; in particular, there need be no indication of congressional purpose to benefit the would be plaintiff." Rather, the test was intended to deny standing where "the plaintiff's interests are [only] marginally related to or inconsistent with the purposes implicit in the statute . . .." Still, prudential standing can be a barrier to judicial review. In *Hazardous Waste Treatment Council v. Thomas*, 885 F.2d 918 (D.C. Cir. 1989), the court found that a trade association and its member companies lacked prudential standing because they did not fall within the zone of interests protected by the statute under which the agency issued the challenged regulations. The statute, the Resource Conservation and Recovery Act (RCRA), requires the EPA to promulgate strict standards for the permissible concentrations of certain hazardous chemicals in waste placed in land disposal facilities. The plaintiff represented companies that treat waste prior to disposal to reduce the concentrations of the hazardous chemicals. Citing *Clarke* for the proposition that the zone of interests test is basically an inquiry into congressional intent, the court denied standing. *Id.* at 922. Critical to the decision were the findings that both: (1) Congress did not mean to protect the commercial interests of hazardous waste treatment firms by improving their competitiveness as a result of increased demand for treatment services; and (2) the plaintiff's interests did not coincide with the intended beneficiaries of the statute, those citizens who are threatened with degradation of their health and environment. Judge Wald dissented by arguing that the majority had not analyzed the zone of interests question in the liberal spirit of *Clarke* and *Data Processing*. In addition, she criticized the majority for dismissing the plaintiff's best claim for standing: that lax EPA regulations harm member companies who operate disposal facilities at or near sites receiving waste with higher concentrations of hazardous chemicals than allowed by RCRA.

5. In *Bennett v. Spear*, 520 U.S. 154, 137 L. Ed. 2d 281 (1997), the Court unanimously granted standing to a group of ranchers who sought to maintain their water deliveries from a federal reclamation project. The plaintiffs challenged a decision by the Fish & Wildlife Service, which found the operation of the reclamation project, at historic levels of water delivery, to jeopardize the continued existence of endangered fishes in violation of the Endangered Species Act (ESA). Water made available to conserve the habitat for fishes is water unavailable for delivery to the ranchers for irrigation. Although the explicit overall purpose of the ESA is to conserve endangered species, and the ranchers

are not themselves regulated by the statute, the Court nonetheless found that the plaintiffs satisfied the prudential requirements of standing. For claims brought under the citizen suit provision of the ESA, the Court found that Congress had effectively negated the zone of interests test. For a separate claim that did not fall within the scope of the citizen suit provision, however, but for which a plaintiff might nonetheless seek review under the general requirements of § 702 of the APA, the Court ruled that the zone of interests test should be applied to the specific provision of the Act whose violation forms the legal basis of the complaint. In this case, the plaintiffs alleged that the Fish & Wildlife Service violated the portion of the ESA requiring it to use the "best scientific and commercial data available" in deciding whether an agency action would jeopardize an endangered species. The Court found that the purpose of this specific requirement is twofold. First, the purpose "is to ensure that the ESA not be implemented haphazardly, on the basis of speculation or surmise." *Id.* at 304. But, also, the Court found a second "readily apparent" purpose "is to avoid needless economic dislocation produced by agency officials zealously but unintelligently pursuing their environmental objectives." *Id.* The Court cited no legislative history, other statutory provisions, regulations, or cases to support this interpretation of the purpose of the requirement. Do you agree that the purpose of avoiding economic dislocation is "readily apparent"? You might return to this question after you have reviewed the ESA in more detail in Chapters 4 and 5 of this casebook.

Should courts impose the prudential restriction on standing by requiring plaintiffs to show that their injuries fall within a zone of interests? How does Congress express its intent when legislating to protect certain interests but not others?

6.   Citizen suit provisions, such as those described at Note 3, were dealt a blow by the Supreme Court's decision in *Steel Co. v. Citizens for a Better Environment,* 523 U.S. 83 (1998). *Steel Co.* involved the Emergency Planning and Community Right to Know Act (EPCRA), 42 U.S.C. §§ 11001 *et seq.,* which requires companies that release certain toxic pollutants into the environment to file annual reports regarding those releases. The company sued in the *Steel Co.* case had failed to file the required reports for seven consecutive years. As required by the statute, the plaintiffs sent to the defendant a notice of its intent to file suit under EPCRA's citizen suit provision. After the notice of intent to sue was sent, but before the plaintiffs filed their lawsuit, the company filed the reports. The plaintiffs then sued for injunctive relief, civil penalties, and their costs, including attorney's fee. In an opinion by Justice Scalia, the Court held that the plaintiffs lacked standing to sue for the wholly past EPCRA violations, since the plaintiffs suffered no continuing injury that judicial review could redress. In dictum, the Court appeared to go even further, suggesting that plaintiffs lack standing to sue even if the violations of the law are not corrected until after the filing of the complaint but before trial, because the same redressability problem arises at that stage in the case. At least one commentator has suggested, however, that this reading of the case is not consistent with the Court's prior holding in *Chesapeake Bay Foundation v. Gwaltney of Smithfield, Ltd.,* 484 U.S. 49 (1987). Jim Hecker, *EPCRA Citizen Suits After* Steel Co. v. Citizens for a Better Environment, 28 ENVTL. L. REP. 10306 (1998). Assuming that plaintiffs lack standing under traditional citizen suit provisions to maintain a lawsuit once the statutory violations have been corrected, how might Congress change those provisions to overcome this problem?

7. In Part IV-A of the majority opinion in *Lujan v. National Wildlife Federation*, the Court finds that, irrespective of standing, this case is not ripe for judicial review. Why not? Under what circumstances, if any, can a person challenge programmatic agency decisions?

8. Courts often tie together ripeness with standing. If a case is not ripe, then there is no injury in fact on which to base standing. The National Forest Management Act (NFMA) 16 U.S.C. §§ 1600-14, requires the Forest Service to prepare Land and Resource Management Plans (LRMPs) for its administrative units. An LRMP divides a national forest into zones which limit the uses of the forest to those specified for the particular zone. The LRMP, however, does not approve particular proposals for use. Individual proposals require project-level analyses and decisions. These individual decisions may be appealed by interested persons. Suppose, however, that a plaintiff wants to challenge an LRMP; is such a challenge ripe under *Lujan v. National Wildlife Federation*? In *Ohio Forestry Association v. Sierra Club,* 118 S. Ct. 1665 (1998), the Supreme Court resolved a split in the circuit courts, holding that a challenge to an LRMP is not ripe for review where the plaintiffs fail to show "significant practical harm" to their interests. According to the Court:

> The Sierra Club . . . will have ample opportunity later to bring its legal challenge at a time when harm is more imminent and more certain. Any such later challenge might also include a challenge to the lawfulness of the present Plan if (but only if) the Plan then matters; *i.e.*, if the Plan plays a causal role with respect to future, then-imminent harm from logging.

Id. at 1670.

PARK COUNTY RESOURCE COUNCIL V. UNITED STATES DEPARTMENT OF AGRICULTURE
817 F.2d 609 (10th Cir. 1987)

McKAY, Circuit Judge.

Section 102(2)(C) of the National Environmental Policy Act of 1969 (NEPA), requires that all federal agencies prepare a detailed environmental impact statement (EIS) "in every recommendation or report on proposals for legislation and other major Federal actions significantly affecting the quality of the human environment." 42 U.S.C. § 4332(2)(C). The plaintiffs in this suit contend that the Bureau of Land Management (BLM) unlawfully issued an oil and gas lease, and thereafter unlawfully approved an Application for Permit to Drill (APD) filed by the Marathon Oil Company, in contravention of both NEPA and the Endangered Species Act of 1973. They appeal the district court's denial of a preliminary injunction enjoining the issuance of the permit to drill as well as its dismissal of their suit with prejudice.

I. FACTS

In 1979, the Forest Service prepared an extensive environmental assessment (EA) exceeding 100 pages and addressing issuance of federal oil and gas leases in the Shoshone and other forests in the Rocky Mountain Region. The EA explores various leasing alternatives, including issuance of leases without stipulations, issuance of leases with stipulations, and issuance of no leases. It examines the potential effects of each of these alternatives on energy use and conservation, on national forest administration, and, as its name indicates, on the environment. It concludes that "[o]il and gas lease issuance, as such, creates no environmental impacts. The imposition of appropriate stipulatory controls for operations subsequent to lease issuance can, in most cases, prevent or satisfactorily mitigate unacceptable environmental impacts." Consequently, the Forest Service's announced preferred alternative is to recommend lease issuance with appropriate stipulations. The EA specifically notes that prior to any drilling activity, the need for a site-specific, much more comprehensive EIS must be examined.

On November 9, 1979, the Regional Forester issued a Finding of No Significant Impact (FONSI) with respect to lease issuance. The FONSI indicated that issuance of oil and gas leases would have no significant impact on the human environment, meaning that the preparation of an EIS pursuant to NEPA would not be necessary at this stage.

On November 5, 1980, May Petroleum, Inc., filed with BLM an oil and gas lease offer which encompassed 10,174 acres of non-wilderness, multiple-use land in the Shoshone National Forest. As is routine with such offers, BLM requested the Forest Service to advise whether the lease should issue, and, if so, to recommend appropriate stipulations to protect the environment. The Regional Forester recommended lease issuance, and BLM issued the lease on July 9, 1982, with an effective date of August 1, 1982.

* * *

On June 21, 1983, Marathon Oil, the lessee's operator, submitted an APD in order to drill an exploratory well (North Fork Well) in the leased area. BLM announced in August of 1983 that it, in conjunction with the Forest Service, would prepare an EIS with respect to the drilling application.

* * *

Although evaluating several alternatives, the final EIS recommended allowing the drilling of the North Fork Well, and permitting water transport to the site through a temporary pipeline, but restricting access to the drill site to helicopter access only, as opposed to temporary roads. It concluded that this proposal best permitted a valid test for oil and gas potential while minimizing adverse environmental impacts. On May 9, 1985, the BLM district manager issued a record of decision approving the APD on the condition that several additional mitigation measures to protect the environment be imposed.

The record and briefs on appeal extensively explore the procedural adequacy of the EIS and the Biological Assessment. However, in light of our disposition of that issue, *see infra* section III, we need not recount such evidence here.

II. PROCEDURAL HISTORY

On May 31, 1985, plaintiffs appealed the APD approval to the Interior Board of Land Appeals (IBLA). On June 3, 1985, before IBLA rendered its decision, plaintiffs filed this action requesting an injunction prohibiting oil exploration and drilling at the North Fork Well and all future sites until the Government complied with NEPA by preparing an adequate EIS. They also challenged for the first time the underlying 1982 lease issuance and requested a declaratory judgment stating "that the issuance of a lease which may be used to drill for oil and establish a wildcat well on National Forest Service Lands constitutes a major federal action which significantly affects the quality of the human environment, and thereby requires the preparation of an EIS." They also prayed for an order "requiring defendants to withdraw their approval on any leases or permits previously given pending their compliance with the provisions and requirements of NEPA."

Thereafter, plaintiffs filed an application for a temporary restraining order and for a preliminary injunction. The district court denied the TRO after an evidentiary hearing. With the consent of all parties, the court consolidated the preliminary injunction hearing with the trial on the merits, at which eleven witnesses testified. At the conclusion of the proceedings, the court orally denied the preliminary injunction and dismissed plaintiffs' complaint with prejudice. A written opinion was issued shortly thereafter.

The district court barred as untimely the claim that an EIS, rather than an EA, was required prior to the lease issuance itself, citing the ninety-day statute of limitations contained in the Mineral Lands Leasing Act, 30 U.S.C. § 226-2 (1982). Alternatively, the court found the claim to be barred by the equitable defense of laches, as well as by failure to exhaust administrative remedies. In an abundance of caution, however, the court further held that even if the challenge of the FONSI with respect to the lease issuance was not barred, the claim failed on the merits.

* * *

Plaintiffs unsuccessfully sought, both from this court and the Supreme Court, a stay of the drilling activities pending appeal. Since the district court's judgment was rendered, drilling of the North Fork Well has been completed, resulting in a dry hole. Reclamation work at the site has also been completed and is now being monitored.

* * *

IV. LEASE ISSUANCE CHALLENGE

Plaintiffs' challenge to the validity of the 1982 lease issuance, unlike their challenge to the APD, has not been mooted by Marathon Oil's abandonment of the North Fork Well site. The lease remains extant, and, under its authority, Marathon Oil has represented that it "may in the future seek approval from federal defendants to drill an additional well in the North Fork Well Area." The suit dismissed by the district court prayed for a declaratory judgment that the issuance of an oil and gas lease on National Forest Service Lands requires the preparation of an EIS pursuant to NEPA and also asked the court to order the defendants to withdraw their approval to the lease in question pending compliance with NEPA. Reversal of the district court's dismissal would result in redress of plaintiffs' grievance. Moreover, since the lease remains operative at present, issuance of the requested declaratory judgment and order would not constitute "an advisory opinion upon a hypothetical basis, but . . . an adjudication of present right upon established facts."

A.

Prior to addressing the merits of plaintiffs' challenge, the district court held that plaintiffs were barred on three distinct grounds from maintaining their cause of action. Thus, we must first address these three bases before reaching the merits.

First, the district court ruled that the present action was time-barred under the ninety-day statute of limitations found in the Mineral Lands Leasing Act, 30 U.S.C. § 226-2 (1982) (MLLA). That statute provides: "No action contesting a decision of the Secretary involving any oil and gas lease shall be maintained unless such action is commenced or taken within ninety days after the final decision of the Secretary relating to such matter." *Id.* While the subject lease was issued in 1982, suit was not instituted until 1985. No other court has addressed the issue of whether the MLLA statute of limitations applies to NEPA challenges that happen to involve an oil and gas lease. We disagree with the trial court and hold that this statute is inapplicable in such cases.

The thrust of our reasoning parallels that of the Ninth Circuit in *Jones v. Gordon*, 792 F.2d 821 (9th Cir. 1986). In that case, plaintiffs challenged the issuance by the National Marine

Fisheries Service (Service) of a permit that authorized Sea World to capture killer whales. The plaintiffs alleged that the Service's issuance of the permit without prior preparation of an EIS violated NEPA. The general act prescribing the procedure for issuance of such permits is the Marine Mammal Protection Act of 1972, 16 U.S.C. §§ 1361-1407 (1982) (MMPA).

The Ninth Circuit rejected Sea World's claim that plaintiffs' challenge, brought six months after the permit's issuance, was time-barred by the sixty-day statute of limitations found in the MMPA itself for "judicial review of the terms and conditions of any permit issued by the Secretary under this section or of his refusal to issue such a permit." 16 U.S.C. § 1374(d)(6). The court found that, rather than disputing the substantive "terms and conditions" of the permit, plaintiffs were challenging the procedural failure to comply with NEPA. While recognizing that a NEPA procedural challenge can indirectly implicate some terms and conditions—even the validity—of the permit, the court held that plaintiffs' challenge was essentially procedural in character and thus not controlled by the statute of limitations found in the MMPA.

Similarly, the MLLA statute of limitations at issue here applies only to actions contesting either the lease issuance or substantive decisions relating to the lease itself. It applies in cases challenging lack of compliance with all the intricate requirements of Subchapter IV of the MLLA which deals with oil and gas leasing. The present action is not one "contesting decisions of the Secretary of the Interior *under the Mineral Leasing Act.*" It is an action contesting a decision under NEPA, challenging defendants' decision to forego preparation of an EIS that plaintiffs contend is statutorily mandated.

The standards applicable to any effort to enforce NEPA should apply here. Otherwise, the singular NEPA claim—that a contemplated federal action is a "major" one "significantly affecting the quality of the human environment," thus requiring preparation of an EIS under NEPA—would be time-barred at any number of times, depending upon which statute the underlying agency action is based. A NEPA challenge to a permit issued under the MMPA would be barred at sixty days, while that same NEPA challenge would be barred at ninety days if it happened to involve an oil and gas lease. Still other identical NEPA claims could technically remain alive for decades if the challenged federal action was not subject to a statute of limitations.

We decline to impute to Congress the intention that such an arbitrary and inconsistent approach to NEPA claims should prevail. The mere happenstance that the present NEPA action involves an oil and gas lease does not remove it from general NEPA principles regarding the timeliness of suit and has no bearing on NEPA enforcement. A contrary holding would be no more than a blind application of a statute of limitations in a context in which its application was not envisioned and would result in illogical and capricious administration of an important environmental statute. Therefore, we hold that a NEPA challenge to the issuance of an oil and gas lease on federal forest land without prior preparation of an EIS is not subject to the ninety-day statute of limitations found in the MLLA.

NEPA itself does not contain a statute of limitations. Thus, timeliness challenges to NEPA actions have routinely involved analysis under the doctrine of laches. The district court in this case invoked this doctrine as the second ground for holding this action barred.

An environmental action may be barred by the equitable defense of laches if (1) there has been unreasonable delay in bringing suit, and (2) the party asserting the defense has been prejudiced by the delay. *Jicarilla Apache Tribe v. Andrus*, 687 F.2d 1324, 1338 (10th Cir. 1982). The district court found that plaintiffs were aware of the lease issuance without preparation of an EIS no later than the fall of 1983 and that their delay in filing suit until May of 1985 was unreasonable. It also found that the approximately $1 million spent on both EIS preparation and other preparatory measures for the North Fork Well drilling constituted sufficient prejudice to warrant application of the bar of laches. Plaintiffs now claim that their decision to wait until BLM acted on the APD to challenge issuance of the lease should not be subject to laches.

Nearly every circuit, including this one, and numerous district courts have recognized the salutary principle that "[l]aches must be invoked sparingly in environmental cases because ordinarily the plaintiff will not be the only victim of alleged environmental damage. A less grudging application of the doctrine might defeat Congress's environmental policy." *Preservation Coalition, Inc. v. Pierce,* 667 F.2d 851, 854 (9th Cir. 1982).

The application of laches involves a discretionary decision of the district court. *Jicarilla Apache Tribe,* 687 F.2d at 1338. Thus, we review to determine whether the district court has abused its discretion in invoking the doctrine of laches. In environmental litigation one measure of abuse of discretion is whether the district court recognized that laches must be invoked sparingly in order to facilitate Congress's environmental policy. The opinion of the district court in this case fails to consider the legal standard disfavoring laches. This failure amounts to an abuse of discretion. * * *

This court has held that the "[m]ere lapse of time does not amount to laches." [*Id.*] The delay must be "unreasonable." The district court found plaintiffs' delay to be unreasonable, because they "were so convinced that the APD would never be granted that they decided to sit on the lease EIS issue until after the decision on the APD."

We do not perceive the sinister motive or dilatory tactics apparently seen by the district court in plaintiffs' conscious decision to initially concentrate their energies and resources on participating in the EIS preparation for the North Fork Well drilling, believing APD approval would be unlikely based on their view that the EIS was inadequate. Their tactical decision to fight the APD rather than the lease issuance, because it appeared to be the most efficient way to press their substantive objectives, standing alone, raises no implication of bad faith. The general public, whose interests plaintiffs essentially represent in environmental cases, should not be penalized for plaintiffs' decision to pursue the avenue that they thought to be most fruitful in vindicating their concerns.

"The defense of laches is bottomed on the principle that equity aids the vigilant, not those who sleep on their rights." *Dalsis,* 424 F. Supp. at 788. The nearly two-year delay in challenging the lease issuance in this case was not due to a lack of vigilance; rather, plaintiffs expected that their strategic decision to focus on the APD approval would render challenge to the underlying lease issuance superfluous. Their strategy proved to be ill-destined, but we should not chastise their efforts to selectively minimize litigation. Otherwise, we discourage such thoughtful preparation and encourage rote litigation at the time of every agency action, even though successful challenge of only one action in the series would result in obtaining the benefits sought.

We also fail to agree that the prejudice prong was sufficiently satisfied. The $1 million expense cited by the district court as constituting adequate prejudice relates primarily to preparation of the EIS for APD approval as well as other drilling expenditures—costs that would have been incurred whether the district court ordered preparation of an additional EIS with respect to the lease issuance itself or not. Any increased costs from delay in drilling while an EIS is being prepared on the lease issuance is not sufficient to establish prejudice, because NEPA contemplates just such a delay.

Furthermore, even if pertinent, the expenditures here may not satisfy the prejudice test. Although $1 million seems to most an exorbitant amount, such expenditure has been held insufficient to establish prejudice. Rather than absolute dollars already spent, the more salient inquiry explores what percentage of total costs has already been committed. The record is completely void of any such projection.

Moreover, and more important, this is not a case where the project is so substantially completed that significant environmental effects are irreversible, even if an EIS would now be ordered on the lease issuance. * * * In most of the cases in which laches has been applied in the NEPA context, the project allegedly significantly affecting the quality of the human environment was nearly completed, rendering preparation of an EIS redundant. * * * While technically the "federal action" we are examining—lease issuance—is completed in this case, preparation of an EIS at this point in time could still reasonably be expected to ameliorate any feared environmental harm emanating from the lease issuance. For example, additional and more tailored lease stipulations might be devised in light of the more probing information found in an EIS as opposed to an EA.

In short, having concluded there is neither unreasonable delay nor sufficient prejudice, we hold that the defense of laches does not bar plaintiffs' claim contesting the lease issuance without preparation of an EIS.

Finally, the district court held the present action barred for failure to exhaust administrative remedies. Plaintiffs did not, as they may have if they so chose, appeal the lease issuance to the Interior Board of Land Appeals within thirty days under 43 C.F.R. §§ 4.410-.411 (1986). Whether to apply the exhaustion doctrine is a matter within the trial court's discretion, *Rocky Mountain Oil & Gas Ass'n v. Watt*, 696 F.2d 734, 743 n.12 (10th Cir. 1982), but we hold that the trial court abused its discretion in applying the doctrine on the present facts.

In *McKart v. United States*, 395 U.S. 185 (1969), the Supreme Court articulated several rationales supporting the exhaustion doctrine, including (1) avoidance of premature interruption of the administrative process, (2) deference to bodies possessing expertise in areas outside the conventional experience of judges, (3) recognition of executive and administrative autonomy, and (4) development of a factual record. *Id.* at 193-94. When these interests would not be promoted by application of the exhaustion doctrine, it is error to indiscriminately dismiss in its name. * * *

Dismissal here did not avoid *interruption* of the administrative process; there was no administrative process available to plaintiffs at the time of dismissal. Exhaustion doctrine presupposes an adequate administrative remedy. Neither the IBLA nor any other administrative forum was available to plaintiffs at the time of suit. Just as we should not penalize plaintiffs' strategy decision to contest the APD approval rather than the lease issuance by applying the doctrine of laches to bar this environmental claim, neither should we foreclose plaintiffs from having any forum to litigate their claim because that same strategy decision resulted in no appeal to the IBLA within thirty days of lease issuance. This circuit has held that the improbability of obtaining adequate relief by pursuing administrative remedies justifies dispensing with the exhaustion requirement. *New Mexico Ass'n for Retarded Citizens v. New Mexico*, 678 F.2d 847, 850 (10th Cir. 1982).

Furthermore, deference to agency expertise is inapplicable in the NEPA context. The deference envisioned under this rationale is appropriate when the disputed issue is one expressly delegated to an agency that deals exclusively with the area and so has refined an expertise in its nuances. All federal agencies are required under NEPA to prepare an EIS if a proposed action meets the statutory criteria. No single agency has expertise in determining whether an EIS is statutorily mandated in a given instance. NEPA *imposes* duties on agencies; agencies do not exist to administer NEPA. Hence, courts are equally well-suited to examine the issue of whether a proposed action is a major federal action significantly affecting the environment.

Because ensurance of NEPA compliance is not within the special province of administrative agencies, executive and administrative autonomy and development of a factual record are likewise irrelevant considerations under NEPA. Simply put, the *McKart* factors apply in the prototypical case of an agency issuing an order within its delegated area of expertise that a potential plaintiff would rather dispute in the court system than with the particular agency. Whether an agency needs to draft an EIS before pursuing a proposed action is unlike other administrative decisions. We are reticent to apply the traditional exhaustion doctrine to this untraditional administrative decision when the underlying goals which prompted the doctrine's development would not be served thereby. Therefore, we hold that the district court erred when it ruled that the present action was barred under the exhaustion doctrine.

* * *

NOTES

1. On the merits, the court was less generous to the plaintiffs, finding that the agency's NEPA analysis was adequate given the very small possibility that lease development would actually occur. Compare the holding in *Park County* with *Conner v. Burford*, 848 F.2d 1441 (9th Cir. 1988), *cert. denied*, 489 U.S. 1012 (1989), *infra* at Chapter 6.

2. The Mineral Leasing Act provides as follows:

> No action contesting a decision of the Secretary involving any oil and gas lease shall be maintained unless such action is commenced or taken within ninety days after the final decision of the Secretary relating to such matter. No such action contesting such a decision of the Secretary rendered prior to enactment of the Mineral Leasing Act Revision of 1960 . . . shall be maintained unless the same be commenced or taken within ninety days after such enactment.

30 U.S.C. § 226-2. Why does the court determine that this provision is inapplicable to the facts of this case? Do you find the court's argument persuasive?

3. Defendants may use the defense of laches to prevent plaintiffs from securing a remedy for a legal claim. The *Park County* court states the rule that claims may be barred where the plaintiff has unreasonably delayed bringing the suit and the defendant has been prejudiced by the delay. At what point in the course of a major federal action is a NEPA challenge foreclosed by laches? *See Save Our Wetlands v. U.S. Army Corps of Engineers*, 549 F.2d 1021 (5th Cir.), *reh'g denied*, 553 F.2d 100 (5th Cir.), *cert. denied*, 434 U.S. 836 (1977); *Ecology Center of Louisiana v. Coleman*, 515 F.2d 860 (5th Cir. 1975); *Inman Park Restoration v. Urban Mass Transp. Admin.*, 414 F. Supp. 99 (N.D. Ga. 1976), *aff'd. sub nom. Save Our Sycamore v. Metropolitan Atlantic Transit Authority*, 576 F.2d 573 (5th Cir. 1978).

4. In addition to laches, the government may be able to bar NEPA claims on the grounds that they violate the six year statute of limitations for commencing civil actions against the United States. 28 U.S.C. § 2401(a). In *Sierra Club v. Slater*, 120 F.3d 623 (6th Cir. 1997), the plaintiffs challenged a highway project that had been approved by the Federal Highway Administration (FHWA) in 1984. Many years later, the plaintiffs requested that the FHWA prepare a supplemental EIS on the project. That request was denied in 1995. The Court of Appeals for the Sixth Circuit held that the cause of action arose in 1984 when the decision was made, and that accordingly, the six-year statute of limitations set out at 28 U.S.C. § 2401(a) barred plaintiffs' cause of action. The plaintiffs had argued that the cause of action did not arise until 1995 when the agency denied plaintiffs' request for a supplemental EIS. The Court found, however, that the plaintiffs' position "defies logic" "because they complain of actions taken by the FHWA at the time of the final EIS was approved and the ROD [record of decision] was issued." *Id.* at 631.

5.   *Park County* found that the doctrine of exhaustion of administrative remedies was inapplicable because "[n]either the IBLA nor any other administrative forum was available to the plaintiffs at the time of suit." 817 F.2d at 619. Why was the remedy of seeking review from the IBLA unavailable? Should Park County be allowed to avail itself of the claim that no adequate administrative remedy was available simply because it failed to invoke the remedy within the time authorized by law? *See* 4 KENNETH CULP DAVIS, ADMINISTRATIVE LAW § 26 (2d ed. 1984) (discussing the flexibility with which courts apply the doctrine of exhaustion of administrative remedies).

PROBLEM #1: STANDING AND RIPENESS

Dr. Jane Green, an assistant professor of biology at Indiana University, is an expert on raptor species. Dr. Green received her Ph.D from the University of Wyoming in 1990. She wrote her thesis on the northern goshawk, a raptor that lives in the lodgepole pine forests of the western United States. Despite its rejection of a petition to list the northern goshawk as an endangered species in 1992, the U.S. Fish and Wildlife Service continues to study the bird for possible future listing.

Since moving to Indiana, Dr. Green has continued to work on raptor species in the western United States, although she does not focus exclusively on the goshawk. Recently, she has learned about a plan by the U.S. Forest Service to clear-cut log in an area of the Shoshone National Forest where she had identified several goshawk nesting sites during her field work for her thesis. This field work was completed five years ago. Dr. Green believes that logging will be detrimental to the survival of the goshawk. She would like to see the plan prohibit logging for both personal and professional reasons. She has come to you for assistance in determining whether she has legal grounds to pursue a case.

Assume that the U.S. Forest Service failed to analyze the cumulative impacts of all past, present and reasonably foreseeable future logging in the area as required by NEPA, and that this is the only legal deficiency that you have been able to identify. Does Dr. Green have standing to sue under NEPA? What facts should she allege in her complaint to support her claim of standing? Is there anything she can do to enhance her chances to show that she has standing? Describe the legal basis for her standing claim.

B. Judicial Review of Agency Action

CITIZENS TO PRESERVE OVERTON PARK, INC. V. VOLPE
401 U.S. 402 (1971)

Opinion of the Court by Mr. Justice MARSHALL.

The growing public concern about the quality of our natural environment has prompted Congress in recent years to enact legislation designed to curb the accelerating destruction of our country's natural beauty. We are concerned in this case with § 4(f) of the Department of Transportation Act of 1966, as amended, and § 18(a) of the Federal-Aid Highway Act of 1968, 23 U.S.C. § 138 (hereafter § 138). These statutes prohibit the Secretary of Transportation from authorizing the use of federal funds to finance the construction of highways through public parks if a "feasible and prudent" alternative route exists. If no such route is available, the statutes allow him to approve construction through parks only if there has been "all possible planning to minimize harm" to the park.

Petitioners, private citizens as well as local and national conservation organizations, contend that the Secretary has violated these statutes by authorizing the expenditure of federal funds for the construction of a six-lane interstate highway through a public park in Memphis, Tennessee. Their claim was rejected by the District Court, which granted the Secretary's motion for summary judgment, and the Court of Appeals for the Sixth Circuit affirmed. After oral argument, this Court granted a stay that halted construction and, treating the application for the stay as a petition for certiorari, granted review. 400 U.S. 939. We now reverse the judgment below and remand for further proceedings in the District Court.

Overton Park is 342-acre city park located near the center of Memphis. The park contains a zoo, a nine-hole municipal golf course, an outdoor theater, nature trails, a bridle path, an art academy, picnic areas, and 170 acres of forest. The proposed highway, which is to be a six-lane, high-speed, expressway, will sever the zoo from the rest of the park. Although the roadway will be depressed below ground level except where it crosses a small creek, 26 acres of the park will be destroyed. The highway is to be a segment of Interstate Highway I-40, part of the National System of Interstate and Defense Highways. I-40 will provide Memphis with a major east-west expressway which will allow easier access to downtown Memphis from the residential areas on the eastern edge of the city.

Although the route through the park was approved by the Bureau of Public Roads in 1956 and by the Federal Highway Administrator in 1966, the enactment of § 4(f) of the Department of Transportation Act prevented distribution of federal funds for the section of the highway designated to go through Overton Park until the Secretary of Transportation determined whether the requirements of § 4(f) had been met. Federal funding for the rest of the project was, however, available; and the state acquired a right-of-way on both sides of the park. In April 1968, the Secretary announced that he concurred in the judgment of local officials that I-40 should be built through the park. And in September 1969 the State acquired the right-of-way inside Overton Park from the city. Final approval for the project—the route as well as the design—was not announced until November 1969, after Congress had reiterated in § 138 of the Federal-Aid Highway Act that highway construction through public parks was to be restricted. Neither announcement approving the route and design of I-40 was accompanied by a statement of the Secretary's factual findings. He did not indicate why he believed there were no feasible and prudent alternative routes or why design changes could not be made to reduce the harm to the park.

Petitioners contend that the Secretary's action is invalid without such formal findings and that the Secretary did not make an independent determination but merely relied on the judgment of the Memphis City Council. They also contend that it would be "feasible and prudent" to route I-40 around Overton Park either to the north or to the south. And they argue that if these alternative routes are not "feasible and prudent," the present plan does not include "all possible" methods for reducing harm to the park. Petitioners claim that I-40 could be built under the park by using either of two possible tunneling methods, and they claim that, at a minimum, by using advanced drainage techniques the expressway could be depressed below ground level along the entire route through the park including the section that crosses the small creek.

Respondents argue that it was unnecessary for the Secretary to make formal findings, and that he did, in fact, exercise his own independent judgment which was supported by the facts. In the District Court, respondents introduced affidavits, prepared specifically for this litigation, which indicated that the Secretary had made the decision and that the decision was supportable. These affidavits were contradicted by affidavits introduced by petitioners, who also sought to take the deposition of a former Federal Highway Administrator who had participated in the decision to route I-40 through Overton Park.

The District Court and the Court of Appeals found that formal findings by the Secretary were not necessary and refused to order the deposition of the former Federal Highway Administrator because those courts believed that probing of the mental processes of an administrative decisionmaker was prohibited. And, believing that the Secretary's authority was wide and reviewing courts' authority narrow in the approval of highway routes, the lower courts held that the affidavits contained no basis for a determination that the Secretary had exceeded his authority.

We agree that formal findings were not required. But we do not believe that in this case judicial review based solely on litigation affidavits was adequate.

A threshold question—whether petitioners are entitled to any judicial review—is easily answered. Section 701 of the Administrative Procedure Act, 5 U.S.C. § 701, provides that the action of "each authority of the Government of the United States," which includes the Department of Transportation, is subject to judicial review except where there is a statutory prohibition on review or where "agency action is committed to agency discretion by law." In this case, there is no indication that Congress sought to prohibit judicial review and there is most certainly no "showing of 'clear and convincing evidence' of a . . . legislative intent" to restrict access to judicial review. *Abbott Laboratories v. Gardner*, 387 U.S. 136, 141 (1967). *Brownell v. We Shung*, 352 U.S. 180, 185 (1956).

Similarly, the Secretary's decision here does not fall within the exception for action "committed to agency discretion." This is a very narrow exception. Berger, *Administrative Arbitrariness and Judicial Review*, 65 COLUM. L. REV. 55 (1965). The legislative history of the Administrative Procedure Act indicates that it is applicable in those rare instances where "statutes are drawn in such broad terms that in a given case there is no law to apply." S. Rep. No. 752, 79th Cong., 1st Sess., 26 (1945).

Section 4(f) of the Department of Transportation Act and § 138 of the Federal-Aid Highway Act are clear and specific directives. Both the Department of Transportation Act and the Federal-Aid to Highway Act provide that the Secretary "shall not approve any program or project" that requires the use of any public parkland "unless (1) there is no feasible and prudent alternative to the use of such land, and (2) such program includes all possible planning to minimize harm to such park . . .." 23 U.S.C. § 138; 49 U.S.C. § 1653(f). This language is a plain and explicit bar to the use of federal funds for construction of highways through parks—only the most unusual situations are exempted.

Despite the clarity of the statutory language, respondents argue that the Secretary has wide discretion. They recognize that the requirement that there be no "feasible" alternative route admits of little administrative discretion. For this exemption to apply the Secretary must find that as a matter of sound engineering it would not be feasible to build the highway along any other route. Respondents argue, however, that the requirement that there be no other "prudent" route requires the Secretary to engage in a wide-ranging balancing of competing interests. They contend that the Secretary should weigh the detriment resulting from the destruction of parkland against the cost of other routes, safety considerations, and other factors, and determine on the basis of the importance that he attaches to these other factors whether, on balance, alternative feasible routes would be "prudent."

But no such wide-ranging endeavor was intended. It is obvious that in most cases considerations of cost, directness of route, and community disruption will indicate that parkland should be used for highway construction whenever possible. Although it may be necessary to transfer funds from one jurisdiction to another, there will always be a smaller outlay required from the public purse when parkland is used since the public already owns the land and there will be no need to pay for right-of-way. And since people do not live or work in parks, if a highway is built on parkland no one will have to leave his home or give up his business. Such factors are common to substantially all highway construction. Thus, if Congress intended these factors to be on an equal footing with preservation of parkland there would have been no need for the statutes.

Congress clearly did not intend that cost and disruption of the community were to be ignored by the Secretary. But the very existence of the statutes indicates that protection of parkland was to be given paramount importance. The few green havens that are public parks were not to be lost unless there were truly unusual factors present in a particular case or the cost or community disruption resulting from alternative routes reached extraordinary magnitudes. If the statutes are to have any meaning, the Secretary cannot approve the destruction of parkland unless he finds that alternative routes present unique problems.

Plainly, there is "law to apply" and thus the exemption for action "committed to agency discretion" is inapplicable. But the existence of judicial review is only the start: the standard for review must also be determined. For that we must look to § 706 of the Administrative Procedure Act, 5 U.S.C. § 706, which provides that a "reviewing court shall . . . hold unlawful and set aside agency action, findings, and conclusions found" not to meet six separate standards.[5] In all cases agency action must be set aside if the action was "arbitrary, capricious, an abuse of

---

[5]   "To the extent necessary to decision and when presented, the reviewing court shall decide all relevant questions of law, interpret constitutional and statutory provisions, and determine the meaning or applicability of the terms of an agency action. The reviewing court shall—

(1)   compel agency action unlawfully withheld or unreasonably delayed; and
(2)   hold unlawful and set aside agency action, findings, and conclusions found to be—
    (A)   arbitrary, capricious, an abuse of discretion, or otherwise not in accordance with law;
    (B)   contrary to constitutional right, power, privilege, or immunity;
    (C)   in excess of statutory jurisdiction, authority, or limitations, or short of statutory right;
    (D)   without observance of procedure required by law;
    (E)   unsupported by substantial evidence in a case subject to sections 556 and 557 of this title or otherwise reviewed on the record of an agency hearing provided by statute; or
    (F)   unwarranted by the facts to the extent that the facts are subject to trial de novo by the reviewing court.

"In making the foregoing determinations, the court shall review the whole record or those parts of it cited by a party, and due account shall be taken of the rule of prejudicial error." 5 U.S.C. § 706 (1964 ed., Supp. V).

discretion, or otherwise not in accordance with law" or if the action failed to meet statutory, procedural, or constitutional requirements. 5 U.S.C. §§ 706(2)(A), (B), (C), (D). In certain narrow, specifically limited situations, the agency action is to be set aside if the action was not supported by "substantial evidence." And in other equally narrow circumstances the reviewing court is to engage in a *de novo* review of the action and set it aside if it was "unwarranted by the facts." 5 U.S.C. §§ 706(2)(E), (F).

Petitioners argue that the Secretary's approval of the construction of I-40 through Overton Park is subject to one or the other of these latter two standards of limited applicability. First, they contend that the "substantial evidence" standard of § 706(2)(E) must be applied. In the alternative, they claim that § 706(2)(F) applies and that there must be a *de novo* review to determine if the Secretary's action was "unwarranted by the facts." Neither of these standards is, however, applicable.

Review under the substantial-evidence test is authorized only when the agency action is taken pursuant to a rulemaking provision of the Administrative Procedure Act itself, 5 U.S.C. § 553, or when the agency action is based on a public adjudicatory hearing. *See* 5 U.S.C. §§ 556, 557. The Secretary's decision to allow the expenditure of federal funds to build I-40 through Overton Park was plainly not an exercise of a rulemaking function. *See* 1 K. Davis, Administrative Law Treatise § 5.01 (1958). And the only hearing that is required by either the Administrative Procedure Act or the statutes regulating the distribution of federal funds for highway construction is a public hearing conducted by local officials for the purpose of informing the community about the proposed project and eliciting community views on the design and route. 23 U.S.C. § 128. The hearing is nonadjudicatory, quasi-legislative in nature. It is not designed to produce a record that is to be the basis of agency action—the basic requirement for substantial-evidence review. *See* H.R. Rep. No. 1980, 79th Cong., 2d Sess.

Petitioners' alternative argument also fails. *De novo* review of whether the Secretary's decision was "unwarranted by the facts" is authorized by § 706(2)(F) in only two circumstances. First, such *de novo* review is authorized when the action is adjudicatory in nature and the agency factfinding procedures are inadequate. And, there may be independent judicial factfinding when issues that were not before the agency are raised in a proceeding to enforce nonadjudicatory agency action. H.R. Rep. No. 1980, 79th Cong., 2d Sess. Neither situation exists here.

Even though there is no *de novo* review in this case and the Secretary's approval of the route of I-40 does not have ultimately to meet the substantial-evidence test, the generally applicable standards of § 706 require the reviewing court to engage in a substantial inquiry. Certainly, the Secretary's decision is entitled to a presumption of regularity. But that presumption is not to shield his action from a thorough, probing, in-depth review.

The court is first required to decide whether the Secretary acted within the scope of his authority. *Schilling v. Rogers*, 363 U.S. 666, 676-77 (1960). This determination naturally begins with a delineation of the scope of the Secretary's authority and discretion. L. JAFFE, JUDICIAL CONTROL OF ADMINISTRATIVE ACTION 359 (1965). As has been shown, Congress has specified only a small range of choices that the Secretary can make. Also involved in this initial inquiry is a determination of whether on the facts the Secretary's decision can reasonably be said to be within that range. The reviewing court must consider whether the Secretary properly construed his authority to approve the use of parkland as limited to situations where there are no feasible alternative routes or where feasible alternative routes involve uniquely difficult problems. And the reviewing court must be able to find that the Secretary could have reasonably believed that in this case there are no feasible alternatives or that alternatives do involve unique problems.

Scrutiny of the facts does not end, however, with the determination that the Secretary has acted within the scope of his statutory authority. Section 706(2)(A) requires a finding that the actual choice made was not "arbitrary, capricious, an abuse of discretion, or otherwise not in accordance with law." 5 U.S.C. § 706(2)(A). To make this finding the court must consider whether the decision was based on a consideration of the relevant factors and whether there has been a clear error of judgment. Although this inquiry into the facts is to be searching and careful, the ultimate standard of review is a narrow one. The court is not empowered to substitute its judgment for that of the agency.

The final inquiry is whether the Secretary's action followed the necessary procedural requirements. Here the only procedural error alleged is the failure of the Secretary to make formal findings and state his reason for allowing the highway to be built through the park.

Undoubtedly, review of the Secretary's action is hampered by his failure to make such findings, but the absence of formal findings does not necessarily require that the case be remanded to the Secretary. Neither the Department of Transportation Act nor the Federal-Aid Highway Act requires such formal findings. Moreover, the Administrative Procedure Act requirements that there be formal findings in certain rulemaking and adjudicatory proceedings do not apply to the Secretary's action here. *See* 5 U.S.C. §§ 553(a)(2), 554(a). And, although formal findings may be required in some cases in the absence of statutory directives when the nature of the agency action is ambiguous, those situations are rare. Plainly, there is no ambiguity here; the Secretary has approved the construction of I-40 through Overton Park and has approved a specific design for the project.

Petitioners contend that although there may not be a statutory requirement that the Secretary make formal findings and even though this may not be a case for the reviewing court to impose a requirement that findings be made, Department of Transportation regulations require them. This argument is based on DOT Order 5610.1, which requires the Secretary to make formal findings when he approves the use of parkland for highway construction but which was issued after the route for I-40 was approved. Petitioners argue that even though the order was not in effect at the time approval was given to the Overton Park project and even though the order was not intended to have retrospective effect the order represents the law at the time of this Court's decision and under *Thorpe v. Housing Authority*, 393 U.S. 268, 281-82 (1969), should be applied to this case.

* * *

While we do not question that DOT Order 5610.1 constitutes the law in effect at the time of our decision, we do not believe that *Thorpe* compels us to remand for the Secretary to make formal findings. Here, unlike the situation in *Thorpe*, there has been a change in circumstances—additional right-of-way has been cleared and the 26-acre right-of-way inside Overton Park has been purchased by the State. Moreover, there is an administrative record that allows the full, prompt review of the Secretary's action that is sought without additional delay which would result from having a remand to the Secretary.

That administrative record is not, however, before us. The lower courts based their review on the litigation affidavits that were presented. These affidavits were merely "post hoc" rationalizations, *Burlington Truck Lines v. United States*, 371 U.S. 156, 168-69 (1962), which have traditionally been found to be an inadequate basis for review. *Burlington Truck Lines v. United States, supra*; *SEC v. Chenery Corp.*, 318 U.S. 80, 87 (1943). And they clearly do not constitute the "whole record" compiled by the agency: the basis for review required by § 706 of the Administrative Procedure Act. *See* n.30, *supra*.

Thus it is necessary to remand this case to the District Court for plenary review of the Secretary's decision. That review is to be based on the full administrative record that was before the Secretary at the time he made his decision. But since the bare record may not disclose the factors that were considered or the Secretary's construction of the evidence it may be necessary for the District Court to require some explanation in order to determine if the Secretary acted within the scope of his authority and if the Secretary's action was justifiable under the applicable standard.

The court may require the administrative officials who participated in the decision to give testimony explaining their action. Of course, such inquiry into the mental processes of administrative decisionmakers is usually to be avoided. *United States v. Morgan*, 313 U.S. 409, 422 (1941). And where there are administrative findings that were made at the same time as the decision, as was the case in *Morgan*, there must be a strong showing of bad faith or improper behavior before such inquiry may be made. But here there are no such formal findings and it may be that the only way there can be effective judicial review is by examining the decisionmakers themselves.

The District Court is not, however, required to make such an inquiry. It may be that the Secretary can prepare formal findings including the information required by DOT Order 5610.1 that will provide an adequate explanation for his action. Such an explanation will, to some extent, be a "post hoc rationalization" and thus must be viewed critically. If the District Court decides that additional explanation is necessary, that court should consider which method will prove the most expeditious so that full review may be had as soon as possible.

Reversed and remanded.

Separate opinion of Mr. Justice BLACK, with whom Mr. Justice BRENNAN joins.

I agree with the Court that the judgment of the Court of Appeals is wrong and that its action should be reversed. I do not agree that the whole matter should be remanded to the District Court. I think the case should be sent back to the Secretary of Transportation. It is apparent from the Court's opinion today that the Secretary of Transportation completely failed to comply with the duty imposed upon him by Congress not to permit a federally financed public highway to run through a public park "unless (1) there is no feasible and prudent alternative to the use of such land, and (2) such program includes all possible planning to minimize harm to such park . . .." 23 U.S.C. § 138; 49 U.S.C. § 1653(f). That congressional command should not be taken lightly by the Secretary or by this Court. It represents a solemn determination of the highest law-making body of this Nation that the beauty and health-giving facilities of our parks are not to be taken away for public roads without hearings, factfindings, and policy determinations under the supervision of a Cabinet officer—the Secretary of Transportation. The Act of Congress in connection with other federal highway aid legislation, it seems to me, calls for hearings—hearings that a court can review, hearings that demonstrate more than mere arbitrary defiance by the Secretary. Whether the findings growing out of such hearings are labeled "formal" or "informal" appears to me to be no more than an exercise in semantics. Whatever the hearing requirements might be, the Department of Transportation failed to meet them in this case. I regret that I am compelled to conclude for myself that, except for some too-late formulations, apparently coming from the Solicitor General's office, this record contains not one word to indicate that the Secretary raised even a finger to comply with the command of Congress. It is our duty, I believe, to remand this whole matter back to the Secretary of Transportation for him to give this matter the hearing it deserves in full good-faith obedience to the Act of Congress. That Act was obviously passed to protect our public parks from forays by road builders except in the most extraordinary and imperative circumstances. This record does not demonstrate the existence of such circumstances. I dissent from the Court's failure to send the case back to the Secretary, whose duty has not yet been performed.

NOTES

1. Under what circumstances may judicial review be denied, according to the *Overton Park* decision? Consider the case where "statutes are drawn in such broad terms that in a given case, there is no law to apply." If a statute is drawn so broadly, might it constitute an unlawful delegation of legislative authority by Congress? *See* 1 KENNETH DAVIS, ADMINISTRATIVE LAW TREATISE § 3 (2d ed. 1978 and Supp. 1989). Does the denial of judicial review raise due process problems? *See Ortwein v. Schwab*, 410 U.S. 656 (1973); BERNARD SCHWARTZ, ADMINISTRATIVE LAW §§ 2.2-2.8 (3rd ed. 1991).

2. The scope of review varies depending on the type of action being reviewed. When does the "substantial evidence" test apply? Does Justice Marshall correctly state the law regarding the application of this test? When does *de novo* review apply? *See* 5 JACOB STEIN ET AL., ADMINISTRATIVE LAW § 51 (1993).

3. The Court makes clear that, in this case, "formal findings" were not required, although in other cases, such as those involving formal hearings under 5 U.S.C. § 554, formal findings may be required. Whether or not an agency makes formal findings, judicial review of agency action is normally based solely upon the administrative record that was before the agency when it made the decision. Thus, when facing the prospect of litigation, government agencies must anticipate the need to present to the court all relevant documents which were considered in making a decision. If these documents reveal that the agency failed to consider relevant information in making its decision, or if the documents do not support the decision that was made, the court may well strike down the agency action as arbitrary and capricious. Many agencies recognize the importance of developing a thorough administrative record, particularly when dealing with complex issues, which often arise in environmental regulation. For this reason, agencies often use formal docketing procedures to track all documents that are associated with informal rulemaking proceedings under 5 U.S.C. § 553. If such rules are challenged in court, the agency can then make the complete docket available to the court and to all parties.

4. The decision in *Overton Park* involves an "informal adjudication," and the APA provides little guidance to agencies regarding the process to be followed in such proceedings. At a minimum, however, persons seeking agency action on a matter generally have the right to appear before an agency "for the presentation, adjustment, or determination of an issue, request, or controversy in a proceeding * * * or in connection with an agency function." 5 U.S.C. § 555(b). Agencies are required to conclude matters presented to them "within a reasonable time." *Id.*; *see also* 5 U.S.C. § 706(1). Moreover, where an agency denies a request it must give notice to interested parties and "a brief statement of the grounds for denial." 5 U.S.C. § 555(e). This latter requirement is designed, in part, to insure that courts will have an adequate record upon which to conduct judicial review of agency decisions. *City of Gillette v. Federal Energy Regulatory Comm.*, 737 F.2d 883, 886 (10th Cir. 1984).

5. What was wrong with the record in this case? Do you agree with Justice Marshall or Justice Black about the proper disposition of an action where the administrative record is found wanting? *Overton Park* involved the situation where a contemporaneous agency explanation was not provided to the court in the administrative record. In *Camp v. Pitts*, 411 U.S. 138 (1973), the Court clarified *Overton Park* and held that where no contemporaneous explanation exists, the decisionmaker may be required to provide an explanation for the decision in court. Because agency decisionmakers rarely prefer this latter option, *Overton Park* and *Camp v. Pitts* promote the preparation of complete administrative records that include full explanations of the bases for their decisions.

6.   *United States v. Morgan*, 313 U.S. 409 (1941), was the culmination of a series of Supreme Court cases which ultimately led to the Court's pronouncement that a complaining party may not "probe the mental processes" of an agency head to help determine the reasons for its decision. *Id.* at 422. *See also* BERNARD SCHWARTZ, ADMINISTRATIVE LAW, §§ 7.21-22 (3rd ed. 1991). How does the rule limit litigants who are challenging agency action? What relevance does this rule have to the requirement that review be based upon an administrative record?

7.   Prior to the filing of the *Overton Park* litigation, the highway authorities:

> proceeded to condemn homes, bulldoze them, and build the highway right-of-way right up to the boundary of the Park. They also built a multimillion dollar bridge across the Mississippi River on the Park highway alignment. It was only then that they turned to the Secretary to ask approval for the Park route on the grounds that there was no longer any feasible and prudent alternative.

ZYGMUNT PLATER ET AL., ENVIRONMENTAL LAW AND POLICY 553 n.16 (1992). Why would the highway authorities invest all that money into the Park route before secretarial approval? Secretary Volpe reversed his decision on remand and refused to approve the Park route. The Tennessee Department of Highways ultimately lost its challenge of the Secretary's denial of funds. *Citizens to Preserve Overton Park v. Brinegar*, 494 F.2d 1212 (6th Cir. 1974), *cert. denied*, 421 U.S. 991 (1975). Interstate highway traffic now loops around the city, avoiding Overton Park. Both Oliver A. Houck, *The Secret Opinions of the United States Supreme Court on Leading Cases in Environmental Law, Never Before Published!*, 65 U. COLO. L. REV. 459, 477-83 (1994), and Peter L. Strauss, *Revisiting* Overton Park: *Political and Judicial Controls Over Administrative Actions Affecting the Community*, 39 UCLA L. REV. 1251 (1992), describe the prior and subsequent events that framed the *Overton Park* controversy.

8.   *Scenic Hudson Preservation Conference v. Federal Power Comm'n*, 354 F.2d 608 (2d Cir. 1965), *cert. denied*, 384 U.S. 941 (1966), stands with *Sierra Club v. Morton* and *Overton Park* as an early landmark in citizen-group use of judicial review of agency action to delay, and ultimately stop, development projects on environmental grounds. *Scenic Hudson* has been called the Grandmother of Environmental Lawsuits. *Comment, Calm After the Storm: Grandmother of Environmental Lawsuits Settled by Mediation*, 11 Envtl. L. Rep. (Envtl. L. Inst.) 10074 (1981). In *Scenic Hudson*, the court granted standing to a conservation association to challenge the Federal Power Commission's (FPC's) grant of a license to Consolidated Edison to build a huge pumped storage hydroelectric facility on Storm King mountain along the Hudson River. A pumped storage hydroelectric facility generates power during peak load periods by releasing water that has been pumped into a high reservoir during off-peak times. Plaintiffs complained that the FPC failed to take account of scenic, historic, recreation, and conservation concerns (the term "environmental" was not widely used in its current sense at the time) in the licensing proceedings. The statute authorizing the FPC to issue licenses required projects to be, in the judgment of the FPC, "best adapted to a comprehensive plan for improving or developing a waterway" for commerce, waterpower, and "other beneficial public uses, including recreational purposes." 354 F.2d at 612. The court held that the FPC failed to produce an adequate record to support its decision because it did not take certain affirmative steps to develop and consider information about alternative sources of power and the effects of the project on fisheries and aesthetic values. The seriousness with which the court took the citizen-plaintiff's grievances against the licensing agency was unusual for its time. Litigation over the Storm King project continued in state and federal courts for nearly twenty years. In December 1980, Consolidated Edison agreed to surrender its license to build the Storm King facility and donate the 500-acre site for use as a park.

VERMONT YANKEE NUCLEAR POWER CORP. V. NATURAL RESOURCES DEFENSE COUNCIL, INC.
435 U.S. 519 (1978)

Justice REHNQUIST delivered the opinion of the Court.

In 1946, Congress enacted the Administrative Procedure Act, which as we have noted elsewhere was not only "a new, basic and comprehensive regulation of procedures in many agencies," *Wong Yang Sung v. McGrath*, 339 U.S. 33 (1950), but was also a legislative enactment which settled "long-continued and hard-fought contentions, and enacts a formula upon which opposing social and political forces have come to rest." *Id.* at 40. Section [553] of the Act, dealing with rulemaking, requires * * * that "notice of proposed rule making shall be published in the Federal Register . . .," describes the contents of that notice, and goes on to require in subsection (c) that after the notice the agency "shall give interested persons an opportunity to participate in the rule making through submission of written data, views, or arguments with or without opportunity for oral presentation. After consideration of the relevant matter presented, the agency shall incorporate in the rules adopted a concise general statement of their basis and purpose." [5 U.S.C. § 553.] Interpreting this provision of the Act in *United States v. Allegheny-Ludlum Steel Corp.*, 406 U.S. 742 (1972), and *United States v. Florida East Coast R. Co.*, 410 U.S. 224 (1973), we held that generally speaking this section of the Act established the maximum procedural requirements which Congress was willing to have the courts impose upon agencies in conducting rulemaking procedures. Agencies are free to grant additional procedural rights in the exercise of their discretion, but reviewing courts are generally not free to impose them if the agencies have not chosen to grant them. This is not to say necessarily that there are no circumstances which would ever justify a court in overturning agency action because of a failure to employ procedures beyond those required by the statute. But such circumstances, if they exist, are extremely rare.

Even apart from the Administrative Procedure Act this Court has for more than four decades emphasized that the formulation of procedures was basically to be left within the discretion of the agencies to which Congress had confided the responsibility for substantive judgments. * * *

It is in the light of this background of statutory and decisional law that we granted certiorari to review two judgments of the Court of Appeals for the District of Columbia Circuit because of our concern that they had seriously misread or misapplied this statutory and decisional law cautioning reviewing courts against engrafting their own notions of proper procedures upon agencies entrusted with substantive functions by Congress. We conclude that the Court of Appeals has done just that in these cases, and we therefore remand them to it for further proceedings. * * *

I

A

Under the Atomic Energy Act of 1954, 42 U.S.C. § 2011 *et seq.*, the Atomic Energy Commission[2] was given broad regulatory authority over the development of nuclear energy. Under the terms of the Act, a utility seeking to construct and operate a nuclear power plant must obtain a separate permit or license at both the construction and the operation stage of the project. In order to obtain the construction permit, the utility must file a preliminary safety analysis report, an environmental report, and certain information regarding the antitrust implications of the proposed project. This application then undergoes exhaustive review by the Commission's staff and by the Advisory Committee on Reactor Safeguards (ACRS), a group of distinguished experts in the field of atomic energy. Both groups submit to the Commission their own evaluations, which then become part of the record of the utility's application. The Commission staff also undertakes the review required by the National Environmental Policy Act of 1969 (NEPA), and prepares a draft environmental impact statement, which, after being circulated for comment, is revised and becomes a final environmental impact statement. Thereupon a three-member Atomic Safety and Licensing Board conducts a public adjudicatory hearing, and reaches a decision[4] which can be appealed to the Atomic Safety and Licensing Appeal Board, and currently, in the Commission's discretion, to the Commission itself. The final agency decision may be appealed to the courts of appeals. The same sort of process occurs when the utility applies for a license to operate the plant, except that a hearing need only be held in contested cases and may be limited to the matters in controversy.[5]

[This case arises] from two separate decisions of the Court of Appeals for the District of Columbia Circuit. In the first, the court remanded a decision of the Commission to grant a license to petitioner Vermont Yankee Nuclear Power Corp. to operate a nuclear power plant. In the second, the court remanded a decision of that same agency to grant a permit to petitioner Consumers Power Co. to construct two pressurized water nuclear reactors to generate electricity and steam.

B

In December 1967, after the mandatory adjudicatory hearing and necessary review, the Commission granted petitioner Vermont Yankee a permit to build a nuclear power plant in Vernon, Vt. Thereafter, Vermont Yankee applied for an operating license. Respondent Natural Resources Defense Council (NRDC) objected to the granting of a license, however, and therefore a hearing on the application commenced on August 10, 1971. Excluded from consideration at the hearings, over NRDC's objection, was the issue of the environmental

---

[2]   The licensing and regulatory functions of the Atomic Energy Commission (AEC) were transferred to the Nuclear Regulatory Commission (NRC) by the Energy Reorganization Act of 1974. * * *

[4]   The Licensing Board issues a permit if it concludes that there is reasonable assurance that the proposed plant can be constructed and operated without undue risk, and that the environmental cost-benefit balance favors the issuance of a permit.

[5]   When a license application is contested, the Licensing Board must find reasonable assurance that the plant can be operated without undue risk and will not be inimical to the common defense and security or to the health and safety of the public. * * *

effects of operations to reprocess fuel or dispose of wastes resulting from the reprocessing operations.[6] This ruling was affirmed by the Appeal Board in June 1972.

In November 1972, however, the Commission, making specific reference to the Appeal Board's decision with respect to the Vermont Yankee license, instituted rulemaking proceedings "that would specifically deal with the question of consideration of environmental effects associated with the uranium fuel cycle in the individual cost-benefit analyses for light water cooled nuclear power reactors." The notice of proposed rulemaking offered two alternatives, both predicated on a report prepared by the Commission's staff entitled Environmental Survey of the Nuclear Fuel Cycle. The first would have required no quantitative evaluation of the environmental hazards of fuel reprocessing or disposal because the Environmental Survey had found them to be slight. The second would have specified numerical values for the environmental impact of this part of the fuel cycle, which values would then be incorporated into a table, along with the other relevant factors, to determine the overall cost-benefit balance for each operating license.

Much of the controversy in this case revolves around the procedures used in the rulemaking hearing which commenced in February 1973. In a supplemental notice of hearing the Commission indicated that while discovery or cross-examination would not be utilized, the Environmental Survey would be available to the public before the hearing along with the extensive background documents cited therein. All participants would be given a reasonable opportunity to present their position and could be represented by counsel if they so desired. Written and, time permitting, oral statements would be received and incorporated into the record. All persons giving oral statements would be subject to questioning by the Commission. At the conclusion of the hearing, a transcript would be made available to the public and the record would remain open for 30 days to allow the filing of supplemental written statements. More than 40 individuals and organizations representing a wide variety of interests submitted written comments. * * * The hearing was held on February 1 and 2, with participation by a number of groups, including the Commission's staff, the United States Environmental Protection Agency, a manufacturer of reactor equipment, a trade association from the nuclear industry, a group of electric utility companies, and a group called Consolidated National Intervenors which represented 79 groups and individuals including respondent NRDC.

After the hearing, the Commission's staff filed a supplemental document for the purpose of clarifying and revising the Environmental Survey. Then the Licensing Board forwarded its report to the Commission without rendering any decision. The Licensing Board identified as the principal procedural question the propriety of declining to use full formal adjudicatory procedures. The major substantive issue was the technical adequacy of the Environmental Survey.

In April 1974, the Commission issued a rule which adopted the second of the two proposed alternatives described above. The Commission also approved the procedures used at the hearing, and indicated that the record, including the Environmental Survey, provided an "adequate data base for the regulation adopted." Finally, the Commission ruled that to the extent the rule differed from the Appeal Board decisions in Vermont Yankee "those decisions have no further

---

[6] The nuclear fission which takes place in light-water nuclear reactors apparently converts its principal fuel, uranium, into plutonium, which is itself highly radioactive but can be used as reactor fuel if separated from the remaining uranium and radioactive waste products. Fuel reprocessing refers to the process necessary to recapture usable plutonium. Waste disposal, at the present stage of technological development, refers to the storage of the very long lived and highly radioactive waste products until they detoxify sufficiently that they no longer present an environmental hazard. There are presently no physical or chemical steps which render this waste less toxic, other than simply the passage of time.

precedential significance," but that since "the environmental effects of the uranium fuel cycle have been shown to be relatively insignificant, . . . it is unnecessary to apply the amendment to applicant's environmental reports submitted prior to its effective date or to Final Environmental Statements for which Draft Environmental Statements have been circulated for comment prior to the effective date."

Respondents appealed from both the Commission's adoption of the rule and its decision to grant Vermont Yankee's license to the Court of Appeals for the District of Columbia Circuit.

* * *

D

With respect to the challenge of Vermont Yankee's license, the court first ruled that in the absence of effective rulemaking proceedings, the Commission must deal with the environmental impact of fuel reprocessing and disposal in individual licensing proceedings. The court then examined the rulemaking proceedings and, despite the fact that it appeared that the agency employed all the procedures required by § 553 and more, the court determined the proceedings to be inadequate and overturned the rule. Accordingly, the Commission's determination with respect to Vermont Yankee's license was also remanded for further proceedings.

* * *

II

A

Petitioner Vermont Yankee first argues that the Commission may grant a license to operate a nuclear reactor without any consideration of waste disposal and fuel reprocessing. We find, however, that this issue is no longer presented by the record in this case. The Commission does not contend that it is not required to consider the environmental impact of the spent fuel processes when licensing nuclear power plants. Indeed, the Commission has publicly stated subsequent to the Court of Appeals' decision in the instant case that consideration of the environmental impact of the back end of the fuel cycle in "the environmental impact statements for individual LWR's [light-water power reactors] would represent a full and candid assessment of costs and benefits consistent with the legal requirements and spirit of NEPA." * * * Thus, at this stage of the proceedings the only question presented for review in this regard is whether the Commission may consider the environmental impact of the fuel processes when licensing nuclear reactors. In addition to the weight which normally attaches to the agency's determination of such a question, other reasons support the Commission's conclusion.

Vermont Yankee will produce annually well over 100 pounds of radioactive wastes, some of which will be highly toxic. The Commission itself, in a pamphlet published by its information office, clearly recognizes that these wastes "pose the most severe potential health hazard . . . ." Many of these substances must be isolated for anywhere from 600 to hundreds of thousands of years. It is hard to argue that these wastes do not constitute "adverse environmental effects which cannot be avoided should the proposal be implemented," or that by operating nuclear power plants we are not making "irreversible and irretrievable commitments of resources." As the Court of Appeals recognized, the environmental impact of the radioactive wastes produced by a nuclear power plant is analytically indistinguishable from the environmental effects of "the stack gases produced by a coal-burning power plant." For these reasons we hold that the Commission acted well within its statutory authority when it considered the back end of the fuel cycle in individual licensing proceedings.

B

We next turn to the invalidation of the fuel cycle rule. But before determining whether the Court of Appeals reached a permissible result, we must determine exactly what result it did reach, and in this case that is no mean feat. Vermont Yankee argues that the court invalidated the rule because of the inadequacy of the procedures employed in the proceedings. Respondents, on the other hand, labeling petitioner's view of the decision a "straw man," argue to this Court that the court merely held that the record was inadequate to enable the reviewing court to determine whether the agency had fulfilled its statutory obligation. * * *

After a thorough examination of the opinion itself, we conclude that while the matter is not entirely free from doubt, the majority of the Court of Appeals struck down the rule because of the perceived inadequacies of the procedures employed in the rulemaking proceedings. The court first determined the intervenors' primary argument to be "that the decision to preclude 'discovery or cross-examination' denied them a meaningful opportunity to participate in the proceedings as guaranteed by due process." The court then went on to frame the issue for decision thus: "Thus, we are called upon to decide whether the procedures provided by the agency were sufficient to ventilate the issues." The court conceded that absent extraordinary circumstances it is improper for a reviewing court to prescribe the procedural format an agency must follow, but it likewise clearly thought it entirely appropriate to "scrutinize the record as a whole to insure that genuine opportunities to participate in a meaningful way were provided. . . ." The court also refrained from actually ordering the agency to follow any specific procedures, but there is little doubt in our minds that the ineluctable mandate of the court's decision is that the procedures afforded during the hearings were inadequate. * * *

In prior opinions we have intimated that even in a rulemaking proceeding when an agency is making a "'quasi-judicial'" determination by which a very small number of persons are "'exceptionally affected, in each case upon individual grounds,'" in some circumstances additional procedures may be required in order to afford the aggrieved individuals due process.[16] *United States v. Florida East Coast R. Co.*, 410 U.S. at 242-45, quoting from *Bi-Metallic Investment Co. v. State Board of Equalization*, 239 U.S. 441, 446 (1915). It might also be true, although we do not think the issue is presented in this case and accordingly do not decide it, that a totally unjustified departure from well-settled agency procedures of long standing might require judicial correction.

But this much is absolutely clear. Absent constitutional constraints or extremely compelling circumstances the "administrative agencies 'should be free to fashion their own rules of procedure and to pursue methods of inquiry capable of permitting them to discharge their multitudinous duties.'" *FCC v. Schreiber*, 381 U.S. 279, 290 (1965), quoting from *FCC v. Pottsville Broadcasting Co.*, 309 U.S. 134, 138 (1940). * * *

* * *

Respondent NRDC argues that § 553 of the Administrative Procedure Act merely establishes lower procedural bounds and that a court may routinely require more than the minimum when an agency's proposed rule addresses complex or technical factual issues or "Issues of Great Public Import." We have, however, previously shown that our decisions reject this view. We also think the legislative history, even the part which it cites, does not bear out its contention. * * * In short, all of this leaves little doubt that Congress intended that the

---

[16] Respondent NRDC does not now argue that additional procedural devices were required under the Constitution. Since this was clearly a rulemaking proceeding in its purest form, we see nothing to support such a view.

discretion of the *agencies* and not that of the courts be exercised in determining when extra procedural devices should be employed.

There are compelling reasons for construing § 553 in this manner. In the first place, if courts continually review agency proceedings to determine whether the agency employed procedures which were, in the court's opinion, perfectly tailored to reach what the court perceives to be the "best" or "correct" result, judicial review would be totally unpredictable. And the agencies, operating under this vague injunction to employ the "best" procedures and facing the threat of reversal if they did not, would undoubtedly adopt full adjudicatory procedures in every instance. Not only would this totally disrupt the statutory scheme, through which Congress enacted "a formula upon which opposing social and political forces have come to rest," but all the inherent advantages of informal rulemaking would be totally lost.

* * *

Finally, and perhaps most importantly, this sort of review fundamentally misconceives the nature of the standard for judicial review of an agency rule. The court below uncritically assumed that additional procedures will automatically result in a more adequate record because it will give interested parties more of an opportunity to participate in and contribute to the proceedings. But informal rulemaking need not be based solely on the transcript of a hearing held before an agency. Indeed, the agency need not even hold a formal hearing. *See* 5 U.S.C. § 553(c). Thus, the adequacy of the "record" in this type of proceeding is not correlated directly to the type of procedural devices employed, but rather turns on whether the agency has followed the statutory mandate of the Administrative Procedure Act or other relevant statutes. If the agency is compelled to support the rule which it ultimately adopts with the type of record produced only after a full adjudicatory hearing, it simply will have no choice but to conduct a full adjudicatory hearing prior to promulgating every rule. In sum, this sort of unwarranted judicial examination of perceived procedural shortcomings of a rulemaking proceeding can do nothing but seriously interfere with that process prescribed by Congress.

Respondent NRDC also argues that the fact that the Commission's inquiry was undertaken in the context of NEPA somehow permits a court to require procedures beyond those specified in § 553 of the APA when investigating factual issues through rulemaking. The Court of Appeals was apparently also of this view, indicating that agencies may be required to "develop new procedures to accomplish the innovative task of implementing NEPA through rulemaking." But we search in vain for something in NEPA which would mandate such a result. We have before observed that "NEPA does not repeal by implication any other statute." In fact, just two Terms ago, we emphasized that the only procedural requirements imposed by NEPA are those stated in the plain language of the Act. Thus, it is clear NEPA cannot serve as the basis for a substantial revision of the carefully constructed procedural specifications of the APA.

In short, nothing in the APA, NEPA, the circumstances of this case, the nature of the issues being considered, past agency practice, or the statutory mandate under which the Commission operates permitted the court to review and overturn the rulemaking proceeding on the basis of the procedural devices employed (or not employed) by the Commission so long as the Commission employed at least the statutory *minima*, a matter about which there is no doubt in this case.

There remains, of course, the question of whether the challenged rule finds sufficient justification in the administrative proceedings that it should be upheld by the reviewing court. Judge Tamm, concurring in the result reached by the majority of the Court of Appeals, thought that it did not. There are also intimations in the majority opinion which suggest that the judges who joined it likewise may have thought the administrative proceedings an insufficient basis upon which to predicate the rule in question. We accordingly remand so that the Court of

Appeals may review the rule as the Administrative Procedure Act provides. We have made it abundantly clear before that when there is a contemporaneous explanation of the agency decision, the validity of that action must "stand or fall on the propriety of that finding, judged, of course, by the appropriate standard of review. If that finding is not sustainable on the administrative record made, then the Comptroller's decision must be vacated and the matter remanded to him for further consideration." *Camp v. Pitts*, 411 U.S. 138, 143 (1973). *See also SEC v. Chenery Corp.*, 318 U.S. 80 (1943). The court should engage in this kind of review and not stray beyond the judicial province to explore the procedural format or to impose upon the agency its own notion of which procedures are "best" or most likely to further some vague, undefined public good.

* * *

Reversed and remanded.

NOTES

1. The following excerpt is from the Court of Appeals decision that the Supreme Court reversed in *Vermont Yankee*. Does Justice Rehnquist accurately characterize the Judge Bazelon opinion?

> The primary argument advanced by the public interest intervenors is that the decision to preclude "discovery or cross-examination" denied them a meaningful opportunity to participate in the proceedings as guaranteed by due process. They do not question the Commission's authority to proceed by informal rulemaking, as opposed to adjudication. They rely instead on the line of cases indicating that in particular circumstances procedures in excess of the bare minima prescribed by the Administrative Procedure Act, 5 U.S.C. § 553, may be required.
>
> The Government concedes that "basic considerations of fairness may under exceptional circumstances" require additional procedures in "legislative-type proceedings," but contends that the procedures here were more than adequate. Thus, we are called upon to decide whether the procedures provided by the agency were sufficient to ventilate the issues.
>
> A few general observations are in order concerning the role of a court in this area. Absent extraordinary circumstances, it is not proper for a reviewing court to prescribe the procedural format which an agency must use to explore a given set of issues. Unless there are statutory directives to the contrary, an agency has discretion to select procedures which it deems best to compile a record illuminating the issues. Courts are no more expert at fashioning administrative procedures than they are in the substantive areas of responsibility which are left to agency discretion. What a reviewing court can do, however, is scrutinize the record as a whole to insure that genuine opportunities to participate in a meaningful way were provided, and that the agency has taken a good, hard look at the major questions before it.

* * *

A prominent feature of the statutory context created by NEPA is the requirement that the agency acknowledge and consider "responsible scientific opinion concerning possible adverse environmental effects" which is contrary to the official agency position. * * *

In order to determine whether an agency has lived up to these responsibilities, a reviewing court must examine the record in detail to determine that a real give and take was fostered on the key issues. This does not give the court a license to judge for itself how much weight should be given particular pieces of scientific or technical data, a task for which it is singularly ill-suited. It does require, however, that the court examine the record so that it may satisfy itself that the decision was based "on a consideration of the relevant factors." Where only one side of a controversial issue is developed in any detail, the agency may abuse its discretion by deciding the issues on an inadequate record.

A reviewing court must assure itself not only that a diversity of informed opinion was heard, but that it was genuinely considered. "[T]he dialogue that the APA's rulemaking section contemplates cannot be a sham." Since a reviewing court is incapable of making a penetrating analysis of highly scientific or technical subject matter on its own, it must depend on the agency's expertise, as reflected in the statement of basis and purpose, to organize the record, to distill the major issues which were ventilated and to articulate its reasoning with regard to each of them.

An agency need not respond to frivolous or repetitive comment it receives. However, where apparently significant information has been brought to its attention, or substantial issues of policy or gaps in its reasoning raised, the statement of basis and purpose must indicate why the agency decided the criticisms were invalid. Boilerplate generalities brushing aside detailed criticism on the basis of agency "judgment" or "expertise" avail nothing; what is required is a reasoned response, in which the agency points to particulars in the record which, when coupled with its reservoir of expertise, support its resolution of the controversy. An agency may abuse its discretion by proceeding to a decision which the record before it will not sustain, in the sense that it raises fundamental questions for which the agency has adduced no reasoned answers.

* * *

In substantial part, the materials uncritically relied on by the Commission in promulgating this rule consist of extremely vague assurances by agency personnel that problems as yet unsolved will be solved. That is an insufficient record to sustain a rule limiting consideration of the environmental effects of nuclear waste disposal to the numerical values in Table S-3. To the extent that uncertainties necessarily underlie predictions of this importance on the frontiers of science and technology, there is a concomitant necessity to confront and explore fully the depth and consequences of such uncertainties. Not only were the generalities relied on in this case not subject to rigorous probing—in any form—but when apparently substantial criticisms were brought to the Commission's attention, it simply ignored them, or brushed them aside without answer. Without a thorough exploration of the problems involved in waste disposal, including past mistakes, and a forthright assessment of the uncertainties and differences in expert opinion, this type of agency action cannot pass muster as reasoned decisionmaking.

Many procedural devices for creating a genuine dialogue on these issues were available to the agency—including informal conferences between intervenors and staff, document discovery, interrogatories, technical advisory committees comprised of outside experts with differing perspectives, limited cross-examination, funding independent research by intervenors, detailed annotation of technical reports, surveys of existing literature, memoranda explaining methodology. We do not presume to intrude on the agency's province by dictating to it which, if any, of these devices it must adopt to flesh out the record. It may be that no combination of the procedures mentioned above will prove adequate, and the agency will be required to develop new procedures to accomplish the innovative task of implementing NEPA through rulemaking. On the other hand, the procedures the agency adopted in this case, if administered in a more sensitive, deliberate manner, might suffice. Whatever techniques the Commission adopts, before it promulgates a rule limiting further consideration of waste disposal and reprocessing issues, it must in one way or another generate a record in which the factual issues are fully developed.

Natural Resources Defense Council v. Nuclear Regulatory Comm'n, 547 F.2d 633 (D.C. Cir. 1976), *rev'd sub nom., Vermont Yankee Nuclear Power Corp. v. NRDC*, 435 U.S. 519 (1978).

2. Upon remand, Judge Bazelon found that the NRC's rule, which assumed no significant environmental risk associated with nuclear waste storage, to be invalid for lack of support in the administrative record. *NRDC v. NRC*, 685 F.2d 459 (D.C. Cir. 1982), *rev'd sub nom., Baltimore Gas & Electric Co. v. NRDC*, 462 U.S. 87 (1983). The Supreme Court revisited this complex issue of nuclear power plant licensing and once again reversed Judge Bazelon in *Baltimore Gas & Electric Co. v. NRDC, infra* Chapter 5 of this book. Vermont Yankee Nuclear Power Corp. reports that it expects its nuclear power station to continue operating "well beyond 2012," when its license expires. James Sinclair, *Mailbag*, 131 PUB. UTIL. FORTNIGHTLY, Mar. 1, 1993, at 6.

3. Do intervenors have the opportunity to discover NRC evidence supporting permit issuance? Do they have the opportunity to cross-examine experts who analyze environmental effects of waste disposal? How important are discovery and cross-examination to effective participation in the administrative process? How can the public monitor the quality of agency decisions that affect the environment?

4. A substantial portion of the *Vermont Yankee* opinion dealing with alternatives analysis under NEPA appears in Chapter 7A, *infra*.

5. Although *Vermont Yankee* marked the beginning of a period of more limited judicial review of agency rulemaking process, the Supreme Court will invalidate agency decisions that are not adequately supported by an administrative record. In finding that the National Highway Transportation Safety Administration's (NHTSA's) revocation of the rule requiring car manufacturers to install passive restraints (*e.g.*, airbags and automatic seatbelts) was arbitrary and capricious, the Court clarified the limits of *Vermont Yankee*:

Petitioners also invoke our decision in *Vermont Yankee* as though it were a talisman under which any agency decision is by definition unimpeachable. Specifically, it is submitted that to require an agency to consider an airbags-only alternative is, in essence, to dictate to the agency the procedures it is to follow. Petitioners both misread *Vermont Yankee* and misconstrue the nature of the remand that is in order. In *Vermont Yankee,* we held that a court may not impose additional procedural requirements upon an agency. We do not require today any specific procedures which NHTSA must follow. * * * We hold only that given the judgment made in 1977 that airbags are an effective and cost-beneficial life-saving technology, the mandatory passive restraint rule may not be abandoned without any consideration whatsoever of an airbags-only requirement.

Motor Vehicle Manufacturers Ass'n v. State Farm Mutual Ins. Co., 463 U.S. 29, 50-51 (1983).

CHEVRON U.S.A., INC. V. NATURAL RESOURCES DEFENSE COUNCIL, INC.
467 U.S. 837 (1984)

Justice STEVENS delivered the opinion of the Court.

In the Clean Air Act Amendments of 1977, Pub. L. 95-95, 91 Stat. 685, Congress enacted certain requirements applicable to States that had not achieved the national air quality standards established by the Environmental Protection Agency (EPA) pursuant to earlier legislation. The amended Clean Air Act required these "nonattainment" States to establish a permit program regulating "new or modified major stationary sources" of air pollution. Generally, a permit may not be issued for a new or modified major stationary source unless several stringent conditions are met. The EPA regulation promulgated to implement this permit requirement allows a State to adopt a plantwide definition of the term "stationary source." Under this definition, an existing plant that contains several pollution-emitting devices may install or modify one piece of equipment without meeting the permit conditions if the alteration will not increase the total emissions from the plant. The question presented by this case is whether EPA's decision to allow States to treat all of the pollution-emitting devices within the same industrial grouping as though they were encased within a single "bubble" is based on a reasonable construction of the statutory term "stationary source."

* * *

II

When a court reviews an agency's construction of the statute which it administers, it is confronted with two questions. First, always, is the question whether Congress has directly spoken to the precise question at issue. If the intent of Congress is clear, that is the end of the matter; for the court, as well as the agency, must give effect to the unambiguously expressed intent of Congress. If, however, the court determines Congress has not directly addressed the precise question at issue, the court does not simply impose its own construction on the statute, as would be necessary in the absence of an administrative interpretation. Rather, if the statute is silent or ambiguous with respect to the specific issue, the question for the court is whether the agency's answer is based on a permissible construction of the statute.

"The power of an administrative agency to administer a congressionally created . . . program necessarily requires the formulation of policy and the making of rules to fill any gap left, implicitly or explicitly, by Congress." *Morton v. Ruiz*, 415 U.S. 199, 231 (1974). If Congress has explicitly left a gap for the agency to fill, there is an express delegation of authority to the agency to elucidate a specific provision of the statute by regulation. Such legislative regulations are given controlling weight unless they are arbitrary, capricious, or manifestly contrary to the statute. Sometimes the legislative delegation to an agency on a particular question is implicit rather than explicit. In such a case, a court may not substitute its own construction of a statutory provision for a reasonable interpretation made by the administrator of an agency.

* * *

IV

The Clean Air Act Amendments of 1977 are a lengthy, detailed, technical, complex, and comprehensive response to a major social issue. A small portion of the statute—42 U.S.C. § 7501-750—expressly deals with nonattainment areas. The focal point of this controversy is one phrase in that portion of the Amendments.

* * *

Most significantly for our purposes, the statute provided that each [state] plan shall: "(6) require permits for the construction and operation of new or modified major stationary sources in accordance with section 173 . . .."

* * *

The 1977 Amendments contain no specific reference to the "bubble concept." Nor do they contain a specific definition of the term "stationary source" * * * . Section 302(j), however, defines the term "major stationary source" as follows:

> "(j) Except as otherwise expressly provided, the terms 'major stationary source' and 'major emitting facility' mean any stationary facility or source of air pollutants which directly emits, or has the potential to emit, one hundred tons per year or more of any air pollutant (including any major emitting facility or source of fugitive emissions of any such pollutant, as determined by rule by the Administrator)."

V

The legislative history of the portion of the 1977 Amendments dealing with nonattainment areas does not contain any specific comment on the "bubble concept" or the question whether a plantwide definition of a stationary source is permissible under the permit program. It does, however, plainly disclose that in the permit program Congress sought to accommodate the conflict between the economic interest in permitting capital improvements to continue and the environmental interest in improving air quality. Indeed, the House Committee Report identified the economic interest as one of the "two main purposes" of this section of the bill.

* * *

VI

* * *

In August 1980, * * * the EPA adopted a regulation that, in essence, applied the basic reasoning of the Court of Appeals in this case. The EPA took particular note of the two then-recent Court of Appeals decisions, which had created the bright-line rule that the bubble concept should be employed in a program designed to maintain air quality but not in one designed to enhance air quality. Relying heavily on those cases, EPA adopted a dual definition of "source" for nonattainment areas that required a permit whenever a change in either the entire plant, or one of its components, would result in a significant increase in emissions even if the increase was completely offset by reductions elsewhere in the plant. The EPA expressed the opinion that this interpretation was "more consistent with congressional intent" than the plantwide definition because it "would bring in more sources or modifications for review" 45 Fed. Reg. 52697 (1980), but its primary legal analysis was predicated on the two Court of Appeals decisions.

In 1981 a new administration took office and initiated a "Government-wide reexamination of regulatory burdens and complexities." 46 Fed. Reg. 16281. In the context of that review, the EPA reevaluated the various arguments that had been advanced in connection with the proper definition of the term "source" and concluded that the term should be given the same definition in both nonattainment areas and PSD [Prevention of Significant Deterioration] areas.

In explaining its conclusion, the EPA first noted that the definitional issue was not squarely addressed in either the statute or its legislative history and therefore that the issue involved an agency "judgment as how to best carry out the Act." *Ibid.* It then set forth several reasons for concluding that the plantwide definition was more appropriate. It pointed out that the dual definition "can act as a disincentive to new investment and modernization by discouraging modifications to existing facilities" and "can actually retard progress in air pollution control by discouraging replacement of older, dirtier processes or pieces of equipment with new, cleaner ones." *Ibid.* Moreover, the new definition "would simplify EPA's rules by using the same definition of 'source' for PSD, nonattainment new source review and the construction moratorium. This reduces confusion and inconsistency." *Ibid.* Finally, the agency explained that additional requirements that remained in place would accomplish the fundamental purposes of achieving attainment with NAAQ's as expeditiously as possible. These conclusions were expressed in a proposed rulemaking in August 1981 that was formally promulgated in October. *See id.* at 50766.

VII

* * * [Respondents] contend that the text of the Act requires the EPA to use a dual definition—if either a component of a plant, or the plant as a whole, emits over 100 tons of pollutant, it is a major stationary source. They thus contend that the EPA rules adopted in 1980, insofar as they apply to the maintenance of the quality of clean air, as well as the 1981 rules which apply to nonattainment areas, violate the statute.

Statutory Language

The definition of the term stationary source in § 111(a)(3) refers to "any building, structure, facility, or installation" which emits air pollution. This definition is applicable only to the NSPS program by the express terms of the statute; the text of the statute does not make this definition applicable to the permit program. Petitioners therefore maintain that there is no statutory language even relevant to ascertaining the meaning of stationary source in the permit program aside from § 302(j), which defines the term major stationary source. We disagree with petitioners on this point.

The definition in § 302(j) tells us what the word "major" means—a source must emit at least 100 tons of pollution to qualify—but it sheds virtually no light on the meaning of the term "stationary source." It does equate a source with a facility—a "major emitting facility" and a "major stationary source" are synonymous under § 302(j). The ordinary meaning of the term facility is some collection of integrated elements which has been designed and constructed to achieve some purpose. Moreover, it is certainly no affront to common English usage to take a reference to a major facility or a major source to connote an entire plant as opposed to its constituent parts. Basically, however, the language of § 302(j) simply does not compel any given interpretation of the term source.

Respondents recognize that, and hence point to § 111(a)(3). Although the definition in that section is not literally applicable to the permit program, it sheds as much light on the meaning of the word source as anything in the statute. As respondents point out, use of the words "building, structure, facility, or installation," as the definition of source, could be read to impose the permit conditions on an individual building that is a part of a plant. A "word may have a character of its own not to be submerged by its association." *Russell Motor Car Co. v. United States*, 261 U.S. 514, 519 (1923). On the other hand, the meaning of a word must be ascertained in the context of achieving particular objectives, and the words associated with it may indicate that the true meaning of the series is to convey a common idea. The language may reasonably be interpreted to impose the requirement on any discrete, but integrated, operation which pollutes. This gives meaning to all of the terms—a single building, not part of a larger operation, would be covered if it emits more than 100 tons of pollution, as would any facility, structure, or installation. Indeed, the language itself implies a bubble concept of sorts: each enumerated item would seem to be treated as if it were encased in a bubble. While respondents insist that each of these terms must be given a discrete meaning, they also argue that § 111(a)(3) defines "source" as that term is used in § 302(j). The latter section, however, equates a source with a facility, whereas the former defines source as a facility, among other items.

We are not persuaded that parsing of general terms in the text of the statute will reveal an actual intent of Congress. We know full well that this language is not dispositive; the terms are overlapping and the language is not precisely directed to the question of the applicability of a given term in the context of a larger operation. To the extent any congressional "intent" can be discerned from this language, it would appear that the listing of overlapping, illustrative terms was intended to enlarge, rather than to confine, the scope of the agency's power to regulate particular sources in order to effectuate the policies of the Act.

* * *

* * * The fact that the agency has from time to time changed its interpretation of the term source does not, as respondents argue, lead us to conclude that no deference should be accorded the agency's interpretation of the statute. An initial agency interpretation is not instantly carved in stone. On the contrary, the agency, to engage in informed rulemaking, must consider varying interpretations and the wisdom of its policy on a continuing basis. Moreover, the fact that the agency has adopted different definitions in different contexts adds force to the argument that the definition itself is flexible, particularly since Congress has never indicated any disapproval of a flexible reading of the statute.

Significantly, it was not the agency in 1980, but rather the Court of Appeals that read the statute inflexibly to command a plantwide definition for programs designed to maintain clean air and to forbid such a definition for programs designed to improve air quality. The distinction the court drew may well be a sensible one, but our labored review of the problem has surely disclosed that it is not a distinction that Congress ever articulated itself, or one that the EPA found in the statute before the courts began to review the legislative work product. We conclude that it was the Court of Appeals, rather than Congress or any of the decisionmakers who are authorized by Congress to administer this legislation, that was primarily responsible for the 1980 position taken by the agency.

Policy

The arguments over policy that are advanced in the parties' briefs create the impression that respondents are now waging in a judicial forum a specific policy battle which they ultimately lost in the agency and in the 32 jurisdictions opting for the bubble concept, but one which was never waged in the Congress. Such policy arguments are more properly addressed to legislators or administrators, not to judges.

In this case, the Administrator's interpretation represents a reasonable accommodation of manifestly competing interests and is entitled to deference: the regulatory scheme is technical and complex, the agency considered the matter in a detailed and reasoned fashion, and the decision involves reconciling conflicting policies. Congress intended to accommodate both interests, but did not do so itself on the level of specificity presented by this case. Perhaps that body consciously desired the Administrator to strike the balance at this level, thinking that those with great expertise and charged with responsibility for administering the provision would be in a better position to do so; perhaps it simply did not consider the question at this level; and perhaps Congress was unable to forge a coalition on either side of the question, and those on each side decided to take their chances with the scheme devised by the agency. For judicial purposes, it matters not which of these things occurred.

Judges are not experts in the field, and are not part of either political branch of the Government. Courts must, in some cases, reconcile competing political interests, but not on the basis of the judges' personal policy preferences. In contrast, an agency to which Congress has delegated policymaking responsibilities may, within the limits of that delegation, properly rely upon the incumbent administration's views of wise policy to inform its judgments. While agencies are not directly accountable to the people, the Chief Executive is, and it is entirely appropriate for this political branch of the Government to make such policy choices—resolving the competing interests which Congress itself either inadvertently did not resolve, or intentionally left to be resolved by the agency charged with the administration of the statute in light of everyday realities.

When a challenge to an agency construction of a statutory provision, fairly conceptualized, really centers on the wisdom of the agency's policy, rather than whether it is a reasonable choice within a gap left open by Congress, the challenge must fail. In such a case, federal judges—who have no constituency—have a duty to respect legitimate policy choices made by those who do. The responsibilities for assessing the wisdom of such policy choices and resolving the struggle between competing views of the public interest are not judicial ones: "Our Constitution vests such responsibilities in the political branches." *TVA v. Hill*, 437 U.S. 153, 195 (1978).

We hold that the EPA's definition of the term "source" is a permissible construction of the statute which seeks to accommodate progress in reducing air pollution with economic growth. "The Regulations which the Administrator has adopted provide what the agency could allowably view as . . . [an] effective reconciliation of these twofold ends . . . ." *United States v. Shimer*, 367 U.S. at 383.

The judgment of the Court of Appeals is reversed.

NOTES

1.   What is the court's role in reviewing an agency's construction of a statute under the *Chevron* case? Should it matter whether the court is reviewing an issue for which the agency has no special expertise? For example, § 522(e) of the Surface Mining Control and Reclamation Act designates certain lands as unsuitable for surface mining, but makes those designations subject to "valid existing rights." The Secretary of the Interior has promulgated several regulations attempting to interpret this phrase. *See* Robert Uram, *A Critical Review of Valid Existing Rights Under SMCRA,* NAT. RESOURCES & ENV'T, Wint. 1991, at 19; 56 Fed. Reg. 33152 (1991). Is the Secretary in a better position than the courts to interpret Congressional intent about the meaning of this phrase?

Professor Sunstein describes *Chevron* as "counter-*Marbury*." Cass Sunstein, *Law and Administration After* Chevron, 90 COLUM. L. REV. 2071, 2075 (1990). Do you think that is an apt characterization?

2. The Court finds that "[t]he fact the agency has from time to time changed its interpretation of the term source does not, as respondents argue, lead us to conclude that no deference should be accorded the agency's interpretation of the statute." On the other hand, the Court has suggested in several other recent cases, that "[a]n agency interpretation of a relevant provision which conflicts with the agency's earlier interpretation is 'entitled to considerably less deference' than a consistently held agency view." *I.N.S. v. Cardoza-Fonseca*, 480 U.S. 421, n.30 (1987), *citing Watt v. Alaska*, 451 U.S. 259, 273 (1981). *See also Motor Vehicle Manufacturers Ass'n v. State Farm Mutual Ins. Co.*, 463 U.S. 29 (1983).

3. *Chevron* is one of the most commonly cited cases in the field of administrative law. Nonetheless, many commentators are critical of its basic holding. Consider, for example, the following comments of Timothy Dyk:

> [S]urely one of the most important developments in administrative law in the last several decades has been the Supreme Court's *Chevron* decision, under which the Supreme Court will defer to the agency's interpretation of its own governing statute when the statute is ambiguous and the agency's construction is reasonable. This reflects a conscious refusal on the part of the Supreme Court to play its traditional role in interpreting federal statutes. * * *
>
> Then-Judge Starr described *Chevron* as "a case which all appellate judges these days bear firmly in mind in reading statutes." And they do. *Chevron* has had an enormous impact upon challenges to agencies: two terms after *Chevron*, Judge Starr noted that in the Supreme Court "*Chevron* has been employed with regularity, and in all cases save one the agency won the case." While the agency record in the past two terms is more mixed, the centrality of *Chevron* to review of administrative agencies continues.
>
> *Chevron* receives not only the attention of law professors and the courts. Congress itself has held hearings to consider whether the *Chevron* interpretive principle should be altered, and even the public pays attention to *Chevron*. On July 18, I was present when Walter Dellinger condemned *Chevron* before a cheering throng of several hundred. That might have been due to the use of *Chevron* in *Rust v. Sullivan*, since those assembled were about to lobby for a legislative change to the law upheld in that case, but I like to think that the opposition was more broadly based.
>
> I place myself firmly in the camp of those who believe that *Chevron* was wrong, and who view it as an abdication of the function of judicial review conferred by the Constitution and by the Administrative Procedure Act. As one who practices both before the Supreme Court and in the area of administrative law, I have special concerns about the wisdom of reposing trust in administrative agencies with respect to issues of statutory construction. This mistrust arises from several sources.
>
> (1) The political agenda of the Executive Branch is largely controlling at administrative agencies. This influence stems in part from the ability of the

incumbent administration to appoint agency chairmen and their role in setting the agency agenda, appointing staff, and formulating policy.

* * *

(2) Many agency members, even if they have no ambition for higher political office, often conduct themselves at their agencies with a view to later employment opportunities in the private sector.

(3) To the extent that agencies pay attention to the Legislative Branch, and they do, they are likely to be far more interested in the views of the current congressional appropriations and oversight committees than they are likely to care about the views of some past Congress.

* * *

(4) One of the justifications for *Chevron* is that members of the administrative agencies are supposedly expert in construing their organic statute. In fact, the agency members often have no real claim to expertise. Because of conflict problems, some come to the agency with little or no background in the area of the agency's authority. The job is not sufficiently prestigious to regularly attract the best and the brightest. And, again, the short tenure discourages the intellectual commitment that would be necessary to understand the complex issues of statutory construction. The expertise of the agency usually resides in the agency bureaucracy rather than in the members who formulate policy.

This not only calls into question the concept of agency expertise. It also suggests that the agencies will not be responsive to the Congress that passed legislation and the President that signed it but to the current administration, the current congressional committees and the affected industries. Justice Scalia, in his talk before this Section on the subject of legislative history at the Justice Department last March 11, said not to worry. The result will be that "the dead hand of an ancient congressional committee" will be supplanted in influence by a "current congressional committee" with the agency in its sway. To me this is exactly wrong.

Timothy Dyk, *The Supreme Court's Role in Shaping Administrative Law,* 17 ADMIN. L. NEWS 1, 13 (1991) [Reprinted with permission—Eds.]. Mr. Dyk goes on to suggest that the *Chevron* decision may be a product of the "lack of competence" of our federal courts in dealing with complex regulatory matters. He offers four suggestions for addressing this problem. First, establishing an independent research office within the Supreme Court. Second, allowing divided oral arguments before the Court by private parties and amicus participants. Third, requiring that *amicus* briefs be consolidated. And finally, selecting more experienced law clerks. Do you agree with his criticism and suggested solutions?

4. The same year that *Chevron* was decided, Judge Scalia (now Justice Scalia) wrote an opinion which suggests that the degree of deference owed an agency interpretation of a statute varies with the circumstances. *Center for Auto Safety v. Ruckelshaus,* 747 F.2d 1 (D.C. Cir. 1984), concerned a requirement in the Clean Air Act that manufacturers of vehicles that do not conform to the vehicle emission standards established under that law "remedy" the non-conformity. The EPA had decided to allow General Motors to "remedy" certain nonconforming vehicles by offsetting the excess pollution emitted from the non-conforming vehicles with lower emission standards for vehicles that would be sold in the future. In response to the agency's claim to deference in construing the term "remedy," Judge Scalia noted:

> [T]he degree of deference [accorded to agency interpretations of statutes] is not uniform. A high degree is appropriate, for example, when the agency's expertise can help in assessing the effects of competing interpretations upon the policies of the statute * * * A high degree of deference is also called for when the text to be interpreted is a statutory provision that directs an agency to apply "a standard of such inherent imprecision * * * that a discretion of almost legislative scope was necessarily contemplated." * * * Finally, the degree of deference is also high when the agency presses upon us an administrative construction that is both "contemporaneous" with the statute's enactment * * * and "longstanding" * * *.

Id. at 5. After finding that none of these situations applied, he concluded:

> The degree of deference appropriate here, therefore, is modest—no more than that thoughtful respect we should give to the views of the officers of another branch who have been officially presented with the issue and who, like us, have taken an oath to apply the law that Congress enacted.

Id. at 6. Is Scalia's position in *Center for Auto Safety* consistent with the decision in *Chevron*, decided four months earlier? The Supreme Court itself has been criticized for inconsistently applying the *Chevron* rule. Thomas Merrill, *Judicial Deference to Executive Precedent,* 101 YALE L.J. 969 (1992).

5.   *Chevron* accorded deference to an agency regulation that construed language in a statute. Suppose, however, that an agency's interpretation of a statute is offered following a less formal process. Is deference owed to such an interpretation? *See Southern Ute Indian Tribe v. Amoco Production Company,* 119 F.3d 816, 832-33 (10th Cir. 1997), *aff'd en banc,* 151 F.3d 1251 (10th Cir. 1998), *rev'd on other grounds, Amoco Production Co. v. Southern Ute Indian Tribe,* 67 U.S.L.W. 4397 (1999) (denying deference to a Department of the Interior legal opinion that was not promulgated with the procedural protections of either legislative rules or adjudications).

6.   Even when *Chevron* deference is not owed, courts may accord a lesser form of deference as articulated in *Skidmore v. Swift & Co.*, 323 U.S. 134, 140 (1944):

> We consider that the rulings, interpretations and opinions of the Administrator * * *, while not controlling upon the courts by reason of their authority, do constitute a body of experience and informed judgment to which courts and litigants may properly resort for guidance. The weight of such a judgment in a particular case will depend upon the thoroughness evident in its consideration, the validity of its reasoning, its consistency with earlier and later pronouncements, and all of those factors which give it power to persuade, if lacking power to control.

4 ENVIRONMENTAL DECISIONMAKING STATUTES

A. *The National Environmental Policy Act*

INTRODUCTION TO THE NATIONAL ENVIRONMENTAL POLICY ACT

Compared with most other environmental legislation, the National Environmental Policy Act (NEPA) is exceptionally brief and straightforward. Despite its unremarkable appearance, however, by many yardsticks, it is one of the most significant of all the statutes passed by Congress to protect the nation's environment.

By the end of 1991, over 2100 lawsuits had been filed challenging federal actions as violating NEPA. A large portion of these are cases of major consequence—to the parties and to society. NEPA has been used by litigants to frustrate, if not block completely, the Alaska pipeline, federal coal leasing on western lands, logging old-growth forests, the Nuclear Regulatory Commission's fast breeder reactor program, the relocation of several military installations, as well as numerous individual dams, nuclear power plants, highways, and federal oil and gas lease sales. The reported decisions, moreover, are but the tip of the iceberg. Over 20,000 environmental impact statements (EISs) have been written since NEPA became law on January 1, 1970. And, if the Act has been obeyed, it has influenced every decision by every federal agency which might have affected the environment since its enactment.

Despite its fundamental impact on all levels of federal governmental action, the bill which became NEPA aroused very little controversy when introduced. Besides creating the Council on Environmental Quality (CEQ), the legislation seemed to be little more than a "motherhood bill" to the casually-observing lawmaker. Indeed, a large portion of the first section, § 101, is devoted to a detailed legislative expression that the federal government is in favor of a good clean environment. The second section, § 102, begins with a general directive that "to the fullest extent possible" all federal agencies are to consider the environment in making and implementing their plans. This mandate perhaps should have alerted those familiar with administrative law to the potential enforceability of the ambitious intent of the Act, but there is little indication that it did.

The most important provision, contained in § 102(2)(C), also appeared to float through both houses without full appreciation of its requirements, at least by its potential opponents. This subsection requires that all federal agencies prepare detailed statements on environmental impacts whenever taking "major federal action significantly affecting the quality of the human environment." At first glance this requirement may have seemed innocuous enough; but it has bred the familiar environmental impact statements now securely internalized in federal bureaucratic action, a powerful weapon in the environmentalist's litigation arsenal, and the bane of any industry desiring to expedite projects requiring federal approval. What many people apparently failed to foresee when NEPA was enacted was: (1) what would be deemed "major federal action significantly affecting the quality of the human environment" (*e.g.,* B-1 bomber programs, new jails, new post offices); (2) what would be required to go into an EIS (*e.g.,* specific and detailed analysis of potential adverse environmental effects of alternatives to the program under consideration); (3) that truly major federal action could be enjoined "temporarily" until the EIS process was followed to the letter; and (4) that the EIS process, once incorporated into agency decisionmaking, would have some substantive effect.

Unfortunately, there are many common misconceptions about NEPA. Before delving into the materials, let us address these misconceptions.

First, NEPA does not apply to purely private or purely state action. If there is no "federal handle," a private or state project of any size and environmental impact may proceed without preparation of an EIS or otherwise complying with NEPA. However, if any federal agency furnishes funds or issues a necessary permit, license, etc., for the otherwise private or state action, such dispersal of federal funds or issuance of a federal permit is federal action which may well necessitate an EIS covering the project—and without which the project may be enjoined. It may, therefore, be understandable how people get the notion that NEPA applies to anything of consequence.

Second, the EPA's role in preparing environmental impact statements is relatively minimal. Each federal agency prepares its own. Indeed, the EPA has been exempted by statute and by judicial decision from preparing EISs for almost all of its own functions. The EPA does have the duty under § 309 of the Clean Air Act to review and comment in writing on the environmental impacts of action to be taken by other federal agencies and departments; but it has no general power to block action by other agencies whose impact statements it considers defective or revealing of environmental dangers ahead.

Third, NEPA does not require that a project with serious environmental effects be abandoned; it merely requires that the effects and alternatives to the project be considered. Preparation of the EIS, however, may cause the agency voluntarily to abandon or modify the project in light of the problems revealed. The EIS reviewers in other executive agencies and offices—the EPA, CEQ, or the Office of Management and Budget (OMB)—may bring pressure to bear, occasionally through the President, against the proposal. The public, which by statute and agency regulation has access to draft and final EISs may react so strongly that the executive branch or Congress responds and halts the project. Such results are all within the purpose of the Act: to inform the agency, the other parts of government, and the public—then allow good faith and the political process to do the rest. Of course, NEPA may halt, delay, or modify proposed federal action in another manner: through administrative challenge and civil litigation. There is, however, much more to NEPA than lawsuits based upon its breach.

Nevertheless, enormous federal programs can be tied up for months, and even years, by injunction. When the Natural Resources Defense Council and other plaintiffs challenged the Interior Department's EIS covering leasing of coal on federal lands, Secretary Andrus estimated in proposing settlement that rectification of deficiencies would take at least three years. When no settlement occurs, it is not unusual for an injunction—against proceeding with a project while errors or omissions remain in the EIS or its preparation procedures—to remain in effect for over a year. In large part because of litigation and the threat of litigation, the quality of EISs has improved significantly since the early seventies, when many agencies treated NEPA's requirements lightly. The regulations promulgated by the Council on Environmental Quality in 1978 did much to clarify NEPA's requirements.

Courts have seemed increasingly inclined to allow action to proceed pending rectification of deficiencies, so long as irreparable environmental damage can be avoided in the interim.

Perhaps the ultimate evidence of NEPA's impact on society is its growing influence on the culture within federal agencies. As NEPA has evolved, and as the pressure to integrate environmental values into agency decisionmaking has increased, federal agencies have had to rely less on employees with expertise in resource extraction, and more on employees with backgrounds in the environmental sciences. A good example of this evolution—some might say revolution—in agency culture is the U.S. Forest Service. Historically dominated by personnel with expertise in timber and range management, over the past 25 years, the agency has hired many more biologists, ecologists, hydrologists, and recreation specialists. In substantial part, these specialists were hired to assist the agency in its efforts to comply with NEPA. Over time, however, these environmental scientists have begun to infiltrate the ranks of Forest Service management, and have brought with them a new perspective on national forest use. This new perspective appears to emphasize environmental protection and disfavor resource extraction that interferes with important ecological values.

NEPA's ability to influence agency culture, however, is substantially dependent upon the willingness of federal agencies to take on the responsibility for NEPA compliance. Many agencies have done so, but others appear to be relying increasingly on private consultants to prepare environmental documents for them. Over time, the increasing use of outside consultants may reduce the need for an agency to hire its own environmental experts, thereby undermining one of the most important, if subtle, influences that NEPA has had on agency decisionmaking. Indeed, in most foreign countries that have adopted NEPA-like statutes, environmental analyses are prepared exclusively by private consultants, often at the behest of a private project proponent. In this situation, private developers will not likely hire environmental consultants who fail to prepare documents that support the outcome preferred by the developer. A comprehensive alternatives analysis—especially one that considers alternatives not supported by the developer—is perhaps the most significant casualty of this process. Moreover, since the agencies in such circumstances generally lack sufficient expertise to evaluate the environmental analysis critically, the environmental assessment process seems far less likely to influence agency decisions.

NOTES

1.   Over the years since NEPA's passage, several efforts have been made to assess NEPA's impact. A 1997 Council on Environmental Quality study concludes that NEPA has had mixed success. According to the authors, NEPA's "most enduring legacy is as a framework for collaboration between federal agencies and those who will bear the environmental, social and economic impacts of agency decisions." THE NATIONAL ENVIRONMENTAL POLICY ACT: A STUDY OF ITS EFFECTIVENESS AFTER TWENTY-FIVE YEARS at ix (1997). *See also*, Federico Cheever, *Decision Making and Judicial Review of Agency Decisions Under NEPA, in* THE NEPA LITIGATION MANUAL (Karin Sheldon & Mark Squillace eds., 1999). As one commentator has noted, however,

* * * NEPA's success is difficult to measure. While one can track the number of EISs filed and the number of judicial decisions based on NEPA claims, an assessment of NEPA's influence on policy is much more subjective and often reflects the values of the viewer. Certainly, making an objective evaluation of NEPA is quite different from measuring the pollutant content of a river over time.

Dinah Bear, *The National Environmental Policy Act: Its Origins and Evolution,* 10 NAT. RES. & ENV'T 3 (1995). Even in the 1997 CEQ Report acknowledged that NEPA does not always work as Congress intended:

Notwithstanding these benefits, the Study determined that frequently NEPA takes too long and costs too much, agencies make decisions before hearing from the public, documents are too long and technical for many people to use, and training for agency officials, particularly senior leadership, is inadequate. According to many federal agency NEPA liaisons, the EIS process is still frequently viewed as merely a compliance requirement rather than as a tool to effect better decision-making. Because of this, millions of dollars, years of time, and tons of paper have been spent on documents that have little effect on decision making.

THE NATIONAL ENVIRONMENTAL POLICY ACT: A STUDY OF ITS EFFECTIVENESS AFTER TWENTY-FIVE YEARS, at 7 (1997).

2.   Substantial legal resources since NEPA's inception have been spent in hammering out the meaning of relatively few words in § 102(2)(C). Look at the introductory phrase alone. Does "every recommendation or report * * * on major federal actions" require an EIS? Or do only "proposals" necessitate EISs? If so, what is a "proposal"? On its face, the Act requires an EIS for "proposals for legislation," but how is such a requirement to be enforced? When is an action "major"? When is it "federal"? When is the environment "significantly" affected? What constitutes the "human environment"? How "detailed" must the statement be? How strictly should we interpret the requirement that the EIS be prepared "by the responsible official"? Such threshold issues may appear at the outset to involve little more than nitpicking, but they have been the critical issues in many important lawsuits.

The following case, *Calvert Cliffs*, was NEPA's first comprehensive judicial interpretation, and it helped define the discourse over the statute that continues today.

CALVERT CLIFFS' COORDINATING COMMITTEE, INC. V. UNITED STATES ATOMIC ENERGY COMMISSION
449 F.2d 1109 (D.C. Cir. 1971)

J. SKELLY WRIGHT, Circuit Judge:

These cases are only the beginning of what promises to become a flood of new litigation— litigation seeking judicial assistance in protecting our natural environment. Several recently enacted statutes attest to the commitment of the Government to control, at long last, the destructive engine of material "progress." But it remains to be seen whether the promise of this legislation will become a reality. Therein lies the judicial role. In these cases, we must for the first time interpret the broadest and perhaps most important of the recent statutes: the National Environmental Policy Act of 1969 (NEPA). We must assess claims that one of the agencies charged with its administration has failed to live up to the congressional mandate. Our duty, in short, is to see that important legislative purposes, heralded in the halls of Congress, are not lost or misdirected in the vast hallways of the federal bureaucracy.

NEPA, like so much other reform legislation of the last 40 years, is cast in terms of a general mandate and broad delegation of authority to new and old administrative agencies. It takes the major step of requiring all federal agencies to consider values of environmental preservation in their spheres of activity, and it prescribes certain procedural measures to ensure that those values are in fact fully respected. Petitioners argue that rules recently adopted by the Atomic Energy Commission to govern consideration of environmental matters fail to satisfy the rigor demanded by NEPA. The Commission, on the other hand, contends that the vagueness of the NEPA mandate and delegation leaves much room for discretion and that the rules challenged by petitioners fall well within the broad scope of the Act. We find the policies embodied in NEPA to be a good deal clearer and more demanding than does the Commission. We conclude that the Commission's procedural rules do not comply with the congressional policy. Hence we remand these cases for further rule making.

I

We begin our analysis with an examination of NEPA's structure and approach and of the Atomic Energy Commission rules which are said to conflict with the requirements of the Act. The relevant portion of NEPA is Title I, consisting of five sections. Section 101 sets forth the Act's basic substantive policy: that the federal government "use all practicable means and measures" to protect environmental values. Congress did not establish environmental protection as an exclusive goal; rather, it desired a reordering of priorities, so that environmental costs and benefits will assume their proper place along with other considerations. In Section 101(b), imposing an explicit duty on federal officials, the Act provides that "it is the continuing responsibility of the Federal Government to use all practicable means, consistent with other essential considerations of national policy," to avoid environmental degradation, preserve "historic, cultural, and natural" resources, and promote "the widest range of beneficial uses of the environment without * * * undesirable and unintended consequences."

Thus the general substantive policy of the Act is a flexible one. It leaves room for a responsible exercise of discretion and may not require particular substantive results in particular problematic instances. However, the Act also contains very important "procedural" provisions— provisions which are designed to see that all federal agencies do in fact exercise the substantive discretion given them. These provisions are not highly flexible. Indeed, they establish a strict standard of compliance.

NEPA, first of all, makes environmental protection a part of the mandate of every federal agency and department. The Atomic Energy Commission, for example, had continually asserted, prior to NEPA, that it had no statutory authority to concern itself with the adverse environmental effects of its actions.[4] Now, however, its hands are no longer tied. It is not only permitted, but compelled, to take environmental values into account. Perhaps the greatest importance of NEPA is to require the Atomic Energy Commission and other agencies to *consider* environmental

---

[4]   Before the enactment of NEPA, the Commission did recognize its separate statutory mandate to consider the specific radiological hazards caused by its actions; but it argued that it could not consider broader environmental impacts. Its position was upheld in *State of New Hampshire v. Atomic Energy Commission*, 406 F.2d 170 (1st Cir.), *cert. denied*, 395 U.S. 962 (1969).

issues just as they consider other matters within their mandates. This compulsion is most plainly stated in Section 102. There, "Congress authorizes and directs that, to the fullest extent possible: (1) the policies, regulations, and public laws of the United States shall be interpreted and administered in accordance with the policies set forth in this Act * * *." Congress also "authorizes and directs" that "(2) all agencies of the Federal Government shall" follow certain rigorous procedures in considering environmental values.[5] * * *

The sort of consideration of environmental values which NEPA compels is clarified in Section 102(2)(A) and (B). In general, all agencies must use a "systematic, interdisciplinary approach" to environmental planning and evaluation "in decisionmaking which may have an impact on man's environment." In order to include all possible environmental factors in the decisional equation, agencies must "identify and develop methods and procedures * * * which will insure that presently unquantified environmental amenities and values may be given appropriate consideration in decisionmaking along with economic and technical considerations." "Environmental amenities" will often be in conflict with "economic and technical considerations." To "consider" the former "along with" the latter must involve a balancing process. In some instances environmental costs may outweigh economic and technical benefits and in other instances they may not. But NEPA mandates a rather finely tuned and "systematic" balancing analysis in each instance.

To ensure that the balancing analysis is carried out and given full effect, Section 102(2)(C) requires that responsible officials of all agencies prepare a "detailed statement" covering the impact of particular actions on the environment, the environmental costs which might be avoided, and alternative measures which might alter the cost-benefit equation. The apparent purpose of the "detailed statement" is to aid in the agencies' own decision making process and to advise other interested agencies and the public of the environmental consequences of planned federal action. Beyond the "detailed statement," Section 102(2)(D)[†] requires all agencies specifically to "study, develop, and describe appropriate alternatives to recommended courses of action in any proposal which involves unresolved conflicts concerning alternative uses of available resources." This requirement, like the "detailed statement" requirement, seeks to ensure that each agency decision maker has before him and takes into proper account all possible approaches to a particular project (including total abandonment of the project) which would alter the environmental impact and the cost-benefit balance. Only in that fashion is it likely that the most intelligent, optimally beneficial decision will ultimately be made. Moreover, by compelling a formal "detailed statement" and a description of alternatives, NEPA provides evidence that the mandated decision making process has in fact taken place and, most importantly, allows those removed from the initial process to evaluate and balance the factors on their own.

Of course, all of these Section 102 duties are qualified by the phrase "to the fullest extent possible." We must stress as forcefully as possible that this language does not provide an escape hatch for footdragging agencies; it does not make NEPA's procedural requirements somehow "discretionary." Congress did not intend the Act to be such a paper tiger. Indeed, the

---

[5]   Only once—in § 102(2) (B)—does the Act state, in terms, that federal agencies must give full "consideration" to environmental impact as part of their decision making processes. However, a requirement of consideration is clearly implicit in the substantive mandate of § 101, in the requirement of § 102(1) that all laws and regulations be "interpreted and administered" in accord with that mandate, and in the other specific procedural measures compelled by § 102(2). * * * Thus a purely mechanical compliance with the particular measures required in § 102(2)(C) & (D) will not satisfy the Act if they do not amount to full good faith consideration of the environment. * * *

[†]   Editors' note: This provision now appears at § 102(2)(E).

requirement of environmental consideration "to the fullest extent possible" sets a high standard for the agencies, a standard which must be rigorously enforced by the reviewing courts.

Unlike the substantive duties of Section 101(b), which require agencies to "use all practicable means consistent with other essential considerations," the procedural duties of Section 102 must be fulfilled to the "fullest extent possible." This contrast, in itself, is revealing. But the dispositive factor in our interpretation is the expressed views of the Senate and House conferees who wrote the "fullest extent possible" language into NEPA. They stated:

> "* * * The purpose of the new language is to make it clear that each agency of the Federal Government shall comply with the directives set out in * * * [Section 102(2)] unless the existing law applicable to such agency's operations expressly prohibits or makes full compliance with one of the directives impossible. * * *"

Thus the Section 102 duties are not inherently flexible. They must be complied with to the fullest extent, unless there is a clear conflict of statutory authority. Considerations of administrative difficulty, delay or economic cost will not suffice to strip the section of its fundamental importance.

We conclude, then, that Section 102 of NEPA mandates a particular sort of careful and informed decisionmaking process and creates judicially enforceable duties. The reviewing courts probably cannot reverse a substantive decision on its merits, under Section 101, unless it be shown that the actual balance of costs and benefits that was struck was arbitrary or clearly gave insufficient weight to environmental values. But if the decision was reached procedurally without individualized consideration and balancing of environmental factors—conducted fully and in good faith—it is the responsibility of the courts to reverse. * * *

In the cases before us now, we do not have to review a particular decision by the Atomic Energy Commission granting a construction permit or an operating license. Rather, we must review the Commission's recently promulgated rules which govern consideration of environmental values in all such individual decisions. The rules were devised strictly in order to comply with the NEPA procedural requirements—but petitioners argue that they fall far short of the congressional mandate.

The period of the rules' gestation does not indicate overenthusiasm on the Commission's part. NEPA went into effect on January 1, 1970. * * * Finally, on December 3, 1970, the Commission terminated its long rule making proceeding by issuing a formal amendment, labelled Appendix D, to its governing regulations * * * and, at last, commits the Commission to consider environmental impact in its decision making process.

The procedure for environmental study and consideration set up by the Appendix D rules is as follows: Each applicant for an initial construction permit must submit to the Commission his own "environmental report," presenting his assessment of the environmental impact of the planned facility and possible alternatives which would alter the impact. When construction is completed and the applicant applies for a license to operate the new facility, he must again submit an "environmental report" noting any factors which have changed since the original report. At each stage, the Commission's regulatory staff must take the applicant's report and prepare its own "detailed statement" of environmental costs, benefits and alternatives. The statement will then be circulated to other interested and responsible agencies and made available to the public. After comments are received from those sources, the staff must prepare a final "detailed statement" and make a final recommendation on the application for a construction permit or operating license.

Up to this point in the Appendix D rules petitioners have raised no challenge. However, they do attack four other, specific parts of the rules which, they say, violate the requirements of Section 102 of NEPA. Each of these parts in some way limits full consideration and individualized balancing of environmental values in the Commission's decision making process. (1) Although environmental factors must be considered by the agency's regulatory staff under the rules, such factors need not be considered by the hearing board conducting an independent review of staff recommendations, unless affirmatively raised by outside parties or staff members. * * * (3) Moreover, the hearing board is prohibited from conducting an independent evaluation and balancing of certain environmental factors if other responsible agencies have already certified that their own environmental standards are satisfied by the proposed federal action. * * * [Editors' Note: The other two issues involved the retroactive effect of the AEC regulations on proceedings that began before the passage of NEPA.]

II

NEPA makes only one specific reference to consideration of environmental values in agency review processes. Section 102(2)(C) provides that copies of the staff's "detailed statement" and comments thereon "shall accompany the proposal through the existing agency review processes." The Atomic Energy Commission's rules may seem in technical compliance with the letter of that provision. They state:

> "12. If any party to a proceeding * * * raises any [environmental] issue * * * the Applicant's Environmental Report and the Detailed Statement will be offered in evidence. The atomic safety and licensing board will make findings of fact on, and resolve, the matters in controversy among the parties with regard to those issues. Depending on the resolution of those issues, the permit or license may be granted, denied, or appropriately conditioned to protect environmental values."

> "13. When no party to a proceeding * * * raises any [environmental] issue * * * such issues will not be considered by the atomic safety and licensing board. Under such circumstances, although the Applicant's Environmental Report, comments thereon, and the Detailed Statement will accompany the application through the Commission's review processes, they will not be received in evidence, and the Commission's responsibilities under the National Environmental Policy Act of 1969 will be carried out *in toto* outside the hearing process."

The question here is whether the Commission is correct in thinking that its NEPA responsibilities may "be carried out *in toto* outside the hearing process"—whether it is enough that environmental data and evaluations merely "accompany" an application through the review process, but receive no consideration whatever from the hearing board.

We believe that the Commission's crabbed interpretation of NEPA makes a mockery of the Act. What possible purpose could there be in the Section 102(2)(C) requirement (that the "detailed statement" accompany proposals through agency review processes) if "accompany" means no more than physical proximity—mandating no more than the physical act of passing certain folders and papers, unopened, to reviewing officials along with other folders and papers? What possible purpose could there be in requiring the "detailed statement" to be before hearing boards, if the boards are free to ignore entirely the contents of the statement? NEPA was meant to do more than regulate the flow of papers in the federal bureaucracy. The word "accompany" in Section 102(2)(C) must not be read so narrowly as to make the Act ludicrous. It must, rather, be read to indicate a congressional intent that environmental factors, as compiled in the "detailed statement," be *considered* through agency review processes.

Beyond Section 102(2)(C), NEPA requires that agencies consider the environmental impact of their actions "to the *fullest* extent possible." The Act is addressed to agencies as a whole, not only to their professional staffs. Compliance to the "fullest" possible extent would seem to demand that environmental issues be considered at every important stage in the decision making process concerning a particular action—at every stage where an overall balancing of environmental and nonenvironmental factors is appropriate and where alterations might be made in the proposed action to minimize environmental costs. Of course, consideration which is entirely duplicative is not necessarily required. But independent review of staff proposals by hearing boards is hardly a duplicative function. A truly independent review provides a crucial check on the staff's recommendations. The Commission's hearing boards automatically consider nonenvironmental factors, even though they have been previously studied by the staff. Clearly, the review process is an appropriate stage at which to balance conflicting factors against one another. And, just as clearly, it provides an important opportunity to reject or significantly modify the staff's recommended action. Environmental factors, therefore, should not be singled out and excluded, at this stage, from the proper balance of values envisioned by NEPA.

* * * In uncontested hearings, the board need not necessarily go over the same ground covered in the "detailed statement." But it must at least examine the statement carefully to determine whether "the review * * * by the Commission's regulatory staff has been adequate." And it must independently consider the final balance among conflicting factors that is struck in the staff's recommendation.

The rationale of the Commission's limitation of environmental issues to hearings in which parties affirmatively raise those issues may have been one of economy. It may have been supposed that, whenever there are serious environmental costs overlooked or uncorrected by the staff, some party will intervene to bring those costs to the hearing board's attention. Of course, independent review of the "detailed statement" and independent balancing of factors in an uncontested hearing will take some time. If it is done properly, it will take a significant amount of time. But all of the NEPA procedures take time. Such administrative costs are not enough to undercut the Act's requirement that environmental protection be considered "to the fullest extent possible." It is, moreover, unrealistic to assume that there will always be an intervenor with the information, energy and money required to challenge a staff recommendation which ignores environmental costs. NEPA establishes environmental protection as an integral part of the Atomic Energy Commission's basic mandate. The primary responsibility for fulfilling that mandate lies with the Commission. Its responsibility is not simply to sit back, like an umpire, and resolve adversary contentions at the hearing stage. Rather, it must itself take the initiative of considering environmental values at every distinctive and comprehensive stage of the process beyond the staff's evaluation and recommendation.

* * *

IV

The sweep of NEPA is extraordinarily broad, compelling consideration of any and all types of environmental impact of federal action. However, the Atomic Energy Commission's rules specifically exclude from full consideration a wide variety of environmental issues. First, they provide that no party may raise and the Commission may not independently examine any problem of water quality—perhaps the most significant impact of nuclear power plants. Rather, the Commission indicates that it will defer totally to water quality standards devised and administered by state agencies and approved by the federal government under the Federal Water Pollution Control Act. Secondly, the rules provide for similar abdication of NEPA authority to the standards of other agencies:

"With respect to those aspects of environmental quality for which environmental quality standards and requirements have been established by authorized Federal, State, and regional agencies, proof that the applicant is equipped to observe and agrees to observe such standards and requirements will be considered a satisfactory showing that there will not be a significant, adverse effect on the environment. Certification by the appropriate agency that there is reasonable assurance that the applicant for the permit or license will observe such standards and requirements will be considered dispositive for this purpose."

The most the Commission will do is include a condition in all construction permits and operating licenses requiring compliance with the water quality or other standards set by such agencies. The upshot is that the NEPA procedures, viewed by the Commission as superfluous, will wither away in disuse, applied only to those environmental issues wholly unregulated by any other federal, state or regional body.

We believe the Commission's rule is in fundamental conflict with the basic purpose of the Act. NEPA mandates a case-by-case balancing judgment on the part of federal agencies. In each individual case, the particular economic and technical benefits of planned action must be assessed and then weighed against the environmental costs; alternatives must be considered which would affect the balance of values. The magnitude of possible benefits and possible costs may lie anywhere on a broad spectrum. Much will depend on the particular magnitudes involved in particular cases. In some cases, the benefits will be great enough to justify a certain quantum of environmental costs; in other cases, they will not be so great and the proposed action may have to be abandoned or significantly altered so as to bring the benefits and costs into a proper balance. The point of the individualized balancing analysis is to ensure that, with possible alterations, the optimally beneficial action is finally taken.

Certification by another agency that its own environmental standards are satisfied involves an entirely different kind of judgment. Such agencies, without overall responsibility for the particular federal action in question, attend only to one aspect of the problem: the magnitude of certain environmental costs. They simply determine whether those costs exceed an allowable amount. Their certification does not mean that they found no environmental damage whatever. In fact, there may be significant environmental damage (*e.g.*, water pollution), but not quite enough to violate applicable (*e.g.*, water quality) standards. Certifying agencies do not attempt to weigh that damage against the opposing benefits. Thus the balancing analysis remains to be done. It may be that the environmental costs, though passing prescribed standards, are nonetheless great enough to outweigh the particular economic and technical benefits involved in the planned action. The only agency in a position to make such a judgment is the agency with overall responsibility for the proposed federal action—the agency to which NEPA is specifically directed.

The Atomic Energy Commission, abdicating entirely to other agencies' certifications, neglects the mandated balancing analysis. Concerned members of the public are thereby precluded from raising a wide range of environmental issues in order to affect particular Commission decisions. And the special purpose of NEPA is subverted.

Arguing before this court, the Commission has made much of the special environmental expertise of the agencies which set environmental standards. NEPA did not overlook this consideration. Indeed, the Act is quite explicit in describing the attention which is to be given to the views and standards of other agencies. Section 102(2)(C) provides:

"Prior to making any detailed statement, the responsible Federal official shall consult with and obtain the comments of any Federal agency which has jurisdiction by law or special expertise with respect to any environmental impact involved. Copies of such statement and the comments and views of the appropriate Federal, State, and local agencies, which are authorized to develop and enforce environmental standards, shall be made available to the President, the Council on Environmental Quality and to the public * * * "

Thus the Congress was surely cognizant of federal, state and local agencies "authorized to develop and enforce environmental standards." But it provided, in Section 102(2)(C), only for full consultation. It most certainly did not authorize a total abdication to those agencies. Nor did it grant a license to disregard the main body of NEPA obligations.

Of course, federal agencies such as the Atomic Energy Commission may have specific duties, under acts other than NEPA, to obey particular environmental standards. Section 104 of NEPA makes clear that such duties are not to be ignored. * * *

* * *

As to water quality, Section 104 and WQIA [Water Quality Improvement Act of 1970] clearly require obedience to standards set by other agencies. But obedience does not imply total abdication. Certainly, the language of Section 104 does not authorize an abdication. It does not suggest that other "specific statutory obligations" will entirely replace NEPA. Rather, it ensures that three sorts of "obligations" will not be undermined by NEPA: (1) the obligation to "comply" with certain standards, (2) the obligation to "coordinate" or "consult" with certain agencies, and (3) the obligation to "act, or refrain from acting contingent upon" a certification from certain agencies. WQIA imposes the third sort of obligation. It makes the granting of a license by the Commission "contingent upon" a water quality certification. But it does not require the Commission to grant a license once a certification has been issued. It does not preclude the Commission from demanding water pollution controls from its licensees which are *more strict* than those demanded by the applicable water quality standards of the certifying agency. It is very important to understand these facts about WQIA. For all that Section 104 of NEPA does is to reaffirm other "specific statutory obligations." Unless those obligations are plainly mutually exclusive with the requirements of NEPA, the specific mandate of NEPA must remain in force. In other words, Section 104 can operate to relieve an agency of its NEPA duties only if other "specific statutory obligations" clearly preclude performance of those duties.

Obedience to water quality certifications under WQIA is not mutually exclusive with the NEPA procedures. It does not preclude performance of the NEPA duties. Water quality certifications essentially establish a *minimum condition* for the granting of a license. But they need not end the matter. The Commission can then go on to perform the very different operation of balancing the overall benefits and costs of a particular proposed project, and consider alterations (above and beyond the applicable water quality standards) which would further reduce environmental damage. Because the Commission can still conduct the NEPA balancing analysis, consistent with WQIA, Section 104 does not exempt it from doing so. And it, therefore, *must* conduct the obligatory analysis under the prescribed procedures.

* * *

VI

We hold that, in the four respects detailed above, the Commission must revise its rules governing consideration of environmental issues. We do not impose a harsh burden on the Commission. For we require only an exercise of substantive discretion which will protect the environment "to the fullest extent possible." No less is required if the grand congressional purposes underlying NEPA are to become a reality.

Remanded for proceedings consistent with this opinion.

NOTES

1. Read §§ 101 and 102 of NEPA. Where does NEPA make environmental protection a part of the mandate of every federal agency and department? Do you agree with Judge Wright's interpretation of the terms "all practical means consistent with other essential considerations" (§ 101(b)) and "fullest extent possible" (§ 102)? Does NEPA stress process more than substance?

2. In Part IV of *Calvert Cliffs*, Judge Wright states that NEPA requires that "the particular economic and technical benefits of planned action must be assessed and then weighed against the environmental costs; alternatives must be considered which would affect the balance of values." Does NEPA require an economic cost-benefit analysis? *See* 40 C.F.R. § 1502.23.

On September 30, 1993, President Clinton issued Executive Order 12866 which requires agencies to "adopt a regulation only upon a reasoned determination that the benefits of the intended regulation justify its costs." 58 Fed. Reg. 51735. The Office of Information and Regulatory Affairs within the Office of Management and Budget (OMB) reviews the cost-benefit analyses of all significant proposed regulations to ensure that agencies comply with the Executive Order. This centralized review is very similar to the Regulatory Impact Analysis (RIA) established under President Reagan's Executive Order 12291, 46 Fed. Reg. 13193 (1981), which governed the rulemaking process until 1993. The RIA had been criticized as a tool that delayed the implementation of rules under environmental laws. *See* ENVIRONMENTAL POLICY UNDER REAGAN'S EXECUTIVE ORDER (V. Kerry Smith ed. 1984). How does the OMB cost-benefit review differ from the analysis requirements of NEPA?

3. Consider the *Calvert Cliffs* court's rejection of the AEC's argument that the licensing board had no obligation to consider environmental factors covered in the EIS when no party raised such issues. Does the holding require an agency to expend time and energy on inconsequential matters? Does it invite abuse by opponents of agency action who might hang back in administrative proceedings and watch for agency oversights or defects in an EIS which could be raised for the first time on judicial review?

4. Was it proper for the AEC to exclude from consideration environmental effects permitted by other responsible agencies, *e.g.*, discharges of effluent into the water or emissions into the air within the express terms of permits issued by state and/or federal agencies? If another agency with special responsibility and expertise in the area says that a given level of discharge is permissible, should the AEC, or any other agency licensing a project, second-guess it?

5. The most important provision of NEPA is §102(2)(C), which requires a detailed statement of impacts and alternatives that has come to be known as an environmental impact statement (EIS). The EIS requirement is more an accident of history than a carefully conceived policy. The original idea for the EIS is generally credited to Dr. Lynton K. Caldwell, a professor at Indiana University. Professor Caldwell worked closely with Senator Henry "Scoop" Jackson in 1968 and 1969 to lay the groundwork for NEPA. *See, e.g., A National Policy for the Environment*, A Special Report to the Committee on Interior and Insular Affairs, U.S. Senate, 90th Cong., 2d Sess. (July 11, 1968) (laying out the elements of a national environmental policy, including the need to consider the total human environment and to create a new federal entity to coordinate environmental policy). In testimony before the Senate Committee for Interior and Insular Affairs, Dr. Caldwell urged that Senator Jackson's proposed National Environmental Policy Act be amended to require federal agencies to evaluate the environmental impact of actions that they proposed to take. *Hearings on S. 1075, S. 237 and S. 1752 Before the Senate Committee on Interior and Insular Affairs*, 91st Cong., 1st Sess. at 116 (April 1969). While Senator Jackson was sympathetic to this idea, the law was redrafted to require only that federal agencies make a "finding" concerning the probable environmental impacts of any proposed major federal actions. The bill passed the Senate in this form.

When the bill reached the House, Congressman Wayne Aspinall introduced an amendment that would have emasculated the "finding" requirement. While it did not actually change the "finding" requirement, it incorporated new language to clarify that NEPA would not "increase, decrease, or change any responsibility or authority of any federal official or agency." 115 CONG. REC. 26569, 26586-26590 (1969). The House bill was passed with Congressman Aspinall's amendment. In the meantime, Senators Jackson and Edmund Muskie had agreed to replace the "finding" requirement with the current §102(2)(C) provision for a "detailed statement." The conference committee retained the Senate version of §102(2)(C) and both houses passed the bill in late December, 1969. President Nixon signed NEPA on January 1, 1970. The legislative history of NEPA is detailed in FREDERICK ANDERSON, NEPA IN THE COURTS 1-14 (1973), and RICHARD ANDREWS, ENVIRONMENTAL POLICY AND ADMINISTRATIVE CHANGE: IMPLEMENTATION OF THE NATIONAL ENVIRONMENTAL POLICY ACT 7-19 (1976).

Virtually all of the thousands of lawsuits that have been filed to challenge a federal action as violating NEPA base their claims, at least in part, on § 102(2)(C).

6. As noted previously in Chapter 1, § 202 of NEPA establishes the Council on Environmental Quality (CEQ or Council). The Council's most prominent role has been as the agency primarily responsible for interpreting NEPA. Pursuant to a directive from President Carter, the CEQ used this authority to adopt regulations that are binding on all federal agencies. *Robertson v. Methow Valley Citizens Council*, 490 U.S. 332, 354 (1989). These regulations, which appear at 40 C.F.R. Part 1500, are reproduced in their entirety in an appendix to this book. They will be referenced regularly in the cases and the notes which follow the cases. Students of NEPA are well-advised to study the CEQ rules with care.

7. A tribute to NEPA's success is the fact that requirements for environmental impact analysis are now commonplace throughout the world. Nicholas Robinson, *International Trends in Environmental Impact Assessment*, 19 B.C. ENVTL. AFF. L. REV. 591, 611-16 (listing over 50 foreign statutes). Sixteen states and the District of Columbia have adopted their own "little-NEPA" statutes. ENVIRONMENTAL QUALITY: 22ND ANNUAL REPORT OF THE COUNCIL ON ENVIRONMENTAL QUALITY 373 (1992). *See, e.g.,* Cal. Pub. Res. Code §§ 21000 *et seq.* (West 1985 & Supp. 1993); Ind. Code Ann. §§ 13-1-10-1 to 13-1-10-8 (West 1990); N.Y. Envtl. Conserv. §§ 8-0101 to 8-0117 (McKinney 1981 & Supp. 1992).

Still, NEPA has its share of critics. Some simply view the required environmental analyses as "the essence of bureaucratic red tape, sand in the gears of progress." Patrick Parenteau, *NEPA at Twenty: Shining Knight or Tilting at Windmills?*, ENVTL. F., Sept./Oct. 1989, at 14, 15. But, not all critics are concerned about NEPA's effects on development:

The tragedy of NEPA is that it turned energy, attention, and effort away from a redefinition of agency authorities and spent it on proliferating paper. It truncated discussion of environmental protection * * * and it directed attention to the preparation and filing of reports. Environmentalists tried to find substantive requirements in the process of writing and circulating impact statements, while turning their backs on agencies' authorizing legislations which clearly have substantive content.

Sally K. Fairfax, *A Disaster in the Environmental Movement,* 199 SCIENCE 743, 747 (1978). Furthermore, not all of the criticism concerns NEPA's lack of a substantive mandate:

Many politicians have been quick to grasp that the quickest way to silence critical "ecofreaks" is to allocate a small proportion of funds for any engineering project for ecological studies. Someone is inevitably available to receive these funds, conduct the studies regardless of how quickly results are demanded, write large, diffuse reports containing reams of uninterpreted and incomplete descriptive data, and in some cases, construct "predictive" models, irrespective of the quality of the data base. These reports have formed a "gray literature" so diffuse, so voluminous, and so limited in distribution that its conclusions and recommendations are never scrutinized by the scientific community at large. Often the author's only scientific credentials are an impressive title in a government agency, university, or consulting firm. * * * [I]mpact statements seldom receive the hard scrutiny that follows the publication of scientific findings in a reputable scientific journal.

D.W. Schindler, *The Impact Statement Boondoggle,* 192 SCIENCE 509 (1976). In the opinion of the authors, most of the criticisms of NEPA leveled by Fairfax and Schindler were more true when written in the late 1970s than they are today. Some of the improvement can be attributed to citizen activists who convinced friendly scientists to read and critique the documents, and where necessary, educated themselves about the pertinent scientific literature. Also, in 1978 the Council on Environmental Quality promulgated binding regulations for NEPA compliance that stressed brevity. *See, e.g.,* 40 C.F.R. § 1500.1 (1992) ("NEPA's purpose is not to generate paperwork—even excellent paperwork—but to foster excellent action.").

Furthermore, the threat and reality of litigation over the years has provided agencies with incentives and experience to improve not only their NEPA documentation, but their decisions as well. *See* Lance Wood, *In Preparing, Using, and Defending Environmental Impact Statements, Do Federal Agencies Exalt Form Over Substance?,* THE PREPARATION AND REVIEW OF ENVIRONMENTAL IMPACT STATEMENTS: WORKING PAPERS 267, 272-73 (Council on Environmental Quality and Environmental Law Section of the New York State Bar Association 1987) (observing that although "many—and probably the majority" of EISs prepared in the 1970s were post-hoc, paper exercises, in the 1980s agencies reversed the trend and used the EIS as a "substantive tool for environmentally responsible agency planning and decisionmaking."). In 1980, the EPA found that over half of the EISs evaluating the impacts of wastewater treatment facilities resulted in changes in the location of facilities, their capacity, and the areas served. United States Environmental Protection Agency Office of Environmental Review, Evaluation of EPA's EIS Program for Wastewater Treatment Facilities (Nov. 1980). Also, over 70% of the EISs resulted in greater improvement of water quality than the original design proposal. *Id.* The EPA study attributed an average additional cost of six million dollars to a project for EIS preparation but found that the average EIS also resulted in a savings of over six million dollars after design plans were altered. *Id.*

Throughout its stormy history, NEPA has never lacked supporters. *See, e.g.,* William Rodgers, *NEPA at Twenty: Mimicry and Recruitment in Environmental Law,* 20 ENVTL. L. 485 (1990); Nicholas Yost, *NEPA—The Law that Works,* ENVTL. F., Jan. 1985, at 38. A recent report from the Environmental Law Institute, Rediscovering the National Environmental Policy Act (1995), argues that NEPA's untapped potential as a monitoring, planning, and coordinating mandate provides opportunities for constructive administrative reform.

8.   The CEQ's annual reports contain information and describe trends regarding NEPA compliance among federal agencies. For example, the 1991 annual report notes a continuing downward trend in EIS preparation by agencies. Federal agencies filed 456 EISs in that year. This is less than one half the number of EISs filed in 1979. What does this trend suggest (if anything) about NEPA compliance? *See* ENVIRONMENTAL QUALITY: 22ND ANNUAL REPORT OF THE COUNCIL ON ENVIRONMENTAL QUALITY 141, 147 (1992).

9.   Pursuant to Section 309 of the Clean Air Act, 42 U.S.C. § 7609, the EPA reviews every draft and final EIS. The EPA rates the quality of the EIS and often negotiates improvements in the document and the preferred alternative selected by the action agency. Where the EPA is not able to negotiate a solution with the action agency that is satisfactory from an environmental standpoint, the EPA refers the matter to the Council on Environmental Quality for resolution at the Executive level.

10.   Probably the most important part of the *Calvert Cliffs* decision was its distinction between the substantive and procedural provisions of NEPA, between the amount of discretion accorded an agency in carrying out these two obligations, and between the respective standards of judicial review of each type of agency action.

Without question, except in the case of irreconcilable conflict, NEPA expands the substantive authority of every federal agency to include protection of environmental values. As explained in *Calvert Cliffs,* "NEPA, first of all, makes environmental protection a part of the mandate of every federal agency and department." Indeed, this basic proposition was announced in the very first circuit court decision construing NEPA, *Zabel v. Tabb,* 430 F.2d 199 (5th Cir. 1970) (upholding the Corps of Engineers' authority, after enactment of NEPA, to deny a dredge and fill permit for ecological reasons even though the project would not interfere with navigation or other matters within its underlying statutory authority); and, since then, it has been reiterated whenever challenges have been made to measures taken by an agency to protect environmental values. *See, e.g., New England Power Co. v. Goulding,* 486 F. Supp. 18 (D.D.C. 1979) (GSA's authority to transfer excess naval property to federal and local agencies for wildlife and park purposes rather than to a utility for a nuclear power plant upheld).

Therefore, as emphasized in *Calvert Cliffs,* federal agencies are permitted and, indeed, required by NEPA to take environmental factors into account in their decisionmaking. A more difficult issue, however, is what role, if any, does a court play in reviewing such substantive decisions. Clearly, the court may vacate an administrative decision if the agency failed to follow the procedures required by NEPA or procedurally failed to give any consideration to environmental effects or alternatives to the proposed action. But, if an agency goes through all the required motions for "consideration," can a court overturn the agency decision if there was no substance to that consideration—that is, if it gave no significant weight to environmental effects? In other words, given that an agency must place environmental factors on the scales, can it ever be reversed for acting arbitrarily and capriciously in striking the balance? Section 706(2)(A) of the Administrative Procedure Act and basic principles of judicial review expressed in *Citizens to Preserve Overton Park v. Volpe, supra* page 122, would seem to indicate that it can. As you read the cases in Chapter 5, consider whether the courts have shown a willingness to engage in arbitrary and capricious review of agency decisions made after the agency followed the NEPA process.

B. *The Endangered Species Act*

Although NEPA is the flagship federal statute requiring environmental impact analysis and consideration of alternatives before an agency may proceed with an action, it is not the only one. The Endangered Species Act (ESA), with roots in the federal wildlife conservation laws of the early twentieth century, has in the past two decades become an important authority driving environmental impact analysis. Indeed, with almost 200,000 federal actions reviewed for effects on threatened and endangered species, the ESA has developed an extensive regulatory body of law on impact analysis. On that basis alone, it would be important to examine the ESA in any study of environmental decisionmaking.

However, the ESA serves another important role in this casebook. It provides a regulatory system with which to compare NEPA. This casebook considers similar provisions of NEPA and the ESA side-by-side to aid students of the field to see a range of possible solutions to the difficult problems of environmental decisionmaking. It also highlights those areas of the law that intertwine in real factual settings. After this introduction, the following chapters seek to establish a comparative basis for critical analysis of both laws.

THE ENDANGERED SPECIES ACT:
A GUIDE TO ITS PROTECTIONS AND IMPLEMENTATION[*]
DANIEL J. ROHLF

* * *

For millions of years, Earth has been a storehouse of life. First in Precambrian seas and later on more hostile land surfaces, an abundance of life forms appeared and thrived. Creatures capable of adapting to harsh environments not only survived, but diversified and evolved.

This dynamic process of evolution continues today, but with an added twist. Within a relatively tiny fraction of earth's history, humans have acquired the power to determine which organisms survive and which cease to exist. Unfortunately, decisions of life and death—made for eons by the impartial process of natural selection on the basis of adaptability and efficiency—are increasingly made by humans with indifference or in ignorance.

I. THE EARTH'S SPECIES

Species are generally defined on the basis of similar morphological and behavioral characteristics. Estimates of the number of species existing on earth today vary from five million to twenty million, with the most widely accepted figure pegged at about ten million. Though this figure represents little more than an educated guess, it illustrates that the overwhelming majority of earth's species are as yet unknown to science. Only about 1.5 million species have actually been identified, suggesting that five out of six species remain to be discovered.

Insects make up the majority of all species, with up to six million types. Plants comprise between one-tenth and one-thirtieth of Earth's life forms. The remainder are made up of mammals, other vertebrates and protozoa.

Geographical distribution of species is heavily weighted in favor of the tropics. Between two-thirds and three-fourths of all species live in tropical habitats; tropical moist forests probably support between forty and fifty percent of earth's species. For example, La Amistad National Park in the tropical forests of Costa Rica supports more bird species than the entire North American continent.

Because life on earth is part of a dynamic process of survival and adaptation, few of the species that existed in the geologic past are present today. Scientists estimate that only about two percent of organisms that have ever lived on earth are now alive. Extinctions are thus historically commonplace and represent an important element of natural selection and evolution. Rates of extinction in the distant past were variable. Fossil records contain evidence of several periods of rapid extinction, including the sudden disappearance of most dinosaurs approximately seventy million years ago in the late Cretaceous period.

The natural causes of extinction are numerous. Some theories of extinction, particularly those attempting to explain rapid extinctions, embody elements of catastrophism and are highly conjectural. These include many recently proposed explanations for the demise of the dinosaurs, including those which attribute that event to comet strikes or to huge volcanic eruptions. Most causes of extinction, however, are less spectacular. Extirpation of a given species often results from biological succession or ecological relationships with other species. For example, a competitor that appropriates the food source of another species may eliminate that species; disappearance of an insect vital for pollinating a certain plant will likely also result in the disappearance of the plant. Habitat changes also cause extinctions. Climatic upheavals associated with past ice ages, for instance, wiped out many species. Organisms unable to adapt to changing ecosystems were eliminated or succeeded by those that could.

II. Mankind And the Extinction of Species

In recent history, humans have accelerated the pace of species extinctions. The rate of extinction within the past four hundred years—a minute fraction of the 1.4 billion year history of life on this planet—is unprecedented. For example, during a three thousand year period in the Pleistocene, a period that included the most recent ice ages, North America lost fifty mammalian species and forty birds. In comparison, over five hundred species and subspecies that inhabited the same area have become extinct since the Pilgrims arrived at Plymouth in 1620, a rate of extinction estimated at between five and fifty times greater than in the geologic past. This rate, however, is increasing rapidly. Naturalist Norman Myers predicts that species will be vanishing at a rate of one hundred per day by the turn of the century.

A. Direct Human-Caused Mortality

Homo Sapiens have become a sort of super-predator. At our disposal are an incredibly vast array of efficient killing devices, from firearms to poison. Whether killed for food or sport or to make various consumer products, many species have been hunted to extinction or to near extinction. Disappearances of the great auk and the passenger pigeon provide examples of North American species that are now extinct due to direct, human-caused mortality.

The well-known demise of the North American bison illustrates the swiftness and scope of human ability to wipe out a species. One conservative estimate places the number of bison inhabiting the North American continent at the time of U.S. westward expansion at approximately thirty million. After an unparalleled twenty years of carnage and slaughter (1865-1885), the entire bison population was reduced to only a few score. By 1894, only about twenty-five bison remained in the wild, the size of the protected herd in Yellowstone National Park. A species whose numbers were thought to be inexhaustible was practically eliminated within thirty years.

B. Ecological Changes

Human alteration of the delicate equilibrium between all living organisms in a given environment also plays a large role in eliminating species. Plants serve as an excellent example of how human-caused ecological changes contribute to extinctions. Approximately one-quarter of the flora present today in the northeastern United States was actually introduced from other geographical areas by human action. Competition from these alien species has contributed to the decline of native plants. Imported diseases have also taken a heavy toll on native American plants. Tremendous tree mortality has been caused by Dutch Elm disease of European origin, and by Chestnut Blight, accidentally introduced from Asia.

More subtly, species are endangered when humans adversely affect other organisms on which they depend. For example, the loss or displacement of pollinators threatens many American plants. If a pollinator insect is eliminated by human action or displaced by an introduced competitor, the particular plant species dependent on that pollinator for reproduction may face extinction. The extinction of one plant may also imperil other species in an ecosystem. Extinction of a single plant species may lead to the same fate for other organisms that depend in some way on that plant, further demonstration, that a threat to one constituent of an ecological web is a threat to many others as well.

C. Habitat Destruction and Modification

Direct mortality and ecological disruptions are critical problems, but human destruction or alteration of habitats necessary for species survival causes most extinctions. Habitat degradation detrimental to flora and fauna results from many human activities that eliminate, change, or pollute the natural environment.

Humans often simply destroy habitat critical to a species' existence. The most striking example of such destruction is the systematic cutting of tropical forests. Presently, the world's forests are disappearing at the rate of eighteen to twenty million hectares a year—an area approximately one-half the size of California. Most of these losses occur in tropical forests that are cleared for agriculture and stock grazing or that are lumbered for valuable hardwoods. Since up to one-half of all species on earth depend on tropical forest habitats, the implications of the continuing elimination of such areas are frightening.

Modification of habitats, though less noticeable, also threatens many species. For example, to a casual observer in the West or Midwest, miles of unbroken rangelands essentially remain in a "natural" state. But domesticated livestock has changed the ecologically rich tall grass prairie to a much less diverse biota capable of supporting far fewer wild species.

Potentially the most harmful and most difficult to control of all forms of habitat disruption is pollution. Though this problem is often discussed in terms of effects on human health or aesthetic values, pollution and environmental poisons can have devastating effects on all life forms. The precipitous decline of a wide variety of bird species due to a chemical byproduct of the pesticide DDT serves as a particularly notorious example. Use of DDT was finally banned in the United States in 1972, but many more toxins with equally harmful effects are still released into the environment. Recent discoveries in the American west of high levels of selenium, which may be linked to a serious drop in numbers of waterfowl, are yet another example in this dismal litany. Unfortunately, such discoveries may represent only the tip of the proverbial pollution iceberg, as knowledge of the consequences of pollution slowly catches up with the rate at which humans are dumping pollutants into the environment.

III. WHY PRESERVE ENDANGERED SPECIES?

The Global 2000 Report, commissioned by President Carter in 1977, does not mince words in evaluating future prospects for a great many species. The report bleakly concludes that "[e]xtinctions of plant and animal species will increase dramatically." The study predicts that as many as twenty percent of earth's species will be driven to extinction by the turn of the century—a total of perhaps two million unique life forms.

Immediate preventative action could help avert such an occurrence, but the processes that jeopardize species are increasing rather than diminishing. In less developed countries, where most tropical forests are located, all physically accessible forest will likely be cut within thirty-five years, if present deforestation rates continue. More deserts will be created as more livestock graze fewer acres. Pollution and poisoning may also worsen in an overcrowded world that relies increasingly on "dirty" energy sources, including coal and other fossil fuels, and on a tremendous variety of potentially hazardous agricultural and industrial chemicals.

Modern societies must face many problems—economic stagnation, various social ills, political strife, even hunger and lack of physical necessities. Loss of species is obviously occurring, but should this be a cause for concern? Aren't there more pressing problems? Why should we preserve species?

A. Aesthetic and Moral Justifications

Many people attach aesthetic value to species because of their beauty, their ability to inspire or serve as symbols, or simply because certain unusual characteristics make them interesting. Bald eagles, for example, once carried bounties on their heads and were systematically shot as dangerous predators. Today, however, bald eagles symbolize freedom and the United States itself, and Americans often go to great lengths to protect them. Similarly, conservation of many species enjoys support principally because people find certain species appealing for one reason or another.

Aesthetic justifications for preserving species, however, have little relevance to the fate of obscure plants and animals whose existence, if known at all, is recognized only in the volumes of taxonomic journals. Many people therefore justify conservation of all life forms, no matter how seemingly humble or insignificant, on moral grounds. For example, Professor David Ehrenfeld writes that species should be conserved "because they exist and because this existence is itself but the present expression of a continuing historical process of immense antiquity and majesty." Long-standing existence in Nature is deemed to carry with it the unimpeachable right to continued existence. This type of non-utilitarian, non-homocentric view of conserving species is becoming increasingly prevalent as a justification for preserving endangered species.

B. Economic Benefits of Species Preservation

Policy decisions are increasingly made based on quantitative cost-benefit analyses. Some commentators even advocate assigning dollar values to such intangibles as clear views or clean water to assess the cost effectiveness of environmental regulation. Surprisingly, preserving even obscure species can often be justified on this type of economic basis due to their direct benefits or potential benefits to humans.

The medical uses of plants provide an excellent example of an economic argument for species preservation. The overall value of plant-derived drugs and pharmaceuticals sold in the United States tops tens of billions of dollars annually. The value of drugs derived from animals and microbes approaches this figure. The uses of such drugs range from laxatives to cardiovascular regulation. Plant and animal-derived drugs are also used in the battle against cancer. Two compounds derived from alkaloids of the Rosy Periwinkle—a flower found in tropical regions—are vital constituents of a chemotherapy treatment that has increased the remission rate of lymph system cancer in Hodgkin's Disease patients from 19 percent to 80 percent. The same drugs have also increased the remission rates of several other forms of cancer. In addition to their tremendous life-saving properties, these compounds account for sales of over one hundred million dollars annually. Despite these enormous benefits, less than one percent of the earth's plant species have been thoroughly studied for their possible usefulness to humans. Consequently, preservation of the vast storehouse of potentially life-saving species in the wild may be justified.

Plants and animals are not only useful for directly extracted agents, but as scientific models as well. The cheetah, for example, is a sort of living cardiovascular experiment. It can accelerate to speeds in excess of seventy miles per hour and maintain that pace over several hundred meters. Since the cheetah can obviously withstand sudden and severe oxygen debt, it may harbor vital clues for treatment of heart disease, blood pressure, and circulatory disorders in humans.

Industrial uses of plant and animal derived materials are extensive and wide-ranging. Chemical producers are increasingly looking toward plants as an important source of raw materials for manufactured chemicals due to the increasing scarcity and price of petroleum. Other non-traditional industrial uses of species becoming increasingly prominent include fuel production from conversion of plant biomass, production of rubber from a shrub native to the American Southwest, and use of species as research models for mechanical engineers.

One of the most important utilitarian benefits of species diversity is as a "genetic bank." Industrialized agriculture points to the importance of genetic preservation. Fewer than twenty plants cultivated on a large-scale basis produce the overwhelming majority of the world's current food supply. This situation is attributable to the remarkable gains in the productivity of certain grains during the last half-century. Since 1930, for example, corn production per acre in the United States has increased in certain cases by a factor of ten. Approximately half of this increase stems from selective breeding to alter the corn's genetic codes. Huge plantings of the same type of corn, while extremely productive, are nevertheless highly vulnerable to catastrophe, including disease or insect infestations. In 1970, an estimated fifteen percent of the entire U.S. corn crop was wiped out by a leaf blight, causing losses of two billion dollars to farmers and consumers. This epidemic was halted only with the aid of blight resistant germ plasm of unique genetic ancestry that originated in Mexico.

Another recent discovery in Mexico of a wild strain of perennial corn may make possible a commercial hybrid corn that grows every year without plowing and replanting. The wild corn species survives in three remnant patches covering only four hectares. If nearby settlement and timber cutting had destroyed this unique strain before it was discovered, a potentially invaluable genetic property would have been lost.

The genetic resource represented by the ten million species on earth is of inestimable worth. Losing one-fifth of this resource by the year 2000, before many of its potential benefits are explored, is a sobering prospect.

C. Ecological Benefits of Species Preservation

Species diversity is also important to humans in more subtle ways. The following events illustrate how human-caused ecological disturbances often have unintended results:

Malaria once infected nine out of ten people on the island of North Borneo, now a state of Indonesia. In 1955, the World Health Organization (WHO) began spraying dieldrin (a pesticide similar to DDT) to kill malaria-carrying mosquitoes. The program was very successful, almost eliminating this dreaded disease. But other things happened. The dieldrin killed other insects besides mosquitoes, including flies and cockroaches inhabiting the houses. The islanders applauded. But then small lizards that also lived in the houses died after gorging themselves on dead insects. Then cats began dying after feeding on the dead lizards. Without cats, rats flourished and began overrunning the villages. Now people were threatened by sylvatic plague carried by fleas on the rats. Fortunately, this situation was brought under control when WHO had the Royal Air Force parachute cats into Borneo.

On top of everything else, the thatched roofs of some houses began to fall in. The dieldrin also killed wasps and other insects that fed on a type of caterpillar that either avoided or was not affected by the insecticide. With most of their predators eliminated, the caterpillar population exploded. The larvae munched their way through one of their favorite foods, the leaves that made up the roofs.[25]

Within an ecosystem, everything is in some way interconnected. A sudden change in even a seemingly minor constituent can disturb the balance of the entire system, greatly affecting humans as well.

Ecosystems are structured in a pyramidal fashion, with multitudes of plants at the base and a relatively small number of carnivores at the top. Energy flows along food webs from plant to herbivore to carnivore, with many interconnections along the way. Generally, a reduction of species diversity within an ecosytem will lead to increased instability of that system. This trend occurs within an unpredictable range, however. An ecosystem may be able to sustain the loss of several species with no noticeable disruption; alternatively, one organism may be the "key-stone" species in its community, affecting all others. In many cases the importance of any one species in an ecosystem simply cannot be accurately foreseen.

Ecosystem stability is important to humans because of a wide variety of what may be termed ecosystem services. Such services include maintenance of atmospheric quality, control and amelioration of climate, soil generation and preservation, waste disposal, and pest and disease control. For example, systematic destruction of tropical forests reduces recycling of water from plant to atmosphere and increases the reflectivity of the earth's surface. Such alterations could lead to local or even regional climatic changes to the detriment of the agricultural development for which the forest was cleared. Devastating chains of events within ecosystems can also be set in motion by seemingly minor causes, such as the elimination of a few insect or plant species. Thus, human-caused extinction of any organism is tantamount to a planetary game of ecological "Russian Roulette."

This idea has attained perhaps its most compelling expression in the writings of naturalist Aldo Leopold. Leopold envisioned a biotic pyramid of which humans are merely a part. He advocated ecological awareness through development of a "land ethic:" "[A] land ethic changes the role of Homo Sapiens from conqueror of the land-community to plain member and citizen of it. It implies respect for his fellow-members, and also respect for the community as such."[26] Leopold saw all ethics as resting on the premise that the individual is a member of a community of interdependent parts. Within the human community, Leopold argued, an elaborate set of ethics differentiates social from anti social conduct. Leopold's land ethic simply enlarges the notion of community to include, in his words, soils, waters, plants, and animals, or collectively:

---

[25] G. MILLER, LIVING IN THE ENVIRONMENT: AN INTRODUCTION TO ENVIRONMENTAL SCIENCE 82-83 (4th ed. 1975).

[26] A. LEOPOLD, A SAND COUNTY ALMANAC 240 (1949).

the land.[27] Leopold saw such a community as appropriate and useful, and viewed disturbing this interrelated community, particularly disturbances committed in ignorance, as folly:

> If the land mechanism as a whole is good, then every part is good, whether we understand it or not. If the biota, in the course of aeons, has built something we like but do not understand, then who but a fool would discard seemingly useless parts? To keep every cog and wheel is the first precaution of intelligent tinkering.[28]

* * *

NOTE

Does Rohlf make a case for endangered species protection, ecosystem protection, or both? What is the difference between the two? Which is more important?

INTRODUCTION TO THE ENDANGERED SPECIES ACT

The Endangered Species Act (ESA) has had a profound impact on the manner in which federal, state and even private entities carry out their activities. Although the ESA is less rigid than it is sometimes characterized by its opponents,[1] it is perhaps rightfully criticized for focusing on protection of individual species rather than the preservation of natural processes.[2] Extinction of species occurred long before humans appeared on Earth and is a part of natural selection. However, human activities have greatly accelerated the rate of species extinction, and it is for this reason that Congress enacted the ESA. The ecological underpinnings of the ESA were endorsed by a 1995 National Academy of Sciences report, Science and the Endangered Species Act.

Under the ESA, all federal agencies must use their authorities to help recover species listed as threatened or endangered. The federal government is generally precluded from taking any action that would jeopardize the continued existence of any listed species. Moreover, federal agencies may not generally take any action that will result in the destruction or adverse modification of habitat that has been designated as critical to the survival of a listed species. The determination that a federal action may jeopardize a species

---

[27]   *Id.* at 239.

[28]   *Id.* at 190.

[1]   See Oliver A. Houck, *The Endangered Species Act and Its Implementation by the U.S. Departments of Interior and Commerce*, 64 U. COLO. L. REV. 277 (1993), for an excellent description of how agencies interpret the ESA to accommodate desired projects.

[2]   *See* Reed F. Noss, *From Endangered Species to Biodiversity*, and J. Michael Scott *et al.*, *Gap Analysis of Species Richness and Vegetation Cover: An Integrated Biodiversity Conservation Strategy*, in BALANCING ON THE BRINK OF EXTINCTION 227, 282 (Kathryn A. Kohm ed. 1991).

or adversely modify critical habitat is made through a process called *consultation,* in accordance with § 7 of the ESA.

In addition to regulating federal actions, the ESA makes it unlawful for any person (defined to include government agencies) to "take" an animal listed as endangered. Similar prohibitions may apply to animals listed as threatened. Endangered and threatened plants receive less protection.

Subject to defenses, the ESA can be enforced with civil penalties up to $25,000 for each violation. § 11(a). A person who "knowingly violates" a provision of the ESA may face criminal prosecution, resulting in fines up to $50,000 and imprisonment for up to a year. § 11(b). Unlike NEPA, the ESA contains a provision authorizing citizen suits to compel compliance or enjoin noncompliance of any person or governmental agency. § 11(g).

Set forth below are brief descriptions of the four principal mechanisms for achieving the goals established by the ESA.

A. Listing of Endangered or Threatened Species

The strictures of the ESA apply only to listed species, critical habitat, and species or habitat that have been formally proposed for listing. *See e.g.,* 50 C.F.R. § 402.10. Thus, the decision to list a species as threatened or endangered is itself a key decision. All listings and designations are promulgated through notice and comment, informal rulemaking under the Administrative Procedure Act. While *endangered species* are in danger of extinction throughout all or a significant portion of their range, *threatened species* face a somewhat less imminent prospect of extinction but are likely to become endangered in the foreseeable future. § 3(6) & (20). Note that the term "species" is broadly defined to include "any subspecies of fish or wildlife or plants, and any distinct population segment of any species of vertebrate fish or wildlife which interbreeds when mature." § 3(16).

A listing decision must be based solely on the best scientific and commercial data available. Significantly, however, the ESA requires the Secretary to take into account the conservation efforts that are being made by any state or other political entity. § 4(b)(1)(A). Thus, a state may substantially reduce the possibility of having a species listed if it has established its own effective plan for reducing threats to the species.

Generally, *critical habitat* must be designated for all listed species on the basis of the best scientific data available. "Critical habitat" is defined by the statute as that habitat which is essential to the conservation of a threatened or endangered species. Unlike the decision to list, however, designation of critical habitat must also take into account economic and other relevant impacts of the designation. Unless extinction is likely to result, the Secretary may exclude any area from critical habitat if the benefits of exclusion outweigh the benefits of designation. § 4(b)(2).

Over 1100 domestic species have been listed by the U.S. Fish and Wildlife Service (FWS) as threatened or endangered. Nearly 4000 other species were designated candidates to be considered for listing by the agency in 1996, when the FWS announced that it was eliminating its largest official candidate category. This category contained species for which current information suggested that listing was appropriate, but for which conclusive data was not yet available. Although the FWS no longer officially acknowledges this evidence indicating thousands of species may qualify for protection under the ESA, the backlog of species to be considered for proposed listing is great. The remaining candidate category now consists of about 200 species for which the FWS has sufficient information to justify listing but that are currently preempted from being proposed by higher priority listing activities. The listing queue lengthened during the years 1995–1996, when a succession of appropriations acts imposed moratoria on the § 4 process. The FWS updates the species lists on the World Wide Web at *http://www.fws.gov/~r9endspp/boxscore.html.*

Species (or critical habitat) may be proposed for listing or delisting at the initiative of the FWS or by petition from any interested person. § 4(b)(3)(A). Within a year after being petitioned, the Secretary must determine whether the petitioned action is warranted. If a listing petition is warranted, the Secretary must either promptly initiate the listing process by publishing a proposed rule, or find that action is warranted but precluded by other pending listing actions and place the candidate species in Category I. § 4(b)(3)(B).

B. Consultation

As noted above, the ESA precludes federal agencies from taking any action that might jeopardize the continued existence of a listed species or adversely modify habitat designated as critical to the survival of the species. Congress established a seldom-used process in 1978 to allow agencies to apply for exemptions from this substantive restriction. The exemption process has been invoked only three times and on two of those occasions federal actions received exemptions: the Grayrocks dam construction on the Laramie River in 1979, and thirteen timber sales in northern spotted owl habitat in 1992.

Whenever an agency action involves a major construction activity (defined as a major federal action under NEPA), the action agency must request information from the FWS about the presence of listed or proposed species. If such species are not present, the action is allowed to proceed. If, however, a listed species is or may be present, the action agency must prepare a *biological assessment* (BA) to ascertain whether the species or its critical habitat is likely to be adversely affected by the proposed action.[3]

If a BA *concludes* that adverse affects are likely, the action agency must enter into *formal consultation* with the FWS.[4] For proposed actions that do not require a BA, agencies must intiate formal consultation if the action may affect a listed species or critical habitat. After formal consultation concludes, the FWS prepares a *biological opinion* (BO), which determines whether the proposed action is likely to jeopardize the continued existence of a listed species or result in the destruction or adverse modification of its critical habitat. If no jeopardy will result, the action may proceed. If no jeopardy will result but individuals of listed species might be "taken" within the meaning of § 9 of the ESA, then FWS may issue an *incidental take statement* which protects the agency against § 9 liability for a stated number of "takes" so long as the agency employs specified precautionary measures.

---

[3]   For species proposed for listing, a separate "conference" process is established by regulation for such species. 50 C.F.R. § 402.10. Agencies frequently avoid findings of adverse imputs on listed species through a process developed by regulation called *informal consultation. Informal consultation* is an optional process to assist the action agency in deciding whether formal consultation is necessary. 50 C.F.R. § 402.13. During informal consultation, the FWS may suggest modifications to a proposed project that will avoid adverse impacts to protected species, and thus the need to engage in formal consultation.

[4]   An applicant may also request *early consultation,* "to reduce the likelihood of conflicts between listed species * * * and proposed actions." 50 C.F.R. § 402.11. Early consultation leads to a "preliminary biological opinion" which may be made final if the applicant decides to go forward with the proposal action. *Id.* at § 402.11(e). The advantage of early consultation is that the applicant can determine whether a proposed action may cause jeopardy before substantial capital investments are made.

If FWS determines that jeopardy will result then it must suggest *reasonable and prudent alternatives* that will not jeopardize the species. § 7(b)(3)(A). Generally, actions that may jeopardize a listed species, or that will result in the destruction or adverse modification of their critical habitat, may not go forward unless an exemption is received. As suggested above, the exemption process is cumbersome, and exemptions are difficult to obtain. In particular, an exemption may not be granted unless five members of a committee of seven presidential appointees find that: (1) there are no reasonable and prudent alternatives to the proposed action; (2) the benefits of the action clearly outweigh the benefits of alternative courses of action which would not jeopardize the species; (3) the action is of regional or national significance; and (4) neither the Federal Agency involved or the exemption applicant made any irreversible or irretrievable commitment of resources with respect to the proposed action.

Despite its importance, public involvement in the ESA process is often limited because of the strict timetables established by federal regulation for preparing the various reports required by the ESA. Nonetheless, interested persons often can and frequently do comment on ESA documents or issues because of their relevance to environmental documents prepared in accordance with NEPA.[5] The action agency's biological assessment is often incorporated into the relevant NEPA document. Indeed, the CEQ regulations require agencies "[t]o the fullest extent possible, [to] prepare draft environmental impact statements concurrently with environmental impact analyses and related surveys and studies required by * * * the Endangered Species Act * * * and other environmental review laws." 40 C.F.R. § 1502.25. Usually, a biological assessment must be completed within 180 days from its inception. Formal consultation usually must be completed within 90 days from its initiation. Then, 45 days after concluding a formal consultation, the FWS issues the biological opinion.

C. Conservation

Conservation is defined under the statute as "the use of all methods and procedures necessary to bring any endangered or threatened species back to the point at which the measures provided [under the ESA] are no longer necessary." Although all federal agencies have a general obligation to conserve listed species, the principle vehicle for doing so is the *recovery plan*. Recovery plans are required for all listed species unless the Secretary finds that such a plan will not promote conservation of the species. § 4(f)(1). As of June, 1998, 771 listed species had approved recovery plans. Of the 78 species contained in the first official endangered species list, which the federal government published in 1967, only one (the American Alligator) has fully recovered.[6]

---

[5]   A federal action which triggers § 7 consultation necessarily triggers preparation of a NEPA document as well. Generally, the public has an opportunity to comment and participate in the preparation of NEPA documents before they become final.

[6]   David Wilcove *et al., Whatever Happened to the Class of '67?*, 2 (Environmental Defense Fund 1993). The authors note, however, that twice as many species on the 1967 list show positive trends toward recovery than show negative trends. *Id.*

D. Takings

Section 9 of the ESA makes it unlawful to take, import, export, possess, sell, deliver, transport or ship in interstate commerce any endangered animal. The ESA defines the word "take" to mean "harass, harm, pursue, hunt, shoot, wound, kill, trap, capture, or collect, or to attempt to engage in any such conduct." § 3(19). Similar restrictions may be imposed for threatened animals in accordance with the pertinent regulations listing those species.

Endangered plant species are protected by special, generally less stringent prohibitions under § 9(a)(2). For example, endangered plants on federal lands are protected from: (1) removal and possession, and (2) malicious damage or destruction. Other prohibitions make it illegal to import to or export from United States an endangered plant.

Although the "takings" prohibitions can be onerous, the ESA incorporates provisions that allow limited takings of listed species without risk of violating the law. Under § 10 of the ESA, any person who proposes an activity that may "incidentally" result in the "taking" of a listed species may prepare and seek approval of a *habitat conservation plan* (HCP). The HCP must describe the impact that will likely result from the taking, the steps that will be taken to minimize and mitigate that impact, the funding that will be available to carry out the mitigation, and the alternatives to the proposed plan that were considered. The Secretary is required to approve a permit that authorizes the incidental taking of a listed species if he finds that the applicant will minimize and mitigate the impacts to the maximum extent practical, that adequate funding is available to carry out the mitigation, and that the taking will not appreciably reduce the likelihood of survival of the species. One of the most important developments in ESA implementation over the past four years is the dramatic increase in permit applications and HCPs. As of November 30, 1998, 243 incidental take permits have been issued and approximately 200 HCPs were in various stages of development. Current information on HCPs is available at *http://www.fws.gov/rgendspp/hcp/heptable.pdf.* Chapter 10 of this casebook discusses the recent developments in this rapidly emerging program.

NORTHERN SPOTTED OWL v. HODEL
716 F. Supp. 479 (W.D. Wash. 1988)

ZILLY, District Judge.

A number of environmental organizations bring this action against the United States Fish & Wildlife Service ("Service") and others, alleging that the Service's decision not to list the northern spotted owl as endangered or threatened under the Endangered Species Act ("ESA" or "the Act") was arbitrary and capricious or contrary to law.

Since the 1970s the northern spotted owl has received much scientific attention, beginning with comprehensive studies of its natural history by Dr. Eric Forsman, whose most significant discovery was the close association between spotted owls and old-growth forests. This discovery raised concerns because the majority of remaining old-growth owl habitat is on public land available for harvest.

In January 1987, plaintiff Greenworld, pursuant to Sec. 4(b)(3) of the ESA petitioned the Service to list the northern spotted owl as endangered. In August 1987, 29 conservation organizations filed a second petition to list the owl as endangered both in the Olympic Peninsula in Washington and in the Oregon Coast Range, and as threatened throughout the rest of its range.

The ESA directs the Secretary of the Interior to determine whether any species have become endangered or threatened due to habitat destruction, overutilization, disease or predation, or other natural or manmade factors. 16 U.S.C. § 1533(a)(1). The Act was amended in 1982 to ensure that the decision whether to list a species as endangered or threatened was based solely on an evaluation of the biological risks faced by the species, to the exclusion of all other factors.

The Service's role in deciding whether to list the northern spotted owl as endangered or threatened is to assess the technical and scientific data in the administrative record against the relevant listing criteria in section 4(a)(1) and then to exercise its own expert discretion in reaching its decision.

In July 1987, the Service announced that it would initiate a status review of the spotted owl and requested public comment. 52 Fed. Reg. 34396 (Sept. 11, 1987). The Service assembled a group of Service biologists, including Dr. Mark Shaffer, its staff expert on population viability, to conduct the review. The Service charged Dr. Shaffer with analyzing current scientific information on the owl. Dr. Shaffer concluded that:

> the most reasonable interpretation of current data and knowledge indicate continued old growth harvesting is likely to lead to the extinction of the subspecies in the foreseeable future which argues strongly for listing the subspecies as threatened or endangered at this time.

The Service invited a peer review of Dr. Shaffer's analysis by a number of U.S. experts on population viability, all of whom agreed with Dr. Shaffer's prognosis for the owl, although each had some criticisms of his work.

The Service's decision is contained in its 1987 Status Review of the owl ("Status Review") and summarized in its Finding on Greenworld's petition ("Finding"). The Status Review was completed on December 14, 1987, and on December 17 the Service announced that listing the owl as endangered under the Act was not warranted at that time. 52 Fed. Reg. 48552, 48554 (Dec. 23, 1987). This suit followed. Both sides now move for summary judgment on the administrative record before the Court.

* * *

This Court reviews the Service's action under the "arbitrary and capricious" standard of the Administrative Procedure Act ("APA"), 5 U.S.C. § 706(2)(A). This standard is narrow and presumes the agency action is valid, but it does not shield agency action from a "thorough, probing, in-depth review," *Citizens to Preserve Overton Park v. Volpe*, 401 U.S. 402, 415 (1971). * * * Agency action is arbitrary and capricious where the agency has failed to "articulate a satisfactory explanation for its action including a 'rational connection between the facts found and the choice made.'" *Motor Vehicle Mfrs. Ass'n v. State Farm Mut. Auto Ins.*, 463 U.S. 29, 43 (1983).

The Status Review and the Finding to the listing petition offer little insight into how the Service found that the owl currently has a viable population. Although the Status Review cites extensive empirical data and lists various conclusions, it fails to provide any analysis. The Service asserts that it is entitled to make its own decision, yet it provides no explanation for its findings. An agency must set forth clearly the grounds on which it acted. Judicial deference to agency expertise is proper, but the Court will not do so blindly. The Court finds that the Service has not set forth the grounds for its decision against listing the owl.

The Service's documents also lack any expert analysis supporting its conclusion. Rather, the expert opinion is entirely to the contrary. The only reference in the Status Review to an actual opinion that the owl does not face a significant likelihood of extinction is a mischaracterization of a conclusion of Dr. Mark Boyce:

> Boyce (1987) in his analysis of the draft preferred alternative concluded that there is a low probability that the spotted owls will go extinct. He does point out that population fragmentation appears to impose the greatest risks to extinction.

Dr. Boyce responded to the Service:

> I did not conclude that the Spotted Owl enjoys a low probability of extinction, and I would be very disappointed if efforts to preserve the Spotted Owl were in any way thwarted by a misinterpretation of something I wrote.

M. Boyce, letter of February 18, 1988, to Rolf Wallenstrom, U.S. Fish and Wildlife Service, Region 1, exhibit 7 to Complaint.

Numerous other experts on population viability contributed to or reviewed drafts of the Status Review, or otherwise assessed spotted owl viability. Some were employed by the Service; others were independent. None concluded that the northern spotted owl is not at risk of extinction. For example, as noted above, Dr. Shaffer evaluated the current data and knowledge and determined that continued logging of old growth likely would lead to the extinction of the owl in the foreseeable future. This risk, he concluded, argued strongly for immediate listing of the subspecies as threatened or endangered.

The Service invited a peer review of Dr. Shaffer's analysis. Drs. Michael Soule, Bruce Wilcox, and Daniel Goodman, three leading U.S. experts on population viability, reviewed and agreed completely with Dr. Shaffer's prognosis for the owl.

For example, Dr. Soule, the acknowledged founder of the discipline of "conservation biology" (the study of species extinction), concluded:

> I completely concur with your conclusions, and the methods by which you reached them. The more one hears about *Strix occidentalis caurina,* the more concern one feels. Problems with the data base and in the models notwithstanding, and politics notwithstanding, I just can't see how a responsible biologist could reach any other conclusion than yours.

M. Soule, letter of November 1, 1987, to Dr. Mark Shaffer.

The Court will reject conclusory assertions of agency "expertise" where the agency spurns unrebutted expert opinions without itself offering a credible alternative explanation. Here, the Service disregarded all the expert opinion on population viability, including that of its own expert, that the owl is facing extinction, and instead merely asserted its expertise in support of its conclusions.

The Service has failed to provide its own or other expert analysis supporting its conclusions. Such analysis is necessary to establish a rational connection between the evidence presented and the Service's decision. Accordingly, the United States Fish and Wildlife Service's decision not to list at this time the northern spotted owl as endangered or threatened under the Endangered Species Act was arbitrary and capricious and contrary to law.

The Court further finds that it is not possible from the record to determine that the Service considered the related issue of whether the northern spotted owl is a threatened species. This failure of the Service to review and make an express finding on the issue of threatened status is also arbitrary and capricious and contrary to law.

In deference to the Service's expertise and its role under the Endangered Species Act, the Court remands this matter to the Service, which has 90 days from the date of this order to provide an analysis for its decision that listing the northern spotted owl as threatened or endangered is not currently warranted. Further, the Service is ordered to supplement its Status Review and petition Finding consistent with this Court's ruling.

IT IS SO ORDERED.

NOTES

1.   Notice that, despite the caption of this case, the plaintiff is identified by the court as "environmental organizations," not the northern spotted owl. Given the holding of *Sierra Club v. Morton*, why did the environmental organizations name as a plaintiff the northern spotted owl?

2.   As described previously, the U.S. Fish and Wildlife Service can respond to a petition to list in three ways: (1) that the petitioned action is not warranted; (2) that the action is warranted, in which case the Secretary must promptly initiate the listing process by publishing a proposed rule; or (3) that the action is warranted but precluded by other pending listing actions. ESA § 4(b)(3)(B). Suppose the Secretary had chosen the third of these responses in this case. How likely is it that the Secretary's action would have been overturned on appeal?

3.   A decision that listing is not warranted, or warranted but precluded by another pending listing decisions, is subject to judicial review; but a decision that listing is warranted may not be reviewed. § 4(b)(3)(C)(ii). Why not?

4.   In the instant case, scientific opinion was generally consistent in suggesting that the owl faced extinction in the foreseeable future. While the Fish and Wildlife Service relied on the opinions of Dr. Mark Boyce, Dr. Boyce himself repudiated the characterization of his view that was offered by the Service. In many cases, however, a true conflict does in fact exist among scientific opinion. How should the court resolve a case where widely disparate professional opinions are offered? Note that the decision to list or not list a species is an informal rulemaking proceeding under APA § 553. Should judicial review in such cases be limited to the administrative record? What problems can you foresee if additional testimony is not allowed?

5.   The *Spotted Owl* decision has been offered as an example of how plaintiffs use the Endangered Species Act to achieve broader environmental goals—in this case, protection of the ancient forests of the Pacific Northwest. Assuming this is true, is it an appropriate use of the ESA? *See* E. Charles Meslow, *Spotted Owl Protection: Unintentional Evolution Toward Ecosystem Management*, ENDANGERED SPECIES UPDATE, Nos. 3 & 4 1993, at 34 (noting that "the northern spotted owl now serves as the surrogate for * * * the old-growth forest ecosystem"). Professor Oliver Houck applauds this surrogate role for endangered species:

> Endangered species are useful, though incomplete, indicators of the health of their ecosystems and of the earth we share. While the best indicators may often be mollusks, plants, and lower life forms, the decline of the bald eagle from the

effects of chlorinated hydrocarbons is a good indication of the impact of those chemicals on human life. As water quality becomes inadequate to protect the delta smelt, it will also become inadequate for human uses. * * * We accept wildlife indicator thresholds for impacts on water, air, and soil—separate components of the whole. What remains is to test the whole. Endangered species are such a test. The ESA serves in this fashion as an "Earth Pollution Act." It is admittedly an incomplete test whose results need careful interpretation, but the fate of listed species * * * help draw the line.

Why Do We Protect Endangered Species, and What Does That Say About Whether Restrictions on Private Property to Protect Them Constitute "Takings"?, 80 IOWA L. REV. 297, 327-28 (1995). Is it improper for a plaintiff to use the ESA to advance broader environmental policy goals?

6. In February 1989, a General Accounting Office report concluded that FWS officials had altered scientific evidence and considered non-biological factors in their original determination that listing was not warranted for the northern spotted owl. U.S. GENERAL ACCOUNTING OFFICE, ENDANGERED SPECIES: SPOTTED OWL PETITION EVALUATION BESET BY PROBLEMS (Feb. 1989). Two months later the FWS proposed listing the owl as a threatened species. On June 22, 1990, the FWS made the listing final. 55 Fed. Reg. 26114 (1990).

The final listing, however, only sparked further rounds of controversy. In both the proposed and final listing notices, the FWS followed its common practice when it stated without explanation that "critical habitat * * * is not presently determinable." 55 Fed. Reg. 26192 (1990). In February 1991, Judge Zilly again found a FWS spotted owl decision arbitrary and capricious. *Northern Spotted Owl v. Lujan*, 758 F. Supp. 621 (W.D. Wash. 1991). Zilly explained that when Congress amended the ESA in 1982 to allow for a one-year delay of designation of critical habitat, it nonetheless expressed a preference for designation concurrent with listing. ESA §§ 4(a)(3)(A), 4(b)(6)(C). However, Congress did not want an inability to designate critical habitat to hold up listing decisions. The court found that the FWS was not entitled to an automatic extension merely by invoking indeterminacy. The FWS could delay designation of critical habitat only by explaining why it could not fulfill the statute's preference for concurrent designation. The court suggested that an adequate explanation would show why critical habitat is not determinable, what effort was made to determine the habitat, and what additional information is needed. In January 1992, after proposing critical habitat twice, the FWS promulgated a final rule designating critical habitat. 57 Fed. Reg. 1796 (1992). Why were the environmental organizations concerned about critical habitat? How does the ESA treat critical habitat differently from undesignated habitat occupied by a listed species? The final designation excluded all non-federal lands from critical habitat. Why do you think the FWS ultimately limited critical habitat to federal lands?

7. Does the FWS need to prepare an EIS for its ESA-related activities? After the FWS published its second proposed critical habitat designation for the northern spotted owl, Douglas County, an area of Oregon economically dependent on the timber industry, sued the agency for violating NEPA by failing to develop a range of alternatives for critical habitat and failing to discuss the cumulative impact of the designation in conjunction with other actions. In *Douglas County v. Lujan*, 810 F. Supp. 1470 (D. Or. 1992), the court found that the FWS, though exempt from NEPA's EIS requirement for listing decisions, must comply with § 102(2)(C) for critical habitat designation. The court reasoned that, unlike listing, designation of critical habitat permits the FWS to consider a wide range of possible impacts. *See* § 4(b)(2). The court also rejected the notion that NEPA does not apply to agencies whose function is to protect the environment. 810 F. Supp. at 1481; *cf. Pacific Legal Foundation v. Andrus*, 657 F.2d 829, 838 n.11 (6th Cir. 1981). The appeals court, however, reversed the district court and found that Congress intended the ESA critical habitat designation procedures to displace NEPA procedures. *Douglas County v. Babbitt*, 48 F.3d 1495 (9th Cir. 1995), *cert. denied*, 516 U.S. 1042 (1996). If you represented an environmental organization, would you have submitted an *amicus* brief supporting the Oregon county or the federal government? The more recent decision of *Catron County Board of Commissioners v. U.S. Fish and Wildlife Service*, 75 F.3d 1429 (10th Cir. 1996), finding that NEPA procedures do apply to designation of critical habitat, now creates a circuit split that the Supreme Court may need to resolve. In Chapter 8, we will discuss in further detail the application of both NEPA and the ESA in situations of statutory conflict.

Why did Douglas County have standing to challenge the FWS in this case? What claims do you suppose the County asserted that fell within the "zone of interests" sought to be protected by NEPA? *See* 810 F. Supp. at 1475-76.

We will return to the spotted owl issue, which Secretary of the Interior Bruce Babbitt is fond of calling "a national train wreck," in Chapter 5 when we discuss the ESA § 7 exemption process in more detail.

Does the FWS need to prepare an EIS before issuing an incidental take statement? *See Ramsey v. Kantor*, 96 F.3d 434 (9th Cir. 1996) (finding issuance of an incidental take statement to constitute a major federal action under NEPA).

8.   Section 4(b)(6)(C) of the ESA generally requires the Secretary to designate critical habitat for a listed species at the same time that the final regulation listing the species is promulgated. If, however, the critical habitat of such species is "not then determinable," the Secretary may extend the period for designating critical habitat for "not more than one additional year." § 4(b)(6)(C)(ii). In *Forest Guardians v. Babbitt*, 164 F.3d 1261 (10th Cir. 1998), the plaintiffs challenged the Secretary's failure to meet the deadline for designating critical habitat for the silvery minnow. The case reached the Court of Appeals for more than three and one-half years after the deadline had passed. The Secretary admitted that he had failed to perform a non-discretionary duty, but claimed that he lacked adequate resources to designate the habitat because of a moratorium that had been imposed on listing actions by the Congress during 1995. After the moratorium was lifted, the Secretary faced a significant backlog of listing actions and inadequate resources to address the backlog quickly. Accordingly, he published a rule establishing priorities among the listing actions that were pending. This "Final Listing Priority Guidance" established three tiers of actions and relegated all critical habitat designations to the third tier on the theory that such designations afforded only limited additional protection to listed species. *Id.* at 1266. Nonetheless, the Court of Appeals held that the Secretary's "inadequate resources defense" did not excuse his failure to meet the statutory deadline for designating critical habitat for the silvery minnow. Accordingly, the court remanded the case to the district court with instructions to order the Secretary to designate critical habitat as soon as possible without regard for the Secretary's "preferred priorities." How should courts address legitimate agency resource problems? Assuming that the time and resources needed to address critical habitat designations will make it more difficult for the Secretary to make timely listing decisions is this an appropriate trade-off? Who is in the best position to make this choice—the Congress? The courts? The plaintiffs?

9.   The FWS's listing program continues to receive criticism. *See, e.g.,* U.S. GENERAL ACCOUNTING OFFICE, ENDANGERED SPECIES: FACTORS ASSOCIATED WITH DELAYED LISTING DECISIONS (Aug. 1993).

In a review of all species listed between 1985 and 1991, the Environmental Defense Fund determined that the median population size at the time of listing was 1,075 individuals for vertebrate animals, 999 for invertebrates, and fewer than 120 for plants. David Wilcove et al., *What Exactly Is an Endangered Species?,* 7 CONSERVATION BIOLOGY 87 (1993). These researchers conclude that the FWS has difficulty meeting the ESA recovery goal because it is not protecting imperiled species soon enough. *Id.* at 92. The prospects for improvement are bleak. The Department of the Interior estimates that the FWS will require $4.6 billion to achieve the recovery goal for domestic listed species. U.S. DEPARTMENT OF THE INTERIOR, OFFICE OF INSPECTOR GENERAL, Rep. No. 90-98, AUDIT REPORT: THE ENDANGERED SPECIES PROGRAM 11 (Sept. 1990). In addition, there are over 3,000 candidate species awaiting further study to determine whether they ought to be proposed for listing. Annual appropriations for the FWS have averaged about $10 million over the past several years. It is extremely unlikely that Congress will appropriate the money necessary to list all qualified species and recover them. How does the ESA set priorities on listing and recovery? *See* §§ 4(b)(3)(C)(iii), 4(b)(7), 4(f)(1)(A), 4(h)(3), 4(h)(4). How should it?

DEFENDERS OF WILDLIFE V. ANDRUS
428 F. Supp. 167 (D.D.C. 1977)

GESELL, District Judge.

Plaintiff claims that regulations of the Department of the Interior governing the hours during which sport hunting of migratory game birds may occur violate a number of treaties, the Migratory Bird Treaty Act, 16 U.S.C. § 704, the Endangered Species Act of 1973, 16 U.S.C. §§ 1531, *et seq.*, and the Administrative Procedure Act, 5 U.S.C. § 706. The parties have filed cross-motions for summary judgment and the issues have been briefed and argued.

Pursuant to the Migratory Bird Treaty Act, the Fish and Wildlife Service, acting for the Secretary of the Interior, annually issues regulations setting the conditions under which certain migratory birds may be hunted. Among the conditions imposed are the hours during the day when game shooting is permitted. For some years now the Service has permitted shooting from one-half hour before sunrise until sunset. *See* 50 C.F.R. 20, as amended. It permitted game shooting of certain species during these hours for the 1976-77 hunting season, and it is this decision that is under immediate attack here.

Under the Migratory Bird Treaty Act the Secretary must implement the migratory bird treaties and has determined that his regulations should "limit the taking of protected species where there is a reasonable possibility of hunter identification error between game and protected species." 41 Fed. Reg. 9177 (1973). In addition, the Endangered Species Act of 1973 prohibits the hunting of endangered species, 16 U.S.C. § 1538(a)(1)(B), and requires the Secretary of the Interior to act to ensure the conservation of protected species.

Shooting of endangered species during the hunting hours is prohibited. Plaintiff contends, however, that the shooting hour regulations violate the Secretary's duties under the above acts, submitting numerous well-prepared affidavits indicating that because visibility is low one-half hour before sunrise and one-half hour before sunset, protected species cannot be readily distinguished from game species. Thus they assert that regulations which allow shooting at these times do not protect threatened and endangered species as required by law. The defendants have countered with some affidavits indicating that visibility during the contested hours is not so impaired that misidentification is likely to occur and that, in any case, such hours are required to provide adequate opportunities for game hunters.

This action challenges an administrative decision made under the notice and comment provisions of the Administrative Procedure Act, 5 U.S.C. § 553. The scope of review is set by that Act, 5 U.S.C. § 706, and it is therefore necessary to examine the record of the agency proceedings on which the challenged regulation is based. In so doing it appears that when proposed regulations were published permitting shooting from one-half hour before sunrise until sunset, 41 Fed. Reg. 9177-82 (1973), plaintiff and other organizations and individuals protested, raising the issue of hunter misidentification of protected species. Neither plaintiff nor defendants presented any data which would indicate how many misidentifications occur during the contested hours compared with those that occur during full daylight. The administrative record contained no studies of the effects on protected species of early morning and late afternoon shooting, nor studies on the amount of light necessary to make the identifications needed to distinguish between species. The administrative record is virtually barren of any information regarding the impact of the contested shooting hours on birds that should not be taken.

The Fish and Wildlife Service contends that it was not required to carry out any such studies or to create a more complete administrative record. Its position is that the Endangered Species Act only requires that the regulations "do not jeopardize the continued existence of these (protected) species." Based on evidence that the most important factor affecting the population of a given species is the quality of its habitat, the Service concluded that it was unlikely that a minor alteration in shooting hours would jeopardize a species.

The Service has misinterpreted the Endangered Species Act of 1973. The Act requires that

> whenever any species is listed as a threatened species pursuant to subsection (c) of this section, the Secretary shall issue such regulations as he deems necessary and advisable to provide for the conservation of such species. 16 U.S.C. § 1533(d).

It also provides that:

> The Secretary shall review other programs administered by him and utilize such programs in furtherance of the purposes of this chapter. 16 U.S.C. § 1536.

A major purpose of the Act is the "conservation" of endangered and threatened species, 16 U.S.C. § 1531, and "conservation" is strictly defined as:

. . . the use of all methods and procedures which are necessary to bring any endangered species or threatened species to the point at which the measures provided pursuant to this chapter are no longer necessary. 16 U.S.C. § 1532.

It is clear from the face of the statute that the Fish and Wildlife Service, as part of Interior, must do far more than merely avoid the elimination of protected species. It must bring these species back from the brink so that they may be removed from the protected class, and it must use all methods necessary to do so. The Service cannot limit its focus to what it considers the most important management tool available to it, *i.e.*, habitat control, to accomplish this end.

It is also clear from the legislative history that Congress considered hunting regulations among the more important weapons in the fight to save vanishing species of wildlife since the Senate Report on the legislation contained the explicit finding that: "The two major causes of extinction are hunting and destruction of the natural habitat." S. Rep. No. 93-307, 93d Cong., 1st Sess. 2 (1973), U.S. Code Cong. & Admin. News 1973, pp. 2989, 2990.

Under the Endangered Species Act of 1973, the agency has an affirmative duty to increase the population of protected species. The regulations permitting twilight shooting of game birds undoubtedly occasions some killing of protected species. The rulemaking proceedings did not concern themselves with the amount, extent or nature of such killing and, especially since plaintiff by its affidavits presents a substantial argument that the destruction of protected species may be considerable, it is apparent that the rulemaking process was not adequately focused upon the obligation of the Fish and Wildlife Service to conserve and increase the population of these species. In this sense, then, the regulations must be said to be arbitrary.

At this stage, however, this question is somewhat academic. The 1976-77 hunting season is over and the agency has now commenced processing comparable proposed regulations for the coming hunting season. The Fish and Wildlife Service recently has indicated, in papers filed with the Court, that some useful computerized data may exist which will more precisely indicate the impact of twilight shooting upon the populations of protected species. In the course of the present regulatory proceeding this and other relevant data must be made forthcoming and subjected to critical analysis. This is not to say that twilight shooting must be prohibited if protected species are subject to any killing by inadvertent action of hunters or otherwise. But there must be evidence in the record that hunting hours under the new regulations are so fixed that such killing is kept to the minimum consistent with other obligations imposed on the Service by Congress. In short, the development of the regulations should more sharply focus on the problem of twilight shooting, and plaintiff's objections must be carefully considered and weighed on the record.

Accordingly, declaratory judgment is issued on behalf of plaintiff to the effect that the regulations for the 1976-77 hunting season were arbitrary and unlawful and defendant is directed to proceed with the current rulemaking proceedings in accordance with its statutory obligations as set forth above. A Declaration and Order are filed herewith.

NOTES

1.   Suppose Defenders of Wildlife had not participated in the administrative process and thus had not commented on the proposed rule. Would it still be able to challenge the final regulation in court?

2.   Section 7(a)(1) of the ESA has received far less attention than the consultation requirement of ESA § 7(a)(2), but an agency's duty to "conserve" listed species remains a powerful source of authority. Although courts consistently hold that the duty to conserve is affirmative, they seldom set out precisely what it requires or rely on it as the sole basis for overturning an agency's decision. *See, e.g., Pyramid Lake Paiute Tribe of Indians v. U.S. Department of the Navy*, 898 F.2d 1410, 1416-17 (9th Cir. 1990); *Carson-Truckee Water Conservancy Dist. v. Clark*, 741 F.2d 257, 261 (9th Cir. 1984), *cert. denied*, 470 U.S. 1083 (1985); *Connor v. Andrus*, 453 F. Supp. 1037, 1041 (W.D. Tex. 1978). The duty falls equally on all agencies, and is not the special province of the Department of the Interior. *Pyramid Lake Paiute Tribe of Indians*, 898 F.2d at 1416 n.15. Professor J.B. Ruhl notes that § 7(a)(1) may be used as a shield by an agency or as a sword by an agency's critic. J.B. Ruhl, *Section 7(a)(1) of the "New" Endangered Species Act: Rediscovering and Redefining the Untapped Power of Federal Agencies' Duty to Conserve Species*, 25 ENVTL. L. 1107, 1129-35 (1995).

As a shield, § 7(a)(1) can be used by an agency to defend a decision that advances the recovery of a listed species. In *Carson-Truckee Water Conservancy Dist. v. Clark, supra*, the court upheld the Interior Department's decision to refuse to sell water from a federal reservoir to Nevada cities. The Interior Department believed the water should be allowed to flow farther downstream to help replenish listed fish species. Although the statute governing allocation of reservoir water was silent on the issue of species conservation, the court found that § 7(a)(1) supplemented the agency's mission. This use of § 7(a)(1) is analogous to the way NEPA supplements agencies' authorities to consider environmental concerns, generally, before making decisions.

As a sword, § 7(a)(1) cannot compel an agency to protect species under all circumstances, but, "if an alternative to the challenged action would be equally as effective at serving the government's interest, and at the same time would enhance conservation to an equal or greater degree than does the challenged action, then the agency must adopt the alternative." *Pyramid Lake Paiute Tribe of Indians v. U.S. Department of the Navy, supra* at 1417. The § 7(a)(1) sword does not, however, go so far as to override an agency's statutory limitations. *Platte River Whooping Crane Trust v. Federal Energy Regulatory Commission*, 962 F.2d 27, 34 (D.C. Cir. 1992), *reh'g denied*, 972 F.2d 1362 (D.C. Cir. 1992) (FERC may not take a conservation action if it would violate the Federal Power Act by altering a license without the mutual consent of the licensee). Still, the duty is affirmative and "imposes substantial and continuing obligations." *Defenders of Wildlife v. Administrator, E.P.A.*, 882 F.2d 1294, 1299 (8th Cir. 1989). Recently, the Fifth Circuit Court of Appeals upheld a district court order based on ESA § 7(a)(1) requiring the U.S. Dept. of Agriculture to consult with the FWS to develop an organized program for using the department's authorities for the conservation of listed species threatened by certain agricultural and water management practices above Texas' Edwards Aquifer. *Sierra Club v. Glickman*, 156 F.3d 606 (5th Cir. 1998). In the strongest judicial interpretation of ESA § 7(a)(1) to date, the court rejected the conventional view of the conversation duty:

At first blush, this section appears to suggest that federal agencies have only a generalized duty to confer and develop programs for the benefit of endangered and threatened species—*i.e.*, not with respect to any particular species. * * * When read in the context of the ESA as a whole, however, we find that the agencies' duties under § 7(a)(1) are much more specific and particular.

Id. at 615.

3.   In *Connor v. Andrus*, 453 F. Supp. 1037 (W.D. Tex. 1978), the court found arbitrary and capricious a portion of the annual FWS migratory waterfowl hunting season framework regulations, which set out season lengths, shooting hours, and bag and possession limits. The portion of the regulations found illegal by the court prohibited hunting in designated areas of Arizona, New Mexico, and Texas. The FWS had justified its closing these areas on its § 7(a)(1) conservation duty to protect the endangered Mexican duck, but the court failed to find a rational relation between the area closures and the recovery of listed species. The court observed that the administrative record showed that hunting presented no threat to the endangered species. Is the burden on an agency to show that a proposed action is justified by the ESA conservation duty the same as the burden to show that a proposed action does not violate the conservation duty?

C. The National Historic Preservation Act

Although it receives much less attention than either NEPA or the ESA, the National Historic Preservation Act (NHPA) of 1966, 16 U.S.C. §§ 470 *et seq.,* establishes important, NEPA-like procedures for protecting historic properties. The Act establishes a National Register of Historic Places maintained by the Secretary of the Interior. 16 U.S.C. § 470a(a)(1)(A). The Register includes both listed properties and (some, but not all) properties eligible for listing. *Id.* at § 470a(a)(2). Eligible properties are those that meet the detailed listing criteria established at 36 C.F.R. § 60.4. *See also,* 36 C.F.R. § 800.2(e). Properties may be nominated for inclusion in the Register either by a state which has an approved State Historic Preservation Program, or by any other person or local government in states without an approved program. 16 U.S.C. § 470a(a)(3), (4). Nominations must be made on a standard form available from the National Park Service in the Department of the Interior. 36 C.F.R. § 60.5.

Under § 106 of the Act, "any Federal agency having direct or indirect jurisdiction over a proposed Federal or federally-assisted undertaking and * * * any Federal * * * agency having authority to license any undertaking shall * * * take into account the effect of the undertaking on any district, site, building, structure, or object that is included in or eligible for inclusion in the National Register." 16 U.S.C. § 470f. Once an agency determines that the threshold for an "undertaking" has been met, it must then establish the undertaking's "area of potential effect." *See* 36 C.F.R. § 800.2(c); 800.4(a). It then identifies and evaluates historic properties within the area of potential effect. "Historic property" is defined to include: "any prehistoric or historic district, site, building, structure, or object, included in, or eligible for inclusion in, the National Register." 36 C.F.R. § 800.2(e). The rules require the agency to make a "reasonable and good faith effort to identify historic properties that may be affected by the undertaking" in consultation with the State Historic Preservation Officer (SHPO). 36 C.F.R. § 800.4(b)

If the agency finds that the undertaking will have "no effect" on historic properties then it must notify the SHPO of its finding. 36 C.F.R. § 800.5(b). The SHPO has 15 days to object to this finding. *Id.* If it does not object, no further action need be taken. If the SHPO objects, or if the agency finds an effect on a historic property, then it must consult with the SHPO to determine whether the effect of the undertaking should be considered adverse. 36 C.F.R. § 800.5(c).

If the agency finds that the undertaking will have an effect but that the effect is not adverse, then it must obtain the concurrence of the SHPO and notify the Advisory Council on Historic Preservation (Council) of its finding. 36 C.F.R. § 800.5(d). This finding must be documented in accordance with the regulations at 36 C.F.R. § 800.8(a). The Council then has 30 days to object to the finding. If the Council does not object, or if the Council objects but proposes changes to the undertaking acceptable to the agency, no further action need be taken. 36 C.F.R. § 800.5(d)(2). If the Council objects, and acceptable changes cannot be found, then the effect must be considered adverse. *Id.*

Where an adverse effect on historic properties is found the agency must notify the Council and consult with the SHPO to seek ways to avoid or reduce the adverse effects. 36 C.F.R. § 800.5(e). A finding of adverse effect must be documented in accordance with 36 C.F.R. § 800.8(b). An undertaking is considered to have an adverse effect when the effect on the historic property may diminish the integrity of the property's location design, setting, materials, workmanship, feeling, or association. 36 C.F.R. § 800.9(b). If the agency and SHPO agree on how to address the adverse effects then they execute a Memorandum of Agreement. 36 C.F.R. § 800.5(e)(4). If the Council has participated in the negotiations it too may sign the Agreement. If not then it has 30 days to review the Agreement. Following review, the Council has three choices: (1) it can concur in the Agreement; (2) it can concur conditionally, subject to acceptable changes; or (3) it can decide to comment on the Agreement within 60 days. 36 C.F.R. § 800.5(a)(1). If the Council concurs or conditionally concurs and the Agreement is accepted, the agency must adhere to the Agreement.

Where no Agreement is submitted, the agency must ask the Council for comments within 60 days. 30 C.F.R. § 800.6(b)(1). In making this request, the agency must "provide the Council with sufficient information to make an independent review of the undertaking's effects on historic properties * * * ." 36 C.F.R. § 800.8(d). In this "the agency official shall consider the Council's comments in reaching a final decision," and "if possible" report that decision to the Council before initiating the undertaking. 36 C.F.R. § 800.6(c)(2).

Any person may ask the Council to consider an agency finding regarding the identification or evaluation of historic properties, or a finding that on undertaking would have "no effect." 36 C.F.R. § 800.6(e)(1). The agency "should" reconsider the finding in light of the Council's view but the Council's inquiry does not delay the undertaking. *Id.* at § 800.6(e)(2). Issues concerning the eligibility of properties for listing must be referred to the Secretary but the Secretary's responsibilities following referral are unclear. *Id.* at § 800.6(e)(3).

In addition to SHPO and the Council, the rules encourage the participation of other "consulting parties" in the process. These are defined to include permit applicants, local governments, Indian tribes, and interested members of the public. 36 C.F.R. § 800.1(c). Also, the SHPO may seek Secretarial approval of a process to substitute a State review process for Council review. 36 C.F.R. § 800.7. The State, however, must afford an opportunity to appeal its decisions to the Council. 36 C.F.R. § 800.7(a)(4)(iv).

PUEBLO OF SANDIA V. UNITED STATES
50 F.3d 856 (10th Cir. 1995)

SEYMOUR, Chief Judge.

The Pueblo of Sandia and various environmental groups brought suit for declaratory and injunctive relief against the United States and a National Forest Service supervisor, alleging that the Forest Service failed to comply with the National Historic Preservation Act (NHPA), 16 U.S.C. §§ 470 *et seq.,* in its evaluation of Las Huertas Canyon in the Cibola National Forest. The Pueblo asserts that the New Mexico canyon contains numerous sites of religious and cultural significance to the tribe, qualifying the canyon as a "traditional cultural property" eligible for inclusion in the National Register of Historic Places. The Forest Service, however, concluded that the canyon did not constitute a traditional cultural property and instituted a new management strategy for it. The district court granted summary judgment for the Forest Service, finding that it had made a reasonable and good faith effort to identify historic properties. Because we conclude that the Forest Service's efforts were neither reasonable nor in good faith, we reverse and remand.

I.

Las Huertas Canyon is located in the Sandia Mountains northeast of Albuquerque, New Mexico. Lying within the Cibola National Forest, the canyon is under the supervision of the Forest Service. The Sandia Pueblo reservation is nearby, and tribal members visit the canyon to gather evergreen boughs for use in significant private and public cultural ceremonies. They also harvest herbs and plants along the Las Huertas Creek which are important for traditional healing practices. The canyon contains many shrines and ceremonial paths of religious and cultural significance to the Pueblo.

In July 1988, the Forest Service released a Draft Environmental Impact Statement (DEIS) detailing eight alternative management strategies for Las Huertas Canyon. After an extended comment period, the Forest Service selected a ninth alternative, Alternative I, as the preferred strategy. Alternative I required the realignment and reconstruction of the Las Huertas Canyon Road and additional improvements to the area, including the rehabilitation and expansion of several picnic grounds and the installation of sanitary facilities at other locations.

Voicing concerns that the strategy would adversely impact traditional cultural properties and practices in the canyon by encouraging additional traffic and visitation to the area, the Pueblo filed an administrative appeal of the decision. The Deputy Regional Forester affirmed the decision, altering the snow plowing and road closure provisions of Alternative I in response to complaints from other appellants. The decision became administratively final in January 1990 when the Chief of the Forest Service declined to review it.

The Pueblo filed this suit in federal court, alleging numerous statutory violations. The Pueblo subsequently amended the complaint to plead a violation of the NHPA. The Pueblo alleged that the Forest Service failed to comply with section 106 of the NHPA when it refused to evaluate the canyon as a traditional cultural property eligible for inclusion on the National Register.

The parties filed cross motions for summary judgment on the issue of NHPA compliance. By the time the district court heard the motions, the State Historic Preservation Officer (SHPO) had concurred in the Forest Service's conclusion that certain specific sites near the roadway and picnic grounds were not eligible for the National Register. In a Memorandum Opinion and Order entered April 30, 1993, the district court noted that "[t]he administrative record is silent as to whether any of the sites found were evaluated [by the Forest Service] against the National Register Criteria as required by [the NHPA], and whether the sites met the criteria." The court accepted the SHPO's concurrence as "evidence that the Forest Service met the substantive requirements with respect to the roadway and the picnic area."

Although concerned that the Forest Service "does not appear to have taken the requirements of [the NHPA] very seriously," the court relied on the agency's assertion that it would diligently pursue information on the potential historic value of other individual sites within the canyon. On that basis, the court granted summary judgment for defendants, and plaintiffs filed this appeal.

On May 13, 1993, the SHPO concurred in the Forest Service's final conclusion that "there is no evidence that there are Pueblo Indian traditional cultural properties in Las Huertas Canyon." Plaintiffs filed this appeal on June 19, 1993. Significantly, nine months later the SHPO withdrew his concurrence upon receiving evidence suggesting that traditional cultural properties existed in Las Huertas Canyon. The SHPO stated:

> We were surprised to see the [affidavits of Dr. Elizabeth Brandt and Phillip Lauriano] since we had been informed that the Cibola National Forest had received no comments on [Traditional Cultural Properties] from the [All Indian Pueblo Council] or from any pueblos. Our previous consultations on this undertaking were based on Dr. Tainter's report. This documentation is relevant to our consultations on this undertaking. I am concerned that our not having received the affidavits has affected our ability to consult appropriately under Section 106 of the National Historic Preservation Act.

Id. The SHPO concluded that the withheld information had a substantial impact on the inquiry into the canyon's eligibility for the Historic Register. * * * Consequently, the SHPO recommended an ethnographic analysis of the canyon to further evaluate the possibility that it contained traditional cultural properties. * * *

We review the district court's summary judgment de novo. *Housing Authority v. United States,* 980 F.2d 624, 628 (10th Cir.1992).

II.

The NHPA requires the Forest Service to "take into account the effect of [any] undertaking on any district, site, building, structure, or object that is included in or eligible for inclusion in the National Register." NHPA, § 106, 16 U.S.C. § 470f (1993). Section 106 also mandates that the agency afford the Advisory Council on Historic Preservation "a reasonable opportunity to comment" on the undertaking. *Id.*

The Advisory Council has established regulations for federal agencies to follow in complying with section 106. *See* 36 C.F.R. § 800. The process is designed to foster communication and consultation between agency officials, the SHPO, and other interested parties such as Indian tribes, local governments, and the general public.

First, the Agency Official must review all existing information on the site, request the SHPO's views on ways to identify historic properties, and seek information from interested parties likely to have knowledge about historic properties in the area. 36 C.F.R. § 800.4(a). In light of this information, the agency determines any need for further investigation.

In consultation with the SHPO, the agency then must make a "reasonable and good faith effort to identify historic properties that may be affected by the undertaking and gather sufficient information to evaluate the eligibility of these properties for the National Register." 36 C.F.R. § 800.4(b). Finally, for each property identified, the agency official and the SHPO must evaluate the property on the basis of the National Register criteria to determine its eligibility for inclusion. 36 C.F.R. § 800.4(c).

The Pueblo claims that the sites within the Las Huertas Canyon are traditional cultural properties which are thus eligible for inclusion in the National Register. The Pueblo asserts that the Forest Service's conclusion to the contrary stems from that agency's failure to make a "reasonable and good faith effort" to identify historical properties.

A. Reasonable Effort

The Forest Service contends that it engaged in reasonable efforts to identify historic properties in Las Huertas Canyon. The record reveals that the Forest Service did request information from the Sandia Pueblo and other local Indian tribes, but a mere request for information is not necessarily sufficient to constitute the "reasonable effort" section 106 requires. Because communications from the tribes indicated the existence of traditional cultural properties and because the Forest Service should have known that tribal customs might restrict the ready disclosure of specific information, we hold that the agency did not reasonably pursue the information necessary to evaluate the canyon's eligibility for inclusion in the National Register.

During the assessment phase of the section 106 process, the Forest Service mailed letters to local Indian tribes, including the Sandia Pueblo, and individual tribal members who were known to be familiar with traditional cultural properties. The letters requested detailed information describing the location of the sites, activities conducted there, and the frequency of the activities. They also asked tribes to provide maps of the sites, drawn at a scale of 1:24,000 or better, as well as documentation of the historic nature of the property.

In addition to mailing form letters to the tribes and individuals, Forest Service officials also addressed meetings of the All Indian Pueblo Council and the San Felipe Pueblo. The officials informed the groups that traditional cultural properties are eligible for inclusion in the National Register and requested the same specific information required in the letters.

None of the tribes or individuals provided the Forest Service with the type of information requested in the letters and meetings. We conclude, however, that the information the tribes did communicate to the agency was sufficient to require the Forest Service to engage in further investigations, especially in light of regulations warning that tribes might be hesitant to divulge the type of information sought.

Prior to its final determination on April 29, 1993 that Las Huertas Canyon contained no traditional cultural properties, the Forest Service was aware of numerous claims to the contrary. As early as January 5, 1987, the Governor of the Sandia Pueblo informed the Forest Service that the Las Huertas Canyon was an area "of great religious and traditional importance to the people of Sandia Pueblo." The minutes of a Las Huertas Canyon Work Group meeting on March 10, 1987 reveal that the group knew that Native Americans used the canyon area for a number of ceremonial, religious, and medicinal purposes. During the period of public comment on the eight alternatives, the Sandia Pueblo supported alternative C, which it believed would be most likely "to permit the Sandia members to perform secret, traditional activities in more seclusion."

On August 9, 1989, the Regional Forester took the affidavit of Philip Lauriano, an elder and religious leader of the Sandia Pueblo. Mr. Lauriano listed several "long-standing religious and traditional practices" which take place in the canyon and alluded to sacred sites which it contains. In 1992, Dr. Elizabeth Brandt, a highly qualified anthropologist who is an expert on the Sandia Pueblo, provided a detailed ethnographic overview of the tribe's religious and cultural connections to the canyon. Dr. Brandt noted the canyon's significance to the Pueblo as a source of herbs and evergreen boughs, which have been an integral part of certain Pueblo ceremonies for at least 60 years. She also described certain ceremonial paths and sites in the canyon which "serve as gateways for access to the spirit world," concluding that

> [t]hese sites and their functions would be significantly impaired if not totally destroyed as a result of the planned development of the Canyon, thus cutting off spiritual access for religious leaders and those responsible for the actions which occur at these shrines. These sites are critical to the religious practice, cultural identity, and overall well-being of the Pueblo.

Noting the secrecy which is crucial to Pueblo religious and cultural practices, Dr. Brandt expressed concern that the proposed development would allow the outside world to intrude upon and negatively impact these practices. Based on these factors, she concluded that "Las Huertas Canyon constitutes a Traditional Cultural District with multiple Sites for the Sandia Tribe."

Furthermore, the Forest Service received communications clearly indicating why more specific responses were not forthcoming. At the meeting with the San Felipe Pueblo, tribal members indicated that "[t]hey did not want to disclose any specific details of site locations or activities." A representative of the Sandia Pueblo made the same claim at the All Indian Pueblo Council meeting. Dr. Brandt also commented upon the Pueblo people's general unwillingness "to divulge any information regarding their religious practices."

This reticence to disclose details of their cultural and religious practices was not unexpected. National Register Bulletin 38 warns that "knowledge of traditional cultural values may not be shared readily with outsiders" as such information is "regarded as powerful, even dangerous" in some societies. * * *

Determining what constitutes a reasonable effort to identify traditional cultural properties "depends in part on the likelihood that such properties may be present." National Bulletin 38. Based on the information contained in the Lauriano and Brandt affidavits, the SHPO ultimately concluded that the "properties [ ] may be eligible to the National Register of Historic Places" but "we do not have enough information to make a determination of eligibility." We agree. The information communicated to the Forest Service as well as the reasons articulated for the lack of more specific information clearly suggest that there is a sufficient likelihood that the canyon contains traditional cultural properties to warrant further investigation. We thus hold that the Forest Service did not make a reasonable effort to identify historic properties.

B. Good Faith Effort

The Pueblo also claims that the Forest Service failed to make the requisite good faith effort to identify traditional cultural properties in Las Huertas Canyon. It bases this assertion on the fact that the Forest Service withheld relevant information from the SHPO during the required consultation process. The district court expressed concern about the Forest Service's commitment to the section 106 process and placed great weight upon the SHPO's concurrence in granting summary judgment. Thus, the withdrawal of that concurrence upon discovery of the withheld information suggests that the Forest Service did not put forth a good faith effort to identify historic properties.

The regulations require that "[i]n consultation with the [SHPO], the Agency Official shall make a reasonable and good faith effort to identify historic properties." 36 C.F.R. § 800.4(b). Indeed, consultation with the SHPO is an integral part of the section 106 process. *See Attakai v. United States,* 746 F. Supp. 1395, 1407 (D. Ariz. 1990) * * * . Affording the SHPO an opportunity to offer input on potential historic properties would be meaningless unless the SHPO has access to available, relevant information. Thus, "consultation" with SHPO mandates informed consultation. The Forest Service did not provide the SHPO copies of the Lauriano and Brandt affidavits until after the consultation was complete and the SHPO had concurred. In fact, the Forest Service informed the SHPO during consultation that "[c]onsultations with pueblo officials and elders, and other users of the Las Huertas Canyon area, disclosed no evidence that the . . . area contains traditional cultural properties." The SHPO's initial concurrence was based on this report. Once the SHPO acquired access to the withheld information, he withdrew his concurrence, noting the relevance of the documents and his concern that "our not having received [them] has affected our ability to consult appropriately under Section 106 of the [NHPA]."

* * *

Because we conclude that the Forest Service did not make a reasonable and good faith effort in its evaluation of Las Huertas Canyon, we REVERSE the judgment of the district court and REMAND for further proceedings in accordance with this opinion.

NOTES

1.   Is the National Historic Preservation Act a substantive statute, more like the ESA, or is it "essentially procedural," like NEPA?

2.   If the Forest Service finds that the proposed undertaking will adversely affect cultural properties eligible for listing in the National Register, what must it do? Is either the SHPO or the Council in a position to prevent an agency from commencing an undertaking that may adversely affect historic properties?

3.   Suppose the Forest Service signs an Agreement with a SHPO describing how it plans to avoid and reduce adverse effects of an action. If the Forest Service later fails to comply with the Agreement who would have standing to sue to force compliance? Can a court compel an agency to comply with a NHPA Agreement?

5 SUBSTANTIVE EFFECTS ON DECISIONMAKING

STRYCKER'S BAY NEIGHBORHOOD COUNCIL, INC. V. KARLEN
444 U.S. 223 (1980)

PER CURIAM

The protracted nature of this litigation is perhaps best illustrated by the identity of the original federal defendant, "George Romney, Secretary of the Department of Housing and Urban Development." At the center of this dispute is the site of a proposed low-income housing project to be constructed on Manhattan's Upper West Side. In 1962, the New York City Planning Commission (Commission), acting in conjunction with the United States Department of Housing and Urban Development (HUD), began formulating a plan for the renewal of 20 square blocks known as the "West Side Urban Renewal Area" (WSURA) through a joint effort on the part of private parties and various government agencies. As originally written, the plan called for a mix of 70% middle-income housing and 30% low-income housing and designated the site at issue here as the location of one of the middle-income projects. In 1969, after substantial progress toward completion of the plan, local agencies in New York determined that the number of low-income units proposed for WSURA would be insufficient to satisfy an increased need for such units. In response to this shortage the Commission amended the plan to designate the site as the future location of a high-rise building containing 160 units of low-income housing. HUD approved this amendment in December 1972.

Meanwhile, in October 1971, the Trinity Episcopal School Corp. (Trinity), which had participated in the plan by building a combination school and middle-income housing development at a nearby location, sued in the United States District Court for the Southern District of New York to enjoin the Commission and HUD from constructing low-income housing on the site. The present respondents, Roland N. Karlen, Alvin C. Hudgins, and the Committee of Neighbors To Insure a Normal Urban Environment (CONTINUE), intervened as plaintiffs, while petitioner Strycker's Bay Neighborhood Council, Inc., intervened as a defendant.

The District Court entered judgment in favor of petitioners. It concluded, *inter alia*, that petitioners had not violated the National Environmental Policy Act of 1969 (NEPA), 42 U.S.C. § 4321 *et seq.*

On respondents' appeal, the Second Circuit affirmed all but the District Court's treatment of the NEPA claim. While the Court of Appeals agreed with the District Court that HUD was not required to prepare a full-scale environmental impact statement under § 102(2)(C) of NEPA, 42 U.S.C. § 4332(2)(C), it held that HUD had not complied with § 102(2)(E), which requires an agency to "study, develop, and describe appropriate alternatives to recommended courses of action in any proposal which involves unresolved conflicts concerning alternative uses of available resources." 42 U.S.C. § 4332(2)(E). According to the Court of Appeals, any consideration by HUD of alternatives to placing low-income housing on the site "was either highly limited or nonexistent." Citing the "background of urban environmental factors" behind HUD's decision, the Court of Appeals remanded the case, requiring HUD to prepare a "statement of possible alternatives, the consequences thereof and the facts and reasons for and against. . . ." The statement was not to reflect "HUD's concept or the Housing Authority's views as to how these agencies would choose to resolve the city's low income group housing situation," but rather was to explain "how within the framework of the Plan its objective of economic integration can best be achieved with a minimum of adverse environmental impact." The Court of Appeals believed that, given such an assessment of alternatives, "the agencies with the cooperation of the interested parties should be able to arrive at an equitable solution."

On remand, HUD prepared a lengthy report entitled Special Environmental Clearance (1977). After marshaling the data, the report asserted that, "while the choice of Site 30 for development as a 100 percent low-income project has raised valid questions about the potential social environmental impacts involved, the problems associated with the impact on social fabric and community structures are not considered so serious as to require that this component be rated as unacceptable." The last portion of the report incorporated a study wherein the Commission evaluated nine alternative locations for the project and found none of them acceptable. While HUD's report conceded that this study may not have considered all possible alternatives, it credited the Commission's conclusion that any relocation of the units would entail an unacceptable delay of two years or more. According to HUD, "[m]easured against the environmental costs associated with the minimum two-year delay, the benefits seem insufficient to justify a mandated substitution of sites."

After soliciting the parties' comments on HUD's report, the District Court again entered judgment in favor of petitioners. * * *

On appeal, the Second Circuit vacated and remanded again. The appellate court focused upon that part of HUD's report where the agency considered and rejected alternative sites, and in particular upon HUD's reliance on the delay such a relocation would entail. The Court of Appeals purported to recognize that its role in reviewing HUD's decision was defined by the Administrative Procedure Act (APA), 5 U.S.C. § 706(2)(A), which provides that agency actions should be set aside if found to be "arbitrary, capricious, an abuse of discretion, or otherwise not in accordance with law . . .." Additionally, however, the Court of Appeals looked to "[t]he provisions of NEPA" for "the substantive standards necessary to review the merits of agency decisions . . .." The Court of Appeals conceded that HUD had "given 'consideration' to alternatives" to redesignating the site. Nevertheless, the court believed that "'consideration' is not an end in itself." Concentrating on HUD's finding that development of an alternative location would entail an unacceptable delay, the appellate court held that such delay could not be "an overriding factor" in HUD's decision to proceed with the development. According to the court, when HUD considers such projects, "environmental factors, such as crowding low-income housing into a concentrated area, should be given determinative weight." The Court of Appeals therefore remanded the case to the District Court, instructing HUD to attack the shortage of low-income housing in a manner that would avoid the "concentration" of such housing on Site 30.

In *Vermont Yankee Nuclear Power Corp. v. NRDC*, 435 U.S. 519, 558 (1978), we stated that NEPA, while establishing "significant substantive goals for the Nation," imposes upon agencies duties that are "essentially procedural." As we stressed in that case, NEPA was designed "to insure a fully informed and well-considered decision," but not necessarily "a decision the judges of the Court of Appeals or of this Court would have reached had they been members of the decisionmaking unit of the agency." *Ibid.* *Vermont Yankee* cuts sharply against the Court of Appeals' conclusion that an agency, in selecting a course of action, must elevate environmental concerns over other appropriate considerations. On the contrary, once an agency has made a decision subject to NEPA's procedural requirements, the only role for a court is to insure that the agency has considered the environmental consequences; it cannot "'interject itself within the area of discretion of the executive as to the choice of the action to be taken.'" *Kleppe v. Sierra Club*, 427 U.S. 390, 410, n.21 (1976).[2]

In the present litigation there is no doubt that HUD considered the environmental consequences of its decision to redesignate the proposed site for low-income housing. NEPA requires no more. The petitions for certiorari are granted, and the judgment of the Court of Appeals is therefore

Reversed.

Mr. Justice MARSHALL, dissenting.

The issue raised by these cases is far more difficult than the *per curiam* opinion suggests.
* * *

Vermont Yankee does not stand for the broad proposition that the majority advances today. The relevant passage in that opinion was meant to be only a "further observation of some relevance to this case," *id.* at 557. That "observation" was a response to this Court's perception that the Court of Appeals in that case was attempting "under the guise of judicial review of agency action" to assert its own policy judgment as to the desirability of developing nuclear energy as an energy source for this Nation, a judgment which is properly left to Congress. *Id.* at 558. The Court of Appeals had remanded the case to the agency because of "a single alleged oversight on a peripheral issue, urged by parties who never fully cooperated or indeed raised the issue below." It was in this context that the Court remarked that "NEPA does set forth significant substantive goals for the Nation, but its mandate to the agencies is *essentially* procedural" (emphasis supplied). Accordingly, "[a]dministrative decisions should be set aside in this context, *as in every other*, only for substantial procedural *or substantive* reasons as mandated by statute," *ibid.* (emphasis supplied). Thus *Vermont Yankee* does not stand for the proposition that a court reviewing agency action under NEPA is limited solely to the factual issue of whether the agency "considered" environmental consequences. The agency's decision must still be set aside if it is "arbitrary, capricious, an abuse of discretion, or otherwise not in accordance with law," 5 U.S.C. § 706(2)(A), and the reviewing court must still insure that the agency "has taken a 'hard look' at environmental consequences," *Kleppe v. Sierra Club*, 427 U.S. 390, 410, n.21 (1976).

In the present case, the Court of Appeals did not "substitute its judgment for that of the agency as to the environmental consequences of its actions," for HUD in its Special Environmental Clearance Report acknowledged the adverse environmental consequences of its proposed action: "the choice of Site 30 for development as a 100 percent low-income project has raised valid questions about the potential social environmental impacts involved." * * * The sole reason for rejecting the environmentally superior site was the fact that if the location were shifted to Site 9, there would be a projected delay of two years in the construction of the housing.

The issue before the Court of Appeals, therefore, was whether HUD was free under NEPA to reject an alternative acknowledged to be environmentally preferable solely on the ground that any change in sites would cause delay. This was hardly a "peripheral issue" in the case. Whether

---

[2]   If we could agree with the dissent that the Court of Appeals held that HUD had acted "arbitrarily" in redesignating the site for low-income housing, we might also agree that plenary review is warranted. But the District Court expressly concluded that HUD had not acted arbitrarily or capriciously and our reading of the opinion of the Court of Appeals satisfies us that it did not overturn that finding. Instead, the appellate court required HUD to elevate environmental concerns over other, admittedly legitimate, considerations. Neither NEPA nor the APA provides any support for such a reordering of priorities by a reviewing court.

NEPA, which sets forth "significant substantive goals," *Vermont Yankee Nuclear Power Corp. v. NRDC, supra*, 435 U.S. at 558, permits a projected two-year time difference to be controlling over environmental superiority is by no means clear. Resolution of the issue, however, is certainly within the normal scope of review of agency action to determine if it is arbitrary, capricious, or an abuse of discretion.[1] The question whether HUD can make delay the paramount concern over environmental superiority is essentially a restatement of the question whether HUD in considering the environmental consequences of its proposed action gave those consequences a "hard look," which is exactly the proper question for the reviewing court to ask. *Kleppe v. Sierra Club, supra*, 427 U.S. at 410, n.21.

The issue of whether the Secretary's decision was arbitrary or capricious is sufficiently difficult and important to merit plenary consideration in this Court. Further, I do not subscribe to the Court's apparent suggestion that *Vermont Yankee* limits the reviewing court to the essentially mindless task of determining whether an agency "considered" environmental factors even if that agency may have effectively decided to ignore those factors in reaching its conclusion. Indeed, I cannot believe that the Court would adhere to that position in a different factual setting. Our cases establish that the arbitrary-or-capricious standard prescribes a "searching and careful" judicial inquiry designed to ensure that the agency has not exercised its discretion in an unreasonable manner. *Citizens To Preserve Overton Park, Inc. v. Volpe*, 401 U.S. 402, 416 (1971). Believing that today's summary reversal represents a departure from that principle, I respectfully dissent.

It is apparent to me that this is not the type of case for a summary disposition. We should at least have a plenary hearing.

NOTES

1. Was NEPA intended to provide a vehicle for contesting the construction of low income housing in urban areas? *See* 40 C.F.R. § 1508.14 (1992).

2. What was the error committed by the Court of Appeals in its second remand decision? How might that court have recast its analysis to avoid this error?

3. How does NEPA, as construed by the Court in *Strycker's Bay*, constrain the substantive decisions of administrative agencies? In this regard, consider the Court's concession in note 2 of the per curiam opinion.

4. In his dissent, Justice Marshall notes that the "[t]he sole reason for rejecting the environmentally preferable site was the fact that if the location were shifted to Site 9, there would be a projected delay of two years in the construction of the housing." Had HUD complied with NEPA at the outset, what is the likelihood that HUD would have faced the same delay in choosing Site 9? Does *Stryker's Bay* allow an agency to claim its own failure to comply with NEPA as the sole excuse for rejecting the environmentally preferable alternative?

---

[1] The Secretary concedes that if an agency gave little or no weight to environmental values its decision might be arbitrary or capricious.

5. *Strycker's Bay* involved a dispute over alternatives to a proposed agency action. NEPA requires an agency to describe alternatives under both § 102(2)(C) and § 102(2)(E). Are these two provisions redundant?

6. As you will soon see, *Strycker's Bay* is but one of the Supreme Court's many decisions rejecting what it apparently views as over-extensions of NEPA by the lower courts. Another one, also involving elements of substantive judicial review, follows.

BALTIMORE GAS & ELECTRIC CO. V. NATURAL RESOURCES DEFENSE COUNCIL, INC.
462 U.S. 87 (1983)

Justice O'CONNOR delivered the opinion of the Court.

Section 102(2)(C) of the National Environmental Policy Act, 42 U.S.C. § 4332(2)(C) (NEPA), requires federal agencies to consider the environmental impact of any major federal action. As part of its generic rulemaking proceedings to evaluate the environmental effects of the nuclear fuel cycle for nuclear power plants, the Nuclear Regulatory Commission (Commission) decided that licensing boards should assume, for purposes of NEPA, that the permanent storage of certain nuclear wastes would have no significant environmental impact and thus should not affect the decision whether to license a particular nuclear power plant. We conclude that the Commission complied with NEPA and that its decision is not arbitrary or capricious within the meaning of § 10(e) of the Administrative Procedure Act (APA), 5 U.S.C. § 706.

I

The environmental impact of operating a light-water nuclear power plant[4] includes the effects of offsite activities necessary to provide fuel for the plant ("front end" activities), and of offsite activities necessary to dispose of the highly toxic and long-lived nuclear wastes generated by the plant ("back end" activities). The dispute in these cases concerns the Commission's adoption of a series of generic rules to evaluate the environmental effects of a nuclear power plant's fuel cycle. At the heart of each rule is Table S-3, a numerical compilation of the estimated resources used and effluents released by fuel cycle activities supporting a year's operation of a typical light-water reactor.[5] The three versions of Table S-3 contained similar numerical values, although the supporting documentation has been amplified during the course of the proceedings.

---

[4]   A light-water nuclear power plant is one that uses ordinary water (H_2O), as opposed to heavy water (D_2O), to remove the heat generated in the nuclear core. *See* D. Considine & G. Considine, Van Nostrand's Scientific Encyclopedia 1998, 2008 (6th ed. 1983). The bulk of the reactors in the United States are light-water nuclear reactors. U.S. Nuclear Regulatory Commission, 1980 Annual Report App. 6.

[5]   For example, the tabulated impacts include the acres of land committed to fuel cycle activities, the amount of water discharged by such activities, fossil fuel consumption, and chemical and radiological effluents (measured in curies), all normalized to the annual fuel requirement for a model 1000 megawatt light-water reactor.

The Commission first adopted Table S-3 in 1974, after extensive informal rulemaking proceedings. 39 Fed. Reg. 14188 *et seq.* (1974). This "original" rule, as it later came to be described, declared that in environmental reports and impact statements for individual licensing proceedings the environmental costs of the fuel cycle "shall be as set forth" in Table S-3 and that "[n]o further discussion of such environmental effects shall be required." *Id.* at 14191. The original Table S-3 contained no numerical entry for the long-term environmental effects of storing solidified transuranic and high-level wastes,[7] because the Commission staff believed that technology would be developed to isolate the wastes from the environment. The Commission and the parties have later termed this assumption of complete repository integrity as the "zero-release" assumption: the reasonableness of this assumption is at the core of the present controversy.

The Natural Resources Defense Council (NRDC), a respondent in the present cases, challenged the original rule and a license issued under the rule to the Vermont Yankee Nuclear Power Plant. The Court of Appeals for the District of Columbia Circuit affirmed Table S-3's treatment of the "front end" of the fuel cycle, but vacated and remanded the portion of the rule relating to the back end because of perceived inadequacies in the rulemaking procedures. *Natural Resources Defense Council, Inc. v. NRC*, 547 F.2d 633 (1976). Judge Tamm disagreed that the procedures were inadequate, but concurred on the ground that the record on waste storage was inadequate to support the zero-release assumption. *Id.* at 658.

In *Vermont Yankee Nuclear Power Corp. v. NRDC*, 435 U.S. 519 (1978), this Court unanimously reversed the Court of Appeals' decision that the Commission had used inadequate procedures, finding that the Commission had done all that was required by NEPA and the APA and determining that courts generally lack the authority to impose "hybrid" procedures greater than those contemplated by the governing statutes. We remanded for review of whether the original rule was adequately supported by the administrative record, specifically stating that the court was free to agree or disagree with Judge Tamm's conclusion that the rule pertaining to the back end of the fuel cycle was arbitrary and capricious within the meaning of § 10(e) of the APA, 5 U.S.C. § 706. *Id.* at 536, n.14.

While *Vermont Yankee* was pending in this Court, the Commission proposed a new "interim" rulemaking proceeding to determine whether to adopt a revised Table S-3. The proposal explicitly acknowledged that the risks from long-term repository failure were uncertain, but suggested that research should resolve most of those uncertainties in the near future. 41 Fed. Reg. 45849, 45850-45851 (1976). After further proceedings, the Commission promulgated the interim rule in March 1977. Table S-3 now explicitly stated that solidified high-level and transuranic wastes would remain buried in a federal repository and therefore would have no effect on the environment. Like its predecessor, the interim rule stated that "[n]o further discussion of such environmental effects shall be required." The NRDC petitioned for review of the interim rule, challenging the zero-release assumption and faulting the Table S-3 rule for failing to consider the health, cumulative, and socioeconomic effects of the fuel cycle activities. The Court of Appeals stayed proceedings while awaiting this Court's decision in *Vermont Yankee*. In April 1978, the Commission amended the interim rule to clarify that health effects were not covered by Table S-3 and could be litigated in individual licensing proceedings. 43 Fed. Reg. 15613 *et seq.* (1978).

---

[7]   High-level wastes, which are highly radioactive, are produced in liquid form when spent fuel is reprocessed. Transuranic wastes, which are also highly toxic, are nuclides heavier than uranium that are produced in the reactor fuel.

In 1979, following further hearings, the Commission adopted the "final" Table S-3 rule. 44 Fed. Reg. 45362 *et seq.* (1979). Like the amended interim rule, the final rule expressly stated that Table S-3 should be supplemented in individual proceedings by evidence about the health, socioeconomic, and cumulative aspects of fuel cycle activities. The Commission also continued to adhere to the zero-release assumption that the solidified waste would not escape and harm the environment once the repository was sealed. It acknowledged that this assumption was uncertain because of the remote possibility that water might enter the repository, dissolve the radioactive materials, and transport them to the biosphere. Nevertheless, the Commission predicted that a bedded-salt repository would maintain its integrity, and found the evidence "tentative but favorable" that an appropriate site would be found. *Id.* at 45368. The Commission ultimately determined that any undue optimism in the assumption of appropriate selection and perfect performance of the repository is offset by the cautious assumption, reflected in other parts of the Table, that all radioactive gases in the spent fuel would escape during the initial 6 to 20 year period that the repository remained open, *ibid,* and thus did not significantly reduce the overall conservatism of the S-3 Table. *Id.* at 45369.

The Commission rejected the option of expressing the uncertainties in Table S-3 or permitting licensing boards, in performing the NEPA analysis for individual nuclear plants, to consider those uncertainties. It saw no advantage in reassessing the significance of the uncertainties in individual licensing proceedings:

> "In view of the uncertainties noted regarding waste disposal, the question then arises whether these uncertainties can or should be reflected explicitly in the fuel cycle rule. The Commission has concluded that the rule should not be so modified. On the individual reactor licensing level, where the proceedings deal with fuel cycle issues only peripherally, the Commission sees no advantage in having licensing boards repeatedly weigh for themselves the effect of uncertainties on the selection of fuel cycle impacts for use in cost-benefit balancing. This is a generic question properly dealt with in the rulemaking as part of choosing what impact values should go into the fuel cycle rule. The Commission concludes, having noted that uncertainties exist, that for the limited purpose of the fuel cycle rule it is reasonable to base impacts on the assumption which the Commission believes the probabilities favor, *i.e.*, that bedded-salt repository sites can be found which will provide effective isolation of radioactive waste from the biosphere." 44 Fed. Reg. 45362, 45369 (1979).

The NRDC and respondent State of New York petitioned for review of the final rule. The Court of Appeals consolidated these petitions for all purposes with the pending challenges to the initial and interim rules. By a divided panel, the court concluded that the Table S-3 rules were arbitrary and capricious and inconsistent with NEPA because the Commission had not factored the consideration of uncertainties surrounding the zero-release assumption into the licensing process in such a manner that the uncertainties could potentially affect the outcome of any decision to license a particular plant. The court first reasoned that NEPA requires an agency to consider all significant environmental risks from its proposed action. If the zero-release assumption is taken as a finding that long-term storage poses no significant environmental risk, which the court acknowledged may not have been the Commission's intent, it found that the assumption represents a self-evident error in judgment and is thus arbitrary and capricious. As the evidence in the record reveals and the Commission itself acknowledged, the zero-release assumption is surrounded with uncertainty.

Alternatively, reasoned the Court of Appeals, the zero-release assumption could be characterized as a decisionmaking device whereby the Commission, rather than individual licensing boards, would have sole responsibility for considering the risk that long-lived wastes will not be disposed of with complete success. The court recognized that the Commission could use generic rulemaking to evaluate environmental costs common to all licensing decisions. Indeed, the Commission could use generic rulemaking to balance generic costs and benefits to produce a generic "net value." These generic evaluations could then be considered together with case-specific costs and benefits in individual proceedings. The key requirement of NEPA, however, is that the agency consider and disclose the actual environmental effects in a manner that will ensure that the overall process, including both the generic rulemaking and the individual proceedings, brings those effects to bear on decisions to take particular actions that significantly affect the environment. The Court of Appeals concluded that the zero-release assumption was not in accordance with this NEPA requirement because the assumption prevented the uncertainties—which were not found to be insignificant or outweighed by other generic benefits—from affecting any individual licensing decision. Alternatively, by requiring that the licensing decision ignore factors that are relevant under NEPA, the zero-release assumption is a clear error in judgment and thus arbitrary and capricious.

We granted certiorari. We reverse.

II

We are acutely aware that the extent to which this Nation should rely on nuclear power as a source of energy is an important and sensitive issue. Much of the debate focuses on whether development of nuclear generation facilities should proceed in the face of uncertainties about their long-term effects on the environment. Resolution of these fundamental policy questions lies, however, with Congress and the agencies to which Congress has delegated authority, as well as with state legislatures and, ultimately, the populace as a whole. Congress has assigned the courts only the limited, albeit important, task of reviewing agency action to determine whether the agency conformed with controlling statutes. As we emphasized in our earlier encounter with these very proceedings, "[a]dministrative decisions should be set aside in this context, as in every other, only for substantial procedural or substantive reasons as mandated by statute . . . , not simply because the court is unhappy with the result reached." *Vermont Yankee*, 435 U.S. 519, at 558.

The controlling statute at issue here is the National Environmental Policy Act. NEPA has twin aims. First, it "places upon an agency the obligation to consider every significant aspect of the environmental impact of a proposed action." *Vermont Yankee, supra*, at 553. Second, it ensures that the agency will inform the public that it has indeed considered environmental concerns in its decisionmaking process. *Weinberger v. Catholic Action of Hawaii*, 454 U.S. 139, 143 (1981). Congress in enacting NEPA, however, did not require agencies to elevate environmental concerns over other appropriate considerations. Rather, it required only that the agency take a "hard look" at the environmental consequences before taking a major action. The role of the courts is simply to ensure that the agency has adequately considered and disclosed the environmental impact of its actions and that its decision is not arbitrary or capricious.

In its Table S-3 Rule here, the Commission has determined that the probabilities favor the zero-release assumption, because the Nation is likely to develop methods to store the wastes with no leakage to the environment. The NRDC did not challenge and the Court of Appeals did not decide the reasonableness of this determination, 685 F.2d at 478, n.96, and no party seriously challenges it here. The Commission recognized, however, that the geological, chemical, physical and other data it relied on in making this prediction were based, in part, on assumptions which involve substantial uncertainties. Again, no one suggests that the uncertainties are trivial or the potential effects insignificant if time proves the zero-release assumption to have been seriously wrong. After confronting the issue, though, the Commission has determined that the uncertainties concerning the development of nuclear waste storage facilities are not sufficient to affect the outcome of any individual licensing decision.

It is clear that the Commission, in making this determination, has made the careful consideration and disclosure required by NEPA. The sheer volume of proceedings before the Commission is impressive. Of far greater importance, the Commission's Statement of Consideration announcing the final Table S-3 Rule shows that it has digested this mass of material and disclosed all substantial risks. 44 Fed. Reg. 45362, 45367-45369 (1979). The Statement summarizes the major uncertainty of long-term storage in bedded-salt repositories, which is that water could infiltrate the repository as a result of such diverse factors as geologic faulting, a meteor strike, or accidental or deliberate intrusion by man. The Commission noted that the probability of intrusion was small, and that the plasticity of salt would tend to heal some types of intrusions. The Commission also found the evidence "tentative but favorable" that an appropriate site could be found. Table S-3 refers interested persons to staff studies that discuss the uncertainties in greater detail. Given this record and the Commission's statement, it simply cannot be said that the Commission ignored or failed to disclose the uncertainties surrounding its zero-release assumption.

Congress did not enact NEPA, of course, so that an agency would contemplate the environmental impact of an action as an abstract exercise. Rather, Congress intended that the "hard look" be incorporated as part of the agency's process of deciding whether to pursue a particular federal action. It was on this ground that the Court of Appeals faulted the Commission's action, for failing to allow the uncertainties potentially to "tip the balance" in a particular licensing decision. As a general proposition, we can agree with the Court of Appeals' determination that an agency must allow all significant environmental risks to be factored into the decision whether to undertake a proposed action. We think, however, that the Court of Appeals erred in concluding the Commission had not complied with this standard.

As *Vermont Yankee* made clear, NEPA does not require agencies to adopt any particular internal decisionmaking structure. Here, the agency has chosen to evaluate generically the environmental impact of the fuel cycle and inform individual licensing boards, through the Table S-3 rule, of its evaluation. The generic method chosen by the agency is clearly an appropriate method of conducting the hard look required by NEPA. *See Vermont Yankee, supra*, 435 U.S. 519, at 535, n.13. The environmental effects of much of the fuel cycle are not plant specific, for any plant, regardless of its particular attributes, will create additional wastes that must be stored in a common long-term repository. Administrative efficiency and consistency of decision are both furthered by a generic determination of these effects without needless repetition of the litigation in individual proceedings, which are subject to review by the Commission in any event. *See generally Ecology Action v. AEC*, 492 F.2d 998, 1002, n.5 (2d. Cir. 1974) (Friendly, J.) (quoting Administrative Conference Proposed Recommendation 73-6).

The Court of Appeals recognized that the Commission has discretion to evaluate generically the environmental effects of the fuel cycle and require that these values be "plugged into" individual licensing decisions. The court concluded that the Commission nevertheless violated NEPA by failing to factor the uncertainty surrounding long-term storage into Table S-3 and precluding individual licensing decisionmakers from considering it.

The Commission's decision to affix a zero value to the environmental impact of long-term storage would violate NEPA, however, only if the Commission acted arbitrarily and capriciously in deciding generically that the uncertainty was insufficient to affect any individual licensing decision. In assessing whether the Commission's decision is arbitrary and capricious, it is crucial to place the zero-release assumption in context. Three factors are particularly important. First is the Commission's repeated emphasis that the zero-risk assumption—and, indeed, all of the Table S-3 rule—was made for a limited purpose. The Commission expressly noted its intention to supplement the rule with an explanatory narrative. It also emphasized that the purpose of the rule was not to evaluate or select the most effective long-term waste disposal technology or develop site selection criteria. A separate and comprehensive series of programs has been undertaken to serve these broader purposes. In the proceedings before us, the Commission's staff did not attempt to evaluate the environmental effects of all possible methods of disposing of waste. Rather, it chose to analyze intensively the most probable long-term waste disposal method—burial in a bedded-salt repository several hundred meters below ground—and then "estimate its impact conservatively, based on the best available information and analysis." 44 Fed. Reg. 45362, 45363 (1979). The zero-release assumption cannot be evaluated in isolation. Rather, it must be assessed in relation to the limited purpose for which the Commission made the assumption.

Second, the Commission emphasized that the zero-release assumption is but a single figure in an entire Table, which the Commission expressly designed as a risk-averse estimate of the environmental impact of the fuel cycle. It noted that Table S-3 assumed that the fuel storage canisters and the fuel rod cladding would be corroded before a repository is closed and that all volatile materials in the fuel would escape to the environment. Given that assumption, and the improbability that materials would escape after sealing, the Commission determined that the overall Table represented a conservative (*i.e.*, inflated) statement of environmental impacts. It is not unreasonable for the Commission to counteract the uncertainties in post-sealing releases by balancing them with an overestimate of pre-sealing releases. A reviewing court should not magnify a single line item beyond its significance as only part of a larger Table.

Third, a reviewing court must remember that the Commission is making predictions, within its area of special expertise, at the frontiers of science. When examining this kind of scientific determination, as opposed to simple findings of fact, a reviewing court must generally be at its most deferential. *See, e.g., Industrial Union Department v. American Petroleum Institute*, 448 U.S. 607, 656 (1980).

With these three guides in mind, we find the Commission's zero-release assumption to be within the bounds of reasoned decisionmaking required by the APA. We have already noted that the Commission's Statement of Consideration detailed several areas of uncertainty and discussed why they were insubstantial for purposes of an individual licensing decision. The Table S-3 Rule also refers to the staff reports, public documents that contain a more expanded discussion of the uncertainties involved in concluding that long-term storage will have no environmental effects. These staff reports recognize that rigorous verification of long-term risks for waste repositories is not possible, but suggest that data and extrapolation of past experience allow the Commission to identify events that could produce repository failure, estimate the probability of those events, and calculate the resulting consequences.[8] The Commission staff also modelled the consequences of repository failure by tracing the flow of contaminated water, and found them to be insignificant. Ultimately, the staff concluded that

---

[8]   For example, using this approach the staff estimated that a meteor the size necessary to damage a repository would hit a given square kilometer of the earth's surface only once every 50 trillion years, and that geologic faulting through the Delaware Basin in southeast New Mexico (assuming that were the site of the repository) would occur once in 25 billion years. The staff determined that a surface burst of a 50 megaton nuclear weapon, far larger than any currently deployed, would not breach the repository. The staff also recognized the possibility that heat generated by the waste would damage the repository, but suggested this problem could be alleviated by decreasing the density of the stored waste. In recognition that this suggestion would increase the size of the repository, the Commission amended Table S-3 to reflect the greater acreage required under these assumptions.

"[t]he radiotoxic hazard index analyses and the modeling studies that have been done indicate that consequences of all but the most improbable events will be small. Risks (probabilities times consequences) inherent in the long term for geological disposal will therefore also be small."

* * *

In sum, we think that the zero-release assumption—a policy judgment concerning one line in a conservative Table designed for the limited purpose of individual licensing decisions—is within the bounds of reasoned decisionmaking. It is not our task to determine what decision we, as Commissioners, would have reached. Our only task is to determine whether the Commission has considered the relevant factors and articulated a rational connection between the facts found and the choice made. *Bowman Transportation, Inc. v. Arkansas-Best Freight System, Inc.*, 419 U.S. 281, 285-86 (1974); *Citizens to Preserve Overton Park v. Volpe, supra.* Under this standard, we think the Commission's zero-release assumption, within the context of Table S-3 as a whole, was not arbitrary and capricious.

* * *

IV

For the foregoing reasons, the judgment of the Court of Appeals for the District of Columbia Circuit is

Reversed.

NOTES

1. Note that the Court of Appeals in *Baltimore Gas* recognized NRC's discretion to evaluate generically the environmental effects of the fuel cycle and to require that such values be "plugged into" individual licensing decisions. However, the court found that NRC violated NEPA by failing to factor the uncertainty of the effect of long-term nuclear waste storage into the plant licensing process. The court believed that the risks of long term storage, although uncertain, were relevant factors which could affect a licensing decision, and therefore must be considered according to NEPA requirements.

Should reviewing courts permit agencies to "round off" assessments of environmental effects so long as it is not arbitrary and capricious to do so? Should it ever be arbitrary and capricious for an agency to require that an effect, or risk, be disregarded as insignificant when it might be significant in a close case?

2. Regulations developed by the Council of Environmental Quality (CEQ) address the problem of uncertainty in agency EIS procedures. When an agency is evaluating "reasonably foreseeable significant adverse effects" and the information essential to making a decision is unavailable or incomplete, the agency must obtain the information if the cost of doing so is not exorbitant. However, if the information is unknown or would be extremely costly to obtain, the agency must state in the EIS that the information is unavailable, and must explain the relevance of the missing information, summarize the relevant information which the agency can obtain, and evaluate the impacts theoretically. *See* 40 C.F.R. § 1502.22 (1992).

3. How uncertain is the "zero release" assumption adopted by the NRC in rulemaking proceedings? Note that the NRC adopted its zero release assumption in 1979, amid claims that a permanent storage site could be found. Almost fifteen years later, controversy still continues over the location of a permanent storage site. Yucca Mountain, Nevada, has been identified as a site following a lengthy selection process which Congress established in the Nuclear Waste Policy Act of 1982, 42 U.S.C. §§ 10101-10226 (1988). The Yucca Mountain site does not consist of the underground salt beds assumed to be the geologic storage environment by the NRC in its Table S-3 rulemaking. For an explanation of the site selection process, see Charles H. Montagne, *The Initial Environmental Assessments for the Nuclear Waste Repository Under Section 112 of the Nuclear Waste Policy Act,* 4 UCLA J. ENVTL. L. & POL'Y 187 (1985).

4.   Can agencies use (and courts require) market analysis of issues like the zero release assumption? Suppose that the NRDC had gathered evidence during the rulemaking proceedings about the cost of insuring a permanent storage site against the risk of releases. Is it likely that insurance for such a site would be free? Isn't that what the agency's decision suggests? How might an economist assess the zero release assumption?

5.   The dilemma of nuclear waste disposal is complicated by the "not in my backyard" (NIMBY) phenomenon. Unified local resistance has been effective in preventing the selection of a disposal site. Such opposition may force the government to seek locations in communities where there is little political resistance. These locations, however, may not be the most suitable sites from a scientific point of view, thus creating greater potential for physical problems with the storage site. They also raise environmental justice concerns.

6.   Is the decision in *Baltimore Gas* consistent with the *per curiam* opinion in *Strycker's Bay* on the important question of a court's authority to engage in a arbitrary and capricious review of an agency decision under NEPA?

7.   Do you agree with the Court's description of NEPA's "twin aims" in the second paragraph of Part II of *Baltimore Gas and Electric*? Contrast the Court's interpretation of NEPA with Judge Wright's in *Calvert Cliffs, supra* Chapter 4. Do you agree with Patrick Parenteau's characterization of the Court's interpretation of NEPA as a "balance sheet with no bottom line"? Patrick A. Parenteau, *NEPA at Twenty: Shining Knight or Tilting at Windmills?,* ENVTL. F., Sept./Oct. 1989, at 14, 16. Does NEPA § 101 provide any "law to apply" that would trigger the *Overton Park* searching analysis under the APA?

8.   It is now clear that courts will enforce only the procedural, not the substantive aspects of NEPA. Can substantive requirements, like those in NEPA § 101, be considered binding on agencies if courts will not provide oversight? Consider the following affirmative argument:

> While * * * judicial decisions limit the courts' ability to overturn agency decisions on the basis of NEPA's provisions, they do not abrogate the other commands of the law itself—commands directed at the agencies and the President. The fact that Congress enacted and the President signed NEPA means that the commands contained therein must be adhered to as the commands of the republic expressed through its representative institutions. They are not simply expressions of opinion, letters to the editor, or petitions seeking the favor of federal officials.
>
> There are, in fact, many laws on the books that cannot be enforced by injunctions in court, but that nevertheless provide affirmative direction to the

conduct of federal officers. The Administrative Procedure Act itself recognizes that many final governmental actions prescribed by law are not subject to judicial review—specifically, where "statutes preclude judicial review, or . . . agency action is committed to agency discretion by law." * * *

To treat a statutory obligation as non-binding unless a court can order a government official to comply * * * mocks the Constitutional obligation of the President to "take Care that the Laws be faithfully executed." Such a crabbed view of NEPA's authority implies that those charged with carrying out the law are free to evade what cannot be compelled—that the President and the executive branch are presumed to act like Justice Oliver Wendell Holmes's hypothetical "bad man" who cares for nothing in ordering his affairs but the prospect of punishment. * * *

Moreover, even if one were to take the view that only sanctions make a law "legal" in character, there are other consequences than orders by the judicial branch. For example, an official's failure to follow the dictates of law—even where not enforceable by court order—may provide a basis for discipline or dismissal from federal service.

Environmental Law Institute, Rediscovering the National Environmental Policy Act 25–26 (1995).

The status of law that cannot be enforced through a judiciary is a perennial challenge for international law. *See, e.g.,* Mary Ellen O'Connell, *Enforcement and the Success of International Environmental Law*, 3 IND. J. GLOBAL L. STUD. 47 (Fall 1995).

9.   Lynton Caldwell, a political scientist and principal architect of NEPA, has lamented the failure of the courts to enforce NEPA's substantive goals. He recommends a constitutional amendment, or perhaps an international treaty on environmental protection, as a means for securing substantive adherence to NEPA's goals. Lynton K. Caldwell, *A Constitutional Law for the Environment: Twenty Years With NEPA Indicates the Need,* 31 ENV'T 6 (1989), and Lynton K. Caldwell, *Beyond NEPA: Future Significance of the National Environmental Policy Act*, 22 HARV. ENVTL. L. REV. 203 (1998). How might a constitutional amendment that affords people a right to a clean environment change judicial interpretations of NEPA?

10.   Like NEPA, the Endangered Species Act requires federal agencies to analyze the effects of their actions on the environment before those actions proceed. The following case, however, illustrates the marked contrast in the Court's interpretation of the substantive effect of these two laws.

TENNESSEE VALLEY AUTHORITY V. HILL
437 U.S. 153 (1978)

Mr. Chief Justice BURGER delivered the opinion of the Court.

The questions presented in this case are (a) whether the Endangered Species Act of 1973 requires a court to enjoin the operation of a virtually completed federal dam—which had been authorized prior to 1973—when, pursuant to authority vested in him by Congress, the Secretary of the Interior has determined that operation of the dam would eradicate an endangered species; and (b) whether continued congressional appropriations for the dam after 1973 constituted an implied repeal of the Endangered Species Act, at least as to the particular dam.

I

The Little Tennessee River originates in the mountains of northern Georgia and flows through the national forest lands of North Carolina into Tennessee, where it converges with the Big Tennessee River near Knoxville. The lower 33 miles of the Little Tennessee takes the river's clear, free-flowing waters through an area of great natural beauty. Among other environmental amenities, this stretch of river is said to contain abundant trout. Considerable historical importance attaches to the areas immediately adjacent to this portion of the Little Tennessee's banks. To the south of the river's edge lies Fort Loudon, established in 1756 as England's southwestern outpost in the French and Indian War. Nearby are also the ancient sites of several Native American villages, the archeological stores of which are to a large extent unexplored. These include the Cherokee towns of Echota and Tennase, the former being the sacred capital of the Cherokee Nation as early as the 16th century and the latter providing the linguistic basis from which the State of Tennessee derives its name.

In this area of the Little Tennessee River the Tennessee Valley Authority, a wholly owned public corporation of the United States, began constructing the Tellico Dam and Reservoir Project in 1967, shortly after Congress appropriated initial funds for its development. Tellico is a multipurpose regional development project designed principally to stimulate shoreline development, generate sufficient electric current to heat 20,000 homes, and provide flatwater recreation and flood control, as well as improve economic conditions in "an area characterized by underutilization of human resources and outmigration of young people." Of particular relevance to this case is one aspect of the project, a dam which TVA determined to place on the Little Tennessee, a short distance from where the river's waters meet with the Big Tennessee. When fully operational, the dam would impound water covering some 16,500 acres—much of which represents valuable and productive farmland—thereby converting the river's shallow, fast-flowing waters into a deep reservoir over 30 miles in length.

The Tellico Dam has never opened, however, despite the fact that construction has been virtually completed and the dam is essentially ready for operation. Although Congress has appropriated monies for Tellico every year since 1967, progress was delayed, and ultimately stopped, by a tangle of lawsuits and administrative proceedings. After unsuccessfully urging TVA to consider alternatives to damming the Little Tennessee, local citizens and national conservation groups brought suit in the District Court, claiming that the project did not conform to the requirements of the National Environmental Policy Act of 1969 (NEPA), 42 U.S.C. § 4321 *et seq*. After finding TVA to be in violation of NEPA, the District Court enjoined the dam's completion pending the filing of an appropriate environmental impact statement. The injunction remained in effect until late 1973, when the District Court concluded that TVA's final environmental impact statement for Tellico was in compliance with the law.

A few months prior to the District Court's decision dissolving the NEPA injunction, a discovery was made in the waters of the Little Tennessee which would profoundly affect the Tellico Project. Exploring the area around Coytee Springs, which is about seven miles from the mouth of the river, a University of Tennessee ichthyologist, Dr. David A. Etnier, found a previously unknown species of perch, the snail darter, or *Percina (Imostoma) tanasi*. This three-inch, tannish-colored fish, whose numbers are estimated to be in the range of 10,000 to 15,000, would soon engage the attention of environmentalists, the TVA, the Department of the Interior, the Congress of the United States, and ultimately the federal courts, as a new and additional basis to halt construction of the dam.

Until recently the finding of a new species of animal life would hardly generate a cause celebre. This is particularly so in the case of darters, of which there are approximately 130 known species, 8 to 10 of these having been identified only in the last five years.[9] The moving force behind the snail darter's sudden fame came some four months after its discovery, when the Congress passed the Endangered Species Act of 1973 (Act), 16 U.S.C. § 1531 *et seq.* This legislation, among other things, authorizes the Secretary of the Interior to declare species of animal life "endangered"[10] and to identify the "critical habitat" of these creatures. When a species or its habitat is so listed, the following portion of the Act—relevant here—becomes effective:

> "The Secretary [of the Interior] shall review other programs administered by him and utilize such programs in furtherance of the purposes of this chapter. All other Federal departments and agencies shall, in consultation with and with the assistance of the Secretary, utilize their authorities in furtherance of the purposes of this chapter by carrying out programs for the conservation of endangered species and threatened species listed pursuant to section 1533 of this title and *by taking such action necessary to insure that actions authorized, funded, or carried out by them do not jeopardize the continued existence of such endangered species and threatened species or result in the destruction or modification of habitat of such species* which is determined by the Secretary, after consultation as appropriate with the affected States, to be critical." 16 U.S.C. § 1536 (emphasis added).

In January 1975, the respondents in this case and others petitioned the Secretary of the Interior to list the snail darter as an endangered species. After receiving comments from various interested parties, including TVA and the State of Tennessee, the Secretary formally listed the snail darter as an endangered species on October 8, 1975. 40 Fed. Reg. 47505-47506. In so acting, it was noted that "the snail darter is a living entity which is genetically distinct and reproductively isolated from other fishes." 40 Fed. Reg. 47505. More important for the purposes of this case, the Secretary determined that the snail darter apparently lives only in that portion of the Little Tennessee River which would be completely inundated by the reservoir created as a consequence of the Tellico Dam's completion. *Id.* at 47506. The Secretary went on to explain the significance of the dam to the habitat of the snail darter:

> "[T]he snail darter occurs only in the swifter portions of shoals over clean gravel substrate in cool, low-turbidity water. Food of the snail darter is almost exclusively snails which require a clean gravel substrate for their survival. *The proposed*

---

[9]   In Tennessee alone there are 85 to 90 species of darters [citation omitted], of which upward to 45 live in the Tennessee River system. New species of darters are being constantly discovered and classified—at the rate of about one per year. This is a difficult task for even trained ichthyologists since species of darters are often hard to differentiate from one another.

[10]   An "endangered species" is defined by the Act to mean "any species which is in danger of extinction throughout all or a significant portion of its range other than a species of the Class Insecta determined by the Secretary to constitute a pest whose protection under the provisions of this chapter would present an overwhelming and overriding risk to man." 16 U.S.C. § 1532(4) (1976 ed.).

"'The act covers every animal and plant species, subspecies, and population in the world needing protection. There are approximately 1.4 million full species of animals and 600,000 full species of plants in the world. Various authorities calculate as many as 10% of them—some 200,000—may need to be listed as Endangered or Threatened. When one counts in subspecies, not to mention individual populations, the total could increase to three to five times that number.'" Keith Shreiner, Associate Director and Endangered Species Program Manager of the U.S. Fish and Wildlife Service * * * .

impoundment of water behind the proposed Tellico Dam would result in total destruction of the snail darter's habitat." Ibid. (emphasis added).

Subsequent to this determination, the Secretary declared the area of the Little Tennessee which would be affected by the Tellico Dam to be the "critical habitat" of the snail darter. 41 Fed. Reg. 13926-13928 (1976). Using these determinations as a predicate, and notwithstanding the near completion of the dam, the Secretary declared that pursuant to § 7 of the Act, "all Federal agencies must take such action as is necessary to insure that actions authorized, funded, or carried out by them do not result in the destruction or modification of this critical habitat area." 41 Fed. Reg. 13928 (1976). This notice, of course, was pointedly directed at TVA and clearly aimed at halting completion or operation of the dam.

During the pendency of these administrative actions, other developments of relevance to the snail darter issue were transpiring. Communication was occurring between the Department of the Interior's Fish and Wildlife Service and TVA with a view toward settling the issue informally. These negotiations were to no avail, however, since TVA consistently took the position that the only available alternative was to attempt relocating the snail darter population to another suitable location. To this end, TVA conducted a search of alternative sites which might sustain the fish, culminating in the experimental transplantation of a number of snail darters to the nearby Hiwassee River. However, the Secretary of the Interior was not satisfied with the results of these efforts, finding that TVA had presented "little evidence that they have carefully studied the Hiwassee to determine whether or not" there were "biological and other factors in this river that [would] negate a successful transplant."[11] 40 Fed. Reg. 47506 (1975).

Meanwhile, Congress had also become involved in the fate of the snail darter. Appearing before a Subcommittee of the House Committee on Appropriations in April 1975—some seven months before the snail darter was listed as endangered—TVA representatives described the discovery of the fish and the relevance of the Endangered Species Act to the Tellico Project. At that time TVA presented a position which it would advance in successive forums thereafter, namely, that the Act did not prohibit the completion of a project authorized, funded, and substantially constructed before the Act was passed. TVA also described its efforts to transplant the snail darter, but contended that the dam should be finished regardless of the experiment's success. Thereafter, the House Committee on Appropriations, in its June 20, 1975, Report, stated the following in the course of recommending that an additional $29 million be appropriated for Tellico:

> "The *Committee* directs that the project, for which an environmental impact statement
> has been completed and provided the Committee, should be completed as promptly
> as possible . . .." H.R. Rep. No. 94-319, p. 76 (1975). (Emphasis added.)

Congress then approved the TVA general budget, which contained funds for continued construction of the Tellico Project. In December 1975, one month after the snail darter was declared an endangered species, the President signed the bill into law.

In February 1976, pursuant to § 11(g) of the Endangered Species Act, 16 U.S.C. § 1540(g), respondents filed the case now under review, seeking to enjoin completion of the dam and impoundment of the reservoir on the ground that those actions would violate the Act by directly

---

[11]   The Fish and Wildlife Service and Dr. Etnier have stated that it may take from 5 to 15 years for scientists to determine whether the snail darter can successfully survive and reproduce in this new environment. In expressing doubt over the long-term future of the Hiwassee transplant, the Secretary noted: "That the snail darter does not already inhabit the Hiwassee River, despite the fact that the fish has had access to it in the past, is a strong indication that there may be biological and other factors in this river that negate a successful transplant." 40 Fed. Reg. 47506 (1975).

causing the extinction of the species *Percina (Imostoma) tanasi*. The District Court denied respondents' request for a preliminary injunction and set the matter for trial. Shortly thereafter the House and Senate held appropriations hearings which would include discussions of the Tellico budget.

At these hearings, TVA Chairman Wagner reiterated the agency's position that the Act did not apply to a project which was over 50% finished by the time the Act became effective and some 70% to 80% complete when the snail darter was officially listed as endangered. It also notified the Committees of the recently filed lawsuit's status and reported that TVA's efforts to transplant the snail darter had "been very encouraging."

Trial was held in the District Court on April 29 and 30, 1976, and on May 25, 1976, the court entered its memorandum opinion and order denying respondents their requested relief and dismissing the complaint. The District Court found that closure of the dam and the consequent impoundment of the reservoir would "result in the adverse modification, if not complete destruction, of the snail darter's critical habitat," making it "highly probable" that "the continued existence of the snail darter" would be "jeopardize[d]." Despite these findings, the District Court declined to embrace the plaintiffs' position on the merits: that once a federal project was shown to jeopardize an endangered species, a court of equity is compelled to issue an injunction restraining violation of the Endangered Species Act.

In reaching this result, the District Court stressed that the entire project was then about 80% complete and, based on available evidence, "there [were] no alternatives to impoundment of the reservoir, short of scrapping the entire project." The District Court also found that if the Tellico Project was permanently enjoined, "[s]ome $53 million would be lost in nonrecoverable obligations," meaning that a large portion of the $78 million already expended would be wasted. The court also noted that the Endangered Species Act of 1973 was passed some seven years after construction on the dam commenced and that Congress had continued appropriations for Tellico, with full awareness of the snail darter problem. Assessing these various factors, the District Court concluded:

> "At some point in time a federal project becomes so near completion and so incapable of modification that a court of equity should not apply a statute enacted long after inception of the project to produce an unreasonable result. . . ." * * *

Less than a month after the District Court decision, the Senate and House Appropriations Committees recommended the full budget request of $9 million for continued work on Tellico. * * * On June 29, 1976, both Houses of Congress passed TVA's general budget, which included funds for Tellico; the President signed the bill on July 12, 1976.

Thereafter, in the Court of Appeals, respondents argued that the District Court had abused its discretion by not issuing an injunction in the face of "a blatant statutory violation." *Hill v. TVA*, 549 F.2d 1064, 1069 (6th Cir. 1977). The Court of Appeals agreed, and on January 31, 1977, it reversed, remanding "with instructions that a permanent injunction issue halting all activities incident to the Tellico Project which may destroy or modify the critical habitat of the snail darter." *Id.* at 1075. The Court of Appeals directed that the injunction "remain in effect until Congress, by appropriate legislation, exempts Tellico from compliance with the Act or the snail darter has been deleted from the list of endangered species or its critical habitat materially redefined." *Ibid.*

* * *

Following the issuance of the permanent injunction, members of TVA's Board of Directors appeared before Subcommittees of the House and Senate Appropriations Committees to testify in support of continued appropriations for Tellico. The Subcommittees were apprised of all aspects of Tellico's status, including the Court of Appeals' decision. TVA reported that the dam stood "ready for the gates to be closed and the reservoir filled," Hearings on Public Works for Water and Power Development and Energy Research Appropriation Bill, 1978, before a Subcommittee of the House Committee on Appropriations, 95th Cong., 1st Sess., pt. 4, p. 234 (1977), and requested funds for completion of certain ancillary parts of the project, such as public use areas, roads, and bridges. As to the snail darter itself, TVA commented optimistically on its transplantation efforts, expressing the opinion that the relocated fish were "doing well and ha[d] reproduced." *Id.* at 235, 261-62.

Both Appropriations Committees subsequently recommended the full amount requested for completion of the Tellico Project. * * * As a solution to the problem, the House Committee advised that TVA should cooperate with the Department of the Interior "to relocate the endangered species to another suitable habitat so as to permit the project to proceed as rapidly as possible." * * * Much the same occurred on the Senate side, with its Appropriations Committee recommending both the amount requested to complete Tellico and the special appropriation for transplantation of endangered species. Reporting to the Senate on these measures, the Appropriations Committee took a particularly strong stand on the snail darter issue:

> "This *committee has not viewed* the Endangered Species Act as preventing the completion and use of these projects which were well under way at the time the affected species were listed as endangered. If the Act has such an effect which is contrary to *the Committee's understanding* of the intent of Congress in enacting the Endangered Species Act, funds should be appropriated to allow these projects to be completed and their benefits realized in the public interest, the Endangered Species Act notwithstanding." S. Rep. No. 95-301, p. 99 (1977). (Emphasis added.)

TVA's budget, including funds for completion of Tellico and relocation of the snail darter, passed both Houses of Congress and was signed into law on August 7, 1977.

We granted certiorari to review the judgment of the Court of Appeals.

II

We begin with the premise that operation of the Tellico Dam will either eradicate the known population of snail darters or destroy their critical habitat. Petitioner does not now seriously dispute this fact. In any event, under § 4(a)(1) of the Act, 16 U.S.C. § 1533(a)(1), the Secretary of the Interior is vested with exclusive authority to determine whether a species such as the snail darter is "endangered" or "threatened" and to ascertain the factors which have led to such a precarious existence. By § 4(d) Congress has authorized—indeed commanded—the Secretary to "issue such regulations as he deems necessary and advisable to provide for the conservation of such species." 16 U.S.C. § 1533(d). As we have seen, the Secretary promulgated regulations which declared the snail darter an endangered species whose critical habitat would be destroyed by creation of the Tellico Dam. Doubtless petitioner would prefer not to have these regulations on the books, but there is no suggestion that the Secretary exceeded his authority or abused his discretion in issuing the regulations. Indeed, no judicial review of the Secretary's determinations has ever been sought and hence the validity of his actions are not open to review in this Court.

Starting from the above premise, two questions are presented: (a) Would TVA be in violation of the Act if it completed and operated the Tellico Dam as planned? (b) If TVA's actions would offend the Act, is an injunction the appropriate remedy for the violation? For the reasons stated hereinafter, we hold that both questions must be answered in the affirmative.

A

It may seem curious to some that the survival of a relatively small number of three-inch fish among all the countless millions of species extant would require the permanent halting of a virtually completed dam for which Congress has expended more than $100 million. The paradox is not minimized by the fact that Congress continued to appropriate large sums of public money for the project, even after congressional Appropriations Committees were apprised of its apparent impact upon the survival of the snail darter. We conclude, however, that the explicit provisions of the Endangered Species Act require precisely that result.

One would be hard pressed to find a statutory provision whose terms were any plainer than those in § 7 of the Endangered Species Act. Its very words affirmatively command all federal agencies "to *insure* that actions *authorized, funded,* or *carried out* by them do not *jeopardize* the continued existence" of an endangered species or "*result* in the destruction or modification of habitat of such species . . .." 16 U.S.C. § 1536. (Emphasis added.) This language admits of no exception. Nonetheless, petitioner urges, as do the dissenters, that the Act cannot reasonably be interpreted as applying to a federal project which was well under way when Congress passed the Endangered Species Act of 1973. To sustain that position, however, we would be forced to ignore the ordinary meaning of plain language. It has not been shown, for example, how TVA can close the gates of the Tellico Dam without "carrying out" an action that has been "authorized" and "funded" by a federal agency. Nor can we understand how such action will "*insure*" that the snail darter's habitat is not disrupted. Accepting the Secretary's determinations, as we must, it is clear that TVA's proposed operation of the dam will have precisely the opposite effect, namely the *eradication* of an endangered species.

Concededly, this view of the Act will produce results requiring the sacrifice of the anticipated benefits of the project and of many millions of dollars in public funds.[12] But examination of the language, history, and structure of the legislation under review here indicates beyond doubt that Congress intended endangered species to be afforded the highest of priorities.

* * *

As it was finally passed, the Endangered Species Act of 1973 represented the most comprehensive legislation for the preservation of endangered species ever enacted by any nation. Its stated purposes were "to provide a means whereby the ecosystems upon which endangered species and threatened species depend may be conserved," and "to provide a program for the conservation of such . . . species . . .." 16 U.S.C. § 1531(b). In furtherance of these goals, Congress expressly stated in § 2(c) that "all Federal departments and agencies *shall* seek *to conserve endangered species* and threatened species . . .." 16 U.S.C. § 1531(c). (Emphasis added.) Lest there be any ambiguity as to the meaning of this statutory directive, the Act specifically defined "conserve" as meaning "to use and the use of *all methods and procedures which are necessary* to bring *any endangered species* or threatened species to the point at which the measures provided pursuant to this chapter are no longer necessary." § 1532(2). (Emphasis added.) Aside from § 7, other provisions indicated the seriousness with which Congress viewed this issue: Virtually all dealings with endangered species, including taking, possession, transportation, and sale, were prohibited, 16 U.S.C. § 1538, except in

---

[12]   The District Court determined that failure to complete the Tellico Dam would result in the loss of some $53 million in nonrecoverable obligations. Respondents dispute this figure, and point to a recent study by the General Accounting Office, which suggests that the figure could be considerably less. The GAO study also concludes that TVA and Congress should explore alternatives to impoundment of the reservoir, such as the creation of a regional development program based on a free-flowing river. None of these considerations are relevant to our decision, however; they are properly addressed to the Executive and Congress.

extremely narrow circumstances, *see* § 1539(b). The Secretary was also given extensive power to develop regulations and programs for the preservation of endangered and threatened species. § 1533(d). Citizen involvement was encouraged by the Act, with provisions allowing interested persons to petition the Secretary to list a species as endangered or threatened, § 1533(c)(2), *see* n.11, *supra*, and bring civil suits in United States district courts to force compliance with any provision of the Act, §§ 1540(c) and (g).

Section 7 of the Act, which of course is relied upon by respondents in this case, provides a particularly good gauge of congressional intent. * * *

* * * In explaining the expected impact of this provision in H.R. 37 on federal agencies, the House Committee's Report states:

> "This subsection *requires* the Secretary and the heads of all other Federal departments and agencies to use their authorities in order to carry out programs for the protection of endangered species, and it further *requires* that those agencies take the *necessary action* that will *not jeopardize* the continuing existence of endangered species or result in the destruction of critical habitat of those species." H.R. Rep. No. 93-412, p. 14 (1973). (Emphasis added.)

* * * [T]he House manager of the bill, Representative Dingell, provided an interpretation of what the Conference bill would require, making it clear that the mandatory provisions of § 7 were not casually or inadvertently included:

> "[Section 7] substantially amplifie[s] the obligation of [federal agencies] to take steps within their power to carry out the purposes of this act. A recent article . . . illustrates the problem which might occur absent this new language in the bill. It appears that the whooping cranes of this country, perhaps the best known of our endangered species, are being threatened by Air Force bombing activities along the gulf coast of Texas. Under existing law, the Secretary of Defense has some discretion as to whether or not he will take the necessary action to see that this threat disappears. . . . [O]nce the bill is enacted, [the Secretary of Defense] *would be required to take the proper steps*. . . .
>
> "Another example . . . [has] to do with the continental population of grizzly bears which may or may not be endangered, but which is surely threatened. . . . Once this bill is enacted, the appropriate Secretary, whether of Interior, Agriculture or whatever, *will have to take action* to see that this situation is not permitted to worsen, and that these bears are not driven to extinction. The purposes of the bill included the conservation of the species and of the ecosystems upon which they depend, and *every agency of government is committed* to see that those purposes are carried out. . . . [T]he agencies of Government can no longer plead that they can do nothing about it. *They can, and they must. The law is clear.*" 119 Cong. Rec. 42913 (1973). (Emphasis added.)

It is against this legislative background that we must measure TVA's claim that the Act was not intended to stop operation of a project which, like Tellico Dam, was near completion when an endangered species was discovered in its path. While there is no discussion in the legislative history of precisely this problem, the totality of congressional action makes it abundantly clear that the result we reach today is wholly in accord with both the words of the statute and the intent of Congress. The plain intent of Congress in enacting this statute was to halt and reverse the trend toward species extinction, whatever the cost. This is reflected not only in the stated policies of the Act, but in literally every section of the statute. All persons, including federal agencies, are specifically instructed not to "take" endangered species, meaning that no one is "to harass, harm, pursue, hunt, shoot, wound, kill, trap, capture, or collect" such life forms. 16

U.S.C. §§ 1532(14), 1538(a)(1)(B). Agencies in particular are directed by §§ 2(c) and 3(2) of the Act to "use . . . *all methods* and procedures which are necessary" to preserve endangered species. 16 U.S.C. §§ 1531(c), 1532(2) (emphasis added). In addition, the legislative history undergirding § 7 reveals an explicit congressional decision to require agencies to afford first priority to the declared national policy of saving endangered species. The pointed omission of the type of qualifying language previously included in endangered species legislation reveals a conscious decision by Congress to give endangered species priority over the "primary missions" of federal agencies.

* * *

Notwithstanding Congress' expression of intent in 1973, we are urged to find that the continuing appropriations for Tellico Dam constitute an implied repeal of the 1973 Act, at least insofar as it applies to the Tellico Project. In support of this view, TVA points to the statements found in various House and Senate Appropriations Committees' Reports; as described in Part I, *supra*, those Reports generally reflected the attitude of the Committees either that the Act did not apply to Tellico or that the dam should be completed regardless of the provisions of the Act. Since we are unwilling to assume that these latter Committee statements constituted advice to ignore the provisions of a duly enacted law, we assume that these Committees believed that the Act simply was not applicable in this situation. But even under this interpretation of the Committees' actions, we are unable to conclude that the Act has been in any respect amended or repealed.

There is nothing in the appropriations measures, as passed, which states that the Tellico Project was to be completed irrespective of the requirements of the Endangered Species Act. These appropriations, in fact, represented relatively minor components of the lump-sum amounts for the entire TVA budget. To find a repeal of the Endangered Species Act under these circumstances would surely do violence to the "'cardinal rule . . . that repeals by implication are not favored.'" *Morton v. Mancari*, 417 U.S. 535, 549 (1974), quoting *Posadas v. National City Bank*, 296 U.S. 497, 503 (1936). In *Posadas* this Court held, in no uncertain terms, that "the intention of the legislature to repeal must be clear and manifest." In practical terms, this "cardinal rule" means that "[i]n the absence of some affirmative showing of an intention to repeal, the only permissible justification for a repeal by implication is when the earlier and later statutes are irreconcilable." *Mancari, supra*, 417 U.S. at 550.

The doctrine disfavoring repeals by implication * * * applies with even greater force when the claimed repeal rests solely on an Appropriations Act. We recognize that both substantive enactments and appropriations measures are "Acts of Congress," but the latter have the limited and specific purpose of providing funds for authorized programs. When voting on appropriations measures, legislators are entitled to operate under the assumption that the funds will be devoted to purposes which are lawful and not for any purpose forbidden. Without such an assurance, every appropriations measure would be pregnant with prospects of altering substantive legislation, repealing by implication any prior statute which might prohibit the expenditure. Not only would this lead to the absurd result of requiring Members to review exhaustively the background of every authorization before voting on an appropriation, but it would flout the very rules the Congress carefully adopted to avoid this need. House Rule XXI(2), for instance, specifically provides: "No appropriation shall be reported in any general appropriation bill, or be in order as an amendment thereto, for any expenditure not previously authorized by law, unless in continuation of appropriations for such public works as are already in progress. *Nor shall any provision in any such bill or amendment thereto changing existing law be in order.*" (Emphasis added.)

* * *

B

Having determined that there is an irreconcilable conflict between operation of the Tellico Dam and the explicit provisions of § 7 of the Endangered Species Act, we must now consider what remedy, if any, is appropriate. It is correct, of course, that a federal judge sitting as a chancellor is not mechanically obligated to grant an injunction for every violation of law. This Court made plain in *Hecht Co. v. Bowles*, 321 U.S. 321, 329 (1944), that "[a] grant of jurisdiction to issue compliance orders hardly suggests an absolute duty to do so under any and all circumstances." As a general matter it may be said that "[s]ince all or almost all equitable remedies are discretionary, the balancing of equities and hardships is appropriate in almost any case as a guide to the chancellor's discretion." D. Dobbs, Remedies 52 (1973). Thus, in *Hecht Co.* the Court refused to grant an injunction when it appeared from the District Court findings that "the issuance of an injunction would have 'no effect by way of insuring better compliance in the future' and would [have been] 'unjust' to [the] petitioner and not 'in the public interest.'" 321 U.S. at 326.

But these principles take a court only so far. Our system of government is, after all, a tripartite one, with each branch having certain defined functions delegated to it by the Constitution. While "[i]t is emphatically the province and duty of the judicial department to say what the law is," *Marbury v. Madison*, 1 Cranch 137, 177 (1803), it is equally—and emphatically—the exclusive province of the Congress not only to formulate legislative policies and mandate programs and projects, but also to establish their relative priority for the Nation. Once Congress, exercising its delegated powers, has decided the order of priorities in a given area, it is for the Executive to administer the laws and for the courts to enforce them when enforcement is sought.

Here we are urged to view the Endangered Species Act "reasonably," and hence shape a remedy "that accords with some modicum of common sense and the public weal." But is that our function? We have no expert knowledge on the subject of endangered species, much less do we have a mandate from the people to strike a balance of equities on the side of the Tellico Dam. Congress has spoken in the plainest of words, making it abundantly clear that the balance has been struck in favor of affording endangered species the highest of priorities, thereby adopting a policy which it described as "institutionalized caution."

Our individual appraisal of the wisdom or unwisdom of a particular course consciously selected by the Congress is to be put aside in the process of interpreting a statute. Once the meaning of an enactment is discerned and its constitutionality determined, the judicial process comes to an end. We do not sit as a committee of review, nor are we vested with the power of veto. The lines ascribed to Sir Thomas More by Robert Bolt are not without relevance here:

> "The law, Roper, the law. I know what's legal, not what's right. And I'll stick to what's legal. . . . I'm *not* God. The currents and eddies of right and wrong, which you find such plain-sailing, I can't navigate, I'm no voyager. But in the thickets of the law, oh there I'm a forester. . . . What would you do? Cut a great road through the law to get after the Devil? . . . And when the last law was down, and the Devil turned round on you where would you hide, Roper, the laws all being flat? . . . This country's planted thick with laws from coast to coast—Man's laws, not God's—and if you cut them down . . . d'you really think you could stand upright in the winds that would blow then? . . . Yes, I'd give the Devil benefit of law, for my own safety's sake." R. Bolt, A Man for All Seasons, Act I, p. 147 (Three Plays, Heinemann ed. 1967).

We agree with the Court of Appeals that in our constitutional system the commitment to the separation of powers is too fundamental for us to pre-empt congressional action by judicially decreeing what accords with "common sense and the public weal." Our Constitution vests such responsibilities in the political branches.

Affirmed.

Mr. Justice POWELL, with whom Mr. Justice BLACKMUN joins, dissenting.

The Court today holds that § 7 of the Endangered Species Act requires a federal court, for the purpose of protecting an endangered species or its habitat, to enjoin permanently the operation of any federal project, whether completed or substantially completed. This decision casts a long shadow over the operation of even the most important projects, serving vital needs of society and national defense, whenever it is determined that continued operation would threaten extinction of an endangered species or its habitat. This result is said to be required by the "plain intent of Congress" as well as by the language of the statute.

In my view § 7 cannot reasonably be interpreted as applying to a project that is completed or substantially completed when its threat to an endangered species is discovered. Nor can I believe that Congress could have intended this Act to produce the "absurd result"—in the words of the District Court—of this case. If it were clear from the language of the Act and its legislative history that Congress intended to authorize this result, this Court would be compelled to enforce it. It is not our province to rectify policy or political judgments by the Legislative Branch, however egregiously they may disserve the public interest. But where the statutory language and legislative history, as in this case, need not be construed to reach such a result, I view it as the duty of this Court to adopt a permissible construction that accords with some modicum of common sense and the public weal.

* * *

I have little doubt that Congress will amend the Endangered Species Act to prevent the grave consequences made possible by today's decision. Few, if any, Members of that body will wish to defend an interpretation of the Act that requires the waste of at least $53 million, and denies the people of the Tennessee Valley area the benefits of the reservoir that Congress intended to confer. There will be little sentiment to leave this dam standing before an empty reservoir, serving no purpose other than a conversation piece for incredulous tourists.

* * *

Mr. Justice REHNQUIST, dissenting.

In the light of my Brother POWELL's dissenting opinion, I am far less convinced than is the Court that the Endangered Species Act of 1973, 16 U.S.C. § 1531 *et seq.,* was intended to prohibit the completion of the Tellico Dam. But the very difficulty and doubtfulness of the correct answer to this legal question convinces me that the Act did not prohibit the District Court from refusing, in the exercise of its traditional equitable powers, to enjoin petitioner from completing the Dam. Section 11(g)(1) of the Act, 16 U.S.C. § 1540(g)(1), merely provides that "any person may commence a civil suit on his own behalf . . . to enjoin any person, including the United States and any other governmental instrumentality or agency . . . who is alleged to be in violation of any provision of this chapter." It also grants the district courts "jurisdiction, without regard to the amount in controversy or the citizenship of the parties, to enforce any such provision."

This Court had occasion in *Hecht Co. v. Bowles,* 321 U.S. 321 (1944), to construe language in an Act of Congress that lent far greater support to a conclusion that Congress intended an injunction to issue as a matter of right than does the language just quoted. There the Emergency Price Control Act of 1942 provided that "[u]pon a showing by the Administrator that [a] person has engaged or is about to engage in any [acts or practices violative of this Act] a permanent or temporary injunction, restraining order, or other order *shall be granted* without bond." 56 Stat. 33 (emphasis added).

But in *Hecht* this Court refused to find even in such language an intent on the part of Congress to require that a district court issue an injunction as a matter of course, without regard to established equitable considerations * * * .

Only by sharply retreating from the principle of statutory construction announced in *Hecht Co.* could I agree with the Court of Appeals' holding in this case that the judicial enforcement provisions contained in § 11(g)(1) of the Act require automatic issuance of an injunction by the district courts once a violation is found. I choose to adhere to *Hecht Co.'s* teaching * * *.

Since the District Court possessed discretion to refuse injunctive relief even though it had found a violation of the Act, the only remaining question is whether this discretion was abused in denying respondents' prayer for an injunction. *Locomotive Engineers v. Missouri, K. & T.R. Co.*, 363 U.S. 528, 535 (1960). The District Court denied respondents injunctive relief because of the significant public and social harms that would flow from such relief and because of the demonstrated good faith of petitioner. * * *

* * * Here the District Court recognized that Congress, when it enacted the Endangered Species Act, made the preservation of the habitat of the snail darter an important public concern. But it concluded that this interest on one side of the balance was more than outweighed by other equally significant factors. These factors, further elaborated in the dissent of my Brother POWELL, satisfy me that the District Court's refusal to issue an injunction was not an abuse of its discretion. I therefore dissent from the Court's opinion holding otherwise.

NOTES

1. Justice Rehnquist, in his dissent, argues that the district court did not abuse its discretion in refusing to enjoin a dam 80 percent complete. At what point during the course of a project, if any, should courts balance the equities in fashioning relief for the violation of an environmental statute? As you will see in Chapter 9, the Court has been considerably more generous in allowing lower courts to exercise discretion in tailoring or denying injunctive relief for violations of environmental laws other than the ESA, especially where it finds that an injunction would not further the purposes of the underlying statute. *See, e.g., Weinberger v. Romero-Barcelo*, 456 U.S. 305 (1982) (upholding a district court decision requiring U.S. Navy to obtain a permit for the discharge of ordinance in violation of the Clean Water Act but refusing to enjoin the discharge pending compliance since the discharge was not polluting waters).

2. Suppose the dam had been completed and the gates closed *before* Dr. Etnier discovered the endangered snail darter. What would the TVA have to do to comply with the ESA once the discovery was made? Would TVA have to destroy the dam? *See Alabama Power Co. v. Federal Energy Regulatory Comm'n*, 979 F.2d 1561 (D.C. Cir. 1992) (discussing ESA compliance for a dam built in 1928 that provides stream flow for an endangered mollusk thought to have been extirpated by a series of dams in the 1960s but rediscovered in 1988).

3.   In finding that appropriations measures for the Tellico Dam did not modify the ESA, the *TVA v. Hill* Court quotes the *Morton v. Mancari*, 417 U.S. 535, 550 (1974), holding that "the only permissible justification for a repeal by implication is when the earlier and later statutes are irreconcilable." Why weren't the repeated appropriations by Congress to fund the Tellico Dam in spite of the presence of the snail darter "later statutes" irreconcilable with the earlier ESA?

4.   The Court revisited the interpretation of appropriations measures in a situation involving the threatened northern spotted owl in *Robertson v. Seattle Audubon Society*, 503 U.S. 429 (1992). In *Seattle Audubon*, the question was not whether the appropriations language exempted projects (in this case, timber sales) from environmental laws, including NEPA. That clearly was Congress' intent. Rather, the issue was whether Congress ran afoul of constitutional separation of powers in enacting a provision stating "Congress hereby determines and directs that management of areas according to [restrictions set out elsewhere] * * * is adequate consideration for the purpose of meeting the statutory requirements that are the basis for" two ongoing cases for which judges had issued injunctions stopping timber sales. Department of Interior and Related Agencies Appropriations Act (Northwest Timber Compromise), § 318(b)(6)(A), 103 Stat. 745 (1990). The Court unanimously overturned the Ninth Circuit's decision that the provision unconstitutionally directed courts to reach specific results under existing law in connection with the two pending cases. The Court found that the appropriations language merely changed the law, not findings or results under old law. Is this result consistent with *TVA v. Hill*? Why do you think Congress exempted the controversial timber sales from environmental laws in such a roundabout way? *See* House Rule XXII, quoted in the *TVA* decision.

5.   Chief Justice Burger, in closing his majority opinion, refers to the policy of "institutionalized caution" as a basis for the ESA. Reconsider the perspectives materials in Chapter 1. Is the primary aim of environmental law to slow or stop development? Is environmental law an expression of aversion to the risks of "progress"?

6.   Although the *TVA v. Hill* decision focuses on the ESA, the underlying controversy was about the construction of Tellico Dam, which was opposed by a coalition of environmental, farmer, sport, and Native American groups. Litigation to stop the dam began before the ESA suit and continued after the ESA issues were exhausted. Is the snail darter being used by the plaintiffs as a surrogate for a larger issue? Should it matter whether the plaintiffs were genuinely concerned about the darter or whether they were mostly concerned with rafting the white-water segments of the Little Tennessee River? Or, whether they were farmers in the valley trying to save their land?

Marc Reisner argues that:

> the big story was not the dam at all but the TVA itself, an agency that had evolved from a benevolent paternalism into the biggest power producer, biggest strip miner, and single biggest polluter in the United States. Unaccountable to the public, largely unaccountable to Congress, the TVA was an elephantine relic of the age of public works; it had undoubtedly done its region some good, but by the 1970s it had passed the uncharted point in an agency's career * * * when it confronts new challenges with barnacled precepts and, in a sense, turns on the constituency it was created to help.

MARC REISNER, CADILLAC DESERT 326 (rev. ed. 1993). *See also* FRED POWLEDGE, WATER 311-24 (1982).

7.   Just a few months after the Court decided *TVA v. Hill*, Congress responded by amending § 7 of the ESA to create the exemption process described in the Introduction to the ESA in Chapter 4. ESA § 7(g) describes the administrative prerequisites for bringing an application before the seven member committee empowered to grant projects exemptions from the Act. This Exemption Committee is sometimes called the "God Squad." To expedite the cumbersome exemption process for the two large projects that faced ESA hurdles in 1978, Congress provided for special, streamlined Exemption Committee review of both the Grayrocks Dam and the Tellico Dam. MICHAEL J. BEAN & MELANIE J. ROWLAND, THE EVOLUTION OF NATIONAL WILDLIFE LAW 242 (3d ed. 1997); *The 1978 Amendments to the Endangered Species Act: Evaluating the New Exemption Process Under § 7*, 9 ENVTL. L. REP. 10031 (1979).

The Grayrocks Dam on the Laramie River in Wyoming was poised to dry up critical habitat for the endangered whooping crane downstream on the Platte River in Nebraska. In 1978, environmental groups and the State of Nebraska were able to enjoin construction of the dam relying on NEPA and the ESA. *Nebraska v. Rural Electrification Admin.*, 8 Envtl. L. Rep. (Envtl. L. Inst.) 20789 (D. Neb. 1978); *Nebraska v. Ray*, 8 Envtl. L. Rep. (Envtl. L. Inst.) 20666 (D. Neb. 1978). Prior to the meeting of the Exemption Committee on Jan. 23, 1979, however, the parties agreed to a settlement that allowed the dam to go forward, guaranteed minimum water flows, and established a fund to improve habitat along the river. The Exemption Committee endorsed the settlement in its exemption decision.

But it was Tellico that remained controversial to the end. Marc Reisner observes that the composition of the Exemption Committee "suggested a predisposition toward completing stalled projects, especially in the case of a dam." REISNER at 327. Read ESA § 7(e), which describes the Committee and consider whether Reisner is correct.

The Exemption Committee voted unanimously to reject the Tellico exemption solely on the basis of economics.

> "Here is a project that is 95 percent complete," said Charles Schultz[e], the chairman of the Council of Economic Advisers, "and if one takes just the cost of finishing it against the [total] benefits . . . it doesn't pay." [Secretary of the Interior] Cecil Andrus added, "Frankly, I hate to see the snail darter get the credit for delaying a project that was so ill-conceived and uneconomic in the first place."

REISNER at 327-28; POWLEDGE at 321.

Determined still to provide public works money for his state, Senator Howard Baker of Tennessee continued to lead Congressional efforts to exempt the Tellico Dam. Later in 1979, Congress legislatively exempted the dam from all federal law through an appropriations rider. By the end of the year, the dam gates were closed. The snail darter population in the Little Tennessee River ultimately perished. Subsequently, however, other small populations were discovered downstream, and these remain. BEAN at 365.

8.   Since the January 1979 Exemption Committee decisions, the Department of the Interior has received four exemption applications. UNITED STATES GENERAL ACCOUNTING OFFICE, ENDANGERED SPECIES ACT: TYPES AND NUMBER OF IMPLEMENTING ACTIONS 37-38 (GAO/RCED-92-131BR 1992). However, only one application has survived the § 7(g) administrative process to receive consideration on its merits by the Exemption Committee

under § 7(h). Recall that under § 7(h), the Committee may not grant an exemption unless five of the seven members find that: (1) there are no reasonable and prudent alternatives to the proposed action; (2) the benefits of the action clearly outweigh the benefits of alternative courses of action which would not jeopardize the species; (3) the action is of regional or national significance; and (4) neither the federal agency involved or the exemption applicant made any irreversible or irretrievable commitment of resources with respect to the proposed action.

In May 1992, the Committee met to consider an application to exempt 44 Bureau of Land Management (BLM) timber sales that the FWS found would jeopardize the continued existence of the northern spotted owl. By a vote of five to two, the Committee exempted 13 of the sales, subject to certain conditions. Environmentalist criticism of the decision included serious allegations of bias in the ESA § 7(g) administrative process conducted by the Department of the Interior. Oliver Houck, *The Endangered Species Act and Its Implementation by the U.S. Departments of Interior and Commerce,* 64 U. COLO. L. REV. 277, 338-44 (1993). Subsequent litigation involved claims that the President and his staff engaged in *ex parte* communications with some Committee members in violation of the APA. *Portland Audubon Society v. Endangered Species Committee,* 984 F.2d 1534 (9th Cir. 1993) (holding that the Committee and the President are subject to the APA *ex parte* restrictions). When the Clinton Administration took office, it withdrew the timber sales, thus ending the exemption litigation. Ultimately, the new administration adopted a comprehensive management plan to guide logging for all public forests in spotted owl habitat. *See Seattle Audubon Soc'y v. Moseley,* 80 F.3d 1401 (9th Cir. 1996) (upholding the comprehensive plan).

The rarity of exemptions reflects the small number of projects that the ESA blocks. According to the FWS (which posts updated statistics at *http://www.fws.gov/~r9endspp/esastats.html*), from 1987 through 1995, of the approximately 186,000 federal actions reviewed by agencies for impacts on listed species, only 2.7% required formal consultation. Of these 5,046 formal consultations, only 600 received "jeopardy" opinions. Of these jeopardy opinions, the FWS identified reasonable and prudent alternatives for all but 100 projects. Of these 100 projects, all but 13 were related to timber sales in spotted owl habitat. Reasonable and prudent alternatives included changes in the timing of construction, modifications to the project's design, adjustments in site location, and emission restrictions. *See* Oliver Houck, *The Endangered Species Act and Its Implementation by the U.S. Departments of Interior and Commerce,* 64 U. COLO. L. REV. 277, 318 (1993) (finding eighteen jeopardy-without-alternatives opinions out of 73,500 informal and formal consultations).

Professor Houck reviewed 99 jeopardy opinions and found that all but a few involving "small-scale, private development directly in habitat essential to the [listed] species" contained reasonable and prudent alternatives that allowed the project to proceed. *Id.* at 320. Houck observed:

> A common theme to all the opinions reviewed was the Service's determination to find an alternative within the economic means, authority, and ability of the applicant. Alternative measures which were clearly more protective, but also more difficult to implement, were ruled out; alternatives strongly favored by the applicant and opposed by the Service were, albeit grudgingly, accepted.

Of the ninety-nine opinions reviewed, the only actions for which reasonable and prudent alternatives were *not* identified involved a beachfront hotel, a number of powerboat piers, and a small secondary road (for which the suggested alternative was the development of a conservation plan for the Florida Key Deer before additional roads in its diminishing habitat were approved).

Id. at 320-21.

9. Two processes that help avoid endangered species conflicts are *early consultation* and *informal consultation*. Early consultation is a process initiated by a prospective applicant who "has reason to believe that the prospective action may affect listed species or critical habitat * * * ." 50 C.F.R. § 402.11(b). The process is essentially the same as with formal consultation except that the Fish and Wildlife Service issues a "preliminary biological opinion" which can be confirmed as a final biological opinion if the applicant decides to go forward with its proposed activity. *Id.* at § 402.11(e). Early consultation allows a prospective applicant to find alternative approaches for carrying out a proposal action before substantial capital is invested in an approach that is more likely to cause jeopardy.

Informal consultation is an optional process that allows the federal action agency and Fish and Wildlife Service to consider modification to a proposed action that will avoid the likelihood of adverse effects to a listed species or critical habitat. 50 C.F.R. § 402.13. If successful, informal consultation makes formal consultation unnecessary. Professor Houck points out that the vast majority of consultations are resolved informally.

The counterpart to informal consultation in the NEPA process is an EA that includes sufficient mitigation measures to allow an agency to avoid a finding of significant impact. The Court of Appeals for the District of Columbia Circuit approved this process in *Cabinet Mountains Wilderness v. Peterson*, 685 F.2d 678, 682-83 (D.C. Cir. 1982); *see also* John Shepard, *Range of Proposals Covered by NEPA* at Ch. 2, V. D., E.; and William Cohen & Andrea Berlowe, *Litigating NEPA Cases* at Ch. 9, V. F. *in* THE NEPA LITIGATION MANUAL, CH. 9, V.F. (KARIN SHELDON & MARK SQUILLACE, eds. 1999).

10. Should environmental laws provide procedures for exemptions or should project proponents be forced to go to Congress for special legislative exemptions? Why doesn't NEPA have an exemption procedure akin to the ESA?

11. Do not confuse exemptions (for individual activities normally covered by an environmental law) with exceptions (for categories of activities excluded by Congress from the reach of an environmental law). Most exceptions to the ESA are found in § 10 and are available for experimental populations (§ 10(j)), activities covered by incidental take permits (§ 10(a)), activities covered by incidental take statements (§ 7(b)(4)), certain subsistence activities of Alaska Natives (§ 10(e)), certain activities for which application of the prohibitions would cause undue economic hardship (§ 10(b)), and takings to protect against bodily harm to oneself or others (§ 11(a)(3)).

12. Courts have found that many EPA activities that involve environmental review and public participation already provide for the "functional equivalent" of NEPA review and therefore are not subject to the EIS requirement. *See, e.g., Merrell v. Thomas*, 807 F.2d 776 (9th Cir. 1986), *cert. denied*, 484 U.S. 848 (1987) (no EIS necessary for EPA registration of pesticides); *Portland Cement Ass'n v. Ruckelshaus*, 486 F.2d 375 (D.C. Cir.

1973), *cert. denied*, 417 U.S. 921 (1974) (no EIS necessary for EPA adoption of air pollution standards). Congress has explicitly created exceptions to NEPA's EIS requirement for certain EPA actions. 33 U.S.C. § 1371 (any action under the Clean Water Act except for issuance of wastewater treatment construction grants and new source discharge permits); 15 U.S.C. § 793(c)(1) (any action under the Clean Air Act). *See also* notes following *Flint Ridge Development Co. v. Scenic Rivers Ass'n, infra* Chapter 8. Should the EPA and FWS be subject to NEPA and the ESA for actions taken to *protect* the environment?

Note that 40 C.F.R. § 1506.11 allows any agency responding to an emergency to work with the CEQ without strict NEPA compliance. Note 8 following *Northern Spotted Owl v. Hodel, supra* Chapter 4, discusses the application of NEPA to ESA listing decisions.

13. Compare the degree of environmental review and substantive control provided by the following Michigan law with NEPA and the ESA.

MICHIGAN ENVIRONMENTAL PROTECTION ACT OF 1970

AN ACT to provide for actions for declaratory and equitable relief for protection of the air, water and other natural resources and the public trust therein; to prescribe the rights, duties and functions of the attorney general, any political subdivision of the state, any instrumentality or agency of the state or of a political subdivision thereof, any person, partnership, corporation, association, organization or other legal entity; and to provide for judicial proceedings relative thereto.

* * *

324.1701. Actions for declaratory and equitable relief; parties; standards for pollution or anti-pollution devices or procedure: Sec. 2. (1) The attorney general, any political subdivision of the state, any instrumentality or agency of the state or of a political subdivision thereof, any person, partnership, corporation, association, organization or other legal entity may maintain an action in the circuit court having jurisdiction where the alleged violation occurred or is likely to occur for declaratory and equitable relief against the state, any political subdivision thereof, any instrumentality or agency of the state or of a political subdivision thereof, any person, partnership, corporation, association, organization or other legal entity for the protection of the air, water and other natural resources and the public trust therein from pollution, impairment or destruction.

(2) In granting relief provided by subsection (1) where there is involved a standard for pollution or for an anti-pollution device or procedure, fixed by rule or otherwise, by an instrumentality or agency of the state or a political subdivision thereof, the court may:

(a) Determine the validity, applicability and reasonableness of the standard.

(b) When a court finds a standard to be deficient, direct the adoption of a standard approved and specified by the court.

324.1703. Prima facie showing of pollution, rebuttal; affirmative defenses; burden of proof; weight of evidence; masters or referees; apportionment of costs: Sec. 3. (1) When the plaintiff in the action has made a prima facie showing that the conduct of the defendant has, or is likely to pollute, impair or destroy the air, water or other natural resources or the public trust therein, the defendant may rebut the prima facie showing by the submission of evidence to the contrary. The defendant may also show, by way of an affirmative defense, that there is no feasible and prudent alternative to defendant's conduct and that such conduct is consistent with the promotion of the public health, safety and welfare in light of the state's paramount concern for the protection of its natural resources from pollution, impairment or destruction. Except as to the affirmative defense, the principles of burden of proof and weight of the evidence generally applicable in civil actions in the circuit courts shall apply to actions brought under this act.

(2) The court may appoint a master or referee, who shall be a disinterested person and technically qualified, to take testimony and make a record and a report of his findings to the court in the action.

(3) Costs may be apportioned to the parties if the interests of justice require.

324.1704. Granting equitable relief; imposition of conditions; remitting parties to other proceedings; judicial review: Sec. 4. (1) The court may grant temporary and permanent equitable relief, or may impose conditions on the defendant that are required to protect the air, water and other natural resources or the public trust therein from pollution, impairment or destruction.

(2) If administrative, licensing or other proceedings are required or available to determine the legality of the defendant's conduct, the court may remit the parties to such proceedings, which proceedings shall be conducted in accordance with and subject to the provisions of Act No. 306 of the Public Acts of 1969, being sections 24.201 to 24.313 of the Compiled Laws of 1948. In so remitting the court may grant temporary equitable relief where necessary for the protection of the air, water and other natural resources or the public trust therein from pollution, impairment or destruction. In so remitting the court shall retain jurisdiction of the action pending completion thereof for the purpose of determining whether adequate protection from pollution, impairment or destruction has been afforded.

(3) Upon completion of such proceedings, the court shall adjudicate the impact of the defendant's conduct on the air, water or other natural resources and on the public trust therein in accordance with this act. In such adjudication the court may order that additional evidence be taken to the extent necessary to protect the rights recognized in this act.

(4) Where, as to any administrative, licensing or other proceeding, judicial review thereof is available, notwithstanding the provisions to the contrary of Act No. 306 of the Public Acts of 1969, pertaining to judicial review, the court originally taking jurisdiction shall maintain jurisdiction for purposes of judicial review.

324.1705. Intervention; determination as to pollution; collateral estoppel; res judicata: Sec. 5. (1) Whenever administrative, licensing or other proceedings, and judicial review thereof are available by law, the agency or the court may permit the attorney general, any political subdivision of the state, any instrumentality or agency of the state or of a political subdivision thereof, any person, partnership, corporation, association, organization or other legal entity to intervene as a party on the filing of a pleading asserting that the proceeding or action for judicial review involves conduct which has, or which is likely to have, the effect of polluting, impairing or destroying the air, water or other natural resources or the public trust therein.

(2) In any such administrative, licensing or other proceedings, and in any judicial review thereof, any alleged pollution, impairment or destruction of the air, water or other natural resources or the public trust therein, shall be determined, and no conduct shall be authorized or approved which does, or is likely to have such effect so long as there is a feasible and prudent alternative consistent with the reasonable requirements of the public health, safety and welfare.

(3) The doctrines of collateral estoppel and res judicata may be applied by the court to prevent multiplicity of suits.

* * *

WEST MICHIGAN ENVIRONMENTAL ACTION COUNCIL, INC. V. NATURAL RESOURCES COMMISSION
275 N.W.2d 538 (Mich. 1979)

MOODY, Justice.

The issue is whether plaintiffs have made a prima facie showing under the Michigan environmental protection act, M.C.L. § 691.1201 *et seq.* [now codified at § 324.1701 *et seq.*] that the drilling of ten exploratory wells in the Pigeon River Country State Forest will constitute a likely impairment or destruction of natural resources.

* * *

FACTS

In 1968 the Department of Natural Resources (DNR) sold oil and gas leases covering 546,196.89 acres of state-owned land, including 57,669 acres in what is now known as the Pigeon River Country State Forest (Pigeon River Forest or Forest). Since that time, 19 oil and gas wells have been drilled in the Forest, five of which have been and are now producing wells.

Over a period of years, various plans to provide for controlled oil and gas development in the Forest were considered by the DNR. A management plan (the "limited development plan"), allowing oil and gas development in the southern one-third of the Forest while prohibiting development in the northern two-thirds, was submitted by the Director of the DNR, Howard Tanner, to the Natural Resources Commission (NRC). The DNR was asked to prepare an Environmental Impact Statement with respect to this management plan. In December, 1975, the Environmental Impact Statement (EIS) was completed.

The DNR then commenced negotiations with oil companies holding leases in the Forest in an attempt to have them agree to the development scheme set forth in the proposed management plan. On June 11, 1976, the NRC entered into an agreement entitled "Stipulation Consent Order" with Shell Oil Company, Amoco Production Company, and Northern Michigan Exploration Company. The consent order adopted the limited development plan allowing oil and gas development in the southern one-third of the Forest, subject to certain enumerated conditions and restrictions.

* * *

II

Plaintiffs allege that the trial court deferred to the DNR's conclusion that no pollution, impairment or destruction of the air, water or other natural resources or the public trust therein was likely to result from the contemplated drilling. Plaintiffs claim that such deference constituted error by the trial court and that the court had a responsibility to independently determine whether such pollution, impairment or destruction would occur. We agree that the trial court so erred.

While we understand the trial judge's reluctance to substitute his judgment for that of an agency with experience and expertise, the Michigan Environmental Protection Act requires independent, *de novo* determinations by the courts.

* * *

* * * We find, however, no need to order remand because we conclude that a judgment in favor of plaintiffs is required on the record presented.

III

Defendants in this case have not sought to raise any affirmative defenses under M.C.L. § 324.1703; but, rather, have rested their case on a denial that plaintiffs have made a prima facie showing that the conduct of defendants has, or is likely to pollute, impair or destroy the air, water or other natural resources or the public trust therein. We find that plaintiffs have demonstrated a likelihood of impairment or destruction of natural resources, specifically of elk, as a result of the proposed drilling of ten exploratory wells.

There is little, if any, dispute that the drilling of the exploratory wells will have some adverse impact upon some wildlife, particularly elk, bobcat and bear. The trial court found that "[t]here appears to be no question that adverse impacts will be visited upon particularly the elk, and to some lesser extent, bear and bobcat. * * * It is clear that an adverse impairment of the herd is likely for some unknown period to some unknown degree."

Perhaps the single most revealing piece of evidence is the Environmental Impact Statement for Potential Hydrocarbon Development in the Pigeon River Country State Forest, prepared by the DNR. Some of this statement concerns the impact of production of oil and is not relevant for present purposes. However, many of the EIS's conclusions directly apply to the effects of exploratory drilling.

Testimony before the trial court indicated that six of the ten proposed sites were not adjacent to any road, requiring that roads be built to such sites. The EIS cites studies in Montana, by the Intermountain Forestry and Range Experiment Station, 1973, which concluded that "[e]lk avoid roads even when there is no traffic." The EIS also observed that "[w]hether the elk will return to their former range following completion of the last seismic survey work is unknown."

Seismic survey work precedes exploratory drilling and it is designed to determine whether oil might be in an area; exploratory wells are then drilled to determine if production efforts are warranted. Seismic survey work occurs over a less prolonged period than exploratory drilling and yet, apparently, may result in an extended absence of the elk to the extent that it is uncertain whether or not they will return.

Exploratory drilling obviously exacerbates this problem and, in fact, the EIS notes, "with the possibility of drilling and production development following the survey, an early return by the elk is doubtful."

The EIS observes that "[t]he most pressing need of Michigan elk is to protect their range against further human intrusion for purposes other than timber or wildlife management," and that the last remaining sanctuaries against the disturbance of oil and gas development have now disappeared. It concludes:

> "Additional disturbances from hydrocarbon development, new roads, initial drilling activities, and the presence of facility sites will significantly reduce elk numbers in the proposed area. It is likely that much of the existing herd will not remain in revised Unit 1, but will spread out to the northern areas of the PRCSF and to private lands. However, private lands also may be impacted by hydrocarbon development. *An unknown number will not survive since habitat is finite.* A viable population *may* survive, however, *if* intensive management efforts are established in priority areas in the northern PRCSF *and if* poaching can be substantially decreased throughout the elk range." (Emphasis supplied.)

The EIS also found that bobcats are "expected to retreat in the face of hydrocarbon development. The history of this species indicates a high degree of incompatibility with the works of man." With respect to bears, the EIS states "[b]ears have been pressed into wild areas of diminishing size by the increasing pressures of land development and other human disturbances throughout much of the northern Lower Peninsula. * * * It is expected that the one to two percent of the land which will be intensively developed as sites will have less impact on bears than will the development of service roads with resultant multiplied human activities and increased human contact."

Some quantification of the adverse impact of exploratory drilling on the elk can be gained from comparing the EIS's Matrix for Proposed Hydrocarbon Development in the Southern Portion of the Forest with Dr. Inman's testimony. Dr. Inman, who participated in the development of the EIS, testified that a slow recovery time is considered to be 40 to 50 years or more, a short recovery time less than 20 years, and a great recovery time is about 100 years or more.

The Environmental Impact Matrix predicts that elk will be adversely affected by the development of roads and pads. These are associated with even exploratory drilling. The Environmental Impact Matrix defines a significant adverse impact as "a change in the element that is impacted from its present status to a status that may take a *long time for recovery*, at least during the duration of the project." Applying Dr. Inman's definitions of what constitutes a slow recovery time to the matrix predictions, it would appear that elk would avoid the impacted areas for 40 to 50 years.

As noted above, the trial court conceded that the exploratory drilling would have an adverse effect upon wildlife. However, the trial court determined that this adverse impact did not constitute impairment or destruction of a natural resource because such adverse impacts are

"commonly the result of management decisions. Improving deer habitat by cutting trees to allow the sun to shine on the forest floor for the purpose of new growth, certainly has an adverse impact upon the animals, birds, so forth, using the trees. Eradicating the entire fish population in a lake or stream to destroy unwanted trash species in order to plant more acceptable fish certainly has an adverse impact on the fish killed but is an acceptable management technique. * * * These animals, along with the trees that will be cut, harvested, or otherwise removed, are the innocent victims of the discovery of oil in their forest domain."

This determination reveals a fundamental misconception. If nature is allowed to pursue its own course, the growth and expansion of some species will inevitably result in the diminution and possible extinction of others. Faced with a situation where an adverse impact will occur naturally unless some action is taken, it is a management decision to determine whether such natural processes should proceed or whether, through human intervention, the adverse impact should artificially be shifted to other species. The choice is not whether an adverse impact will occur, but, rather, upon what.

* * *

We recognize that virtually all human activities can be found to adversely impact natural resources in some way or other. The real question before us is when does such impact rise to the level of impairment or destruction?

The DNR's environmental impact statement recognizes that "[e]lk are *unique* to this area of Michigan" and that the herd is "the *only* sizable wild herd east of the Mississippi River. Several attempts to introduce elk elsewhere in Michigan have been unsuccessful."

It is estimated that the herd's population, which numbered in excess of 1500 in 1963, now probably lies between 170 and 180. Expert testimony has established that the Pigeon River Country State Forest, particularly unit 1 in which the exploratory drilling is to take place, provides excellent habitat for elk and that the elk frequent this area. Furthermore, it is clear from the record that available habitat is shrinking. The result of a further shrinkage of this habitat by the intrusion of exploratory drilling and its concomitant developments is that "an unknown number [of elk] will not survive."

In light of the limited number of the elk, the unique nature and location of this herd, and the apparently serious and lasting, though unquantifiable, damage that will result to the herd from the drilling of the ten exploratory wells, we conclude that defendants' conduct constitutes an impairment or destruction of a natural resource.

Accordingly, we reverse and remand to the trial court for entry of a permanent injunction prohibiting the drilling of the ten exploratory wells pursuant to permits issued on August 24, 1977.

NOTES

1. How does the Michigan Environmental Protection Act (MEPA) differ from NEPA? What are its essential goals, as compared to the goals of NEPA? Does the Michigan statute serve as a substitute for NEPA-type statutes, or should it work along side such laws? Do you see any parallels between MEPA and the ESA?

2. As illustrated in *West Michigan Environmental Action Council*, MEPA requires the court to determine if the environmental impact of an activity rises to the level of impairment necessary to justify declaratory or equitable relief. Another case in which the impairment standard was at issue is *Kimberly Hill Neighborhood Ass'n v. Dion*, 320 N.W.2d 668 (Mich. Ct. App. 1982). There, the court concluded that the proposed development of 9.2 acres of diverse wetlands serving as wildlife habitat did not rise to the requisite level of impairment. The court stated that "impairment" must be considered from a statewide rather than local perspective, and that the impairment analysis must go beyond an examination of individual animals or neighborhoods to consider entire populations and ecological communities. Additionally, the court asserted that the impairment standard does not limit resource conservation to only those resources which are "biologically unique" or "endangered." On the basis of these considerations, the court held that the proposed development of the wetlands would not interfere with wildlife habitat from a statewide perspective and accordingly refused to enjoin the development.

3. In *City of Portage v. Kalamazoo County Road Commission*, 355 N.W.2d 913 (Mich. Ct. App. 1984), the defendant sought to remove 74 trees along a city road. The trial court analyzed the impairment standard by weighing the environmental risk of removing the trees against the benefit accomplished by their removal. The appellate court rejected this analysis, stating that the impairment analysis should compare the environmental situation prior to the proposed action with the probable condition of the environment afterwards. Four factors were considered by the court:

> (1) whether the natural resource involved is rare, unique, endangered, or has historical significance, (2) whether the resource is easily replaceable * * * , (3) whether the proposed action will have any significant consequential effect on other natural resources, * * * and (4) whether the direct or consequential impact on animals or vegetation will affect a critical number, considering the nature and location of the wildlife affected.

Id. at 916. According to the court, there was no evidence showing that the trees were unique or that removal of the trees would have any significant consequential effects on other natural resources. Additionally, the environmental damage from removing the trees could be easily repaired. The court concluded that removal of the trees did not rise to the level of impairment necessary for MEPA protection.

4. MEPA § 324.1701(1) allows "any person" to maintain an action "for the protection of the air, water, and other natural resources and the public trust therein * * * ." Can a Canadian citizen invoke its protections? If MEPA were adopted as federal law, what constitutional constraints might limit application of this provision? *See Lujan v. Defenders of Wildlife*, 504 U.S. 555 (1992), *supra* at Chapter 3.

5. How does the MEPA § 324.1701(2) standard of review differ from the APA? Would a federal court applying the *Chevron* test arrive at the same conclusion as the Michigan Supreme Court in *West Michigan Environmental Action Council*? Does the MEPA place judges in an inappropriate role?

6. By now you may conclude that some constraints may not be neatly classified as either procedural or substantive, but rather fall in a continuum between the two. Further complicating the picture is the interplay between procedure and outcome. Are there certain decisionmaking procedures that systematically result in certain kinds of outcomes?

7. In 1992, Canada adopted federal environmental impact assessment legislation which imposes substantive controls on agencies in two ways: First, if the "responsible authority" finds that a proposed project "is likely to cause significant adverse environmental effects that cannot be justified in the circumstances," the responsible authority cannot approve the project. Canadian Environment Protection Act, R.S.C. Ch. 37, §§ 20(1)(b), 37(1)(b). While the agency obviously has wide discretion in deciding what can be "justified," this provision signals that the Canadian Parliament intended that EIA should encompass more than mere process. Second, and perhaps more importantly, the Canadian law specifically requires the responsible authority, in approving a project, to ensure that appropriate mitigation measures are implemented. *Id.* at §§ 20(1)(a), 37(1)(a). In addition, the responsible authority must design and arrange for the implementation of an appropriate "follow-up program" for any such approved project. *Id.* at § 38. For a comparative analysis of U.S. and Australian environmental impact assessment, read Mark Squillace, *An American Perspective on Environmental Impact Assessment in Australia*, 20 COLUM. J. ENVTL. L. 43 (1995).

PROBLEM # 2: SUBSTANTIVE EFFECTS ON AGENCY DECISIONMAKING

Martina Goldbrick, a prominent real estate developer, has proposed to build a new shopping mall on land she owns in Fairfax, Virginia, a suburb of Washington, D.C. The proposed mall will be adjacent to an existing shopping mall, which was built about twenty years ago by Donald Grump, Goldbrick's chief competitor. The existing mall is very popular. It has ample parking and a wide range of stores. Most experts believe that the community will not support two similar malls in the same vicinity and many in the business community suspect that Goldbrick's primary motive in deciding to build a new mall adjacent to the Grump Mall is to force the Grump Mall to close down.

Construction of the Goldbrick Mall will require filling about thirty acres of wetlands, and as a result, Goldbrick must obtain a permit from the U.S. Army Corps of Engineers in accordance with § 404 of the Clean Water Act. The Corps has prepared a draft and final EIS on the project and has decided to issue the permit.

Save Our Swamps (SOS), a local conservation group, opposes the Goldbrick Mall. It points out that the area that will be filled by the new mall is an important part of a unique wetlands ecosystem which supports a wide variety of plant and animal life. SOS further notes that there is no demand for a new mall, and that the only way the new mall will succeed is if it forces the existing mall out of business. The final EIS acknowledged these essential facts. The economic analysis prepared by the Corps on the project shows a benefit/cost ratio for the project of .10. This means that for every dollar spent constructing the mall and every dollar value of wetlands lost, the project will return only 10 cents in benefits to society. The Corps nonetheless decided to approve the project on the grounds that the project itself was a viable, profitable enterprise for Goldbrick and there were no alternative sites available for another mall.

Grump has recently become a member of SOS and is preparing to challenge the Corps' decision on the grounds that it violated NEPA. Assuming the Corps made no procedural errors, what are his chances for success?

Section 404(c) of the Clean Water Act authorizes the U.S. Environmental Protection Agency to veto Corp permits. Was the EPA's decision not to object to the Corps' decision an "action" requiring either an EA or an EIS? *See Chesapeake Bay Foundation v. Virginia State Water Control Board*, 453 F. Supp. 122 (E.D. Va. 1978). Can the EPA play any other role in this NEPA dispute?

While Grump's lawsuit was pending, a biologist for SOS discovered on the Goldbrick site a rare plant, the velvet lousewort, that is listed as endangered under the ESA. How is this likely to affect the proposed project? How is it likely to affect Grump's chances for success in the litigation? Would the discovery of an endangered animal change your analysis?

Suppose that Virginia had adopted legislation identical to the Michigan Environmental Protection Act. How might the existence of such legislation affect Grump's chances for success?

6 THE DECISION TO PREPARE ENVIRONMENTAL DOCUMENTS

A. Significance

HANLY V. KLEINDIENST [HANLY II]
471 F.2d 823 (2d Cir. 1972), *cert. denied*, 412 U.S. 908 (1973)

[The following facts are taken from a prior decision in this controversy. *Hanly v. Mitchell* [*Hanly I*] 460 F.2d 640 (2d Cir. 1972), *cert. denied*, 409 U.S. 990.]

Plaintiffs, including Reverend Denis Hanly, Pastor of Transfiguration Church, 29 Mott Street, sue for themselves and on behalf of a class of "residents, merchants, businessmen, institutions, religious organizations and other members of the public living within the area." * * * *Although that area contains many government buildings, including several courthouses, surprisingly at least 50,000 people live there and in adjacent Chinatown. Included in that group are over 3,000 persons living in approximately 660 cooperative apartments in two buildings called Chatham Towers and Chatham Green. These directly face the proposed new jail, some 100-150 feet away. The apartments, constructed in the last decade, have many individual terraces, and there are lawns and play areas around the buildings.*

*   *   * *The proposed construction is called the Foley Square Courthouse Annex, but it actually consists of two nine-story buildings. One, on the southerly portion of the site, will be a conventional office building containing about 127,000 square feet of interior space. It will house the relocated offices of the United States Attorney and the United States Marshal for the Southern District of New York and the Joint Strike Force Against Organized Crime. The other building, on the northerly portion of the site, will contain about 200,000 square feet and will be the Metropolitan Correction Center (MCC). Although plaintiffs formally attack the entire project, this building draws most of their fire. The MCC is designed to provide modern detention facilities for 449 prisoners, including an infirmary, a diagnostic center for psychiatric problems and a community treatment center for outpatients as well as inmates. Since the MCC is intended to replace the overcrowded and inadequate Federal Detention Center now located at West Street in Manhattan, it is probable that the new building will service not only prisoners involved in prosecutions in the Southern District but also prisoners from the Eastern District, and perhaps from New Jersey.*

*   *   *

[The court found that a brief memorandum prepared by the GSA did not satisfy NEPA and remanded the case to the agency for further NEPA compliance.]

MANSFIELD, Circuit Judge:

*   *   * Following the district court's denial for the second time of a preliminary injunction against construction of a jail and other facilities known as the Metropolitan Correction Center ("MCC") we are called upon to decide whether a redetermination by the General Services

Administration ("GSA") that the MCC is not a facility "significantly affecting the quality of the human environment" * * * satisfies the requirements of NEPA and thus renders it unnecessary for GSA to follow the procedure prescribed by § 102(2)(C) of NEPA, 42 U.S.C. § 4332(2)(C), which requires a formal, detailed environmental impact statement. In view of the failure of the GSA, upon redetermination, to make findings with respect to certain relevant factors and to furnish an opportunity to appellants to submit relevant evidence, the case is again remanded.

* * *

Following the remand a new threshold determination in the form of a 25-page "Assessment of the Environmental Impact" ("Assessment" herein) was made by the GSA and submitted to the district court on June 15, 1972. This document * * * reflects a detailed consideration of numerous relevant factors. Among other things, it analyzes the size, exact location, and proposed use of the MCC; its design features, construction, and aesthetic relationship to its surroundings; the extent to which its occupants and activities conducted in it will be visible by the community; the estimated effects of its operation upon traffic, public transit and parking facilities; its approximate population, including detainees and employees; its effect on the level of noise, smoke, dirt, obnoxious odors, sewage and solid waste removal; and its energy demands. It also sets forth possible alternatives, concluding that there is none that is satisfactory. Upon the basis of this Assessment the Acting Commissioner of the Public Building Service Division of the GSA, who is the responsible official in charge, concluded on June 7, 1972, that the MCC was not an action significantly affecting the quality of the human environment.

* * *

Discussion

At the outset we accept and agree with the decision of the *Hanly I* panel that the agency in charge of a proposed federal action (in this case the GSA) is the party authorized to make the threshold determination whether an action is one "significantly affecting the quality of the human environment" as that phrase is used in § 102(2)(C). * * *

* * *

Upon attempting * * * to interpret the amorphous term "significantly," as it is used in § 102(2)(C), we are faced with the fact that almost every major federal action, no matter how limited in scope, has some adverse effect on the human environment. It is equally clear that an action which is environmentally important to one neighbor may be of no consequence to another. Congress could have decided that every major federal action must therefore be the subject of a detailed impact statement prepared according to the procedure prescribed by § 102(2)(C). By adding the word "significantly," however, it demonstrated that before the agency in charge triggered that procedure, it should conclude that a greater environmental impact would result than from "any major federal action." Yet the limits of the key term have not been adequately defined by Congress or by guidelines issued by the CEQ and other responsible federal agencies vested with broad discretionary powers under NEPA. Congress apparently was willing to depend principally upon the agency's good faith determination as to what conduct would be sufficiently serious from an ecological stand-point to require use of the full-scale procedure.

Guidelines issued by the CEQ, which are echoed in rules for implementation published by the Public Buildings Service, the branch of GSA concerned with the construction of the MCC, suggest that a formal impact statement should be prepared with respect to "proposed actions, the environmental impact of which is likely to be highly controversial." However, the term "controversial" apparently refers to cases where a substantial dispute exists as to the size, nature or effect of the major federal action rather than to the existence of opposition to a use, the effect of which is relatively undisputed. This Court in *Hanly I*, for instance, did not require a formal impact statement with respect to the office building portion of the Annex despite the existence of neighborhood opposition to it. * * *

In the absence of any Congressional or administrative interpretation of the term, we are persuaded that in deciding whether a major federal action will "significantly" affect the quality of the human environment the agency in charge, although vested with broad discretion, should normally be required to review the proposed action in the light of at least two relevant factors: (1) the extent to which the action will cause adverse environmental effects in excess of those created by existing uses in the area affected by it, and (2) the absolute quantitative adverse environmental effects of the action itself, including the cumulative harm that results from its contribution to existing adverse conditions or uses in the affected area. Where conduct conforms to existing uses, its adverse consequences will usually be less significant than when it represents a radical change. Absent some showing that an entire neighborhood is in the process of redevelopment, its existing environment, though frequently below an ideal standard, represents a norm that cannot be ignored. For instance, one more highway in an area honeycombed with roads usually has less of an adverse impact than if it were constructed through a roadless public park.

Although the existing environment of the area which is the site of a major federal action constitutes one criterion to be considered, it must be recognized that even a slight increase in adverse conditions that form an existing environmental milieu may sometimes threaten harm that is significant. One more factory polluting air and water in an area zoned for industrial use may represent the straw that breaks the back of the environmental camel. Hence the absolute, as well as comparative, effects of a major federal action must be considered.

Chief Judge Friendly's thoughtful dissent, while conceding that we (and governmental agencies) face a difficult problem in determining the meaning of the vague and amorphous term "significantly" as used in § 102(2)(C), offers no solution other than to suggest that an impact statement should be required whenever a major federal action might be "arguably" or "potentially" significant and that such an interpretation would insure the preparation of impact statements except in cases of "true" insignificance. In our view this suggestion merely substitutes one form of semantical vagueness for another. By failure to use more precise standards it would leave the agency, which admittedly must make the determination, in the very quandary faced in this case and only serve to prolong and proliferate uncertainty as to when a threshold determination should be accepted. The problem is not resolved by use of terms as "*obviously* insignificant," "minor," "*arguably* significant," a "*fairly arguable*" adverse impact, or the like, or by reference to "grey" areas or characterization of our opinion as "raising the floor" to permit agencies to escape an impact statement.

We agree with Chief Judge Friendly that an impact statement should not be required where the impact will be minor or unimportant, or where "there is no sensible reason for making one," and that such a statement should be required where the action may fairly be said to have a potentially significant adverse effect. But these conclusions merely pose the problem which cannot be solved by an interchange of adjectives. In our view such a morass can be avoided only by formulation of more precise factors that must be considered in making the essential threshold determination. This we have attempted to do.

* * *

Although this Court in *Hanly I* did not expressly articulate the standards we have used, its decision that the proposed office building portion of the Annex would not be environmentally significant conforms to the rationale. The office building would not differ substantially from the makeup of the surrounding area. Nor would it in absolute terms give rise to sizeable adverse environmental effects. Most of the employees occupying the building would merely be transferred from the existing Courthouse where the newly created space will be used primarily for courtrooms and desperately needed office space for court personnel. On the other hand, the proposed jail, for reasons set forth in detail in *Hanly I,* might have adverse effects differing both qualitatively and quantitatively from those associated with existing uses in the area. Moreover there was insufficient evidence that the absolute environmental effect with respect to the jail had been analyzed and considered by the GSA. Thus the matter was remanded for reappraisal. Now that the GSA has made and submitted its redetermination in the form of a 25-page "Assessment," our task is to determine (1) whether it satisfies the foregoing tests as to environmental significance, and (2) whether GSA, in making its assessment and determination, has observed "procedure required by law" as that term is used in § 10 of the APA, 5 U.S.C. § 706(2)(D).

The Assessment closely parallels in form a detailed impact statement. The GSA's finding that the MCC would harmonize architecturally with existing buildings in the area, and even enhance the appearance of the neighborhood, is supported by details of the proposed building, architectural renditions, and photographs of the area. The facade of the MCC and of the Annex office building are designed to reflect the first cornice height of the Municipal Building, a prominent architectural feature of both the United States Courthouse and the New York Supreme Court, and to blend closely in appearance and geometry with the surrounding buildings, including the newly constructed New York City Police Headquarters. The windows, which will be glazed with unbreakable polycarbonate plastic shatter-proof sheets will be recessed and will be of a dark gray color designed to insulate the community from visual contact with the detainees. Moreover, there will be no fortress walls or unsightly steel-barred windows. In short, the building will not look like a correctional center.

The Assessment further describes efforts that will be made to minimize any contact between detainees and members of the community. In addition to the recessed, darkened windows, all prisoners will enter the building through an entrance on Cardinal Hayes Place, located on the side opposite from and out of view of neighborhood residential apartments. Although there will be a roof-top recreational area for detainees, a 20-foot wall will minimize their visibility from the apartments.

The Assessment further notes that any increase in traffic from MCC will be extremely slight. One van will take and return detainees on one daily round trip during weekdays to the Eastern District Courthouse and to the Newark District Courthouse. However, this traffic will be offset by the fact that two vans currently used to bring prisoners from West Street to the Courthouse in Foley Square daily will be eliminated since these prisoners will be transported from the MCC across enclosed bridges connecting it with the Courthouse.

Visiting hours at the MCC will be permitted between 8:00 A.M. and 4:00 P.M. and between 7:00 P.M. and 9:00 P.M. The GSA Assessment projected on the basis of past experience that approximately 130 visitors will arrive per day with no more than 20 on the premises at any one time. This would not impose any excessive burden on mass transportation facilities, which are nearby, numerous and include several subway lines and bus routes described in detail. In addition to limited parking during the day on certain nearby streets, there are at least six garages or lots available for parking in the area, also identified by location and capacity. There will be only four truck deliveries of supplies per day to the premises.

The windows of the MCC are designed to minimize any noise from within the premises, in addition to which detainees will be under constant supervision when outside on the roof-top for recreational purposes. During the past five years there have been only two small inside disturbances at the present detention facility at West Street, Manhattan, and three outside disturbances, the latter confined to non-violent picketing, marching and the like, incidents which have been common occurrence in the Foley Square area during the same period.

The Assessment makes clear that the MCC will not produce any unusual or excessive amounts of smoke, dirt, obnoxious odors, solid waste, or other forms of pollution. The utilities required to heat and air-condition the building are readily available and the MCC is designed to incorporate energy-saving features, so that no excessive power demands are posed. The GSA further represents that the building will conform to all local codes, use and zoning, and attaches a letter from the New York City Office of Lower Manhattan Development dated August 4, 1971, indicating approval of the Annex, which includes the MCC.

Appellants contend that the Assessment is merely a "rewrite" of GSA's earlier February 23, 1971 "Environmental Statement" found inadequate in *Hanly I*, and that GSA has failed to take into consideration certain adverse facts. A comparison of the 25-page detailed Assessment with the earlier statement reveals that the former is far more than a "rewrite" and that it furnishes detailed findings with respect to most of the relevant factors unmentioned in the earlier statement. On its face the Assessment indicates that GSA has redetermined the environmental impact of the MCC with care and thoroughness. In the absence of contrary factual proof, we would have no hesitancy in upholding it, whether it is reviewed by the "arbitrary, capricious" standard or the "rational basis" test. Judged by the comparative uses in the area and according to its quantitative environmental effects, the MCC should not have a significant effect upon the human environment.

Appellants offer little or no evidence to contradict the detailed facts found by the GSA. For the most part their opposition is based upon a psychological distaste for having a jail located so close to residential apartments, which is understandable enough. It is doubtful whether psychological and sociological effects upon neighbors constitute the type of factors that may be considered in making such a determination since they do not lend themselves to measurement. However we need not decide that issue because these apartments were constructed within two or three blocks of another existing jail, The Manhattan House of Detention for Men, which is much larger than the proposed MCC and houses approximately 1,200 prisoners. Furthermore the area in which the MCC is located has at all times been zoned by the City of New York as a commercial district designed to provide for a wide range of uses, specifically including "*Prisons*."

Despite the GSA's scrupulous efforts the appellants do present one or two factual issues that merit further consideration and findings by the GSA. One bears on the possibility that the MCC will substantially increase the risk of crime in the immediate area, a relevant factor as to which the Assessment fails to make an outright finding despite the direction to do so in *Hanly I*. Appellants urge that the Community Treatment Program and the program for observation and study of non-resident out-patients will endanger the health and safety of the immediate area by exposing neighbors and passersby to drug addicts visiting the MCC for drug maintenance and to drug pushers and hangers-on who would inevitably frequent the vicinity of a drug maintenance center. If the MCC were to be used as a drug treatment center, the potential increase in crime might tip the scales in favor of a mandatory detailed impact statement. The Government has assured us by postargument letter addressed to the Court that:

> "Neither the anticipated nonresident pre-sentence study program nor any program to be conducted within the Metropolitan Correction Center will include drug maintenance."

While we do not question the Government's good faith, a finding in the matter by GSA is essential, since the Assessment is ambiguous as to the scope of the non-resident out-patient observation program and makes no finding on the subject of whether the MCC will increase the risk of crime in the community. * * *

Appellants further contend that they have never been given an opportunity to discuss the MCC with any governmental agency prior to GSA's submission of its Assessment, which raises the question whether the agency acted "without observance of procedure required by law," *see Citizens to Preserve Overton Park v. Volpe,* 401 U.S. 402 (1971). We do not share the Government's view that the procedural mandates of § 102(A), (B), and (D), 42 U.S.C. § 4332(2)(A), (B) and (D), apply only to actions found by the agency itself to have a significant environmental effect. While these sections are somewhat opaque, they are not expressly limited to "major Federal actions significantly affecting the quality of the human environment." Indeed if they were so limited § 102(D) [now § 102(2)(E)], which requires the agency to develop appropriate alternatives to the recommended course of action, would be duplicative since § 102(C), which does apply to actions "significantly affecting" the environment, specifies that the detailed impact statement must deal with "alternatives to the proposed action." 42 U.S.C. § 4332(2)(C)(iii). However, in our view the Assessment does, in fact, satisfy the requirement of § 102(2)(A) that an interdisciplinary approach taking into account the "natural and social sciences and the environmental design arts" be used. The GSA has retained architects familiar with the design requirements of the Civic Center and consulted with the Office of Lower Manhattan Development in an effort to harmonize the MCC with the Civic Center. The Assessment scrupulously takes into account the aesthetics and the tangible factors involved in the designing and planning of the MCC. Furthermore we find that § 102(2)(D) was complied with insofar as the GSA specifically considered the alternatives to continuing operation at the present facility at West Street and evaluated the selected site as compared with other specified possibilities. Although the assessment of the alternative sites was not as intensive as we might hope, its failure to analyze them in further detail does not warrant reversal.

A more serious question is raised by the GSA's failure to comply with § 102(2)(B), which requires the agency to "identify and develop methods and procedures . . . which will insure that presently unquantified environmental amenities and values may be given appropriate consideration in decision-making along with economic and technical considerations." 42 U.S.C. § 4332 (2)(B). Since an agency, in making a threshold determination as to the "significance" of an action, is called upon to review in a general fashion the same factors that would be studied in depth for preparation of a detailed environmental impact statement, § 102(2)(B) requires that some rudimentary procedures be designed to assure a fair and informed preliminary decision. Otherwise the agency, lacking essential information, might frustrate the purpose of NEPA by a threshold determination that an impact statement is unnecessary. Furthermore, an adequate record serves to preclude later changes in use without consideration of their environmental significance as required by NEPA.

Where a proposed major federal action may affect the sensibilities of a neighborhood, the prudent course would be for the agency in charge, before making a threshold decision, to give notice to the community of the contemplated action and to accept all pertinent information proffered by concerned citizens with respect to it. Furthermore, in line with the procedure usually followed in zoning disputes, particularly where emotions are likely to be aroused by fears, or rumors of misinformation, a public hearing serves the dual purpose of enabling the agency to obtain all relevant data and to satisfy the community that its views are being considered. However, neither NEPA nor any other federal statute mandates the specific type of procedure to be followed by federal agencies. * * *

Notwithstanding the absence of statutory or administrative provisions on the subject, this Court has already held in *Hanly I* that federal agencies must "affirmatively develop a reviewable environmental record . . . even for purposes of a threshold section 102(2)(C) determination." We now go further and hold that before a preliminary or threshold determination of significance is made the responsible agency must give notice to the public of the proposed major federal action and an opportunity to submit relevant facts which might bear upon the agency's threshold decision. We do not suggest that a full-fledged formal hearing must be provided before each such determination is made, although it should be apparent that in many cases such a hearing would be advisable for reasons already indicated. The necessity for a hearing will depend greatly upon the circumstances surrounding the particular proposed action and upon the likelihood that a hearing will be more effective than other methods in developing relevant information and an understanding of the proposed action. The precise procedural steps to be adopted are better left to the agency, which should be in a better position than the court to determine whether solution of the problems faced with respect to a specific major federal action can better be achieved through a hearing or by informal acceptance of relevant data.

* * *

The case is remanded for further proceedings not inconsistent with this opinion. The mandate shall issue forthwith.

FRIENDLY, Chief Judge (dissenting):

The learned opinion of my brother MANSFIELD gives these plaintiffs, and environmental advocates in future cases, both too little and too much. It gives too little because it raises the floor of what constitutes "major Federal actions significantly affecting the quality of the human environment," 42 U.S.C. § 4332 (2)(C), higher than I believe Congress intended. It gives too much because it requires that before making a threshold determination that no impact statement is demanded, the agency must go through procedures which I think are needed only when an impact statement must be made. The upshot is that a threshold determination that a proposal does not constitute major Federal action significantly affecting the quality of the human environment becomes a kind of mini-impact statement. The preparation of such a statement under the conditions laid down by the majority is unduly burdensome when the action is truly minor or insignificant. On the other hand, there is a danger that if the threshold determination is this elaborate, it may come to replace the impact statement in the grey area between actions which, though "major" in a monetary sense, are obviously insignificant (such as the construction of the proposed office building) and actions that are obviously significant (such as the construction of an atomic power plant). We would better serve the purposes of Congress by keeping the threshold low enough to insure that impact statements are prepared for actions in this grey area and thus to permit the determination that no statement is required to be made quite informally in cases of true insignificance.

While I agree that determination of the meaning of "significant" is a question of law, one must add immediately that to make this determination on the basis of the dictionary would be impossible. Although all words may be "chameleons, which reflect the color of their environment," *C.I.R. v. National Carbide Corp.*, 167 F.2d 304, 306 (2d Cir. 1948) (L. Hand, J.), "significant" has that quality more than most. It covers a spectrum ranging from "not trivial" through "appreciable" to "important" and even "momentous." If the right meaning is at the lower end of the spectrum, the construction of the MCC comes within it; *per contra* if the meaning is at the higher end.

The scheme of the National Environmental Policy Act argues for giving "significant" a reading which places it toward the lower end of the spectrum. * * *

* * * What Congress was trying to say was "You don't need to make an impact statement, with the consequent expense and delay, when there is no sensible reason for making one." I thus agree with Judge J. Skelly Wright's view that "a statement is required whenever the action

arguably will have an adverse environmental impact," with the qualification, doubtless intended, that the matter must be *fairly* arguable. * * *

* * *

I thus reach the question whether, with the term so narrowed, the GSA's refusal to prepare an impact statement for the MCC can be supported. Accepting the majority's standard of review, I would think that, even with the fuller assessment here before us, the GSA could not reasonably conclude that the MCC does not entail potentially significant environmental effects. * * *

* * *

* * * The energies my brothers would require GSA to devote to still a third assessment designed to show that an impact statement is not needed would better be devoted to making one.

I would reverse and direct the issuance of an injunction until a reasonable period after the making of an impact statement.

NOTES

1.   The majority in *Hanly II* holds that "before a * * * threshold determination of significance is made the responsible agency must give notice to the public of the proposed major federal action and an opportunity to submit relevant facts which might bear upon the agency's threshold decision." 471 F.2d at 836. Is this requirement consistent with the subsequent decision of the U.S. Supreme Court in *Vermont Yankee*, *supra* at Chapter 3? What is the basis for the court's determination that these procedures are necessary? Why does Judge Friendly dissent?

2.   What are the plaintiffs' "environmental" concerns regarding the proposed project? Are these concerns within the scope of the "human environment" as defined at 40 C.F.R. § 1508.14?

3.   Whether an agency should prepare an EIS may not be obvious at first blush. What choices are available to an agency facing a proposed action when it is unsure as to whether an EIS is necessary? Under 40 C.F.R. § 1501.4, an agency faced with a proposed action may make one of only three choices: (1) it may decide to prepare an EIS; (2) it may decide that the proposed action is "categorically excluded" from NEPA; or (3) it may prepare an environmental assessment (EA).

4.   What are "categorical exclusions"? *See* 40 C.F.R. §§ 1501.4(a)(2); 1508.4. What requirements are imposed on an agency that seeks to categorically exclude certain actions from NEPA review? *See, e.g., Jones v. Gordon*, 792 F.2d 821, 827-29 (9th Cir. 1986) (invalidating the National Marine Fisheries Service's (NMFS's) use of a categorical exclusion for a permit authorizing capture of killer whales by Sea World because NMFS did not adequately explain why the permit does not fall under an exception to the agency's categorical exclusions for uncertain environmental impacts or unknown risks); *City of Alexandria v. Federal Highway Admin.*, 756 F.2d 1014 (4th Cir. 1985) (upholding the application of a categorical exclusion to the construction of entrance ramp meters and other traffic management systems for the Shirley Highway outside of Washington, D.C.).

5.   How does an "environmental assessment" differ from an EIS? What are the purposes of an EA as opposed to an EIS? *See* 40 C.F.R. §§ 1501.4(b-c); 1508.9.

6. When an agency prepares an environmental assessment it must either make a "finding of no significant impact" (FONSI), 40 C.F.R. § 1508.13, or it must decide to prepare an EIS. As a result of decisions like *Chevron, supra* Chapter 3, agencies are generally accorded a great deal of discretion by courts reviewing a decision not to prepare an EIS. Some courts have articulated specific standards for reviewing FONSIs:

> This court has established four criteria for reviewing an agency's decision to forego preparation of an EIS. First, the agency must have accurately identified the relevant environmental concern. Second, once the agency has identified the problem it must have taken a "hard look" at the problem in preparing the EA. Third, if a finding of no significant impact is made, the agency must be able to make a convincing case for its finding. Last, if the agency does find an impact of true significance, an EIS can be avoided only if the agency finds that changes or safeguards in the project sufficiently reduce the impact to a minimum.

Sierra Club v. United States Dep't of Transportation, 753 F.2d 120 (D.C. Cir. 1985) (upholding a Federal Aviation Administration FONSI for an order allowing airlines to operate out of Jackson Hole Airport in Grand Teton National Park).

In a few cases, however, courts have rejected as unreasonable an agency FONSI, or some other statement that an EIS is not necessary because the proposed action lacks significance. *See, e.g., Save the Yaak Committee v. Block*, 840 F.2d 714 (9th Cir. 1988) (road reconstruction and related timber sales); *Citizen Advocates for Responsible Expansion v. Dole*, 770 F.2d 423 (5th Cir. 1985) (interstate highway expansion in downtown Fort Worth); *Foundation on Economic Trends v. Heckler*, 756 F.2d 143 (D.C. Cir. 1985) (approval of university experiment to release genetically engineered, recombinant-DNA-containing organisms); *Natural Resources Defense Council v. Herrington*, 768 F.2d 1355 (D.C. Cir. 1985) (final rule finding that mandatory energy efficiency standards are not justified for certain types of household appliances); *Thomas v. Peterson*, 753 F.2d 754 (9th Cir. 1985) (road construction and related timber sales); *Foundation for North American Wild Sheep v. U.S. Dep't of Agriculture*, 681 F.2d 1172 (9th Cir. 1982) (road reopening).

Frequently, an agency defending a FONSI will argue that restrictions or mitigation measures included in the proposed action reduce the impacts to the point of insignificance. *See, e.g., Louisiana v. Lee*, 758 F.2d 1081 (5th Cir. 1985), *cert. denied*, 475 U.S. 1044 (1986) (renewal of permits for shell dredging); *Cabinet Mountains Wilderness v. Peterson*, 685 F.2d 678 (D.C. Cir. 1982) (approval of plan for exploratory drilling in a wilderness area). We will devote more attention to mitigation in Chapter 7.

Just as frequently, the basis for the plaintiff's challenge to an agency FONSI is that the scope of the proposed action is much broader than that suggested by the agency. *See, e.g., Thomas v. Peterson, infra* Chapter 7. The expansive definition of "scope" at 40 C.F.R. § 1508.25 lends support for such an argument in many cases. The scope of NEPA and ESA documents is addressed in detail *infra* Chapter 7.

7. Do you think that Chief Judge Friendly was justified in warning that formalized "threshold determinations," today's FONSIs, might come to replace true impact statements in cases in which the environmental effects are debatable? If so, would there be any harm? In 1992, the CEQ surveyed 45,000 EAs prepared by federal agencies that year and found that:

Agencies rarely use an EA to determine whether an EIS is necessary;

Agencies prepare EAs that are often quite lengthy and correspondingly costly; Agencies appear to rely heavily on mitigation measures to justify EAs and FONSIs.

COUNCIL ON ENVIRONMENTAL QUALITY, ENVIRONMENTAL QUALITY: THE TWENTY-THIRD ANNUAL REPORT 153 (1993). In its Twenty-Fifth Anniversary Report, the CEQ estimated that by 1993, federal agencies were preparing approximately 50,000 ESA annually, and averaging 488 EISs annually during the five year period between 1990 and 1994. COUNCIL ON ENVIRONMENTAL QUALITY, THE TWENTY-FIFTH ANNIVERSARY REPORT 51 (1997). Are the procedural requirements for preparation, consideration, and public input for an EA as thorough and specific as for an EIS? Is the content for such an EA as clearly defined?

8. The Council on Environmental Quality regulations now provide detailed guidance to administrative agencies which are trying to determine how NEPA may apply to a particular action. Note, for example, the various definitions of key terms which help to guide agencies in deciding whether to prepare an EIS, and if so, the extent to which issues should be addressed. These include: "affecting," 40 C.F.R. § 1508.3; "cumulative impact," 40 C.F.R. § 1508.7; "effects," 40 C.F.R. § 1508.8; "human environment," 40 C.F.R. § 1508.14; "major federal action," 40 C.F.R. § 1508.18; "proposal," 40 C.F.R. § 1508.23; "scope," 40 C.F.R. § 1508.25; and "significantly," 40 C.F.R. § 1508.27. Does the CEQ definition of the crucial term "significantly" differ from the *Hanly II* court's interpretation? Is the CEQ discussion of the relationship between "major" and "significantly" at 40 C.F.R. § 1508.18 consistent with the Second Circuit's interpretation of the two terms as separate requirements? *See Sierra Club v. Hodel*, 848 F.2d 1068, 1089 (10th Cir. 1988) ("'[M]ajor' federal action does not have a meaning completely independent of significant impact.")

9. What is the threshold standard for an agency deciding whether to prepare a biological assessment under the ESA? How is this decision linked to the NEPA process? *See* 50 C.F.R. § 402.12. Under what circumstances does an agency need to initiate formal consultation with the FWS? *See* 50 C.F.R. § 402.14. Should courts apply the same level of deference in reviewing ESA threshold questions as NEPA threshold questions?

CONNER V. BURFORD
848 F.2d 1441 (9th Cir. 1988), *cert. denied*, 489 U.S. 1012 (1989)

NORRIS, Circuit Judge:

This appeal presents the question whether federal agencies violated the National Environmental Policy Act of 1969 (NEPA), 42 U.S.C. § 4321 *et seq.*, or the Endangered Species Act of 1973 (ESA), 16 U.S.C. § 1531 *et seq.*, by selling oil and gas leases on 1,300,000 acres of national forest land in Montana without preparing either an environmental impact statement (EIS) or a comprehensive biological opinion encompassing the impact of post-leasing activities on threatened or endangered species. The district court ruled that the sale of the leases without an EIS or a comprehensive biological opinion violated both NEPA and the ESA, 605 F.Supp. 107. We affirm the judgment of the district court in part, reverse in part, and remand for further proceedings.

I
FACTS AND PROCEDURAL HISTORY

The Flathead National Forest in northwestern Montana is a vast tract of rugged mountainous wilderness. Its many lakes and rivers provide exceptionally pure surface water, prized for trout fishing, and its undisturbed ecosystem is a sustaining habitat not only for game animals, but also for the bald eagle, the peregrine falcon, the gray wolf, and the grizzly bear—all listed as threatened or endangered species under the ESA. The Gallatin National Forest in south-central Montana provides a tremendous diversity of natural resources. Its rugged landscape of mountains, valleys, and rivers supports abundant fish and wildlife populations, while portions of the forest also provide important timber reserves for the local logging industry. Bordered on the south by Yellowstone National Park, the Gallatin is the watershed for some of the nation's most important trout waters, including the blue-ribbon Madison River. Big game populations also teem in the wilds of the Gallatin, and 30,000 acres there have been identified as essential grizzly bear habitat.

Beneath the surface of these vast and beautiful national forests lies the reason for this litigation. Both forests are located in the geologic zone known as the Overthrust Belt, a formation running north-south from Canada to Mexico and thought to be a rich source of petroleum deposits. Since 1970, preliminary seismic explorations as well as oil seeps discovered in the area have triggered an avalanche of applications to the Bureau of Land Management (BLM) for oil and gas leases within the boundaries of the two forests.

In February and March of 1981, the United States Forest Service issued environmental assessments (EAs) recommending that a total of 1,300,000 acres of land in the Flathead and Gallatin National Forests be leased for oil and gas development. Based on these EAs, the Forest Service also issued Decision Notices and Findings of No Significant Impact (FONSIs), which conclude that the mere sale of oil and gas leases in the forests will have no significant impact on the human environment. The issuance of the FONSIs obviated the need for EISs at the lease sale phase of the project. *See* 40 C.F.R. § 1508.13 (1985).

Following the preparation of the EAs and the FONSIs, the BLM sold over 700 leases for oil and gas exploration, development, and production on 1,350,000 acres within the two forests. The leases fall into two basic categories depending on the nature of the stipulations written into the lease to ameliorate the environmental impact of oil and gas activities. Some of the leases contain "no surface occupancy" (NSO) stipulations. On their face, these NSO stipulations appear to prohibit lessees from occupying or using the surface of the leased land without further specific approval from the BLM. Leases fully governed by an NSO stipulation are referred to herein as "NSO leases." Leases not governed by an NSO stipulation, which we refer to as "non-NSO leases," contain the Forest Service's standard stipulations for environmental protection and, in some cases, special stipulations to protect particularly sensitive areas. These standard and special stipulations, which we refer to collectively as "mitigation stipulations," authorize the government to impose reasonable conditions on drilling, construction, and other surface-disturbing activities; unlike NSO stipulations, however, they do not authorize the government to preclude such activities altogether.

In addition to issuing the EAs and FONSIs under NEPA, the Forest Service also initiated formal consultations with the Fish and Wildlife Service (FWS), as required under the ESA, 16 U.S.C. § 1536(b), for the purpose of determining whether the surface-disturbing activities of the oil and gas lessees might jeopardize the continued existence of threatened or endangered species. Both the Forest Service and the FWS decided there was insufficient information about the nature of post-leasing oil and gas activities to render a comprehensive biological opinion considering anything more than the lease sale itself. Instead the FWS proposed ongoing consultation and preparation of additional biological opinions at various stages of post-leasing activities.

Following the issuance of the FONSIs, the EAs, and the biological opinions, administrative appeals were filed by James Conner, the Montana Wildlife Federation, and the Madison-Gallatin Alliance (appellees). *See* 36 C.F.R. § 211.19 (1980). Protests were also filed with the BLM in order to prevent leasing before the administrative proceedings were concluded. *See* 43 C.F.R. § 4.450-2 (1980). These appeals and protests were rejected and in 1982 leasing began in both the Flathead and Gallatin Forests.

Having exhausted their administrative remedies, the appellees then filed this action in federal district court in Montana, claiming that the sale of the leases without an EIS violated NEPA and that the sale of the leases without a biological opinion assessing the impact of post-leasing activities on the threatened and endangered species violated the ESA.

* * *

II

The NEPA Issues

Section 102(2)(C) of NEPA requires federal agencies to file an EIS before undertaking "major Federal actions significantly affecting the quality of the human environment." 42 U.S.C. § 4332(2)(C); 40 C.F.R. § 1508.11 (1985). If the agency finds, based on a less formal and less rigorous "environmental assessment," that the proposed action will not significantly affect the environment, the agency can issue a Finding of No Significant Impact (FONSI) in lieu of the EIS. 40 C.F.R. § 1508.13 (1985). We will uphold an agency decision that a particular project does not require an EIS unless that decision is unreasonable. *Friends of Endangered Species v. Jantzen*, 760 F.2d 976, 985 (9th Cir. 1985); *Foundation for North Am. Wild Sheep v. United States*, 681 F.2d 1172, 1177 (9th Cir. 1982). The reviewing court must assure, however, that the agency took a "hard look" at the environmental consequences of its decision. *Kleppe v. Sierra Club*, 427 U.S. 390, 410 n.21 (1976); *California v. Block*, 690 F.2d 753, 761 (9th Cir. 1982).

The purpose of an EIS is to apprise decisionmakers of the disruptive environmental effects that may flow from their decisions at a time when they "retain[ ] a maximum range of options." *Sierra Club v. Peterson*, 717 F.2d 1409, 1414 (D.C. Cir. 1983); *see also* 40 C.F.R. §§ 1501.2, 1502.1 (1985); *Thomas v. Peterson*, 753 F.2d 754, 760 (9th Cir. 1985); *Environmental Defense Fund v. Andrus*, 596 F.2d 848, 852-53 (9th Cir. 1979) (*EDF v. Andrus*). Toward this end, the courts have attempted to define a "point of commitment" at which the filing of an environmental impact statement is required. *Sierra Club v. Peterson*, 717 F.2d at 1414. *See* 40 C.F.R. § 1502.5(a) (1985) (EIS must be prepared at the go/no go stage). Our circuit has held that an EIS must be prepared before any irreversible and irretrievable commitment of resources. *EDF v. Andrus*, 596 F.2d at 852. *Accord Sierra Club v. Peterson*, 717 F.2d at 1414 (citing cases). Thus, in this case we must decide whether the sale of any of the oil and gas leases within the two forests constituted an irreversible and irretrievable commitment of federal forest land to surface-disturbing oil and gas activities that could have a significant impact on the environment.

In this case the Forest Service gave three justifications for its finding that none of the proposed leases would have a significant impact on the human environment:

(a) The Environmental Assessment and the analysis it documents conform with the guidance and management requirements given in the [Gallatin and Flathead National Forest Multiple Use Plans].

(b) The resulting action for which this environmental analysis is made will be the granting or denying of leases. This, in and of itself, will have no environmental effect. Surface-disturbing activities that are conducted as a result of granting gas and oil leases will be analyzed on a case-by-case basis, and further environmental analyses will be prepared as required by the National Environmental Policy Act.

(c) Appropriate standard and special stipulations will prevent or mitigate much of the adverse environmental impacts from gas and oil activities.

Gallatin FONSI at 2; *see also* Flathead FONSI at 2. Appellants add that, at the very least, the sale of an NSO lease cannot be considered to have a significant effect on the environment because, absent further government approval, the NSO leases absolutely prohibit surface-disturbing activity. We consider the validity of the agency's findings of no significant environmental impact with respect to the NSO leases separately from the validity of its findings with respect to the non-NSO leases.

A. The NSO Leases

For the purposes of this opinion, NSO leases are those leases that absolutely forbid the lessee from occupying or using the surface of the leased land unless a modification of the NSO stipulation is specifically approved by the BLM. Without approval of specific surface-disturbing activity, development of the oil and gas reserves underlying the surface of an NSO lease can only occur through directional (slant) drilling from a parcel not burdened by an NSO stipulation or by well spacing over a large reservoir such that no wells are located on the NSO leasehold. Of approximately 709 leases sold thus far, only 57 are governed by NSO stipulations in their entirety, but around 500 leases contain NSO stipulations covering a portion of the leased property.

Appellants argue that the sale of an NSO lease has *no* effect on the environment, let alone a significant one. They assert that such leases make no commitment of any part of the national forests to surface-disturbing activities by the lessees because the government retains *absolute* authority to decide whether any such activities will ever take place on the leased lands.[16] The district court disagreed, holding that the issuance of an NSO lease was an irreversible commitment of national forest land. The court reasoned, "The issuance of a lease with an NSO stipulation does not guarantee an EIS before any development would occur. In fact, NSO stipulations can be modified or removed without an EIS." 605 F. Supp. at 109.

We disagree with the district court's ruling that the sale of an NSO lease is an irreversible commitment of resources requiring the preparation of an EIS. In ruling that the NSO stipulation could be modified without the preparation of an EIS, the district court evidently relied on a provision in the NSO stipulation which reads: "The [NSO stipulation] may be modified when specifically approved in writing by the District Engineer, Geological Survey with concurrence of the authorized officer of the surface management agency." The mere inclusion of such a clause in the lease has no effect, however, on the obligation of the surface management agency to comply with NEPA. Modification or removal of an NSO stipulation would have the same effect as the sale of a non-NSO lease, which, as discussed below, would constitute an irretrievable commitment of resources requiring the preparation of an EIS. Contrary to the assumptions of the district court, NSO provisions cannot be freely altered without an EIS. We cannot assume that government agencies will not comply with their NEPA obligations in later stages of development. *Cf. Citizens to Preserve Overton Park v. Volpe*, 401 U.S. 402, 415

---

[16]   Despite this absolute control by the government, NSO leases have economic value because they give the lessees the exclusive right of development, should development be allowed. In this sense, an NSO lease is effectively a right of first refusal to produce oil and gas on the leased premises. Moreover, oil and gas reserves may be tapped without disturbing the surface (and thus without governmental approval under an NSO provision), through directional drilling or well spacing.

(1971) (agency action entitled to presumption of regularity). Thus, we believe that piecemeal invasion of the forests will be avoided because, as the federal appellants concede, government evaluation of surface-disturbing activity on NSO leases must include consideration of the potential for further connected development and cumulative impacts from all oil and gas development activities pursuant to the federal leases. *See Thomas v. Peterson*, 753 F.2d 754, 757-61 (9th Cir. 1985); 40 C.F.R. §§ 1508.7, 1508.8, 1508.25(a)(1), (2) (1985).

* * *

In sum, we hold that the sale of an NSO lease cannot be considered the go/no go point of commitment at which an EIS is required. What the lessee really acquires with an NSO lease is a right of first refusal, a priority right much like the one granted in *Sierra Club v. FERC*. This does not constitute an irretrievable commitment of resources. *Cf. Colorado River Water Conservation District v. United States*, 593 F.2d 907, 909-10 (10th Cir. 1977) (contract to supply water, contingent upon subsequent preparation of EIS and approval by Secretary of the Interior, does not constitute an irretrievable commitment of resources). Thus, we reverse the district court's judgment as it relates to NSO leases and remand with instructions for the court to determine which leases were NSO leases within the meaning of this opinion.

B. The Non-NSO Leases

We next consider whether the sale of non-NSO leases without an EIS violates NEPA. The mitigation stipulations in non-NSO leases permit reasonable regulation of surface-disturbing activities to reduce their impact on the environment. These stipulations do not, however, preclude the lessees from engaging in surface-disturbing activities altogether. They may, for example, build roads and drill for oil, subject only to reasonable mitigation measures. Accordingly, we must decide whether the government's right to regulate, rather than preclude, surface-disturbing activities protects the forest environment from significant adverse effects, obviating the need for an EIS at the lease sale stage.

The identical question was decided by the District of Columbia Circuit in *Sierra Club v. Peterson*, 717 F.2d 1409, 1412-15 (D.C. Cir. 1983). In that case, the government sold oil and gas leases on lands within the Targhee and Bridger-Teton National Forests of Idaho and Wyoming without first preparing an EIS. All leases contained standard and special mitigation stipulations for the protection of the environment, many of which were identical to the stipulations used in this case. *Sierra Club v. Peterson*, 717 F.2d at 1411 & nn. 4 & 5. Standard stipulations provide that any surface-disturbing activity on the leases is conditional on compliance with additional NEPA analysis, including an EIS if appropriate. Special stipulations provide for the protection of particularly sensitive areas through various restrictions as to (1) timing of surface occupancy (to prevent human activity during critical periods in animal lifecycles), (2) frequency of road use (to minimize human/animal contact), or (3) location of surface activity (to avoid activity near recreation areas, steep slopes, unstable soils, or occupied wildlife habitat). The Forest Service may also require that operators mitigate detrimental effects on the environment through relocation, testing, and salvage. Thus, in *Sierra Club v. Peterson*, the Forest Service was able to condition its approval of surface-disturbing activity on the timing, coordination, and extent of exploratory drilling and other post-leasing operations. The District of Columbia Circuit concluded, however, that "[o]n land leased without a No Surface Occupancy Stipulation the Department cannot deny the permit to drill; it can only impose 'reasonable' conditions which are designed to mitigate the environmental impacts of the drilling operations." 717 F.2d at 1411; *cf. EDF v. Andrus*, 596 F.2d at 852 (Interior Department cannot execute option contracts without preparing an EIS because once granted, the contracts prohibit government from "unilaterally changing its mind.").

The District of Columbia Circuit found the distinction between the NSO and non-NSO leases critical. Even though the standard and special mitigation stipulations provided a modicum of protection for the environment, the court held that the sale of non-NSO leases entailed an irrevocable commitment of land to significant surface-disturbing activities, including drilling and roadbuilding, and that such a commitment could not be made under NEPA without an EIS. 717 F.2d at 1414-15.

* * * Because the purpose of the leases sold in the Flathead and Gallatin National Forests is oil and gas exploration, development, and production, it would clearly be inconsistent with the purpose of the leases if the government prevented all drilling, roadbuilding, pipe-laying, and other lease-related surface-disturbing activities. Yet it is also clear that those activities are likely, if not certain, to significantly affect the environment. As the Flathead EA specifically notes, "It is generally acknowledged that in areas where substantial oil and gas reserves are discovered, the effects of development and production become broad in extent." Flathead EA at 8.

We are unpersuaded by appellants' argument that the mitigation measures reduce the effects of even oil and gas exploration, development, and production activities to environmental insignificance. We understand that the mitigation stipulations enable the government to regulate many of the adverse environmental impacts of oil and gas activities. We seriously question, however, whether the ability to subject such highly intrusive activities to reasonable regulation can reduce their effects to insignificance. NEPA does not require that mitigation measures completely compensate for the adverse environmental effects of post-leasing oil and gas activities, *see Friends of Endangered Species v. Jantzen*, 760 F.2d 976, 987 (9th Cir. 1985), but an EIS must be prepared as long as "substantial questions" remain as to whether the measures will completely preclude significant environmental effects. *Friends of the Earth v. Hintz*, 800 F.2d 822, 836 (9th Cir. 1986); *Foundation for North Am. Wild Sheep v. United States*, 681 F.2d 1172, 1180-81 (9th Cir. 1982). Thus, even if there is a chance that regulation of surface-disturbing activities will render insignificant the impacts of those activities, that possibility does not dispel substantial questions regarding the government's ability to adequately regulate activities which it cannot absolutely preclude. In sum, we agree with the district court that the government violated NEPA by selling non-NSO leases without preparing an EIS.

Appellants also complain that the uncertain and speculative nature of oil exploration[21] makes preparation of an EIS untenable until lessees present precise, site-specific proposals for development. The government's inability to fully ascertain the precise extent of the effects of mineral leasing in a national forest is not, however, a justification for failing to estimate what those effects might be before irrevocably committing to the activity. *Cf. EDF v. Andrus*, 596 F.2d at 851 (uncertainty about environmental impact of use of water diverted pursuant to option contract "does not obviate the importance of the decision to divert and the necessity to evaluate the environmental consequences of that decision"). Appellants' suggestion that we approve now and ask questions later is precisely the type of environmentally blind decision-making NEPA was designed to avoid.

Moreover, we agree with the District of Columbia Circuit in *Sierra Club v. Peterson* that the option of selling NSO leases rather than non-NSO leases provides a reasonable alternative approach for oil and gas leasing in the face of uncertainty * * *.

In sum, the sale of a non-NSO oil or gas lease constitutes the "point of commitment;" after the lease is sold the government no longer has the ability to prohibit potentially significant inroads on the environment. By relinquishing the "no action" alternative without the preparation

---

[21]   Less than 10 percent, on average, of non-competitive leases yield an oil strike and less than 2 percent lead to actual development.

of an EIS, the government subverts NEPA's goal of insuring that federal agencies infuse in project planning a thorough consideration of environmental values. The "heart" of the EIS—the consideration of reasonable alternatives to the proposed action—requires federal agencies to consider seriously the "no action" alternative before approving a project with significant environmental effects. 40 C.F.R. § 1502.14(d) (1985). That analysis would serve no purpose if at the time the EIS is finally prepared, the option is no longer available. We agree with the District of Columbia Circuit that unless surface-disturbing activities may be absolutely precluded, the government must complete an EIS before it makes an irretrievable commitment of resources by selling non-NSO leases. *See Sierra Club v. Peterson*, 717 F.2d at 1412-15; *see also Cady v. Morton*, 527 F.2d 786, 793-95 (9th Cir. 1975) (EIS required for decision to issue coal leases); Dept. of the Interior, 516 Dept.Manual 4.3A, promulgated at 45 Fed.Reg. 27,541, 27,546 (1980) ("The feasability analysis (go/no-go) state, at which time an EIS is to be completed, is to be interpreted as the stage prior to the first point of major commitment to the proposal. For example, this would normally be at . . . the leasing stage for mineral resource proposals."); *cf. South Dakota v. Andrus*, 614 F.2d 1190, 1194-95 (8th Cir.1980) (issuance of mineral patent not a major federal action, because *unlike a lease*, mineral patent not a precondition to initiation of mining operations). We therefore affirm the district court's ruling on the NEPA issues with respect to those leases which, on remand, it determines are not NSO leases within the meaning of this opinion.

* * *

[Portions of the opinion dealing with the adequacy of the biological opinion are reproduced, *infra* Chapter 7.]

We hereby AFFIRM the judgment in part, REVERSE in part, and REMAND with instructions that the district court determine which leases are NSO leases within the meaning of this opinion.

Costs are awarded to appellees.

[The opinion of Judge Wallace, concurring in part and dissenting in part, is omitted.]

NOTES

1. Is the fact situation in *Conner* ripe for judicial review under the standard established in *Lujan v. National Wildlife Federation*, 497 U.S. 871 (1990), *supra* Chapter 3? Does it matter whether this case involves a challenge to "the FONSIs, EAs, and biological opinions" or to the individual leases issued after these documents were prepared?

2. In *Park County Resource Council v. Department of Agriculture*, 817 F.2d 609 (10th Cir. 1987), the Court of Appeals for the Tenth Circuit confronted the same NEPA issues that were addressed by the Ninth Circuit in the *Conner* case. *Park County*, however, upheld the BLM's decision not to prepare an EIS for a single 10,174 acre oil and gas lease. The lease required prior approval from the government before the lessee could conduct any surface-disturbing actions. Other stipulations in the lease mentioned particular environmental concerns. One stipulation, for instance, required all reasonable steps to prevent unnecessary soil erosion or timber damage. It may surprise some readers that the Ninth Circuit never cited the earlier opinion in *Park County*. Conversely, the *Park County* court never cited the earlier opinion in *Sierra Club v. Peterson*, 717 F.2d 1409 (D.C. Cir.

1983), which was decided by the Court of Appeals for the District of Columbia, and which was cited to support the Ninth Circuit's decision in *Conner*.

3.   Both *Park County* and *Sierra Club* involved oil and gas leases in Wyoming. What problems do these conflicting decisions present for the public land managers in Wyoming? Which case should the agencies follow to avoid further conflict? Recent Forest Service regulations appear to resolve the conflict in favor of the *Conner* and *Sierra Club* cases. *See* 55 Fed. Reg. 10445 (1990), *codified at* 36 C.F.R. § 228.102(c). *Cf.* GEORGE COGGINS, PUBLIC NATURAL RESOURCES LAW § 23.02[4][b] (1992) (arguing that the circuit split "is more apparent than real" and that the opinions can all be reconciled).

4.   Oil and gas development on public lands occurs in several phases. First, lands are leased by the Bureau of Land Management (BLM) in accordance with the Mineral Leasing Act. 30 U.S.C. §§ 181 *et seq*. Generally, lands are leased through an auction system to the highest bidder and, as suggested in *Conner,* these leases may contain stipulations that restrict activities on the leased lands. If the lessee chooses to explore potential oil and gas deposits through drilling, an application for a permit to drill (APD) must be filed with and approved by the BLM. If the exploration wells show promise, commercial or "full field" development may occur through further APDs. *See* 43 C.F.R. Part 3100 (1992). As note 21 of the *Conner* decision suggests, only a small percentage of leased lands reach the development stage. How is this fact relevant to the agency's obligation to comply with NEPA?

5.   In *Michael Gold*, 108 IBLA 231 (1989), the Interior Board of Land Appeals held that the *Park County* decision requires the BLM to prepare an EIS to analyze the cumulative environmental impacts of full field development whenever an initial application for a permit to drill to begin development has been filed. The *Michael Gold* decision provoked an uproar in the oil and gas industry. Following a motion for reconsideration, the Board affirmed its earlier decision requiring an EIS in the circumstances of the *Michael Gold* case, but acknowledged that an EA rather than an EIS might be sufficient in other cases. 115 IBLA 218 (1990). The oil and gas industry remained dissatisfied with the result, and two representatives of the industry, the Amoco Corporation and the Rocky Mountain Oil and Gas Association, requested secretarial review of the Board's decision under the seldom used authority at 43 C.F.R. § 4.5. On June 26, 1991, Secretary of the Interior Manuel Lujan reversed the decision of the Board. In his decision, the Secretary stated that past NEPA litigation "does not provide an appropriate foundation for the issuance of general rules regarding the preparation of EISs in development situations." *Decision on Review in Michael Gold (On Reconsideration)*, 50-1, G.F.S. (O&G) (1991). Assuming that an EIS is not required at the leasing stage, should it be required at the exploration stage? At the development stage?

MARSH V. OREGON NATURAL RESOURCES COUNCIL
490 U.S. 360 (1989)

Justice STEVENS delivered the opinion of the Court.

This case is a companion to *Robertson v. Methow Valley Citizens Council*, 490 U.S. 332 (1989) [*infra* Chapter 7]. It arises out of a controversial decision to construct a dam at Elk Creek in the Rogue River Basin in southwest Oregon. In addition to the question whether an Environmental Impact Statement (EIS) prepared pursuant to the National Environmental Policy Act of 1969 (NEPA), 42 U.S.C. § 4321 *et seq.*, must contain a complete mitigation plan and a "worst case analysis," which we answered in *Robertson*, it presents the question whether information developed after the completion of the EIS requires that a supplemental EIS be prepared before construction of the dam may continue.

I

In the 1930's in response to recurring floods in the Rogue River Basin, federal and state agencies began planning a major project to control the water supply in the Basin. In 1961 a multi-agency study recommended the construction of three large dams: the Lost Creek Dam on the Rogue River, the Applegate Dam on the Applegate River, and the Elk Creek Dam on the Elk Creek near its confluence with the Rogue River. The following year, Congress authorized the Army Corps of Engineers (the Corps) to construct the project in accordance with the recommendations of the 1961 study. The Lost Creek Dam was completed in 1977 and the Applegate Dam was completed in 1981.

Plans for the Elk Creek Dam describe a 238-foot-high concrete structure that will control the run-off from 132-square-miles of the 135-square-mile Elk Creek watershed. When full, the artificial lake behind the dam will cover 1,290 acres of land, will have an 18-mile shoreline, and will hold 101,000 acre-feet of water. The dam will cost approximately $100 million to construct and will produce annual benefits of almost $5 million. It will be operated in coordination with the nearby Lost Creek Dam, where the control center for both dams will be located. Its "multiport" structure, which will permit discharge of water from any of five levels, makes it possible to regulate, within limits, the temperature, turbidity,[2] and volume of the downstream flow. Although primarily designed to control flooding along the Rogue River, additional project goals include enhanced fishing, irrigation, and recreation.

In 1971, the Corps completed its EIS for the Elk Creek portion of the three-dam project and began development by acquiring 26,000 acres of land and relocating residents, a county road, and utilities. Acknowledging incomplete information, the EIS recommended that further studies concerning the project's likely effect on turbidity be developed. The results of these studies were discussed in a draft supplemental EIS completed in 1975. However, at the request of the Governor of Oregon, further work on the project was suspended and the supplemental EIS was not filed to make it possible to analyze the actual consequences of the construction of the Lost Creek Dam, which was nearing completion, before continuing with the Elk Creek project. Following that analysis and the receipt of a statement from the Governor that he was "extremely

---

[2]   "Turbidity is an expression of the optical property of water which causes light to be scattered and absorbed rather than transmitted through in straight lines. Turbidity is caused by the presence of suspended matter." This optical property of water is most commonly measured using the Jackson Turbidity Unit (JTU). "A general rule of thumb guideline is that 5 JTU is the limit for drinking water, 10 JTU impairs flyfishing, 20 JTU impairs other fishing methods, and long-term 50 JTU water alters fish behavior."

interested in pursuing construction of the Elk Creek Dam," the Corps completed and released its Final Environmental Impact Statement, Supplement No. 1 [FEISS], in December 1980.

Because the Rogue River is one of the Nation's premier fishing grounds, the FEISS paid special heed to the effects the dam might have on water quality, fish production, and angling. In its chapter on the environmental effects of the proposed project, the FEISS explained that water quality studies were prepared in 1974 and in 1979 and that "[w]ater temperature and turbidity have received the most attention." FEISS 33. Using computer simulation models, the 1974 study predicted that the Elk Creek Dam might, at times, increase the temperature of the Rogue River by one to two degrees Fahrenheit and its turbidity by one to three JTU's. *Ibid.* The 1979 study took a second look at the potential effect of the Elk Creek Dam on turbidity and, by comparing the 1974 study's predictions concerning the effects of the Lost Creek Dam with actual measurements taken after that dam became operational, it "increased technical confidence in the mathematical model predictions . . . and reinforced the conclusions of the 1974 [study]." *Id.* at 33-34. Based on these studies, the FEISS predicted that changes in the "turbidity regime" would not have any major effect on fish production, but that the combined effect of the Lost Creek and Elk Creek Dams on the turbidity of the Rogue River might, on occasion, impair fishing.

Other adverse effects described by the FEISS include the displacement of wildlife population—including 100 black-tailed deer and 17 elk—and the loss of forest land and vegetation resulting from the inundation of 1,290 acres of land with the creation of the artificial lake. *Id.* at 26, 38, 46. Most significantly, it is perfectly clear that the dam itself would interfere with the migration and spawning of a large number of anadromous fish, but this effect has been mitigated by the construction of a new hatchery. *Id.* at 35. Finally, the FEISS found that no endangered or threatened species would be affected by the project. *Id.* at 27.

On February 19, 1982, after reviewing the FEISS, the Corps' Division Engineer made a formal decision to proceed with construction of the Elk Creek Dam, "subject to the approval of funds by the United States Congress." In his decision, he identified the mitigation measures that had already been taken with respect to the loss of anadromous fish spawning habitat, as well as those that would "most likely" be taken to compensate for the loss of other wildlife habitat. He concluded that the benefits that would be realized from the project "outweigh the economic and environmental costs" and that completion would serve "the overall public interest." In August 1985, Congress appropriated the necessary funds.[3] The dam is now about one-third completed and the creek has been rechanneled through the dam.

II

In October 1985, four Oregon nonprofit corporations filed this action in the United States District Court for the District of Oregon seeking to enjoin construction of the Elk Creek Dam. Their principal claims were that the Corps violated NEPA by failing (1) to consider the cumulative effects of the three dams on the Rogue River Basin in a single EIS; (2) adequately to describe the environmental consequences of the project; (3) to include a "worst case analysis" of uncertain effects; and (4) to prepare a second supplemental EIS to review information developed after 1980.

After conducting a hearing on respondents' motion for a preliminary injunction, the District Judge denied relief on each of the NEPA claims. * * *

---

[3]   In the Report accompanying this legislation the Senate Appropriations Committee stressed that it "included specific language in the legislation directing the Secretary of the Army, acting through the Chief of Engineers, to award a continuing contract for construction of the main dam for the Elk Creek Lake project." S. Rep. No. 99-82, p. 97 (1985).

The new information relied upon by respondents is found in two documents. The first, an internal memorandum prepared by two Oregon Department of Fish and Wildlife (ODFW) biologists based upon a draft ODFW study, suggested that the dam will adversely affect downstream fishing, and the second, a soil survey prepared by the United States Soil Conservation Service (SCS), contained information that might be taken to indicate greater downstream turbidity than did the FEISS. As to both documents, the District Judge concluded that the Corps acted reasonably in relying on the opinions of independent and Corps experts discounting the significance of the new information. * * *

The Court of Appeals reversed. 832 F.2d 1489 (9th Cir. 1987). Applying the same "reasonableness" standard of review employed by the District Court, the Court of Appeals reached a contrary conclusion, holding that the Corps had not adequately evaluated the cumulative environmental impact of the entire project. *Id.* at 1497. Since the Corps did not seek review of that holding, we do not discuss it. The court also held that the FEISS was defective because it did not include a complete mitigation plan and because it did not contain a "worst case analysis." *Id.* at 1493-94, 1496-97. These holdings were erroneous for the reasons stated in our opinion in *Robertson v. Methow Valley Citizens Council*, 490 U.S. 332 (1989) [*infra* Chapter 7], and will not be further discussed. With regard to the failure to prepare a second supplemental EIS, the Court of Appeals concluded that the ODFW and SCS documents brought to light "significant new information" concerning turbidity, water temperature, and epizootic[12] fish disease; that this information, although "not conclusive," is "probably accurate;" and that the Corps' experts failed to evaluate the new information with sufficient care. 832 F.2d at 1494-96. The court thus concluded that a second supplemental EIS should have been prepared. * * *

III

The subject of post-decision supplemental environmental impact statements is not expressly addressed in NEPA. Preparation of such statements, however, is at times necessary to satisfy the Act's "action-forcing" purpose. NEPA does not work by mandating that agencies achieve particular substantive environmental results. Rather, NEPA promotes its sweeping commitment to "prevent or eliminate damage to the environment and biosphere" by focusing government and public attention on the environmental effects of proposed agency action. 42 U.S.C. § 4321. By so focusing agency attention, NEPA ensures that the agency will not act on incomplete information, only to regret its decision after it is too late to correct. *See Robertson*, 490 U.S. 332, 349 (1989) [*infra* Chapter 7]. Similarly, the broad dissemination of information mandated by NEPA permits the public and other government agencies to react to the effects of a proposed action at a meaningful time. *Robertson*, Ante at 349-50. It would be incongruous with this approach to environmental protection, and with the Act's manifest concern with preventing uninformed action, for the blinders to adverse environmental effects, once unequivocally removed, to be restored prior to the completion of agency action simply because the relevant proposal has received initial approval. As we explained in *TVA v. Hill*, 437 U.S. 153, 188, n.34, (1978), although "it would make sense to hold NEPA inapplicable at some point in the life of a project, because the agency would no longer have a meaningful opportunity to *weigh* the benefits of the project versus the detrimental effects on the environment," up to that point, "NEPA cases have generally required agencies to file [EISs] when the remaining governmental action would be environmentally 'significant.'"

---

[12]   An epizootic disease is one that affects many animals of the same kind at the same time. *See* 832 F.2d at 1496, n.5.

This reading of the statute is supported by Council on Environmental Quality (CEQ) and Corps regulations, both of which make plain that at times supplementation is required. The CEQ regulations, which we have held are entitled to substantial deference, *see Robertson, ante* 355-56; *Andrus v. Sierra Club*, 442 U.S. 347, 358 (1979), impose a duty on all federal agencies to prepare supplements to either draft or final EIS's if there "are significant new circumstances or information relevant to environmental concerns and bearing on the proposed action or its impacts." Similarly, the Corps' own NEPA implementing regulations require the preparation of a supplemental EIS if "new significant impact information, criteria or circumstances relevant to environmental considerations impact on the recommended plan or proposed action." [*See* 40 CFR § 1502.9(c)(1) and 33 C.F.R. § 230.11(b).]

The parties are in essential agreement concerning the standard that governs an agency's decision whether to prepare a supplemental EIS. They agree that an agency should apply a "rule of reason," and the cases they cite in support of this standard explicate this rule in the same basic terms. These cases make clear that an agency need not supplement an EIS every time new information comes to light after the EIS is finalized. To require otherwise would render agency decisionmaking intractable, always awaiting updated information only to find the new information outdated by the time a decision is made.[13] On the other hand, and as the petitioners concede, NEPA does require that agencies take a "hard look" at the environmental effects of their planned action, even after a proposal has received initial approval. Application of the "rule of reason" thus turns on the value of the new information to the still pending decisionmaking process. In this respect the decision whether to prepare a supplemental EIS is similar to the decision whether to prepare an EIS in the first instance: If there remains "major Federal actio[n]" to occur, and if the new information is sufficient to show that the remaining action will "affec[t] the quality of the human environment" in a significant manner or to a significant extent not already considered, a supplemental EIS must be prepared. *Cf.* 42 U.S.C. § 4332(C).

The parties disagree, however, on the standard that should be applied by a court that is asked to review the agency's decision. [The Government] argues that the reviewing court need only decide whether the agency decision was "arbitrary and capricious," whereas respondents argue that the reviewing court must make its own determination of reasonableness to ascertain whether the agency action complied with the law. In determining the proper standard of review, we look to § 10(e) of the Administrative Procedure Act (APA), 5 U.S.C. § 706, which empowers federal courts to "hold unlawful and set aside agency action, findings, and conclusions" if they fail to conform with any of six specified standards. We conclude that review of the narrow question before us of whether the Corps' determination that the FEISS need not be supplemented should be set aside is controlled by the "arbitrary and capricious" standard of § 706(2)(A).

Respondents contend that the determination of whether the new information suffices to establish a "significant" effect is either a question of law or, at a minimum, a question of ultimate fact and, as such, "deserves no deference" on review. * * * We disagree.

---

[13]   In other contexts we have observed: "'Administrative consideration of evidence . . . always creates a gap between the time the record is closed and the time the administrative decision is promulgated. . . . If upon the coming down of the order litigants might demand rehearing as a matter of law because some new circumstance has arisen, some new trend has been observed, or some new fact discovered, there would be little hope that the administrative process could ever be consummated in an order that would not be subject to reopening.'" *Vermont Yankee Nuclear Power Corp. v. Natural Resources Defense Council, Inc.*, 435 U.S. 519, 554-555, (1978) (*quoting ICC v. Jersey City*, 322 U.S. 503, 514, (1944)). *See also Northern Lines Merger Cases*, 396 U.S. 491, 521, (1970).

The question presented for review in this case is a classic example of a factual dispute the resolution of which implicates substantial agency expertise. Respondents' claim that the Corps' decision not to file a second supplemental EIS should be set aside primarily rests on the contentions that the new information undermines conclusions contained in the FEISS, that the conclusions contained in the ODFW memorandum and the SCS survey are accurate, and that the Corps' expert review of the new information was incomplete, inconclusive, or inaccurate. The dispute thus does not turn on the meaning of the term "significant" or on an application of this legal standard to settled facts. Rather, resolution of this dispute involves primarily issues of fact. Because analysis of the relevant documents "requires a high level of technical expertise," we must defer to "the informed discretion of the responsible federal agencies." *Kleppe v. Sierra Club*, 427 U.S. 390, 412 (1976). *See also Baltimore Gas & Electric Co. v. Natural Resources Defense Council, Inc.*, 462 U.S. 87, 103 (1983) ("When examining this kind of scientific determination . . . a reviewing court must generally be at its most deferential"). Under these circumstances, we cannot accept respondents' supposition that review is of a legal question and that the Corps' decision "deserves no deference." Accordingly, as long as the Corps' decision not to supplement the FEISS was not "arbitrary or capricious," it should not be set aside.[23]

* * *

IV

Respondents' argument that significant new information required the preparation of a second supplemental EIS rests on two written documents. The first of the documents is the so-called "Cramer Memorandum," an intra-office memorandum prepared on February 21, 1985 by two scientists employed by ODFW. * * * The second document is actually a series of maps prepared in 1982 by SCS to illustrate the composition of soil near the Elk Creek shoreline. The information was provided to the Corps for use in managing the project. Although respondents contend that the maps contained data relevant to a prediction of the dam's impact on downstream turbidity, the maps do not purport to shed any light on that subject. Nor do they purport to discuss any conditions that had changed since the FEISS was completed in 1980. The Corps responded to the claim that these documents demonstrate the need for supplementation of the FEISS by preparing a formal Supplemental Information Report, dated January 10, 1986. *See* U.S. Army Corps of Engineers, Portland District, Elk Creek Lake Supplemental Information Report No. 2, p. 7a (hereinafter SIR). The SIR explained, "[w]hile it is clear based upon our review that this information does not require additional NEPA documentation, Corps regulations

---

[23]   Respondents note that several Courts of Appeals, including the Court of Appeals for the Ninth Circuit as articulated in this and other cases, have adopted a "reasonableness" standard of review, *see, e.g., Sierra Club v. Froehlke*, 816 F.2d 205, 210 (5th Cir. 1987); *Enos v. Marsh*, 769 F.2d 1363, 1373 (9th Cir. 1985); *National Wildlife Federation v. Marsh*, 721 F.2d 767, 782 (11th Cir. 1983); *Massachusetts v. Watt*, 716 F.2d 946, 948 (1st Cir. 1983); *Monarch Chemical Works, Inc. v. Thone*, 604 F.2d 1083, 1087-1088 (8th Cir. 1979), and argue that we should not upset this well-settled doctrine. This standard, however, has not been adopted by all of the Circuits. *See, e.g., Wisconsin v. Weinberger*, 745 F.2d 412, 417 (7th Cir. 1984) (adopting "arbitrary and capricious" standard). Moreover, as some of these courts have recognized, the difference between the "arbitrary and capricious" and "reasonableness" standards is not of great pragmatic consequence. *See Manasota-88, Inc. v. Thomas*, 799 F.2d 687, 692, n.8 (11th Cir. 1986) ("As a practical matter, . . . the differences between the 'reasonableness' and 'arbitrary and capricious' standards of review are often difficult to discern"); *River Road Alliance, Inc. v. Corps of Engineers of United States Army*, 764 F.2d 445, 449 (7th Cir. 1985) ("we are not sure how much if any practical difference there is between 'abuse of discretion' and 'unreasonable'"), *cert. denied*, 475 U.S. 1055 (1986). Accordingly, our decision today will not require a substantial reworking of long-established NEPA law.

provide that a Supplemental Information Report can be used to disseminate information on points of concern regarding environmental impacts set forth in the EIS."

The significance of the Cramer Memorandum and the SCS survey is subject to some doubt. Before respondents commenced this litigation in October 1985, no one had suggested that either document constituted the kind of new information that made it necessary or appropriate to supplement the FEISS. Indeed, the record indicates that the Corps was not provided with a copy of the Cramer Memorandum until after the lawsuit was filed. Since the probative value of that document depends largely on the expert qualification of its authors, the fact that they did not see fit to promptly apprise the Corps of their concern—or to persuade ODFW to do so—tends to discount the significance of those concerns. Similarly, the absence of any pretrial expression of concern about the soil characteristics described in the 1982 SCS survey is consistent with the view that it shed little, if any, new light on the turbidity potential of the dam. Yet, even if both documents had given rise to prompt expressions of concern, there are good reasons for concluding that they did not convey significant new information requiring supplementation of the FEISS.

The Court of Appeals attached special significance to two concerns discussed in the Cramer Memorandum: the danger that an increase in water temperature downstream during fall and early winter will cause an early emergence and thus reduce survival of spring chinook fry and the danger that the dam will cause high fish mortality from an epizootic disease. Both concerns were based partly on fact and partly on speculation.

With respect to the first, the Cramer Memorandum reported that the authors of the draft ODFW study had found that warming of the Rogue River caused by the Lost Creek Dam had reduced the survival of spring chinook fry; however, the extent of that reduction was not stated, nor did the memorandum estimate the extent of warming to be expected due to closure of the Elk Creek Dam. Instead, the memorandum estimated that an increase of only one degree centigrade in river temperature in January would decrease survival of spring chinook "from by 60-80%." Cramer Memorandum 3a. The authors of the memorandum concluded that because the Elk Creek Dam is likely to increase the temperature of the Rogue River, further evaluation of this effect should be completed "before ODFW sets its final position on this project." *Ibid.*

The Corps' response to this concern in its SIR acknowledged that the "biological reasoning is sound and has been recognized for some time," but then explained why the concern was exaggerated. The SIR stressed that because the model employed by ODFW had not been validated, its predictive capability was uncertain. Indeed, ODFW scientists subsequently recalculated the likely effect of a one degree centigrade increase in temperature, adjusting its estimate of a 60 to 80 percent loss downward to between 30 and 40 percent. Moreover, the SIR supplied a variable missing in the Cramer Memorandum, suggesting that the Elk Creek Dam would, in most cases, either reduce or leave unchanged the temperature of the Rogue River. Discernible increases were only found in July, August, and December of the study year, and even during those months the maximum temperature increase was only 0.6 degrees centigrade. Finally, the SIR observed that the Cramer Memorandum failed to take into account the dam's beneficial effects, including its ability to reduce peak downstream flow during periods of egg incubation and fry rearing and its ability to reduce outflow temperature through use of the multiport structure. Given these positive factors, the Corps concluded that any adverse effects of the 0.6 degree temperature increase can be offset.

With respect to the second concern emphasized by the Court of Appeals, the Cramer Memorandum reported the fact that "an unprecedented 76% of the fall chinook in 1979 and 32% in 1980 were estimated to have died before spawning" and then speculated that the Lost Creek Dam, which had been completed in 1977, was a contributing cause of this unusual mortality. The Corps responded to this by pointing out that the absence of similar epizootics after the closure of the Applegate Dam and the evidence of pre-spawning mortality in the Rogue River prior to the closing of the Lost Creek Dam were inconsistent with the hypothesis suggested in the Cramer Memorandum. In addition, the Corps noted that certain diseased organisms thought to have been the cause of the unusually high mortality rates were not found in the outflow from the Lost Creek Dam.

In thus concluding that the Cramer Memorandum did not present significant new information requiring supplementation of the FEISS, the Corps carefully scrutinized the proffered information. Moreover, in disputing the accuracy and significance of this information, the Corps did not simply rely on its own experts. Rather, two independent experts hired by the Corps to evaluate the ODFW study on which the Cramer Memorandum was premised found significant fault in the methodology and conclusions of the study. We also think it relevant that the Cramer Memorandum did not express the official position of ODFW. In preparing the memorandum, the authors noted that the agency had "adopted a neutral stand on Elk Creek Dam" and argued that new information raised the question whether "our agency should continue to remain neutral." The concerns disclosed in the memorandum apparently were not sufficiently serious to persuade ODFW to abandon its neutral position.

* * *

There is little doubt that if all of the information contained in the Cramer Memorandum and SCS survey was both new and accurate, the Corps would have been required to prepare a second supplemental EIS. It is also clear that, regardless of its eventual assessment of the significance of this information, the Corps had a duty to take a hard look at the proffered evidence. However, having done so and having determined based on careful scientific analysis that the new information was of exaggerated importance, the Corps acted within the dictates of NEPA in concluding that supplementation was unnecessary. Even if another decisionmaker might have reached a contrary result, it was surely not "a clear error of judgment" for the Corps to have found that the new and accurate information contained in the documents was not significant and that the significant information was not new and accurate. As the SIR demonstrates, the Corps conducted a reasoned evaluation of the relevant information and reached a decision that, although perhaps disputable, was not "arbitrary or capricious."

The judgment of the Court of Appeals is accordingly reversed and the case is remanded for further proceedings consistent with this opinion.

It is so ordered.

NOTES

1.   *Marsh,* along with the Court's decision in the companion case, *Robertson v. Methow Valley Citizens Council,* 490 U.S. 332 (1989), *infra* Chapter 7, continues a perfect string of Supreme Court decisions narrowly construing NEPA. *See* Antonio Rossmann, *NEPA: Not So Well at Twenty,* 20 Envtl. L. Rep. (Envtl. L. Inst.) 10174 (1990); Karin P. Sheldon, *NEPA in the Supreme Court,* 25 LAND & WATER L. REV. 83 (1990). Professor Rodgers calls the Supreme Court NEPA cases "the dirty dozen" and argues that NEPA remains strong in spite of:

> Court decisions consistently rejecting interpretations advanced by environmental groups and accepting the narrower accounts espoused by the government as the NEPA defendant. In few walks of legal life has the Court demonstrated such a decided tilt in its choice of prevailing parties.

William H. Rodgers, *NEPA at Twenty: Mimicry and Recruitment in Environmental Law,* 20 ENVTL. L. 485, 497 (1990).

2.   A key issue in *Marsh* was the standard of review applied by the Court. Be sure to distinguish an agency's obligation to take a "hard look" at the environmental impacts of a proposed action, and to consider all "reasonable" alternatives to the proposed action, from the standard applied by the Court in reviewing an agency's actions under NEPA. In *Marsh,* the parties disagreed over whether the Court ought to use an arbitrary and capricious standard or a standard of reasonableness to review the Corps' decision. Do you agree with the Court's assessment that there is little difference between the two standards? What does the arbitrary and capricious standard of review involve in this case? *Sierra Club v. Lujan,* 949 F.2d 362, 367-68 (10th Cir. 1991) (applying the *Marsh* arbitrary and capricious standard to uphold an agency FONSI), discusses some problems courts have had in applying the *Marsh* standard of review to other NEPA disputes. *See also Puerto Rico Conservation Foundation v. Larson,* 797 F. Supp. 1074 (D.P.R. 1992) (discussing the application of the *Marsh* standard of review in finding that agencies failed to comply with NEPA by relying on a ten year old EA and failing to prepare an EIS for highway reconstruction).

3.   What was the purpose of the "Supplemental Information Report" prepared by the Corps following the disclosure of new information regarding the environmental impacts from the proposed Elk Creek Dam? Are agencies obliged to prepare such a report whenever they are presented with new information about a project?

4.   The CEQ regulations describe two circumstances where agencies are obliged to prepare a supplemental statement—(1) where the agency makes substantial changes in the proposed action that are relevant to environmental concerns; and (2) where there are significant new circumstances or information relevant to environmental concerns and bearing on the proposed action or its impacts. 40 C.F.R. § 1502.9(c). At what point during the course of construction of a dam is it too late to prepare an SEIS? If new, conclusive evidence showing more severe impacts on fish in the Rogue River system comes to light the day before the Corps is ready to close the flood gates on the Elk Creek Dam, does the agency have to prepare an SEIS?

5.   In *Friends of the Bow v. Thompson,* 124 F.3d 1210 (10th Cir. 1997), the plaintiffs argued that a 55% reduction in the volume available for a timber sale approved following preparation of an EA was a "substantial change" that required preparation of a supplemental EA. Among other things, Friends claimed that the reduced sale volume had changed a profitable sale to one that would lose money, and that according to the agency's own analysis the proposed alternative no longer had the highest benefit-cost ratio of the alternatives considered. The high benefit-cost ratio was one of three "key" reasons offered by the agency to support its choice of the high timber volume alternative. Are *Friends* allegations sufficient to require a supplemental EA? Note that 40 C.F.R § 1502.9(c) applies to EISs and makes no mention of EAs. Should courts require agencies to prepare supplemental EAs on the same basis as supplemental EISs? (After the Forest Service prepared a supplemental information report, the Court found that a supplemental EA was not required.)

6.   The Army Corps has now abandoned the half-completed Elk Creek Dam, $70 million short of completion.

PROBLEM #3: THE SUPPLEMENTAL EIS

In March 1992, the U.S. Forest Service approved the Fallen Pines Timber Sale in the Leopold National Forest. The proposed sale is located in the Sleeping Giant Roadless Area, an area of great scenic beauty and a likely candidate for wilderness designation if the proposed timber sale falls through. The EIS prepared for the sale discusses the impact of the logging on scenery and wilderness as well as the effects on wildlife. The EIS considered a no action alternative but the agency ultimately rejected this option because of the overwhelming need to supply timber to local communities.

Under the terms of its decision, the Forest Service has proposed to let a contract for the timber in November, 1992. During the summer of 1992, John Audubon, a wildlife photographer, observed and photographed a Mexican spotted owl in a portion of the Sleeping Giant Roadless Area where logging is proposed. The Mexican spotted owl is listed as a threatened species under the ESA. A wildlife biologist verified the sighting and offered her opinion that the owl may be nesting in the roadless area. The Sleeping Giant Wilderness Advocates, a local conservation group, has submitted this information to the Forest Service and asked that the agency prepare a supplemental EIS before the timber sale goes forward. Assume that the deadline has passed for an administrative appeal of the decision approving the sale. How should the agency respond? Of what relevance is the fact that the Mexican spotted owl is listed as a threatened species?

Suppose that the Forest Service had already let the contract at the time that the new information came to light. How might this change your analysis of the problem?

B. Federal Action

DEFENDERS OF WILDLIFE V. ANDRUS
627 F.2d 1238 (D.C. Cir. 1980)

MCGOWAN, Circuit Judge:

This is an appeal from an order of the District Court granting a preliminary injunction against the Secretary of the Interior. It raises the question of whether, under the circumstances of this case, the National Environmental Policy Act obligates the Secretary to prepare and circulate an environmental impact statement when he does not act to prevent the State of Alaska from conducting, as part of a wildlife-management program, a wolf hunt on certain federal land. Because the Secretary's conduct here does not constitute a "major Federal action" within the meaning of the Act, we hold that the Secretary is not so obligated, and we reverse.

I

The Background of this Action

On February 16, 1979, the Alaska Department of Fish and Game (ADFG) announced a program whose aim was to kill from aircraft 170 wolves (approximately sixty percent of the wolf population) in an area of 35,000 square miles in the interior part of the state. Many, perhaps most, of the wolves were to be killed on federal lands for which the Department of the Interior is responsible. On February 23, counsel for one of the appellees, Natural Resources Defense Council, Inc., asked the Department to prepare an environmental impact statement for Alaska's program before allowing it to begin. The Department, however, did not exercise whatever authority it may have to stop the program and did not prepare an impact statement. On March 12, appellees—organizations and individuals interested in the preservation of the environment in general and of wildlife in particular—filed a complaint asking for declaratory and injunctive relief against appellants—the Secretary and two other officials of the Department of the Interior.

The complaint predicted that, although the wolf hunt was proposed in order to increase the number of moose in the region by decreasing the numbers of their major predator, it would in fact weaken the moose herds by ending a "culling process [which] is natural selection in action, and [which] assures survival of the fittest moose . . ." and would devastate the wolf packs even beyond the ADFG's estimates. This interference with these two major species, the complaint continued, would disrupt the ecology of the entire area.

The complaint asserted that the Federal Land Policy and Management Act (FLPMA), 43 U.S.C. § 1701 *et seq.,* authorizes the Secretary of the Interior to prevent the killing of wildlife on federal lands and requires him to evaluate whether he must intervene if he is fully to serve the environmental concerns of the Act. The complaint claimed as one of its "Violations of Law" that appellants failed to make that evaluation. The other violation of law the complaint alleged is that appellants had, but failed to meet, an obligation under § 102(2)(C) of the National Environmental Policy Act (NEPA), 42 U.S.C. 4321 *et seq.,* to prepare an environmental impact statement before deciding not to prevent Alaska from killing wolves on Federal land.

On March 13, 1979, the United States District Court for the District of Columbia issued a temporary restraining order which enjoined appellants to "take all steps necessary to halt the aerial killing of wolves by agents of the State of Alaska" on the relevant federal lands. Although Alaska has apparently continued to kill wolves on its own lands, it has discontinued doing so on federal lands.

On March 23, 1979, the District Court acted on appellees' motion for a preliminary injunction. It first denied appellants' requests to transfer the action to the District of Alaska, pursuant to 28 U.S.C. § 1404(a), and to dismiss the action for failure to join Alaska as an indispensable party, pursuant to Fed. R. Civ. P. 19(a). The Court said that it would inconvenience both parties to transfer the action to Alaska and that, "[a]lthough Alaska has an interest in the outcome in this matter, the Court notes that the interest is not so great as to prompt a motion to intervene."

The District Court then weighed the merits of the motion for a preliminary injunction in the scales this court constructed in *Virginia Petroleum Jobbers Association v. Federal Power Commission,* 259 F.2d 921 (1958). The District Court came to the following conclusions: (1) Plaintiffs would be irreparably harmed if no injunction were issued, since without one, the killing of wolves would soon begin and the natural environment of the federal lands would thereby be damaged. Further, plaintiffs' rights under NEPA to an impact statement would be irretrievably lost if the wolves were killed before the statement was written. (2) An injunction would not unduly injure the defendants, since they had not invested time or resources in the program to hunt wolves. (3) "There exists a strong public interest under NEPA in having federal officials consider the potential environmental effects on national lands and resources prior to the occurrence of a highly controversial and potentially devastating wolf control program." (4) There was a substantial likelihood plaintiffs would win on the merits.

As to those merits, the District Court believed it was "confronted with a simple question: Does NEPA require the Secretary of the Interior to prepare an EIS prior to permitting an extensive wolf kill to take place on federal lands?" The District Court reasoned that FLPMA requires the Secretary "to manage and plan the use of federal lands" and that "[c]learly, an environmental assessment of the wolf elimination program must be part of the decisionmaking process." The District Court therefore issued a preliminary injunction which required appellants "to prevent any such killing of wolves pending preparation of an environmental impact statement on the potential effects of the wolf control program."

* * *

IV

The Secretary's Obligations Under NEPA

* * *

A

* * * Does NEPA require that the Secretary prepare and circulate an environmental impact statement in the circumstances of this case?

Our discussion of that question must center around the fact that, while the plain language of the statute calls for an impact statement when there is "major Federal action," here it is the Secretary's inaction which is complained of. Appellees, as we understand them, respond that (1) the environmental consequences of inaction may be greater than the consequences of action, and (2) the purpose of the statute is to ensure that environmentally informed decisions are made, not simply that the environmental consequences of all federal programs are considered. We acknowledge the truth of the first response, but we do not understand it to change the language of the statute.

As to the second response, we agree that a purpose of the statute is to ensure that environmentally informed decisions are made. Nevertheless, as it is written, NEPA only refers to decisions which the agency anticipates will lead to actions. This common-sense reading of the statute is confirmed by the statutory directive that the impact statement is to be part of a "recommendation or report" on a "proposal" for action. That is, only when an agency reaches the point in its deliberations when it is ready to propose a course of action need it be ready to produce an impact statement. As the Supreme Court said in *Andrus v. Sierra Club*, "Of course an EIS need not be promulgated unless an agency's planning ripens into a 'recommendation or report on proposals for legislation [or] other major Federal actions significantly affecting the quality of the human environment.'" 442 U.S. 347, 350 n.2 (1979). Logically, then, if the agency decides not to act, and thus not to present a proposal to act, the agency never reaches a point at which it need prepare an impact statement.

* * *

B

Appellees argue that, by not inhibiting an action of a private party or a state or local government, the federal government makes that action its own within the meaning of NEPA. However, in no published opinion of which we have been made aware has a court held that there is "federal action" where an agency has done nothing more than fail to prevent the other party's action from occurring. Even here courts have not abandoned the requirement that it must be a specifically federal action which triggers the preparation of an impact statement. To borrow from the language of the criminal law of conspiracy, we may say that federal "approval" of another party's action does not make that action federal unless the federal government undertakes some "overt act" in furtherance of that other party's project. Thus, when the Supreme Court discussed two circuit court decisions which held that private actions permitted by the federal government might necessitate the preparation of an impact statement, the Court's examples of federal "permission" were such concrete acts as decisions "to issue a lease, approve a mining plan, issue a right-of-way permit, or *take other action to allow private activity . . .*." *Kleppe v. Sierra Club*, 427 U.S. 390, 399 (1976) (emphasis added).

Appellees quote language from our decision in *Scientists' Institute for Public Information, Inc. (SIPI) v. Atomic Energy Commission*, 481 F.2d 1079, 1088-89 (1973):

> [T]here is "Federal action" within the meaning of the statute not only when an agency proposes to build a facility itself, but also whenever an agency makes a decision which permits action by other parties which will affect the quality of the environment. NEPA's impact statement procedure has been held to apply where . . . the federal agency took action affecting the environment in the sense that the agency made a decision which permitted some other party private or governmental to take action affecting the environment.

However, an examination of the material which appellees deleted reveals that nothing in the quotation can legitimately be construed as saying that there can be "Federal action" without an "overt act." In the deleted material, the court gave instances of the kind of federal approval of a non-federal project which constitutes "Federal action." The second sentence of the above quotation reads in full:

> NEPA's impact statement procedure has been held to apply where a federal agency approves a lease of land to private parties, grants licenses and permits to private parties, or approves and funds state highway projects.

SIPI, 481 F.2d at 1088.

* * *

C

* * *

* * * No agency could meet its NEPA obligations if it had to prepare an environmental impact statement every time the agency had power to act but did not do so. Nor does it suffice to say that an agency's burden would be kept to a reasonable level by the fact that no impact statement is needed when the inaction could have no significant environmental results, for we have held that an agency which decides not to issue an impact statement must provide a written explanation of its reasons for that decision. *See, e.g., SIPI,* 481 F.2d at 1094. This requirement is necessary to ensure that the agency's decision is well-considered and to provide a basis for the judicial review of the agency's decision. It would be an imaginative and vigorous agency indeed which could identify and prepare all the statements and explanations appellees' reading of NEPA would have the statute demand.

In a letter to the Department of Justice, the General Counsel of the Council on Environmental Quality (CEQ) the agency established in part to oversee the implementation of NEPA recognized that an over-expansive interpretation of section 102(2)(C) could create

> a serious administrative burden on Federal agencies. There are literally thousands of decisions which Federal officials are authorized to and could conceivably make under existing law. If the mere existence of this authority was a basis for invoking NEPA regardless of whether a Federal decision was required to be or had been made the scope of the environmental review process would be vastly expanded.

* * *

V

The Relationship of NEPA and FLPMA

The District Court and appellees believe that the above analysis of the Secretary's duty under NEPA is insufficient. They reason that FLPMA imposes such supervisory duties on the Secretary that every failure to prohibit a state wildlife program which is carried out on Federal land and which may have significant environmental consequences must be accounted for with an impact statement. The District Court decided

> that the Secretary has a nondiscretionary duty to plan for and manage federal land and resources. In view of this responsibility, the Secretary must prohibit any major actions significantly affecting the human environment from occurring on federal lands until an environmental impact statement has been prepared and circulated. Accordingly, until an EIS has been prepared, the Secretary must take appropriate action to prevent aerial wolf killing on federal lands by the State of Alaska and its agents.

FLPMA, which is also referred to as the Bureau of Land Management Organic Statute, was enacted "to provide the first comprehensive, statutory statement of purposes, goals, and authority for the use and management of about 448 million acres of federally-owned lands administered by the Secretary of the Interior through the Bureau of Land Management." S. Rep. No. 94-583, 94th Cong., 1st Sess. 24 (1975). As such, it certainly imposes on the Secretary a general duty "to plan for and manage federal land and resources." However, the District Court's reasoning seems to us to upset an allocation of functions Congress carefully and explicitly made in FLPMA, for Congress there assigned the states the primary responsibility for the management of wildlife programs within their boundaries.

It is unquestioned that "the States have broad trustee and police powers over wild animals within their jurisdictions," *Kleppe v. New Mexico,* 426 U.S. 529, 545 (1976). Neither is it questioned that, because the Property Clause of the Constitution provides that "Congress shall have Power to dispose of and make all needful Rules and Regulations respecting the Territory or other Property belonging to the United States," U.S. Const., Art. IV, § 3, cl. 2, Congress may, if it wishes, pre-empt state management of wildlife on federal lands. *Kleppe v. New Mexico,* 426 U.S. at 539-41. Despite its ability to take control into its own hands, Congress has traditionally allotted the authority to manage wildlife to the states. For instance, in the Multiple Use-Sustained Yield Act of 1960, Congress declared:

> It is the policy of the Congress that the national forests are established and shall be administered for outdoor recreation, range, timber, watershed, and wildlife and fish purposes. . . . Nothing herein shall be construed as affecting the jurisdiction or responsibilities of the several States with respect to wildlife and fish in the national forests. . . .

16 U.S.C. § 528.

Even in writing specifically "environmental" legislation, Congress has adhered to that allocation. Thus, Congress stated in the National Wildlife Refuge System Administration Act, "The Provisions of this Act shall not be construed as affecting the authority, jurisdiction, or responsibility of the several States to manage, control, or regulate fish and resident wildlife under State law or regulations in any area within the System." 16 U.S.C. § 668dd(c). Similarly, the Wild and Scenic Rivers Act provides that "[n]othing in this chapter shall affect the jurisdiction or responsibilities of the States with respect to fish and wildlife." 16 U.S.C. § 1284(a).

Far from attempting to alter the traditional division of authority over wildlife management, FLPMA broadly and explicitly reaffirms it. Section 302(b) of FLPMA begins by directing that the Secretary shall regulate "the use, occupancy, and development of the public lands." After a proviso relating to the use of lands by federal agencies, section 302(b) continues:

> *Provided further,* That *nothing in this Act* shall be construed as authorizing the Secretary concerned to require Federal permits to hunt and fish on public lands or on lands in the National Forest System and adjacent waters *or as enlarging or diminishing the responsibility and authority of the States for management of fish and resident wildlife.* However, the Secretary concerned *may* designate areas of public land and of lands in the National Forest System where, and establish periods when, no hunting or fishing will be permitted for reasons of public safety, administration, or compliance with provisions of applicable law. Except in emergencies, any regulations of the Secretary concerned relating to hunting and fishing pursuant to this section shall be put into effect only after consultation with the appropriate State fish and game department.

43 U.S.C. § 1732(b) (emphasis added.)

The first quoted sentence of section 302(b) self-evidently places the "responsibility and authority" for state wildlife management precisely where Congress has traditionally placed it—in the hands of the states. The second quoted sentence of the section arguably permits ("may"), but certainly does not require ("shall"), the Secretary to supersede a state program, and even when he does so, it must be after consulting state authorities. We are simply unable to read this cautious and limited permission to intervene in an area of state responsibility and authority as imposing such supervisory duties on the Secretary that each state action he fails to prevent becomes a "Federal action." A state wildlife-management agency which must seek federal approval for each program it initiates can hardly be said to have "responsibility and authority" for its own affairs.

Appellees remind us that FLPMA directs the Secretary to "manage the public lands under principles of multiple use and sustained yield," 43 U.S.C. § 1732(a), and that "'multiple use' means . . . a combination of balanced and diverse resource uses that takes into account the long-term needs of future generations for renewable and nonrenewable resources, including, but not limited to, recreation, range, timber, minerals, watershed, wildlife and fish, and natural scenic, scientific and historical values . . .." 43 U.S.C. § 1702(c). Appellees also remind us that, pursuant to his authority under FLPMA, 43 U.S.C. § 1714(e), the Secretary has ordered that some of the lands on which wolves are to be killed "are withdrawn from settlement, sale, location, entry or selection under the operation of the public land laws, including but not limited to the mining laws . . . and are reserved and appropriated for the public purpose of preserving, protecting, and maintaining the resource values of said lands which would otherwise be lost . . .." 43 Fed. Reg. 59756 (December 21, 1978).

Nevertheless, the statutory provisions of which appellees remind us are all part of FLPMA. Section 302(b) of that Act expressly commands that "nothing in this Act" enlarges or diminishes the state's responsibility for managing wildlife. We are therefore unable to conclude that appellees' citations to FLPMA should alter our understanding of the Secretary's obligation to prepare an environmental impact statement when he declines to exercise the power which FLPMA arguably gives him to preempt state wildlife-management programs.

The order of the District Court granting a preliminary injunction is reversed.

It is so ordered.

NOTES

1.   This opinion was the culmination of a four-year legal battle fought in the federal district courts in the District of Columbia and Alaska between conservation organizations and the State of Alaska. The history of this heated litigation is summarized more fully in the unedited text of D.C. Circuit's decision above.

In an earlier proceeding in this matter, Judge Gasch described the wolf kill at issue:

The wolf kill which is the subject of the instant action is being undertaken by the Alaska Department of Fish and Game (hereinafter ADFG). The goal of the program is to kill 80 percent of the wolf population, about 1,000 wolves * * * during the winter of 1976-77. The killing will be done from airplanes by hunters licensed by ADFG. ADFG has determined to issue 30 such hunting permits, of which about 16 have been issued. This wolf kill is currently underway, and approximately 30 wolves have already been killed.

The wolf kill was undertaken to halt the sharp decline in the caribou population in this region; it does not involve sport or subsistence hunting. The caribou population in this area has sharply declined in the last six years, from about 244,000 in 1970 to about 60,000 in 1976. The wolves are one of the principal predators of the caribou. Also as a part of ADFG's efforts to halt the decline in this caribou population, ADFG curtailed caribou hunting by man in August of 1976 and limited the native subsistence hunters to an annual take of 3,000 bull caribou. * * *

The Arctic region where this wolf kill is occurring is a particularly fragile ecosystem. The wolf and the caribou are two of the dominant life forms in this region and have coexisted for at least 10,000 years. There are also several native groups in this region who depend on caribou hunting for part of their food supply.

The wolves prey on old, sick, injured, and young caribou, thereby culling the weakest members from the caribou herd and keeping the caribou's habitat and food supply from being overburdened. The elimination of a substantial portion of the predator population may cause the caribou population to oscillate widely and, in the long term, decline significantly. When weak members of the herd are not eliminated, the health of the entire population may be adversely affected and the habitat and food supply may be overburdened. This, in turn, may cause a marked decline in the caribou population. This has occurred as a result of other predator control programs.

The wolves depend on the pack structure for survival, and the dominant male is of critical importance to the maintenance of the pack structure. The random killing of 80 percent of the wolves may have dire secondary effects on the surviving 20 percent of the wolves through potential destruction of the pack structure. When caribou populations decline, the wolf populations also decline naturally. The survival of those wolves least fit for survival, such as the older wolves and wolf pups, is reduced when hunting success becomes low. Wolves also postpone procreation during such times.

Defenders of Wildlife v. Andrus, 9 Env't Rep. Cas. (BNA) 2111, 2112-13 (D.D.C. 1977).

2.   The *Defenders of Wildlife v. Andrus* court admits in Section IV.C. of its opinion that its reading of NEPA may seem literal and formalistic. Does it seem that way to you? Compare the court's interpretation of NEPA with Judge Wright's decision in *Calvert Cliffs*, *supra* Chapter 4.

The *Defenders of Wildlife v. Andrus* court expressed concern about diluting the effect of NEPA by spreading its mandate too widely. Is this the same concern that Judge Friendly described in his dissent to *Hanly II*? Should the same considerations that apply to the interpretation of "significantly" also apply to "federal action"?

3.   Compare the court's holding with the definition of "major federal action" at 40 C.F.R. § 1508.18. Note also the definition of "agency action" in the Administrative Procedure Act—"agency action includes the whole or a part of an agency rule, order, license, sanction, relief, or the equivalent or denial thereof, or failure to act." 5 U.S.C. § 551(13). Is the decision in *Defenders of Wildlife v. Andrus* consistent with the language of these provisions?

4.   To sustain the lower court, was it necessary for the Court of Appeals to find that an EIS is required whenever an agency with the appropriate authority refuses to act in a manner protective of the environment? How might the court have limited its decision?

5.   How might the plaintiffs have used the Administrative Procedure Act to force "agency action" sufficient to require NEPA compliance? Consider the language of 5 U.S.C. § 555(b):

So far as the orderly conduct of public business permits, an interested person may appear before an agency or its responsible employees for the presentation, adjustment, or determination of an issue, request, or controversy in a proceeding, whether interlocutory, summary, or otherwise, or in connection with an agency function. With due regard for the convenience and necessity of the parties or their representatives and within a reasonable time, each agency shall proceed to conclude a matter presented to it.

6.   When a state or private party applies for a federal grant or permit, the federal agency may want the applicant to do as much of the work as possible in preparing the EIS, in order to save money and labor. The applicant may want to do as much as possible in order to present the facts in a favorable light, or in order to make sure the EIS is properly prepared and therefore "injunction proof." But environmentalists may fear bias in such products. How should these considerations be balanced? The CEQ regulations allow responsible federal agencies to hire contractors to prepare EISs; however, the rules seek to prevent bias by requiring contractors to execute disclosure statements indicating the absence of financial or other interests in the outcome of the proposed project. 40 C.F.R. § 1506.5(c). Applicants may play a more direct role in preparing EAs. 40 C.F.R. § 1506.5(b).

7.   Agency preparation of NEPA documents is a unique feature of the American experience with environmental impact assessment. The CEQ rules expressly require that EISs be prepared by the agency, or by a disinterested contractor selected by the agency. 40 C.F.R. § 1506.5(c). An EA may be prepared by the applicant, but the agency must "make its own evaluation of the environmental issues and take responsibility for the scope and content of the environmental assessment." *Id.* at § 1506.5(b). Since agencies must take responsibility for the scope and content of the EA, they usually choose to simply prepare the document themselves. Although NEPA has been emulated by many countries throughout the world, in virtually all of these countries, a private project applicant (or a consultant hired by the applicant) prepares the environmental analysis. What problems or benefits do you see with this approach? What is the role of the agency decision-maker where the environmental analysis is prepared by the project applicant? How would you expect an applicant-prepared EIS to differ from an agency EIS with respect to the alternatives analysis? Suppose, for example, that an applicant in the business of operating hydro-electric power stations seeks approval from the Federal Energy Regulatory Commission to construct a new dam on a navigable river. The sole purpose of the dam is to provide a new source of electricity. How well would you expect the environmental analysis to address an energy conservation alternative, or alternative sources of electrical power? For a criticism of applicant-prepared environmental analyses in Australia *see* Mark Squillace, *An American Perspective on Environmental Impact Assessment in Australia,* 20 COLUM. J. ENVTL. L. 43, 101-03 (1995).

8.   The United States is a member of the International Whaling Convention. Suppose the Convention decides that in order to protect a severely endangered species of whale it must ban the last remaining permissible type of killing: subsistence hunting by Eskimos. By treaty and statute the Secretary of State has ninety days in which to formally object to the ban. If he objects, the ban will not become effective against the United States. If he does not, the Convention action will make hunting by Alaskan Eskimos a criminal offense. Does the Secretary of State have to prepare an EIS in deciding whether or not to object? Does he have to consult with the Secretary of the Interior under the ESA? *See Adams v. Vance,* 570 F.2d 950 (D.C. Cir. 1978) (describing Secretary of State's decision, after preparing an EIS, not to object to a Convention ban on subsistence hunting of bowhead whales).

9. In *Gemeinschaft zum Schutz des Berliner v. Marienthal*, 12 ENV'T REP. CAS. (BNA) 1337 (D.D.C. 1978), a German group sued to block a U.S. Army decision allowing the German government to construct an apartment complex in the American sector of West Berlin, because of the Army's failure to prepare an EIS. In response to the plaintiff's contention that federal action was involved in the Army's decision not to order a halt to construction and in its refusal to permit a local Berlin court to hear a challenge to the project, the court held:

> In order to qualify as federal action there must be some affirmative conduct on the part of the government, not simply a failure to prevent what the government has the power to prevent. * * * Merely because the Army has declined to intervene and exercise its authority to halt construction is insufficient to transform action by the German government into federal action. If the Court were to accept the plaintiffs' argument that a failure to intervene is sufficient to constitute federal action, all major actions by the German government would be subject to review by the American courts because technically, the U.S. Army has the ultimate authority in the American sector to modify local law. Plainly, such a rule of law would be unacceptable.

Id. at 1337-38.

10. In December 1977, the Nuclear Regulatory Commission (NRC) announced a two year suspension of its rulemaking and related licensing proceedings on proposals to build facilities that would recycle nuclear waste into plutonium. The agency also suspended preparation of a generic EIS (GESMO) on the subject that it had been working on for three years. During this two-year hiatus, pending applications to construct and operate nuclear recycling facilities would be held in abeyance so that the government could re-examine alternatives to such facilities, and the risks posed by them, including sabotage. The Westinghouse Electric Corporation challenged the decision for, among other reasons, the NRC's failure to prepare an EIS on the decision to delay the GESMO and other proceedings. The Court of Appeals for the Third Circuit rejected Westinghouse's challenge on the grounds that the NRC's moratorium was not a proposed action triggering NEPA. *Westinghouse Electric Corp. v. U.S. Nuclear Regulatory Comm'n*, 598 F.2d 759 (3d Cir. 1970). Is there a "proposed action" here? Could Westinghouse argue that a two-year moratorium was itself a major action? Suppose, for example, that the two-year delay in licensing nuclear waste recycling facilities substantially increased the risks associated with the storage of these nuclear wastes. Should it matter that the agency's decision was not yet final?

11. *Defenders of Wildlife v. Andrus* did not end the controversy over wolf management by the State of Alaska. Throughout the 1980s, Alaska controlled wolves through state sharpshooters and sport hunters. The ADFG fought with environmentalists over the use of research radio collars to track wolves for state kills and the practice of allowing sport hunters to spot wolves aerially, land, and then shoot. By the late 1980s, however, fiscal constraints and political changes temporarily ended the wolf killing. In 1990, the state elected Walter Hickel governor. Governor Hickel appointed supporters of the wolf kill to key positions, and in November 1992, the Alaska Game Board decided to resume state-funded shooting from airplanes. The decision unleashed a national protest causing thousands of people to notify the Governor of their opposition. Environmental groups organized a tourism and convention boycott of the state. As a result, Governor Hickel tabled the planned wolf kill. State control of the wolf population through shooting, trapping, and birth control continued to generate annual controversies throughout the 1990s under Governor Hickel and his successor, Governor Tony Knowles.

12. Distinguishing between agency action and inaction may be important even where a clear cause of action exists in either case. Many pollution control statutes give federal district courts jurisdiction over citizen suits challenging an agency's failure to perform a non-discretionary act; but federal courts of appeals are given jurisdiction over challenges to final agency actions. Daniel P. Selmi, *Jurisdiction to Review Agency Inaction under Federal Environmental Law*, 72 IND. L.J. 65, 68 (1996), explores the tangles that result from this "bifurcated jurisdictional structure."

13. NEPA documents are commonly prepared on federal aid highway projects. In such cases, however, the statute authorizes the state agency supervising the project to actually prepare the NEPA document. *See* § 102(2)(D). This procedure, which applies generally to all federal grant programs to states, "shall not relieve the Federal official of his responsibilities for the scope, objectivity, and content of the entire statement." *Id.*

14. Note that states generally have some flexibility in choosing where to spend federal aid highway money. Can a state avoid NEPA compliance on controversial projects simply by choosing to spend its grant money on other highway projects? Perhaps so, but a state that chooses this route will likely face some obstacles. For one thing, once a state chooses to accept grant money for a particular project, it may be difficult to "de-federalize" the project. In *Scottsdale Mall v. Indiana*, 549 F.2d 484, 489 (7th Cir. 1977), *cert. denied*, 434 U.S. 1008 (1978), the court found that "Indiana's seeking and receiving federal approval at various stages of the project and receiving preliminary financial benefits so imbued the highway project with a federal character that, notwithstanding the state's withdrawal of the project from federal funding consideration, compliance with federal environmental statutes was necessary." *See also Ross v. Federal Highway Administration*, 162 F.3d 1046 (10th Cir. 1998); *Many Named Individual Members of the San Antonio Conservation Society v. Texas Highway Dep't*, 446 F.2d 1013, 1027 (5th Cir. 1971).

Another problem with the policy of avoiding federal funding for controversial highway segments arises from the definition of "scope" at 40 C.F.R. § 1508.25. Under that definition, the scope of the NEPA document encompasses all "connected actions" and all "cumulative actions." Thus, all connected highway segments and highway segments that have cumulative environmental impacts would have to be analyzed in a single EIS, even if they were not all "federal" projects. *See, e.g., Citizens for Responsible Growth v. Adams*, 477 F. Supp. 994 (D.N.H. 1979); *see also* 40 C.F.R. § 1508.7 which defines "cumulative impacts" to encompass "the incremental impact of the action when added to other past, present or reasonably foreseeable future actions, regardless of what agency . . . or person undertakes such other actions." Nonetheless, in *Bennett v. Taylor*, 505 F. Supp. 800 (M.D. La. 1980), the court upheld construction of a 4.5 mile "state" segment of a 25 mile highway project without NEPA compliance on the grounds that the 4.5 mile segment had independent utility. The issue of segmentation is addressed in greater detail in Chapter 7, *infra*.

15. The CEQ regulations specifically exempt federal assistance in the form of general revenue sharing funds from the definition of "major federal action." 40 C.F.R. § 1508.18(a).

Beyond that, courts have found some other programs that are funded by federal grants to be outside the scope of NEPA. *See, e.g., Centralia Prison Opposition Group, Inc. v. Department of Justice*, 12 Env't Rep. Cas. (BNA) 1447 (S.D. Ill. 1978) (denying motion for preliminary injunction against state construction of a new jail despite substantial federal funding of the state prison system as a whole because no federal approval was required for construction or dispersal of funds).

C. The Human Environment

METROPOLITAN EDISON CO. V. PEOPLE AGAINST NUCLEAR ENERGY
460 U.S. 766 (1983)

Justice REHNQUIST delivered the opinion of the Court.

The issue in these cases is whether petitioner Nuclear Regulatory Commission (NRC) complied with the National Environmental Policy Act, 42 U.S.C. § 4321 *et seq.* (NEPA), when it considered whether to permit petitioner Metropolitan Edison Co. to resume operation of the Three Mile Island Unit 1 nuclear power plant (TMI-1). The Court of Appeals for the District of Columbia Circuit held that the NRC improperly failed to consider whether the risk of an accident at TMI-1 might cause harm to the psychological health and community well-being of residents of the surrounding area. 678 F.2d 222 (D.C. Cir. 1982). We reverse.

Metropolitan owns two nuclear power plants at Three Mile Island near Harrisburg, Pennsylvania. Both of these plants were licensed by the NRC after extensive proceedings, which included preparation of Environmental Impact Statements (EIS). On March 28, 1979, TMI-1 was not operating; it had been shut down for refueling. TMI-2 was operating, and it suffered a serious accident that damaged the reactor. Although, as it turned out, no dangerous radiation was released, the accident caused widespread concern. The Governor of Pennsylvania recommended an evacuation of all pregnant women and small children, and many area residents did leave their homes for several days.

After the accident, the NRC ordered Metropolitan to keep TMI-1 shut down until it had an opportunity to determine whether the plant could be operated safely. 44 Fed. Reg. 40461 (1979). The NRC then published a notice of hearing specifying several safety related issues for consideration. The notice stated that the Commission had not determined whether to consider psychological harm or other indirect effects of the accident or of renewed operation of TMI-1. It invited interested parties to submit briefs on this issue.

Petitioner People Against Nuclear Energy (PANE) intervened and responded to this invitation. PANE is an association of residents of the Harrisburg area who are opposed to further operation of either TMI reactor. PANE contended that restarting TMI-1 would cause both severe psychological health damage to persons living in the vicinity, and serious damage to the stability, cohesiveness, and well-being of the neighboring communities.[2]

---

2   Specifically, PANE contended:

1.) Renewed operation of . . . [TMI-1] would cause severe psychological distress to PANE's members and other persons living in the vicinity of the reactor. The accident at [TMI-2] has already impaired the health and sense of well being of these individuals, as evidenced by their feelings of increased anxiety, tension and fear, a sense of helplessness and such physical disorders as skin rashes, aggravated ulcers, and skeletal and muscular problems.   Such manifestations of psychological distress have been seen in the aftermath of other disasters. The possibility that [TMI-1] will reopen severely aggravates these problems. As long as this possibility exists, PANE's members and other persons living in the communities around the plant will be unable to resolve and recover from the trauma which they have suffered. Operation of [TMI-1] would be a constant reminder of the terror which they felt during the accident, and of the possibility that it will happen again. The distress caused by this ever present spectre of disaster makes it impossible . . . to operate TMI-1 without endangering the public health and safety.

2.) Renewed operation of TMI-1 would cause severe harm to the stability, cohesiveness and well being of the communities in the vicinity of the reactor. Community institutions have already been weakened as a result of a loss of citizen confidence in the ability of these institutions to

The NRC decided not to take evidence concerning PANE's contentions. PANE filed a petition for review in the Court of Appeals, contending that both NEPA and the Atomic Energy Act, 42 U.S.C. § 2011 *et seq.,* require the NRC to address its contentions. Metropolitan intervened on the side of the NRC.

The Court of Appeals concluded that the Atomic Energy Act does not require the NRC to address PANE's contentions. It did find, however, that NEPA requires the NRC to evaluate "the potential psychological health effects of operating" TMI-1 which have arisen since the original EIS was prepared. It also held that, if the NRC finds that significant new circumstances or information exist on this subject, it shall prepare a "supplemental [EIS] which considers not only the effects on psychological health but also effects on the well being of the communities surrounding Three Mile Island." We granted certiorari.

All the parties agree that effects on human health can be cognizable under NEPA, and that human health may include psychological health. The Court of Appeals thought these propositions were enough to complete a syllogism that disposes of the case: NEPA requires agencies to consider effects on health. An effect on psychological health is an effect on health. Therefore, NEPA requires agencies to consider the effects on psychological health asserted by PANE. PANE, using similar reasoning, contends that because the psychological health damage to its members would be caused by a change in the environment (renewed operation of TMI-1), NEPA requires the NRC to consider that damage. Although these arguments are appealing at first glance, we believe they skip over an essential step in the analysis. They do not consider the closeness of the relationship between the change in the environment and the "effect" at issue.

* * *

To paraphrase the statutory language in light of the facts of this case, where an agency action significantly affects the quality of the human environment, the agency must evaluate the "environmental impact" and any unavoidable adverse environmental effects of its proposal. The theme of § 102 is sounded by the adjective "environmental": NEPA does not require the agency to assess *every* impact or effect of its proposed action, but only the impact or effect on the environment. If we were to seize the word "environmental" out of its context and give it the broadest possible definition, the words "adverse environmental effects" might embrace virtually any consequence of a governmental action that someone thought "adverse." But we think the context of the statute shows that Congress was talking about the physical environment—the world around us, so to speak. NEPA was designed to promote human welfare by alerting governmental actors to the effect of their proposed actions on the physical environment.

The statements of two principal sponsors of NEPA, explaining to their colleagues the Conference Report that was ultimately enacted, illustrate this point:

> What is involved [in NEPA] is a declaration that we do not intend as a government or as a people to initiate actions which endanger the continued existence or the health

---

function properly and in a helpful manner during a crisis. The potential for a reoccurrence of the accident will further stress the community infrastructure, causing increased loss of confidence and a breakdown of the social and political order. Sociologists such as Kai Erikson have documented similar phenomena in other communities following disasters.

The perception, created by the accident, that the communities near Three Mile Island are undesirable locations for business and industry, or for the establishment of law or medical practice, or homes compounds the damage to the viability of the communities. Community vitality depends upon the ability to attract and keep persons, such as teachers, doctors, lawyers, and businesses critical to economic and social health. The potential for another accident, should TMI-1 be allowed to operate, would compound and make permanent the damage, trapping the residents in disintegrating and dying communities and discouraging . . . essential growth.

of mankind: That *we will not intentionally initiate actions which do irreparable damage to the air, land and water* which support life on earth." 115 Cong. Rec. 40416 (1969) (Remarks of Sen. Jackson) (emphasis supplied). "[W]e can now move forward *to preserve and enhance our air, aquatic, and terrestrial environments . . .* to carry out the policies and goals set forth in the bill to provide each citizen of this great country a healthful environment." 115 Cong. Rec. 40924 (1969) (Remarks of Rep. Dingell) (emphasis supplied).

Thus, although NEPA states its goals in sweeping terms of human health and welfare, these goals are ends that Congress has chosen to pursue by means of protecting the physical environment.

To determine whether § 102 requires consideration of a particular effect, we must look at the relationship between that effect and the change in the physical environment caused by the major federal action at issue. For example, if the Department of Health and Human Services were to implement extremely stringent requirements for hospitals and nursing homes receiving federal funds, many perfectly adequate hospitals and homes might be forced out of existence. The remaining facilities might be so limited or so expensive that many ill people would be unable to afford medical care and would suffer severe health damage. Nonetheless, NEPA would not require the Department to prepare an EIS evaluating that health damage because it would not be proximately related to a change in the physical environment.

Some effects that are "caused by" a change in the physical environment in the sense of "but for" causation, will nonetheless not fall within § 102 because the causal chain is too attenuated. For example, residents of the Harrisburg area have relatives in other parts of the country. Renewed operation of TMI-1 may well cause psychological health problems for these people. They may suffer "anxiety, tension and fear, a sense of helplessness," and accompanying physical disorders, n. 2, *supra,* because of the risk that their relatives may be harmed in a nuclear accident. However, this harm is simply too remote from the physical environment to justify requiring the NRC to evaluate the psychological health damage to these people that may be caused by renewed operation of TMI-1.

Our understanding of the congressional concerns that led to the enactment of NEPA suggests that the terms "environmental effect" and "environmental impact" in § 102 be read to include a requirement of a reasonably close causal relationship between a change in the physical environment and the effect at issue. This requirement is like the familiar doctrine of proximate cause from tort law. *See generally* W. PROSSER, LAW OF TORTS, ch. 7 (4th ed. 1971). The issue before us, then, is how to give content to this requirement. This is a question of first impression in this Court.

The federal action that affects the environment in this case is permitting renewed operation of TMI-1. The direct effects on the environment of this action include release of low-level radiation, increased fog in the Harrisburg area (caused by operation of the plant's cooling towers), and the release of warm water into the Susquehanna River. The NRC has considered each of these effects in its EIS, and again in the EIA. Another effect of renewed operation is a risk of a nuclear accident. The NRC has also considered this effect.

PANE argues that the psychological health damage it alleges "will flow directly from the risk of [a nuclear] accident." But a risk of an accident is not an effect on the physical environment. A risk is, by definition, unrealized in the physical world. In a causal chain from renewed operation of TMI-1 to psychological health damage, the element of risk and its perception by PANE's members are necessary middle links. We believe that the element of risk lengthens the causal chain beyond the reach of NEPA.

Risk is a pervasive element of modern life; to say more would belabor the obvious. Many of the risks we face are generated by modern technology, which brings both the possibility of major accidents and opportunities for tremendous achievements. Medical experts apparently agree that risk can generate stress in human beings, which in turn may rise to the level of serious health damage. For this reason, among many others, the question whether the gains from any technological advance are worth its attendant risks may be an important public policy issue. Nonetheless, it is quite different from the question whether the same gains are worth a given level of alteration of our physical environment or depletion of our natural resources. The latter question rather than the former is the central concern of NEPA.

Time and resources are simply too limited for us to believe that Congress intended to extend NEPA as far as the Court of Appeals has taken it. *See Vermont Yankee Nuclear Power Corp. v. Natural Resources Defense Council, Inc.,* 435 U.S. 519, 551 (1978). The scope of the agency's inquiries must remain manageable if NEPA's goal of "insur[ing] a fully informed and well considered decision," *id.* at 558, is to be accomplished.

If contentions of psychological health damage caused by risk were cognizable under NEPA, agencies would, at the very least, be obliged to expend considerable resources developing psychiatric expertise that is not otherwise relevant to their congressionally assigned functions. The available resources may be spread so thin that agencies are unable adequately to pursue protection of the physical environment and natural resources. As we said in another context in *United States v. Dow,* 357 U.S. 17, 25 (1958), "[w]e cannot attribute to Congress the intention to . . . open the door to such obvious incongruities and undesirable possibilities."

* * *

* * * [The Court of Appeals] thought PANE raised an issue of health damage, [as opposed to] questions of fear or policy disagreement. We do not believe this line is so easily drawn. Anyone who fears or dislikes a project may find himself suffering from "anxiety, tension[,] fear, [and] a sense of helplessness." N. 2, *supra.* Neither the language nor the history of NEPA suggest that it was intended to give citizens a general opportunity to air their policy objections to proposed federal actions. The political process, and not NEPA, provides the appropriate forum in which to air policy disagreements.

We do not mean to denigrate the fears of PANE's members, or to suggest that the psychological health damage they fear could not, in fact, occur. Nonetheless, it is difficult for us to see the differences between someone who dislikes a government decision so much that he suffers anxiety and stress, someone who fears the effects of that decision so much that he suffers similar anxiety and stress, and someone who suffers anxiety and stress that "flow directly," from the risks associated with the same decision. It would be extraordinarily difficult for agencies to differentiate between "genuine" claims of psychological health damage and claims that are grounded solely in disagreement with a democratically adopted policy. Until Congress provides a more explicit statutory instruction than NEPA now contains, we do not think agencies are obliged to undertake the inquiry.

The Court of Appeals' opinion seems at one point to acknowledge the force of these arguments, but seeks to distinguish the situation suggested by the related cases. First, the Court of Appeals thought the harm alleged by PANE is far more severe than the harm alleged in other cases. It thought the severity of the harm is relevant to whether NEPA requires consideration of an effect. This cannot be the case. NEPA addresses environmental effects of federal actions. The gravity of harm does not change its character. If a harm does not have a sufficiently close connection to the physical environment, NEPA does not apply.

Second, the Court of Appeals noted that PANE's claim was made "in the wake of a unique and traumatic nuclear accident." We do not understand how the accident at TMI-2 transforms

PANE's contentions into "environmental effects." The Court of Appeals "cannot believe that the psychological aftermath of the March 1979 accident falls outside" NEPA. On the contrary, NEPA is not directed at the effects of past accidents and does not create a remedial scheme for past federal actions. It was enacted to require agencies to assess the future effects of future actions. There is nothing in the language or the history of NEPA to suggest that its scope should be expanded "in the wake of" any kind of accident.

For these reasons, we hold that the NRC need not consider PANE's contentions. NEPA does not require agencies to evaluate the effects of risk, *qua* risk. The judgment of the Court of Appeals is reversed, and the case is remanded with instructions to dismiss the petition for review.

It is so ordered.

Justice BRENNAN, concurring.

I join the opinion of the Court. There can be no doubt that psychological injuries are cognizable under NEPA. As the Court points out, however, the particular psychological injury alleged in this case did not arise, for example, out of the direct sensory impact of a change in the physical environment, *cf. Chelsea Neighborhood Assns. v. United States Postal Service,* 516 F.2d 378, 388 (2d Cir. 1975), but out of a perception of risk. In light of the history and policies underlying NEPA, I agree with the Court that this crucial distinction "lengthens the causal chain beyond the reach" of the statute.

NOTES

1.   TMI-1 resumed operation in 1985 and is expected to run until 2014. In 1993, Metropolitan Edison completed cleanup of the 1979 TMI-2 accident. *14-Year Cleanup at Three Mile Island Concludes,* N.Y. TIMES, Aug. 15, 1993, at A19.

2.   Justice Rehnquist interprets NEPA to require an analysis of only those effects where there exists a "reasonably close causal relationship between a change in the physical environment and the effect at issue." Why do the risks allegedly suffered by PANE's members fail to meet the Court's test?

3.   What kinds of psychological effects are covered by NEPA? Consider for example the following:

   a.   Does NEPA encompass the psychological effects from neurological damage caused by increased lead in the environment?

   b.   Does NEPA encompass the aesthetic (i.e. psychological) impacts from the construction of high voltage transmission towers through a wilderness area?

   c.   Does NEPA encompass the increased risk of crime caused by the construction of a new jail in an urban area?

For one interpretation, see Victor B. Flatt, *The Human Environment of the Mind: Correcting NEPA Implementation by Treating Environmental Philosophy and Environmental Risk Allocation as Environmental Values under NEPA,* 46 HASTINGS L.J. 85 (1994).

4. Does NEPA encompass the risk of a "meltdown" from the TMI reactor? The increased risk of cancer from low-level radiation exposure?

5. Suppose the psychological effects of risk associated with living near the Three Mile Island reactor (which are not covered by NEPA) force property values to decline by 50 percent. Is the real decline in property values, and its attendant impact on the environment, an effect which must be addressed under NEPA?

6. Suppose that the Department of Defense proposes to collect plutonium from decommissioned nuclear weapons and store it at the high-security Crane Naval Weapons Support Center in rural southern Indiana. Plutonium, besides being the most toxic substance known to humans, is coveted by terrorists and some nations around the world for use in bombs. Will the EIS that accompanies its proposal have to address:

a. the increased risk of terrorist attack on that area?
b. the fear of local residents about the increased risk of a terrorist attack?
c. the decline in population likely to be caused by the desire of people not to live near stored plutonium?
d. the risk of a leak or accident that might cause the release of plutonium into the environment?

7. Under the CEQ's definition of "human environment" social and economic impacts will not by themselves require preparation of an EIS. Where an EIS is otherwise required, however, agencies must discuss these impacts when they are interrelated with environmental effects. 40 C.F.R. § 1508.14. Federal courts have held that a plaintiff must allege a *primary* ecological impact in order to have standing to complain of the government's failure to consider *secondary*, "socio-economic" effects. *See, e.g., Lake Erie Alliance v. Corps of Engineers*, 486 F. Supp. 707 (W.D. Pa. 1980).

Social and economic concerns are often the motivation for NEPA challenges by both persons who don't want to lose a government facility in their community and those who don't want to gain one. An example of the typical disposition of a casually-drafted NEPA complaint against reduction in force at a military base is *Image of Greater San Antonio v. Brown*, 570 F.2d 517 (5th Cir. 1978). There all of plaintiffs' evidence related to the adverse socio-economic effects of the discharge of some 1200 civilian employees at Kelly AFB in San Antonio—specifically on the discharged employees and generally on the San Antonio area. The court refused to find sufficient a broad allegation in the complaint that the reduction would have a "profound effect upon the environment, the health and welfare of man, and the natural resources of the greater San Antonio area." *Id.* at 522.

The plaintiffs in *City of Rochester v. United States Postal Service*, 541 F.2d 967 (2d Cir. 1976), fared better. There the court held that before the Postal Service moved the Rochester mail processing facility from the inner city to an outlying suburban area it had to consider not only the possible "urban" environmental effects of abandonment of the inner-city facility, but also the potential loss of jobs by employees who could not commute to the new facility.

D. Programmatic Proposals and Legislation

The following two early NEPA cases consider the extent to which an EIS is required for programmatic actions. The cases should be read and discussed together.

SCIENTISTS' INSTITUTE FOR PUBLIC
INFORMATION, INC. v. ATOMIC ENERGY COMMISSION [SIPI]
481 F.2d 1079 (D.C. Cir. 1973)

J. SKELLY WRIGHT, Circuit Judge.

Appellant claims that the Atomic Energy Commission's Liquid Metal Fast Breeder Reactor program involves a "recommendation or report on proposals for legislation and other major Federal actions significantly affecting the quality of the human environment" under Section 102(C) of the National Environmental Policy Act (NEPA), 42 U.S.C. § 4332(C) (1970), and that the Commission is therefore required to issue a "detailed statement" for the program. The District Court held that no statement was presently required since, in its view, the program was still in the research and development stage and no specific implementing action which would significantly affect the environment had yet been taken. Taking into account the magnitude of the ongoing federal investment in this program, the controversial environmental effects attendant upon future widespread deployment of breeder reactors should the program fulfill present expectations, the accelerated pace under which this program has moved beyond pure scientific research toward creation of a viable, competitive breeder reactor electrical energy industry, and the manner in which investment in this new technology is likely to restrict future alternatives, we hold that the Commission's program comes within both the letter and the spirit of Section 102(C) and that a detailed statement about the program, its environmental impact, and alternatives thereto is presently required. Since the Commission has not yet issued such a statement, we reverse and remand the case to the District Court for entry of appropriate declaratory relief.

I. FACTUAL BACKGROUND:
THE LIQUID METAL FAST BREEDER REACTOR PROGRAM

Although more than a superficial understanding of the technology underlying this case is beyond the layman's ken, a brief summary will prove helpful. Nuclear reactors use nuclear fission—the splitting of the atom—to produce heat which may be used to generate electricity in nuclear power plants. Only a few, relatively rare, naturally occurring substances—primarily Uranium-235—can maintain the nuclear fission chain reaction necessary for operation of these reactors. There are thus severe constraints on the long run potential of nuclear energy for generating electricity unless new nuclear fuel is "artificially" produced. Such fuel can be produced through the process of "breeding" within a "fast breeder reactor." The fast breeder reactor differs from the now common light water nuclear reactor in that the neutrons which split atoms in the fuel (thereby releasing new neutrons and heat energy) travel much faster than the neutrons in ordinary reactors. The reactor breeds new fuel through what has aptly been termed "a sort of modern alchemy." Some neutrons leave the inner core of the reactor, which is made up of fissionable Uranium-235, and enter a blanket of nonfissionable Uranium-238. When atoms in this blanket are struck by neutrons, they are transmuted into Plutonium-239, itself a fissionable fuel which can be removed from the reactor and used in other installations. It is estimated that after about 10 years of operation the typical fast breeder reactor will produce enough fissionable Plutonium-239 not only to refuel itself completely, but also to fuel an additional reactor of comparable size. The Liquid Metal Fast Breeder Reactor (henceforth LMFBR) is simply a fast breeder reactor that uses a liquid metal, sodium, as a coolant and heat transfer agent.

Because the breeding principle makes possible vast expansion of fuel available for nuclear reactors (Uranium-238 is many times more common than Uranium-235), it has been the subject of considerable interest since the earliest days of atomic energy. The Commission demonstrated the feasibility of breeder reactors by constructing several experimental breeder reactors in the 1950's. In its 1962 Report to the President on Civilian Nuclear Power, the Commission specifically recommended that future Government programs include vigorous development and timely introduction of economic breeder reactors which, in the Commission's view, were essential to long-range major use of nuclear energy. By 1967, when the Commission supplemented its Report to the President, the LMFBR had been singled out as a priority program representing the largest civilian power development area. The Commission's focus expanded beyond solving the technical problems posed by the LMFBR, and began to embrace efforts to build an industrial base and obtain acceptance for LMFBR plant types by utilities, primarily through planned Government-assisted construction of commercial scale LMFBR electrical power plants. In sum, the Commission came to see its program as serving "as the key to effecting the transition of the fast breeder program from the technology development stage to the point of large-scale commercial utilization."

In furtherance of these objectives the Commission, in 1968, issued a 10-volume LMFBR Program Plan, the dual objectives of which were (1) to achieve, through research and development, the necessary technology, and (2) "to assure maximum development and use of a competitive, self-sustaining industrial LMFBR capability." With growing concern about a possible energy crisis, rapid commercial implementation of LMFBR technology has become a national mission. In the style of President Kennedy's 1960 commitment to put an American on the moon by the end of the decade, President Nixon, in his June 4, 1971 Energy Message to Congress, announced as the highest priority item of his program "[a] commitment to complete the successful demonstration of the liquid metal fast breeder reactor by 1980," and this goal has obtained the concurrence of Congress' Joint Committee on Atomic Energy. Statutory authorization has been obtained to proceed with the first demonstration plant, financed in large part by the federal government, and the Commission has entered into negotiations with the Tennessee Valley Authority and Commonwealth Edison aimed at concluding construction contracts for the plant. On September 26, 1971 the President announced his intention to seek the necessary legislative authority for a second demonstration plant. The Congress supports the program through annual appropriations and, at a time of general budgetary restraint, LMFBR program funds have recently mushroomed to $90.3 million in fiscal 1971 and $130 million in fiscal 1972. The Commission expects future federal expenditures for the program to be over $2 billion. These funds have been in the past, and will continue in the future to be, matched with sizable financial commitments from the private sector.

The LMFBR's prospects are sufficiently bright to have led President Nixon to say: "Our best hope today for meeting the Nation's growing demand for economical clean energy lies with the fast breeder reactor." And the Commission has recently predicted that by the year 2000 LMFBR capacity will equal total electrical generating capacity in the United States today.

II. APPLICATION OF NEPA TO TECHNOLOGY
DEVELOPMENT PROGRAMS

NEPA requires federal agencies to include a detailed environmental impact statement "in every recommendation or report on proposals for legislation and other major Federal actions significantly affecting the quality of the human environment * * *." That the Commission must issue a detailed statement for each of the major test facilities and demonstration plants encompassed by the LMFBR program is conceded by the Commission and not at issue in this case. The Commission has already issued an impact statement for its Fast Flux Test Facility to be constructed in Hanford, Washington, and, at the President's request, has completed a statement for the first demonstration plant prior to the time such a statement would normally be issued. Nor is the adequacy of either of these statements as they pertain to their respective individual facilities an issue on this appeal. The question raised, instead, is basically twofold: whether at some point in time the Commission must issue a statement for the research and development program as a whole, rather than simply for individual facilities, and, assuming an affirmative answer to this question, whether a statement covering the entire program should be drafted now.

Our consideration of this case has been somewhat complicated by the Commission's ambivalent position with respect to these already difficult questions. The Commission's basic position seems to be that NEPA requires detailed statements only for particular facilities, and that no separate NEPA analysis of an entire research and development program is required. In the words of then Chairman James Schlesinger: "These environmental statements are intended to deal with the particular facility or a particular project." * * *

Elsewhere in its brief, however, the Commission seems to concede that at some point in time a NEPA statement for the entire program would be required. "Most assuredly, the AEC is not declaring its intention to never file a detailed statement for the overall program." In this context the Commission argues that the program has not yet reached that stage where a NEPA statement on the overall program would be either feasible or meaningful. "[T]he remote and speculative nature of the project" and the fact that it "remains uncrystallized in form and undetermined in application," lead the Commission to conclude that any detailed analysis at the present time of the overall program, its environmental effects, and alternatives thereto would require the Commission "to look into the crystal ball" and "would be meaningless in terms of content."

The remainder of this section will focus on the Commission's first line of defense—the applicability of NEPA to technology research and development programs and the possibility of substituting an "environmental survey" for a NEPA statement. The following section will discuss the Commission's second argument—the timing of a NEPA statement on the overall program.

The Commission takes an unnecessarily crabbed approach to NEPA in assuming that the impact statement process was designed only for particular facilities rather than for analysis of the overall effects of broad agency programs. Indeed, quite the contrary is true.

> "Individual actions that are related either geographically or as logical parts in a chain of contemplated actions may be more appropriately evaluated in a single, program statement. Such a statement also appears appropriate in connection with * * * the development of a new program that contemplates a number of subsequent actions. * * * [T]he program statement has a number of advantages. It provides an occasion for a more exhaustive consideration of effects and alternatives than would be practicable in a statement on an individual action. It ensures consideration of cumulative impacts that might be slighted in a case-by-case analysis. And it avoids duplicative reconsideration of basic policy questions. * * *"

* * *

The statutory phrase "actions significantly affecting the quality of the environment" is intentionally broad, reflecting the Act's attempt to promote an across-the-board adjustment in federal agency decision making so as to make the quality of the environment a concern of every federal agency. The legislative history of the Act indicates that the term "actions" refers not only to construction of particular facilities, but includes "project proposals, proposals for new legislation, regulations, policy statements, or expansion or revision of ongoing programs * * *." Thus there is "Federal action" within the meaning of the statute not only when an agency proposes to build a facility itself, but also whenever an agency makes a decision which permits action by other parties which will affect the quality of the environment. NEPA's impact statement procedure has been held to apply where a federal agency approves a lease of land to private parties, grants licenses and permits to private parties, or approves and funds state highway projects. In each of these instances the federal agency took action affecting the environment in the sense that the agency made a decision which permitted some other party—private or governmental—to take action affecting the environment. The Commission does precisely the same thing here by developing a technology which will permit utility companies to take action affecting the environment by building LMFBR power plants. Development of the technology serves as much to affect the environment as does a Commission decision granting a construction permit for a specific plant. Development of the technology is a necessary precondition of construction of any plants.

* * *

NEPA's objective of controlling the impact of technology on the environment cannot be served by all practicable means, see 42 U.S.C. § 4331(b) (1970), unless the statute's action forcing impact statement process is applied to ongoing federal agency programs aimed at developing new technologies which, when applied, will affect the environment. To wait until a technology attains the stage of complete commercial feasibility before considering the possible adverse environmental effects attendant upon ultimate application of the technology will undoubtedly frustrate meaningful consideration and balancing of environmental costs against economic and other benefits. Modern technological advances typically stem from massive investments in research and development, as is the case here. Technological advances are therefore capital investments and, as such, once brought to a stage of commercial feasibility the investment in their development acts to compel their application. Once there has been, in the terms of NEPA, "an irretrievable commitment of resources" in the technology development stage, the balance of environmental costs and economic and other benefits shifts in favor of ultimate application of the technology. * * * [B]ecause of the long lead times necessary for development of new commercially feasible technologies for production of electrical energy, the decisions our society makes today as to the direction of research and development will determine what technologies are available 10, 20, or 30 years hence when we must apply some new means of producing electrical energy or face the alternative of energy rationing, through higher prices or otherwise. The manner in which we divide our limited research and development dollars today among various promising technologies in effect determines which technologies will be available, and what type and amount of environmental effects will have to be endured, in the future when we must apply some new technology to meet projected energy demand.

In a very practical sense, then, the Commission's LMFBR program affects the quality of the environment. That the effects will not begin to be felt for several years, perhaps over a decade, is not controlling, for the Act plainly contemplates consideration of "both the long- and short-range implications to man, his physical and social surroundings, and to nature, * * * in order to avoid to the fullest extent practicable undesirable consequences for the environment." * * *

We thus tread firm ground in holding that NEPA requires impact statements for major federal research programs, such as the Commission's LMFBR program, aimed at development of new technologies which, when applied, will significantly affect the quality of the human environment. To the extent the Commission's "environmental survey" would not be issued in accordance with NEPA's procedures for preparation and distribution, it is not an adequate substitute for a NEPA statement. * * *

* * *

Certainly NEPA does not require the Commission to forecast the deployment and effects of LMFBR power reactors in the year 2000 in the same detail or with the same degree of accuracy as another agency might have to forecast the increased traffic congestion likely to be caused by a proposed highway. Conversely, the Commission may well be expected to devote more resources toward preparation of an impact statement for its multi-billion-dollar program than it would for a project involving a federal investment many times smaller.

Similarly, Section 102(C)'s requirement that the agency describe the anticipated environmental effects of proposed action is subject to a rule of reason. The agency need not foresee the unforeseeable, but by the same token neither can it avoid drafting an impact statement simply because describing the environmental effects of and alternatives to particular agency action involves some degree of forecasting. And one of the functions of a NEPA statement is to indicate the extent to which environmental effects are essentially unknown. It must be remembered that the basic thrust of an agency's responsibilities under NEPA is to predict the environmental effects of proposed action before the action is taken and those effects fully known. Reasonable forecasting and speculation is thus implicit in NEPA, and we must reject any attempt by agencies to shirk their responsibilities under NEPA by labeling any and all discussion of future environmental effects as "crystal ball inquiry." * * *

Accordingly, if the Commission's environmental survey is prepared and issued in accordance with NEPA procedures, and if the Commission makes a good faith effort in the survey to describe the reasonably foreseeable environmental impact of the program, alternatives to the program and their reasonably foreseeable environmental impact, and the irreversible and irretrievable commitment of resources the program involves, we see no reason why the survey will not fully satisfy the requirements of Section 102(C). The resulting document may look very different from the impact statement the Commission is used to issuing for a particular nuclear power plant, but this variance should be accepted as a healthy reflection of NEPA's broad scope. It should not be twisted into an excuse for not complying with NEPA at all.

* * *

III. TIMING THE NEPA STATEMENT

Whether a statement on the overall LMFBR program should be issued now or at some uncertain date in the future is the most difficult question presented by this case. * * *

In our view, the timing question can best be answered by reference to the underlying policies of NEPA in favor of meaningful, timely information on the effects of agency action. In the early stages of research, when little is known about the technology and when future application of the technology is both doubtful and remote, it may well be impossible to draft a meaningful impact statement. Predictions as to the possible effects of application of the technology would tend toward uninformative generalities, arrived at by guesswork rather than analysis. NEPA requires predictions, but not prophecy, and impact statements ought not to be modeled upon the works of Jules Verne or H. G. Wells. At the other end of the spectrum, by the time commercial feasibility of the technology is conclusively demonstrated, and the effects of application of the technology certain, the purposes of NEPA will already have been thwarted. Substantial investments will have been made in development of the technology and options will have been precluded without consideration of environmental factors. Any statement prepared at such a late date will no doubt be thorough, detailed and accurate, but it will be of little help in ensuring that decisions reflect environmental concerns. Thus we are pulled in two directions. Statements must be written late enough in the development process to contain meaningful information, but they must be written early enough so that whatever information is contained can practically serve as an input into the decision making process.

Determining when to draft an impact statement for a technology development program obviously requires a reconciliation of these competing concerns. Some balance must be struck, and several factors should be weighed in the balance. How likely is the technology to prove commercially feasible, and how soon will that occur? To what extent is meaningful information presently available on the effects of application of the technology and of alternatives and their effects? To what extent are irretrievable commitments being made and options precluded as the development program progresses? How severe will be the environmental effects if the technology does prove commercially feasible?

Answers to questions like these require agency expertise, and therefore the initial and primary responsibility for striking a balance between the competing concerns must rest with the agency itself, not with the courts. At the same time, however, some degree of judicial scrutiny of an agency's decision that the time is not yet ripe for a NEPA statement is necessary in order to ensure that the policies of the Act are not being frustrated or ignored. Agency decisions in the environmental area touch on fundamental personal interests in life and health, and these interests have always had a special claim to judicial protection.

The first function of judicial review in this area should be to require the agency to provide a framework for principled decision making. Agencies engaging in long-term technology research and development programs should develop either formal or informal procedures for regular, perhaps annual, evaluation of whether the time for drafting a NEPA statement has arrived.

* * *

* * * Fortunately, a substantial record was made before the District Court, consisting in large part of analyses and reports completed by the Commission itself. Our examination of this record leads us to conclude that the Commission could have no rational basis for deciding that the time is not yet ripe for drafting an impact statement on the overall LMFBR program. Consideration of each of the facts set out in our balancing test point in the direction of drafting an impact statement now.

To begin with, commercial implementation of LMFBR technology is far from speculative. The massive amounts of money being pumped into this program by Congress and the Presidential Energy Policy statement committing the nation to completion of the first commercialized demonstration plant by 1980 both indicate widespread confidence that the program will succeed in its twin goals of demonstrating the commercial feasibility of the breeder reactor and producing an industrial infrastructure ready, willing and able to construct such reactors on a commercial basis. * * * Nor do we think completion of the program may be termed remote. While 10 years may seem a long time in other contexts, by 1968 the Commission already had a carefully planned and detailed schedule for the LMFBR program through the year 1980.

Secondly, the Commission's own documents indicate that there already exists much meaningful information on the reasonably foreseeable environmental impact of development of LMFBR technology. The impact statement for the first demonstration plant, for example, contains detailed estimates of the radioactive wastes produced annually by a single commercial-scale LMFBR electrical power plant. It also contains estimates of the amount of land area necessary for short-and long-term storage of such wastes. Other studies completed by the Commission contain reasonable estimates of the expected deployment of LMFBR power plants through the year 2000 if the program proceeds on schedule. The overall environmental effects of the program could thus be extrapolated from already existing data. We see no reason why the Commission could not, from information already before us, explore in a NEPA statement such vital matters as, for example, the total amounts of radioactive wastes which will be produced by development of this technology and the total amounts of land area needed for long-and short-term storage of these wastes. The Commission's continual references to "crystal ball inquiry" have a hollow ring in light of the fact that the Commission has already prepared a complex cost-benefit analysis of the LMFBR program, involving projections through and beyond the year 2000. * * * The Commission evidently believes its cost-benefit forecasts are accurate enough for use in convincing Congress to fund the program and for use in planning various supporting facilities and fuel production requirements. * * *

It also seems clear that the Commission has available much information on alternatives to the program and their environmental effects. The Commission's own answer to the complaint in this case states:

> "Alternatives to the LMFBR program have received serious national attention, study and debate. This reactor concept has been under continual review since its conception in the late 1940's. Alternative energy systems have been studied and compared by both governmental and private groups and the conclusion always has been that the LMFBR merits the highest priority within the nation's energy program. * * *"

* * * One would be hard pressed to give a better description of what the discussion of alternatives in a NEPA statement on the overall LMFBR program should look like.

Moving to another factor in our balancing test, it is evident that there are sizable irretrievable commitments of resources taking place in the program. As indicated in the introduction, the federal commitment to this program is now over $100 million per year. The Commission itself admits that one of the results of this commitment has been to slow down development of other new technologies, such as alternative breeder reactor concepts, which would also require a large investment to move from the stage of technical and theoretical research into a stage of commercial feasibility.

Finally, we cannot ignore the fact that the anticipated effects of the LMFBR program on the environment are among the most significant, and most controversial, of all federal programs. We deal here with a radical change in the manner in which our entire nation produces electricity. In many respects, no doubt, this new technique of producing electricity will be less harmful to the environment than present fossil fuel generating plants. But it is evident that the program presents unique and unprecedented environmental hazards. The Commission itself concedes it is expected that by the year 2000 some 600,000 cubic feet of high-level concentrated radioactive wastes will have been generated. These wastes will pose an admitted hazard to human health for hundreds of years, and will have to be maintained in special repositories. The environmental problems attendant upon processing, transporting and storing these wastes, and the other environmental issues raised by widespread deployment of LMFBR power plants, warrant the most searching scrutiny under NEPA.

Of course, some of the environmental impacts of the program are still shrouded in uncertainty. But one of the functions of an impact statement is to point up uncertainties where they exist. And whatever statement is drafted by the Commission can be amended to reflect newly obtained information as the program progresses.

IV. CONCLUSION

At this point it is appropriate that we emphasize the limited nature of the issue under review in this case. By our holding we do not intend in any way to question either the wisdom of the Commission's LMFBR program or the Commission's dedication to protection of the public health and safety. * * *

* * * [T]he judgment of the District Court is reversed and the case is remanded to the District Court for entry of appropriate declaratory relief.

So ordered.

KLEPPE V. SIERRA CLUB
427 U.S. 390 (1976)

Mr. Justice POWELL delivered the opinion of the Court.

* * *

I

Respondents, several organizations concerned with the environment, brought this suit in July 1973 in the United States District Court for the District of Columbia. The defendants in the suit, petitioners here, were the officials of the Interior Department and other federal agencies responsible for issuing coal leases, approving mining plans, granting rights-of-way, and taking the other actions necessary to enable private companies and public utilities to develop coal reserves on land owned or controlled by the Federal Government. Citing widespread interest in the reserves of a region identified as the "Northern Great Plains region," and an alleged threat from coal-related operations to their members' enjoyment of the region's environment, respondents claimed that the federal officials could not allow further development without preparing a "comprehensive environmental impact statement" under § 102(2)(C) on the entire region. They sought declaratory and injunctive relief.

The District Court, on the basis of extensive findings of fact and conclusions of law, held that the complaint stated no claim for relief and granted the petitioners' motions for summary judgment. Respondents appealed. * * * In June 1975 the Court of Appeals ruled on the merits and, for reasons discussed below, reversed the District Court and remanded for further proceedings. 514 F.2d 856. The court continued its injunction in force.

* * *

II

* * *

The Northern Great Plains region identified in respondents' complaint encompasses portions of four States—northeastern Wyoming, eastern Montana, western North Dakota, and western South Dakota. There is no dispute about its richness in coal, nor about the waxing interest in developing that coal, nor about the crucial role the federal petitioners will play due to the significant percentage of the coal to which they control access. The Department has initiated, in this decade, three studies in areas either inclusive of or included within this region. The North Central Power Study was addressed to the potential for coordinated development of electric power in an area encompassing all or part of 15 States in the North Central United States. It aborted in 1972 for lack of interest on the part of electric utilities. The Montana-Wyoming Aqueducts Study, intended to recommend the best use of water resources for coal development in southeastern Montana and northeastern Wyoming, was suspended in 1972 with the initiation of the third study, the Northern Great Plains Resources Program (NGPRP).

While the record does not reveal the degree of concern with environmental matters in the first two studies, it is clear that the NGPRP was devoted entirely to the environment. It was carried out by an interagency, federal-state task force with public participation, and was designed "to assess the potential social, economic and environmental impacts" from resource development in five States—Montana, Wyoming, South Dakota, North Dakota, and Nebraska. Its primary objective was "to provide an analytical and informational framework for policy and planning decisions at all levels of government" by formulating several "scenarios" showing the probable consequences for the area's environment and culture from the various possible techniques and levels of resource development. The final interim report of the NGPRP was issued August 1, 1975, shortly after the decision of the Court of Appeals in this case.

In addition, since 1973 the Department has engaged in a complete review of its coal-leasing program for the entire Nation. On February 17 of that year the Secretary announced the review and announced also that during study a "short-term leasing policy" would prevail, under which new leasing would be restricted to narrowly defined circumstances and even then allowed only when an environmental impact statement had been prepared if required under NEPA. The purpose of the program review was to study the environmental impact of the Department's entire range of coal-related activities and to develop a planning system to guide the national leasing program. The impact statement, known as the "Coal Programmatic EIS," went through several drafts before issuing in final form on September 19, 1975—shortly before the petitions for certiorari were filed in this case. The Coal Programmatic EIS proposed a new leasing program based on a complex planning system called the Energy Minerals Activity Recommendation System (EMARS), and assessed the prospective environmental impact of the new program as well as the alternatives to it. We have been informed by the parties to this litigation that the Secretary is in the process of implementing the new program.

Against this factual background, we turn now to consider the issues raised by this case in the status in which it reached this Court.

III

The major issue remains the one with which the suit began: whether NEPA requires petitioners to prepare an environmental impact statement on the entire Northern Great Plains region. Petitioners, arguing the negative, rely squarely upon the facts of these and the language of § 102(2)(C) of NEPA. We find their reliance well placed.

* * * [Section] 102(2)(C) [of NEPA] requires an impact statement "in every recommendation or report on proposals for legislation and other major Federal actions significantly affecting the quality of the human environment." Since no one has suggested that petitioners have proposed legislation on respondents' region, the controlling phrase in this section of the Act, for this case, is "major Federal actions." Respondents can prevail only if there has been a report or recommendation on a proposal for major federal action with respect to the Northern Great Plains region. Our statement of the relevant facts shows there has been none; instead, all proposals are for actions of either local or national scope.

The local actions are the decisions by the various petitioners to issue a lease, approve a mining plan, issue a right-of-way permit, or take other action to allow private activity at some point within the region identified by respondents. Several Courts of Appeals have held that an impact statement must be included in the report or recommendation on a proposal for such action if the private activity to be permitted is one "significantly affecting the quality of the human environment" within the meaning of § 102(2)(C). The petitioners do not dispute this requirement in this case, and indeed have prepared impact statements on several proposed actions of this type in the Northern Great Plains during the course of this litigation. Similarly, the federal petitioners agreed at oral argument that § 102(2)(C) required the Coal Programmatic EIS that was prepared in tandem with the new national coal-leasing program and included as part of the final report on the proposal for adoption of that program. Their admission is well made, for the new leasing program is a coherent plan of national scope, and its adoption surely has significant environmental consequences.

But there is no evidence in the record of an action or a proposal for an action of regional scope. The District Court, in fact, expressly found that there was no existing or proposed plan or program on the part of the Federal Government for the regional development of the area described in respondents' complaint. It found also that the three studies initiated by the Department in areas either included within or inclusive of respondents' region that is, the Montana-Wyoming Aqueducts Study, the North Central Power Study, and the NGPRP were not parts of any plan or program to develop or encourage development of the Northern Great Plains. That court found no evidence that the individual coal development projects undertaken or proposed by private industry and public utilities in that part of the country are integrated into a plan or otherwise interrelated. These findings were not disturbed by the Court of Appeals, and they remain fully supported by the record in this Court.

Quite apart from the fact that the statutory language requires an impact statement only in the event of a proposed action, respondents' desire for a regional environmental impact statement cannot be met for practical reasons. In the absence of a proposal for a regional plan of development, there is nothing that could be the subject of the analysis envisioned by the statute for an impact statement. * * *

IV

A

The Court of Appeals, in reversing the District Court, did not find that there was a regional plan or program for development of the Northern Great Plains region. It accepted all of the District Court's findings of fact, but concluded nevertheless that the petitioners "contemplated" a regional plan or program. The court thought that the North Central Power Study, the Montana-Wyoming Aqueducts Study, and the NGPRP all constituted "attempts to control development" by individual companies on a regional scale. It also concluded that the interim report of the NGPRP, then expected to be released at any time, would provide the petitioners with the information needed to formulate the regional plan they had been "contemplating." The Court therefore remanded with instructions to the petitioners to inform the District Court of their role in the further development of the region within 30 days after the NGPRP interim report issued; if they decided to control that development, an impact statement would be required.

We conclude that the Court of Appeals erred in both its factual assumptions and its interpretation of NEPA. We think the court was mistaken in concluding, on the record before it, that the petitioners were "contemplating" a regional development plan or program. * * *

Moreover, at the time the Court of Appeals ruled there was no indication in the record that the NGPRP was aimed toward a regional plan or program, and subsequent events have shown that this was not its purpose. The interim report of the study, issued shortly after the Court of Appeals ruled, described the effects of several possible rates of coal development but stated in its preface that the alternatives "are for study and comparison only; they do not represent specific plans or proposals." All parties agreed in this Court that there still exists no proposal for a regional plan or program of development.

Even had the record justified a finding that a regional program was contemplated by the petitioners, the legal conclusion drawn by the Court of Appeals cannot be squared with the Act.

The court recognized that the mere "contemplation" of certain action is not sufficient to require an impact statement. But it believed the statute nevertheless empowers a court to require the preparation of an impact statement to begin at some point prior to the formal recommendation or report on a proposal. The Court of Appeals accordingly devised its own four-part "balancing" test for determining when during the contemplation of a plan or other type of federal action, an agency must begin a statement. The factors to be considered were identified as the likelihood and imminence of the program's coming to fruition, the extent to which information is available on the effects of implementing the expected program and on alternatives thereto, the extent to which irretrievable commitments are being made and options precluded "as refinement of the proposal progresses," and the severity of the environmental effects should the action be implemented.

The Court of Appeals thought that as to two of these factors—the availability of information on the effects of any regional development program, and the severity of those effects—the time already was "ripe" for an impact statement. It deemed the record unclear, however, as to the likelihood of the petitioners' actually producing a plan to control the development, and surmised that irretrievable commitments were being avoided because petitioners had ceased approving most coal-related projects while the NGPRP study was underway. The court also thought that the imminent release of the NGPRP interim report would provide the officials with sufficient information to define their role in development of the region, and it believed that as soon as the NGPRP was completed the petitioners would begin approving individual projects in the region, thus permitting irrevocable commitments of resources. It was for this reason that the court in its remand required the petitioners to report to the District Court their decision on the federal role with respect to the Northern Great Plains as a region within 30 days after issuance of the NGPRP report.

The Court's reasoning and action find no support in the language or legislative history of NEPA. The statute clearly states when an impact statement is required, and mentions nothing about a balancing of factors. Rather, as we noted last Term, under the first sentence of § 102(2)(C) the moment at which an agency must have a final statement ready "is the time at which it makes a recommendation or report on a *proposal* for federal action." *Aberdeen & Rockfish R. C. v. SCRAP,* 422 U.S. 289, 320 (1975) (*SCRAP II*) (emphasis in original). The procedural duty imposed upon agencies by this section is quite precise, and the role of the courts in enforcing that duty is similarly precise. A court has no authority to depart from the statutory language and, by a balancing of court-devised factors, determine a point during the germination process of a potential proposal at which an impact statement *should be prepared.* Such an assertion of judicial authority would leave the agencies uncertain as to their procedural duties under NEPA, would invite judicial involvement in the day-to-day decisionmaking process of the agencies, and would invite litigation. As the contemplation of a project and the accompanying study thereof do not necessarily result in a proposal for major federal action, it may be assumed that the balancing process devised by the Court of Appeals also would result in the preparation of a good many unnecessary impact statements.

* * *

V

Our discussion thus far has been addressed primarily to the decision of the Court of Appeals. It remains, however, to consider the contention now urged by respondents. They have not attempted to support the Court of Appeals' decision. Instead, respondents renew an argument they appear to have made to the Court of Appeals, but which that court did not reach. Respondents insist that, even without a comprehensive federal plan for the development of the

Northern Great Plains, a "regional" impact statement nevertheless is required on all coal-related projects in the region because they are intimately related.

There are two ways to view this contention. First, it amounts to an attack on the sufficiency of the impact statements already prepared by the petitioners on the coal-related projects that they have approved or stand ready to approve. As such, we cannot consider it in this proceeding, for the case was not brought as a challenge to a particular impact statement and there is no impact statement in the record. It also is possible to view the respondents' argument as an attack upon the decision of the petitioners not to prepare one comprehensive impact statement on all proposed projects in the region. This contention properly is before us, for the petitioners have made it clear they do not intend to prepare such a statement.

We begin by stating our general agreement with respondents' basic premise that § 102(2)(C) may require a comprehensive impact statement in certain situations where several proposed actions are pending at the same time. NEPA announced a national policy of environmental protection and placed a responsibility upon the Federal Government to further specific environmental goals by "all practicable means, consistent with other essential considerations of national policy." § 101(b), 42 U.S.C. § 4331(b). Section 102(2)(C) is one of the "action-forcing" provisions intended as a directive to "all agencies to assure consideration of the environmental impact of their actions in decisionmaking." Conference Report on NEPA, 115 Cong. Rec. 40416 (1969). By requiring an impact statement Congress intended to assure such consideration during the development of a proposal or—as in this case—during the formulation of a position on a proposal submitted by private parties. A comprehensive impact statement may be necessary in some cases for an agency to meet this duty. Thus, when several proposals for coal-related actions that will have cumulative or synergistic environmental impact upon a region are pending concurrently before an agency, their environmental consequences must be considered together. Only through comprehensive consideration of pending proposals can the agency evaluate different courses of action.

Agreement to this extent with respondents' premise, however, does not require acceptance of their conclusion that all proposed coal-related actions in the Northern Great Plains region are so "related" as to require their analysis in a single comprehensive impact statement. Respondents informed us that the Secretary recently adopted an approach to impact statements on coal-related actions that provides:

> "A. As a general proposition, and as determined by the Secretary, when action is proposed involving coal development such as issuing several coal leases or approving mining plans in the same region, such actions will be covered by a single EIS rather than by multiple statements. In such cases, the region covered will be determined by basin boundaries, drainage areas, areas of common reclamation problems, administrative boundaries, areas of economic interdependence, and other relevant factors."

* * * [T]he Department has decided to prepare comprehensive impact statements of the type contemplated by § 102(2)(C), although it has not deemed it appropriate to prepare such a statement on all proposed actions in the region identified by respondents.

Respondents conceded at oral argument that to prevail they must show that petitioners have acted arbitrarily in refusing to prepare one comprehensive statement on this entire region, and we agree. The determination of the region, if any, with respect to which a comprehensive statement is necessary requires the weighing of a number of relevant factors, including the extent of the interrelationship among proposed actions and practical considerations of feasibility. Resolving these issues requires a high level of technical expertise and is properly left to the informed discretion of the responsible federal agencies. Absent a showing of arbitrary action, we must assume that the agencies have exercised this discretion appropriately. Respondents have made no showing to the contrary.

Respondents' basic argument is that one comprehensive statement on the Northern Great Plains is required because all coal-related activity in that region is "programmatically," "geographically," and "environmentally" related. Both the alleged "programmatic" relationship and the alleged "geographic" relationship resolve, ultimately, into an argument that the region is proper for a comprehensive impact statement because the petitioners themselves have approached environmental study in this area on a regional basis. * * * As for the alleged "environmental" relationship, respondents contend that the coal-related projects "will produce a wide variety of cumulative environmental impacts" throughout the Northern Great Plains region. They described them as follows: Diminished availability of water, air and water pollution, increases in population and industrial densities, and perhaps even climatic changes. Cumulative environmental impacts are, indeed, what require a comprehensive impact statement. But determination of the extent and effect of these factors, and particularly identification of the geographic area within which they may occur, is a task assigned to the special competency of the appropriate agencies. Petitioners dispute respondents' contentions that the interrelationship of environmental impacts is regionwide and, as respondents' own submissions indicate, petitioners appear to have determined that the appropriate scope of comprehensive statements should be based on basins, drainage areas, and other factors. We cannot say that petitioners' choices are arbitrary. * * *

In sum, respondents' contention as to the relationships between all proposed coal-related projects in the Northern Great Plains region does not require that petitioners prepare one comprehensive impact statement covering all before proceeding to approve specific pending applications. As we already have determined that there exists no proposal for regionwide action that could require a regional impact statement, the judgment of the Court of Appeals must be reversed, and the judgment of the District Court reinstated and affirmed. The case is remanded for proceedings consistent with this opinion.

So ordered.

Mr. Justice MARSHALL, with whom Mr. Justice BRENNAN joined, concurring in part and dissenting in part.

* * *

Because an early start in preparing an impact statement is necessary if an agency is to comply with NEPA, there comes a time when an agency that fails to begin preparation of a statement on a contemplated project is violating the law. It is this fact, which is not disputed by the Court today, that was recognized by the Court of Appeals and that formed the basis of its remedy. The Court devised a four-part test to enable a reviewing court to determine when judicial intervention might be proper in such cases. The questions formulated by the Court of Appeals were:

> "How likely is the program to come to fruition, and how soon will that occur? To what extent is meaningful information presently available on the effects of implementation of the program, and of alternatives and their effects? To what extent are irretrievable commitments being made and options precluded as refinement of the proposal progresses? How severe will be the environmental effects if the program is implemented?"

514 F.2d 856, 880 (1975).

* * *

I believe the Court of Appeals' test is a sensible way to approach enforcement of NEPA, and none of the Court's reasons for concluding otherwise are, for me, persuasive.

The Court begins its rejection of the four-part test by announcing that the procedural duty imposed on the agencies by § 102(2)(C) is "quite precise" and leaves a court "no authority to depart from the statutory language . . . .." Given the history and wording of NEPA's impact statement requirement, this statement is baffling. A statute that imposes a complicated procedural requirement on all "proposals" for "major Federal actions significantly affecting the quality of the human environment" and then assiduously avoids giving any hint, either expressly or by way of legislative history, of what is meant by a "proposal" or by a "major Federal action" can hardly be termed precise. In fact, this vaguely worded statute seems designed to serve as no more than a catalyst for development of a "common law" of NEPA. To date, the courts have responded in just that manner and have created such a "common law." 514 F.2d at 870-72. Indeed, that development is the source of NEPA's success. Of course, the Court is correct that the courts may not dart from NEPA's language. They must, however, give meaning to that language if there is to be anything in NEPA to enforce at all. And that is all the Court of Appeals did in this case.

But, claims the Court, judicial intervention of the sort approved by the Court of Appeals would leave the agencies uncertain about their procedural duties under NEPA. There is no basis for this claim. The agencies already know their duties under NEPA and the Court of Appeals did not alter them. All it did was create a mechanism to allow it to enforce those pre-existing duties.

Next, the Court fears, the four-part test, would "invite judicial involvement in the day-to-day decisionmaking process of the agencies. . . ." This concern is in part untrue and in part exaggerated. The test would certainly result in judicial involvement with the single decision whether the time is right to begin an impact statement. But this is hardly a day-to-day process, and the involvement even in that decision would be limited to timing alone. The Court of Appeals made clear that, so long as their decision was not arbitrary or capricious, "definition of the proper region for comprehensive development and, therefore, the comprehensive impact statement should be left in the hands of the federal appellees," 514 F.2d at 881 n.33, a position which the Court adopts today. And, most important, a federal court would intervene at all only when the four-part test indicated an abdication of the agency's statutory duty and the necessity for judicial intervention.

The Court is also concerned that the proposed rule would invite litigation. But the recognition of any right invites litigation, and it is a curious notion of statutory construction that makes substantive rights depend on whether persons would seek to enforce them in court. In any case, to the extent the litigation is the result of agency noncompliance with NEPA, the Court can hardly complain about it. And to the extent the litigation is frivolous, the four-part test is a stiff one and "the plaintiff can be hastened from [the] court by summary judgment."

Lastly, the Court complains, since some contemplated projects might never come to fruition, the Court of Appeals' test might result "in the preparation of a good many unnecessary impact statements." Even bypassing the instances in which a project is dropped as a result of environmental considerations discovered in the course of preparing an impact statement, the Court's concerns are exaggerated. The Court of Appeals showed great sensitivity to the need for federal officials to be able "to dream out loud without filing an impact statement," 514 F.2d at 879, and did not seek to disturb that freedom. Indeed, a major point of the four-part test is to avoid wasted effort including the wasted effort of enjoining an already proposed project to allow the belated preparation of an impact statement and the Court suggests, and I can imagine, no reason why the test is unlikely to be successful in achieving that goal.

In short, the Court offers nothing but speculation, misconception, and exaggeration to reject a reasonably designed test for enforcing the duty NEPA imposes upon the federal agencies. Whatever difficulties the Court may have with the initial application of the test in this case and I agree that an injunction was not warranted on the facts before the Court of Appeals the Court has articulated no basis for interring the test before it has been given a chance to breathe.

NOTES

1. Does the proposed action in the *SIPI* case satisfy the criteria for "ripeness" set out in *Lujan v. National Wildlife Federation, supra* Chapter 3?

2. When, if ever, are programmatic EISs required under NEPA? The CEQ regulations state that an EIS may be and sometimes is required for "broad Federal actions," which may include programs or regulations. 40 C.F.R. § 1502.4(b). The regulations define a program as a group of actions to implement a specific policy or plan. 40 C.F.R. § 1508.18(b)(3). A "proposal" exists when an agency has a goal and is preparing to make a decision on the means of accomplishing the goal, and when the effects can be meaningfully evaluated. 40 C.F.R. § 1508.23. Three approaches for evaluating a proposal which represents a broad federal action are suggested—geographically, generically (i.e., by relevant similarities), or by stage of technological development. 40 C.F.R. § 1502.4(c). An EIS must be prepared as closely as possible to the development of a proposal, so that the final EIS can be included in the recommendation or report on the proposal, and can contribute to decisionmaking, rather than rationalizing or justifying the decision. 40 C.F.R. § 1502.5. How do the CEQ regulations compare with the holdings in *SIPI* and *Kleppe*? For a survey of many of the issues that bear on programmatic proposals, see Jon C. Cooper, *Broad Programmatic, Policy and Planning Assessments Under the National Environmental Policy Act and Similar Devices: A Quiet Revolution in an Approach to Environmental Considerations*, 11 PACE ENVTL. L. REV. 89 (1993).

3. Does *Kleppe* reject Judge Wright's four-part *SIPI* test? If so, on what basis is a court supposed to determine whether a programmatic EIS is necessary? Are the CEQ rules helpful? Does *Kleppe* require a plaintiff to find a specific "report or recommendation on a proposal" before a claim exists under NEPA? Note that Judge Wright also delivered the opinion of the D.C. Court of Appeals that the Court reversed in *Kleppe*. Recall that it was Wright who interpreted NEPA expansively in *Calvert Cliffs*.

4. Disputes over the need for a programmatic EIS sometimes are litigated on the issue of timing. When does an agency study or preliminary plan ripen into a proposal? *See Natural Resources Defense Council v. Hodel*, 435 F. Supp. 590 (D. Or. 1977), *aff'd on other grounds sub nom. Natural Resources Defense Council v. Munro*, 626 F.2d 134 (9th Cir. 1980) (requiring a programmatic EIS for a cooperative plan to develop electric power to meet forecasted needs for the Pacific Northwest).

Alternatively, litigation over whether an agency must prepare a programmatic EIS sometimes hinges on whether component activities of the alleged program are somehow interdependent. *See Foundation on Economic Trends v. Lyng*, 817 F.2d 882 (D.C. Cir. 1987) (Agriculture Department's Agricultural Research Service animal productivity research consists of projects too diverse and discrete to require a programmatic EIS—agency policy to promote productive efficiency does not rise to the level of "concerted" or "systematic and connected" actions required by 40 C.F.R. § 1508.18(b)(3).) This issue may overlap with the question of adequacy of an EIS for one of the individual projects that plaintiffs claim is a segmented part of a broader program. *See Thomas v. Peterson, supra* Chapter 7.

5.   What is the scope of the EIS that will be required when the first coal mine is proposed for the Northern Great Plains Region? In this context, consider the definition of "scope" at 40 C.F.R. § 1508.25. What does this suggest about the utility of a programmatic EIS as sought by the Sierra Club?

6.   Note that the CEQ regulations require agencies to apply NEPA early in the process. 40 C.F.R. § 1501.2. Why? In the context of coal development in the Northern Great Plains, when should federal agencies consider the potential ramifications of large-scale coal development—at the stage when the first mine is proposed, or at an earlier stage?

7.   The National Forest Management Act (NFMA) requires the Forest Service to prepare land and resource management plans for individual forests in the National Forest System. 16 U.S.C. § 1604. The forest plans contain a summary of the current resource management situation, a description of the multiple use goals and objectives for the forest, prescriptions and associated standards and guidelines for each management area zoned in the plan, and monitoring requirements that can be used to evaluate implementation of the plan. Like Euclidian zoning, forest plans prohibit certain uses within areas of the forest, but permissible uses may or may not occur. The NFMA and its implementing regulations provide for public participation in the preparation of forest plans through such means as notice, public meetings, the dissemination of information, and requests for written comments. *See* Bradley Bobertz & Robert Fischman, *Administrative Appeal Reform: The Case of the Forest Service,* 64 U. COLO. L. REV. 371, 378 (1993). The NFMA also requires the Forest Service to engage in specific environmental analyses. *See, e.g.,* 16 U.S.C. § 1604(g)(3)(E) (requiring the Forest Service to insure that timber harvesting occurs only on land physically suitable for the prescribed logging techniques). Traditionally, the agency has prepared EISs to accompany the forest plans in tandem with the required NFMA environmental analyses. Does NEPA apply to the promulgation of forest plans? Is a forest plan the "functional equivalent" of an EIS? *See Texas Committee on Natural Resources v. Bergland,* 573 F.2d 201 (5th Cir. 1978), *reh'g denied,* 576 F.2d 931 (5th Cir. 1978), *cert. denied,* 439 U.S. 966 (1978) (limiting functional equivalence exception to the EIS requirement to environmental agencies that do not have mandates to produce a yield of resources, such as timber). *See also* DANIEL R. MANDELKER, NEPA LAW AND LITIGATION § 5.03[8] (2d ed. 1992) (criticizing *Texas Committee*). *See generally* Stark Ackerman, *Observations on the Transformation of the Forest Service: The Effects of the National Environmental Policy Act on U.S. Forest Service Decision Making,* 20 ENVTL. L. 703 (1990), for a critique of the application of NEPA to forest management.

8.   Can an interested person challenge an EIS prepared in conjunction with a forest plan in light of the Supreme Court's holding in *Lujan v. National Wildlife Federation*? In *Ohio Forestry Association v. Sierra Club,* 523 U.S. 726, 118 S. Ct. 1665 (1998), the Supreme Court found that judicial review of NEPA and other issues arising from approval of a forest plan was not ripe for review:

> [F]rom the court's perspective, review of the Sierra Club's claim regarding logging and clearcutting now would require time-consuming judicial consideration of the details of an elaborate, technically based plan * * *. That review would have to take place without benefit of the focus that a particular logging proposal could provide * * *. And, of course, depending on the agency's future actions to revise the Plan or modify the expected methods of implementation, review now may turn out to have been unnecessary.

523 U.S. at ___ , 118 S. Ct. at 1672. Does *Ohio Forestry* suggest that programmatic decisions can never be reviewed? The Court appeared to concede at least two situations where review might be appropriate: (1) where Congress has specifically provided for "pre-enforcement" review of agency rules (as it has done in many environmental statutes); and (2) where the programmatic decision allows actions to go forward without further agency process. Can you think of any other situation where a programmatic decision might be "ripe" for judicial review? *See Abbott Laboratories v. Gardner*, 387 U.S. 136 (1967).

9. Frequently, a programmatic EIS forms the basis for a large number of individual activities. When the agency prepares to commence an individual action within the context of a larger program it may prepare another EIS, or perhaps an EA, and "tier" that document to the larger EIS on the program. The practice of "tiering" is encouraged by the CEQ regulations as a means "to eliminate repetitive discussions of the same issues and to focus on the actual issues ripe for decision at each level of environmental review." 40 C.F.R. § 1502.20. The Forest Service, for instance, often tiers the NEPA analysis of development projects, such as timber sales, to the forest plan EIS. Are there any limitations on the kinds of documents prepared for prior environmental analyses that agencies may incorporate by reference into later NEPA documents? What procedural requirements do the CEQ regulations impose on agencies that tier to other documents? *See* 40 C.F.R. §§ 1502.20, 1502.21; *see also* 40 C.F.R. § 1506.6(f).

So, where a programmatic EIS exists, an agency may be able to avoid preparation of another EIS, and instead prepare an EA on a site specific project which otherwise would plainly have required an EIS. What implications does such a practice have for public participation and other aspects of the decisionmaking process?

10. The relationship between programmatic and individual NEPA documents has spawned a fair amount of litigation. For example, in *Natural Resources Defense Council, Inc. v. Morton*, 388 F. Supp. 829 (D.D.C. 1974), *aff'd mem.*, 527 F.2d 1386 (D.C. Cir. 1976), *cert. denied*, 427 U.S. 913 (1976), plaintiffs argued that a programmatic EIS on the Bureau of Land Management's (BLM's) entire national livestock grazing program, covering 171 million acres of public land in eleven western states, did not alone satisfy NEPA since it failed to consider the individualized "on the ground" effects on local environments. The court held that detailed individual statements should be prepared on appropriate administrative district or geographic levels to assess the actual impacts of grazing permits in specific environments. (The plaintiffs did not seek and the court did not require EISs for each of the 24,000 individual permits issued by the BLM.)

> While the programmatic EIS drafted by the BLM provides general policy guidelines as to relevant environmental factors, it in no way insures that the [district manager] decision-maker considers all of the specific and particular

consequences of his actions, or the alternatives available to him. The proposed EIS does not provide the detailed analysis of local geographic conditions necessary for the decision-maker to determine what course of action is appropriate under the circumstances.

Id. at 838-39.

Similar site-specific issues arise in the ESA. Recently, a district court held that the Forest Service must complete § 7(a)(2) consultation on individual grazing allotments before issuing permits. *Pacific Rivers Council v. Thomas*, 936 F. Supp. 738 (D. Idaho 1996).

11. In *California v. Block*, 690 F.2d 753 (9th Cir. 1982), the court held that a Forest Service programmatic EIS for the Roadless Area Review and Evaluation (RARE II) process for proposing wilderness designation was not sufficient to release roadless lands not recommended for wilderness from a development ban without individual, site-specific analyses. Under RARE II, the Forest Service studied and then classified 2,918 roadless areas (about 62 million acres) in three categories: "wilderness" areas, which would be recommended to the Congress for legislative protection; "nonwilderness" areas, which would be "released" (open to development without further consideration as wilderness); and "further planning" areas, whose future would be decided under ordinary forest planning procedures. In upholding the district court's injunction against the Forest Service's allowing any development in the 47 California areas released as nonwilderness, the Ninth Circuit agreed that the RARE II process had violated NEPA in several ways. The part of the opinion imposing the greatest burden on the Forest Service was the court's holding that the site-specific impacts of opening each of these areas to development through the nonwilderness designation had to be individually assessed. This, the court reasoned, was required because the designation meant, under Forest Service regulations, that forest plans over the next ten to fifteen years would not consider wilderness features or uses for the area as an alternative to development. *Id.* at 762.

12. NEPA applies to rulemaking proceedings, 40 C.F.R. §§ 1502.4(b), 1502.5(d) and 1508.18(a), and litigation challenging final rules often includes claims under NEPA. *See, e.g.*, *Natural Resources Defense Council, Inc. v. Herrington*, 768 F.2d 1355 (D.C. Cir. 1985) (rule rejecting mandatory energy efficiency standards for certain types of household appliances); *Calvert Cliffs' Coordinating Committee v. Atomic Energy Comm'n*, 449 F.2d 1109 (D.C. Cir. 1971), *supra* Chapter 4 (rules for licensing nuclear power plants); *American Public Transit Ass'n v. Goldschmidt*, 485 F. Supp. 811 (D.D.C. 1980), *rev'd on other grounds*, 655 F.2d 1272 (D.C. Cir. 1981) (rules governing accessibility of federally-assisted mass transit program vehicles to the disabled).

13. NEPA does not apply to actions by administrative agencies to bring judicial or administrative, civil or criminal enforcement proceedings. 40 C.F.R. § 1508.18(a). What are the likely reasons for this policy? Suppose an agency were to adopt an inspection and enforcement program to guide the agency in its enforcement responsibilities. Is such a program subject to NEPA? *See generally* DANIEL R. MANDELKER, NEPA LAW AND LITIGATION § 8.05[4] (2d ed. 1992).

14. The principal purpose of NEPA is to assist agencies in making sound decisions. 40 C.F.R. § 1500.1(c). How well does the preparation of a programmatic EIS serve this goal? Are programmatic decisions likely to be less or more political than discrete actions?

Some countries have adopted legislation which provides for inquiries into broad programmatic issues such as the one addressed in the *SIPI* case. Under this model, an independent commission is typically appointed to conduct an inquiry into a proposed program and is asked to issue a report that includes information and recommendations about the proposal. The Commission generally has much broader powers than those available to an agency engaged in preparing a NEPA document, including the power to subpoena witnesses, and to compel their testimony. The Commission may also have the authority to obtain a warrant to enter and inspect private property. *See, e.g.*, §§ 11-24, Environmental Protection (Impact of Proposals) Act, 1974 (Australia). Australia has taken this idea one step further and chartered a new agency called the Resource Assessment Commission whose sole purpose is to "hold inquiries and make reports to the Prime Minister on specific resource use matters referred to it." RESOURCE ASSESSMENT COMMISSION, ANNUAL REPORT, 1991-92; Resource Assessment Commission Act, 1989 (Australia). Is the inquiry process preferable to the EIS process for programmatic proposals?

LANE COUNTY AUDUBON SOCIETY V. JAMISON
958 F.2d 290 (9th Cir. 1992)

SCHROEDER, Circuit Judge:

In June of 1989, the United States Fish & Wildlife Service (FWS) proposed listing the northern spotted owl as a threatened species under the Endangered Species Act, 16 U.S.C. §§ 1531 *et seq.* (ESA). In addition, in October of 1989, the Interagency Scientific Committee to Address the Conservation of the Northern Spotted Owl (the ISC) was formed to "develop a scientifically credible conservation strategy for the northern spotted owl." In May of 1990, the ISC issued its Final Report, concluding that the lack of a consistent planning strategy has resulted in a high risk of extinction for the owl. In June of 1990, the FWS listed the northern spotted owl as a threatened species pursuant to the ESA. The FWS based its decision to list the owl on its finding that "[e]xisting regulatory mechanisms are insufficient to protect either the northern spotted owl or its habitat."

In response to these events, the Bureau of Land Management (BLM), which manages approximately 1,149,954 acres of the remaining old growth forests suitable for spotted owl habitat in western Oregon, promulgated a document entitled "Management Guidelines for the Conservation of the Northern Spotted Owl, FY 1991 through FY 1992", commonly known as the "Jamison Strategy" ("the Strategy"). In this Strategy, the BLM essentially sets forth the criteria for selection of land for logging in the millions of acres administered by the BLM in Washington, Oregon and California. The BLM described the Jamison Strategy as "a four-phase plan . . . which will direct BLM management of western forest lands into FY 1994 and beyond." The Strategy contains management guidelines for fiscal years 1991 and 1992, including a program to offer 750 million board feet of timber for sale each year. The Strategy was designed to be implemented immediately.

On December 4, 1990, Lane County Audubon Society and various environmental groups (Lane County), filed the requisite 60-day notice of their intention to file an ESA citizen suit to challenge the BLM's failure to consult with the FWS on the Strategy pursuant to 16 U.S.C. § 1536 ("Section 7") of the ESA. *See* 16 U.S.C. § 1540(g)(2)(A)(i). In January of 1991, the BLM submitted about 174 proposed timber sales to be conducted in fiscal 1991 to the FWS for consultation pursuant to section 7 of the ESA, but did not submit the Jamison Strategy itself.

Lane County then filed this action in United States District Court for the District of Oregon seeking an injunction barring the conduct of any sales until the Jamison Strategy had undergone the consultation process. The district court agreed with Lane County that the Jamison Strategy is an "action" within the meaning of section 7 of the ESA and held that the BLM had violated that section by failing to consult with the FWS to obtain that agency's biological opinion regarding the effects of the Strategy on the northern spotted owl before implementing the Strategy. The district court on April 4, 1991, enjoined the BLM from implementing the Strategy pending compliance with section 7, but stated in its order that the 1991 sales were not affected by its order. At the time of the district court's order, the FWS had reviewed 174 of the proposed 1991 sales and had declared that 122 of these would not be likely to jeopardize the owls' habitat, provided the remaining 52, the so called "jeopardy sales," would take place only within the strict limitations provided for in the FWS' biological opinion. In reviewing the 1991 sales, FWS had before it the Jamison Strategy and found its criteria insufficient to protect owl habitat. It applied instead the criteria recommended in the ISC Final Report.

Lane County now appeals the district court's refusal to enjoin the 1991 timber sales. It seeks an injunction, pending completion of consultation on the Jamison Strategy, prohibiting all future sales on BLM lands in the affected area, including the 1992 sales and the remaining 1991 sales that have not yet been awarded.

The BLM cross-appeals the district court's order holding that the Jamison Strategy is "agency action" and requiring the BLM to submit the Strategy for consultation. The BLM contends that the Jamison Strategy is not an "action" requiring consultation and that it is merely a voluntarily created "policy statement." Moreover, the BLM contends that it has in fact substantially complied with the ESA by submitting the individual 1991 sales for section 7 consultation, and so, an injunction is unwarranted.

* * *

I

We turn first to the Jamison Strategy itself. It is intended to establish interim timber management standards to replace standards set forth in the old Timber Management Plans (TMPs) pending issuance of new TMPs. TMPs are discussed in some detail in *Portland Audubon Soc'y v. Lujan,* 884 F.2d 1233, 1234-35 (9th Cir. 1989), *cert. denied,* 494 U.S. 1026 (1990) ("*PAS*"). The TMPs are 10-year plans that "designate commercial forest land under BLM management in [each] district for one of several uses." TMPs do not designate specific timber-sale boundaries, or require that any particular area be harvested. Rather, they decide land-use allocation and set the "annual allowable harvest" for each district.

The BLM itself described its Jamison Strategy as an "interim strategy" to be carried out while new management plans are prepared. The Strategy outlines in detail the various criteria that will be used to develop the 1991 and 1992 timber sales. It develops a "detailed management strategy" to be carried out in four phases to cover fiscal years 1990 through 1994 "and beyond." Like the TMPs, it establishes total annual allowable harvests. The impact of each individual sale on owl habitat cannot be measured without reference to the management criteria established in the TMPs and the Jamison Strategy.

Section 7(a)(2) of the ESA requires the Secretary of the Interior to ensure that an action of a federal agency is not likely to jeopardize the continued existence of any threatened or endangered species. To this end, section 7(b) sets out a process of consultation whereby the agency with jurisdiction over the protected species issues to the Secretary a "biological opinion" evaluating the nature and extent of jeopardy posed to that species by the agency action. 16

U.S.C. § 1536(b). In order to maintain the status quo, section 7(d) forbids "irreversible or irretrievable commitment of resources" during the consultation period. *Id.* § 1536(d).

Section 7 specifically provides that a federal agency (the "action" agency) shall "in consultation with . . . the Secretary [of the Interior], insure that any action authorized, funded, or carried out by such agency . . . is not likely to jeopardize the continued existence of any endangered species or threatened species . . . ." *Id.* § 1536(a)(2) (emphasis added).

Procedural guidelines for complying with this consultation requirement are codified at 50 C.F.R. Part 402. The FWS implementing regulations under the ESA require agencies to review their action "at the earliest possible time to determine whether any action may affect listed species." *Id.* § 402.14(a). The FWS defines agency "action" broadly to include "all activities or programs of any kind authorized, funded, or carried out, in whole or in part, by Federal agencies . . . ." *Id.* § 402.02. Examples include but are not limited to:

(a) actions intended to conserve listed species or their habitat; * * *

(d) actions directly or indirectly causing modifications to the land, water, or air.

Id. This court also interprets the term "agency action" broadly.

We agree with the district court that "without a doubt," the Jamison Strategy as announced was to be an agency action "authorized, funded or carried out by the BLM." Moreover, the Jamison Strategy is action that "may affect" the spotted owl, since it sets forth criteria for harvesting owl habitat. It falls squarely within the definition of agency action set forth in 50 C.F.R. § 402.02. Accordingly, the BLM must submit the Jamison Strategy to the FWS for consultation before the Jamison Strategy can be implemented through the adoption of individual sale programs. In implementing the Jamison Strategy before consultation with the FWS, the BLM has violated the ESA. The district court properly enjoined implementation of the Strategy.

II

This brings us to Lane County's appeal regarding sales. Lane County asks that all sales be enjoined pending consultation on the Jamison Strategy. The government acknowledges that sales are "actions" under section 7 and require ESA consultation. The government contends, however, that despite the district court's injunction against implementation of the Jamison Strategy, individual sales may nevertheless go forward under the TMPs promulgated between 1979 and 1983 rather than the Jamison Strategy. The TMPs were, of course, not submitted for consultation at the time they were promulgated, because the owl was not listed as a threatened species until 1990. The government argues that the sales may go forward because Lane County has not challenged the TMPs under the ESA.

This is not a tenable position, for if the Jamison Strategy is an "action" requiring consultation, then clearly the BLM's reinstatement of the TMPs would also constitute such action. The two documents serve the same function with respect to sales. Moreover, in adopting the Jamison Strategy in the first place, the government recognized that a new, interim underlying strategy was necessary after the owls were listed pursuant to the ESA, because the old TMPs were inadequate to meet the requirements of that Act.

In addition, in previous appearances before this court, the BLM has successfully argued that because its decision on an individual sale necessarily implicated the underlying programmatic EIS for the TMPs to which the individual sale decisions were tiered, a challenge to individual sales would be barred by Section 312 of the 1990 Appropriations Act. *See PAS,* 884 F.2d at 1239-40. The BLM should not now be able to claim that the individual sales at issue here exist in total isolation from the Strategy to which they are similarly tiered.

In sum, neither the underlying TMPs nor the Jamison "interim management strategy" has ever been submitted to FWS for consultation pursuant to the mandate of the ESA. Accordingly, the individual sales cannot go forward until the consultation process is complete on the underlying plans which BLM uses to drive their development.

The district court's order, however, did not make it clear that pending the completion of the consultation process, the BLM should be enjoined from conducting any new sales. Such an injunction is necessary because until consultation is satisfactorily concluded with respect to the Jamison Strategy, or indeed any other conservation strategy intended to establish the criteria under which sites for sales are to be selected, the sales cannot lawfully go forward. The ESA prohibits the "irreversible or irretrievable commitment of resources" during the consultation period. 16 U.S.C. § 1536(d). The sales are such commitments.

AFFIRMED IN PART, REMANDED IN PART for entry of an injunction barring future announcement or conduct of additional sales and for reconsideration of whether the 1991 sales already announced but not awarded should be enjoined.

NOTES

1.   How does the definition of "action" under the Endangered Species Act differ from the definition of the same term under NEPA? *Compare* 50 C.F.R. § 402.02 *with* 40 C.F.R. § 1508.18. Does NEPA apply to all situations where the Endangered Species Act applies? How might NEPA and the ESA complement each other in the context of government decisionmaking?

2.   Did the BLM violate NEPA by failing to prepare a programmatic EIS for the Jamison Strategy? *See Portland Audubon Soc'y v. Lujan*, 795 F. Supp. 1489 (D. Or. 1992), *aff'd sub nom., Portland Audubon Soc'y v. Babbitt*, 998 F.2d 705 (9th Cir. 1993) (failure to prepare supplemental EISs for existing Timber Management Plans violated NEPA).

3.   Suppose the BLM had never proposed the Jamison Strategy. Would the BLM still be vulnerable to suit under the ESA? What about under NEPA?

4.   By the time the Ninth Circuit enjoined the BLM timber sales in March 1992, the BLM had already applied for exemptions from the ESA for 44 of the 52 fiscal year 1991 timber sales that received jeopardy opinions. The BLM secured ESA exemptions for 13 of the 44 sales in May 1992. But a federal district court enjoined the sales in June 1992 because they were based on plans whose EISs were not supplemented as required by NEPA to account for new information. *See Portland Audubon Soc'y, supra* Note 2.

5.   Consider the following facts. In 1990, the Forest Service approved a land and resource management plan (LRMP) for a national forest. The LRMP establishes forest-wide and area-specific standards to which all projects, permits, and contracts involving the forest must adhere. In 1992, the National Marine Fisheries Service (NMFS) listed an anadromous fish dependent on rivers in the forest as a threatened species. As a result, the Forest Service began consultation on all ongoing and proposed projects, but not on the underlying LRMP. Does the Forest Service need to reinitiate consultation on the LRMP? Is the LRMP an action under § 7(a)(2), as interpreted by 50 C.F.R. § 402.02, at all times, or only when adopted, revised, or amended? *See Pacific Rivers Council v. Thomas*, 30 F.3d 1050 (9th Cir. 1994) (relying on *Lane County Audubon Soc'y v. Jamison*, 958 F.2d 290 (9th Cir. 1992), to find that an existing LRMP constitutes an ongoing action authorized for the purposes of § 7(a)(2)). Can the Forest Service continue ongoing projects that have satisfied the § 7(a)(2) requirements? *See id.* (injunction barring all ongoing activities that may affect the threatened fish until the agencies complete consultation on the LRMP).

6.   NEPA seldom applies to EPA programmatic decisions, but the ESA has caused more problems for the EPA. Consider, for example, the problem described in the following case:

> Congress enacted the Federal Insecticide, Fungicide, and Rodenticide Act (FIFRA) to regulate the use of pesticides in this country. *See* 7 U.S.C. §§ 136-136y (1982 & Supp. IV 1986). Under FIFRA, pesticides must be registered with the EPA before they may be sold or distributed. *Id.* §§ 136a(a), 136j(a)(1)(A) (1982). The EPA may approve an application for registration only after determining that when used in compliance with "commonly recognized practice," the pesticide will "perform its intended function without unreasonable adverse effects on the environment." *Id.* § 136a(c)(5)(C)-(D) (1982). If, at any time, the EPA believes a registered pesticide fails to meet this standard, the EPA may initiate an administrative process to cancel the registration. The EPA does so by publishing a Notice of Intent to Cancel. *See id.* § 136d(b)(1) (1982). Registrants and users of the pesticides may request an administrative hearing and later obtain judicial review of the EPA's final decision on cancellation. *See id.* §§ 136d(b), 136n (1982 & Supp. IV 1986).
>
> With that statutory background, we turn to the present case. Strychnine is an active ingredient in several pesticides registered with the EPA. This poison is highly toxic and kills both target and nontarget species of wildlife. In midwestern and western states, farmers and ranchers use strychnine to control rodents that may harm their land or crops. These users often place strychnine in grain bait, and the bait attracts the target species. Nontarget species die when they eat either the bait or the poisoned rodent. Thus, environmental groups have become concerned about the threat strychnine poses to protected species of wildlife.

Defenders of Wildlife v. Administrator, E.P.A., 882 F.2d 1294, 1296 (8th Cir. 1989). Among the protected species that the plaintiffs claimed were harmed were the endangered black-footed ferret and bald eagle. Clearly, the EPA must consult with the FWS for new registrations that may affect a listed species. But, what obligation does the EPA have under § 7 of the ESA to review existing registrations for adverse effects on protected species? The court found that EPA had violated § 9 of the ESA by failing to obtain an incidental taking statement before registering certain pesticides. *Id.* at 1301. Since the late 1970s, the EPA has tried a number of approaches to ESA compliance for the pesticide program that have generated a great deal of controversy. Jim Serfis, *Pesticide Regulation, in* BALANCING ON THE BRINK OF EXTINCTION: THE ENDANGERED SPECIES ACT AND LESSONS FOR THE FUTURE 214 (Kathryn A. Kohm ed. 1991). For instance:

> [I]n 1982 the EPA adopted a new method referred to as the "cluster approach." Under this new system, pesticides with the same use pattern (pesticides used on grain crops, on forests, as mosquito larvicide, or on rangeland, for example) were considered at the same time. The FWS then prepared a biological opinion that included all of the endangered species that might be affected by a particular use pattern. Although the cluster approach seemed to speed up the process initially, it was not without problems. The major crop uses of pesticides were covered

under the system, but other minor uses escaped review altogether. * * * Paradoxically, another problem was the time it took to complete a cluster analysis. Although the cluster approach was designed to facilitate the process, final versions of the cluster packages sometimes took two or three years to complete.

Id. at 216-17. Can you think of any alternatives to a "cluster approach" for programmatic consultation? *See* 54 Fed. Reg. 27,984-28,002 (1989) (describing the cluster and other approaches). Recall that NEPA does not apply to EPA pesticide registration under the "functional equivalent" doctrine. *Merrell v. Thomas*, 807 F.2d 776 (9th Cir. 1986), *cert. denied*, 484 U.S. 848 (1987).

More recently, the EPA programs under the Clean Water Act have been criticized for lax ESA compliance. For instance, the EPA and FWS recently agreed to a memorandum of understanding to guide consultation for EPA approval of state permit decisions, state regulations, and state water quality standards under the Clean Water Act. The memorandum was at least partly a result of a challenge to the EPA's failure to consult in approving a number of programs for Alabama. *Mudd v. Reilly*, CV-91-P-1392-S (N.D. Ala. June 19, 1991) (complaint). *See* John W. Steiger, *The Consultation Provision of Section 7(a)(2) of the Endangered Species Act and Its Application to Delegable Federal Programs*, 21 ECOLOGY L.Q. 243 (1994). However, the Fifth Circuit invalidated part of the new EPA-FWS approach when it overturned the EPA's attempt to condition delegation of a Clean Water Act permit program to a state on the state's willingness to consult with the Service before issuing permits. *American Forest and Paper Ass'n v. U.S. EPA*, 28 Envtl. L. Rep. 21122 (Envtl. L. Inst.) (5th Cir. 1998). The court found that the EPA had insufficient authority under the Clean Water Act to place such a condition on a state. This case is discussed in more detail in Note 4 following *Riverside Irrigation District v. Andrews* in Chapter 8.

ATCHISON, TOPEKA & SANTA FE RAILWAY CO. V. CALLAWAY
431 F. Supp. 722 (D.D.C. 1977)

CHARLES R. RICHEY, District Judge.

[The *Atchison* case involved a challenge to the final EIS prepared by the U.S. Army Corps Engineers to accompany a proposal to Congress to authorize the replacement of Locks and Dam 26 on the Mississippi River. The railroad opposed the project fearing it would promote barge traffic at the expense of the railroads.]

Section 102(2)(C) of NEPA, 42 U.S.C. 4332(2)(C), "directs that, to the fullest extent possible . . . all agencies of the Federal Government shall . . . include in every recommendation or report on proposals for legislation and other major Federal actions significantly affecting the quality of the human environment" an environmental impact statement. To comply with this mandate and with the Corp of Engineers' own implementing regulation, which specifically requires the preparation of an EIS for "[r]ecommendations or reports to the Congress for legislation affecting Corps of Engineers programs including proposals to authorize projects (survey, review, and authorization reports) and other legislation, exclusive of appropriations," 33 C.F.R. § 209.410(e)(1) (1976); *see also* 40 C.F.R. §§ 1500.5(a)(1), 1500.12 (1976), defendants prepared a final EIS which they submitted to Congress along with the proposed legislation. Plaintiffs now seek a declaratory judgment that this final EIS is inadequate and does not satisfy the requirements of section 102(2)(C).

Defendants argue that "[s]ince the Secretary of the Army has committed that Department to take no action toward (the reconstruction of Locks and Dam 26) unless expressly authorized by Congress," and since Congress has not yet authorized any such construction, "there is, at this time, no case or controversy which is subject to judicial review, nor is there any effective relief which this Court could conceivably grant." Similarly, defendants argue that plaintiffs have no standing to challenge the adequacy of the final EIS since they suffer no "injury in fact" as a result of the Secretary's action in proposing legislation. The essence of defendants' argument is that a court can *never* review the adequacy of an EIS for a legislative proposal unless and until Congress takes action on the proposal.

This issue is apparently one of first impression; no case of which the Court is aware has addressed the question of whether the adequacy of an EIS for a legislative proposal can be reviewed by a court before Congress has acted on the proposal. In fact, surprisingly few cases have even considered whether the total failure of an agency to prepare an EIS for a legislative proposal can be challenged. The majority of the cases that have considered the question have held, though without substantial analysis, that an agency's total failure to prepare an EIS for a legislative proposal can be reviewed by a court at the behest of a private plaintiff. However, one case in this district recently held that section 102(2)(C) "was designed solely to aid the Congress and was not intended to create a right of action in a private party to claim injury in some fashion from the ongoing legislative process." *Wingfield v. Office of Management and Budget,* Civil Action No. 77-489, Transcript at 6 (D.D.C. 1977).

Upon careful consideration of section 102(2)(C), the policies underlying its enactment, and the numerous cases that have analyzed the purposes of the EIS requirement for "recommendation[s] and report[s] for . . . other major Federal actions significantly affecting the quality of the human environment," 42 U.S.C. § 4332(2)(C), the Court concludes that (1) the section 102(2)(C) EIS requirement for legislative proposals is enforceable by a private right of action, and that private right of action includes challenges to the adequacy of, as well as to the absence of, an EIS; (2) plaintiffs in the present case have standing to maintain such a challenge to the adequacy of the EIS for the proposed legislation authorizing the construction of Lock and Dam 26; and (3) this case is justiciable in that the Court has the power to enter a declaratory judgment as to the adequacy of the EIS and such a judgment would provide effective relief to the plaintiffs.

In ruling that the section 102(2)(C) EIS requirement for legislative proposals was not enforceable by a private right of action, the *Wingfield* court emphasized that

> Congress has within its own investigatory and other resources ample means to obtain from the Executive whatever information it desires relating to environmental impact prior to taking action. It is clear, of course, that Congress did not intend to stultify itself by this legislation (NEPA) if at any point it was satisfied it had enough information to proceed in a given situation.[5]

---

[5]   One significant difference between *Wingfield* and the instant case is that plaintiff Wingfield sought to enjoin various agencies and departments from transmitting recommendations to Congress before an EIS was prepared. He also sought to enjoin the Secretary of the Interior from testifying before the House Committee on Interior and Insular Affairs. Of course, such relief would have interfered substantially with the legislative process. This Court agrees with that decision that, in the absence of express legislative direction, it should not be inferred from section 102(2)(C) that Congress so intended "to stultify itself." This Court would never so interfere with the legislative process. In the instant case, on the other hand, plaintiffs seek no relief that would

The Court does not doubt that Congress imposed the EIS requirement for proposed legislation to ensure that all agencies would provide Congress with detailed environmental information that could be considered by the legislators along with the agencies' proposals for legislation. The Court concludes, however, that the EIS requirement, both on "proposals for legislation" and on "other major Federal actions," was also intended by Congress to provide detailed environmental information to the public to permit them to participate in a meaningful way in further decisionmaking both at the administrative and legislative levels. In this way, NEPA was intended to ensure that both Congress and the public will be advised of the predicted consequences of the proposed legislation and the alternatives thereto, and they will therefore be able to act responsibly thereon.

* * *

This interpretation of section 102(2)(C) leads the Court to conclude that the requirement of an adequate EIS for legislative proposals can be enforced by a private right of action. It is beyond peradventure that the requirement of an adequate EIS for "other major Federal actions" is enforceable by a private right of action. Although *Wingfield* concludes that no corollary right of action exists to enforce the EIS requirement for legislative proposals, and while defendants contend that at least the adequacy of an EIS for a legislative proposal cannot be challenged by a private action pending congressional consideration of the proposal, this Court can discern no such distinction between the two EIS requirements of section 102(2)(C). Neither the language of section 102(2)(C) itself nor the purposes served by the two types of EIS suggests that Congress intended to distinguish between the two requirements.

Moreover, in the absence of an express legislative directive to the contrary, this Court must presume that judicial review of the defendants' alleged failure to comply with NEPA's EIS requirement is available to plaintiffs: Judicial review of final agency action is presumptively available under the Administrative Procedure Act (APA), 5 U.S.C. §§ 701-06 (1976). *See Dunlop v. Bachowski,* 421 U.S. 560, 567 (1975). * * *

The Court further concludes that plaintiffs herein are proper parties to seek such judicial review by a private action. Section 10(a) of the APA, 5 U.S.C. § 702, provides that persons "adversely affected or aggrieved by agency action within the meaning of a relevant statute" are "entitled to judicial review thereof." As concluded above, one major purpose of the EIS requirement for legislative proposals (and for other major Federal actions) is to provide the public with information about the environmental impacts of proposed projects to permit meaningful participation by interested parties in the decisionmaking processes. Plaintiffs herein are indisputably interested in participating in the legislative consideration of the proposed authorizing legislation for Lock and Dam 26, and accordingly they are "adversely affected" and "aggrieved" by the defendants' alleged failure to prepare and to make available an adequate EIS. Thus, pursuant to 5 U.S.C. § 702, plaintiffs are entitled to judicial review of the agency's alleged failure to prepare an adequate EIS to accompany its proposed legislation.

The Court also concludes that plaintiffs herein have alleged sufficient "injury in fact" to satisfy the constitutional "case and controversy" limitations on standing. *See Warth v. Seldin,*

---

in any way interfere with the legislative process.

In fact, the declaratory relief sought by plaintiffs, if ultimately granted by the Court, would likely aid the legislative process. First, it would enable interested parties, both governmental and nongovernmental, to participate more fully and effectively in the process. Second, it would enable the Congress to know before voting on the authorizing legislation whether the final EIS complies with NEPA, as interpreted by the courts. In that way, Congress will be informed before and when it votes as to whether it is necessary to consider exempting the proposal from NEPA's EIS requirement. * * *

422 U.S. 490, 498 (1975). Defendants' alleged failure to prepare an adequate EIS in accordance with section 102(2)(C) would have an adverse effect on plaintiffs' ability to participate in the legislative process by denying them access to important environmental information about the proposed construction of Lock and Dam 26. A comparable allegation of injury to various plaintiffs' "informational interests" was held to be sufficient to confer standing by the Court of Appeals for this Circuit in *Scientists' Institute for Public Information, Inc. v. AEC,* 481 F.2d 1079, 1087 n.29 (1973). As that court reasoned,

> Any other approach to standing in the context of suits to enforce compliance with NEPA for [proposals] not yet resulting in injury to discrete economic, aesthetic or environmental interests would insulate administrative action from judicial review, prevent the public interest from being protected through the judicial process, and frustrate the policies Congress expressed in NEPA, a result clearly inconsistent with the Supreme Court's approach to standing. *Id.*

In other words, NEPA creates "a statutory right or entitlement" to environmental information, and the alleged deprivation of such information clearly confers on plaintiffs "standing to sue even where the plaintiff[s] would have suffered no judicially cognizable injury in the absence of statute." *Warth v. Seldin,* 422 U.S. at 514.

Finally, the Court concludes that this case is justiciable in that the Court is capable of molding "effective relief for resolving this case." *Powell v. McCormack,* 395 U.S. 486, 517 (1969). Plaintiffs herein seek a declaratory judgment as to the adequacy of the final EIS. As the *Powell* Court made clear, "The Declaratory Judgment Act, 28 U.S.C. § 2201, provides that a district court may 'declare the rights . . . of any interested party . . . whether or not further relief is or could be sought.' . . . [A] request for declaratory relief may be considered independently of whether other forms of relief are appropriate." 395 U.S. at 517-18. Thus, there can be no doubt that this Court has the power to issue a declaratory judgment as to the adequacy of the final EIS here in question. There can also be no doubt that such a declaratory judgment would provide effective relief to the plaintiffs. While most cases challenging the absence or the adequacy of EIS's have sought both declaratory and injunctive relief, the Court of Appeals, for this Circuit has at least twice affirmed that declaratory relief alone is sufficient to enforce NEPA's EIS requirement. Certainly the Court can assume that if it determines that the final EIS here in issue is inadequate, then the defendants would correct the deficiencies in the EIS "without the coercion of a court order."

* * *

* * * [T]he Court concludes that * * * NEPA requires the Corps of Engineers to submit to Congress with its proposal for legislation authorizing construction on the proposed Lock and Dam 26 a final EIS that complies with the requirements of section 102(2)(C). * * *

* * *

NOTES

1.   In a later ruling in the same case, the D.C. District Court held that when Congress subsequently approved Locks and Dam 26 it did not repeal NEPA requirements for the project. Accordingly, a private right of action to enforce compliance with NEPA survived congressional authorization, and a party could still seek judicial review of the adequacy of

the legislative EIS. *Atchison, Topeka & Santa Fe Railway Co. v. Callaway*, 480 F. Supp. 972 (D.D.C. 1979).

When the case finally came to trial on the merits, the court was far less sympathetic to the plaintiffs' NEPA claims than it was to their right to assert them. Judge Richey held that, although congressional authorization did not destroy the NEPA claims, it did have a bearing on the required scope of the EIS and on the range of reasonable alternatives to be considered in the EIS. After Congress had specifically authorized investment in the waterways system, the Corps did not have to engage in additional analyses of alternative investments in other transportation modes. Similarly, the court held that the plaintiffs' complaint stating that the EIS failed to consider the environmental impacts of related projects on the river no longer had merit, since in the same legislation Congress had expressly precluded such additional development pending further Congressional authorization. Finally, the court found adequate the EIS's analysis of the environmental impacts of Locks and Dam 26, and concluded that the Corps' final decision to build it was not arbitrary or capricious. The only defect found by the court was the Corps' failure to hold a public meeting as required by its own regulations. But that failure, the court decided, was not cause for injunctive relief. Instead, the court "urged" the Corps to "re-evaluate their own conduct" and to "hold a meeting if they find that one may reasonably be scheduled." *Atchison, Topeka & Santa Fe Railway Co. v. Alexander*, 480 F. Supp. 980 (D.D.C. 1979).

2.   Recall *Lujan v. Defenders of Wildlife, supra* at Chapter 3, in which the Supreme Court held that the Defenders of Wildlife did not have standing to sue because they could not show injury-in-fact. How does the Court's reasoning in *Defenders* compare to Judge Richey's statement in *Atchison* that "NEPA creates a 'statutory right or entitlement' to environmental information, and the alleged deprivation of such information clearly confers on plaintiffs 'standing to sue even where the plaintiff[s] would have suffered no judicially cognizable injury in the absence of statute'"? 431 F. Supp. 722 at 730.

3.   In *Andrus v. Sierra Club*, 442 U.S. 347 (1979), the Court held that NEPA does not require a federal agency to prepare an EIS to accompany an appropriation (or budget) request. The Sierra Club brought the claim on the basis that proposed curtailments in the budget of the National Wildlife Refuge System would significantly affect the quality of the human environment by reducing the operation, maintenance and staffing of the Refuge System. The Court concluded, however, that an EIS on the budget cuts was not required because appropriation requests do not constitute "proposals for legislation" or a "proposal for * * * major federal actions" under § 102(2)(c) of NEPA. *Id.* at 361-62. Did the Sierra Club have standing to challenge the alleged failure to prepare an EIS on appropriation requests? Was the case ripe for review under the test established in *Lujan v. National Wildlife Federation, supra* at Chapter 3? When should NEPA compliance be required in such cases? When would it offer the greatest benefits?

4.   Suppose the Environmental Protection Agency decided to request zero funding for enforcing the environmental programs it administers. What purpose would an EIS serve in evaluating such a proposal? Suppose alternatively that the Department of the Interior proposed a substantial increase in funding for mineral leasing activities, or that the Department of Agriculture proposed a similar increase for logging and road building. Would it "trivialize NEPA" to require preparation of an EIS in these circumstances?

5.   NEPA applies to administrative agencies. It does not apply to the President, Congress or the judiciary. 40 C.F.R. § 1508.12. Thus, Congress can lawfully enact legislation proposed by an agency even where the agency unlawfully failed to comply with NEPA. Furthermore, as a practical matter there may be no adequate remedy available when challenging an agency's decision not to comply with NEPA when submitting a legislative proposal.

6.   Although NEPA does not apply to the President (*see* 40 C.F.R. § 1508.12), the boundary between a presidential action and an agency action is not always clear. Consider the case of the North American Free Trade Agreement (NAFTA), negotiated by the Office of the U.S. Trade Representative (OTR) under the active supervision of the President. The environmental effects of the NAFTA regime are potentially pervasive and highly contentious. *See Environmental Aspects of the North American Free Trade Agreement: Hearings Before the Senate Comm. on Environment and Public Works,* 103d Cong., 1st Sess. (1993). Does NEPA apply to the NAFTA as it would to any legislative proposal submitted by an agency to Congress? This is the question addressed by recent litigation summarized in the following article.

THE LEGISLATIVE ENVIRONMENTAL IMPACT STATEMENT:
AN ANALYSIS OF
PUBLIC CITIZEN V. OFFICE OF THE U.S. TRADE REPRESENTATIVE
Joseph Mendelson III & Andrew Kimbrell
23 Envtl. L. Rep. (Envtl. L. Inst.) 10653 (1993)[*]

At its heart, the National Environmental Policy Act (NEPA) is an informational statute. Designed to make Congress and the public the beneficiaries of environmental impact information for all major federal projects, NEPA §102(2)(C) requires all federal government agencies to "include in every recommendation or report on proposals for legislation and other major Federal actions significantly affecting the quality of the human environment, a detailed statement by the responsible official on the environmental impact of the proposed action." NEPA's requirement that federal agencies perform environmental impact statements (EISs) before undertaking specific major federal actions has been publicized, analyzed, and enforced relatively thoroughly. In contrast, Congress and the executive branch have largely ignored NEPA's mandate that agencies prepare legislative environmental impact statements (LEISs) to help the legislative branch predict, prevent, and analyze environmental impacts of broader, proposed programs. As a result of this indifference, federal agencies usually prepare NEPA documents about legislative programs, if at all, only after initiating them and responding to legal challenges. At that point, Congress may have already committed substantial resources to the programs, limiting the usefulness of environmental impact information.

A recent ruling by the U.S. District Court for the District of Columbia initially transformed the LEIS requirement's moribund status. In *Public Citizen v. Office of the U.S. Trade Representative* [822 F. Supp. 21 (D.D.C. 1993)], the court issued a declaratory judgment that

---

the Office of the United States Trade Representative (OTR) violated NEPA by failing to prepare a legislative EIS to accompany the completed North American Free Trade Agreement (NAFTA). The decision was promptly overturned by the U.S. Court of Appeals for the District of Columbia Circuit. [5 F.3d 549 (D.C. Cir. 1993).] The decisions have renewed interest in NEPA's role in improving legislation, the use of LEIS deficiency as a cause of action, and the judicial remedies available when agencies fail to perform LEISs * * *.

BACKGROUND

In 1991, the United States, Canada, and Mexico began negotiations to establish a North American free trade zone. These negotiations resulted in NAFTA, a comprehensive agreement affecting every aspect of trade between the three countries, which their trade representatives signed on October 7, 1992.

NAFTA is subject to the Trade Act of 1974 (Trade Acts), which mandate that the OTR serve as the President's chief negotiator in trade matters. Congress has assured that the agreement will be submitted under the so-called fast track approval process. Under the fast track process, the President will submit NAFTA to Congress along with implementing legislation and an explanation of any changes to current law. Both the House of Representatives and the Senate must then approve the trade agreement and implementing legislation. Under the fast track provisions, Congress has a limited time to debate NAFTA and may not change the implementing legislation or the agreement. Although the President can abandon his pursuit of NAFTA's approval, he is expected to submit the trade agreement to Congress for approval this fall.

In August of 1991, three nonprofit environmental organizations, Public Citizen, Sierra Club, and Friends of the Earth, brought a challenge to NAFTA, asserting that the OTR violated NEPA by failing to prepare an LEIS to accompany the submission of NAFTA to Congress. At that time the negotiations on the trade agreement had not yet concluded and the participating countries had not signed the agreement. In holding that it lacked the ability to rule on the case, the court noted that because the agreement was not yet complete, there was no final agency action on NAFTA.

After the treaty had been completed, however, the plaintiffs filed *Public Citizen*. The district court held that final agency action was then present because the treaty had been signed, negotiations completed, and, under the congressional fast track negotiating authority, the agreement could not be changed before submission to Congress. Ultimately, the court held that the agreement came under the plain language of NEPA §102(2)(C). Noting that the completion of an LEIS could only aid Congress in its decisionmaking, the U.S. District Court for the District of Columbia ordered the OTR to complete an LEIS "with all deliberate speed."

On September 24, 1993, the U.S. Court of Appeals overturned the District Court's decision, holding that "the final agency action challenged in this case is the submission of NAFTA to Congress by the President. . . . [H]is action, and not that of the OTR, will directly affect Public Citizen's members." Because the President is not an agency, the D.C. Circuit held that his actions are not reviewable under the Administrative Procedure Act.

IGNORING THE IMPACT—THE EARLY LEIS YEARS

The courts' decisions in *Public Citizen* are the culmination of a long judicial debate over the relevance and applicability of the LEIS requirement. Early interpretations of NEPA suggested that the LEIS would play a significant role in the future of the Nation's environmental lawmaking. The Council for Environmental Quality (CEQ), which is responsible for promulgating NEPA's regulations, initially took the position that almost every type of legislative proposal or report was subject to the LEIS requirement. In its 1970 NEPA guidelines, the CEQ defined "legislation" as "(i) agency recommendations on their own proposals for legislation and

(ii) agency reports on legislation initiated elsewhere. (In the latter case only the agency which has primary responsibility for the subject matter involved will prepare an environmental statement.)" Congress apparently had a similar view of the LEIS requirement. * * *

Despite this history, congressional response to the LEIS process has been less then overwhelming. Early in NEPA's implementation, the House Committee on Merchant Marine and Fisheries estimated that if the LEISs were being prepared as they should be, 800 statements would be submitted during each session of Congress. In 1971, the Committee reported that federal agencies had introduced over 4,000 bills related to the environment in the 91st Congress but had prepared only a total of seven LEISs. * * *

SECOND GENERATION RESPONSES BY THE EXECUTIVE AND THE JUDICIARY

Despite Congress' and the executive agencies initial hesitancy to use the powerful LEIS requirement as a decisionmaking tool, NEPA's supporters and opponents alike feared that widespread application of §102(2)(C) could delay important legislative initiatives. These fears were spurred in 1975, when the U.S. District Court for the District of Columbia, in *Sierra Club v. Morton* [395 F. Supp. 1187 (D.D.C. 1975), *rev'd sub nom. Sierra Club v. Andrus*, 581 F.2d 895 (D.C. Cir. 1978), *rev'd sub nom. Andrus v. Sierra Club*, 442 U.S. 347 (1979)], ruled that budget proposals for financing the National Wildlife Refuge System were recommendations or reports on proposals for legislation that required an LEIS. The decision was the first to suggest that all proposals affecting the human environment, including appropriations, were potential subjects of NEPA's litigation.

Similar decisions followed. In *Realty Income Trust v. Eckerd* [564 F.2d 447 (D.C. Cir. 1977)], the U.S. Court of Appeals for the District of Columbia Circuit further expanded the definition of "legislative proposals." The court ruled that the General Service Administration (GSA) violated NEPA by failing to present the House and Senate Committees on Public Works with an LEIS to accompany a prospectus for constructing a $25 million building in Jackson, Mississippi. Although the GSA's prospectus only required the approval of the two committees, rather than a full congressional vote, the court noted that "it is at a critical juncture like this, when the Committees are weighing the final Congressional judgments about whether to proceed with these projects at all, that the 'environmental source material' provided by a EIS, would appear to be particularly needed in making relevant decisions." The Federal District Court for the District of Hawaii extended this broad definition of "legislative proposals" still further when the court ruled that the Navy's appropriation for bombing activities on the island of Kahoolawe required an accompanying LEIS every year.

The growing reach of the LEIS' provisions prompted the CEQ to redefine the type of actions that required an LEIS. In its 1977 NEPA implementing regulations, the CEQ defined legislation as "a bill or legislative proposal to Congress developed by or with the significant support of a Federal agency, but [not] requests for appropriations." In *Andrus v. Sierra Club* [442 U.S. 347 (1979)], the U.S. Supreme Court quickly adopted the new CEQ definition and held unanimously that appropriation requests are not proposals for legislation within the meaning of NEPA §102(2)(C). Using the traditional distinction Congress had drawn between legislation and appropriation and the rules of both Houses prohibiting legislation from being added to an appropriation bill, the court reasoned that appropriations did not meet the threshold definition of legislation. The court explained, "Section 102(2)(C) is thus best interpreted as applying to those recommendations or reports that actually propose programmatic actions, rather than those which merely suggest how such actions may be funded." Following the U.S. Supreme Court decision, the U.S. Court of Appeals for the Ninth Circuit overturned the district court decision requiring the Navy to submit annual LEISs for the Kahoolawe island bombing activity, and another district court held the LEIS requirement inapplicable to a proposal for the modification of a state and federal water project cost sharing program.

Although these decisions clarified that appropriation proposals are beyond NEPA's grasp, they did not exempt other forms of legislation from the LEIS requirement. The recent *Public Citizen* decisions are consistent with continued application of the LEIS requirement to all final agency legislative proposals or reports that are not appropriation proposals or constitutionally or statutorily required to be submitted by the President.

In *Public Citizen*, the district court pointed out that although NAFTA is a trade agreement, not a proposed piece of legislation, and is not required to be submitted to Congress, it has all of the earmarks of a final legislative proposal. The agreement was signed by the three participating countries, the OTR functions as an executive agency with its own statutory basis for authority, and NAFTA will be submitted to Congress for approval in its current form. Citing *Realty Income Trust* and *Trustees for Alaska v. Hodel* [806 F.2d 1378 (9th Cir. 1986)], the district court held that NAFTA does constitute final agency action on a proposal, that "an EIS must be prepared once such a proposal is completed and that its submission to Congress is not required." By focusing on NAFTA itself instead of the finalized implementing legislation that the OTR submitted with it, the district court expanded the applicability of the LEIS requirement to include trade agreements and similar actions.

However, the expanded scope of the LEIS requirement was short-lived. The D.C. Circuit reversed the district court, holding that despite the OTR's completion of its role as NAFTA negotiator, the final agency action needed to trigger NEPA's requirements was not present. Relying on the recent Supreme Court decision in *Franklin v. Massachusetts* [505 U.S. 788 (1992)], the D.C. Circuit determined that it is the action of the President submitting NAFTA to congress, not the OTR completing negotiations, that has the required "direct effect" on the plaintiffs. However, because the President is not an agency, his actions are not reviewable under the Administrative Procedure Act.

In dicta, the D.C. Circuit stressed its view that the LEIS requirement remains enforceable:

> Although we acknowledge the stringency of *Franklin's* "direct effect" requirement, *we disagree that it represents the death knell of the legislative EIS. Franklin* is limited to those cases in which the President has final constitutional or statutory responsibility for the final step necessary for the agency action directly to affect the parties. . . . *When the President's role is not essential to the integrity of the process, however, APA review of otherwise final agency actions may well be available.* [Slip op. at 7.]

The court noted that *Franklin* emphasizes the importance of the President's role in the integrity of the process at issue. Here, Congress specifically required that the President, and not the OTR, submit NAFTA and its implementing legislation, indicating that Congress deems the President's involvement essential to the integrity of the international trade negotiations. Thus, the court's analysis would not insulate from judicial review an effort by the executive branch to end run the LEIS requirement by having the President, rather than an agency, submit legislation in situations where the U.S. Constitution or Congress has not recognized an essential presidential role in the submission. Whether a president would even cooperate in an agency's effort to bypass NEPA is also, of course, questionable. Because most legislative proposals do not require presidential involvement, and are in fact submitted by the agencies directly, not by the President, this restriction on NEPA should have fairly limited application. Thus the *Public Citizen* decisions, while not expanding the scope of the LEIS requirement, do not interfere with its application to all final agency proposals for legislation that are not appropriations or constitutionally or statutorily required to be submitted by the President.

* * *

RECOMMENDATIONS

Properly functioning, the LEIS requirement will inform lawmakers of environmental pitfalls that lay ahead, will provide a foundation for substantive environmental debate, and will result in better crafted legislation. Despite the outcome of *Public Citizen*, several courses of action can and should be pursued to ensure that the LEIS requirement continues to play an active role in our national decisionmaking.

First, environmental advocates must make a habit of asking congressional delegations to request LEISs with proposed legislation. Such requests affirm the basic informational role of NEPA. The LEIS is a procedural requirement developed explicitly to aid congressional decisionmaking. The *Public Citizen* district court ruled for the plaintiffs because, among other things, the LEIS process was not followed despite congressional requests for documentation of environmental impacts. Environmentalists should not allow Congress to forget its important role in enforcing the LEIS process. Moreover, Congress should make a habit of withholding action on legislation pending submission of an accompanying LEIS, as it recently did when it reportedly refused to debate the opening of the Arctic National Wildlife Refuge to oil exploration until the completion of an LEIS.

Second, the OMB should require agencies to file the LEIS' documentation during its legislative clearing process. While its legislative clearing procedures include the requirement of environmental documentation "to the maximum extent possible," the OMB should formalize this requirement to mean the filing of the LEISs. The OMB is in a unique position to oversee the LEIS' compliance with finalized legislation.

Finally, the environmental community must make a regular habit of challenging agency legislative proposals that omit LEISs. *Public Citizen* does not prevent private parties from seeking declaratory judgements. Such actions place further public scrutiny on the development of pending legislation and serve to direct agency efforts toward compliance with NEPA. Active outside enforcement of these requirements can only serve to revitalize this long overlooked provision of law.

NOTES

1.   The Supreme Court denied *certiorari* in *Public Citizen*, 510 U.S. 1041 (1994).

2.   For an excellent discussion of the legal and policy issues involved in applying NEPA to the NAFTA in particular and international agreements in general, see *The National Environmental Policy Act and the North American Free Trade Agreement: Hearing before the Senate Comm. on Environment and Public Works,* 103d Cong., 1st Sess. (1993).

3.   Do you agree with Mendelson and Kimbrell that *Public Citizen* will not interfere with NEPA's "application to all final agency proposals for legislation that are not appropriations or constitutionally or statutorily required to be submitted by the President"? Judge Randolph, in his concurring opinion in *Public Citizen,* questioned this view. He noted that an action cannot be considered final under the Administrative Procedure Act, as interpreted by *Franklin*, unless it will directly affect the parties. Judge Randolph expressed skepticism about whether the act of proposing legislation could ever generate direct effects on plaintiffs.

4. The decision in *Public Citizen* may have been inevitable following the Supreme Court's decision in *Franklin v. Massachusetts*, 505 U.S. 788 (1992). *Franklin* involved a challenge to a Presidential decision which calculated population for purposes of apportioning congressional representatives among the states. The State of Massachusetts and others sought review of the President's actions under the judicial review provisions of the APA. The APA defines "agency" as "each authority of the Government of the United States * * * ", but specifically excludes from this definition—(1) the Congress; (2) the courts of the United States; (3) territorial governments; and (4) the District of Columbia government. No mention is made of the President. Nonetheless, Justice O'Connor held that "[o]ut of respect for the separation of powers and the unique constitutional position of the President, we find that factual silence is not enough to subject the President to the provisions of the APA." *Id.* at 800-01. Is O'Connor's opinion consistent with general rules of statutory construction?

5. Would legislation amending NEPA to allow direct citizen suit enforcement of § 102(2)(C) solve the enforcement problems presented by *Public Citizen* and *Franklin*?

E. Extraterritorial Activities

EXECUTIVE ORDER 12114
ENVIRONMENTAL EFFECTS ABROAD OF MAJOR FEDERAL ACTIONS

By virtue of the authority vested in me by the Constitution and the laws of the United States, and as President of the United States, in order to further environmental objectives consistent with the foreign policy and national security policy of the United States, it is ordered as follows:

SECTION 1

1-1. *Purpose and Scope.* The purpose of this Executive Order is to enable responsible officials of Federal agencies having ultimate responsibility for authorizing and approving actions encompassed by this Order to be informed of pertinent environmental considerations and to take such considerations into account, with other pertinent considerations of national policy, in making decisions regarding such actions. While based on independent authority, this Order furthers the purpose of the National Environmental Policy Act and the Marine Protection Research and Sanctuaries Act and the Deepwater Port Act consistent with the foreign policy and national security policy of the United States, and represents the United States government's exclusive and complete determination of the procedural and other actions to be taken by Federal agencies to further the purpose of the National Environmental Policy Act, with respect to the environment outside the United States, its territories and possessions.

SECTION 2

2-1. *Agency Procedures.* Every Federal agency taking major Federal actions encompassed hereby and not exempted herefrom having significant effects on the environment outside the geographical borders of the United States and its territories and possessions shall within eight months after the effective date of this Order have in effect procedures to implement this Order. Agencies shall consult with the Department of State and the Council on Environmental Quality concerning such procedures prior to placing them in effect.

2-2. *Information Exchange.* To assist in effectuating the foregoing purpose, the Department of State and the Council on Environmental Quality in collaboration with other interested Federal agencies and other nations shall conduct a program for exchange on a continuing basis of information concerning the environment. The objectives of this program shall be to provide information for use by decisionmakers, to heighten awareness of and interest in environmental concerns and, as appropriate, to facilitate environmental cooperation with foreign nations.

2-3. *Actions Included.* Agencies in their procedures under Section 2-1 shall establish procedures by which their officers having ultimate responsibility for authority and approving actions in one of the following categories encompassed by this Order, take into consideration in making decisions concerning such actions, a document described in Section 2-4(a):

(a) major Federal actions significantly affecting the environment of the global commons outside the jurisdiction of any nation (*e.g.*, the oceans or Antarctica);

(b) major Federal actions significantly affecting the environment of a foreign nation not participating with the United States and not otherwise involved in the action;

(c) major Federal actions significantly affecting the environment of a foreign nation which provide to that nation:

(1) a product, or physical project producing a principal product or an emission of effluent, which is prohibited or strictly regulated by Federal law in the United States because its toxic effects on the environment create a serious public health risk; or

(2) a physical project which in the United States is prohibited or strictly regulated by Federal law to protect the environment against radioactive substances.

(d) major Federal actions outside the United States, its territories and possessions which significantly affect natural or ecological resources of global importance designated for protection under this subsection by the President, or, in the case of such a resource protected by international agreement binding on the United States, by the Secretary of State. Recommendations to the President under this subsection shall be accompanied by the views of the Council on Environmental Quality and the Secretary of State.

2-4. *Applicable Procedures.*

(a) There are the following types of documents to be used in connection with actions described in Section 2-3:

(i) environmental impact statements (including generic, program and specific statements);

(ii) bilateral or multilateral environmental studies, relevant or related to the proposed action, by the United States and one or more foreign nations, or by an international body or organization in which the United States is a member or participant; or

(iii) concise reviews of the environmental issues involved, including environmental assessments, summary environmental analyses or other appropriate documents.

* * *

2.5. *Exemptions and Considerations.*

(a) Notwithstanding Section 2-3, the following actions are exempt from this Order:

(i) actions not having a significant effect on the environment outside the United States as determined by the agency;

(ii) actions taken by the President;

(iii) actions taken by or pursuant to the direction of the President or Cabinet officer when the national security or interest is involved or when the action occurs in the course of an armed conflict;

(iv) intelligence activities and arms transfers;

(v) export licenses or permits or export approvals, and actions relating to nuclear activities except actions providing to a foreign nation a nuclear production or utilization facility as defined in the Atomic Energy Act of 1954, as amended, or a nuclear waste management facility;

(vi) votes and other actions in international conferences and organizations;

(vii) disaster and emergency relief action.

* * *

SECTION 3

3-1. *Rights of Action.* This Order is solely for the purpose of establishing internal procedures for Federal agencies to consider the significant effects of their actions on the environment outside the United States, its territories and possessions, and nothing in this Order shall be construed to create a cause of action.

3-2. *Foreign Relations.* The Department of State shall coordinate communications by agencies with foreign governments concerning environmental agreements and other arrangements in implementation of this Order.

* * *

3-4. *Certain Terms.* For purposes of this Order, "environment" means the natural and physical environment and excludes social, economic and other environments; and an action significantly affects the environment if it does significant harm to the environment even though on balance the agency believes the action to be beneficial to the environment. The term "export approvals" in Section 2-5(a)(v) does not mean or include direct loans to finance exports.

3-5. *Multiple Impacts.* If a major Federal action having effects on the environment of the United States or the global commons requires preparation of an environmental impact statement, and if the action also has effects on the environment of the foreign nation, an environmental impact statement need not be prepared with respect to the effects on the environment of the foreign nation.

JIMMY CARTER
THE WHITE HOUSE
January 4, 1979

ENVIRONMENTAL DEFENSE FUND, INC. V. MASSEY
986 F.2d 528 (D.C. Cir. 1993)

MIKVA, Chief Judge:

The Environmental Defense Fund ("EDF") appeals the district court's order dismissing its action seeking declaratory and injunctive relief under the National Environmental Policy Act ("NEPA"). EDF alleges that the National Science Foundation ("NSF") violated NEPA by failing to prepare an environmental impact statement ("EIS") in accordance with Section 102(2)(C) before going forward with plans to incinerate food wastes in Antarctica. The district court dismissed EDF's action for lack of subject matter jurisdiction. The court explained that while Congress utilized broad language in NEPA, the statute nevertheless did not contain "a clear expression of legislative intent through a plain statement of extraterritorial statutory effect;" consequently, the court was compelled by the recent Supreme Court decision in *Equal Employment Opportunity Commission v. Arabian American Oil Co.*, 111 S. Ct. 1227 (1991) ("*Aramco*") to conclude that NEPA does not apply to NSF's decision to incinerate food wastes in Antarctica. *See Environmental Defense Fund, Inc. v. Massey*, 772 F. Supp. 1296, 1297 (D.D.C. 1991).

We reverse the district court's decision, and hold that the presumption against the extraterritorial application of statutes described in *Aramco* does not apply where the conduct regulated by the statute occurs primarily, if not exclusively, in the United States, and the alleged extraterritorial effect of the statute will be felt in Antarctica—a continent without a sovereign, and an area over which the United States has a great measure of legislative control. We therefore remand to the district court for a determination of whether NSF actually failed to comply with Section 102(2)(C) of NEPA, as EDF alleges in its complaint.

I.

As both parties readily acknowledge, Antarctica is not only a unique continent, but somewhat of an international anomaly. Antarctica is the only continent on earth which has never been, and is not now, subject to the sovereign rule of any nation. Since entry into force of the Antarctic Treaty in 1961, the United States and 39 other nations have agreed not to assert any territorial claims to the continent or to establish rights of sovereignty there. *See* The Antarctica

Treaty, 12 U.S.T. 794 (Dec. 1, 1959). Hence, Antarctica is generally considered to be a "global commons" and frequently analogized to outer space. *See Beattie v. United States*, 756 F.2d 91, 99 (D.C. Cir. 1984).

Under the auspices of the United States Antarctica Program, NSF operates the McMurdo Station research facility in Antarctica. McMurdo Station is one of three year-round installations that the United States has established in Antarctica, and over which NSF exercises exclusive control. All of the installations serve as platforms or logistic centers for U.S. scientific research; McMurdo Station is the largest of the three, with more than 100 buildings and a summer population of approximately 1200.

Over the years, NSF has burned food wastes at McMurdo Station in an open landfill as a means of disposal. In early 1991, NSF decided to improve its environmental practices in Antarctica by halting its practice of burning food wastes in the open by October, 1991. After discovering asbestos in the landfill, however, NSF decided to cease open burning in the landfill even earlier, and to develop quickly an alternative plan for disposal of its food waste. NSF stored the waste at McMurdo Station from February, 1991 to July, 1991, but subsequently decided to resume incineration in an "interim incinerator" until a state-of-the-art incinerator could be delivered to McMurdo Station. EDF contends that the planned incineration may produce highly toxic pollutants which could be hazardous to the environment, and that NSF failed to consider fully the consequences of its decision to resume incineration as required by the decisionmaking process established by NEPA.

Section 102(2)(C) of NEPA requires "all federal agencies" to prepare an EIS in connection with any proposal for a "major action significantly affecting the quality of the human environment." 42 U.S.C. § 4332(2)(C). The EIS requirement, along with the many other provisions in the statute, is designed to "promote efforts which will prevent or eliminate damage to the environment and biosphere." 42 U.S.C. § 4321. Following the passage of NEPA, NSF promulgated regulations applying the EIS requirement to its decisions regarding proposed actions in Antarctica. *See* 29 Fed. Reg. 3544, 3547 (Jan. 28, 1974) (codified at 45 C.F.R. § 640.3(e) (1977)). Since the issuance of Executive Order 12114, however, NSF has contended that proposed action affecting the environment in Antarctica is governed by the Executive Order, not NEPA. *See* Exec. Order 12114, 3 C.F.R. 356 (1980) [hereinafter cited as E.O. 12114].

Executive Order 12114 declares that federal agencies are required to prepare environmental analyses for "major Federal actions significantly affecting the environment of the global commons outside the jurisdiction of any nation (*e.g.*, the oceans or Antarctica)." E.O. 12114 § 2-3(a). According to the Executive Order, major federal actions significantly affecting the environment of foreign countries may also require environmental analyses under certain circumstances. *Id.* Although the procedural requirements imposed by the Executive Order are analogous to those under NEPA, the Executive Order does not provide a cause of action to a plaintiff seeking agency compliance with the EIS requirement. The Executive Order explicitly states that the requirements contained therein are "solely for the purpose of establishing internal procedures for Federal agencies . . . and nothing in [the Order] shall be construed to create a cause of action." E.O. 12114 § 3-1. Thus, what is at stake in this litigation is whether a federal agency may decide to take actions significantly affecting the human environment in Antarctica without complying with NEPA and without being subject to judicial review.

II.
A. The Presumption Against Extraterritoriality

As the district court correctly noted, the Supreme Court recently reaffirmed the general presumption against the extraterritorial application of statutes in *Equal Employment Opportunity*

Commission v. Arabian American Oil Co., 111 S.Ct. 1227 (1991) ("*Aramco*"). Extraterritoriality is essentially, and in common sense, a jurisdictional concept concerning the authority of a nation to adjudicate the rights of particular parties and to establish the norms of conduct applicable to events or persons outside its borders. More specifically, the extraterritoriality principle provides that "[r]ules of the United States statutory law, whether prescribed by federal or state authority, apply only to conduct occurring within, or having effect within, the territory of the United States." RESTATEMENT (SECOND) OF FOREIGN RELATIONS LAW OF THE UNITED STATES § 38 (1965) [hereinafter RESTATEMENT (SECOND)]; RESTATEMENT (THIRD) OF FOREIGN RELATIONS LAW OF THE UNITED STATES § 403, com. (g) (1987) [hereinafter RESTATEMENT (THIRD)]. As stated by the Supreme Court in *Aramco*, the primary purpose of this presumption against extraterritoriality is "to protect against the unintended clashes between our laws and those of other nations which could result in international discord." *Aramco*, 111 S. Ct. at 1230.

An early example of the application of the extraterritoriality principle is *American Banana Co. v. United States Fruit Co.*, 213 U.S. 347 (1909). In that case, the plaintiff alleged that the defendant, a U.S. corporation, had violated United States antitrust laws by inducing a foreign government to take actions within its own territory which were adverse to the plaintiff's business. The Supreme Court refused, in the absence of a clear statement of extraterritorial scope, to infer congressional intent to apply the federal statute to the conduct of a foreign government because enforcement would have interfered with the exercise of foreign sovereignty.

Similarly, in *Foley Bros. v. Filardo*, 336 U.S. 281, 282 (1949), the Supreme Court declined to give extraterritorial effect to the Eight Hour Law, a labor statute applying to "[e]very contract made to which the United States . . . is a party." The Court recognized that extraterritorial application of the statute would have "extend[ed] its coverage beyond places over which the United States has sovereignty or has some measure of legislative control," and therefore held that the intention "to regulate labor conditions, which are the primary concern of a foreign country, should not be attributed to Congress in the absence of a clearly expressed purpose." *Id.* at 285-286.

Most recently, in *Aramco*, the Supreme Court held that Title VII of the 1964 Civil Rights Act does not apply extraterritorially to regulate the employment practices of United States firms that employ American citizens abroad. *Aramco*, 111 S. Ct. at 1236. In that case, the discriminatory conduct that allegedly violated Title VII occurred within the jurisdiction of another sovereign, although perpetrated by a U.S. firm. Since the petitioners were advancing a construction of Title VII that would logically result in the statute's application to foreign as well as American employers, the Court held that the presumption against extraterritoriality was necessary to avoid the inevitable clash between foreign and domestic employment laws. *Id.* 111 S. Ct. at 1234.

There are at least three general categories of cases for which the presumption against the extraterritorial application of statutes clearly does not apply. First, as made explicit in *Aramco*, the presumption will not apply where there is an "affirmative intention of the Congress clearly expressed" to extend the scope of the statute to conduct occurring within other sovereign nations. *Id.* 111 S. Ct. at 1230 (quoting *Benz v. Compania Naviera Hidalgo, S.A.*, 353 U.S. 138, 147 (1957)).

Second, the presumption is generally not applied where the failure to extend the scope of the statute to a foreign setting will result in adverse effects within the United States. Two prime examples of this exception are the Sherman Anti-Trust Act, 15 U.S.C. §§ 1-7 (1976), and the Lanham Trade-Mark Act, 15 U.S.C. § 1051 *et seq.* (1976), which have both been applied extraterritorially where the failure to extend the statute's reach would have negative economic consequences within the United States.

Finally, the presumption against extraterritoriality is not applicable when the conduct regulated by the government occurs within the United States. By definition, an extraterritorial application of a statute involves the regulation of conduct beyond U.S. borders. Even where the significant effects of the regulated conduct are felt outside U.S. borders, the statute itself does not present a problem of extraterritoriality, so long as the conduct which Congress seeks to regulate occurs largely within the United States. *See generally Laker Airways*, 731 F.2d at 921; RESTATEMENT (SECOND) § 38 (rules of U.S. statutory law apply "to conduct occurring within, or having effect within the territory of the United States"); RESTATEMENT (SECOND) § 17 (1965); RESTATEMENT (THIRD) § 492(1)(a), (b) (1987).

* * *

B. Regulated Conduct Under NEPA

NEPA is designed to control the decisionmaking process of U.S. federal agencies, not the substance of agency decisions. By enacting NEPA, Congress exercised its statutory authority to determine the factors an agency must consider when exercising its discretion, and created a process whereby American officials, while acting within the United States, can reach enlightened policy decisions by taking into account environmental effects. In our view, such regulation of U.S. federal agencies and their decisionmaking processes is a legitimate exercise of Congress' territoriality-based jurisdiction, and does not raise extraterritoriality concerns.

Section 102(2)(C) lies at the heart of NEPA and is often considered the "action-forcing" element of the statute. *See* S. Rep. No. 91-296, 91st Cong., 1st Sess. 19 (1969); *Robertson v. Methow Valley Citizens Council*, 490 U.S. 332, 350 (1989). This section requires "all agencies of the Federal Government" to prepare a detailed environmental impact statement for every "major Federal action[ ]" which has the potential to significantly affect the human environment. 42 U.S.C. § 4332(2)(C). Section 102(2)(C) binds only American officials and controls the very essence of the government function: decisionmaking. Because the decisionmaking processes of federal agencies take place almost exclusively in this country and involve the workings of the United States government, they are uniquely domestic. *See* Mary A. McDougall, *Extraterritoriality and the Endangered Species Act of 1973*, 80 GEO. L. J. 435, 445 (1991).

NEPA, unlike many environmental statutes, does not dictate agency policy or determine the fate of contemplated action. *Robertson*, 490 U.S. at 350; *Strycker's Bay Neighborhood Council, Inc. v. Karlen*, 444 U.S. 223, 227-228, (1980) (per curiam). NEPA simply mandates a particular process that must be followed by a federal agency before taking action significantly affecting the human environment. After weighing environmental considerations, an agency decisionmaker remains free to subordinate the environmental concerns revealed in the EIS to other policy concerns. * * *

In many respects, NEPA is most closely akin to the myriad laws directing federal decisionmakers to consider particular factors before extending aid or engaging in certain types of trade. *See* Comment, *NEPA's Role in Protecting the World Environment*, 131 U. PA. L. REV. 353, 371 (1982). For example, the Foreign Assistance Act of 1961 requires the Agency for International Development, before approving developmental assistance, to consider the degree to which programs integrate women into the economy, as well as the possibility of using aid to "support democratic and social political trends in recipient countries." 22 U.S.C. §§ 2151k, 2218(c) (1976). Similarly, the Nuclear Nonproliferation Act requires the Nuclear Regulatory Commission to consider a nation's willingness to cooperate with American nonproliferation objectives before approving a nuclear export license. 22 U.S.C. §§ 3201-3282 (1976); 42 U.S.C. §§ 2156, 2157 (Supp. III 1979). Just as these statutes fall short of prescribing action in foreign jurisdictions, and are instead directed at the regulation of agency decisionmaking, NEPA also creates no substantive environmental standards and simply prescribes by statute the factors an agency must consider when exercising its discretionary authority.

Moreover, NEPA would never require enforcement in a foreign forum or involve "choice of law" dilemmas. This factor alone is powerful evidence of the statute's domestic nature, and distinguishes NEPA from Title VII as well as the Federal Tort Claims Act—two statutes that have been limited in their effect by the presumption against extraterritoriality. See Aramco, 111 S. Ct. at 1234 (presumption against extraterritoriality applies where Congress failed to provide for overseas enforcement and failed to address the potential conflicts of law issue); Smith v. United States, 932 F.2d 791, 793 (9th Cir. 1991) (an "indication that the [statute] was not intended to apply to Antarctica is the choice of law problem"), cert. granted, 112 S. Ct. 2963 (1992).

In sum, since NEPA is designed to regulate conduct occurring within the territory of the United States, and imposes no substantive requirements which could be interpreted to govern conduct abroad, the presumption against extraterritoriality does not apply to this case.

C. The Unique Status of Antarctica

Antarctica's unique status in the international arena further supports our conclusion that this case does not implicate the presumption against extraterritoriality. The Supreme Court explicitly stated in Aramco that when applying the presumption against extraterritoriality, courts should look to see if there is any indication that Congress intended to extend the statute's coverage "beyond places over which the United States has sovereignty *or some measure of legislative control.*" Aramco, 111 S. Ct. at 1230, (quoting Foley Bros., 336 U.S. at 285 (emphasis added)). Thus, where the U.S. has some real measure of legislative control over the region at issue, the presumption against extraterritoriality is much weaker. See, e.g., Sierra Club v. Adams, 578 F.2d 389 (D.C. Cir. 1978) (NEPA assumed to be applicable to South American highway construction where the United States had two-thirds of the ongoing financial responsibility and control over the highway construction); People of Enewetak v. Laird, 353 F. Supp. 811 (D. Hawaii 1973) (concluding that NEPA applies to the United States trust territories in the Pacific). And where there is no potential for conflict "between our laws and those of other nations," the purpose behind the presumption is eviscerated, and the presumption against extraterritoriality applies with significantly less force. Aramco, 111 S. Ct. at 1230.

Indeed, it was the general understanding that Antarctica "is not a foreign country," but rather a continent that is most frequently analogized to outer space, that led this Court to conclude in Beattie v. United States, 756 F.2d 91 (D.C. Cir. 1984), that the presumption against extraterritoriality should not apply to cases arising in Antarctica. But cf. Smith v. United States, 932 F.2d 791 (9th Cir. 1991). The Beattie Court noted that Antarctica is not a "country" at all, as it has no sovereign, and stated that "to the extent that there is any assertion of governmental authority in Antarctica, it appears to be predominately that of the United States." Beattie, 756 F.2d at 99.

Even aside from this Court's holding in Beattie, it cannot be seriously suggested that the United States lacks some real measure of legislative control over Antarctica. The United States controls all air transportation to Antarctica and conducts all search and rescue operations there. Moreover, the United States has exclusive legislative control over McMurdo Station and the other research installations established there by the United States Antarctica Program. This legislative control, taken together with the status of Antarctica as a sovereignless continent, compels the conclusion that the presumption against extraterritoriality is particularly inappropriate under the circumstances presented in this case. As stated aptly by a State Department official in congressional testimony shortly following the enactment of NEPA, application of [NEPA] to actions occurring outside the jurisdiction of any State, including the United States, would not conflict with the primary purpose underlying this venerable rule of interpretation—to avoid ill-will and conflict between nations arising out of one nation's encroachments upon another's sovereignty. . . . There are at least three general areas: The high seas, outer space, and Antarctica.

See Memorandum of C. Herter, Special Assistant to the Secretary of State for Environmental Affairs, *reprinted in Administration of the National Environmental Policy Act: Hearing Before the Subcommittee on Fisheries and Wildlife Conservation of the House Committee on Merchant Marine and Fisheries,* 91st Cong., 2d Sess. 551 (1970) [hereinafter cited as State Dept. Memo].

While the State Department memo is hardly a part of appropriate legislative history, and is not entitled to any particular deference, the memo does reflect the general understanding by those intimately involved in the creation and execution of U.S. foreign policy that the global commons, including Antarctica, do not present the challenges inherent in relations between sovereign nations. Thus, in a sovereignless region like Antarctica, where the United States has exercised a great measure of legislative control, the presumption against extraterritoriality has little relevance and a dubious basis for its application.

D. Foreign Policy Considerations

Although NSF concedes that NEPA only seeks to regulate the decisionmaking process of federal agencies, and that this case does not present a conflict between U.S. and foreign sovereign law, NSF still contends that the presumption against extraterritoriality controls this case. In particular, NSF argues that the EIS requirement will interfere with U.S. efforts to work cooperatively with other nations toward solutions to environmental problems in Antarctica. In NSF's view, joint research and cooperative environmental assessment would be "placed at risk of NEPA injunctions, making the U.S. a doubtful partner for future international cooperation in Antarctica." Appellee's Brief at 45.

NSF also argues that the Protocol on Environmental Protection to the Antarctic Treaty, which was adopted and opened for signature on October 4, 1991, would, if adopted by all the proposed signatories, conflict with the procedural requirements adopted by Congress for the decisionmaking of federal agencies under NEPA. *See* Protocol on Environmental Protection to the Antarctic Treaty, with Annexes, XI ATSCM, *reprinted in* 30 Int'l Legal Materials 1461 (1991). According to NSF, since NEPA requires the preparation of an EIS for actions with potentially "significant" impacts, while the Protocol requires an environmental analysis even for actions with "minor or transitory" impacts on the Antarctic environment, the two regulatory schemes are incompatible and will result in international discord.

We find these arguments unpersuasive. First, it should be noted that the Protocol is not in effect in any form and is years away from ratification by the United States and all 26 signatories. Second, we are unable to comprehend the difficulty presented by the two standards of review. It is clear that NSF will have to perform fewer studies under NEPA than under the Protocol, and where an EIS is required under NEPA, it would not strain a researcher's intellect to indicate in a single document how the environmental impact of the proposed action is more than "minor" and also more than "significant."

More importantly, we are not convinced that NSF's ability to cooperate with other nations in Antarctica in accordance with U.S. foreign policy will be hampered by NEPA injunctions. We made clear in *Natural Resources Defense Council v. Nuclear Regulatory Commission,* 647 F.2d 1345, 1366 (D.C. Cir. 1981) ("*NRDC*"), that where the EIS requirement proves to be incompatible with Section 102(2)(F), federal agencies will not be subject to injunctions forcing compliance with Section 102(2)(C). Section 102(2)(F) specifically requires all federal agencies to "recognize the worldwide and long-range character of environmental problems and, where consistent with the foreign policy of the United States, lend appropriate support to initiatives, resolutions, and programs designed to maximize international cooperation. . . ." 42 U.S.C. § 4332(F). While there was no majority opinion in *NRDC*, Judge Wilkey, writing for the Court, concluded that because U.S. foreign policy interests in the area of nuclear exportation were unique and delicate, the EIS requirement had to give way to the explicit directive in Section 102(2)(F) requiring agencies to cooperate with other nations where consistent with U.S. foreign policy. *NRDC*, 647 F.2d at 1348. Judge Robinson, in his concurrence, echoed this theme in many respects, and noted that the EIS requirement did not actually present an issue of extraterritoriality since "the licensing procedure takes place entirely within the United States, and domestic law completely expends its force then and there." *Id.* at 1384 n.138.

NRDC was not the first case to hold that NEPA's EIS requirement must yield where overriding policy concerns are present. In *Committee for Nuclear Responsibility v. Seaborg*, 463 F.2d 796 (D.C. Cir. 1971), for example, we refused to issue an injunction under NEPA, despite the real potential for significant harm to the environment, because the government made "assertions of harm to national security and foreign policy." *Id.* at 798. In that case, conservation groups sought to enjoin an underground nuclear test on the grounds that the Atomic Energy Commission failed to comply fully with NEPA. Although there was reason to believe that the petitioners would succeed on the merits of their claim, we denied the requested injunction in light of the foreign policy concerns.

NRDC and *Seaborg* illustrate that the government may avoid the EIS requirement where U.S. foreign policy interests outweigh the benefits derived from preparing an EIS. Since NEPA imposes no substantive requirements, U.S. foreign policy interests in Antarctica will rarely be threatened, except perhaps where the time required to prepare an EIS would itself threaten international cooperation, *see Flint Ridge Development Co. v. Scenic Rivers Association*, 426 U.S. 776, 791, (1976) (EIS requirement must yield where a clear conflict in statutory authority is unavoidable, including conflicts which arise out of timetables imposed by statute), or where the foreign policy interests at stake are particularly unique and delicate. *See NRDC*, 647 F.2d at 1348. Thus, contrary to NSF's assertions, where U.S. foreign policy interests outweigh the benefits of the EIS requirement, NSF's efforts to cooperate with foreign governments regarding environmental practices in Antarctica will not be frustrated by forced compliance with NEPA.

E. NEPA's Plain Language and Interpretation

NSF's final argument is that even if the presumption against extraterritoriality does not apply to this case, the plain language of Section 102(2)(C) precludes its application to NSF's decisionmaking regarding proposed agency action in Antarctica. We read the plain language differently.

Section 102(2)(C), on its face, is clearly not limited to actions of federal agencies that have significant environmental effects within U.S. borders. This Court has repeatedly taken note of the sweeping scope of NEPA and the EIS requirement. *See, e.g., Calvert Cliffs' Coord. Comm. v. United States A.E. Com'n*, 449 F.2d 1109, 1122 (D.C. Cir. 1971) ("[T]he sweep of NEPA is extraordinarily broad, compelling consideration of any and all types of environmental impact of federal action."); *City of Los Angeles v. NHTSA*, 912 F.2d 478, 491 (D.C. Cir. 1990) ("[NEPA] was designed explicitly to take account of impending as well as present crises in this country and *in the world as a whole*.") (emphasis added).

Far from employing limiting language, Section 2 states that NEPA is intended to "encourage productive and enjoyable harmony between *man and his environment*" as well as to "promote efforts which will prevent or eliminate damage to the environment and *biosphere*." 42 U.S.C. § 4321 (emphasis added). Clearly, Congress painted with a far greater brush than

NSF is willing to apply. As stated by the *Enewetak* court, "there appears to have been a conscious effort to avoid the use of restrictive or limiting terminology." *Enewetak*, 353 F. Supp. at 816.

Section 102(2)(F) further supports the conclusion that Congress, when enacting NEPA, was concerned with worldwide as well as domestic problems facing the environment. 42 U.S.C. § 4332(2)(F) (federal agencies required to "recognize the worldwide and long-range character of environmental problems"). NSF acknowledges that Section 102(2)(F) clearly addresses international environmental problems, but argues that this section announces Congress' only requirement for agencies pursuing action in the international arena.

We find nothing in the statute which supports the construction of Section 102 urged by NSF. Apparently, NSF has chosen to ignore the clear interrelationship between the Section 102 subsections and the Section 102 mandate as a whole. Section 102 lists several requirements under NEPA for "*all Federal agencies.*" 42 U.S.C. § 4332(2). Compliance with one of the subsections can hardly be construed to relieve the agency from its duty to fulfill the obligations articulated in other subsections. For example, compliance with Section 102(2)(G), which requires agencies to make environmental information available to the states, does not excuse an agency from preparing an EIS under Section 102(2)(C).

We also note, that prior to the issuance of Executive Order 12114, the Council on Environment Quality ("CEQ") maintained that NEPA applies to the decisionmaking process of federal agencies regarding actions in Antarctica. CEQ is the agency created by Congress to oversee the implementation of NEPA, and its interpretation of that statute is generally entitled to "substantial deference." *See, e.g., Andrus v. Sierra Club*, 442 U.S. 347, 358, (1979). NSF contends that CEQ changed its mind after the issuance of the Executive Order, and therefore its interpretation of NEPA is not entitled to deference. Whether or not NSF is right about CEQ's change of heart, we find CEQ's original conclusion to be not only reasonable, but fully supported by the plain language of the statute.

CONCLUSION

Applying the presumption against extraterritoriality here would result in a federal agency being allowed to undertake actions significantly affecting the human environment in Antarctica, an area over which the United States has substantial interest and authority, without ever being held accountable for its failure to comply with the decisionmaking procedures instituted by Congress—even though such accountability, if it was enforced, would result in no conflict with foreign law or threat to foreign policy. NSF has provided no support for its proposition that conduct occurring within the United States is rendered exempt from otherwise applicable statutes merely because the effects of its compliance would be felt in the global commons. We therefore reverse the district court's decision, and remand for a determination of whether the environmental analyses performed by NSF, prior to its decision to resume incineration, failed to comply with Section 102(2)(C) of NEPA.

We find it important to note, however, that we do not decide today how NEPA might apply to actions in a case involving an actual foreign sovereign or how other U.S. statutes might apply to Antarctica. We only hold that the alleged failure of NSF to comply with NEPA before resuming incineration in Antarctica does not implicate the presumption against extraterritoriality.

Reversed and remanded.

NOTES

1. Did Executive Order 12114 apply to the action proposed by the National Science Foundation (NSF) in this case? If it did apply, is the President's interpretation of NEPA entitled to deference from the court?

2. The Order states that it is based upon independent authority but that it "furthers the purposes of NEPA." Does the Order serve as a government vehicle for *implementing* NEPA? Does the Order represent an executive branch interpretation of NEPA? If so, should the court defer to that interpretation?

3. In *NEPA Coalition of Japan v. Aspin*, 837 F. Supp. 466 (D.D.C. 1993), the court upheld a decision by the Defense Department to refuse to prepare an EIS to analyze the effects on nearby residential neighborhoods of U.S. military installations in Japan. The Japanese neighbors were concerned about aircraft noise and the risk of ship collisions that might spill dangerous substances. The court distinguished *Massey* on the grounds that the Navy's actions were occurring on foreign sovereign territory, not Antarctica or the high seas. The court also found that even if NEPA did apply, the EIS requirement would be waived because of strong foreign policy concerns.

4. If NEPA controls only the decisionmaking process of U.S. federal agencies, why are courts concerned about interfering with the sovereignty of foreign nations?

5. If the United States believes that NEPA compliance is important for good government and for sound agency decisions, how can it justify waiving requirements when, for example, it provides foreign aid for the construction of a large dam? What risks are involved in failing to insist on NEPA compliance?

6. As we noted in Chapter 4, perhaps the best indicator of NEPA's success lies in the fact that over 50 foreign countries have adopted laws and policies which promote environmental impact assessment before major projects may go forward. In 1987, the United Nations Environment Programme published a set of guidelines and principles which strongly endorsed EIA processes for all countries. *See* 9 UNEP ENVIRONMENTAL LAW: GUIDELINES AND PRINCIPLES (1987). *See also,* John E. Bonine, *Environmental Impact Assessment—Principles Developed,* 17 ENVTL. POL'Y & L. 5 (1987). More recently, the 1992 United Nations Framework Convention on Biological Diversity, signed by 150 nations at the Rio Earth Summit (U.N. Conference on Environment and Development), states that each party to the Convention shall:

> (a) Introduce appropriate procedures requiring environmental impact assessment of its proposed projects that are likely to have significant adverse effects on biological diversity with a view to avoiding or minimizing such effects and, where appropriate, allow for public participation in such procedures;

* * *

> (c) Promote, on the basis of reciprocity, notification, exchange of information and consultation on activities under their jurisdiction or control which are likely to significantly affect adversely the biological diversity of other States or areas beyond the limits of national jurisdiction, by encouraging the conclusion of bilateral, regional or multilateral arrangements, as appropriate;

(d) In the case of imminent or grave danger or damage, originating under its jurisdiction or control, to biological diversity within the area under jurisdiction of other States or in areas beyond the limits of national jurisdiction, notify immediately the potentially affected States of such danger or damage, as well as initiate action to prevent or minimize such danger or damage;

* * *

21 INT'L ENVTL. REP. (BNA) 4001, 4003–04 (1992) (Article 14). President Clinton signed the Convention in June 1993, but the Senate has thus far failed to ratify it. If the Convention becomes widely adopted, will the law of most nations be consistent with extraterritorial application of NEPA? Will Congress have to amend NEPA or the ESA if the United States ratifies the Convention? Since the focus of the Convention is biological diversity, consider the effect ratification would have on extraterritorial application of the ESA as you read the following opinion.

LUJAN V. DEFENDERS OF WILDLIFE
504 U.S. 555 (1992)

[This case involved a challenge to a rule promulgated by the Secretary of the Interior which interpreted § 7 of the Endangered Species Act of 1973 (ESA), 16 U.S.C. § 1536. The rule made the Act applicable only to actions within the United States or on the high seas. The plurality opinion, which addressed the plaintiffs' standing to sue, was reproduced in part in Chapter 3, *supra.* Justice Stevens' concurring opinion, reproduced in relevant part below, was the only opinion to address the merits of the plaintiffs' claim.]

Justice STEVENS, concurring in the judgment.

Because I am not persuaded that Congress intended the consultation requirement in § 7(a)(2) of the Endangered Species Act of 1973 (ESA), 16 U.S.C. § 1536(a)(2), to apply to activities in foreign countries, I concur in the judgment of reversal. I do not, however, agree with the Court's conclusion that respondents lack standing because the threatened injury to their interest in protecting the environment and studying endangered species is not "imminent." Nor do I agree with the plurality's additional conclusion that respondents' injury is not "redressable" in this litigation.

* * *
II

Although I believe that respondents have standing, I nevertheless concur in the judgment of reversal because I am persuaded that the Government is correct in its submission that § 7(a)(2) does not apply to activities in foreign countries. As with all questions of statutory construction, the question whether a statute applies extraterritorially is one of congressional intent. *Foley Bros., Inc. v. Filardo,* 336 U.S. 281, 284-285 (1949). We normally assume that "Congress is primarily concerned with domestic conditions," *id.* at 285, and therefore presume that "'legislation of Congress, unless a contrary intent appears, is meant to apply only within the territorial jurisdiction of the United States.'" *EEOC v. Arabian American Oil Co.,* 111 S. Ct. 1227 (1991) (quoting *Foley Bros.,* 336 U.S. at 285).

Section 7(a)(2) provides, in relevant part:

"Each Federal agency shall, in consultation with and with the assistance of the Secretary [of the Interior or Commerce, as appropriate], insure that any action authorized, funded, or carried out by such agency (hereinafter in this section referred to as an 'agency action') is not likely to jeopardize the continued existence of any endangered species or threatened species or result in the destruction or adverse modification of habitat of such species which is determined by the Secretary, after consultation as appropriate with affected States, to be critical, unless such agency has been granted an exemption for such action by the Committee pursuant to subsection (h) of this section. . . ." 16 U.S.C. § 1536(a)(2).

Nothing in this text indicates that the section applies in foreign countries.[2] Indeed, the only geographic reference in the section is in the "critical habitat" clause, which mentions "affected States." The Secretary of the Interior and the Secretary of Commerce have consistently taken the position that they need not designate critical habitat in foreign countries. See 42 Fed. Reg. 4869 (1977) (initial regulations of the Fish and Wildlife Service and the National Marine Fisheries Service on behalf of the Secretary of Interior and the Secretary of Commerce). Consequently, neither Secretary interprets § 7(a)(2) to require federal agencies to engage in consultations to insure that their actions in foreign countries will not adversely affect the critical habitat of endangered or threatened species.

That interpretation is sound, and, in fact, the Court of Appeals did not question it. There is, moreover, no indication that Congress intended to give a different geographic scope to the two clauses in § 7(a)(2). To the contrary, Congress recognized that one of the "major causes" of extinction of endangered species is the "destruction of natural habitat." It would thus be illogical to conclude that Congress required federal agencies to avoid jeopardy to endangered species abroad, but not destruction of critical habitat abroad.

The lack of an express indication that the consultation requirement applies extraterritorially is particularly significant because other sections of the ESA expressly deal with the problem of protecting endangered species abroad. Section 8, for example, authorizes the President to provide assistance to "any foreign country (with its consent) . . . in the development and management of programs in that country which [are] . . . necessary or useful for the conservation of any endangered species or threatened species listed by the Secretary pursuant to section 1533 of this title." 16 U.S.C. § 1537(a). It also directs the Secretary of Interior, "through the Secretary of State," to "encourage" foreign countries to conserve fish and wildlife and to enter into bilateral or multilateral agreements. § 1537(b). Section 9 makes it unlawful to import endangered species into (or export them from) the United States or to otherwise traffic in endangered species "in interstate or foreign commerce." §§ 1538(a)(1)(A), (E), (F). Congress thus obviously thought about endangered species abroad and devised specific sections of the ESA to protect them. In this context, the absence of any explicit statement that the consultation requirement is applicable to agency actions in foreign countries suggests that Congress did not intend that § 7(a)(2) apply extraterritorially.

---

[2]   Respondents point out that the duties in § 7(a)(2) are phrased in broad, inclusive language: "Each Federal agency" shall consult with the Secretary and insure that "any action" does not jeopardize "any endangered or threatened species" or destroy or adversely modify the "habitat of such species." 16 U.S.C. § 1536(a)(2). The Court of Appeals correctly recognized, however, that such inclusive language, by itself, is not sufficient to overcome the presumption against the extraterritorial application of statutes. 911 F.2d 117, 122 (8th Cir. 1990); see also Foley Bros., Inc. v. Filardo, 336 U.S. 281, 282, 287-288 (1949) (statute requiring an eight-hour day provision in "'[e]very contract made to which the United States . . . is a party'" is inapplicable to contracts for work performed in foreign countries).

Finally, the general purpose of the ESA does not evince a congressional intent that the consultation requirement be applicable to federal agency actions abroad. The congressional findings explaining the need for the ESA emphasize that "various species of fish, wildlife, and plants *in the United States* have been rendered extinct as a consequence of economic growth and development untempered by adequate concern and conservation," and that these species "are of aesthetic, ecological, educational, historical, recreational, and scientific value to the *Nation and its people*." §§ 1531(1), (3) (emphasis added). The lack of similar findings about the harm caused by development in other countries suggests that Congress was primarily concerned with balancing development and conservation goals in this country.[7]

In short, a reading of the entire statute persuades me that Congress did not intend the consultation requirement in § 7(a)(2) to apply to activities in foreign countries. Accordingly, notwithstanding my disagreement with the Court's disposition of the standing question, I concur in its judgment.

NOTES

1.   Suppose a federal agency proposes an action that may adversely affect the habitat of a listed species in a foreign nation. Suppose further that the species migrates to the United States. Is the agency required to consult under § 7(a)(2)? Does it matter whether the particular population adversely affected is the same population which migrates to the United States?

2.   How might Justice Stevens' analysis affect species in the global commons?

3.   International concerns regarding endangered species protection are addressed to a limited extent under the ESA in §§ 8 and 8A. 16 U.S.C. §§ 1537, 1537A. Section 8 authorizes the President to provide certain limited forms of aid to other countries to assist them in the development and management of programs designed to conserve endangered or threatened species. Section 8A implements the Convention on International Trade in Endangered Species (CITES) for the United States. CITES focuses strictly on trade in endangered species and species parts. Its utility is thus limited to those species that have or may have some market value. Species are listed under one of three Appendices established under the Convention. The highest protection is accorded species listed under Appendix I. For those species, signatory countries agree to require both import and export permits for any commerce in those species or their parts. For Appendix II species, only an export permit is required. Appendix III species may be unilaterally designated by any party to the Convention, and those countries which have so designated these species must require an export permit.

---

[7]   Of course, Congress also found that "the United States has pledged itself as a sovereign state in the international community to conserve to the extent practicable the various species of fish or wildlife and plants facing extinction, pursuant to [several international agreements]," and that "encouraging the States . . . to develop and maintain conservation programs which meet national and international standards is a key to meeting the Nation's international commitments. . . ." 16 U.S.C. §§ 1531(4), (5). The Court of Appeals read these findings as indicative of a congressional intent to make § 7(a)(2)'s consultation requirement applicable to agency action abroad. *See* 911 F.2d, at 122-123. I am not persuaded, however, that such a broad congressional intent can be gleaned from these findings. Instead, I think the findings indicate a more narrow congressional intent that the United States abide by its international commitments.

4.   Which statute—NEPA or the ESA—offers a more compelling case for international application? Why?

5.   For a fuller discussion of international conservation of biological diversity, see Catherine Tinker, *Responsibility for Biological Diversity Conservation under International Law*, 29 VAND. J. TRANSNAT'L L. 777 (1995); Kal Raustiala & David G. Victor, *Biodiversity Since Rio: The Future of the Convention on Biological Diversity*, ENV'T, May 1996, at 17.

7 THE SCOPE OF NEPA AND ESA DOCUMENTS

A. Alternatives

The CEQ regulations characterize the discussion of alternatives as "the heart of the [EIS]." 40 C.F.R. § 1502.14. Not surprisingly, the adequacy of the alternatives portion of EISs has spawned substantial litigation.

NATURAL RESOURCES DEFENSE COUNCIL, INC. v. MORTON
458 F.2d 827 (D.C. Cir. 1972)

LEVENTHAL, Circuit Judge:

This appeal raises a question as to the scope of the requirement of the National Environmental Policy Act (NEPA) that environmental impact statements contain a discussion of alternatives. Before us is the Environmental Impact Statement filed October 28, 1971, by the Department of Interior with respect to its proposal, under § 8 of the Outer Continental Shelf Lands Act, for the oil and gas general lease sale, of leases to some 80 tracts of submerged lands, primarily off eastern Louisiana. The proposal was finally structured so as to embrace almost 380,000 acres, about 10% of the offshore acreage presently under Federal lease. Opening of bids for the leases was scheduled for December 21, 1971, and three conservation groups brought this action on November 1, to enjoin the proposed sale. On December 16, the District Court held a hearing and granted a preliminary injunction enjoining the sale of these leases pending compliance with NEPA. The Government appealed, and filed a motion in this court for summary reversal and immediate hearing. We granted the immediate hearing * * *. As to the motion for summary reversal, we conclude that this must be denied.

I. BACKGROUND
Chronology and Impact Statements

On June 15, 1971, Secretary of Interior Rogers Morton, a defendant in this litigation, announced that a general oil and gas lease sale of tracts on the Outer Continental Shelf (OCS) off eastern Louisiana would take place in December, 1971. This was responsive to the directive in President Nixon's June 4, 1971, Message on Supply of Energy and Clean Air. On July 31, 1971, Mr. Burton W. Silcock, Director of the Bureau of Land Management, also a defendant, promulgated and circulated for comment a "Draft Environmental Impact Statement" pursuant to § 102(2)(c) of NEPA and § 10(b) of the Guidelines of the Council on Environmental Quality. Plaintiffs submitted comments on this draft statement. * * * On October 28, 1971, Mr. Silcock promulgated the "Final Environmental Impact Statement" (hereafter Statement). On November 20, 1971, the Interior Department announced that the proposed lease sale would take place * * *.

Statement—Adverse Environmental Impact Disclosed

While the Statement presents questions, subsequently delineated, this document—67 pages in length, exclusive of appendices—is not challenged on the ground of failure to disclose the problems of environmental impact of the proposed sale. On the contrary, these problems are set

319

forth in considerable range and detail. Indeed, the complaint voiced by the Audubon Society's witness in testimony was that the draft Statement gives a green light for the sale while its contents seem to cry out for the opposite conclusion. Without purporting to summarize, we identify some of the Statement's highlights:

Adjacent to the proposed lease area is the greatest estuarine coastal marsh complex in the United States, some 7.9 million acres, providing food, nursery habitat and spawning ground vital to fish, shellfish and wildlife, as well as food and shelter for migratory waterfowl, wading birds and fur-bearing animals. This complex provides rich nutrient systems which make the Gulf of Mexico, blessed also with warm waters and shallow depths, the most productive fishing region of the country. * * *

The coastal regions of Louisiana and Mississippi contain millions of acres suitable for outdoor recreation, with a number of state and federal recreation areas, and extensive beach shorelines * * *. These serve millions—not only the residents of the seven state region * * * but visitors attracted to the beaches in increasing numbers * * *.

As to probable impact of issuance of leases on the environment the Statement did not anticipate continuation of debris from drilling operations, in view of recent regulations prohibiting dumping of debris on the OCS. The Statement acknowledged some impact from construction of platforms, pipelines and other structures. A concluding section (III D) on "Unavoidable Adverse Environmental Effects" particularly noted the destruction of marsh and of marine species and plants from dredging incident to pipeline installation, and the effect of pipeline canals in e.g., increasing ratio of water to wetlands and increasing salt water intrusion.

Oil pollution is the problem most extensively discussed in the Statement and its exposition of unavoidable adverse environmental effects. The Statement acknowledges that both short and long term effects on the environment can be expected from spillage, including in that term major spills (like that in the Santa Barbara Channel in 1969); minor spills from operations and unidentified sources; and discharge of waste water contaminated with oil.

These adverse effects relate both to the damage to the coastal region—beaches, water areas and historic sites; and the forecast that oil pollution "may seriously damage the marine biological community"—both direct damage to the larger organisms, visible more easily and sooner, and to smaller life stages which would lead one step removed to damage later in the food chain.

The Statement noted the diverse conclusions and comments in existing reports on oil spills, some minimizing damage done, others stressing that oil spillage has effects beyond the period of visible evidence; that oil may mix with water, especially in a turbulent sea, and disperse downward into the sea; that emulsifiers used to remove surface oil may have toxic consequences, etc.

The Statement asserted that while past major spills in the Gulf resulted in minimal damage, this was due to a fortunate combination of offshore winds and surface currents. The Statement rates blocks in the sale on an estimated probability of impact basis, calculated principally on proximity to high value/critically vulnerable area.

* * *

II. Discussion of Requirement of NEPA as to Alternatives

The pertinent instruction of Congress appears in § 102 of NEPA, 42 U.S.C. § 4332 * * *.

Paragraph (iii) of § 102(2)(C) is a terse notation for: "The alternative ways of accomplishing the objectives of the proposed action and the results of not accomplishing the proposed action."

Congress contemplated that the Impact Statement would constitute the environmental source material for the information of the Congress as well as the Executive, in connection with the making of relevant decisions, and would be available to enhance enlightenment of—and by—the public. The impact statement provides a basis for (a) evaluation of the benefits of the proposed project in light of its environmental risks, and (b) comparison of the net balance for the proposed project with the environmental risks presented by alternative courses of action.

Need to discuss environmental consequences of alternatives

We reject the implication of one of the Government's submissions which began by stating that while the Act requires a detailed statement of alternatives, it "does not require a discussion of the environmental consequences of the suggested alternative." A sound construction of NEPA, which takes into account both the legislative history and contemporaneous executive construction, requires a presentation of the environmental risks incident to reasonable alternative courses of action. The agency may limit its discussion of environmental impact to a brief statement, when that is the case, that the alternative course involves no effect on the environment, or that their effect, briefly described, is simply not significant. A rule of reason is implicit in this aspect of the law as it is in the requirement that the agency provide a statement concerning those opposing views that are responsible.

Alternative as to oil import quotas

We think the Secretary's Statement erred in stating that the alternative of elimination of oil import quotas was entirely outside its cognizance. Assuming, as the Statement puts it, that this alternative "involves complex factors and concepts, including national security, which are beyond the scope of this statement," it does not follow that the Statement should not present the environmental effects of that alternative. While the consideration of pertinent alternatives requires a weighing of numerous matters, such as economics, foreign relations, national security, the fact remains that, as to the ingredient of possible adverse environmental impact, it is the essence and thrust of NEPA that the pertinent Statement serve to gather in one place a discussion of the relative environmental impact of alternatives.

The Government also contends that the only "alternatives" required for discussion under NEPA are those which can be adopted and put into effect by the official or agency issuing the statement. * * *

While we agree with so much of the Government's presentation as rests on the assumption that the alternatives required for discussion are those reasonably available, we do not agree that this requires a limitation to measures the agency or official can adopt. This approach would be particularly inapposite for the lease sale of offshore oil lands hastened by Secretary Morton in response to the directive which President Nixon set forth in his message to Congress on the Supply of Energy and Clean Air, as part of an overall program of development to provide an accommodation of the energy requirements of our country with the growing recognition of the necessity to protect the environment. * * * The Executive's proposed solution to a national problem, or a set of inter-related problems, may call for each of several departments or agencies to take a specific action; this cannot mean that the only discussion of alternatives required in the ensuing environmental impact statements would be the discussion by each department of the particular actions it could take as an alternative to the proposal underlying its impact statement.

When the proposed action is an integral part of a coordinated plan to deal with a broad problem, the range of alternatives that must be evaluated is broadened. While the Department of the Interior does not have the authority to eliminate or reduce oil import quotas, such action is within the purview of both Congress and the President, to whom the impact statement goes. The impact statement is not only for the exposition of the thinking of the agency, but also for the guidance of these ultimate decision-makers, and must provide them with the environmental effects of both the proposal and the alternatives, for their consideration along with the various other elements of the public interest.

An evaluation of the environmental effects of all the alternatives in the area of the energy crisis might have been provided by an impact statement issued by an officer or agency with broad responsibility. This could have been done in June, 1971, when the President abstained from exercising his authority to invoke a change in import quota administration and issued the Message that included the directive as to offshore leasing. * * *

* * *

The need for continuing review of environmental impact of alternatives under NEPA cannot be put to one side on the ground of past determinations by Congress or the President. * * * The OCS leasing was specifically made subject to executive authority to withdraw unleased lands from disposition from time to time. Import controls were from the outset dependent on continuing Presidential findings as to the nature and duration of controls deemed necessary. * * *

* * *

We reiterate that the discussion of environmental effects of alternatives need not be exhaustive. What is required is information sufficient to permit a reasoned choice of alternatives so far as environmental aspects are concerned. As to alternatives not within the scope of authority of the responsible official, reference may of course be made to studies of other agencies—including other impact statements. Nor is it appropriate, as Government counsel argues, to disregard alternatives merely because they do not offer a complete solution to the problem. If an alternative would result in supplying only part of the energy that the lease sale would yield, then its use might possibly reduce the scope of the lease sale program and thus alleviate a significant portion of the environmental harm attendant on offshore drilling.

Other "alternatives"

* * *

We think there is merit to the Government's position insofar as it contends that no additional discussion was requisite for such "alternatives" as the development of oil shale, desulfurization of coal, coal liquefaction and gasification, tar sands and geothermal resources.

The Statement sets forth * * * that while these possibilities hold great promise for the future, their impact on the energy supply will not likely be felt until after 1980, and will be dependent on environmental safeguards and technilogical [sic] developments. Since the Statement also sets forth that the agency's proposal was put forward to meet a near-term requirement, imposed by an energy shortfall projected for the mid-1970's, the possibility of the environmental impact of long-term solutions requires no additional discussion at this juncture. We say "at this juncture" for the problem requires continuing review, in the nature of things, and these alternatives and their environmental consequences may be more germane to subsequent proposals for OCS leases, in the light of changes in technology or in the variables of energy requirements and supply.

Furthermore, the requirement in NEPA of discussion as to reasonable alternatives does not require "crystal ball" inquiry. * * * The statute must be construed in the light of reason if it is not to demand what is, fairly speaking, not meaningfully possible, given the obvious, that the resources of energy and research—and time—available to meet the Nation's needs are not infinite.

Still different considerations are presented by the "alternatives" of increasing nuclear energy development, listed in the Statement, and the possibilities, identified by the District Court as a critical omission, of federal legislation or administrative action freeing current offshore and state-controlled offshore production from state market demand prorationing, or changing the Federal Power Commission's natural gas pricing policies.

The mere fact that an alternative requires legislative implementation does not automatically establish it as beyond the domain of what is required for discussion, particularly since NEPA was intended to provide a basis for consideration and choice by the decisionmakers in the legislative as well as the executive branch. But the need for an overhaul of basic legislation certainly bears on the requirements of the Act. We do not suppose Congress intended an agency to devote itself to extended discussion of the environmental impact of alternatives so remote from reality as to depend on, say, the repeal of the antitrust laws.

In the last analysis, the requirement as to alternatives is subject to a construction of reasonableness, and we say this with full awareness that this approach necessarily has both strengths and weaknesses. Where the environmental aspects of alternatives are readily identifiable by the agency, it is reasonable to state them—for ready reference by those concerned with the consequences of the decision and its alternatives. * * *

There is reason for concluding that NEPA was not meant to require detailed discussion of the environmental effects of "alternatives" put forward in comments when these effects cannot be readily ascertained and the alternatives are deemed only remote and speculative possibilities, in view of basic changes required in statutes and policies of other agencies—making them available, if at all, only after protracted debate and litigation not meaningfully compatible with the time-frame of the needs to which the underlying proposal is addressed.

A final word. In this as in other areas, the functions of courts and agencies, rightly understood, are not in opposition but in collaboration, toward achievement of the end prescribed by Congress. So long as the officials and agencies have taken the "hard look" at environmental consequences mandated by Congress, the court does not seek to impose unreasonable extremes or to interject itself within the area of discretion of the executive as to the choice of the action to be taken.

Informed by our judgment that discussion of alternatives may be required even though the action required lies outside the Interior Department, the Secretary will, we have no doubt, be able without undue delay to provide the kind of reasonable discussion of alternatives and their environmental consequences that Congress contemplated.

Motion denied.

NOTES

1.   Suppose Secretary Morton cured the procedural defects identified in *NRDC v. Morton*. Would a subsequent decision to go forward with the proposed oil and gas leasing off the coast of Louisiana be arbitrary and capricious, or an abuse of discretion? What problems would you foresee in making such an argument? If a plaintiff chose to file a complaint against the government alleging arbitrary and capricious action, or alleging that the government failed to take into account all of the relevant factors, what procedural tools would likely be available in court? Should a plaintiff in this circumstance have the right to introduce new evidence (for example, the testimony of consultants on economic or scientific issues) at a trial? Alternatively, should the case be heard "on the record" before the agency? (Typically, cases which are heard on the record are resolved on cross-motions for summary judgment. Why?) If the plaintiff is afforded an opportunity to introduce new evidence, should the court impose any limits on the government's rebuttal? If the government is allowed to introduce new evidence at a trial to support its decision, how can the public's

right to comment on this evidence be preserved? For one view of these issues, see Susannah T. French, *Judicial Review of the Administrative Record in NEPA Litigation*, 81 CAL. L. REV. 929 (1993).

2. Judge Leventhal's opinion in the *NRDC* OCS leasing case substantially influenced the Council on Environmental Quality regulations as they relate to the alternatives analysis. Compare, for example, the *NRDC* decision with the requirements that agencies: (1) "present the environmental impacts of the proposal and the alternatives in comparative form thus sharply defining the issues and providing a clear basis for choice among options by the decisionmaker and the public"; (2) "rigorously explore and objectively evaluate all reasonable alternatives"; and (3) "[i]nclude [in the EIS] reasonable alternatives not within the jurisdiction of the lead agency." 40 C.F.R. § 1502.14.

3. The importance of the alternatives analysis cannot be overstated. When properly carried out by the agency, it changes the environmental analysis from a document justifying a decision already made, to one that offers real choices to an agency. To be sure, agencies rarely choose the "no action" alternative. More and more, however, agencies appear willing to accept a reasonable alternative to a proposal where the result will be less environmentally damaging. Often, during the EIS process, a new alternative emerges that allows some form of development to go forward with less damaging environmental consequences.

4. Is it appropriate to ask an administrative agency to evaluate political alternatives (such as the elimination of oil import quotas) that are wholly outside of its control? What purpose would it serve? In deciding whether such alternatives are reasonable, should an agency consider political realities? *See* Arthur W. Murphy, *The National Environmental Policy Act and the Licensing Process: Environmentalist Magna Carta or Agency Coup De Grace?*, 72 COLUM. L. REV. 963, 986-87 (1972).

Is Judge Leventhal in *NRDC v. Morton* suggesting that the President should have assigned an agency the task of preparing an EIS on his energy strategy? Recall that NEPA does not apply to the President. 40 C.F.R. § 1508.12. Should NEPA require that *someone* consider reducing the oil import quotas?

5. The requirement that agencies consider alternatives in the context of drafting an EIS appears at §102(2)(C)(iii) of NEPA. A separate requirement at § 102(2)(E), however, requires that agencies "study, develop, and describe appropriate alternatives to recommended courses of action in *any* proposal which involves unresolved conflicts concerning alternative uses of available resources." (Emphasis added.) Assume that the relevant agencies have determined that the following activities do not require an EIS. How might §102(2)(E) be used in the context of the following situations:

(a) a proposal to build a new hiking trail in a national park;
(b) a proposal to log a small quantity of timber in an area that has been subject to frequent logging in the past;
(c) a proposal to renew a grazing permit on public lands managed by the Bureau of Land Management;
(d) a proposal to build a new restaurant at the summit of an existing ski resort located on National Forest lands, and operating under a permit from the U.S. Forest Service.

VERMONT YANKEE NUCLEAR POWER CORP. V. NATURAL RESOURCES DEFENSE COUNCIL, INC.
435 U.S. 519 (1978)

[A substantial portion of this case is excerpted at Chapter 2.B., *supra.*]

Mr. JUSTICE REHNQUIST delivered the opinion of the Court

* * *

I

* * *

C

In January 1969, petitioner Consumers Power Co. applied for a permit to construct two nuclear reactors in Midland, Mich. Consumers Power's application was examined by the Commission's staff and the ACRS [Advisory Committee on Reactor Safeguards]. The ACRS issued reports which discussed specific problems and recommended solutions. It also made reference to "other problems" of a more generic nature and suggested that efforts should be made to resolve them with respect to these as well as all other projects. Two groups, one called Saginaw and another called Mapleton, intervened and opposed the application. Saginaw filed with the Board a number of environmental contentions, directed over 300 interrogatories to the ACRS, attempted to depose the chairman of the ACRS, and requested discovery of various ACRS documents. The Licensing Board denied the various discovery requests directed to the ACRS. Hearings were then held on numerous radiological health and safety issues. Thereafter, the Commission's staff issued a draft environmental impact statement. Saginaw submitted 119 environmental contentions which were both comments on the proposed draft statement and a statement of Saginaw's position in the upcoming hearings. The staff revised the statement and issued a final environmental statement in March 1972. Further hearings were then conducted during May and June 1972. Saginaw, however, choosing not to appear at or participate in these latter hearings, indicated that it had "no conventional findings of fact to set forth" and had not "chosen to search the record and respond to this proceeding by submitting citations of matters which we believe were proved or disproved." But the Licensing Board, recognizing its obligations to "independently consider the final balance among conflicting environmental factors in the record," nevertheless treated as contested those issues "as to which intervenors introduced affirmative evidence or engaged in substantial cross examination."

At issue now are 17 of those 119 contentions which are claimed to raise questions of "energy conservation." The Licensing Board indicated that as far as appeared from the record, the demand for the plant was made up of normal industrial and residential use. It went on to state that it was "beyond our province to inquire into whether the customary uses being made of electricity in our society are 'proper' or 'improper.'" With respect to claims that Consumers Power stimulated demand by its advertising the Licensing Board indicated that "[n]o evidence was offered on this point and absent some evidence that Applicant is creating abnormal demand, the Board did not consider the question." * * * The Appeal Board ultimately affirmed the Licensing Board's grant of a construction permit and the Commission declined to further review the matter.

At just about the same time, the Council on Environmental Quality revised its regulations governing the preparation of environmental impact statements. The regulations mentioned for the first time the necessity of considering in impact statements energy conservation as one of the alternatives to a proposed project. * * * Saginaw then moved the Commission to clarify its ruling and reopen the Consumers Power proceedings.

In a lengthy opinion, the Commission declined to reopen the proceedings. The Commission first ruled it was required to consider only energy conservation alternatives which were "'reasonably available,'" would in their aggregate effect curtail demand for electricity to a level at which the proposed facility would not be needed, and were susceptible of a reasonable degree of proof. It then determined, after a thorough examination of the record, that not all of Saginaw's contentions met these threshold tests. It further determined that the Board had been willing at all times to take evidence on the other contentions. Saginaw had simply failed to present any such evidence. The Commission further criticized Saginaw for its total disregard of even those minimal procedural formalities necessary to give the Board some idea of exactly what was at issue. The Commission emphasized that "[p]articularly in these circumstances, Saginaw's complaint that it was not granted a hearing on alleged energy conservation issues comes with ill grace." And in response to Saginaw's contention that regardless of whether it properly raised the issues, the Licensing Board must consider all environmental issues, the Commission basically agreed, as did the Board itself, but further reasoned that the Board must have some workable procedural rules and these rules

> "in this setting must take into account that energy conservation is a novel and evolving concept. * * *
>
> However, at this emergent stage of energy conservation principles, intervenors also have their responsibilities. They must state clear and reasonably specific energy conservation contentions in a timely fashion. Beyond that, they have a burden of coming forward with some affirmative showing if they wish to have these novel contentions explored further."

Respondents then challenged the granting of the construction permit in the Court of Appeals for the District of Columbia Circuit.

D

* * *

With respect to the permit to Consumers Power, the court first held that the environmental impact statement for construction of the Midland reactors was fatally defective for failure to examine energy conservation as an alternative to a plant of this size. The court also thought the report by ACRS was inadequate, although it did not agree that discovery from individual ACRS members was the proper way to obtain further explication of the report. Instead, the court held that the Commission should have *sua sponte* sent the report back to the ACRS for further elucidation of the "other problems" and their resolution. * * *

* * *

III

A

We now turn to the Court of Appeals' holding "that rejection of energy conservation on the basis of the 'threshold test' was capricious and arbitrary," and again conclude the court was wrong.

The Court of Appeals ruled that the Commission's "threshold test" for the presentation of energy conservation contentions was inconsistent with NEPA's basic mandate to the Commission. The Commission, the court reasoned, is something more than an umpire who sits back and resolves adversary contentions at the hearing stage. And when an intervenor's comments "bring 'sufficient attention to the issue to stimulate the Commission's consideration of it,'" the Commission must "undertake its own preliminary investigation of the proffered alternative sufficient to reach a rational judgment whether it is worthy of detailed consideration in the EIS. Moreover, the Commission must explain the basis for each conclusion that further consideration of a suggested alternative is unwarranted."

While the court's rationale is not entirely unappealing as an abstract proposition, as applied to this case we think it basically misconceives not only the scope of the agency's statutory responsibility, but also the nature of the administrative process, the thrust of the agency's decision, and the type of issues the intervenors were trying to raise.

There is little doubt that under the Atomic Energy Act of 1954, state public utility commissions or similar bodies are empowered to make the initial decision regarding the need for power. The Commission's prime area of concern in the licensing context, on the other hand, is national security, public health, and safety. And it is clear that the need, as that term is conventionally used, for the power was thoroughly explored in the hearings. * * *

NEPA, of course, has altered slightly the statutory balance, requiring "a detailed statement by the responsible official on . . . alternatives to the proposed action." But, as should be obvious even upon a moment's reflection, the term "alternatives" is not self-defining. To make an impact statement something more than an exercise in frivolous boilerplate the concept of alternatives must be bounded by some notion of feasibility. As the Court of Appeals for the District of Columbia Circuit has itself recognized:

> "There is reason for concluding that NEPA was not meant to require detailed discussion of the environmental effects of 'alternatives' put forward in comments when these effects cannot be readily ascertained and the alternatives are deemed only remote and speculative possibilities, in view of basic changes required in statutes and policies of other agencies—making them available, if at all, only after protracted debate and litigation not meaningfully compatible with the time-frame of the needs to which the underlying proposal is addressed." *Natural Resources Defense Council v. Morton,* 458 F.2d 827, 837-38 (1972).

Common sense also teaches us that the "detailed statement of alternatives" cannot be found wanting simply because the agency failed to include every alternative device and thought conceivable by the mind of man. Time and resources are simply too limited to hold that an impact statement fails because the agency failed to ferret out every possible alternative, regardless of how uncommon or unknown that alternative may have been at the time the project was approved.

With these principles in mind we now turn to the notion of "energy conservation," an alternative the omission of which was thought by the Court of Appeals to have been "forcefully pointed out by Saginaw in its comments on the draft EIS." Again, as the Commission pointed out, "the phrase 'energy conservation' has a deceptively simple ring in this context. Taken literally, the phrase suggests a virtually limitless range of possible actions and developments that might, in one way or another, ultimately reduce projected demands for electricity from a particular proposed plant." Moreover, as a practical matter, it is hard to dispute the observation that it is largely the events of recent years that have emphasized not only the need but also a large variety of alternatives for energy conservation. Prior to the drastic oil shortages incurred by the United States in 1973, there was little serious thought in most Government circles of energy conservation alternatives. Indeed, the Council on Environmental Quality did not promulgate regulations which even remotely suggested the need to consider energy conservation in impact statements until August 1, 1973. And even then the guidelines were not made applicable to draft and final statements filed with the Council before January 28, 1974. * * * All this occurred over a year and a half after the draft environmental statement for Midland had been prepared, and over a year after the final environmental statement had been prepared and the hearings completed.

We think these facts amply demonstrate that the concept of "alternatives" is an evolving one, requiring the agency to explore more or fewer alternatives as they become better known and understood. This was well understood by the Commission, which, unlike the Court of Appeals, recognized that the Licensing Board's decision had to be judged by the information then available to it. And judged in that light we have little doubt the Board's actions were well within the proper bounds of its statutory authority. Not only did the record before the agency give every indication that the project was actually needed, but also there was nothing before the Board to indicate to the contrary.

We also think the court's criticism of the Commission's "threshold test" displays a lack of understanding of the historical setting within which the agency action took place and of the nature of the test itself. In the first place, while it is true that NEPA places upon an agency the obligation to consider every significant aspect of the environmental impact of a proposed action, it is still incumbent upon intervenors who wish to participate to structure their participation so that it is meaningful, so that it alerts the agency to the intervenors' position and contentions. This is especially true when the intervenors are requesting the agency to embark upon an exploration of unchartered territory, as was the question of energy conservation in the late 1960's and early 1970's.

> "[C]omments must be significant enough to step over a threshold requirement of materiality before any lack of agency response or consideration becomes of concern. The comment cannot merely state that a particular mistake was made . . .; it must show why the mistake was of possible significance in the results . . .." *Portland Cement Assn. v. Ruckelshaus,* 486 F.2d 375, 394 (1973).

Indeed, administrative proceedings should not be a game or a forum to engage in unjustified obstructionism by making cryptic and obscure reference to matters that "ought to be" considered and then, after failing to do more to bring the matter to the agency's attention, seeking to have that agency determination vacated on the ground that the agency failed to consider matters "forcefully presented." In fact, here the agency continually invited further clarification of Saginaw's contentions. Even without such clarification it indicated a willingness to receive evidence on the matters. But not only did Saginaw decline to further focus its contentions, it virtually declined to participate, indicating that it had "no conventional findings of fact to set forth" and that it had not "chosen to search the record and respond to this proceeding by submitting citations of matter which we believe were proved or disproved."

We also think the court seriously mischaracterized the Commission's "threshold test" as placing "heavy substantive burdens . . . on intervenors . . .." On the contrary, the Commission explicitly stated:

> "We do not equate this burden with the civil litigation concept of a prima facie case, an unduly heavy burden in this setting. But the showing should be sufficient to require reasonable minds to inquire further."

We think this sort of agency procedure well within the agency's discretion.

In sum, to characterize the actions of the Commission as "arbitrary or capricious" in light of the facts then available to it as described at length above, is to deprive those words of any meaning. * * *

We have also made it clear that the role of a court in reviewing the sufficiency of an agency's consideration of environmental factors is a limited one, limited both by the time at which the decision was made and by the statute mandating review.

"Neither the statute nor its legislative history contemplates that a court should substitute its judgment for that of the agency as to the environmental consequences of its actions." *Kleppe v. Sierra Club,* 427 U.S. at 410 n.21 (1976).

We think the Court of Appeals has forgotten that injunction here and accordingly its judgment in this respect must also be reversed.

B

Finally, we turn to the Court of Appeals' holding that the Licensing Board should have returned the ACRS report to ACRS for further elaboration, understandable to a layman, of the reference to other problems.

* * *

Again the Court of Appeals has unjustifiably intruded into the administrative process. * * *

* * *

All this leads us to make one further observation of some relevance to this case. To say that the Court of Appeals' final reason for remanding is insubstantial at best is a gross understatement. Consumers Power first applied in 1969 for a construction permit—not even an operating license, just a construction permit. The proposed plant underwent an incredibly extensive review. The reports filed and reviewed literally fill books. The proceedings took years, and the actual hearings themselves over two weeks. To then nullify that effort seven years later because one report refers to other problems, which problems admittedly have been discussed at length in other reports available to the public, borders on the Kafkaesque. Nuclear energy may some day be a cheap, safe source of power or it may not. But Congress has made a choice to at least try nuclear energy, establishing a reasonable review process in which courts are to play only a limited role. The fundamental policy questions appropriately resolved in Congress and in the state legislatures are not subject to reexamination in the federal courts under the guise of judicial review of agency action. Time may prove wrong the decision to develop nuclear energy, but it is Congress or the States within their appropriate agencies which must eventually make that judgment. In the meantime courts should perform their appointed function. NEPA does set forth significant substantive goals for the Nation, but its mandate to the agencies is essentially procedural. It is to insure a fully informed and well-considered decision, not necessarily a decision the judges of the Court of Appeals or of this Court would have reached had they been members of the decisionmaking unit of the agency. Administrative decisions should be set aside in this context, as in every other, only for substantial procedural or substantive reasons as mandated by statute, not simply because the court is unhappy with the result reached. And a single alleged oversight on a peripheral issue, urged by parties who never fully cooperated or indeed raised the issue below, must not be made the basis for overturning a decision properly made after an otherwise exhaustive proceeding.

Reversed and remanded.

NOTES

1. Why does the Court reject Saginaw's claim that the agency should have considered "energy conservation" as an alternative to building the proposed nuclear power plant? Was "energy conservation" a reasonable alternative? Consider this in regard to recent actions by Southern California Edison to distribute energy-saving, high-efficiency light bulbs at substantial discounts to its customers in order to reduce demand for electricity rather than build new power plants. Michael Parrish, *Homes, Businesses Plug in to Savings on Power Costs*, L.A. TIMES, Mar. 27, 1991, at A1. Pacific Gas and Electric has 30 programs to help customers increase their energy efficiency, and "expects to meet three-quarters of its new energy demand in the next decade through conservation." *Id*. The CEQ regulations now provide that the description of environmental consequences contained in an EIS include a discussion of "[e]nergy requirements and conservation potential of various alternatives and mitigation measures." 40 C.F.R. § 1502.16(e).

2. The Court notes that "the agency continually invited clarification of Saginaw's contentions [that energy conservation was a reasonable alternative.]" 435 U.S. 519 at 554. One might argue that the agency had the responsibility to investigate this issue, not Saginaw. Indeed, one of Saginaw's claims was that the company involved, Consumers Power, had stimulated electrical demand through its advertising. Surely this was a subject that could most easily have been investigated by the agency. Still, as a practical matter, courts have come to expect more of citizen groups than Saginaw offered here. Many groups now hire their own cadre of technical experts and lawyers to assist in cases like this. How difficult would it have been for Saginaw to find support for its arguments regarding energy conservation in 1972, when the EIS was prepared? Assuming it did not have the expertise on its staff, where might a small organization with a meager budget look for assistance?

3. The failure of an organization to file comments and otherwise participate in an administrative process may be grounds for denying that plaintiff an opportunity to seek judicial review. *Compare Nader v. Nuclear Regulatory Comm'n*, 513 F.2d 1045, 1055 (D.C. Cir. 1975) ("those who refrain from participation in rulemaking proceedings may not obtain direct judicial review of the regulations resulting"), *with Natural Resources Defense Council v. U.S. EPA*, 824 F.2d 1146, 1150-52 (D.C. Cir. 1987) (excusing plaintiff from the requirement of raising an issue before the agency where the agency in fact did consider the issue). *See also Atlantic Terminal Urban Renewal Area Coalition v. New York City Department of Environmental Protection*, 740 F. Supp. 989, 992 (S.D.N.Y. 1990) ("[A] number of courts, when confronted with untimely challenges to an EIS, have chosen nevertheless to evaluate the merits of those challenges, which often implicate important public interests, and to consider the plaintiffs' failure to raise the objections earlier as a factor in evaluating those objections."). How important is it that lawyers be involved in these administrative proceedings? Do you think it likely that Saginaw had anticipated that its case would wind up before the U.S. Supreme Court when it filed its comments on the draft EIS in this case?

4. How does NEPA facilitate public participation in agency decisionmaking? The CEQ regulations provide detailed suggestions and mandates for agencies engaged in NEPA compliance. 40 C.F.R. § 1506.6. *See also* 40 C.F.R. § 1501.7 (inviting the participation of interested persons in an open scoping process). The ESA § 7 consultation rules do not afford the public comparable opportunities to participate in the requisite environmental analyses. Why not?

5. One of the most effective times for public participation in the NEPA process is during "scoping." Scoping is defined as "an early and open process for determining the scope of issues to be addressed and for identifying the significant issues related to a proposed action." 40 C.F.R. § 1501.7. In addition to determining the "scope" of an EIS scoping is intended to help the action agency decide, among other things, (1) the significant issues to be analyzed in depth; and (2) which issues are not significant or have previously been analyzed so that the EIS will not have to address them in depth. During scoping agencies typically decide which alternatives to consider and which to eliminate from detailed consideration. Thus, effective public participation during scoping can dramatically impact the development of an EIS. *See generally* Joseph Feller, *Public Participation Under NEPA, in* THE NEPA LITIGATION GUIDE (Karin Sheldon & Mark Squillace, eds, 1999).

6.   The CEQ occasionally publishes guidance to federal agencies that clarifies issues not resolved by the 1978 regulations. The most frequently cited guidance is "Forty Most Asked Questions Concerning CEQ's NEPA Regulations," published after a series of implementation meetings held with federal agencies. 46 Fed. Reg. 18,026 (1981), *amended* 51 Fed. Reg. 15,618 (1986). The text of this guidance document is included in your supplement. Other guidance may be found at 48 Fed. Reg. 34,263 (1983). Are courts bound by the CEQ's interpretation of its own NEPA regulations? Read the questions and answers for questons 1a., 1b., 2a., and 2b. (included in your supplement) before reading the following case.

CITIZENS AGAINST BURLINGTON, INC. V. BUSEY
938 F.2d 190 (D.C. Cir. 1991), *cert. denied,* 502 U.S. 994 (1991)

CLARENCE THOMAS, Circuit Judge:

The city of Toledo decided to expand one of its airports, and the Federal Aviation Administration decided to approve the city's plan. In this petition for review of the FAA's order, an alliance of people who live near the airport contends that the FAA has violated several environmental statutes and regulations. We hold that the FAA has complied with all of the statutes and all but one of the regulations.

I.

The Toledo Express Airport, object of the controversy in this case, lies about twenty-five miles to the west of downtown Toledo. Half a mile to the southwest of the airport, surrounded by four highways and intersected by three more, lies the Oak Openings Preserve Metropark, used by joggers, skiers, and birders, and site of one of the world's twelve communities of oak savannas. Within Oak Openings lies the Springbrook Group Camp, site of a primitive (tents only) campground, and used by hikers and campers, including Richard Van Landingham III, one of the petitioners in this lawsuit. Near the airport live Daniel Kasch, Carol Vaughan, and Professor William Reuter, three of the other petitioners. The Toledo-Lucas County Port Authority, one of the intervenors, wants to make the city of Toledo a cargo hub. Burlington Air Express, Inc., the other intervenor, wants to move its operations to Toledo. Kasch, Vaughan, Reuter, Van Landingham, and others have formed Citizens Against Burlington, Inc. to stop them.

Citizens Against Burlington first materialized about a year after the Port Authority first commissioned an "Airport Noise Compatibility Planning" study (known as a "Part 150 study," *see generally* 14 C.F.R. pt. 150 & apps. A & B) and began to consider the possibility of the airport's expansion. The Port Authority soon heard from Burlington Air Express, which had been flying its planes out of an old World War II hangar at Baer Field, an Air National Guard airport in Fort Wayne. After looking at seventeen sites in four midwestern states, Burlington chose the Toledo Express Airport. Among Burlington's reasons were the quality of Toledo's work force and the airport's prior operating record, zoning advantages, and location (near major highways and close to Detroit and Chicago). For its part, the Port Authority expects the new hub to create one thousand new jobs in metropolitan Toledo and to contribute almost $68 million per year to the local economy after three years of the hub's operation. The Port Authority plans to pay for the new hub with both private and public funds. Much of the money, however, will come from user fees and lease agreements, and more than half will come from local bonds issued to private investors. Grants from the city of Toledo and the state of Ohio will make up another, much smaller portion of the costs. The Port Authority has applied for some federal funds as well, but the FAA has reacted coolly to the Port Authority's feelers.

* * *

On May 11, 1990, the FAA published a final environmental impact statement. The first chapter of the statement explained that the Port Authority needed the FAA's approval for its plan to expand the Toledo Express Airport and described the role in that process that Congress meant for the agency to play. The second chapter of the EIS reviewed the particulars of the Port Authority's plan, listed the fourteen separate federal statutes and regulations that applied to the Port Authority's proposal, briefly described some alternatives to acting on the Port Authority's plan, and explained why the agency had decided not to discuss those possibilities more fully. The FAA then concluded that it had to consider in depth the environmental impacts of only two alternatives: the approval of the Port Authority's plan to expand the airport, and no action. The third chapter of the EIS described the environment affected by the proposal, and the fourth chapter detailed the environmental consequences of the two alternatives. After summarizing the environmental impacts in the fifth chapter, the agency listed in the sixth chapter the statement's preparers. Appendices to the statement collected scientific data and relevant inter-agency correspondence. In the second volume of the statement, the FAA compiled copies of the hundreds of letters concerning the draft EIS, a transcript of the public hearing, and written comments submitted after the hearing had ended.

* * *

II.

* * *

The problem for agencies is that "the term 'alternatives' is not self-defining." *Vermont Yankee Nuclear Power Corp. v. Natural Resources Defense Council, Inc.*, 435 U.S. 519, 551 (1978). Suppose, for example, that a utility applies for permission to build a nuclear reactor in Vernon, Vermont. Free-floating "alternatives" to the proposal for federal action might conceivably include everything from licensing a reactor in Pecos, Texas, to promoting imports of hydropower from Quebec. If the Nuclear Regulatory Commission had to discuss these and other imaginable courses of action, its statement would wither into "frivolous boilerplate," *id.*, if indeed the agency were to prepare an EIS at all and not instead just deny the utility a permit. If, therefore, the consideration of alternatives is to inform both the public and the agency decisionmaker, the discussion must be moored to "some notion of feasibility." *Vermont Yankee*, 435 U.S. at 551, 98 S. Ct. at 1215; *see id.* ("Common sense also teaches us that the 'detailed statement of alternatives' cannot be found wanting simply because the agency failed to include every device and thought conceivable by the mind of man.").

Recognizing the harm that an unbounded understanding of alternatives might cause, CEQ regulations oblige agencies to discuss only alternatives that are feasible, or (much the same thing) reasonable. 40 C.F.R. §§ 1502.14(a)-(c), 1508.25(b)(2); *see* Forty Most Asked Questions

Concerning CEQ's NEPA Regulations, 46 Fed.Reg. 18,026, 18,026 (1981) [hereinafter Forty Questions]. But the adjective "reasonable" is no more self-defining than the noun that it modifies. Consider two possible alternatives to our nuclear reactor in Vernon. Funding research in cold fusion might be an unreasonable alternative by virtue of the theory's scientific implausibility. But licensing a reactor in Lake Placid, New York might also be unreasonable, even though it passes some objective test of scientific worth. In either case, the proposed alternative is reasonable only if it will bring about the ends of the federal action—only if it will do what the licensing of the reactor in Vernon is meant to do. If licensing the Vernon reactor is meant to help supply energy to New England, licensing a reactor in northern New York might make equal sense. If licensing the Vernon reactor is meant as well to stimulate the Vernon job market, licensing a reactor in Lake Placid would be far less effective. The goals of an action delimit the universe of the action's reasonable alternatives.

* * *

We realize, as we stated before, that the word "reasonable" is not self-defining. Deference, however, does not mean dormancy, and the rule of reason does not give agencies license to fulfill their own prophecies, whatever the parochial impulses that drive them. Environmental impact statements take time and cost money. Yet an agency may not define the objectives of its action in terms so unreasonably narrow that only one alternative from among the environmentally benign ones in the agency's power would accomplish the goals of the agency's action, and the EIS would become a foreordained formality. Nor may an agency frame its goals in terms so unreasonably broad that an infinite number of alternatives would accomplish those goals and the project would collapse under the weight of the possibilities.

* * *

In the second chapter of the environmental impact statement, the FAA begins by stating:

> The scope of alternatives considered by the sponsoring Federal agency, where the Federal government acts as a proprietor, is wide ranging and comprehensive. Where the Federal government acts, not as a proprietor, but to approve and support a project being sponsored by a local government or private applicant, the Federal agency is necessarily more limited. In the latter instance, the Federal government's consideration of alternatives may accord substantial weight to the preferences of the applicant and/or sponsor in the siting and design of the project.

* * *

The FAA's reasoning fully supports its decision to evaluate only the preferred and do-nothing alternatives. The agency first examined Congress's views on how this country is to build its civilian airports. As the agency explained, Congress has told the FAA to nurture aspiring cargo hubs. At the same time, however, Congress has also said that the free market, not an ersatz Gosplan for aviation, should determine the siting of the nation's airports. Congress has expressed its intent by statute, and the FAA took both of Congress's messages seriously.

The FAA also took into account the Port Authority's reasons for wanting a cargo hub in Toledo. In recent years, more than fifty major companies have left the Toledo metropolitan area, and with them, over seven thousand jobs. The Port Authority expects the cargo hub at Toledo Express to create immediately more than two hundred permanent and six hundred part-time jobs with a total payroll value of more than $10 million. * * * All of those factors, the Port Authority hopes, will lead to a renaissance in the Toledo metropolitan region.

Having thought hard about these appropriate factors, the FAA defined the goal for its action as helping to launch a new cargo hub in Toledo and thereby helping to fuel the Toledo economy. The agency then eliminated from detailed discussion the alternatives that would not accomplish this goal. Each of the different geometric configurations would mean technological problems and extravagant costs. So would plans to route traffic differently at Toledo Express, or to build a hub at one of the other airports in the city of Toledo. None of the airports outside of the Toledo area would serve the purpose of the agency's action. The FAA thus evaluated the environmental impacts of the only proposal that might reasonably accomplish that goal—approving the construction and operation of a cargo hub at Toledo Express. It did so with the thoroughness required by law. *See* 40 C.F.R. § 1502.16.[7]

We conclude that the FAA acted reasonably in defining the purpose of its action, in eliminating alternatives that would not achieve it, and in discussing (with the required do-nothing option) the proposal that would. The agency has therefore complied with NEPA.

Citizens agrees that the FAA need only discuss reasonable, not all, alternatives to Toledo Express. Relying on *Van Abbema v. Fornell,* 807 F.2d 633 (7th Cir. 1986), however, Citizens argues that "the evaluation of 'alternatives' mandated by NEPA is to be an evaluation of alternative means to accomplish the general goal of an action; it is not an evaluation of the alternative means by which a particular applicant can reach his goals." *Id.* at 638 (construing NEPA § 102(2)(E), 42 U.S.C. § 4332(2)(E)). According to Citizens, the "general goal" of the Port Authority's proposal is to build a permanent cargo hub for Burlington. Since, in Citizens' view, Fort Wayne (and perhaps Peoria) will accomplish this general goal just as well as Toledo, if not better, Baer Field is a reasonable alternative to Toledo Express, and the FAA should have discussed it in depth. Since it did not, this court should force the FAA to prepare a new (or supplemental) environmental impact statement.

We see two critical flaws in *Van Abbema,* and therefore in Citizens' argument. The first is that the *Van Abbema* court misconstrued the language of NEPA. *Van Abbema* involved a private businessman who had applied to the Army Corps of Engineers for permission to build a place to "transload" coal from trucks to barges. *See* 807 F.2d at 635. The panel decided that the Corps had to survey "feasible alternatives . . . to the applicant's proposal," or alternative ways of accomplishing "the general goal [of] deliver[ing] coal from mine to utility." *Id.* at 638; *see also Trout Unlimited v. Morton,* 509 F.2d 1276, 1286 (9th Cir. 1974). In commanding agencies to discuss "alternatives to the proposed action," however, NEPA plainly refers to

---

[7]   Judge Buckley maintains that the FAA, having decided to discuss the socioeconomic impacts of inaction in Toledo on Toledo, was obliged then in its "No Action" section to discuss the socioeconomic impacts of inaction in Toledo on Fort Wayne. As Judge Buckley's dissent reveals, information concerning Fort Wayne's economy is already available for consumption elsewhere in the EIS. [Citation omitted.] In any event, the FAA also discussed the (beneficial) environmental effects of inaction in Toledo on Toledo, so one can infer that it should have discussed the (presumably negative) environmental effects of inaction in Toledo on Fort Wayne. Because Toledo's loss would be many other cities' potential gain, moreover, there would be no reason to limit the FAA's discussion to Fort Wayne: Indeed, one can infer that the FAA should have discussed the socioeconomic and environmental impacts of inaction in Toledo on Peoria, Akron, Detroit, and every other site assessed by Burlington's consultant. The EIS demonstrates that the discussion of the socioeconomic and environmental impacts of inaction is the flip side of the discussion of the impacts of action. If, for example, the FAA were to approve the Port Authority's application, Toledo would lose environmentally but gain socioeconomically, and Peoria and Fort Wayne and the other cities would lose socioeconomically but gain environmentally. If the FAA were to reject the Port Authority's application, Toledo would remain somewhat quieter but lose some jobs, and either Peoria (or another city) might gain noise along with jobs or Fort Wayne might retain some of both. But the FAA was not obliged to discuss the environmental or socioeconomic impacts of approving airport expansions in Peoria or Fort Wayne or any of the other cities: None, as we have explained, would have fulfilled the goal of the agency's action, and all were therefore unreasonable and beyond the scope of the FAA's responsibilities. The upshot of Judge Buckley's approach, it seems to us, would be to force an agency to discuss the socioeconomic and environmental impacts of even unreasonable alternatives—to do the very thing in the section on the do-nothing alternative that the agency need not do in the statement's main body.

alternatives to the "major *Federal* actions significantly affecting the quality of the human environment," and not to alternatives to the applicant's proposal. NEPA § 102(2)(C), 42 U.S.C. § 4332(2)(C) (emphasis added). An agency cannot redefine the goals of the proposal that arouses the call for action; it must evaluate alternative ways of achieving its goals, shaped by the application at issue and by the function that the agency plays in the decisional process. Congress did expect agencies to consider an applicant's wants when the agency formulates the goals of its own proposed action. Congress did not expect agencies to determine for the applicant what the goals of the applicant's proposal should be.

The second problem with *Van Abbema* lies in the court's assertion that an agency must evaluate "alternative means to accomplish the general goal of an action," 807 F.2d at 638 (emphasis deleted)—a statement that troubles us even if we assume that the panel was alluding to the general goals of the federal action instead of to the goals of the private proposal. Left unanswered in *Van Abbema* and Citizens' brief (and at oral argument) is why and how to distinguish general goals from specific ones and just who does the distinguishing. Someone has to define the purpose of the agency action. Implicit in *Van Abbema* is that the body responsible is the reviewing court. As we explained, however, NEPA and binding case law provide otherwise.

In chiding this court for having overreached in construing NEPA, a unanimous Supreme Court once wrote that Congress enacted NEPA "to ensure a fully informed and well-considered decision, not necessarily a decision the judges of the Court of Appeals or of this Court would have reached had they been members of the decisionmaking unit of the agency." *Vermont Yankee,* 435 U.S. at 558. We are forbidden from taking sides in the debate over the merits of developing the Toledo Express Airport; we are required instead only to confirm that the FAA has fulfilled its statutory obligations. Events may someday vindicate Citizens' belief that the FAA's judgment was unwise. *See id.* at 557-58. All that this court decides today is that the judgment was not uninformed. *See Methow Valley,* 490 U.S. at 351.

* * *

BUCKLEY, Circuit Judge, dissenting in part:

Burlington Air Express and the Federal Aviation Administration might be right: On substantial economic and environmental balance, Toledo Express Airport may well be the only suitable site for Burlington's air cargo hub. The public cannot know for certain, however, and neither can the FAA. By refusing to inquire into the feasibility of sites rejected by Burlington, the agency sidestepped its obligation to prepare "a detailed statement . . . on . . . alternatives to the proposed action." 42 U.S.C. § 4332(2)(C) (1988). The majority endorses this evasion. I cannot, and therefore I dissent from part II(A) of the majority opinion. While "the concept of 'alternatives' is an evolving one," *Vermont Yankee Nuclear Power Corp. v. NRDC,* 435 U.S. 519, 552 (1978), judicial evolution may not reduce it to a vermiform appendix.

I.

* * *

The majority would limit the consideration of alternatives to those available to the Toledo-Lucas County Port Authority. As the majority sees it, the FAA "defined the goal for its action as helping to launch a new cargo hub in Toledo and thereby helping to fuel the Toledo economy." As a consequence, airports outside the Toledo area were not to be considered because "[n]one . . . would serve the purpose of the agency's action." I read the EIS differently. Recognizing that Burlington is an essential party to the Port Authority's application, the FAA understands that the EIS must consider any reasonable alternative to Toledo Express Airport that might be available to Burlington, whether it lies within the Toledo area or outside it.

* * *

I cannot fault the FAA for the attention given Burlington and its preferences. While both Toledo and Burlington are indispensable to the enterprise, Burlington is plainly the dominant partner; its requirements and desires shaped the project from the start. * * *

I do fault the agency for failing to attend to its own business, which is to examine all alternatives "that are practical or feasible from the technical and economic standpoint . . . rather than simply desirable from the standpoint of the applicant." Forty Most Asked Questions Concerning CEQ's National Environmental Policy Act Regulations ("Forty Questions"), 46 Fed. Reg. 18,026, 18,027 (1981) (emphasis omitted). As far as I can tell, the FAA never questioned Burlington's assertions that of the ones considered, Toledo Express is the only airport suitable to its purposes. Instead, the agency simply accepted Burlington's "Toledo-or-bust" position. Thus, the EIS notes that Burlington hired consultants to help it choose a new hub site, and that the consultants prepared a confidential report. The impact statement fails to summarize the report; indeed, it does not say whether Burlington made the document available to the FAA. The EIS reports that a letter from the consultants demonstrates that Burlington's Toledo decision rests on "legitimate business interests." Of Burlington's decision to leave Fort Wayne, the FAA's Record of Decision similarly declares: "This is a business decision on the part of Burlington, in which the FAA has not been involved." The FAA thus accepts at face value Burlington's assertion that it had no second choice.

* * *

I do not suggest that Burlington is untrustworthy, only that the FAA had the duty under NEPA to exercise a degree of skepticism in dealing with self-serving statements from a prime beneficiary of the project. It may well be that none of the sixteen other alternatives examined by Burlington and its consultants could be converted into a viable air cargo hub at acceptable cost. That, however, was something that the FAA should have determined for itself instead of accepting as a given. * * *

* * *

II.

Even if the FAA had correctly concluded that the only reasonable alternative was "No Action," its EIS would still be flawed. By viewing the no-action alternative exclusively through Toledo's eyes, it failed to appreciate that that city's gains must necessarily be Fort Wayne's losses. Thus the EIS informs us that whereas the proposed project would produce 750 new jobs and $17 million for the Toledo economy during the first full year of operation, "the no-action alternative would mean foregoing . . . [these] economic benefits."

This analysis suggests that the jobs and dollars will arise spontaneously from the Toledo soil. In reality, Toledo's gains will come at Fort Wayne's expense. * * *

* * *

NOTES

1. Judge (now Justice) Thomas distinguishes cases where a federal agency acts as a proprietor, itself engaging in a land disturbing action, from cases, such as *Citizens Against*

Burlington, where a federal agency's role is simply to approve or disapprove a project of a private applicant. What is the legal basis for this distinction? *See* DANIEL R. MANDELKER, NEPA LAW AND LITIGATION § 9.05[7] (2d ed. 1992) (calling the dual standard for private and public projects set out in a different case an incorrect interpretation of NEPA). Is the distinction consistent with 40 C.F.R. § 1502.14 or Q.2a. from the CEQ Forty Questions guidance? Are there situations where it is important to distinguish the role of an agency as proprietor from its role as regulator?

2.   Is the CEQ Forty Questions guidance binding on federal agencies? On courts? *See Friends of the Earth v. Hintz*, 800 F.2d 822, 837 n.15 (9th Cir. 1986).

3.   What is the proper scope of alternatives? Is it the range of ways to achieve the general goal of an action, as argued by the plaintiffs? Or, is it the available means by which an applicant can reach its goals? Should the FAA have examined alternative means of:

    (a) sparking economic development for Toledo;

    (b) creating a new cargo hub in the midwestern United States;

    (c) creating a new cargo hub at Toledo Express Airport;

    (d) siting a new cargo hub for Burlington?

What role, if any, should the statutory mission of the FAA play in determining the scope of alternatives?

4.   Peter J. Kirsch and Conrad M. Rippy, *Defining the Scope of Alternatives in an EIS After* Citizens Against Burlington, 21 ENVTL. L. REP. 10701 (1991), criticize the court's reasoning but ultimately defend the outcome of *Citizens Against Burlington* because the scope of the alternatives was consistent with the agency's weak but unchallenged statement of need.

5.   The *Citizens Against Burlington* court criticizes the Seventh Circuit's rule in *Van Abbema* requiring that agencies explore alternative ways of achieving the general goal of an action. *Van Abbema v. Fornell*, 807 F.2d 633 (7th Cir. 1986). Does *Van Abbema* ask too much of an agency that must process hundreds of applications annually? How might programmatic EISs help? Would your analysis of *Citizens Against Burlington* change if you learned that the FAA had prepared a programmatic EIS discussing the issue of cargo transportation along with an agency plan that identified Toledo as the best choice for a regional hub?

In *Van Abbema*, the Army Corps did not prepare an EIS. The court found that the Corps violated the NEPA § 102(2)(E) requirement to discuss alternatives, not the requirement in § 102(2)(C). Is it possible to reconcile the two cases on this basis?

6.   What should the FWS consider in determining the scope of the reasonable and prudent alternatives it must provide with a jeopardy opinion? *See* 16 U.S.C. § 1536(b)(3)(A) (ESA § 7(b)(3)(A)). The ESA regulations define "reasonable and prudent alternatives" as:

    alternative actions identified during formal consultation that can be implemented in a manner consistent with the intended purpose of the action, that can be implemented consistent with the scope of the Federal agency's legal authority and jurisdiction, that is economically and technologically feasible, and that the [FWS believes would avoid jeopardy].

50 C.F.R. § 402.02. Will the scope of these ESA alternatives be narrower than those considered in the NEPA process? Should they be?

7.   One of the distinguishing features of NEPA is its requirement that the EIS be prepared by the agency responsible for the decision. In most countries with NEPA-like statutes, the EIS or an equivalent document is prepared by the private proponent of the action. How would you expect a proponent-prepared EIS to analyze alternatives? Note that the CEQ regulations allow a private proponent to prepare an EA, although in this case, an agency must make its own evaluation of the environmental issues and take responsibility for the scope and content of the EA. 40 C.F.R. § 1506.5. Furthermore, an independent contractor can prepare an EIS but the contractor must be chosen "solely by the lead agency" and such contractors must execute a disclosure statement "specifying that they have no financial or other interest in the outcome of the project." *Id.*

8.   The following exercise challenges you to integrate this new material on scope of alternatives with the threshold issues discussed *supra* Chapter 6. We recommend working through this exercise as a simulated negotiation between groups of students representing PNP and FIRE.

PROBLEM #4: ALTERNATIVES AND OTHER EIS ISSUES

The National Park Service (NPS) manages the Portal National Park (PNP) in California. The PNP includes the Greenway Unit in the hills that lie to the east of the city of Ashland. Seven years of drought have left the Greenway Unit brown with bone-dry tinder.

In 1993, state park land in the hills south of Ashland caught fire during a dry thunderstorm and seared 100 acres, including the affluent neighborhood of Phlogiston. Although there were no fatalities, 75 people lost their homes in the blaze. Another thunderstorm season is approaching and there is no rain in the long-term forecasts.

The Portal National Park is notoriously underfunded. It has neither the equipment nor the personnel to fight fires. Furthermore, it has always operated on the assumption that nature knows best. The PNP managers do not try to put out wildfires caused by lightning. The ecosystem self-regulates when nature takes its course. The Greenway Unit contains a large number of inholdings of state and private land. The PNP managers do not believe they could suppress fire even if they had adequate resources because they do not have control over surrounding and inheld property.

The residents in the Thorton neighborhood, just downwind from the Greenway Unit, are upset. The thunderstorm season is sure to set some wildfires and Thortonites worry that these blazes may build, escape into their neighborhood, and cause a disaster like the one that hit Phlogiston in 1993. The anxiety level is so high that many residents suffer fatigue from sleepless nights. Many of the young children who watched the Phlogiston conflagration on television are exhibiting abnormally withdrawn behavior. Property values in Thorton are falling and the community organizations are losing members as residents begin to turn elsewhere to build their futures.

In an effort to prevent the unravelling of their community, the residents of Thorton have organized and founded a group called Friends for an Inhabitable Residential Environment (FIRE). FIRE wants the PNP to consider alternatives to its current laissez faire stance toward wildfire. The citizen group is particularly interested in an alternative of total suppression of wildfire. FIRE wants to persuade the PNP to prepare an EIS that addresses the impacts of wildfire on the Thornton community and the psychological well-being of its residents.

What issues are likely to come up as FIRE and PNP attempt to work together on future management for the park unit?

B. Scope of Analysis and Cumulative Impacts

Perhaps the most difficult part of an environmental analysis is deciding how to assess the consequences of a particular proposed alternative. Cumulative impacts may be far removed in space or time from the action that triggers them. Some form of cumulative effects analysis is required under both NEPA and the ESA. But how far should agencies go in exploring sometimes distant and indeterminate synergistic, ripple effects?

As usual, the CEQ regulations for NEPA afford the best starting point for understanding the scope of analysis and cumulative impacts in environmental decisionmaking. Those regulations define "scope" as follows:

Scope consists of the range of actions, alternatives, and impacts to be considered in an environmental impact statement. The scope of an individual statement may depend on its relationships to other statements (§§ 1502.20 and 1508.28). To determine the scope of environmental impact statements, agencies shall consider 3 types of actions, 3 types of alternatives, and 3 types of impacts. They include:
(a) Actions (other than unconnected single actions) which may be:
(1) Connected actions, which means that they are closely related and therefore should be discussed in the same impact statement. Actions are connected if they:
(i) Automatically trigger other actions which may require environmental impact statements.
(ii) Cannot or will not proceed unless other actions are taken previously or simultaneously.
(iii) Are interdependent parts of a larger action and depend on the larger action for their justification.
(2) Cumulative actions, which when viewed with other proposed actions have cumulatively significant impacts and should therefore be discussed in the same impact statement.
(3) Similar actions, which when viewed with other reasonably foreseeable or proposed agency actions, have similarities that provide a basis for evaluating their environmental consequences together, such as common timing or geography. An agency may wish to analyze these actions in the same impact statement. It should do so when the best way to assess adequately the combined impacts of similar actions or reasonable alternatives to such actions is to treat them in a single impact statement.
(b) Alternatives, which include:
(1) No action alternative.
(2) Other reasonable courses of actions.
(3) Mitigation measures (not in the proposed action).
(c) Impacts, which may be:
(1) Direct;
(2) Indirect;
(3) Cumulative.

The CEQ rules further define "cumulative impact" as the impact on the environment which results from the incremental impact of the action when added to other past, present, and reasonably foreseeable future actions regardless of what agency (Federal or non-Federal) or person undertakes such other actions. Cumulative impacts can result from individually minor but collectively significant actions taking place over a period of time. 40 C.F.R. § 1508.7. "Effects" are defined to include:

(a) Direct effects, which are caused by the action and occur at the same time and place; [and]

(b) Indirect effects, which are caused by the action and are later in time or farther removed in distance, but are still reasonably foreseeable. Indirect effects may include growth inducing effects and other effects related to induce changes in the pattern of land use, population density or growth rate, and related effects on air and water and other natural systems, including ecosystems.

Effects and impacts as used in these regulations are synonymous. Effects include ecological (such as the effects on natural resources and on the components, structures, and functioning of affected ecosystems), aesthetic, historic, cultural, economic, social, or health, whether direct, indirect, or cumulative. Effects may also include those resulting from actions which may have both beneficial and detrimental effects, even if on balance the agency believes that the effect will be beneficial.

40 C.F.R. § 1508.8. Of course, as some of the materials below suggest, it may not be self-evident what kinds of impacts or effects are "reasonably foreseeable."

As you work through the material in this subchapter, recognize that the cumulative impacts concept is also important in deciding whether to prepare an EIS (covered in Chapter 6). The CEQ regulations make clear that in deciding whether an action *significantly* affects the environment the action agency must consider both the *context* and *intensity* or severity of the impact. In evaluating intensity the rules require the agency to consider:

Whether the action is related to other actions with individually insignificant but cumulatively significant impacts. Significance exists if it is reasonable to anticipate a cumulatively significant impact on the environment. Significance cannot be avoided by terming an action temporary or by breaking it down into small component parts.

40 C.F.R. § 1508.27(b)(7). Thus, an individual, seemingly insignificant action could become significant and require preparation of an EIS where other related actions may cause cumulatively significant impacts.

As the following excerpt makes clear, the Department of the Interior interprets the scope of analysis for the ESA to be different from the scope of NEPA. Read this memorandum and consider whether you agree with its reasoning.

CUMULATIVE EFFECTS UNDER THE ENDANGERED SPECIES ACT
U.S. DEPARTMENT OF THE INTERIOR, OFFICE OF THE SOLICITOR
AUGUST 27, 1981

MEMORANDUM

To: Director, Fish and Wildlife Service

From: Associate Solicitor, Conservation and Wildlife

Subject: Cumulative Effects to be Considered Under Section 7 of the Endangered Species Act

This memorandum sets forth the legal requirements for consideration by federal agencies of the "cumulative effects" of other projects and impacts in determining whether a particular proposed action complies with section 7(a) of the Endangered Species Act (ESA or Act), 16 U.S.C. § 1536(a). The Solicitor has now withdrawn all prior legal opinions[1] on cumulative impacts and section 7. This memorandum shall control the scope of consultation and cumulative impact analysis under the Endangered Species Act.

Section 7 requires all federal agencies, in consultation with the Fish and Wildlife Service (FWS or Service), to insure that their actions are not likely to jeopardize the continued existence of endangered or threatened species, or adversely modify their critical habitats. The Service consults with federal agencies and renders a biological opinion on the effects of agency action upon listed species, pursuant to section 7(b), 16 U.S.C. § 1536(b).

Consideration of the legal requirements for cumulative effects analysis arose in 1978, as the result of section 7 consultations for two water development projects on the North and South Platte Rivers: the Grayrocks Dam and the Narrows Project. As proposed, both projects would affect downstream flows in the Big Bend area of the Platte River in Nebraska, an area designated as critical habitat for the whooping crane. During these consultations, the Service requested a Solicitor's Opinion on whether section 7 requires consideration of the effects of other water projects in the area which were then in the planning or construction phases, would affect the crane's habitat, and would have impacts which might be cumulative to those of the proposal at hand.

An opinion issued on July 19, 1978, concluded that federal agencies must consider the cumulative effects of other projects, whether federal, state or private, during consultations under section 7. Although the July 19 opinion did not expressly define the term "cumulative effects", a July 24, 1978, opinion stated that for any ecosystem upon which an endangered or threatened species depends, all pending project impacts must be considered if those impacts can reasonably be anticipated to occur either before or after the completion of the project which is the subject of consultation.

For the reasons that follow, the definition of cumulative effects used in these prior opinions is inappropriate when applied to section 7.

---

[1]   85 Interior Dec. 275 (July 19, 1978) (supplemented July 24, 1978). * * *

Consideration of Cumulative Effects Under Section 7

The previous Solicitor's Opinions used concepts developed in NEPA law[2] which should not be applied, without modification, to section 7 consultations. The first reason is that the *substantive* consequences of requiring such cumulative effects to be considered under section 7 differ from the *procedural* consequences of environmental planning statutes such as NEPA. Section 7 is a substantive statute which provides:

> Each federal agency shall, in consultation with and with the assistance of the Secretary [of the Interior or Commerce], insure that any action authorized, funded or carried out by such agency . . . is not likely to jeopardize the continued existence of any endangered species or threatened species or result in the destruction or adverse modification of habitat of such species which is determined by the Secretary, after consultation as appropriate with the affected States, to be critical. . . .

16 U.S.C. § 1536(a)(2). The Supreme Court, in interpreting a slightly different, earlier version of section 7, has noted the difference from NEPA:

> NEPA essentially imposes a procedural requirement on agencies, requiring them to engage in an extensive *inquiry* as to the effect of federal actions on the environment; by way of contrast, [section 7 of] the 1973 Act is substantive in effect, designed to *prevent* the loss of any endangered species, regardless of the cost.

Tennessee Valley Authority v. Hill, 437 U.S. 153, 188 n.34 (1978) (Emphasis in original).

A wholesale adoption of the cumulative effects approach under NEPA is thus inappropriate because prerequisite authority for a proposed action subject to consultation could be denied because of the effects of other speculative and unrelated future actions which might be likely to jeopardize a listed species. This substantive result is quite different from that under planning statutes such an NEPA, where an analysis of the cumulative effects of other unrelated future actions means only that such effects be *considered* before proceeding with the proposed action undergoing environmental review. *See, Natural Resources Defense Council v. Calloway*, 524 F.2d 79 (2d Cir. 1979).

The second reason for not adopting NEPA's approach to cumulative effects analysis under section 7 is that all other *future federal* actions will themselves be subject to the restraints of section 7 at some later date. It is, therefore, more appropriate to consider the effects of future federal actions in a given area at the time consultation under section 7 is initiated for those actions. That is, the impact of future federal projects should be addressed sequentially, rather than collectively, since each must be capable at some point of individually satisfying the standards of section 7. Thus for federal projects, section 7 provides a "first-in-time, first-in-right" process whereby the authorization of federal projects may proceed until it is determined that further actions are likely to jeopardize the continued existence of a listed species or adversely modify its critical habitat. Environmental planning statutes such as NEPA do not impose such substantive limitations on future federal conduct, and so it is more appropriate for

---

[2]   The Council on Environmental Quality regulations implementing the National Environmental Policy Act (NEPA), 42 U.S.C. § 4332(2)(C), define the term "cumulative impact" as—

the impact on the environment which results from the incremental impact of the action when added to other past, present, and reasonably foreseeable future actions regardless of what agency (Federal or non-Federal) or person undertakes such other actions. Cumulative impacts can result from individually minor but collectively significant actions taking place over a period of time.

40 CFR 1508.7 (1980).

them to require the collective consideration of reasonably foreseeable, future federal activities. The substantive nature of section 7, however, suggests that a project-by-project sequential review of federal actions is a more appropriate approach for endangered species consultation.

A recent case which considered NEPA and the ESA side by side in a given factual situation implicitly recognized different approaches for cumulative impact analysis under NEPA and the ESA, requiring broad agency consideration of cumulative impacts under NEPA while focusing on a more limited analysis of impacts under section 7.

In *North Slope Borough v. Andrus*, 486 F. Supp. 332 (D.D.C. 1980), *rev'd. on other grounds*, 642 F.2d 589 (D.C. Cir. 1980), the court considered NEPA and ESA compliance for offshore oil and gas leasing. Both the district and appeals courts held that the cumulative effects of "other significant Federal and state energy development projects . . . in progress and planned for the North Slope Region," had to be considered in the EIS. 486 F. Supp. at 347; 642 F.2d at 600. The cumulative effects of these other actions, however, were not mentioned by either court in their discussion of the proper scope of agency review under section 7. Instead, for section 7 purposes, the courts only focused on the impacts of the lease sale itself. 486 F. Supp. at 350-51; 642 F.2d at 608-09. Thus, though both courts required consideration of the cumulative effects of unrelated future state and federal actions for purposes of NEPA, each implicitly endorsed a more limited review of the leasing proposal under section 7.

Section 7 Consultation Process

Having concluded that limited analysis of cumulative effects is required under section 7, we will now discuss how that analysis should occur.

Obviously the first task in consultation is to define the scope of the project under review. In the case of construction activities, a "project" is both the proposed activity itself and any "connected" activity as well. Connected activities are those which are related to (interrelated) or dependent upon (interdependent) a proposed project. Interdependent actions are those which have no independent utility apart from the proposed project. Interrelated actions are those which are part of a larger project and cannot proceed unless other actions are taken previously or simultaneously. Thus, in the case of a reservoir project with a proposed lattice work of irrigation canals, in all likelihood the canals would be considered part of the "project" for purposes of section 7 consultation because it is unlikely that they would have any independent utility *but for* the impoundment.

Once the "project" has been defined, the consultation team should then focus on analyzing the environmental baseline in the affected area. This is necessary for determining what the environmental "status quo" is going to be at the time of consultation on the proposed project. The impacts of the project under review should then be measured against this environmental baseline.

In determining the environmental baseline, the consultation team should consider the *past* and *present* impacts of all projects and human activities in the area, regardless of whether they are federal, state or private in nature. This is logical since the actual impacts of these projects and activities are not dependent upon the origin of their sponsorship; rather, they all are contributing influences which mold the present environmental status quo of any given area.

Furthermore, the consultation team should consider as part of the environmental baseline the anticipated impacts of all *proposed* federal projects in the affected area which have previously been the subject of section 7 consultation and received a favorable biological opinion. This is consistent with the "first-in-time, first-in-right" approach discussed earlier, since a project passing muster under section 7 is in effect allocated the right to consume (and is presumed to utilize) a certain portion of the remaining natural resources of the area. It is this "cushion" of remaining natural resources which is available for allocation to projects until the utilization is such that any future use may be likely to jeopardize a listed species or adversely modify or destroy its critical habitat. At this point, any additional federal activity in the area requiring a further consumption of resources would be precluded under section 7.

However, the consultation team should not consider as part of the environmental baseline the anticipated impacts of future federal projects which have not been previously reviewed under section 7. Those projects are not part of the environmental baseline and have not had their priority set under the first-in-time system. They would undergo separate review by the consultation team and could only be authorized if it was subsequently concluded that a sufficient "resource cushion" still remained or if an exemption was granted by the Endangered Species Committee under subsection 7(h) of the ESA.

The impact of state or private actions which are contemporaneous with the consultation in process should also be factored into the environmental baseline for the project area.

Having thus established an environmental baseline, the consultation team must then determine what the *direct* and *indirect* effects of the project under review will be. Such effects must be analyzed as part of the consultation process. *See Tennessee Valley Authority v. Hill*, 439 U.S. 153 (1978); *National Wildlife Federation v. Coleman*, 529 F.2d 1064 (5th Cir. 1976); *See also North Slope Borough v. Andrus*, 486 F. Supp. 332 (D.D.C.), *aff'd in part and rev'd in part*, 642 F.2d 589 (D.C. Cir. 1980).

Finally, the consultation team should consider the "cumulative impacts" of *future* state or private sections where such actions are *reasonably certain* to occur prior to the completion of the federal project. A non-federal action is "reasonably certain" to occur if the action requires the approval of a state or local resource or land use control agency and such agencies have approved the action, and the project is ready to proceed. Other indicators which may also support such a determination include whether the project sponsors provide assurance that action will proceed, whether contracting has been initiated, whether there is obligated venture capital, or whether State or local planning agencies indicate that grant of authority for the action is imminent. These indicators must show more than the possibility that the non-federal project will occur; they must demonstrate with reasonable certainty that it *will occur*. The more that state or local administrative discretion remains to be exercised before a proposed state or private action can proceed, the less there is reasonable certainty that the project will be authorized. In summary, the consultation team should consider only those state or private projects which satisfy all major land use requirements and which appear to be economically viable.

J. Roy Spradley, Jr.

NOTES

1.   Why does the Associate Solicitor's opinion require that consultation encompass future state and private actions that are reasonably certain to occur, but not federal actions that are equally certain to occur?

2.   What is the Associate Solicitor's basis for distinguishing between the scope of NEPA documents and ESA documents? Does the stricter ESA substantive jeopardy standard militate in favor of a narrower scope of analysis for ESA documents? Do you agree with his view that NEPA is a planning statute and the ESA is not?

3.   Should courts apply *Chevron* or *Skidmore* deference to the interpretation of the ESA offered in the Associate Solicitor's memorandum? *See Southern Ute Indian Tribe v.*

Amoco Production Co., 119 F.3d 816 (10th Cir. 1997), *aff'd en banc*, 151 F.3d 1251 (10th Cir. 1998), *rev'd on other grounds, Amoco Production Co. v. Southern Ute Indian Tribe*, 67 U.S.L.W. 4397 (1999).

4. Compare NEPA's scope of analysis of environmental impacts with the consultation requirements of the ESA. Consider, for example, a proposed national forest timber sale that may adversely affect the red-cockaded woodpecker, a listed species. Which of the following matters must be considered in the NEPA document prepared for the sale? Which of the following matters must be considered in the biological assessment and biological opinion prepared pursuant to § 7 of the ESA?

(a) Past and present logging in the vicinity of the proposed sale.
(b) Proposed future timber sales in the vicinity of the proposed sale that have not yet been approved, but that are viable economically only if the proposed sale (which will provide road access) is approved.
(c) New logging roads planned, but not yet approved, in the area to access future timber sales.
(d) A proposed campground on national forest lands in the vicinity of the sale area.
(e) A proposed campground on private lands in the vicinity of the sale area.

5. In 1986, the FWS codified the policy articulated in the Associated Solicitor's opinion in the ESA consultation regulations. *See* 51 Fed. Reg. 19926-20001 (1986); 50 C.F.R. § 402.02 (definitions of "cumulative effects" and "effects of the action").

6. Keith Hammer, an environmental activist in Montana, has criticized the Associate Solicitor's memorandum because it fails to allow planning to modify and prioritize projects before a species reaches the threshold of jeopardy. Keith Hammer, *Triage in the Forest: How the Fish and Wildlife Service Manages Species on the Knife-Edge of Extinction*, FOREST WATCH, Oct. 1992, at 19, 21. Mr. Hammer goes on to describe the "first-come, first-serve" policy as one that illegally waits for the straw that breaks the camel's back. *Id.* Does the Associate Solicitor's memorandum set out an interpretation of ESA § 7(a)(2) that violates § 7(a)(1)? How should NEPA work to avoid the problem that Mr. Hammer poses?

7. What is the relationship between NEPA and the ESA with respect to public participation? Note that while NEPA broadly promotes and encourages public participation (*see, e.g.*, 40 C.F.R. § 1506.6), the ESA and the ESA rules are basically silent on the public's right to participate in the § 7 consultation process. This does not necessarily mean, however, that the public cannot participate effectively in consultation. On the contrary, the CEQ rules, expressly provide that "[t]o the fullest extent possible, agencies shall prepare draft environmental impact statements concurrently with and integrated with environmental surveys and studies required by * * * the Endangered Species Act and other environmental review laws and executive orders." 40 C.F.R. § 1502.25(a). As a practical matter, agencies usually prepare a draft or final biological assessment (BA) required by § 7(c) of the ESA, in conjunction with the draft EIS. The BA is then appended to the draft EIS, and public comments may be offered on the BA, or on the impact of the proposed action on endangered species generally. The action agency is then responsible for assuring that these comments are adequately addressed. Where public comments are allowed on a draft EA, a similar process is generally followed.

CONNER V. BURFORD
848 F.2d 1441 (9th Cir. 1988), *cert. denied*, 489 U.S. 1012

NORRIS, Circuit Judge:

[The background to this case appears in the excerpt in Chapter 6.]

* * *

III
THE ENDANGERED SPECIES ACT ISSUES

Section 7(a)(2) of the ESA, 16 U.S.C. § 1536(a)(2), requires the Secretary of the Interior to ensure that an action of a federal agency is not likely to jeopardize the continued existence of any threatened or endangered species. Section 7(b) sets out a process of consultation whereby the agency with jurisdiction over the protected species issues to the Secretary a "biological opinion" evaluating the nature and extent of jeopardy posed to that species by the agency action. 16 U.S.C. § 1536(b). The agency proposing the action (action agency) must provide the Secretary with "the best scientific and commercial data available." 16 U.S.C. § 1536(a)(2). If the biological opinion concludes that the proposed action is likely to jeopardize a protected species, the action agency must modify its proposal. In addition, section 7(d) forbids "irreversible or irretrievable commitment of resources" during the consultation process.

In this case, the ESA consultation process was triggered when the Forest Service notified the Secretary that the sale of oil and gas leases in the Flathead and Gallatin National Forests, proposed pursuant to the Mineral Leasing Act of 1920 (MLA), 30 U.S.C. § 181 *et seq.,* might affect threatened and endangered species living there, including the grizzly bear, the bald eagle, the peregrine falcon, and the gray wolf. The Secretary, through the FWS, issued biological opinions assessing the environmental effects of the lease sales. The FWS divided the oil and gas activities into stages and addressed the effects of only the leasing stage, concluding that there was "insufficient information available to render a comprehensive biological opinion beyond the initial lease phase." Thus, the biological opinions of the FWS, which concluded that leasing itself was not likely to jeopardize the protected species, did not assess the potential impact that post-leasing oil and gas activities might have on protected species. Rather the FWS opinions relied on "incremental-step consultation," contemplating that additional biological evaluations would be prepared prior to all subsequent activities and that lessees' development proposals would be modified to protect species: "[A]dditional consultation will be required for each of the subsequent phases of oil and gas activities."

The district court rejected the biological opinions because they were limited to the lease sale stage, holding that the FWS "violated ESA by failing to analyze the consequences of all stages of oil and gas activity on the forests." *Conner v. Burford,* 605 F. Supp. at 109. Appellants had argued that various lease stipulations protected the species by allowing for intervention if subsequent oil and gas activities, such as development and production, should threaten to jeopardize species' continued existence. By indicating that the lease issuance could proceed only on the basis of a "comprehensive" biological opinion which considered not only the leasing stage but leasing and all post-leasing activities, the district court effectively held that incremental-step consultation violates the ESA.

Reviewing *de novo* the district court's grant of summary judgment, we will not reverse the FWS' decision to limit the biological opinion to the lease sale stage unless that decision was "arbitrary, capricious, an abuse of discretion, or otherwise not in accordance with law." *Friends of Endangered Species v. Jantzen,* 760 F.2d 976, 981-82 (9th Cir. 1985). On this record, we agree with the district court that the FWS' decision was not in accordance with the law.

A. The Limited Scope of the Biological Opinions

The parties agree that before any leases could be sold, the FWS was required to prepare a biological opinion. *See, e.g. Thomas v. Peterson,* 753 F.2d 754, 763 (9th Cir. 1985) (Forest Service's failure to prepare biological assessment prior to decision to build road violated ESA). The ESA requires that the biological opinion detail "how the *agency action* affects the species or its critical habitat." 16 U.S.C. § 1536(b)(3)(A) (emphasis added). Thus, the scope of the agency action is crucial because the ESA requires the biological opinion to analyze the effect of the entire agency action. *North Slope Borough v. Andrus,* 642 F.2d 589, 608 (D.C. Cir. 1980), *aff'g in part, rev'g in part,* 486 F. Supp. 332 (D.D.C. 1980) (legal adequacy of a "biological opinion" tested by matching the meaning of "agency action" with a legal definition of term). We interpret the term "agency action" broadly. *TVA v. Hill,* 437 U.S. 153, 173 & n.18 (1978). As the District of Columbia Circuit has noted, "[c]aution can only be exercised if the agency takes a look at all the possible ramifications of the agency action." *North Slope,* 642 F.2d at 608 (*quoting North Slope,* 486 F. Supp. at 351).

In *North Slope,* which involved an offshore oil lease sale under the Outer Continental Shelf Lands Act (OCSLA), 43 U.S.C. § 1331 *et seq.,* the District of Columbia Circuit held that the "agency action" encompassed the entire leasing project, from the issuance of the leases through post-leasing development and production: "'[P]umping oil' and not 'leasing tracts' is the aim of congressional [mineral leasing] policy." *North Slope,* 642 F.2d at 608. Following the District of Columbia Circuit, we hold that agency action in this case entails not only leasing but leasing and all post-leasing activities through production and abandonment. Thus, section 7 of the ESA on its face requires the FWS in this case to consider all phases of the agency action, which includes post-leasing activities, in its biological opinion. Therefore the FWS was required to prepare, at the leasing stage, a comprehensive biological opinion assessing whether or not the agency action was likely to jeopardize the continued existence of protected species, based on "the best scientific and commercial data available." 16 U.S.C. § 1536(a)(2).

Both the Flathead and Gallatin biological opinions pay lip service to this statutory duty. Each contains the statement that the "action" being considered "includes not just final lease issuance but all resulting subsequent activities." However, as noted above, both biological opinions concluded that there was insufficient information pertaining to the specific location and extent of post-leasing oil and gas activities to render a comprehensive biological opinion beyond the initial lease stage.

Appellees argue that the FWS failed to prepare biological opinions based on the best data available. We agree. The FWS took the position that there was insufficient information on post-leasing activities to prepare comprehensive biological opinions. Although we recognize that the precise location and extent of future oil and gas activities were unknown at the time, extensive information about the behavior and habitat of the species in the areas covered by the leases was available. For example, appellees point out that three-fourths of the area studied in the forests had been designated "essential" or "occupied" habitat for protected species. Indeed, the environmental assessments prepared by the Forest Service contained detailed information on the behavior and habitats of the species, and discussed the likely impact of various stages of oil and gas activities.

We agree with appellees that incomplete information about post-leasing activities does not excuse the failure to comply with the statutory requirement of a comprehensive biological opinion using the best information available. 16 U.S.C. § 1536(a)(2). With the post-leasing and biological information that was available, the FWS could have determined whether post-leasing activities in particular areas were fundamentally incompatible with the continued existence of the species. Indeed, by recommending the exclusion of areas where leasing would conflict with the conservation of protected species, the FWS implicitly admitted that even minimal exploration and development would be incompatible with the conservation of the species in some areas that can be identified before any agency action is taken. With the information available, the FWS could also have identified potential conflicts between the protected species and post-leasing activities due to the cumulative impact of oil and gas activities. For example, species like the grizzly and the gray wolf require large home ranges making it critical that ESA review occur early in the process to avoid piecemeal chipping away of habitat.

Furthermore, although the FWS justified the decision to delay completing comprehensive biological opinions on the inexact information about post-leasing activities, Congress, in enacting the ESA, did not create an exception to the statutory requirement of a comprehensive biological opinion on that basis. The First Circuit, for example, has recognized that the Secretary may be required to make projections, based on *potential* locations and levels [of] oil and gas activity, of the impact of production on protected species. *See Roosevelt Campobello Int'l Park Comm'n v. EPA*, 684 F.2d 1041, 1052-55 (1st Cir. 1982) (EPA must prepare "real time simulation" studies of low risk oil spills despite the fact that study will only produce informed estimate of potential environmental effects).

In light of the ESA requirement that the agencies use the best scientific and commercial data available to insure that protected species are not jeopardized, 16 U.S.C. § 1536(a)(2), the FWS cannot ignore available biological information or fail to develop projections of oil and gas activities which may indicate potential conflicts between development and the preservation of protected species. We hold that the FWS violated the ESA by failing to use the best information available to prepare comprehensive biological opinions considering all stages of the agency action, and thus failing to adequately assess whether the agency action was likely to jeopardize the continued existence of any threatened or endangered species, as required by section 7(a)(2). To hold otherwise would eviscerate Congress' intent to "give the benefit of the doubt to the species."

B. Incremental-Step Consultation as a Substitute for Comprehensive Biological Opinions

Appellants argue that the ESA's mandate to protect species is satisfied without a comprehensive biological opinion if an incremental-step consultation process is written into the leases. Specifically, appellants argue that the requirements of the ESA are satisfied by Threatened and Endangered Species (T & E) stipulations contained in each lease which provide:

> The Federal surface management agency is responsible for assuring that the leased land is examined prior to undertaking any surface-disturbing activities to determine effects upon any plant or animal species, listed or proposed for listing as endangered or threatened, or their habitats. The findings of this examination may result in some restrictions to the operator's plans or even disallow use and occupancy that would be in violation of the Endangered Species Act of 1973 by detrimentally affecting endangered or threatened species or their habitats.

Appellants reason that the T & E stipulations ensure that there will be adequate environmental review prior to the initiation of any activity which might jeopardize protected species. They argue that since the T & E stipulations reserve to the government the authority to absolutely preclude any activity likely to jeopardize a species, the need for a comprehensive biological opinion at the initial lease phase is obviated.

Appellants ask us, in essence, to carve out a judicial exception to ESA's clear mandate that a comprehensive biological opinion—in this case one addressing the effects of leasing and all post-leasing activities—be completed before initiation of the agency action. They would have us read into the ESA language to the effect that a federal agency may be excused from this requirement if, in its judgment, there is insufficient information available to complete a comprehensive opinion and it takes upon itself incremental-step consultation such as that embodied in the T & E stipulations. We reject this invitation to amend the ESA. That it is the role of Congress, not the courts.

Appellants argue that their position—that an incremental-step consultation process is consistent with the ESA—is supported by *North Slope*. 642 F.2d 589. However, we read *North Slope* as supporting our view that incremental-step consultation does not vitiate the ESA requirement that the Secretary prepare a comprehensive biological opinion. As noted above, the District of Columbia Circuit recognized that the ESA on its face requires that a biological opinion consider the entire agency action and stressed that OCSLA "does not attenuate ESA's notion of 'agency action.'" *Id.* at 609. The court wrestled with the apparent tension between the ESA, which requires that the entire agency action be considered in a biological opinion, and OCSLA, which provides for a segmented approach to offshore oil projects. It concluded that the two statutes were ultimately complementary because the segmented approach of OCSLA, which requires the Secretary to examine the effect of proposed oil leasing, exploration and drilling prior to their separate initiation, ensures "graduated compliance with environmental and endangered life standards." 642 F.2d at 609; *see also Conservation Law Foundation v. Andrus*, 623 F.2d 712 (1st Cir. 1979). In reaching this conclusion, the court explicitly relied on the OCSLA system of "checks and balances." 642 F.2d at 609. As the Supreme Court later noted, these "checks and balances" include careful review by the Secretary of the Interior of all activity carried out pursuant to OCSLA and "specific requirements for consultation with Congress, between federal agencies, or with the States" at every stage. *See Secretary of Interior v. California*, 464 U.S. 312, 337 (1984). These procedural guarantees led the District of Columbia Circuit to conclude that the segmented approach of OCSLA mitigated the ESA requirement that the biological opinion address all phases of the mineral leasing project.

Similarly, appellants also rely on *Village of False Pass v. Clark*, 733 F.2d 605, 609-12 (9th Cir. 1984), *aff'g*, 565 F. Supp. 1123 (D. Alaska 1983) (*False Pass*), another case involving the proposed sale of oil leases under OCSLA, to support their contention that the FWS is not required to prepare comprehensive biological opinions in this case involving lease sales under the MLA. In *False Pass*, although we acknowledged that "agency action" is broadly construed under the ESA, we concluded that the agency action at issue was limited to the sale of leases. *Id.* at 611. We stressed that the Secretary was obligated to comply with the ESA at each stage of development, *id.* at 611 (*citing Conservation Law Foundation v. Andrus*, 623 F.2d 712, 715 (1st Cir. 1979)), and that the regulations promulgated, in part under OCSLA, made the Secretary's plan to assess the impact on marine life prior to each stage of oil development "a real safeguard." *Id.* at 612. We concluded that the requirements of the ESA were satisfied by a biological opinion that was limited to the lease sale and exploration stages. Thus in *False Pass*, as in *North Slope*, we accepted a limited biological opinion on the basis of the complementary relationship between the ESA's requirements and the segmented approach of OCSLA. However, *False Pass* cannot be interpreted as authority that Congress intended to create an across-the-board exception to the ESA's biological opinion requirement.

Appellants argue that *North Slope* and *False Pass* are authority for using a similar segmented approach, "incremental-step consultation," with respect to oil and gas leases issued under the MLA. The MLA, however, contains no system of "checks and balances" similar to OCSLA's. Thus there is no tension between the MLA and the ESA and hence we find no justification to obviate the ESA's congressional mandate that a comprehensive biological opinion be prepared in this case. We reject both *North Slope* and *False Pass* as controlling authority on this issue.

* * *

We conclude that the ESA does not permit the incremental-step approach under the MLA advocated by appellants. The biological opinions must be coextensive with the agency action and T & E stipulations cannot be substituted for comprehensive biological opinions. We therefore hold in this case that before further leasing occurs in the Flathead and Gallatin National Forests and before any further surface-disturbing activities occur on the lands already leased, the FWS must prepare biological opinions assessing the potential impacts of all post-leasing activities.

* * *

We hereby AFFIRM the judgment in part, REVERSE in part, and REMAND with instructions that the district court determine which leases are NSO leases within the meaning of this opinion.

Costs are awarded to appellees.

[The opinion of Judge Wallace, concurring in part and dissenting in part, is omitted.]

NOTES

1.   In that portion of the *Conner* opinion that addresses the NEPA issues (*supra* at Chapter 6), the court allows the agency to defer preparation of the environmental analysis for the oil and gas development stage, so long as the agency included a "no surface occupancy" stipulation in the lease. Regarding ESA compliance, the agency had included in the lease a stipulation which expressly authorized the agency to re-examine leased land prior to surface disturbance activities and to "disallow use and occupancy that was in violation of the ESA" if any listed species or their habitat were threatened. Why was the NSO stipulation sufficient in the context of NEPA, whereas the species stipulation was not sufficient in the context of the ESA? What is the difference between the two stipulations? What must happen before drilling activities begin on a lease with an NSO stipulation? On a lease without an NSO stipulation, but with a species stipulation? Assuming that the species stipulation was re-drafted to operate like the NSO stipulation, how is the scope of the action different in the context of NEPA and the ESA?

2.   Is *Conner* consistent with the Associate Solicitor's opinion, drafted approximately seven years earlier? Is it consistent with the definitions of "cumulative effects" and "effects of the action" in the ESA regulations at 50 C.F.R. § 402.02, promulgated two years before *Conner*?

3.   Incremental ESA compliance is specifically authorized by the ESA regulations subject to certain specified conditions. 50 C.F.R. § 402.14(k). These regulations were promulgated by the FWS at the same time it altered the definition of "cumulative effects." 51 Fed. Reg. 19926-20001 (1986). How much deference should courts accord these agency rules?

4.   Although deference to the expertise of the FWS or NMFS makes it difficult to challenge the content or conclusion of a biological opinion, *Conner* is not unique in remanding a biological opinion for substantive defects. In *Idaho Dep't of Fish & Game v. NMFS*, 850 F. Supp. 886 (D. Or. 1994), a court found arbitrary and capricious a "no jeopardy" opinion issued by the NMFS on federal dam operations on the Columbia and

Snake rivers. The court found fault with the agency's definition of jeopardy, its choice of baseline data, and its failure to consider certain scientific models of extinction.

5. Section 7(d) of the ESA provides that:

[a]fter initiation of consultation * * * [the Federal agency] shall not make any irreversible or irretrievable commitment of resources with respect to the agency action which has the effect of foreclosing the formulation or implementation of any reasonable and prudent alternative measures which would not violate subsection (a)(2) [the jeopardy provision] of this section.

Does the agency's species stipulation at issue in *Conner* violate this provision?

THOMAS V. PETERSON
753 F.2d 754 (9th Cir. 1985)

SNEED, Circuit Judge:

Plaintiffs sought to enjoin construction of a timber road in a former National Forest roadless area. The District Court granted summary judgment in favor of defendant R. Max Peterson, Chief of the Forest Service, and plaintiffs appealed. We affirm in part, reverse in part, and remand for further proceedings consistent with this opinion.

* * *

I.
STATEMENT OF THE CASE

This is another environmental case pitting groups concerned with preserving a specific undeveloped area against an agency of the United States attempting to obey the commands given it by a Congress which is mindful of both environmentalists and those who seek to develop the nation's resources. Our task is to discern as best we can what Congress intended to be done under the facts before us.

Plaintiffs—landowners, ranchers, outfitters, miners, hunters, fishermen, recreational users, and conservation and recreation organizations—challenge actions of the United States Forest Service in planning and approving a timber road in the Jersey Jack area of the Nezperce National Forest in Idaho. The area is adjacent to the Salmon River, a congressionally-designated Wild and Scenic River, and is bounded on the west by the designated Gospel Hump Wilderness and on the east by the River of No Return Wilderness. The area lies in a "recovery corridor" identified by the U.S. Fish & Wildlife Service for the Rocky Mountain Gray Wolf, an endangered species.

The Jersey Jack area was originally part of the larger Gospel Hump roadless area, but when Congress created the Gospel Hump Wilderness in 1978 it did not include the Jersey Jack area. The Forest Service's Roadless Area Review and Evaluation (RARE II) in 1979 recommended that the Jersey Jack area be managed as non-wilderness. (For a discussion of RARE II, *see California v. Block,* 690 F.2d 753, 758 (9th Cir. 1982).) In 1980, Congress passed the Central Idaho Wilderness Act, Pub. L. 96-312, 94 Stat. 948, which created the River of No Return Wilderness to the east of the Jersey Jack area, but left the Jersey Jack area as non-wilderness. The Act stated as one of its purposes to assure that "adjacent lands better suited for multiple uses other than wilderness will be managed by the Forest Service under existing laws and applicable land management plans." 94 Stat. 948.

* * *

After the passage of the Central Idaho Wilderness Act, the Forest Service, in keeping with its earlier expressed intention, proceeded to plan timber development in the Jersey Jack area. In November, 1980, the Forest Service solicited public comments and held a public hearing on a proposed gravel road that would provide access to timber to be sold. The Forest Service prepared an environmental assessment (EA), *see* 40 C.F.R. § 1508.9 (1984), to determine whether an EIS would be required for the road. Based on the EA, the Forest Service concluded that no EIS was required, and issued a Finding of No Significant Impact (FONSI), *see* 40 C.F.R. § 1508.13. The FONSI and the notice of the Forest Supervisor's decision to go ahead with the road were issued in a single document on February 9, 1981. The decision notice stated that "no known threatened or endangered plant or animal species have been found" within the area, but the EA contained no discussion of endangered species.

The EA for the road discussed only the environmental impacts of the road itself; it did not consider the impacts of the timber sales that the road was designed to facilitate. Subsequently, on November 23, 1981, and on June 30, 1982, the Forest Service issued EA's for, and approved, two of the timber sales. An EA for a third timber sale was also issued prior to the commencement of this action in district court. Each EA covered only the effects of a single timber sale; none discussed cumulative impacts of the sales or of the sales and the road. Each EA resulted in a FONSI, and therefore no environmental impact statements were prepared.

The plaintiffs appealed the Forest Supervisor's decision on the road to the Regional Forester, who affirmed the decision on May 26, 1981. The Regional Forester's decision was then appealed to the Chief of the Forest Service, who affirmed the decision on November 24, 1981.

The plaintiffs filed this action, challenging the Chief's decision, on June 30, 1982. Their three principal allegations are:

(1) NEPA, and regulations issued by the Council on Environmental Quality (CEQ), require the Forest Service to prepare an EIS that analyzes the combined effects of the proposed road and the timber sales that the road is designed to facilitate.

* * *

(3) The road is likely to affect the Rocky Mountain Gray Wolf, an endangered species, and the Forest Service has failed to follow procedures mandated by the Endangered Species Act.

After briefing and oral argument, the district court granted summary judgment for the Forest Service on all claims. * * *

II.
THE NEPA CLAIM

The central question that plaintiffs' NEPA claim presents is whether the road and the timber sales are sufficiently related so as to require combined treatment in a single EIS that covers the cumulative effects of the road and the sales. If so, the Forest Service has proceeded improperly. An EIS must be prepared and considered by the Forest Service before the road can be approved. If not, the Forest Service may go ahead with the road, and later consider the environmental impacts of the timber sales.

Section 102(2)(C) of NEPA requires an EIS for "major Federal actions significantly affecting the quality of the human environment." While it is true that administrative agencies must be given considerable discretion in defining the scope of environmental impact statements, *see Kleppe v. Sierra Club,* 427 U.S. 390, 412-15 (1976), there are situations in which an agency is required to consider several related actions in a single EIS, *see id.* at 409-10. Not to require this would permit dividing a project into multiple "actions," each of which individually has an insignificant environmental impact, but which collectively have a substantial impact. *See Alpine Lakes Protection Society v. Schlapfer,* 518 F.2d 1089, 1090 (9th Cir. 1975).

Since the Supreme Court decided the *Kleppe* case, the Council on Environmental Quality (CEQ) has issued regulations that define the circumstances under which multiple related actions must be covered by a single EIS. The regulations are made binding on federal administrative agencies by Executive Order. *See* Exec. Order No. 11991, 3 C.F.R., 1977 Comp. 123 (1978). The CEQ regulations and this court's precedents both require the Forest Service to prepare an EIS analyzing the combined environmental impacts of the road and the timber sales.

A. CEQ Regulations

1. Connected actions

The CEQ regulations require "connected actions" to be considered together in a single EIS. *See* 40 C.F.R. § 1508.25(a)(1) (1984). "Connected actions" are defined, in a somewhat redundant fashion, as actions that

> "(i) Automatically trigger other actions which may require environmental impact statements.
>
> (ii) Cannot or will not proceed unless other actions are taken previously or simultaneously.
>
> (iii) Are interdependent parts of a larger action and depend on the larger action for their justification." *Id.*

The construction of the road and the sale of the timber in the Jersey Jack area meet the second and third, as well as perhaps the first, of these criteria. It is clear that the timber sales cannot proceed without the road, and the road would not be built but for the contemplated timber sales. This much is revealed by the Forest Service's characterization of the road as a "logging road," and by the first page of the environmental assessment for the road, which states that "[t]he need for a transportation route in the assessment area is to access the timber lands to be developed over the next twenty years." Moreover, the environmental assessment for the road rejected a "no action" alternative because that alternative would not provide the needed timber access. The Forest Service's cost-benefit analysis of the road considered the timber to be the benefit of the road, and while the Service has stated that the road will yield other benefits, it does not claim that such other benefits would justify the road in the absence of the timber sales. Finally, the close interdependence of the road and the timber sales is indicated by an August 1981 letter in the record from the Regional Forester to the Forest Supervisor. It states, "We understand that sales in the immediate future will be dependent on the early completion of portions of the Jersey Jack Road. It would be advisable to divide the road into segments and establish separate completion dates for those portions to be used for those sales."

We conclude, therefore, that the road construction and the contemplated timber sales are inextricably intertwined, and that they are "connected actions" within the meaning of the CEQ regulations.

2. Cumulative Actions

The CEQ regulations also require that "cumulative actions" be considered together in a single EIS. 40 C.F.R. § 1508.25(a)(2). "Cumulative actions" are defined as actions "which when viewed with other proposed actions have cumulatively significant impacts." *Id.* The record in this case contains considerable evidence to suggest that the road and the timber sales will have cumulatively significant impacts. The U.S. Fish & Wildlife Service, the Environmental

Protection Agency, and the Idaho Department of Fish & Game have asserted that the road and the timber sales will have significant cumulative effects that should be considered in an EIS. The primary cumulative effects, according to these agencies, are the deposit of sediments in the Salmon River to the detriment of that river's population of salmon and steelhead trout and the destruction of critical habitat for the endangered Rocky Mountain Gray Wolf. These agencies have criticized the Forest Service for not producing an EIS that considers the cumulative impacts of the Jersey Jack road and the timber sales. For example, the Fish & Wildlife Service has written, "Separate documentation of related and cumulative potential impacts may be leading to aquatic habitat degradation unaccounted for in individual EA's (*i.e.*, undocumented cumulative effects). . . . Lack of an overall effort to document cumulative impacts could be having present and future detrimental effects on wolf recovery potential." These comments are sufficient to raise "substantial questions" as to whether the road and the timber sales will have significant cumulative environmental effects. Therefore, on this basis also, the Forest Service is required to prepare an EIS analyzing such effects.

B. Ninth Circuit Precedents

The conclusion that NEPA requires a single EIS that considers both road and sales is supported by our precedents. In *Trout Unlimited v. Morton,* 509 F.2d 1276 (9th Cir. 1974), we addressed the issue of when subsequent phases of development must be covered in an environmental impact statement on the first phase. We stated that an EIS must cover subsequent stages when "[t]he dependency is such that it would be irrational, or at least unwise, to undertake the first phase if subsequent phases were not also undertaken." *Id.* at 1285. The dependency of the road on the timber sales meets this standard; it would be irrational to build the road and then not sell the timber to which the road was built to provide access.

The same principle is embodied in standards that we have established for determining when a highway may be segmented for purposes of NEPA. In *Daly v. Volpe,* 514 F.2d 1106 (9th Cir. 1975), we held that the environmental impacts of a single highway segment may be evaluated separately from those of the rest of the highway only if the segment has "independent utility." 514 F.2d at 1110. In the light of *Trout Unlimited,* the phrase "independent utility" means utility such that the agency might reasonably consider constructing only the segment in question. The Forest Service has not alleged that the Jersey Jack road has sufficient utility independent from the timber sales to justify its construction. Severance of the road from the timber sales for purposes of NEPA, therefore, is not permissible.

C. Timing of the EIS

The Forest Service argues that the cumulative environmental effects of the road and the timber sales will be adequately analyzed and considered in the EA's and/or EIS's that it will prepare on the individual timber sales. The EA or EIS on each action, it contends, will document the cumulative impacts of that action and all previous actions.

We believe that consideration of cumulative impacts after the road has already been approved is insufficient to fulfill the mandate of NEPA. A central purpose of an EIS is to force the consideration of environmental impacts in the decisionmaking process. That purpose requires that the NEPA process be integrated with agency planning "at the earliest possible time," 40 C.F.R. § 1501.2, and the purpose cannot be fully served if consideration of the cumulative effects of successive, interdependent steps is delayed until the first step has already been taken.

The location, the timing, or other aspects of the timber sales, or even the decision whether to sell any timber at all affects the location, routing, construction techniques, and other aspects of the road, or even the need for its construction. But the consideration of cumulative impacts will serve little purpose if the road has already been built. Building the road swings the balance decidedly in favor of timber sales even if such sales would have been disfavored had road and sales been considered together before the road was built. Only by selling timber can the bulk of the expense of building the road be recovered. Not to sell timber after building the road constitutes the "irrational" result that *Trout Unlimited's* standard is intended to avoid. Therefore, the cumulative environmental impacts of the road and the timber sales must be assessed before the road is approved.

The Forest Service argues that the sales are too uncertain and too far in the future for their impacts to be analyzed along with that of the road. This comes close to saying that building the road now is itself irrational. We decline to accept that conclusion. Rather, we believe that if the sales are sufficiently certain to justify construction of the road, then they are sufficiently certain for their environmental impacts to be analyzed along with those of the road. *Cf. City of Davis v. Coleman,* 521 F.2d 661, 667-76 (9th Cir. 1975) (EIS for a road must analyze the impacts of industrial development that the road is designed to accommodate). Where agency actions are sufficiently related so as to be "connected" within the meaning of the CEQ regulations, the agency may not escape compliance with the regulations by proceeding with one action while characterizing the others as remote or speculative.

Moreover, the record contains substantial evidence that the timber sales were in fact at an advanced stage of planning by the time that the decision to build the road was made. The Forest Service issued EA's for, and approved, two of the timber sales nine and sixteen months after it issued the road EA, and it had issued an EA for a third sale by the time that this action was filed. In fact, one of the Forest Service's own affidavits shows that the Service was preparing the EA on at least one of the sales at the same time that it was preparing the EA on the road. The record plainly establishes that the Forest Service, in accordance with good administrative practices, was planning contemporaneously the timber sales and the building of the road. Either without the other was impractical. The Forest Service knew this and cannot insist otherwise to avoid compliance with NEPA.

We therefore reverse the district court on the NEPA issue and hold that, before deciding whether to approve the proposed road, the Forest Service is required to prepare and consider an environmental impact statement that analyzes the combined impacts of the road and the timber sales that the road is designed to facilitate.

* * *

IV.
THE ENDANGERED SPECIES ACT CLAIM

The plaintiffs' third claim concerns the Forest Service's alleged failure to comply with the Endangered Species Act (ESA) in considering the effects of the road and timber sales on the endangered Rocky Mountain Gray Wolf.

The ESA contains both substantive and procedural provisions. Substantively, the Act prohibits the taking or importation of endangered species, and requires federal agencies to ensure that their actions are not "likely to jeopardize the continued existence of any endangered species or threatened species or result in the destruction or adverse modification" of critical habitat of such species, *see* 16 U.S.C. § 1536(a)(2).

The Act prescribes a three-step process to ensure compliance with its substantive provisions by federal agencies. Each of the first two steps serves a screening function to determine if the successive steps are required. The steps are:

(1) An agency proposing to take an action must inquire of the Fish & Wildlife Service (F & WS) whether any threatened or endangered species "may be present" in the area of the proposed action. *See* 16 U.S.C. § 1536(c)(1).

(2) If the answer is affirmative, the agency must prepare a "biological assessment" to determine whether such species "is likely to be affected" by the action. *Id.* The biological assessment may be part of an environmental impact statement or environmental assessment. *Id.*

(3) If the assessment determines that a threatened or endangered species "is likely to be affected," the agency must formally consult with the F & WS. *Id.* § 1536(a)(2). The formal consultation results in a "biological opinion" issued by the F & WS. *See id.* § 1536(b). If the biological opinion concludes that the proposed action would jeopardize the species or destroy or adversely modify critical habitat, then the action may not go forward unless the F & WS can suggest an alternative that avoids such jeopardization, destruction, or adverse modification. *Id.* § 1536(b)(3)(A). If the opinion concludes that the action will not violate the Act, the F & WS may still require measures to minimize its impact. *Id.* § 1536(b)(4)(ii)-(iii).

Plaintiffs first allege that, with respect to the Jersey Jack road, the Forest Service did not undertake step (1), a formal request to the F & WS. The district court found that to be the case, but concluded that the procedural violation was insignificant because the Forest Service was already aware that wolves may be present in the area. The court therefore refused to enjoin the construction of the road. Plaintiffs insist, based on *TVA v. Hill,* 437 U.S. 153 (1978), that an injunction is mandatory once any ESA violation is found. Defendants respond, citing *Village of False Pass v. Clark,* 733 F.2d 605 (9th Cir. 1984), that TVA applies only to substantive violations of the ESA, and that a court has discretion to deny an injunction when it finds a procedural violation to be *de minimis.*

We need not reach this issue. The Forest Service's failure goes beyond the technical violation cited by the district court, and is not *de minimis.*

Once an agency is aware that an endangered species may be present in the area of its proposed action, the ESA requires it to prepare a biological assessment to determine whether the proposed action "is likely to affect" the species and therefore requires formal consultation with the F & WS. The Forest Service did not prepare such an assessment prior to its decision to build the Jersey Jack road. Without a biological assessment, it cannot be determined whether the proposed project will result in a violation of the ESA's substantive provisions. A failure to prepare a biological assessment for a project in an area in which it has been determined that an endangered species may be present cannot be considered a *de minimis* violation of the ESA.

The district court found that the Forest Service had "undertaken sufficient study and action to further the purposes of the ESA." Its finding was based on affidavits submitted by the Forest Service for the litigation. These do not constitute a substitute for the preparation of the biological assessment required by the ESA.

Given a substantial procedural violation of the ESA in connection with a federal project, the remedy must be an injunction of the project pending compliance with the ESA. The procedural requirements of the ESA are analogous to those of NEPA: under NEPA, agencies are required to evaluate the environmental impact of federal projects "significantly affecting the quality of the human environment," 42 U.S.C. § 4332(2)(C); under the ESA, agencies are required to assess the effect on endangered species of projects in areas where such species may be present. 16 U.S.C. § 1536(c). A failure to prepare a biological assessment is comparable to a failure to prepare an environmental impact statement.

Our cases repeatedly have held that, absent "unusual circumstances," an injunction is the appropriate remedy for a violation of NEPA's procedural requirements. *See Save Our Ecosystems v. Clark,* 747 F.2d 1240, 1250 (9th Cir. 1984); *Alpine Lakes Protection Society v. Schlapfer,* 518 F.2d 1089 (9th Cir. 1975); *Lathan v. Volpe,* 455 F.2d 1111, 1116-17 (9th Cir. 1971). Irreparable damage is presumed to flow from a failure properly to evaluate the environmental impact of a major federal action. *Save Our Ecosystems,* 747 F.2d at 1250;

Friends of the Earth, Inc. v. Coleman, 518 F.2d 323, 330 (9th Cir. 1975). We see no reason that the same principle should not apply to procedural violations of the ESA.

The Forest Service argues that the procedural requirements of the ESA should be enforced less stringently than those of NEPA because, unlike NEPA, the ESA also contains substantive provisions. We acknowledge that the ESA's substantive provisions distinguish it from NEPA, but the distinction acts the other way. If anything, the strict substantive provisions of the ESA justify more stringent enforcement of its procedural requirements, because the procedural requirements are designed to ensure compliance with the substantive provisions. The ESA's procedural requirements call for a systematic determination of the effects of a federal project on endangered species. If a project is allowed to proceed without substantial compliance with those procedural requirements, there can be no assurance that a violation of the ESA's substantive provisions will not result. The latter, of course, is impermissible. *See TVA v. Hill,* 437 U.S. 153.

The district court, citing *Palila v. Hawaii Dept. of Land and Natural Resources,* 639 F.2d 495 (9th Cir. 1981), held that "[a] party asserting a violation of the Endangered Species Act has the burden of showing the proposed action would have some prohibited effect on an endangered species or its critical habitat," and found that the plaintiffs in this case had not met that burden. This is a misapplication of *Palila*. That case concerned the ESA's prohibition of the "taking" of an endangered species, 16 U.S.C. § 1538(a)(1)(B), not the ESA's procedural requirements. Quite naturally, the court in *Palila* found that a plaintiff, in order to establish a violation of the "taking" provision, must show that such a "taking" has occurred. *See* 639 F.2d at 497. The holding does not apply to violations of the ESA's procedural requirements. A plaintiff's burden in establishing a procedural violation is to show that the circumstances triggering the procedural requirement exist, and that the required procedures have not been followed. The plaintiffs in this case have clearly met that burden.

The Forest Service would require the district court, absent proof by the plaintiffs to the contrary, to make a finding that the Jersey Jack road is not likely to effect the Rocky Mountain Gray Wolf, and that therefore any failure to comply with ESA procedures is harmless. This is not a finding appropriate to the district court at the present time. Congress has assigned to the agencies and to the Fish & Wildlife Service the responsibility for evaluation of the impact of agency actions on endangered species, and has prescribed procedures for such evaluation. Only by following the procedures can proper evaluations be made. It is not the responsibility of the plaintiffs to prove, nor the function of the courts to judge, the effect of a proposed action on an endangered species when proper procedures have not been followed. *Cf. City of Davis v. Coleman,* 521 F.2d 661, 671 (9th Cir. 1975) (under NEPA, agency, not plaintiff, is responsible for investigating the environmental effects of a proposed action).

We therefore hold that the district court erred in declining to enjoin construction of the Jersey Jack road pending compliance with the ESA.

Finally, one additional development must be considered. The Forest Service's brief states that now a "biological evaluation" has been completed. The Service's memorandum opposing an injunction pending appeal states that the evaluation was completed on April 15, 1984, *i.e.,* after oral argument in district court but before the court issued its decision. The brief claims that the evaluation concluded that wolves will not be affected if certain mitigation measures are taken. The Forest Service, however, has submitted the evaluation neither to this court nor to the district court, and the plaintiffs state in their brief that the Service has refused to show the evaluation to them. Obviously, therefore, this evaluation cannot serve as a basis for holding that the Forest Service has complied with the ESA. Should the Forest Service wish to enter its biological evaluation into the record, it will be for the district court to determine whether that evaluation is sufficient to satisfy the ESA's requirement of a biological assessment, and whether its preparation after the approval of the road can bring the Forest Service into compliance with the ESA. For this purpose, and for the purpose of fashioning an appropriate remedy for the Service's failure to comply with NEPA, we remand this case to the district court for proceedings consistent with this opinion.

AFFIRMED IN PART, REVERSED IN PART, AND REMANDED.

NOTES

1.   See CHARLES F. WILKINSON, CROSSING THE NEXT MERIDIAN: LAND, WATER, AND THE FUTURE OF THE WEST 1-9 (1992), for a more detailed description of the issues and people involved in the Jersey Jack project challenged in *Thomas v. Peterson.*

2.   In a "strikingly similar" case, *Save the Yaak Committee v. Block*, 840 F.2d 714, 719 (9th Cir. 1988), the court found Forest Service EAs on road segments in the Kootenai National Forest inadequate because they failed to consider the connected timber sales. The court noted that "connected actions and unrelated, but reasonably foreseeable, future actions may result in cumulative impacts." *Id.* at 721.

3.   Unlike the situation in *Conner*, the ESA violation in *Thomas* involved a threshold determination—the decision not to prepare a biological assessment. How would you categorize the NEPA violation in *Thomas*? Was it a failure to prepare a required document or an inadequate scope of analysis in a NEPA document? How useful is the distinction between a threshold issue and a scope issue?

4.   Regarding the project at issue in *Thomas v. Peterson*, what is the scope of the agency action for purposes of consultation under the Associate Solicitor's opinion? Under *Conner v. Burford*? Is the scope of analysis required by NEPA different from the scope of analysis required by the ESA? *Compare* 40 C.F.R. § 1508.7 (cumulative impact) *and* § 1508.25 (scope) (which include *reasonably foreseeable* actions and effects) *with* 50 C.F.R. § 402.02 (effects of the action) (which applies the *reasonably certain* standard).

5.   As new environmental concerns emerge, agencies must keep pace by broadening the scope of analysis in their NEPA documents. For instance, in the past decade, conservation biologists have warned of the Earth's declining biological diversity. Courts are now beginning to recognize the importance of dealing with this issue in reviewing EISs. In *Marble Mountain Audubon Soc'y v. Rice*, 914 F.2d 179, 180-81 n.2 (9th Cir. 1990), the court found a Forest Service EIS for a salvage timber sale inadequate because it did not take a hard look at the impacts of logging activities in a biological corridor which provided an avenue "along which wide-ranging animals can travel, plants can propagate, genetic interchange can occur, populations can move in response to environmental changes and natural disasters, and threat[en]ed species can be replenished from other areas." These concerns did not stem from the survival needs of any listed species but rather from the degradation of biological diversity caused by the fragmentation of large blocks of forest. Recently, the CEQ published non-binding guidelines "to help agencies identify situations where consideration of biodiversity under NEPA is appropriate, and to strengthen their efforts to do so." Council on Environmental Quality, *Incorporating Biodiversity*

Considerations Into Environmental Impact Analysis Under the National Environmental Policy Act (1993).

6. Where a proposed action is a "major construction activity," defined as a major Federal action that requires an EIS, 50 C.F.R. § 402.02, agencies must comply with specific procedures for biological assessments as outlined at 50 C.F.R. § 402.12. Note, however, that § 7 of the ESA may require an agency to prepare a biological assessment whether or not a major construction activity is involved. *See* 16 U.S.C. § 1536(c).

7. Neither the ESA itself nor its implementing regulations specifically address public participation. Nonetheless, any action that requires preparation of a biological assessment or a biological opinion will almost certainly attract public attention during the NEPA process which must accompany that same action. Often, an agency includes the biological assessment in the draft EIS so that the public will have the opportunity to comment on it before the final environmental analysis is completed. Thus, NEPA guarantees that, in most circumstances, the public will have an opportunity to comment on endangered species issues which may be relevant to a proposed action. *See* 40 C.F.R. § 1502.25 (requiring agencies to "prepare draft environmental impact statements concurrently with and integrated with environmental impact analyses and related surveys and studies required by * * * the Endangered Species Act * * * and other environmental laws").

8. The issue of cumulative impacts is linked to the question of whether to prepare a programmatic EIS for a number of individual projects. *See* 40 C.F.R. § 1508.25(a)(2); *City of Tenakee Springs v. Clough*, 915 F.2d 1308, 1312 (9th Cir. 1990) ("Where several foreseeable similar projects in a geographical region have a cumulative impact, they should be evaluated in a single EIS."). How does the requirement to consider cumulative impacts relate to the definition of a proposal? *See* 40 C.F.R. § 1508.23; *Kleppe v. Sierra Club*, 427 U.S. 390 (1976), *supra* Chapter 6.

TAXPAYERS WATCHDOG, INC. V. STANLEY
819 F.2d 294 (D.C. Cir. 1987)

PER CURIAM.

Appellee Ralph Stanley, Administrator of the Urban Mass Transportation Administration ("UMTA") and intervenor Southern California Rapid Transit District ("SCRTD") have each moved this court for summary affirmance of an order of the district court granting summary judgment to UMTA. Because the district court was correct in granting judgment to UMTA, the motions are granted and the order on appeal is summarily affirmed.

On September 3, 1986, appellant Taxpayers Watchdog ("Taxpayers") filed a complaint in the district court seeking to enjoin UMTA from disbursing $225.6 million in federal funds to SCRTD for the construction of a metro rail system in Los Angeles, California. The complaint alleged that UMTA had contracted with SCRTD to release federal funds for construction of a four mile subway system without first complying with the National Environmental Policy Act.

* * *

In 1978, in the hope of securing federal funds to improve public transportation in southern California, SCRTD presented to UMTA a document entitled "Draft Alternatives Analysis/ Environmental Impact Statement/Environmental Impact Report." ("Draft EIS"). The Draft EIS presented eleven mass transit alternatives designed to improve public transportation in and around the city of Los Angeles. The Draft EIS was approved by UMTA in May, 1979, and made available for review and public comment during the following month. In September of that year, the SCRTD adopted "Alternative II" as its "preferred alternative."[1] Alternative II was an 18.6 mile subway line between the Los Angeles central business district and North Hollywood.

In April, 1980, after public hearings, the SCRTD and UMTA adopted the first tier environmental documentation. The SCRTD then began the preliminary engineering phase of the project, analyzing in detail the effects of the preferred alternative.

By November of 1983, the SCRTD published its "second tier" or "final" EIS. The final EIS analyzed four alternative plans for the metro rail project: (a) the locally preferred alternative of 18.6 miles of entirely below ground tracks; (b) the same 18.6 mile system with some aerial components; (c) the "minimum operable segment" of 8.8 miles, and (d) a "no project" alternative. Shortly thereafter, the underground 18.6 mile plan was adopted for final design and construction, and UMTA approved the final EIS.

In 1984, however, the federal government dramatically curtailed the funding available for local transit projects. Thus, UMTA could not commit itself to provide funds for the 18.6 mile or even the 8.8 mile systems. In response, SCRTD developed a fifth alternative. This alternative consisted simply of the first four miles of the 18.6 mile system. It was designated as the truly "minimum operable segment" or MOS-1.

In June, 1984, SCRTD requested immediate funding for MOS-1, and asked UMTA to prepare an Environmental Assessment ("EA") for the project. SCRTD had already prepared its own preliminary environmental study. SCRTD concluded that MOS-1 would make a "viable contribution to the greater Los Angeles urban transportation infrastructure" and would ease congestion in the city's central business district.

UMTA issued its EA in August, 1984. The agency noted that "[b]ecause of continuing uncertainty of federal capital funds, this analysis has been undertaken to insure that the 4 mile project would be an independent operable segment." The EA addressed the impact of a four mile system, particularly the effect of a terminal station at the intersection of Wilshire Boulevard and Alvarado Street. In all other respects, MOS-1 was identical to the first four miles of the previously approved 18.6 mile system. The EA also addressed a "no project" alternative. The agency concluded that even a shortened four mile system was preferable to no rail system at all. UMTA concluded that MOS-1 would be "worth the investment when weighed against the benefits . . . increased accessibility and decreased total number of vehicle miles traveled in the [central business district] area." The environmental review process for MOS-1 was completed in November, 1984, with the issuance of a Finding of No Significant Impact ("FONSI") by UMTA.

---

[1]   The UMTA has developed a two-step procedure for reaching funding decisions. In the first stage, the local transit authority analyzes alternatives and prepares a first tier environmental impact statement ("EIS"). Following this "alternatives analysis," the applicant designates the "preferred alternative" it proposes to implement. A public hearing is then held. Following the hearing, the UMTA may grant federal funds to the local applicant for design and engineering of the preferred alternative. The second stage follows completion of the preliminary design and engineering plan. The applicant prepares a site-specific "second tier" EIS analyzing the effects of the chosen alternative. After UMTA circulates the final EIS for comments, the applicant prepares a capital grant application for the construction of the preferred alternative and holds a public hearing thereon. The UMTA then decides whether to provide funds for the actual construction of the transit system.

Unfortunately, the problems associated with the construction of a rapid rail system in Los Angeles did not end there. Four months after UMTA issued the FONSI for MOS-1, an explosion of methane gas occurred several miles from the proposed terminal station at Wilshire and Alvarado. This explosion occurred in the Fairfax Avenue section of Los Angeles, through which part of the 18.6 mile route beyond MOS-1 was to pass. As a result of the explosion, a local task force report labeled the area a "potential risk zone."

When word of the explosion reached Washington, Congress promptly prohibited the use of any federal funds for construction of any part of the Los Angeles subway system unless SCRTD made a commitment to UMTA that no part of the system would tunnel into or through any risk zone identified by the task force. This congressional action forced SCRTD to scrap the proposed 18.6 mile route and develop a new rail system that would not pass through the Fairfax Avenue area. In June of 1986, SCRTD had identified four potential alternative routes, all of which would utilize MOS-1. The process of developing and choosing a single alternate extension to MOS-1 is still underway. On August 27, UMTA signed a full funding contract with SCRTD, agreeing to release $225 million for the construction of MOS-1.

* * *

Taxpayers does not challenge the "substantive adequacy of the environmental documentation prepared for the original 18.6 mile subway, as that original documentation once related to MOS-1." In addition, it does not claim that UMTA acted arbitrarily or capriciously by failing to issue a separate full-blown EIS on MOS-1 in 1984. Further, it neither challenges the substantive adequacy of the August, 1984 EA, nor suggests that the 1985 methane explosion in any way threatens the safety of the MOS-1 system.

Rather, Taxpayers claims only that the entire, as yet undetermined, subway system must be considered and a "determination . . . made whether the small part of the larger project has been improperly segmented from the whole." It argues that MOS-1 is not an independent project but is now, and always has been, conceived of as the first leg of a rail line extending past the Wilshire/Alvarado station to North Hollywood. Thus, the entire metro rail project is said to be the "major federal action" and MOS-1 is said to have been improperly segmented therefrom, frustrating adequate environmental review.

"Piecemealing" or "Segmentation" allows an agency to avoid the NEPA requirement that an EIS be prepared for all major federal actions with significant environmental impacts by dividing an overall plan into component parts, each involving action with less significant environmental effects. *West Chicago, Ill. v. U.S. Nuclear Regulatory Comm'n,* 701 F.2d at 650. The rule against segmentation was developed to insure that interrelated projects the overall effect of which is environmentally significant, not be fractionalized into smaller, less significant actions.

The rule against segmentation, however, is not required to be applied in every situation. To determine the appropriate scope for an EIS, courts have considered such factors as whether the proposed segment (1) has logical termini; (2) has substantial independent utility; (3) does not foreclose the opportunity to consider alternatives, and (4) does not irretrievably commit federal funds for closely related projects.

The district court concluded that "MOS-1 is an independent project that would make a much needed contribution to Los Angeles' transit system." That conclusion was based upon the uncontradicted evidence offered by SCRTD that MOS-1 would provide a much needed service to the central business district ("CBD") of a city that will shortly face "debilitating daily gridlock."

The unrebutted evidence presented to the district court demonstrated that MOS-1 is a four mile rail system providing service to the CBD of Los Angeles and close-in residential areas. In the Northeast, it will connect with Union Station, the city's main railroad terminal, and from there provide easy access to the El Monte busway which serves the San Gabriel valley. In the South, MOS-1 will connect with the Long Beach and Century Freeway light rail systems. It will intersect major bus lines and provide easier access to the CBD for those who live in the densely populated Wilshire/Alvarado area. Further, it was estimated that MOS-1 will reduce by one fourth the current travel time from one end of the CBD to the other. Based upon this unchallenged evidence, the district court properly concluded that MOS-1 has substantial independent utility and has logical endpoints.

In addition, because of its central location connecting downtown Los Angeles with outlying residential areas, the district court concluded that MOS-1 was particularly well suited for future expansion. Any rapid rail system that would be constructed in the future would have to provide service to the CBD in much the same manner as MOS-1. Thus, MOS-1 does not foreclose alternative routes of expansion, nor does it foreordain a particular choice. This flexibility was demonstrated by the fact that SCRTD currently has under consideration no less than four possible extensions of MOS-1 to the San Fernando Valley. Moreover, although expansion of the rail system may be desirable, the substantial utility of MOS-1 as an independent rail segment serving the CBD does not require the construction of additional rail miles to justify the building of MOS-1 alone. Thus, many alternatives, including a "no-build" option, are preserved by construction of MOS-1.

* * *

Taxpayers is correct when it alleges that MOS-1 has always been, and still is, envisioned as the first leg of a larger system. It is also correct in pointing out the dangers that may arise if a project is segmented into overly narrow portions for environmental review. Environmental assessment on less than a systemwide scope may, in certain situations, lead to evaluation of segments in isolation of one another, thereby creating a misleading picture of the impact of the project as a whole. The record is barren, however, of any facts that would suggest that such a danger exists here.

* * *

NOTES

1.   The MOS-1 segment of the L.A. subway system opened in January 1993. Robert Reinhold, *Subway to Open in Los Angeles (Yes, a Subway)*, N.Y. TIMES, Jan. 28, 1993, at A1. However, the city is still a long way from completing its $75 billion mass transportation plan. James Sterngold, *Betting on Rails in the Realm of Cars*, N.Y. TIMES, Jan. 15, 1996, at A11.

2.   Does *Lujan v. National Wildlife Federation, supra* Chapter 3, support Taxpayers' standing to sue in this case?

3.   Why was the EIS for the proposed rail line prepared by the Southern California Rapid Transit District (SCRTD) rather than the Urban Mass Transit Authority, the federal agency involved in this case? *See* 42 U.S.C. § 4332(2)(D) (NEPA § 102(2)(D)).

4.   In the original EIS, SCRTD deemed the "minimum operable segment" to be 8.8 miles. Subsequently, after SCRTD learned that funding was not available for 8.8 miles, it curtailed the "truly" minimum operable segment to 4 miles, which happened to correspond

with the amount of money that was available. Given these facts, how convincing is SCRTD's claim that the 4-mile segment had independent utility?

5. The district court received evidence on the viability of MOS-1 as an independent subway segment. What kind of evidence should the court allow litigants to introduce? Can SCRTD submit supporting evidence that is not a part of the administrative record? What about the plaintiffs? Should they be subject to the same rules as the agency that controls the record?

Normally, courts will not allow parties to introduce evidence outside of the administrative record. If the record does not contain information adequate for the court to rule, the usual remedy is not introduction of supplementary evidence but rather a remand to the agency. *See, e.g., Citizens to Preserve Overton Park v. Volpe*, 401 U.S. 402, 421-22 (concurring opinion of Justice Black) (1971), *supra* Chapter 3. Exceptions to the general rule arise in cases where plaintiffs allege that the agency has not provided a complete record of its deliberations or where no record can be compiled. Professor Mandelker surveys a number of NEPA cases involving extra-record evidence and concludes that the recent trend is for federal district courts to allow more supplementation where an agency's record is not clear. DANIEL R. MANDELKER, NEPA LAW AND LITIGATION § 4.09[1][b] (2d ed. 1992). For instance, in *County of Suffolk v. Secretary of the Interior*, 562 F.2d 1368, 1384-85 (2d Cir. 1977), *cert. denied*, 434 U.S. 1064 (1978) (citations omitted), the court explained that:

> in NEPA cases, by contrast [to ordinary suits challenging nonadjudicatory, nonrulemaking agency action], a primary function of the court is to insure that the information available to the decision-maker includes an adequate discussion of environmental effects and alternatives, which can sometimes be determined only by looking outside the administrative record to see what the agency may have ignored.
>
> * * *
>
> [A]llegations that an EIS has neglected to mention a serious environmental consequence, failed adequately to discuss some reasonable alternative, or otherwise swept "stubborn problems or serious criticism . . . under the rug," raise issues sufficiently important to permit the introduction of new evidence in the district court, including expert testimony.

Is the Second Circuit correct in its assessment of the need for expert testimony in NEPA cases? How would such a rule affect the responsibility of commenters to provide evidence supporting their arguments during the public comment period on the EIS?

6. The ESA regulations expressly provide for "incremental step" consultation under § 7. Under these rules, the Fish and Wildlife Service is required (if requested by the action agency) to issue "a biological opinion on the incremental step being considered, including its views on the entire action." 50 C.F.R. § 402.14(k). The action agency may proceed with the proposed action if (1) the incremental step would not cause jeopardy; (2) the agency obtains additional biological opinions for each incremental step; (3) the incremental step does not make an irreversible or irretrievable commitment of resources that might foreclose the implementation of reasonable and prudent alternatives that would not cause jeopardy; and (4) it is reasonably likely that the entire action will not cause jeopardy. *Id.* How can you reconcile the policy against segmentation under NEPA with incremental step consultation under the ESA?

PROBLEM #5: SCOPE OF ENVIRONMENTAL DOCUMENTS

The Climax Coal Company proposes to open a new coal mine on federal land in southeastern Montana. Climax currently holds a lease to mine those lands, but the lease will expire in one year unless coal is produced in paying quantities by that deadline. Thus, Climax is interested in securing all necessary approvals and permits as soon as possible. Among other things, Climax needs a mining permit from the federal Office of Surface Mining (OSM) before mining can proceed.[†] Accordingly, Climax filed its application for a permit last week. OSM understands the Company's situation and has indicated that it will act on the permit application as quickly as possible. Among the stumbling blocks, however, is the requirement that the agency prepare an EIS or an EA on the proposed mining operations before the permit decision can be made.

The Big Sky Ranchers Association opposes the new mine for several reasons. First, it will increase dust and air pollution thus adversely affecting visibility in what is now a pristine area. Second, it will result in the loss of lands available for grazing at least until reclamation is completed. Third, the Association believes that Climax has failed to demonstrate the need for additional mining capacity in the region. The proposed Climax Mine will have a capacity of 10 million tons of coal per year. Currently, there are 10 mines in the region which are producing a combined total of 60 million tons per year. These mines have a total capacity, however, of 80 million tons per year. Moreover, in addition to Climax, permit applications are currently pending for two other mines in the region, one located on private land, the other on federal land. Finally, five other federal land sites located in the vicinity of the proposed Climax mine have been proposed for coal leasing by the federal government. If leasing occurs, it will probably take place within the next 12 months.

The Big Sky Ranchers Association has hired your law firm to assist them in opposing the Climax mine. OSM has announced that a preliminary scoping meeting (*see* 40 C.F.R. § 1501.7) will be held next week to discuss the proposed mine and the scope of the environmental analysis to be performed. What arguments should you present on the Association's behalf at this meeting?

In conjunction with the scoping meeting, OSM has announced that it has initiated consultation with the U.S. Fish and Wildlife Service over the interior least tern and piping plover, two listed species which are thought to be present in the vicinity of the proposed mine. To what extent should the scope of the Fish and Wildlife Service's biological opinion differ from the scope of the environmental analysis prepared for the mine?

[†]   The company's obligation to obtain a permit from OSM should be understood to apply to this hypothetical case only. In actuality, mining companies can obtain permits to mine on federal lands in accordance with an agreement between the state and the federal government. The use of this arrangement to avoid "federal action" and thus NEPA compliance raises an interesting legal question. *See National Wildlife Federation v. Hodel*, 839 F.2d 694 (D.C. Cir. 1988).

SYLVESTER V. U.S. ARMY CORPS OF ENGINEERS
871 F.2d 817 (9th Cir. 1989)

SNEED, Circuit Judge:

* * *

I.
FACTS AND PROCEEDINGS BELOW

Perini, [a resort developer and a defendant in this case] has begun building a multi-million dollar resort in Squaw Valley, California. The resort, if completed as planned, will include skiing facilities, a resort village, and a golf course. Perini has decided to locate the golf course on a meadow in Squaw Valley and to locate the resort village and the ski runs on neighboring uplands. The meadow, through which the Squaw Creek flows, contains pockets of wetlands. To make the land suitable for golf, Perini intends to fill eleven acres of these wetlands. Although others already have used the meadow for various purposes, such as farming, waste disposal, and parking, the parties dispute whether these activities have affected the natural state of the wetlands.

Perini has sought to obtain the necessary permits to build the resort for almost five years. It has obtained approval from four government agencies: (1) the Placer County Board of Supervisors, (2) the State Regional Water Control Board—Lahontan Region, (3) the State Water Resources Control Board, and (4) the Corps [the U.S. Army Corps of Engineers]. It also has settled two state court actions challenging the adequacy of the state environmental analyses.

Placer County, which has jurisdiction over all of the resort property, certified an "Environmental Impact Report" for the entire project, pursuant to California law, after analyzing each component of the resort. It then issued a "Conditional Use Permit" that allowed Perini to construct the resort subject to one hundred and twenty-eight conditions. Thirty-seven of these conditions related to the golf course. The State Regional Water Control Board and the State Water Resources Control Board, which have jurisdiction to review and approve compliance with state waste discharge restrictions, have required Perini to adopt additional water quality protective measures.

The Corps believed that it had jurisdiction only over the wetlands and, accordingly, confined its review to the meadow where Perini intends to locate the golf course. The Corps reviewed the records compiled by the state agencies, held a public hearing, and conducted its own evaluation of the environmental effects of constructing the golf course. The Corps also agreed to accept anonymous written comments about the resort because of the possibility that Perini may have curtailed the speech of concerned citizens and organizations by threatening to enforce certain "no further opposition" terms of its state court settlements.

On February 25, 1988, the Corps issued a conditional permit under § 404 of the CWA [Clean Water Act] allowing Perini to build the golf course but requiring it: (1) to construct 12.7 acres of new artificial wetlands, (2) to restore 117 acres of the existing meadow, and (3) to comply with certain conditions imposed by the state agencies. In its "Environmental Assessment" (EA), issued pursuant to its own regulations, *see* 53 Fed. Reg. 3120, 3129 (1988) (to be codified at 33 C.F.R. § 230.10), the Corps stated that it had decided not to prepare an EIS under 42 U.S.C. § 4332(2)(C) (1982), because it found that the federal action of granting the § 404 permit to Perini would not have a significant effect on the quality of the human environment. As already mentioned, the Corps considered only the impact of the golf course and not the impact of the rest of the resort complex in reaching this decision.

Sylvester reacted quickly. On April 28, 1988, he sued Perini and the Federal Defendants in the United States district court below. His complaint raised claims under the NEPA, the

CWA, the Endangered Species Act and the Clean Air Act. The relief he sought included declaratory relief, a writ of mandamus ordering the Corps, among other things, to prepare an EIS and to rescind Perini's § 404 permit, and, finally, a preliminary and permanent injunction restraining the defendants from authorizing or undertaking "work in the Squaw Meadow or in other areas that would affect the wetlands in Squaw Meadow."

On August 4, 1988, the district court granted a temporary restraining order preventing Perini from doing any work in the wetlands. On September 21, 1988, it issued a preliminary injunction halting all work on the entire resort complex. The court accepted Sylvester's claim that the Corps should not have issued the § 404 permit because it failed to comply with the NEPA. It relied, in particular, on Sylvester's assertion that, in deciding whether to prepare an EIS, the Corps improperly limited the scope of its NEPA analysis to the golf course rather than examining the environmental effects of the entire resort complex. After reviewing various Ninth Circuit cases, the court stated that the "plaintiff has at least raised serious questions on the merits, if not a likelihood of success, regarding the proper scope of analysis under his NEPA claim." The court later explained that it would not defer to the Corps' NEPA regulations, which interpreted the NEPA to limit the scope of its analysis to the golf course, because the regulations did not comport with the NEPA and its legislative history. * * *

* * *

IV.
THE ISSUE

The NEPA requires federal agencies to prepare a detailed statement on the environmental impact of "major Federal actions significantly affecting the quality of the human environment." 42 U.S.C. § 4332(2)(C) (1982). The issue before us is whether the Corps' understanding of the term "federal action" that it used in deciding whether to prepare such a statement was correct. The NEPA does not specify the scope of analysis that federal agencies must conduct in determining whether their actions, when combined with private actions, come within the mandate of § 4332(2)(C). The district court, as noted above, looked to Ninth Circuit precedent for guidance. We hold that the district court erred in reaching the conclusion it did.

V.
THE REGULATIONS
A. The Corps' Regulations

The Corps follows its own regulations when determining how to comply with the NEPA. In 1980, the Corps published a version of regulations that did not specify how it should determine the scope of its NEPA analysis when issuing permits for projects combining both federal and non-federal actions. See 45 Fed. Reg. 56760 (1980). In the same year, the Fifth and Eighth Circuits decided to limit this scope to the federally controlled or regulated aspects of such projects. See Winnebago Tribe v. Ray, 621 F.2d 269, 273 (8th Cir.) (NEPA did not require the Corps to consider an entire power line when issuing a permit allowing the line to cross navigable waters), cert. denied, 449 U.S. 836 (1980); Save the Bay, Inc. v. United States Corps of Eng'rs, 610 F.2d 322, 327 (5th Cir.) (NEPA did not require the Corps to consider a chemical plant when issuing a permit allowing construction of a wastewater pipeline from the plant), cert. denied, 449 U.S. 900 (1980).

In 1984, the Corps proposed an amendment to its NEPA regulations that would have codified Winnebago and Save the Bay. The Clean Air Act (CAA), however, requires the Administrator of the Environmental Protection Agency (EPA) to review proposed NEPA compliance regulations. See 42 U.S.C. § 7609(a) (1982). The Administrator did not approve the Corps' amendment and, therefore, had to refer it to the Council of Environmental Quality (CEQ) under § 7609(b) (1982). On June 8, 1987, the CEQ approved the amendment subject to a few proposed modifications. *See* 52 Fed. Reg. 22518, 22520-22 (1987). On February 3, 1988, the Corps revised and published the amendment; the revision adopted the CEQ's proposals. *See* 53 Fed. Reg. 3120, 3121 (1988).

The final set of regulations provides:

b. *Scope of Analysis.*

(1) In some situations, a permit applicant may propose to conduct a specific activity requiring a Department of the Army (DA) permit (*e.g.*, construction of a pier in a navigable water of the United States) which is merely one component of a larger project (*e.g.*, construction of an oil refinery on an upland area). The district engineer should establish the scope of the NEPA document (*e.g.*, the EA or EIS) to address the impacts of the specific activity requiring a DA permit and those portions of the entire project over which the district engineer has sufficient control and responsibility to warrant Federal review.

(2) The district engineer is considered to have control and responsibility for portions of the project beyond the limits of Corps jurisdiction where the Federal involvement is sufficient to turn an essentially private action into a Federal action. These are cases where the environmental consequences of the larger project are essentially products of the Corps permit action.

Typical factors to be considered in determining whether sufficient "control and responsibility" exists include:

(i) Whether or not the regulated activity comprises "merely a link" in a corridor type project (*e.g.*, a transportation or utility transmission project).

(ii) Whether there are aspects of the upland facility in the immediate vicinity of the regulated activity which affect the location and configuration of the regulated activity.

(iii) The extent to which the entire project will be within Corps jurisdiction.

(iv) The extent of cumulative Federal control and responsibility.

Id. at 3135 (to be codified at 33 C.F.R. Part 325, App. B., § 7b).

B. Deference to the Regulations

In *Chevron, U.S.A. Inc. v. National Resources Defense Council, Inc.,* 467 U.S. 837 (1984), the Supreme Court established two rules for reviewing an agency's construction of a statute that it administers. First, the court must follow any unambiguously expressed intent of Congress. Second, when a statute is "silent or ambiguous" with respect to a specific issue, the court must defer to the agency's interpretation if based on a permissible construction of the statute.

* * *

VI.
SYLVESTER'S CONTENTIONS

Sylvester makes four arguments to which we should respond.

The first addresses the deference to which the Corps' regulations are entitled. Sylvester insists that while *Chevron* may require a court to give controlling weight to an agency's construction of a statute that it administers, a court does not have to give deference to an agency's interpretation of a statute outside of its "administrative ken." *See Parola v. Weinberger,* 848 F.2d 956, 959 (9th Cir. 1988). Therefore, Sylvester argues, this court owes no deference to the Corps' NEPA regulations because the Corps does not administer the NEPA. True, but this argument misses the mark. It ignores the role of the EPA and the CEQ. As the

Federal Defendants point out, the CAA requires the EPA to review the Corps' regulations and designates the CEQ as the arbitrator in disputes between federal agencies on environmental issues. *See* 42 U.S.C. § 7609(a)-(b). This is not done as an idle exercise. It is to provide guidance to all who may be concerned, including courts. Thus, even though the Corps actually promulgated the regulations, we believe that the principles underlying *Chevron* entitle them to, and require us to extend, deference.

Second, Sylvester argues that the Corps' regulations are contrary to Congress' clear intention. The NEPA requires agencies to comply with its mandates "to the fullest extent possible." 42 U.S.C. § 4332 (1982). Congress explained that this means that no agency may "utilize an excessively narrow construction of its existing statutory authorizations to avoid compliance." H.R. Conf. Rep. No. 91-765, 91st Cong., 1st Sess. 10, *reprinted in* 1969 U.S. Code Cong. & Admin. News 2751, 2767, 2770. Even expansive language has some limits. These statements cannot expand the areas over which the Corps may exercise control and responsibility beyond its statutory authority. Mindful of this positive restraint, we find that the Corps' regulations fixing the scope of its NEPA analysis strike an acceptable balance between the needs of the NEPA and the Corps' jurisdictional limitations.

* * *

Fourth, Sylvester argues that the Corps' regulations conflict with the CEQ's regulations. The CEQ's regulations provide that in deciding whether to prepare an EIS, an agency must consider significant indirect effects, including "growth inducing effects and other effects relating to induced changes in the pattern of land use, population density or growth rate." 40 C.F.R. § 1508.8(b) (1987). The regulations provide further that an agency cannot avoid finding significant indirect effects by "breaking [an action] down into small component parts." *Id.* § 1508.27(b)(7). The regulations also explain that the cumulative impact of a project consists of the "incremental impact of the action when added to other past, present, and reasonably foreseeable future action regardless of what agency (Federal or non-Federal) or person undertakes such other actions." *Id.* § 1508.7.

Environmental impacts are in some respects like ripples following the casting of a stone in a pool. The simile is beguiling but useless as a standard. So employed it suggests that the entire pool must be considered each time a substance heavier than a hair lands upon its surface. This is not a practical guide. A better image is that of scattered bits of a broken chain, some segments of which contain numerous links, while others have only one or two. Each segment stands alone, but each link within each segment does not.

Drawing our inspiration from this image, we find no conflict in the regulations as applied in this case. Consistent with both its own regulations and the CEQ's regulations, the Corps did analyze the secondary and cumulative impacts of the golf course, but concluded that these impacts did not include the other resort facilities. As we explain below, we cannot find that the golf course and the rest of the resort are two links of a single chain that require the Corps to look further than it did.

VII.
NINTH CIRCUIT PRECEDENTS

Perhaps the district court, in deciding not to defer to the regulations, was swayed by several Ninth Circuit precedents indicating that agencies cannot divide projects to avoid their duties under the NEPA. These cases include *Port of Astoria, Oregon v. Hodel*, 595 F.2d 467, 480 (9th Cir. 1979) (agency's EIS had to consider the supply of federal power and the construction of a private magnesium plant that used the power); *Thomas v. Peterson*, 753 F.2d 754, 761 (9th Cir. 1985) (agency's EIS had to consider both a federal road and the federal timber sales that the road would facilitate); and *Colorado River Indian Tribes v. Marsh*, 605 F. Supp. 1425, 1433

(C.D. Cal. 1985) (agency had to prepare an EIS that considered both the federal action of stabilizing a river bank and the private housing built as a result).

These cases do not conflict with the Corps' decision not to consider the entire resort. The federal and private portions of the projects considered in these cases were joined to each other (links in the same bit of chain) in a way that the golf course and the remainder of the resort complex (a separate segment of chain) are not. Although the parties dispute what Perini has represented about the economic feasibility of building the resort complex without the golf course, we take judicial notice that ski resorts in the Lake Tahoe region of California can and do exist without being located immediately adjacent to golf courses. We do not understand how Perini's desire to place the course in a meadow that contains wetlands can federalize the entire resort complex.

Indeed, we believe that a contrary decision on our part might conflict with *Friends of the Earth v. Hintz,* 800 F.2d 822, 832 (9th Cir. 1986) (agency considered only filled wetlands and not other aspects of a harbor facility in deciding not to prepare an EIS); *Enos v. Marsh,* 769 F.2d 1363, 1371-72 (9th Cir. 1985) (agency's EIS did not have to consider non-federal shore facilities for a new deep draft harbor); and *Friends of Earth, Inc. v. Coleman,* 518 F.2d 323, 328 (9th Cir. 1975) (agency did not have to prepare an EIS for state funded projects in a partially federally funded airport development). Although Sylvester asserts that the projects in these cases were more divisible than Perini's project, and amici curiae point out various other differences, we find the present case to resemble these cases more closely than it resembles *Hodel, Thomas,* or *Colorado River Indian Tribes.*[3]

* * *

NOTES

1.   Re-read the CEQ regulations at 40 C.F.R. §§ 1508.7 and 1508.25. Do you agree with the court's finding that the Corps actions were consistent with these rules? Suppose that the resort complex without the golf course was going to destroy 60 percent of the habitat for the local mule deer herd, and that the golf course would destroy an additional 20 percent. Is it appropriate for the Corps to limit its consideration to the impact of the golf course? Is it lawful?

2.   How clear is the distinction drawn by the court between actions that require a comprehensive analysis because they are "links in the same chain," and actions that do not because they are "separate segments of the chain"? Consider, for example, the following hypothetical proposals. Which would require a comprehensive analysis under the *Sylvester* standard?

   (a)   A 250 megawatt power plant built on private land that requires a federal right-of-way for transmission lines which will cross 300 miles of federal land. *Compare Winnebago Tribe of Nebraska v. Ray,* 621 F.2d 269 (8th Cir.

---

[3]   The parties also have cited *Methow Valley Citizens Council v. Regional Forester,* 833 F.2d 810, 816 (9th Cir.1987) (agency had to assess the commercial development caused by a ski resort), *cert. granted,* 487 U.S. 1217 (1988); and *City of Davis v. Coleman,* 521 F.2d 661, 671 (9th Cir. 1975) (agency had to consider the commercial development caused by an interstate highway interchange). These cases address the impact of federal action rather than the scope of federal action.

1980). (Would it matter if more than half of the capital costs were associated with construction of the transmission lines?)

(b) A 10 mile road through a national forest to access 5 million board feet of timber on private land.

(c) A ski resort on public lands, immediately adjacent to a ski resort that is currently under construction on private lands.

3. The court finds that the resort complex was feasible even without the golf course. Is this a sufficient finding to resolve the question of whether they are "connected actions" within the meaning of the CEQ rules? Should it matter whether the resort complex is viable without the golf course? Is the resort "connected" to the golf course? *See* 40 C.F.R. § 1508.25(a): "Actions are connected if they: * * * (ii) Cannot or will not proceed unless other actions are taken previously or simultaneously; (iii) Are interdependent parts of a larger action and depend on the larger action for their justification."

4. When working on NEPA problems, be sure to supplement the CEQ regulations with the relevant agency's NEPA regulations. As *Sylvester* illustrates, these rules, which are tailored to the agency's routine functions, can be critical in defining the scope of analysis of NEPA documents.

5. Other courts have taken different approaches in determining the degree of federal involvement necessary to federalize a project for the purposes of NEPA. In reviewing these cases, Patrick Parenteau has discerned a recent trend toward limiting the scope of projects subject to NEPA through a "small federal handle." Patrick Parenteau, *Small Handles, Big Impacts: When Do Corps Permits Federalize Private Development?*, 20 ENVTL. L. 747, 748 (1990); *see also* Mary K. Fitzgerald, *Small Handles, Big Impacts: When Should the National Environment Policy Act Require an Environmental Impact Statement?*, 23 B.C. ENVTL. AFF. L. REV. 437 (1996); Christopher H. Meyer, *Small Handles on Big Projects: The Federalization of Private Undertakings*, 41 ROCKY MT. MIN. L. INST. 5-1 (1995). Is this trend consistent with the CEQ's definitions of "cumulative impact" and "scope"? *See* 40 C.F.R. §§ 1508.7, 1508.25.

Still, some courts have taken a more expansive view of NEPA requirements. For instance, in *Colorado River Indian Tribes v. Marsh*, 605 F. Supp. 1425 (C.D. Cal. 1985), the Corps issued a permit allowing a developer to stabilize the shoreline of the Colorado River, which formed the eastern boundary of a 156-acre residential and commercial development. Without the river bank stabilization, the developer would not have been able to get the necessary county permit to proceed with the project. The court held that:

> In limiting the scope of its inquiry, the Corps acted improperly and contrary to the mandates of NEPA. The Corps' decision to assess only those impacts physically dependent upon activities within its redefined jurisdiction, *i.e.,* the river and its immediate banks, was tantamount to limiting its assessment to primary impacts.

Id. at 1433. The court went on to describe indirect and cumulative impacts, such as increased population growth and damage to archeological resources outside of the shoreline area, that the Corps should have analyzed. Can you distinguish *Colorado River Indian Tribes* from *Sylvester*?

In *Sierra Club v. Marsh*, 769 F.2d 868 (1st Cir. 1985), the court held that an EA prepared by the Corps for a permit to build a port on and a causeway to the undeveloped, 940-acre Sears Island in Maine was inadequate to meet the requirements of NEPA. Judge Breyer wrote that an EIS was necessary to consider the growth inducing effects and other consequences of the changes in land use (*see* 40 C.F.R. § 1508.8) that would occur when the causeway and cargo terminal stimulated industrial development. 769 F.2d at 877-78.

6. Professor Mandelker has endorsed what he views as the predominant "substantial contribution" rule in small federal handle cases. He worries that a contrary rule would overextend NEPA to "large numbers of nonfederal actions in which the federal presence is too limited to justify an impact statement." DANIEL R. MANDELKER, NEPA LAW AND LITIGATION § 8.04[2] (2d 2d. 1992). *Cf.* Patrick Parenteau, *Small Handles, Big Impacts: When Do Corps Permits Federalize Private Development?*, 20 ENVTL. L. 747, 756 (1990) (arguing that an impact statement is justified for any project that has a significant environmental effect).

7. The *Sylvester* court notes in Part I of its opinion that the Corps accepted anonymous comments because of the possibility that Perini curtailed the speech of concerned parties. What was going on? After expressing its environmental concerns before the county and Water Quality Board, the Sierra Club and a number of other organizations and individuals signed an agreement with Perini. The accord committed Perini to evaluate any proposed chemical use on the golf course. In return, the environmentalists agreed to withhold further opposition to the development.

At this point in the story, the environmentalists and Perini disagree about what happened. The Sierra Club claims that Rick Sylvester, who did not sign the agreement, continued to oppose the project as an individual. Perini claims that its opponents were supported by monies and organizations connected with the Sierra Club. Perini filed a breach of contract suit against its opponents. Sierra Club characterized the suit as a "SLAPP" (strategic lawsuit against public participation), a term coined by Professors George Pring and Penelope Canan to characterize a growing trend of litigation against citizens who participate in public discourse. Professor Pring describes a SLAPP as "a unilateral effort by one side to transform a public, political dispute into a private, legal adjudication" using such causes of action as defamation or interference with business. George W. Pring & Penelope Canan, *"Strategic Lawsuits Against Public Participation" ("SLAPPs"): An Introduction,* 12 BRIDGEPORT L. REV. 937, 941 (1992). Even though most SLAPP plaintiffs know they will lose on the merits, the point is to impose substantial litigation costs on citizens to discourage activism. Perini claimed that its suit was not a SLAPP; it merely sought to force its opponents to honor their earlier agreement. The litigation (including a counter-suit by Sierra Club), dragged on for over three years before the parties settled. Under the terms of the settlement, Sierra Club agreed to publish statements from attorneys on both sides. The statements make fascinating reading for anyone interested in the anatomy of a dispute over a major development. *See* Phillip S. Berry, *Club SLAPPs Back,* SIERRA, July/Aug. 1993, at 95; James N. Penrod & Barry D. Brown, *Developer Sued Opponents Because It Believed They Failed to Honor Their Word,* SIERRA, July/Aug. 1993, at 96.

Recent developments in SLAPPs are described in Alexandra Dylan Lowe, *The Price of Speaking Out,* A.B.A. J., Sept. 1996, at 48; Judith Miller, *States Have Moved to Keep Plaintiffs from Using Courts to Muzzle Critics,* N.Y. TIMES, June 11, 1996, at A22.

C. Mitigation and Uncertainty

ROBERTSON V. METHOW VALLEY CITIZENS COUNCIL
490 U.S. 332 (1989)

Justice STEVENS delivered the opinion of the Court.

We granted certiorari to decide two questions of law. As framed by petitioners, they are:

"1. Whether the National Environmental Policy Act requires federal agencies to include in each environmental impact statement: (a) a fully developed plan to mitigate environmental harm; and (b) a 'worst case' analysis of potential environmental harm if relevant information concerning significant environmental effects is unavailable or too costly to obtain."

"2. Whether the Forest Service may issue a special use permit for recreational use of national forest land in the absence of a fully developed plan to mitigate environmental harm."

* * *

I

The Forest Service is authorized by statute to manage the national forests for "outdoor recreation, range, timber, watershed, and wildlife and fish purposes." 16 U.S.C. § 528. *See also* 16 U.S.C. § 1600 *et seq.* Pursuant to that authorization, the Forest Service has issued "special use" permits for the operation of approximately 170 alpine and nordic ski areas on federal lands.

The Forest Service permit process involves three separate stages. The Forest Service first examines the general environmental and financial feasibility of a proposed project and decides whether to issue a special use permit. *See* 36 CFR § 251.54(f) (1988). Because that decision is a "major Federal action" within the meaning of NEPA, it must be preceded by the preparation of an Environmental Impact Statement (EIS). 42 U.S.C. § 4332. If the Service decides to issue a permit, it then proceeds to select a developer, formulate the basic terms of the arrangement with the selected party, and issue the permit. The special use permit does not, however, give the developer the right to begin construction. *See* 36 CFR § 251.56(c) (1988). In a final stage of review, the Service evaluates the permittee's "master plan" for development, construction, and operation of the project. Construction may begin only after an additional environmental analysis (although it is not clear that a second EIS need always be prepared) and final approval of the developer's master plan. This case arises out of the Forest Service's decision to issue a special use permit authorizing the development of a major destination alpine ski resort at Sandy Butte in the North Cascades mountains.

Sandy Butte is a 6,000-foot mountain located in the Okanogan National Forest in Okanogan County, Washington. At present Sandy Butte, like the Methow Valley it overlooks, is an unspoiled, sparsely populated area that the district court characterized as "pristine." In 1968, Congress established the North Cascades National Park and directed the Secretaries of Interior and Agriculture to agree on the designation of areas within and adjacent to the park for public uses, including ski areas. 16 U.S.C. §§ 90, 90d-3. A 1970 study conducted by the Forest Service pursuant to this congressional directive identified Sandy Butte as having the highest potential of any site in the State of Washington for development as a major downhill ski resort.

In 1978, Methow Recreation, Inc. (MRI) applied for a special use permit to develop and operate its proposed "Early Winters Ski Resort" on Sandy Butte and an 1,165 acre parcel of land it had acquired adjacent to the National Forest. The proposed development would make use of approximately 3,900 acres of Sandy Butte; would entice visitors to travel long distances to stay at the resort for several days at a time; and would stimulate extensive commercial and residential growth in the vicinity to accommodate both vacationers and staff.

In response to MRI's application, the Forest Service, in cooperation with state and county officials, prepared an EIS known as the Early Winters Alpine Winter Sports Study (Early Winters Study or Study). The stated purpose of the EIS was "to provide the information required to evaluate the potential for skiing at Early Winters" and "to assist in making a decision whether to issue a Special Use Permit for downhill skiing on all or a portion of approximately 3900 acres of National Forest System land." A draft of the Study was completed and circulated in 1982, but release of the final EIS was delayed as Congress considered including Sandy Butte in a proposed wilderness area. When the Washington State Wilderness Act of 1984 was passed, however, Sandy Butte was excluded from the wilderness designation, and the EIS was released.

The Early Winters Study is a printed document containing almost 150 pages of text and 12 appendices. It evaluated five alternative levels of development of Sandy Butte that might be authorized, the lowest being a "no action" alternative and the highest being development of a 16-lift ski area able to accommodate 10,500 skiers at one time. The Study considered the effect of each level of development on water resources, soil, wildlife, air quality, vegetation and visual quality, as well as land use and transportation in the Methow Valley, probable demographic shifts, the economic market for skiing and other summer and winter recreational activities in the Valley, and the energy requirements for the ski area and related developments. The Study's discussion of possible impacts was not limited to on-site effects, but also, as required by Council on Environmental Quality (CEQ) regulations, see 40 CFR § 1502.16(b) (1987), addressed "off-site impacts that each alternative might have on community facilities, socio-economic and other environmental conditions in the Upper Methow Valley." As to off-site effects, the Study explained that "due to the uncertainty of where other public and private lands may become developed," it is difficult to evaluate off-site impacts, and thus the document's analysis is necessarily "not site-specific." Finally, the Study outlined certain steps that might be taken to mitigate adverse effects, both on Sandy Butte and in the neighboring Methow Valley, but indicated that these proposed steps are merely conceptual and "will be made more specific as part of the design and implementation stages of the planning process."

The effects of the proposed development on air quality and wildlife received particular attention in the Study. In the chapter on "Environmental Consequences," the first subject discussed is air quality. As is true of other subjects, the discussion included an analysis of cumulative impacts over several years resulting from actions on other lands as well as from the development of Sandy Butte itself. The Study concluded that although the construction, maintenance, and operation of the proposed ski area "will not have a measurable effect on existing or future air quality," the off-site development of private land under all five alternatives—including the "no action" alternative—"will have a significant effect on air quality during severe meteorological inversion periods." The burning of wood for space heat, the Study explained, would constitute the primary cause of diminished air quality and the damage would increase incrementally with each of the successive levels of proposed development. The Study cautioned that without efforts to mitigate these effects, even under the "no action" alternative, the increase in automobile, fireplace, and wood stove use would reduce air quality below state standards, but added that "[t]he numerous mitigation measures discussed" in the Study "will greatly reduce the impacts presented by the model."

In its discussion of air-quality mitigation measures, the EIS identified actions that could be taken by the county government to mitigate the adverse effects of development, as well as those that the Forest Service itself could implement at the construction stage of the project. The Study suggested that Okanogan County develop an air quality management plan, requiring weatherization of new buildings, limiting the number of wood stoves and fireplaces, and adopting monitoring and enforcement measures. In addition, the Study suggested that the Forest

Service require that the master plan include procedures to control dust and to comply with smoke management practices.

In its discussion of adverse effects on area wildlife, the EIS concluded that no endangered or threatened species would be affected by the proposed development and that the only impact on sensitive species was the probable loss of a pair of spotted owls and their progeny. With regard to other wildlife, the Study considered the impact on 75 different indigenous species and predicted that within a decade after development vegetational change and increased human activity would lead to a decrease in population for 31 species, while causing an increase in population for another 24 species on Sandy Butte. Two species, the pine marten and nesting goshawk, would be eliminated altogether from the area of development.

In a comment in response to the draft EIS, the Washington Department of Game voiced a special concern about potential losses to the State's largest migratory deer herd, which uses the Methow Valley as a critical winter range and as its migration route. The state agency estimated that the total population of mule deer in the area most likely to be affected was "better than 30,000 animals" and that "the ultimate impact on the Methow deer herd could exceed a 50 percent reduction in numbers." The agency asserted that "Okanogan County residents place a great deal of importance on the area's deer herd." In addition, it explained that hunters had "harvested" 3,247 deer in the Methow Valley area in 1981, and "that, since in" 1980 hunters on average spent $1,980 for each deer killed in Washington, they had contributed over $6 million to the State's economy in 1981. Because the deer harvest is apparently proportional to the size of the herd, the state agency predicted that "Washington business can expect to lose over $3 million annually from reduced recreational opportunity." The Forest Service's own analysis of the impact on the deer herd was more modest. It first concluded that the actual operation of the ski hill would have only a "minor" direct impact on the herd, but then recognized that the off-site effect of the development "would noticeably reduce numbers of deer in the Methow [Valley] with any alternative." Although its estimate indicated a possible 15 percent decrease in the size of the herd, it summarized the State's contrary view in the text of the EIS, and stressed that off-site effects are difficult to estimate due to uncertainty concerning private development.

As was true of its discussion of air quality, the EIS also described both on-site and off-site mitigation measures. Among possible on-site mitigation possibilities, the Study recommended locating runs, ski lifts, and roads so as to minimize interference with wildlife, restricting access to selected roads during fawning season, and further examination of the effect of the development on mule deer migration routes. Off-site options discussed in the Study included the use of zoning and tax incentives to limit development on deer winter range and migration routes, encouragement of conservation easements, and acquisition and management by local government of critical tracts of land. As with the measures suggested for mitigating the off-site effects on air quality, the proposed options were primarily directed to steps that might be taken by state and local government.

Ultimately, the Early Winters Study recommended the issuance of a permit for development at the second highest level considered—a 16-lift ski area able to accommodate 8,200 skiers at one time. On July 5, 1984, the Regional Forester decided to issue a special use permit as recommended by the Study. In his decision, the Regional Forester found that no major adverse effects would result directly from the federal action, but that secondary effects could include a degradation of existing air quality and a reduction of mule deer winter range. He therefore directed the supervisor of the Okanogan National Forest, both independently and in cooperation with local officials, to identify and implement certain mitigating measures.

Four organizations (respondents) opposing the decision to issue a permit appealed the Regional Forester's decision to the Chief of the Forest Service. *See* 36 CFR § 211.18 (1988).

After a hearing, he affirmed the Regional Forester's decision. Stressing that the decision, which simply approved the general concept of issuing a 30-year special use permit for development of Sandy Butte, did not authorize construction of a particular ski area and, in fact, did not even act on MRI's specific permit application, he concluded that the EIS's discussion of mitigation was "adequate for this stage in the review process."

* * *

Concluding that the Early Winters Study was inadequate as a matter of law, the Court of Appeals reversed [the decision of a U.S. Magistrate]. *Methow Valley Citizens Council v. Regional Forester,* 833 F.2d 810 (9th Cir. 1987). The court held that the Forest Service could not rely on "'the implementation of mitigation measures'" to support its conclusion that the impact on the mule deer would be minor "since not only has the effectiveness of these mitigation measures not yet been assessed, but the mitigation measures themselves have yet to be developed." *Id.* at 817. It then added that if the agency had difficulty obtaining adequate information to make a reasoned assessment of the environmental impact on the herd, it had a duty to make a so-called "worst case analysis." Such an analysis is "'formulated on the basis of available information, using reasonable projections of the worst possible consequences of a proposed action.' *Save our Ecosystems* [*v. Clark,*] 747 F.2d [1240], at 1244-45 (9th Cir. 1984) (quoting 46 Fed. Reg. 18032 (1981))." *Ibid.*

The court found a similar defect in the EIS['s] treatment of air quality. Since the EIS made it clear that commercial development in the Methow Valley will result in violations of state air quality standards unless effective mitigation measures are put in place by the local governments and the private developer, the Court of Appeals concluded that the Forest Service had an affirmative duty to "develop the necessary mitigation measures *before* the permit is granted." *Id.* at 819 (emphasis in original) (footnote omitted). The court held that this duty was imposed by both the Forest Service's own regulations and § 102 of NEPA. *Ibid.* It read the statute as imposing a substantive requirement that "action be taken to mitigate the adverse effects of major federal actions." *Ibid. (quoting Stop H-3 Assn. v. Brinegar,* 389 F. Supp. 1102, 1111 (Haw. 1974), *rev'd on other grounds,* 533 F.2d 434 (9th Cir.), *cert. denied,* 429 U.S. 999 (1976)). For this reason, it concluded that "an EIS must include a fair discussion of measures to mitigate the adverse environmental impacts of a proposed action." 833 F.2d at 819. The Court of Appeals concluded by quoting this paragraph from an opinion it had just announced:

> "'The importance of the mitigation plan cannot be overestimated. It is a determinative factor in evaluating the adequacy of an environmental impact statement. Without a complete mitigation plan, the decisionmaker is unable to make an informed judgment as to the environmental impact of the project—one of the main purposes of an environmental impact statement.'" *Id.* at 820 (*quoting Oregon Natural Resources Council v. Marsh,* 832 F.2d 1489, 1493 (9th Cir. 1987), *rev'd,* 490 U.S. 360 (1989)).

II

Section 101 of NEPA declares a broad national commitment to protecting and promoting environmental quality. 42 U.S.C. § 4331. To ensure that this commitment is "infused into the ongoing programs and actions of the Federal Government, the act also establishes some important 'action-forcing' procedures." 115 Cong. Rec. 40416 (remarks of Sen. Jackson). * * *

The statutory requirement that a federal agency contemplating a major action prepare such an environmental impact statement serves NEPA's "action-forcing" purpose in two important respects. *See Baltimore Gas & Electric Co. v. Natural Resources Defense Council, Inc.,* 462 U.S. 87, 97 (1983); *Weinberger v. Catholic Action of Hawaii/Peace Education Project,* 454 U.S. 139, 143 (1981). It ensures that the agency, in reaching its decision, will have available and will carefully consider detailed information concerning significant environmental impacts; it also guarantees that the relevant information will be made available to the larger audience that may also play a role in both the decisionmaking process and the implementation of that decision.

Simply by focusing the agency's attention on the environmental consequences of a proposed project, NEPA ensures that important effects will not be overlooked or underestimated only to be discovered after resources have been committed or the die otherwise cast. *See ibid.*; *Kleppe, supra,* 427 U.S. at 409. Moreover, the strong precatory language of § 101 of the Act and the requirement that agencies prepare detailed impact statements inevitably bring pressure to bear on agencies "to respond to the needs of environmental quality." 115 Cong. Rec. 40425 (1969) (remarks of Sen. Muskie).

Publication of an EIS, both in draft and final form, also serves a larger informational role. It gives the public the assurance that the agency "has indeed considered environmental concerns in its decisionmaking process," *Baltimore Gas & Electric Co., supra,* 462 U.S. at 97, and, perhaps more significantly, provides a springboard for public comment, *see* L. CALDWELL, SCIENCE AND THE NATIONAL ENVIRONMENTAL POLICY ACT 72 (1982). Thus, in this case the final draft of the Early Winters Study reflects not only the work of the Forest Service itself, but also the critical views of the Washington State Department of Game, the Methow Valley Citizens Council, and Friends of the Earth, as well as many others, to whom copies of the draft Study were circulated. Moreover, with respect to a development such as Sandy Butte, where the adverse effects on air quality and the mule deer herd are primarily attributable to predicted off-site development that will be subject to regulation by other governmental bodies, the EIS serves the function of offering those bodies adequate notice of the expected consequences and the opportunity to plan and implement corrective measures in a timely manner.

The sweeping policy goals announced in § 101 of NEPA are thus realized through a set of "action-forcing" procedures that require that agencies take a "'hard look' at environmental consequences," *Kleppe, supra,* 427 U.S. at 410 n.21 (citation omitted), and that provide for broad dissemination of relevant environmental information. Although these procedures are almost certain to affect the agency's substantive decision, it is now well settled that NEPA itself does not mandate particular results, but simply prescribes the necessary process. *See Strycker's Bay Neighborhood Council, Inc. v. Karlen,* 444 U.S. 223, 227-28, (1980) (*per curiam*); *Vermont Yankee Nuclear Power Corp. v. Natural Resources Defense Council, Inc.,* 435 U.S. 519, 558 (1978). If the adverse environmental effects of the proposed action are adequately identified and evaluated, the agency is not constrained by NEPA from deciding that other values outweigh the environmental costs. *See ibid.*; *Strycker's Bay Neighborhood Council, Inc., supra,* 444 U.S. at 227-28; *Kleppe,* 427 U.S. at 410, n.21. In this case, for example, it would not have violated NEPA if the Forest Service, after complying with the Act's procedural prerequisites, had decided that the benefits to be derived from downhill skiing at Sandy Butte justified the issuance of a special use permit, notwithstanding the loss of 15 percent, 50 percent, or even 100 percent of the mule deer herd. Other statutes may impose substantive environmental obligations on federal agencies, but NEPA merely prohibits uninformed—rather than unwise—agency action.

To be sure, one important ingredient of an EIS is the discussion of steps that can be taken to mitigate adverse environmental consequences. The requirement that an EIS contain a detailed discussion of possible mitigation measures flows from both the language of the Act and, more expressly, from CEQ's implementing regulations. Implicit in NEPA's demand that an agency prepare a detailed statement on "any adverse environmental effects which cannot be avoided should the proposal be implemented," 42 U.S.C. § 4332(C)(ii), is an understanding that the EIS will discuss the extent to which adverse effects can be avoided. *See* D. MANDELKER, NEPA LAW AND LITIGATION § 10:38 (1984). More generally, omission of a reasonably complete discussion of possible mitigation measures would undermine the "action-forcing" function of NEPA.

Without such a discussion, neither the agency nor other interested groups and individuals can properly evaluate the severity of the adverse effects. An adverse effect that can be fully remedied by, for example, an inconsequential public expenditure is certainly not as serious as a similar effect that can only be modestly ameliorated through the commitment of vast public and private resources. Recognizing the importance of such a discussion in guaranteeing that the agency has taken a "hard look" at the environmental consequences of proposed federal action, CEQ regulations require that the agency discuss possible mitigation measures in defining the scope of the EIS, 40 C.F.R. § 1508.25(b) (1987), in discussing alternatives to the proposed action, § 1502.14(f), and consequences of that action, § 1502.16(h), and in explaining its ultimate decision, § 1505.2(c).

There is a fundamental distinction, however, between a requirement that mitigation be discussed in sufficient detail to ensure that environmental consequences have been fairly evaluated, on the one hand, and a substantive requirement that a complete mitigation plan be actually formulated and adopted, on the other. In this case, the off-site effects on air quality and on the mule deer herd cannot be mitigated unless nonfederal government agencies take appropriate action. Since it is those state and local governmental bodies that have jurisdiction over the area in which the adverse effects need be addressed and since they have the authority to mitigate them, it would be incongruous to conclude that the Forest Service has no power to act until the local agencies have reached a final conclusion on what mitigating measures they consider necessary. Even more significantly, it would be inconsistent with NEPA's reliance on procedural mechanisms—as opposed to substantive, result-based standards—to demand the presence of a fully developed plan that will mitigate environmental harm before an agency can act. Cf. *Baltimore Gas & Electric Co.,* 462 U.S. at 100 ("NEPA does not require agencies to adopt any particular internal decisionmaking structure").

We thus conclude that the Court of Appeals erred, first, in assuming that "NEPA requires that 'action be taken to mitigate the adverse effects of major federal actions,'" 833 F.2d at 819 (*quoting Stop H-3 Assn. v. Brinegar,* 389 F. Supp. at 1111), and, second, in finding that this substantive requirement entails the further duty to include in every EIS "a detailed explanation of specific measures which *will* be employed to mitigate the adverse impacts of a proposed action," 833 F.2d at 819 (emphasis supplied).

III

The Court of Appeals also concluded that the Forest Service had an obligation to make a "worst case analysis" if it could not make a reasoned assessment of the impact of the Early Winters project on the mule deer herd. Such a "worst case analysis" was required at one time by CEQ regulations, but those regulations have since been amended. Moreover, although the prior regulations may well have expressed a permissible application of NEPA, the Act itself does not mandate that uncertainty in predicting environmental harms be addressed exclusively in this manner. Accordingly, we conclude that the Court of Appeals also erred in requiring the "worst case" study.

In 1977, President Carter directed that CEQ promulgate binding regulations implementing the procedural provisions of NEPA. Exec. Order No. 11991, 3 C.F.R. 123 (1977 Comp.). Pursuant to this presidential order, CEQ promulgated implementing regulations. Under § 1502.22 of these regulations—a provision which became known as the "worst case requirement"—CEQ provided that if certain information relevant to the agency's evaluation of the proposed action is either unavailable or too costly to obtain, the agency must include in the EIS a "worst case analysis and an indication of the probability or improbability of its occurrence." 40 C.F.R. § 1502.22 (1985). In 1986, however, CEQ replaced the "worst case" requirement with a requirement that federal agencies, in the face of unavailable information concerning a reasonably foreseeable significant environmental consequence, prepare "a summary of existing credible scientific evidence which is relevant to evaluating the . . . adverse impacts" and prepare an "evaluation of such impacts based upon theoretical approaches or research methods generally accepted in the scientific community." 40 C.F.R. § 1502.22(b) (1987). The amended regulation thus "retains the duty to describe the consequences of a remote, but potentially severe impact, but grounds the duty in evaluation of scientific opinion rather than in the framework of a conjectural 'worst case analysis.'" 50 Fed. Reg. 32237 (1985).

The Court of Appeals recognized that the "worst case analysis" regulation has been superseded, yet held that "[t]his rescission . . . does not nullify the requirement . . . since the regulation was merely a codification of prior NEPA case law." 833 F.2d at 817 n.11. This conclusion, however, is erroneous in a number of respects. Most notably, review of NEPA case law reveals that the regulation, in fact, was not a codification of prior judicial decisions. The cases cited by the Court of Appeals ultimately rely on the Fifth Circuit's decision in *Sierra Club v. Sigler,* 695 F.2d 957 (1983). *Sigler,* however, simply recognized that the "worst case analysis" regulation codified the "judicially created principl[e]" that an EIS must "consider the probabilities of the occurrence of any environmental effects it discusses." *Id.* at 970-71. As CEQ recognized at the time it superseded the regulation, case law prior to the adoption of the "worst case analysis" provision did require agencies to describe environmental impacts even in the face of substantial uncertainty, but did not require that this obligation necessarily be met through the mechanism of a "worst case analysis." *See* 51 Fed. Reg. 15625 (1986). CEQ's abandonment of the "worst case analysis" provision, therefore, is not inconsistent with any previously established judicial interpretation of the statute.

Nor are we convinced that the new CEQ regulation is not controlling simply because it was preceded by a rule that was in some respects more demanding. In *Andrus v. Sierra Club,* 442 U.S. at 358, we held that CEQ regulations are entitled to substantial deference. In that case we recognized that although less deference may be in order in some cases in which the "'administrative guidelines'" conflict "'with earlier pronouncements of the agency,'" *ibid.* (*quoting General Electric Co. v. Gilbert,* 429 U.S. 125, 143 (1976)), substantial deference is nonetheless appropriate if there appears to have been good reason for the change, 442 U.S. at 358. Here, the amendment only came after the prior regulation had been subjected to considerable criticism.[4] Moreover, the amendment was designed to better serve the twin functions of an EIS—requiring agencies to take a "hard look" at the consequences of the proposed action and providing important information to other groups and individuals. CEQ explained that by requiring that an EIS focus on reasonably foreseeable impacts, the new regulation "will generate information and discussion on those consequences of greatest concern to the public and of greatest relevance to the agency's decision," 50 Fed. Reg. 32237 (1985),

---

4   As CEQ explained:

"Many respondents to the Council's Advance Notice of Proposed Rulemaking pointed to the limitless nature of the inquiry established by this requirement; that is, one can always conjure up a worse 'worst case' by adding an additional variable to a hypothetical scenario. Experts in the field of risk analysis and perception stated that the 'worst case analysis' lacks defensible rationale or procedures, and that the current regulatory language stands 'without any discernible link to the disciplines that have devoted so much thought and effort toward developing rational ways to cope with problems of uncertainty. It is, therefore, not surprising that no one knows how to do a worst case analysis . . .', Slovic, P., February 1, 1985, Response to ANPRM.

"Moreover, in the institutional context of litigation over EIS(s) the 'worst case' rule has proved counterproductive, because it has led to agencies being required to devote substantial time and resources to preparation of analyses which are not considered useful to decisionmakers and divert the EIS process from its intended purpose." 50 Fed. Reg. 32236 (1985).

rather than distorting the decisionmaking process by overemphasizing highly speculative harms, 51 Fed. Reg. 15624-15625 (1986); 50 Fed. Reg. 32236 (1985). In light of this well-considered basis for the change, the new regulation is entitled to substantial deference. Accordingly, the Court of Appeals erred in concluding that the Early Winters Study is inadequate because it failed to include a "worst case analysis."

* * *

V

In sum, we conclude that NEPA does not require a fully developed plan detailing what steps will be taken to mitigate adverse environmental impacts and does not require a "worst case analysis." * * * The judgment of the Court of Appeals is accordingly reversed and the case is remanded for further proceedings consistent with this opinion.

It is so ordered.

Justice BRENNAN, concurring.

I write separately to highlight the Court's observation that "one important ingredient of an EIS is the discussion of steps that can be taken to mitigate adverse environmental consequences."

NOTES

1.   The Court describes a three stage process for obtaining the right to develop a ski area on national forest lands. The decision challenged in this case involved the first stage— the decision to issue a special use permit. What is the scope of the EIS required at this stage in the process? Is the agency required to consider the environmental impacts associated with the final two stages?

2.   The Court notes that "NEPA merely prohibits uninformed—rather than unwise— agency action." 490 U.S. 332 at 351. Is this holding consistent with prior case law? Suppose the proposed ski area and associated development would in fact lead to the demise of the entire mule deer herd and the costs of the project exceeded the benefits by a ratio of 10 to 1. How might the Methow Valley Citizens Council have used these facts in an effort to stop this project? *See Baltimore Gas & Electric Co. v. Natural Resources Defense Council*, 462 U.S. 87 (1983), *supra* at Chapter 5. Is it arbitrary and capricious for an agency to refuse to require mitigation of environmental impacts where such mitigation can be done at a reasonable cost, and where the benefits of mitigation plainly exceed those costs?

3.   How did the 1986 CEQ regulations amend the worst case analysis requirement? How should this change affect the analysis of issues where agencies lack adequate information? *See* 40 C.F.R. § 1502.22. Which do you think is the better approach? Does the EIS prepared for the proposed Early Winters Ski Resort meet the requirements of the current CEQ rules regarding uncertainty? *See id.*

Tragically, worst case scenarios sometimes occur. In *Trout Unlimited v. Morton*, 509 F.2d 1276 (9th Cir. 1974), the court rejected a series of challenges to the adequacy of an EIS prepared for the proposed Bureau of Reclamation's Teton Dam and reservoir. A litigator for the Sierra Club Legal Defense Fund recalled that among the issues raised by the plaintiffs was the failure of the Bureau adequately to consider the possibility of catastrophic dam failure given the geologic unsuitability of the site. The court dismissed this concern by characterizing it as remote, highly speculative, and possible but improbable. *Id.* at 1283. "Two years later, as the reservoir was being filled, the Teton Dam burst, flooding over 300 square miles, killing 11 people, and causing an estimated $1 billion in property damage." *Application of the National Environmental Policy Act: Hearing before the Subcomm. on Oversight and Investigations of the Senate Comm. on Energy and Natural Resources*, 104th Cong., 1st Sess. 30 (1995) (statement of Robert G. Dreher, Sierra Club Legal Defense Fund).

4.   The Ninth Circuit's view that NEPA should require a more detailed mitigation plan has its defenders. *See, e.g.,* Debra L. Donahue, Note, *Taking a Hard Look at Mitigation: The Case for the* Northwest Indian *Rule,* 59 U. COLO. L. REV. 687 (1988); Antonio Rossmann, *NEPA: Not So Well at Twenty,* 20 Envtl. L. Rep. (Envtl. L. Inst.) 10174 (1990). Should Congress amend NEPA to require mitigation of environmental impacts where such mitigation can be accomplished at a reasonable cost? *See* H.R. 1113, 101st Cong., 1st Sess. (1989); S. 1089, 101st Cong., 1st Sess. (1989).

5.   Suppose the Forest Service had prepared an EA and a FONSI instead of an EIS in the *Methow Valley* situation. Would the Court have allowed the agency to rely on a discussion of mitigation measures without a plan of implementation? *Compare* Council on Environmental Quality, Forty Most Asked Questions Concerning CEQ's National Environmental Policy Act, 46 Fed. Reg. 18026, 18037-38 (1981), *and Foundation for North American Wild Sheep v. U.S. Dep't of Agriculture,* 681 F.2d 1172 (9th Cir. 1982), *with Friends of the Earth v. Hintz,* 800 F.2d 822 (9th Cir. 1986), *and Cabinet Mountains Wilderness/Scotchman's Peak Grizzly Bears v. Peterson,* 685 F.2d 678 (D.C. Cir. 1982).

CABINET MOUNTAIN WILDERNESS/SCOTCHMAN'S GRIZZLY BEARS V. PETERSON
685 F.2d 678 (D.C. Cir 1982)

ROBB, Senior Circuit Judge.

In this action in the District Court the plaintiffs challenged the decision of the United States Forest Service to approve a plan of operations for exploratory mineral drilling in the Cabinet Mountains Wilderness Area in Northwestern Montana. The plaintiffs alleged the Forest Service action violated the Endangered Species Act (ESA), 16 U.S.C. §§ 1531 *et seq.*, and the National Environmental Policy Act (NEPA), 42 U.S.C. §§ 4321 *et seq.* ASARCO, Inc. intervened as a defendant to protect its interest as the drilling permittee. On cross-motions for summary judgment the District Court upheld the Forest Service's decision. *Cabinet Mountain Wilderness v. Peterson,* 510 F. Supp. 1186 (D.D.C. 1981). The plaintiffs appeal. We affirm the judgment of the District Court.

The Cabinet Mountain Wilderness Area consists of approximately 94,272 acres and is part of the Cabinet-Yaak ecosystem, one of only six ecosystems in the continental United States that supports populations of grizzly bears. The bears are listed as a threatened species under the ESA. *See* 50 C.F.R. § 17.11(h) (1981). Although it is estimated that only about a dozen grizzly bears may inhabit a portion of the Cabinet Mountains area where drilling will take place, the area has been recognized as having a high potential for grizzly bear management.

ASARCO holds a claim block consisting of 149 unpatented mining claims totaling 2,980 acres, most of them located in the Cabinet Mountains Wilderness Area. In 1979 ASARCO submitted a proposal to conduct preliminary exploratory drilling. The Forest Service began an extensive review of the proposal, including an environmental assessment, biological evaluation, and biological opinion. The Forest Service approved the proposal and ASARCO drilled four holes between July and November of that year. On February 4, 1980 ASARCO submitted a proposal for the continuation of the 1979 exploration program to be conducted during 1980-1983. For 1980, 36 drill holes on 22 sites in the Chicago Peak area of the Wilderness were proposed with a similar level of activity expected to take place in each of the three succeeding years. The purpose of the drilling program is to assess the extent of copper and silver deposits in the area. Each drill site is limited to an area of 20 feet by 20 feet. Over a four-year period these sites will occupy a combined area of about one-half acre. Pursuant to 36 C.F.R. § 252.4(f) (1981), the Forest Service prepared an environmental assessment of the proposal, referred to as the Chicago Peak Mining Exploration Project. Copies of the assessment were sent to various individuals for comment and five public meetings were held. In accordance with section 7(c) of the ESA, the Forest Service prepared a biological evaluation, assessing potential effects of the proposal on the grizzly bears. It concluded that the cumulative impact of the drilling together with other activities in the Cabinet Mountains Wilderness Area, such as timber sales, could adversely affect the bears. Therefore fourteen specific recommendations were made which were designed to reduce these potential effects to a minimum. To offset the adverse effects of the drilling activities the evaluation suggested the adoption of compensatory measures which would positively influence grizzly habitat.

Pursuant to section 7(a)(2) of the ESA, the Forest Service initiated formal consultation with the Fish and Wildlife Service of the Department of Interior (FWS). In compliance with section 7(b) of the ESA, the FWS prepared a biological opinion detailing the effects of the ASARCO Chicago Peak project on the grizzlies and suggesting alternatives. This biological opinion was submitted to the Forest Service on June 19, 1980 and stated that the ASARCO proposal was "likely to jeopardize the continued existence of the grizzly bear." The principal factors underlying this conclusion were:

(a) The current precarious status of the Cabinet Mountains grizzly bear population.

(b) Impacts that exploration may have upon denning activities and hence reproductive success.

(c) The level of current and proposed projects that will be occurring simultaneously with the exploration program, further removing the amount of habitat available to the grizzly.

The FWS outlined an alternative course of action which would avoid jeopardizing the continued existence of the Cabinet Mountains grizzly bear population. According to the FWS, the alternative was designed to "completely compensate in specific ways the cumulative adverse effects of the proposed project and other ongoing and proposed Forest Service activities." Three measures were described: (1) limiting ASARCO's proposed annual period of operation so that no drilling or helicopter flights occur after September 30 of each operating season. This was a month earlier than ASARCO proposed; (2) rescheduling or eliminating certain timber sales; and (3) ordering seasonal or permanent road closures so as to provide greater security for the grizzlies' habitat.

In May 1980 the Forest Service completed a final environmental assessment which incorporated the recommendations made by the FWS in its biological opinion. In addition the

Forest Service recommended measures designed to mitigate the adverse effects on the Wilderness Area with particular regard to the grizzly bears, including a prohibition on overnight camping by ASARCO personnel except in emergency situations, daily and seasonal restrictions on helicopter flights to avoid disturbing the grizzlies during the important denning and feeding periods, restrictions on helicopter usage to specified flight corridors, reclamation of drilling sites, seasonal restrictions on drilling activities in specified areas of the Wilderness, and monitoring of ASARCO's operations by Forest Service personnel. The plan devised by the FWS was expressly adopted by the Forest Service.

On June 17, 1980 the Kootenai National Forest Supervisor, William E. Morden, issued a "Decision Notice and Finding of No Significant Impact" which approved the ASARCO plan subject to the modifications contained in the environmental assessment and the complete compensation plan described in the FWS's biological opinion. Morden concluded that the impacts of the proposed activity had been adequately assessed and appropriate measures initiated to ensure that "[t]he continued existence of the grizzly bear is not threatened nor is its critical habitat adversely modified." Because the environmental assessment found there would be no significant impacts from the proposal as modified, Morden stated that an environmental impact statement (EIS) was unnecessary. Approval was expressly limited to the proposed exploratory drilling activities; further activities such as developmental exploration or mineral extraction would require a comprehensive examination of environmental effects.

After an unsuccessful administrative appeal of the decision plaintiffs began this action in the District Court. The plaintiffs averred that the Forest Service had violated its responsibilities under section 7(a)(2) of the ESA, which provides, "[e]ach Federal agency shall . . . insure that any action authorized, funded, or carried out by such agency is not likely to jeopardize the continued existence of any endangered species or threatened species or result in the destruction or adverse modification of habitat of such species. . . ." The plaintiffs also argued that the agency's failure to prepare an EIS violated NEPA. On April 15, 1981 the district judge denied the plaintiffs' motion for summary judgement and granted the summary judgement motions of the Forest Service and ASARCO. The court first concluded that agency actions under the ESA are subject to the arbitrary and capricious standard of review, rather than de novo review, 510 F. Supp. at 1189. It then held that the Forest Service had met its burden under both NEPA and the ESA by showing that its decision was not arbitrary or capricious. *Id.* The court emphasized that the Forest Service had imposed mitigation measures and taken affirmative steps to ensure that the grizzly bears would be protected. *Id.* at 1190. Also the court noted that only exploratory drilling had been approved and that more extensive activities would require further environmental studies and approval. *Id.*

Two issues are presented for review: first, whether the agency erred by failing to prepare an EIS, second, whether the agency's decision to permit the drilling program violated the ESA.

Appellants contend that the Forest Service violated NEPA by failing to prepare an EIS. NEPA requires that an EIS be prepared for major federal actions "significantly affecting the quality of the human environment . . ." § 102(2)(C). Under the statute the administrative agency has the "initial and primary responsibility" to ascertain whether an EIS is required and its decision can be overturned only if it was arbitrary, capricious or an abuse of discretion. *Committee for Auto Responsibility v. Solomon*, 603 F.2d 992, 1002 (D.C. Cir. 1979), *cert. denied*, 445 U.S. 915 (1980).

Both the Forest Service and the FWS concluded that the ASARCO proposal could have an adverse impact upon the grizzly bears, particularly when other concurrent activities in the Cabinet Mountains area were taken into account. Numerous specific recommendations were made to avoid this impact and mitigation measures to protect the grizzly bears were imposed upon the proposal. As we have said these measures were designed to "completely compensate" both the adverse effects of ASARCO proposal and the cumulative effects of other activities on the bears and their habitat. In light of the imposition of these measures, the Forest Service concluded that implementation of ASARCO proposal would not result in "any significant effects upon the quality of the human environment." Therefore an EIS was found to be unnecessary.

This court has established four criteria for reviewing an agency's decision to forego preparation of an EIS: (1) whether the agency took a "hard look" at the problem; (2) whether the agency identified the relevant areas of environmental concern; (3) as to the problems studied and identified, whether the agency made a convincing case that the impact was insignificant; and (4) if there was impact of true significance, whether the agency convincingly established that changes in the project sufficiently reduced it to a minimum. *Maryland-National Park and Planning Comm'n v. United States Postal Service*, 487 F.2d 1029, 1040 (1973). The fourth criterion permits consideration of any mitigation measures that the agency imposed on the proposal. As this court noted, "changes in the project are not legally adequate to avoid an impact statement *unless they permit a determination that such impact as remains, after the change, is not 'significant.'*" *Id.* (emphasis supplied). Other courts have also permitted the effect of mitigation measures to be considered in determining whether preparation of an EIS is necessary. *See e.g., Preservation Coalition, Inc. v. Pierce*, 667 F.2d 851, 860 (9th Cir. 1982); *City & County of San Francisco v. United States*, 615 F.2d 498, 501 (9th Cir. 1980); *Sierra Club v. Alexander*, 484 F. Supp. 445, 468 (N.D.N.Y.), *aff'd men.*, 633 F.2d 206 (2d Cir. 1980). Logic also supports this result. NEPA's EIS requirement is governed by the rule of reason, *Committee for Auto Responsibility v. Solomon*, 603 F.2d at 1003 (D.C. Cir. 1979), and an EIS must be prepared only when significant environmental impacts will occur as a result of the proposed action. If, however, the proposal is modified prior to implementation by adding specific mitigation measures which completely compensate for any possible adverse environmental impacts stemming from the original proposal, the statutory threshold of significant environmental effects is not crossed and an EIS is not required. To require an EIS in such circumstances would trivialize NEPA and would "diminish its utility in providing useful environmental analysis for major federal actions that truly affect the environment." *Id.*

The appellants rely on a recent statement by the Council on Environmetnal Quality (CEQ) concerning the effect of mitigation measures on NEPA's EIS requirement. In a publication entitled "Forty Most Asked Questions Concerning CEQ's National Environmental Policy Act Regulations," 46 Fed. Reg. 18,026 (1981), the CEQ said:

> Mitigation measures may be relied upon to make a finding of no significant impact only if they are imposed by statute or regulation, or submitted by an applicant or agency as part of the original proposal. As a general rule, the regulations contemplate that agencies should use a broad approach in defining significance and should not rely on the possibility of mitigation as an excuse to avoid the EIS requirement.

Id. at 18,038. Because the mitigation measures adopted in the present case were not part of the original proposal and were not imposed by statute or regulation, appellants contend they can not be used to justify the Forest Service's failure to prepare an EIS.

We think the appellants' reliance on the CEQ statement is misplaced. The CEQ is charged with administering NEPA and its interpretations are generally entitled to substantial deference, *Andrus v. Sierra Club*, 442 U.S. 347, 358 (1979), but such deference is neither required nor appropriate here. The NEPA regulations issued by the CEQ are binding on all federal agencies. Exec. Order 11,991, 3 C.F.R. 123, 124 (1978). The "Forty Questions" publication, however, is merely an informal statement, not a regulation, and we do not find it to be persuasive authority. *See General Electric v. Gilbert*, 429 U.S. 125, 141-42, (1976). Unlike the regulations considered in the *Andrus* case, it was not the product of notice and comment procedures and does not impose a mandatory obligation on all federal agencies. Although the introduction to the memorandum states that it does not impose any additional requirements beyond those contained in the NEPA regulations, 46 Fed. Reg. At 18,026, the answer relied on by appellants is "not at all evident from the underlying regulations." *Cabinet Mountains Wilderness v. Peterson*, 510 F. Supp. at 1190, n.4. The sections cited by the CEQ, 40 C.F.R. §§ 1508.8 and 1508.27 (1981), construe the terms "effects" and "significantly" broadly but do not discuss the appropriateness of mitigation measures. Moreover, the CEQ published the "Forty Questions" on March 23, 1981, approximately nine months after the Forest Service approved ASARCO's exploratory drilling program. Fairness would require that it not be accorded binding retroactive effect.

Because the mitigation measures were properly taken into consideration by the agency, we have no difficulty in concluding that the Forest Service's decision that an EIS was unnecessary was not arbitrary or capricious. The record indicates that the Forest Service carefully considered the ASARCO proposal, was well informed on the problems presented, identified the relevant areas of environmental concern, and weighed the likely impacts.

When ASARCO submitted its four-year drilling proposal the agency prepared an environmental assessment, copies were circulated for comment, and public meetings were held. An extensive biological evaluation was conducted which concluded the proposed drilling could potentially affect the grizzly bears in two ways: habitat modification and increased human-bear interactions, including direct encounters and reductions in secure habitat due to human disturbances. The evaluation also pointed out that the cumulative effects of the proposal and other concurrent activities might be significantly greater than the effects of the drilling proposal considered by itself. As to habitat modification, the evaluation concluded the adverse effect would be insignificant. The total area involved in the drilling was estimated to be less than one-half acre and even this estimate was considered high because the drill sites could be reclaimed. The more serious threat was posed by the loss of secure habitat due to increased human activities in the area, particularly the disturbance of important denning and feeding sites. Timber sales and recreational activities were specifically referred to. To reduce such potential adverse effects to a minimum, fourteen recommendations were made, including completion of project activities by October 31 of each year, restrictions of helicopter flights to specified corridors, measures to reduce helicopter noise, seasonal restrictions on the use of helicopters in particular areas, prohibition of project activities in the Copper Gulch area after July 31 in order to protect potentially important late summer and early fall food sources, daily restrictions on helicopter flights during important feeding periods, monitoring of the project by a biological technician, closure of various roads to protect the bears during feeding periods and to enhance their security, prohibiting the carrying of firearms by ASARCO personnel, prohibiting overnight camping by project personnel except in emergency situations, and daily removal of food wrappers, containers and excess food.

The Forest Service also initiated formal consultation with the FWS. In its biological opinion the FWS expressed concern over the cumulative effects of human activities in the area and agreed that displacement of the bears from secure habitats was the most serious impact of the proposal. Although the FWS concluded that the drilling program was likely to jeopardize the bears, it set forth a number of measures which were designed to avoid this result. To reduce adverse effects to a minimum the FWS stated that restrictions set forth in the biological evaluation prepared by the Forest Service must be strictly adhered to. Because the Chicago Peak area is a potentially important denning area, the FWS recommended that September 30, rather than October 31, should be the annual termination date for drilling activities. In assessing the cumulative effects of activities in the area, the FWS used a 10-mile radius for the bears to determine which other activities were relevant. This estimated travel radius was based on several expert studies of grizzly bears' home range. Using this method the FWS determined that certain timber sales and roads were relevant in addressing the problem of cumulative effects. Therefore, in addition to modifying ASARCO's period of operations, the FWS recommended rescheduling or eliminating certain timber sales and implementing specified road closures to provide a more secure habitat for the bears. According to the FWS, this course of action would "completely compensate in specific ways the cumulative adverse effects of the proposed project and other ongoing and proposed Forest Service activities" and would "avoid jeopardizing the continued existence of the grizzly bear." The Forest Service's final environmental assessment incorporated the recommendations made in the biological evaluation and biological opinion and expressly adopted the complete compensation plan devised by the FWS.

Appellants have not demonstrated any deficiencies in the agency's decision making process. They allege that the agency did not address the issue of cumulative impacts, that the effectiveness of the mitigation measures is not factually supported, and that the measures are too vague to be enforced. All these contentions are without merit. As we have noted, the Forest Service carefully considered the cumulative effects of activities in the Cabinet Mountains area. This led to curtailment of timber sales and the closure of several roads. As to the factual basis of the agency's decision, the Forest Service and FWS conducted a comprehensive evaluation of the proposal. Wildlife biologists were consulted and expert studies were referred to. For each identified area of concern, one or more measures were implemented to mitigate potential adverse environmental effects.

* * *

We emphasize that our review of the agency's action is limited to the approval of the four-year exploratory drilling proposal. Similarly, the Forest Service and the FWS expressly limited their findings to the drilling program presented by ASARCO, which is minor in scope and temporary in nature. Any future proposals by ASARCO to conduct drilling activities in the Cabinet Mountains area will require further scrutiny under NEPA and the ESA.

We conclude therefore that the Forest Service's findings that an EIS was unnecessary and that the existence of the Cabinet Mountain grizzly bears was not likely to be jeopardized by the ASARCO drilling project were not arbitrary or capricious. Accordingly, the order of the District Court is

Affirmed.

NOTES

1.   Despite the fact that the decision seems contrary to the CEQ's "Forty Questions" guidance document, the result in *Cabinet Mountain* has proved popular in the courts. *See, e.g.*, *Audubon Society of Central Arkansas v. Dailey*, 977 F.2d 428, 436 (8th Cir. 1992); *Roanoke River Basin Ass'n v. Hudson*, 940 F.2d 58, 62 (4th Cir. 1991); *C.A.R.E. Now, Inc. v. Federal Aviation Administration*, 844 F.2d 1569, 1575 (11th Cir. 1988). Do you agree with the court that any other interpretation would "trivialize NEPA" and "diminish its utility in providing useful environmental analysis for major federal actions that truly affect the environment"? Is the court's dismissal of the CEQ's Forty Questions guidance consistent with the deference required by the Supreme Court under *Skidmore v. Swift & Co.*, 323 U.S. 134 (1944). *See* Chapter 3, *supra*.

2.   Mitigation to avoid preparing an EIS has proved popular with agencies and applicants for agency action since it allows them to avoid the much more onerous standards

of EIS preparation set out at 40 C.F.R. subpart 1502. The CEQ estimates that agencies prepare more than 100 EAs for every EIS they prepare. The Council on Environmental Quality, Twenty-Fifth Anniversary Report 51 (1997).

3. In the same way that agencies may avoid EIS preparation through mitigation, they can also avoid formal consultation through a device established under the Endangered Species Act rules called "informal consultation." 50 C.F.R. § 402.13. "Informal consultation is an optional process * * * designed to assist the Federal agency in determining whether formal consultation * * * is required." *Id.* at § 402.13(a). "During informal consultation, the Service may suggest modifications to the action that the Federal agency and the applicant could implement to avoid the likelihood of adverse effects to the listed species or critical habitat." *Id.* at § 402.13(b). The ratio of "informal" to "formal" consultations under the ESA is even more stark than the ratio of EAs to EISs. One commentator has found that:

> From 1987 to 1994, * * * the FWS carried out nearly 100,000 formal and informal consultations with other federal agencies on projects and activities that potentially jeopardized the continued existence of endangered or threatened species under Section 7 of the ESA. Of these, almost 95,000 were conducted informally and resulted in no project delays or modifications. Of the 2,719 formal consultations, 2,367 resulted in "no jeopardy" findings, allowing the projects to proceed as planned.

Karin P. Sheldon, *Habitat Conservation Planning: Addressing the Achilles Heel of the Endangered Species Act*, 6 N.Y.U. Envtl. L.J. 279, 280 n.8 (1998).

Roosevelt Campobello International Park Comm'n v. United States Environmental Protection Agency
684 F.2d 1041 (1st Cir. 1982)

Coffin, Chief Judge.

In these three consolidated appeals petitioners challenge the final decision of the EPA Administrator to issue a National Pollutant Discharge Elimination System (NPDES) permit to the Pittston Company pursuant to § 402 of the Clean Water Act. The permit authorizes the Pittston Co. to construct and operate a 250,000 barrel per day oil refinery and associated deep water terminal at Eastport, Maine, in accordance with specified effluent limitations, monitoring requirements, and other conditions. Petitioners contend that EPA's actions violated the National Environmental Policy Act (NEPA), the Endangered Species Act, and the Clean Water Act.

Pittston proposes to construct an oil refinery and marine terminal in Eastport, Maine, a relatively pristine area of great natural beauty near the Canadian border. The area is known for being the foggiest on the East Coast, experiencing some 750-1000 hours of fog a year; daily tides approximate twenty feet. The plan contemplates that crude oil shipments will arrive several times a week in supertankers, or Very Large Crude Carriers (VLCCs), as long as four football fields, or slightly less than a quarter of a mile. The tankers will travel through Canadian waters around the northern tip of Campobello Island, where the Roosevelt Campobello International Park is located down Head Harbor Passage to a refinery near Eastport where they will be turned and berthed. Numerous barges and small tankers will carry the refined product from Eastport to destination markets in the Northeast.

The protracted procedural history of this case begins in April 1973, when Pittston applied to the Maine Board of Environmental Protection (BEP) for permission to locate the refinery in Eastport. After public hearings, the BEP approved the proposal under the Maine Site Location of Development Law, 38 M.R.S.A. § 481 *et seq.,* subject to a number of pre-construction and pre-operation conditions designed primarily to reduce the risk of oil spills. Pittston subsequently filed an application with EPA to obtain an NPDES permit, and submitted an Environmental Assessment Report to aid EPA in its duty to prepare an Environmental Impact Statement (EIS) pursuant to NEPA. *See* 33 U.S.C. § 1371(c)(1); 42 U.S.C. § 4332(2)(C). EPA promulgated a draft EIS recommending issuance of the permit as conditioned by the Maine BEP, held a joint public hearing with the Army Corps of Engineers in Eastport, and received approximately 600 responses during a public comment period. In September 1977, the Maine Department of Environmental Protection certified, under § 401(a)(1) of the Clean Water Act that the proposed discharge would satisfy the appropriate requirements of state and federal law. In June 1978, the final EIS was issued, again recommending that the permit be issued pursuant to the BEP conditions.

Several months later, the National Marine Fisheries Service (NMFS) of the Department of Commerce and the Fish and Wildlife Service (FWS) of the Department of Interior initiated consultations with EPA concerning the proposed refinery's impact on endangered species—the right and humpback whales, and the northern bald eagle, respectively—under § 7 of the Endangered Species Act (ESA). In November, the NMFS issued a threshold determination that there were insufficient data to conclude that the project was not likely to jeopardize the continued existence of the endangered whales. In December, the FWS concluded that the project was likely to jeopardize the bald eagle. In light of these opinions and of the value of the natural resources in the Eastport area as noted in the EIS, EPA's Region I issued a notice of determination to deny Pittston's application for an NPDES permit in January 1979. Pittston thereafter sought an adjudicatory hearing and administrative review of this decision.[2]

Prior to the hearing, extensive consultation between EPA, NMFS, FWS, and Pittston took place to consider mitigation measures proposed by Pittston. In May, NMFS concluded on the basis of the best scientific data available that EPA was unable to comply with the statutory mandate that it "insure that [the project] is not likely to jeopardize the continued existence of" endangered whales. 16 U.S.C. § 1536(a)(2). In June FWS reaffirmed its previous determination that the refinery was likely to jeopardize the bald eagle. EPA Region I amended its decision to include these new findings.

The adjudicatory hearing took place over five weeks in January and February of 1980. More than fifty witnesses testified and were cross-examined; several hundred exhibits were introduced. In January 1981, the ALJ rendered EPA's Initial Decision, overturning EPA Region I and ordering that the NPDES permit issue. He concluded that the EIS was adequate to comply with NEPA, and that no supplemental EIS was necessary; that the risk of oil spills was "minute" and that the refinery was therefore not likely to jeopardize any endangered species; and that the conditions imposed by the Maine BEP, and assumed by the EIS, were not required to be conditions of the federal permit. Petitioners subsequently sought review before the EPA Administrator, and also moved to reopen the record to admit a recent study showing an increased number of endangered whales in the Eastport region. Both motions were denied, and

---

[2]   Pittston also sought an exemption from the requirements of the ESA pursuant to 16 U.S.C. § 1536(g)(1), but this application was ruled not ripe for review until final action by EPA denying a permit. *Pittston Co. v. Endangered Species Comm.,* 14 Env't Rep. Cas. (BNA) 1257 (D.D.C. 1980).

in September 1981 EPA Region I issued the NPDES permit to the Pittston Company. Petitioners now seek review in this court pursuant to § 509(b)(1)(F) of the Clean Water Act.

* * *

II. THE ENDANGERED SPECIES ACT

* * *

C. The Administrative Law Judge's Initial Decision

* * *

2. * * *

We now proceed to outline the ALJ's reasoning leading to his finding, crucial to both ESA issues, of the unlikelihood of a significant oil spill.

3. The Finding as to Risk of Oil Spill

The ALJ's conclusion that the risk of a major oil spill was minute was based primarily on three items of evidence. First, the ALJ relied heavily on assurances from the Coast Guard which, after reviewing the testimony of Pittston's witnesses before the BEP and other data, wrote EPA on March 28, 1977, that the channel in Head Harbor Passage was "adequate for safe navigation by 250,000 DWT tankers" if four conditions were met. These conditions were "(1) that the channel passage area depths, configurations and current data shown on nautical charts and surveys be confirmed by hydrographic survey, (2) provision for a navigation system wherein the existence and movement of all traffic in the area could be monitored, communicated with and scheduled, (3) provision for means to control movement of tankers in the event of steering and/or propulsion failure during transit and (4) development and strict adherence to an operating procedure for tanker passage."

In response to a request by the Council on Environmental Quality that the Coast Guard assist Pittston in carrying out "real time simulation" studies[6] in order to ascertain the precise conditions for safe navigation prior to granting the permit, Rear Admiral Fugaro of the Coast Guard responded in August 1977 that it could not divert scarce resources until "final clearance had been granted for construction of a refinery . . . [so that] no possibility exists that these efforts may be wasted." * * *

Second, the ALJ found confirmation of the Coast Guard's assurance in the computer simulation studies of Dr. Eda, who concluded that a loaded 250,000 DWT tanker could maintain a trajectory close to a desired track in Head Harbor Passage without tug assistance in a 60 knot wind. Although these studies could not account for the human factor, *i.e.*, could not test any difficulty on the part of the human pilot in perceiving the location, heading and rate of change of heading of the ship, the ALJ understood there was "an encouraging correlation" between computer simulation and actual sea trial. The ALJ accepted Dr. Eda's statement that "for obtaining an overall perspective of the suitability of a particular channel for ship traffic of specific sizes under particular conditions, off-line computer studies are adequate."

---

[6]   Real time simulation studies are tests run with actual tanker pilots on a device capable of simulating the responses of a ship to certain conditions of wind, tide, fog, current, etc. What it adds to completely computerized tests is the human reaction factor. The Council on Environmental Quality had included in its comments on the draft EIS the recommendations that "EPA complete its analysis of real time tanker simulation studies, and the twelve trial tanker voyages through Head Harbor passage (required by Maine's Board of Environmental Protection as one of the conditions for granting a refinery permit) before making its permit decision."

Also cited with approval by the ALJ was a second study by Frederick R. Harris, Inc. premised on provision for a more adequate turning basin for the VLCCs than an earlier study which had approved the project subject to severe restrictions and "a high order of seamanship and prudence." This study, the ALJ found, deemed the proposed approach "satisfactory for the type and size of vessels specified providing navigational aides are installed, and providing recommended operational procedures were followed." These included tug assistance from entry into channel, lighted buoys and radar reflectors, an electronic guidance system involving land based radar and electronic range finders, confining berthing and deberthing to slack tide, limiting Head Harbor transit to daylight or clearly moonlit hours, proscribing entrance to the Passage if visibility is less than a mile, and barring tankers awaiting a berth from anchoring in Eastport waters.

Finally, the ALJ made rather minute review of testimony concerning prevailing currents and cross-currents, fog, wind, and duration of oil spill effects, concluding in general that currents were not excessive for shipping, that the expected presence of fog was not so great as to bar shipping during most of the time, that winds were in general within tolerable limits, and that the effects of large known oil spills had not been long lasting over a period of years.

D. Analysis of the Assessment of Risks

We have set forth in some detail and full strength all of the strands of the decision of the ALJ because we conclude that, in light of EPA's duty to insure that the project is unlikely to jeopardize endangered whales or eagles, the ALJ's failure to require, at a minimum, that "real time simulation" studies be done to assure the low risk of an oil spill prior to granting the permit violated his duty to "use the best scientific . . . data available." Given the Supreme Court's statement that the ESA is designed to prevent the loss of any endangered species, "regardless of the cost," *TVA v. Hill,* 437 U.S. at 188 n.34, we cannot see how the permit can issue when real time simulation studies, which EPA, the State of Maine, and the Coast Guard all view as being necessary to a final determination of safety, are to be delayed until the Coast Guard has adequate funds to undertake them.

We begin with the linchpin—the Coast Guard opinion. From what we have reported above, we think it quite clear that the Coast Guard was not purporting to do a risk analysis. It was, in effect, signifying its willingness to accept the problem of devising procedures to minimize navigation risks for vessels of certain characteristics transiting via Head Harbor Passage to Eastport. That this is a correct reading is confirmed by the testimony of Rear Admiral Fugaro, who candidly stated of the Coast Guard opinion that "[i]t's not designed to provide a risk analysis." His letter to EPA, which we have quoted, makes clear that he expected any set of Coast Guard orders and procedures to go through the EIS process.

* * *

We cannot presume to know what issues may be posed as the result of real time simulation studies, or, for that matter, real sea trials by VLCCs under ballast. Risks of collisions or grounding may be identified whose assured prevention may entail costs unacceptable to Pittston or measures involving other environmental intrusions or, simply, unacceptable risks which may persist despite the most stringent and expensive procedures and equipment. That those further studies are conceded to be vital is demonstrated by the following testimony of EIS drafter Stickney:

"Q. So, basically, then you decided that that [results of real time simulation studies] wasn't information that was needed to determine whether this refinery should be built or not?

A. We felt the information was needed and that if the facility failed the real time simulation study it would never be built. * * *

Q. It will be too late, will it not, if that study, for example, shows some problems that you haven't anticipated in the final EIS, it will be too late for EPA to say at that point, now the weighing of risk versus benefit is different than we originally thought? Will it not be too late for that?

A. No, sir."

We see absolutely no justification for issuing an NPDES permit before a closer and feasible risk assessment is made.[11]

Additionally, we note the Coast Guard's requirements of a hydrographic survey to make sure that the depth figures on the navigation chart fairly represent the entire length, width, and depth of the channel, face of pinnacles and outcroppings, so that VLCCs with draft beginning at 65 feet may pass without danger of grounding during the lowest of tides. Never, we suspect, has there been occasion to make sure that the bottom is from 70 to 90 or 100 feet under low water at all times of the year at all points beneath a broad channel seven miles long in Head Harbor Passage. Should the hydrographic survey reveal embarrassing obstructions, this fact and ways of dealing with it must receive the most careful scrutiny.

The other grounds relied on by the ALJ leading to his conclusion of small or minute risk are even less persuasive than the Coast Guard undertaking. Dr. Eda's computer simulations were avowedly valuable for obtaining "an overall perspective of . . . suitability"; they could not approach even a rough approximation of risk, nor could they account for human error in confronting diverse weather conditions. The second Harris study merely pronounced a route "acceptable" if fairly rigorous conditions were complied with, but none of these conditions were incorporated in the federal permit. Finally, the ALJ's analyses of current, wind, fog, and duration of spills gave only general assurance that prudence, procedures, and equipment can, most of the time and absent human error, compensate for difficult conditions of tide, current, fog, wind and weather.

We stress that our disagreement with the ALJ does not involve challenging his credibility judgments, although we do not share his view that the "overwhelming weight" of evidence pointed to the feasibility of safe transit.[12] Were the issue whether, by a preponderance of the

---

[11]   We can sympathize with the always penurious Coast Guard in not eagerly volunteering to run costly tests, but we have seen no reason why Pittston has not financed both the hydrographic survey and real time simulation studies and perhaps the real tanker trial runs it will need to comply with the Maine BEP permit. EPA has reported in its responses to comments on the EIS that Pittston has contracted with the National Marine Research Facility of the Department of Commerce for the studies. This seems to us well within the concept of "best scientific . . . data available." Particularly does this seem true when the whole structure of reasoning about the hazard to two endangered species depends on the force of the conclusion that there is an almost complete absence of risk of a catastrophic oil spill.

[12]   In addition to the evidence referred to above, upon which the ALJ primarily relied, a number of witnesses testified favorably both at the adjudicatory hearing and at the hearing before the Maine BEP. These witnesses included a number of Captains, Coast Guard Admirals, and weather observers.

There was substantial negative evidence which the ALJ refused to credit. He rejected efforts to consider world-wide statistics as to oil spills, an approach which has been used in studying other ports, see, e.g., Sierra Club v. Sigler, 532 F. Supp. 1222 (S.D. Tex. 1982), concluding that such statistics were unreliable or meaningless and that a site-specific focus was more appropriate. A study by Engineering Computer Opteconomics, using such data, had calculated a 48% probability of a major oil spill (loss of 365,000 barrels or more) over an assumed 25 year life of the refinery. He did not accept a 1976 report of the Canadian Coast Guard, highly negative as to the feasibility of safe supertanker traffic in Head Harbor Passage, observing that three years earlier the Canadian government had opposed the project. He rejected an adverse rating of the

evidence, it had been established that VLCCs could make the transit through Head Harbor Passage to Eastport with reasonable safety, the ALJ's decision might be accepted. But the issue is a harder one: whether, after using the best data available, it is established that the risk of significant oil spills from the proposed tanker traffic is so small as to insure that there is no likelihood of jeopardizing the two endangered species. All witnesses have agreed that real time simulation studies would contribute a more precise appreciation of risks of collision and grounding. We think the same could be said of a hydrographic survey of the depth of the channel, and perhaps of trial runs by VLCCs in ballast. If so, such methodologies obviously represent as yet untapped sources of "best scientific and commercial data."

It may very well be that, after conducting real time simulation studies and any other tests and studies which are suggested by the best available science and technology, the most informed judgment of risk of a major oil spill will still have a large component of estimate, its quantitative element being incapable of precise verification. But at least the EPA will have done all that was practicable prior to approving a project with such potentially grave environmental costs.

We also conclude, for many of the same reasons, that the real time simulation studies and other new data must be the subject of a supplemental EIS, both to assess the magnitude of risk and, if acceptable, to establish appropriate conditions of navigation. The testimony quoted above demonstrates that EPA and the Coast Guard have acknowledged the need for such a supplemental EIS on this issue. The EIS itself recognizes that "real time simulation studies . . . will help to settle the navigation [safety] issue." Given the importance of the studies to the crucial issue of the risk of oil spills, NEPA provides an additional ground for overturning the issuance of a permit until the studies have been conducted, circulated, and discussed.

* * *

IV. CONCLUSION

Accordingly, we vacate EPA's decision to issue the NPDES permit to Pittston, and remand the case to EPA to conduct further proceedings consistent with this opinion. EPA's jeopardy determination under the Endangered Species Act must be reconsidered in light of the results of real time simulation studies and a hydrographic survey of Head Harbor Passage, and any other studies, such as the 1980 whale study by the New England Aquarium, which EPA determines to be necessary to meet its statutory obligation to use the best scientific data available. If, in light of the studies, EPA decides to recommend approval of the project, this proposal shall be the subject of a supplemental EIS relating to the conditions of navigation necessary to minimize the

---

Atlantic Pilotage Authority for "extreme inconsistency." Two VLCC captains, Huntley and Crook, were discredited for the inaccuracy of their observations and for being too conservative. A contrary witness, Captain Peacock, was credited in his testimony that piloting a VLCC through the Passage was not "insurmountable," but his later testimony that he would want trial runs in ballasted tankers before construction was deemed "inexplicable." A 1972 study by Frederick R. Harris, Inc., a company commissioned by Pittston, which had conditioned its approval on severe restrictions and a "high order of seamanship and prudence," was discounted as a limited budget study based on a premise, since abandoned, of a confined turning area.

Additional negative evidence or critical witnesses included the statement of the Maine Board of Environmental Protection, in issuing its permit, that "the combination of currents, tides, fog, extremes of weather and rocky shores make Eastport one of the more difficult ports of the world. . . . VLCCs are extremely hazardous vessels which ought not to be operated in these difficult waters"; a study by the Corps of Engineers; a study by Arthur D. Little ("severely wanting"); an evaluation by National Bulk Carriers ("more difficult than any other location"); Captain Musse of Texaco ("not feasible"); National Salvage Association ("hairy navigation problem"); Captain Mills ("I can't think of anything to compare with this"); Captain Kennedy ("call[s] for a degree of accuracy . . . heretofore unheard of").

Finally, we note that the EIS itself concluded that the proposed refinery "ultimately will experience its share of severe spills, as have other comparable refineries."

risk of oil spills. Finally, the conditions imposed by the State of Maine in its certification of the proposed discharge must be included in any federal permit unless the conditions are subsequently modified according to law.

NOTES

1.   Following the favorable decision by the administration law judge (ALJ) in 1981 on Pittston's permit application, the EPA issued the NPDES permit challenged in the *Roosevelt Campobello* case. The permit was issued notwithstanding the fact that both the National Marine Fisheries Service and the U.S. Fish and Wildlife Service had issued jeopardy opinions on the right and humpback whales and the bald eagle, respectively. What authority does an action agency have to proceed with a decision notwithstanding a jeopardy opinion? *See National Wildlife Federation v. Coleman,* 529 F.2d 359, 371 (5th Cir.), *cert. denied,* 429 U.S. 979 (1976); Oliver A. Houck, *The Endangered Species Act and Its Implementation by the U.S. Departments of Interior and Commerce,* 64 U. COLO. L. REV. 277, 311 (1993). What authority did the ALJ have to second-guess the jeopardy opinions?

2.   What is the scope of review of the ALJ's decision? What deference should the court give to the EPA's decision?

3.   Suppose there were no listed species involved in the *Roosevelt Campobello* situation. What obtainable but not obtained information would be necessary for an adequate EIS? *See* 40 C.F.R. § 1502.22.

4.   The ESA regulations require the action agency to provide the Fish and Wildlife Service and the National Marine Fisheries Service with "the best scientific and commercial data available or which can be obtained during the consultation for an adequate review of the effects that an action may have on a listed species or critical habitat." 50 C.F.R. § 402.14(d). How might this rule have been used to support the Court's decision?

5.   During the time that the EPA was reconsidering its decision in light of the *Roosevelt Campobello* remand, Pittston withdrew its permit application and abandoned the project.

6.   Which law—NEPA or the ESA—affords a stronger basis for requiring real time simulation studies? Why? On which statute does the court primarily rely?

7.   What mitigation measures should the relevant federal agencies impose if the proposed refinery is built? How can the agency insure that Pittston internalizes the costs associated with a possible accident or spill?

PROBLEM #6: UNCERTAINTY[†]

Electro-magnetic fields (EMF) are generated by high voltage power lines. In 1979, researchers from the University of Colorado reported that children exposed to high EMF had increased risk of leukemia. Subsequently, homeowners who live adjacent to proposed power line routes have used this and a handful of other studies as a basis for opposition.

In the past two years, a number of radiation and cancer researchers have theorized about ways that EMF exposure might lead to cancer. However, the scientific community is divided over whether a relationship exists and, if so, what mechanism triggers EMF-induced cancers. Experimental scientists have exposed mice and pigs to EMF. For very high levels of EMF (approximately 10,000 times the dose received by someone standing directly under a power line 12 hours a day for one year), these animals experience double the expected number of cancers. However, for doses similar to those encountered by someone living directly under a power line, no effects in animal studies have been observed.

Many scientists agree that the best way to determine whether and how EMF from power lines affects humans is to conduct a massive epidemiological study of the tens of thousands of people living adjacent to power lines. Researchers seldom mount such a huge epidemiological effort to determine the relationship between environment and disease. The cost for a comprehensive epidemiological study searching for a possible link between EMF and cancer would total more than $10 million. A substantial minority of scientists maintains that even such a comprehensive cancer study would not conclusively prove or disprove the relationship between EMF and cancer because it could not account for the subtle variations in exposure caused by building materials, amount of time spent at home, and household sources of EMF such as microwave ovens and TVs. Also, an epidemiological study may not be able to detect an increased cancer risk unless it is at least ten-fold.

The Tennessee Valley Authority (TVA) is proposing to build a new high voltage power line between the Tellico Dam and Oak Ridge National Laboratory, 200 miles away. Under current law, how must the TVA address the EMF issue in its EIS? How would you draft language to include in the EIS?

[†]   Although the details of this problem, including some of the description of the studies, are hypothetical, the EMF issue remains contentious for the reasons explored below. For more information on EMF, see NATIONAL RESEARCH COUNCIL, POSSIBLE HEALTH EFFECTS OF EXPOSURE TO RESIDENTIAL ELECTRIC AND MAGNETIC FIELDS (1996); Roy A. Torres, *Causes of Action for EMF Harm*, 5 FORDHAM ENVTL. L.J. 403 (1994); Gary Taubes, *Electrical Emissions: Dangerous or Not?*, N.Y. TIMES, June 22, 1993, at B5; U.S. Environmental Protection Agency, Electric and Magnetic Fields: An EPA Perspective on Research Needs and Priorities for Improving Health Risk Assessment (EPA/600/9-91/016F 1992). *See also Criscuola v. Power Authority of the State of New York*, 81 N.Y.2d 649 (1993) (damages for high voltage power line easement includes the diminution in property values caused by public fear of EMF).

8 CONFLICTS WITH OTHER STATUTES

" * * * Section 102 duties are not inherently inflexible. They must be complied with to the fullest extent, *unless there is a clear conflict of statutory authority*. Considerations of administrative difficulty, delay or economic cost will not suffice to strip the section of its fundamental importance." *Calvert Cliffs' Coordinating Committee, Inc. v. U.S. Atomic Energy Commission*, 449 F.2d 1109, 1115 (D.C. Cir. 1971) (emphasis added).

FLINT RIDGE DEVELOPMENT CO. V. SCENIC RIVERS ASS'N
426 U.S. 776 (1976)

Mr. Justice MARSHALL delivered the opinion of the Court.

Today we must decide whether the National Environmental Policy Act of 1969 (NEPA) requires the Department of Housing and Urban Development [HUD] to prepare an environmental impact statement before it may allow a disclosure statement filed with it by a private real estate developer pursuant to the Interstate Land Sales Full Disclosure Act (Disclosure Act) to become effective.

I

The Disclosure Act, 15 U.S.C. § 1701 *et seq.,* is designed to prevent false and deceptive practices in the sale of unimproved tracts of land by requiring developers to disclose information needed by potential buyers. The Act is based on the full disclosure provisions and philosophy of the Securities Act of 1933, 15 U.S.C. § 77a *et seq.,* which it resembles in many respects. Section 1404(a)(1) of the Disclosure Act makes it unlawful for the developer of a covered subdivision "to make use of any means or instruments of transportation or communication in interstate commerce, or of the mails . . . to sell or lease any lot in any subdivision unless a statement of record with respect to such lot is in effect . . . and a printed property report . . . is furnished to the purchaser in advance of the signing of any contract or agreement for sale or lease by the purchaser." 15 U.S.C. § 1703(a)(1).

The statement of record and the property report, which is a condensed version of the statement of record, are prepared by the developer. They contain information concerning the title of the land; the terms and conditions for disposing of lots; the conditions of the subdivision, including access, noise, safety, sewage, utilities, proximity to municipalities, and the nature of the developer's proposed improvements; various other specified data; and such additional matters "as the Secretary [of HUD] may require as being reasonably necessary or appropriate for the protection of purchasers." * * *

A developer registers a subdivision by filing the statement of record, including the property report, with HUD. The statement, which is effective only with respect to the lots specified therein, becomes effective automatically on the 30th day after filing, or on such earlier date as the Secretary may determine. §§ 1405, 1407(a) of the Disclosure Act, 15 U.S.C. §§ 1704, 1706(a). If the Secretary determines that the statement of record is on its face incomplete or inaccurate in any material respect, and so notifies the developer within 30 days of filing, the effective date is suspended until 30 days after the developer files the information necessary to complete or correct the report. § 1407(b) of the Disclosure Act, 15 U.S.C. § 1706(b). If the statement is on its face complete and accurate, however, it must be permitted to go into effect. The Secretary has no power to evaluate the substance of the developer's proposal; and the Disclosure Act expressly provides: "The fact that a statement of record with respect to a subdivision has been filed or is in effect shall not be deemed a finding by the Secretary that the statement of record is true and accurate on its face, or be held to mean the Secretary has in any way passed upon the merits of, or given approval to, such subdivision." * * *

Petitioner Flint Ridge Development Co. (Flint Ridge) is a private joint venture organized to develop and sell lots in a subdivision located in northeastern Oklahoma adjacent to the Illinois River. In February 1974, the company filed with HUD a statement of record and property report relating to "Flint Ridge No. 1," which consists of approximately 1,000 residential lots on 2,200 acres of company land. The Secretary found the statement to be inaccurate and incomplete on its face, and suspended its effective date. Flint Ridge subsequently filed corrections and the amended statement became effective on May 2, 1974. Sales of lots commenced immediately thereafter.

Respondents Scenic Rivers Association of Oklahoma and Illinois River Conservation Council are nonprofit Oklahoma corporations organized for the purpose of protecting the Illinois River, a state-designated "scenic" river, and its undeveloped environs, which some members use for recreation. After Flint Ridge filed its statement of record, but before it became effective, respondents petitioned HUD to prepare an environmental impact statement on the development prior to allowing the statement of record to go into effect. HUD rejected the request and respondents brought suit in the United States District Court for the Eastern District of Oklahoma against the Secretary of HUD and the Administrator of HUD's Office of Interstate Land Sales Registration. Respondents requested a declaratory judgment and an injunction requiring that the defendants "prior to approval and registration of a statement of record and property report, under the Interstate Land Sales Act, conduct an environmental study in compliance with the National Environmental Policy Act [42 U.S.C. § 4321 et seq.] . . . ." Respondents also sought a preliminary injunction to require the federal defendants to "[w]ithdraw the approval of the Interstate Land Sales filing for the Flint Ridge Development Company. . . ." The District Court permitted Flint Ridge to intervene as a defendant.

After a hearing, the District Court ruled for the respondents. It found that the requirements of NEPA applied to HUD and that its action in allowing Flint Ridge's statement of record to go into effect constituted major federal action significantly affecting the quality of the human environment so as to require the preparation and filing of an environmental impact statement under NEPA. The court thereupon suspended Flint Ridge's statement of record, prohibited public sale thereunder, ordered the preparation of an environmental impact statement, and enjoined HUD "from approving the . . . filing of Flint Ridge Development Co. until such time as the environmental impact study has been prepared and a public hearing held thereon . . . ." 382 F. Supp. 69, 76 (E.D. Okla. 1974).

On appeal, the Court of Appeals for the Tenth Circuit reversed the District Court's holding that a public hearing was necessary on the environmental impact statement, but affirmed the remainder of the District Court's decision. * * *

* * *

II

Section 102(2)(C) of NEPA, 42 U.S.C. § 4332(2)(C), requires all agencies of the United States "to the fullest extent possible" to "include in every recommendation or report on proposals for legislation and other major Federal actions significantly affecting the quality of the human environment" an environmental impact statement analyzing the consequences of, and alternatives to, the proposed action. The Secretary and Flint Ridge offer essentially two theories for exempting HUD from this duty in the administration of the Disclosure Act.

First, they claim, allowing a disclosure statement to become effective is not major federal action significantly affecting the quality of the human environment within the meaning of NEPA. In petitioners' view, NEPA is concerned only with introducing environmental considerations into the decisionmaking processes of agencies that have the ability to react to environmental consequences when taking action. If the agency cannot so act, its action is not "major" and does not fall within the statutory language. Thus, petitioners urge, NEPA should not be read to impose a duty on HUD to prepare an environmental impact statement in this case since the agency, by statute, has no power to take environmental consequences into account in deciding whether to allow a disclosure statement to become effective. To this respondents counter, as did the Court of Appeals, that NEPA's goals are not so narrow and that even if the agency taking action is itself powerless to protect the environment, preparation and circulation of an impact statement serves the valuable function of bringing the environmental consequences of federal actions to the attention of those who are empowered to do something about them— other federal agencies, Congress, state agencies, or even private parties.

Petitioner's second argument is that even if HUD's action in allowing a disclosure statement to become effective constitutes major federal action significantly affecting the quality of the human environment within the meaning of NEPA, HUD is nonetheless exempt from the duty of preparing an environmental impact statement because compliance with that duty is not possible if HUD is also to comply with the Disclosure Act's requirement that statements of record become effective within 30 days of filing, unless incomplete or inaccurate on their face. In response to this claim, respondents contend that the Secretary has an inherent power to suspend the effective date of a statement of record past the 30-day deadline in order to prepare an impact statement. Because we reject this argument of respondents and find that preparation of an impact statement is inconsistent with the Secretary's mandatory duties under the Disclosure Act, we need not resolve petitioners' first contention.

NEPA's instruction that all federal agencies comply with the impact statement requirement—and with all the other requirements of § 102—"to the fullest extent possible," 42 U.S.C. § 4332, is neither accidental nor hyperbolic. * * *

Section 102 recognizes, however, that where a clear and unavoidable conflict in statutory authority exists, NEPA must give way. As we noted in *United States v. SCRAP*, 412 U.S. 669, 694 (1973), "NEPA was not intended to repeal by implication any other statute." And so the question we must resolve is whether, assuming an environmental impact statement would otherwise be required in this case, requiring the Secretary to prepare such a statement would create an irreconcilable and fundamental conflict with the Secretary's duties under the Disclosure Act.

The Disclosure Act provides that a statement of record becomes effective automatically 30 days after filing unless the Secretary acts affirmatively, within that time, to suspend it for inadequate disclosure. 15 U.S.C. § 1706. It is inconceivable that an environmental impact statement could, in 30 days, be drafted, circulated, commented upon, and then reviewed and revised in light of the comments.[2] Respondents do not contend otherwise. Rather, they take the

---

[2]   Draft environmental impact statements on simple projects prepared by experienced personnel take some three to five months to complete, at least in the Department of the Interior. Complex projects prepared by inexperienced personnel may take up to 18 months to prepare. Sixth Annual Report, Council on Environmental Quality 639 (1975).

position, accepted by the Court of Appeals, that the statute does not preclude the Secretary from suspending the effective date of the proposed statement for such time as is necessary to prepare an impact statement.

We find, to the contrary, that the Disclosure Act leaves the Secretary no such discretion. The Act mandates that "[e]xcept as hereinafter provided, the effective date of a statement of record . . . *shall* be the thirtieth day after the filing thereof . . . ." § 1407(a), 15 U.S.C. § 1706(a) (emphasis added). The only exception to this mandatory command that is "hereinafter provided" is the power granted the Secretary to suspend the effective date of a statement "[i]f it appears to the Secretary that a statement of record . . . is on its face incomplete or inaccurate in any material respect . . . ." § 1407(b), 15 U.S.C. § 1706(b). Thus, while the Secretary may unquestionably suspend an effective date in order to allow the developer to remedy an inadequate disclosure statement, there is no basis in the statute to allow the Secretary to order such a suspension so as to give HUD time to prepare an impact statement.

Not only does the Court of Appeals' opinion grant the Secretary a power not conferred by statute, but the exercise of that power ordered by the court would contravene the purpose of the 30-day provision of the Disclosure Act. The 30-day time limit, as the Court of Appeals recognized, is designed to protect developers from costly delays as a result of the need to register with HUD. Yet, the Court of Appeals' reading of the statute would make such delays commonplace, and render the 30-day provision little more than a nullity. Environmental impact statements, and consequent lengthy suspensions, would be necessary in virtually all cases.

In sum, even if the Secretary's action in this case constituted major federal action significantly affecting the quality of the human environment so that an environmental impact statement would ordinarily be required, there would be a clear and fundamental conflict of statutory duty. The Secretary cannot comply with the statutory duty to allow statements of record to go into effect within 30 days of filing, absent inaccurate or incomplete disclosure, and simultaneously prepare impact statements on proposed developments. In these circumstances, we find that NEPA's impact statement requirement is inapplicable.

This is not to say that environmental concerns are irrelevant to the Disclosure Act or that the Secretary has no duties under NEPA. Section 1406(5) of the Disclosure Act recognizes that disclosure of some of the environmental aspects of a subdivision is necessary to protect prospective purchasers and requires such disclosure in the statement of record and property report. 15 U.S.C. § 1705(5). The developer must provide information on such factors as roads, water, sewage, drainage, soil erosion, climate, nuisances, natural hazards, municipal services, and zoning restrictions. Moreover, §§ 1406(12) and 1408(a) confer on the Secretary authority to require "other information" from developers in their statements of record and property reports, both for the "protection of purchasers" and "in the public interest." Therefore, if the Secretary finds it necessary for the protection of purchasers or in the public interest, the Secretary may adopt rules requiring developers to incorporate a wide range of environmental information into property reports to be furnished prospective purchasers; and respondents may request the Secretary to institute a rulemaking proceeding to consider the desirability of ordering such disclosure. 5 U.S.C. § 553(e).

Because the courts below erred in ordering the Secretary to prepare an impact statement before allowing Flint Ridge's statement of record to go into effect, the judgment of the Court of Appeals for the Tenth Circuit is reversed, and the cases are remanded for further proceedings consistent with this opinion.

It is so ordered.

NOTES

1. Suppose the Court had found that the HUD disclosure statement was not exempt from NEPA's impact statement requirement. Is the decision to allow a disclosure statement to become effective a major federal action?

2. The Court finds that "NEPA's impact statement requirement is inapplicable" to HUD's obligations under the Disclosure Act. 426 U.S. at 2440. Does this mean that NEPA does not apply to those actions? What obligations might remain? Are those obligations judicially enforceable? In *1000 Friends of Oregon v. Kreps*, 11 Env't Rep. Cas. (BNA) 1098 (D. Or. 1977), the court suggested that while a 60 day time period for acting on an application for public works projects afforded insufficient time to prepare an EIS, the agency might nonetheless invoke NEPA to reject an application where the potential environmental effects were sufficient to warrant further study.

3. *Natural Resources Defense Council v. TVA*, 367 F. Supp. 122 (E.D. Tenn. 1973), *aff'd*, 502 F.2d 852 (6th Cir. 1974), involved the Tennessee Valley Authority's (TVA's) coal procurement practices for its electrical generating facilities. The TVA had prepared a programmatic EIS on its procurement program, but the NRDC sought additional NEPA documents on individual coal purchase contracts. The court found that a requirement for EISs on individual contracts would conflict with the TVA's statutory obligation to purchase coal through competitive bidding, because the delays inherent in EIS preparation would limit the number of companies able to bid. *Cf. Forelaws on Board v. Johnson*, 743 F.2d 677 (9th Cir. 1984), *cert. denied*, 478 U.S. 1004 (1986) (rejecting claim of Bonneville Power Administration that a nine-month statutory deadline for contract offer and acceptance made compliance with NEPA impossible where the agency chose to implement the law in such a way that permitted only 30 days between offer and acceptance). Assuming that requiring an EIS would conflict with the TVA Act, should the court nonetheless have required a more limited environmental analysis?

4. Emergencies may also excuse EIS preparation. Under the CEQ regulations, however, the agency considering the emergency action "should" first consult with the CEQ about "alternative arrangements." The purpose of these rules is to limit the action to that which is necessary to address the emergency. 40 C.F.R. § 1506.11. In *Valley Citizens for a Safe Environment v. Vest*, 22 Envtl. L. Rep. (Envtl. L. Inst.) 20335 (D. Mass. 1991), *reconsideration denied*, 1991 WL 405184 (D. Mass. 1991), the plaintiffs challenged the validity of the CEQ rules and their application to the commencement of night flights of C-5A transport planes at the Westover Air Force Base in Massachusetts. An EIS had previously been prepared on the environmental impacts from the operation of the C-5A planes from the Air Force Base but it did not address night flights. The CEQ found that an emergency existed within the meaning of its rules and allowed the night flights to commence without NEPA compliance. The court sustained both the validity of the CEQ rules and their application to the facts in this case. *See also Louisiana Power & Light Co. v. FPC*, 557 F.2d 1122 (5th Cir. 1977); *Louisiana v. FPC*, 503 F.2d 844 (5th Cir. 1974), *reh'g denied*, 505 F.2d 1304 (5th Cir. 1974).

5. Congress may, and occasionally has, expressly exempted certain projects from NEPA compliance. For example, the Mineral Leasing Act of 1920 was amended in 1973 to exempt from NEPA the actions needed for approval of the trans-Alaska pipeline. Trans-

Alaska Pipeline Authorization Act, Pub. L. 93-153, § 203(d). In a few cases, Congress has even exempted entire programs from NEPA's reach. For example, § 511(c) of the Clean Water Act exempts the EPA from preparing EISs for actions taken under the CWA, except in two circumstances: (1) grants for publicly owned waste treatment plants (POTWs); and (2) permits for new point sources of pollution. 33 U.S.C. § 1371. All actions under the Clean Air Act are exempt from NEPA in accordance with a provision of the 1974 Energy Supply and Environmental Coordination Act. 15 U.S.C. § 793. Even before this provision was enacted, the Court of Appeals for the D.C. Circuit had held that EIS preparation was not necessary for actions taken by the EPA to protect the environment, since the administrative record required for such actions was essentially the functional equivalent of an EIS. *See, e.g., Environmental Defense Fund, Inc. v. EPA*, 489 F.2d 1247, 1257 (D.C. Cir. 1973); *Portland Cement Ass'n v. Ruckelshaus*, 486 F.2d 375, 384 (D.C. Cir. 1973), *cert. denied*, 417 U.S. 921 (1974). What would a NEPA document look like in the context of an EPA action to promulgate an air emission standard, and how would it likely differ from the administrative record developed outside of NEPA's purview?

6. Given that Congress has shown a willingness to exempt certain projects and programs from NEPA compliance expressly, is it appropriate for the courts to extend exemptions to EPA programs where no express exemptions have been enacted?

7. Does the U.S. Fish and Wildlife Service have an obligation to prepare an EIS when it makes listing decisions under ESA § 4? In *Pacific Legal Foundation v. Andrus*, 657 F.2d 829 (6th Cir. 1981), the court answered no. The case involved the construction of a dam on the Duck River in Tennessee. The proposed dam threatened seven listed species of freshwater mussels and five species of river snails which were proposed for listing. The Pacific Legal Foundation sued to have the mussels removed from the list and to enjoin the listing of new species until an EIS was prepared on these actions. The court held that preparation of an EIS would conflict with the Secretary's statutory duty to consider only specific criteria in determining whether to list a species. Accordingly, the court decided that it would be improper for the Secretary to consider broader environmental concerns. Do you find the court's holding convincing?

The Pacific Legal Foundation is a conservative group that typically supports development activities. Are their interests within the zone sought to be protected by the ESA? *See Bennett v. Spear*, 520 U.S. 154 (1997) (discussed in Note 4 following *National Wildlife Federation* in Chapter 3); *Douglas County v. Babbitt*, 48 F.3d 1495 (9th Cir. 1995), *cert. denied*, 516 U.S. 1042 (1996). To what extent should the plaintiff's motives be relevant to the consideration of the exemption issue? Should the court consider, for example, that the Portland Cement Association's apparent motive in *Portland Cement Ass'n v. Ruckelshaus*, 486 F.2d 375, *supra* Note 5, was to delay the promulgation of certain air emissions standards by demanding that an EIS be prepared first? If it is appropriate for the court to consider this evidence, how should it influence the court's decision on the merits?

8. Assuming that *Pacific Legal Foundation* was correctly decided, does it follow that NEPA compliance is unnecessary for decisions designating critical habitat? What factors are considered in critical habitat designation which change the analysis? *Compare Catron County Bd. of Commissioners v. U.S. Fish & Wildlife Serv.*, 75 F.3d 1429 (10th Cir. 1996) (NEPA does apply to designation of critical habitat), *with Douglas County v. Babbitt*, 48 F.3d 1495 (9th Cir. 1995), *cert. denied*, 516 U.S. 1042 (1996) (NEPA does not apply to designation of critical habitat), discussed in Note 7 following *Northern Spotted Owl* in Chapter 4.

9. Note that if the immediate designation of critical habitat for the northern spotted owl was deemed necessary by the Secretary because of a "significant risk to the well being of [the] species," he could have used his emergency authority under ESA § 4(b)(7); 16 U.S.C. § 1533(b)(7). Under this provision, the designation rules would take effect immediately upon the publication of the rule. Emergency rules under § 4(b)(7) may remain in effect for no more than 240 days, during which time the Secretary can prepare NEPA and ESA documentation as may be necessary to promulgate a final rule. *See also* 40 C.F.R. § 1506.11 (CEQ rule on emergencies).

10. Congress has given the EPA a special role to play in the EIS process. Under § 309 of the Clean Air Act, the EPA is required to review and comment on the environmental impacts of "any matter relating to duties and responsibilities granted" under federal statute. 42 U.S.C. § 7609. Since the passage of NEPA, the EPA has reviewed approximately 20,000 draft and final EISs. U.S. Environmental Protection Agency, Office of Enforcement, *EPA's Section 309 Review: The Clean Air Act and NEPA* (Dec. 1992). If the EPA determines that the matter is "unsatisfactory from the standpoint of public health or welfare or environmental quality * * * the matter shall be referred to the Council on Environmental Quality." *Id.* Where conflicts arise between agencies, the CEQ rules establish a process for handling referrals from the EPA and from other federal agencies. 40 C.F.R. §§ 1504.2, 1504.3.

11. What if, in *Flint Ridge*, the time for disapproval of the developer's disclosure statement had not been too short to reconcile with NEPA's requirement for preparation of an impact statement? Then the Court would have had to address HUD's first defense—that NEPA should not be read to impose a duty to prepare an EIS when the agency had no discretion to reject on environmental grounds an accurate and complete disclosure statement. Does NEPA impose such a duty? Consider the following case.

SOUTH DAKOTA V. ANDRUS

614 F.2d 1190 (8th Cir. 1980), *cert. denied*, 449 U.S. 822

HENLEY, Circuit Judge.

This is an appeal from a judgment entered by The Honorable Andrew W. Bogue of the United States District Court for the District of South Dakota dismissing the State of South Dakota's suit in which the State sought declaratory and injunctive relief to compel the United States Department of Interior to prepare an Environmental Impact Statement (EIS) prior to its issuance of a mineral patent to the Pittsburgh Pacific Company (Pittsburgh). * * *

I

Pittsburgh filed an application under the General Mining Act of 1872, 30 U.S.C. § 21 *et seq.,* for a mineral patent to twelve contiguous twenty acre mining claims located within the Black Hills National Forest in Lawrence County, South Dakota. Pittsburgh claimed discovery of some 160 million tons of relatively low grade iron ore and sought a mineral patent covering the discovery lands. Pittsburgh proposed to mine 96 million tons of the ore through open pit mining at an annual rate of approximately seven million long tons a year. The general plan of operation also included processing the best of this ore into hard pellets as well as loading these pellets into railroad cars for shipping.

In 1971, however, Pittsburgh's application for a mineral patent was contested, at the request of the United States Forest Service, by the Bureau of Land Management. The Bureau contended that Pittsburgh had not discovered a valuable mineral deposit under the 1872 Mining Act. The Administrative Law Judge nonetheless dismissed the complaint and approved the mineral patent.

The Bureau then appealed the decision to the Interior Board of Land Appeals alleging that the Administrative Law Judge erred in his geological and economic analysis in determining whether Pittsburgh had discovered a "valuable" deposit. In addition, the State of South Dakota petitioned to intervene and was permitted to file an amicus brief in which the State argued, *inter alia,* that the Administrative Law Judge had not given proper consideration to the cost of compliance with environmental quality statutes. Recognizing that Pittsburgh's proposed mining project would take 240 to 1,140 acres from a national forest and discard approximately 2.3 million tons of waste annually, the State argued that the Secretary must prepare an EIS before a mineral patent could issue. The Board determined that an EIS need not be prepared prior to the issuance of a mineral patent for these claims. *United States v. Pittsburgh*, 30 IBLA 388 (1977). The Board, however, set aside the decision of the Administrative Law Judge on other grounds and remanded the case for further hearings with respect to the expense of complying with environmental laws as well as any other issue which might arise.

Subsequently, the State filed an original action in federal district court seeking to compel preparation of an EIS prior to the issuance of a mineral patent naming as defendants the United States Department of the Interior and Pittsburgh. Both defendants moved to dismiss contending the issuance of a mineral patent is not a major federal action which requires an EIS, and Judge Bogue granted the motion. *South Dakota v. Andrus*, 462 F. Supp. 905 (D.S.D. 1978).

II

The issue on this appeal is whether the United States Department of the Interior is required by § 102(2)(C) of the National Environmental Policy Act, 42 U.S.C. § 4332(C) to file an EIS prior to the issuance of a mineral patent.

Our starting point is, of course, the statutory language. Section 102(2)(C) provides in part that an EIS is required for "major Federal actions significantly affecting the quality of the human environment." Applied to this case, § 102(2)(C) mandates the filing of an EIS if (1) the issuance of a mineral patent is an "action" within the meaning of the provision, and (2) the alleged federal action is "major" in the sense that it significantly affects the quality of the human environment.

A

We turn first to the question whether the granting of a mineral patent constitutes an "action" within the meaning of NEPA. As the district court noted, it is well established that the issuance of a mineral patent is a ministerial act. Both the Supreme Court, in a series of decisions in the early part of this century, *Wilbur v. United States ex rel. Krushnic*, 280 U.S. 306, 318-19 (1929); *Cameron v. United States*, 252 U.S. 450, 454 (1920); *Roberts v. United States*, 176 U.S.

221, 231 (1900), and, more recently, the Interior Board of Land Appeals, *United States v. Kosanke Sand Corp.*, 12 IBLA 282, 290-91 (1973),[3] have so concluded.

Ministerial acts, however, have generally been held outside the ambit of NEPA's EIS requirement. Reasoning that the primary purpose of the impact statement is to aid agency decisionmaking, courts have indicated that nondiscretionary acts should be exempt from the requirement.

In light of these decisions, it is at least doubtful that the Secretary's nondiscretionary approval of a mineral patent constitutes an "action" under § 102(2)(C).

B

But even if a ministerial act may in some circumstances fall within § 102(2)(C), we still cannot say that the issuance of a mineral patent is a "major" federal action under the statute. This conclusion does not stem from the court's belief that an agency itself must propose to build a facility and directly affect the environment in order to constitute a "major" federal action within the meaning of NEPA. We fully recognize that NEPA's impact statement procedure has been held to apply where the federal government grants a lease, issues a permit or license, or approves or funds state highway projects.

In each of these cases, however, an agency took a "major" federal action because it enabled a private party to act so as to significantly affect the environment. Such enablements have consistently been held subject to NEPA. But in the instant case, the granting of a mineral patent does not enable the private party, Pittsburgh, to do anything. Unlike the case where a lease, permit or license is required before the particular project can begin, the issuance of a mineral patent is not a precondition which enables a party to begin mining operations. 30 U.S.C. § 26.

As the Supreme Court noted in *Union Oil Co. v. Smith*, 249 U.S. 337 (1919), if a qualified locator of a mining claim locates, marks and records his claim to unappropriated public lands in accordance with federal and local law, he has an "exclusive right of possession to the extent of his claim as located, with the right to extract the minerals, even to exhaustion, without paying any royalty to the United States as owner, and without ever applying for a patent . . . ." *Id.* at 348-49. Furthermore, in *Wilbur v. United States ex rel. Krushnic, supra*, 280 U.S. at 316-17, the Court revealed:

> "The rule is established by innumerable decisions of this Court, and of state and lower federal courts, that, when the location of a mining claim is perfected under the law, it has the effect of a grant by the United States of the right of present and exclusive possession . . . so long as he complies with the provisions of the mining laws, his possessory right, for all practical purposes of ownership, is as good as though secured by patent."

---

[3]   As the district court observed, the Board, in *United States v. Kosanke Sand Corp., supra,* concluded:

Upon satisfaction of the requirements of the statute, the holder of a valid mining claim has an absolute right to a patent from the United States conveying fee title to the land within the claim, and the actions taken by the Secretary of the Interior in processing an application for patent by such claimant are not discretionary; issuance of a patent can be compelled by court order. The patent may contain no conditions not authorized by law. The claimant need not, however, apply for patent to preserve his property right in the claim, but may if he chooses continue to extract and freely dispose of the locatable minerals until the claim is exhausted, without ever having acquired full legal title to the land. The patent, if issued, conveys fee simple title to the land within the claim, but does nothing to enlarge or diminish the claimant's right to its locatable mineral resources.

In recent years the mining laws governing the locating of mineral claims have remained unchanged, 30 U.S.C. §§ 22, 26, and modern decisions have continued to allow locators of mining claims to extract minerals without a patent provided they have met the statutory prerequisites. *See, e.g., Lombardo Turquoise Milling & Mining Co. v. Hemanes*, 430 F. Supp. 429 (D. Nev. 1977).

In light of the fact that a mineral patent in actuality is not a federal determination which enables the party to mine, we conclude in present context that the granting of such a patent is not a "major" federal action within the meaning of § 102(2)(C).

III

In reaching this conclusion, we do not decide the question whether an EIS should be required at some point after the mineral patent has issued. While a federal agency need not prepare an EIS during the "germination process of a potential proposal," *Kleppe v. Sierra Club*, 427 U.S. 390, 401 n.12, 406 (1976), this is not to say that at some later date an EIS will not be required. We note that Pittsburgh's proposed mining project is substantial and that if Pittsburgh decides to build the mine many actions may be necessary. For example, the claims at issue will presumedly need permits from the Forest Service for roads, water pipelines and railroad rights of way. 43 U.S.C. § 1761(a)(1) and (a)(6). Moreover, the company may possibly seek to make land exchanges with the Forest Service. We leave to another day the question whether an EIS would be required in connection with any one or more such actions.

It is sufficient for the moment to conclude that in the present case an EIS need not be filed prior to the issuance of a mineral patent. Accordingly, the judgment of the district court is affirmed.

NOTES

1. Under the 1872 Mining Law, which applies to the location of hard rock minerals on public lands, any U.S. citizen who discovers a valuable deposit of minerals may stake a mining claim. A valid mining claim entitles the claimant to develop and market the minerals without the payment of royalties. Traditionally, hard rock mining operations have been subject to very limited environmental controls, though gradually this is changing. As the *South Dakota* case suggests, mining claimants may also apply for a patent which, if granted, transfers fee title to the land. Patentees must pay a nominal fee of between $2.50 and $5.00 per acre to acquire title. As the court notes, however, mining can and often does proceed without a patent. Thus, the patent does not entitle the claimant to perform any additional ground disturbing activities for mining than might otherwise have been performed. Does it follow, however, that the issuance of a patent will not have a significant impact on the environment? Consider, for example, a case where the claim is located in the middle of a national park or wilderness area.

2. The *South Dakota* court further suggests, citing a long line of cases, that the granting of a patent is a ministerial act. While true, this statement does not reflect the complexity of the decision. While the BLM must grant a patent to any person who meets the requirements of the law, one of those requirements is that the claimant prove a valuable discovery of minerals. The traditional test for a "discovery" is whether a prudent person "would be justified in the further expenditure of his labor and means, with a reasonable prospect of success, in developing a valuable mine." *Castle v. Womble*, 19 L.D. 455 (1894);

see also United States v. Coleman, 390 U.S. 599, *reh'g denied*, 391 U.S. 961 (1968). In determining whether the "prudent person" test is met, however, the Department must consider the costs of compliance with environmental laws, as well as a host of other factors that may be peculiar to the site and the individual company seeking the patent. *United States v. Pittsburgh Pacific Co.*, 30 IBLA 388, 84 I.D. 282 (June 15, 1977). Furthermore, the Interior Department has broad discretion regarding the extent of environmental controls that it can impose on a mining operator. Thus, it is conceivable that the federal government's imposition of reasonable environmental controls may be sufficiently costly that the "prudent person" test cannot be met. In light of these facts, how might an EIS assist the agency in deciding whether to grant a patent?

3.   *Natural Resources Defense Council v. Berklund*, 458 F. Supp. 925 (D.D.C. 1978), *aff'd*, 609 F.2d 553 (D.C. Cir. 1979), involved the system of preference-right coal leasing allowed under the pre-1976 provisions of the Mineral Leasing Act. Under that system, a person was granted a prospecting permit to seek coal deposits on federal lands. If commercial quantities of coal were discovered, the permittee had a right to obtain a coal lease for such lands. Although the Federal Coal Leasing Amendments Act in 1976 abolished this system, a plethora of prospecting permits were outstanding and the Department of the Interior had to consider lease applications filed under the old law. The plaintiffs sought a declaration that NEPA gave the Secretary authority to reject the lease applications outright on environmental grounds. The court rejected this claim as inconsistent with the pre-1976 Mineral Leasing Act provisions. But, the court held that an EIS was required before issuance of the preference-right lease, because the lease terms might affect the determination of whether the lease contained commercial quantities of coal. The Court of Appeals for the D.C. Circuit affirmed the trial court's decision as well as its reasoning.

WEINBERGER V. CATHOLIC ACTION OF HAWAII/PEACE EDUCATION PROJECT
454 U.S. 139 (1981)

Justice REHNQUIST delivered the opinion of the Court.

The Court of Appeals for the Ninth Circuit held that § 102(2)(C) of the National Environmental Policy Act of 1969 (NEPA), 42 U.S.C. § 4332(2)(C), requires the Navy to prepare and release to the public a "Hypothetical Environmental Impact Statement" with regard to the operation of a facility capable of storing nuclear weapons. *Catholic Action of Hawaii/ Peace Education Project v. Brown*, 643 F.2d 569, 572 (1980). Because we conclude that the "Hypothetical Environmental Impact Statement" is a creature of judicial cloth, not legislative cloth, and that it is not mandated by any of the statutory or regulatory provisions upon which the Court of Appeals relied, we reverse its decision.

The facts relevant to our decision are not seriously controverted. Pursuant to a decision by the Navy to transfer ammunition and weapons stored at various locations on the island of Oahu, Hawaii, to the West Loch branch of the Lualualei Naval Magazine, the Navy prepared an Environmental Impact Assessment (EIA) concerning how the plan would affect the environment. The assessment concluded that the necessary construction of 48 earth-covered magazines and associated structures would have no significant environmental impact, and therefore no Environmental Impact Statement (EIS) was prepared at the construction stage. Construction contracts were let in March 1977 and in April 1978. Construction of the West Loch facilities has been completed and the magazines are now in use. It is stipulated that the magazines are capable of storing nuclear weapons. Because the information is classified for national security reasons, the Navy's regulations forbid it either to admit or to deny that nuclear weapons are actually stored at West Loch.

In 1978, the Navy prepared a Candidate Environmental Impact Statement (CEIS). This CEIS deals generally with the environmental hazards associated with the storage, handling, and transportation of nuclear weapons, but does not refer to any specific site or storage facility. It concludes that no significant hazards to the environment are present.

In March 1978, respondents brought this action seeking an injunction against the building of the new facilities at West Loch until an EIS had been filed. Their principal complaint was that the Navy's EIA had ignored the enhanced risk of a nuclear accident resulting from West Loch's proximity to three nearby air facilities, the effects of such an accident on the population and environment of Hawaii, and the effects of radiation from the storage of nuclear weapons in a populated area. * * * But given certain national security provisions of the Atomic Energy Act, 42 U.S.C. § 2011 *et seq.* (1976 ed. and Supp. IV), and the Navy's own regulations concerning nuclear weapons, the District Court concluded that petitioners had complied with NEPA "to the fullest extent possible." We find it unnecessary to reach the question posed by the District Court's reliance on the security provisions of the Atomic Energy Act, since respondents have made no showing in this case that the Navy has failed to comply, or even need comply, with NEPA's requirements regarding the preparation and public disclosure of an EIS.

* * *

The decisionmaking and public disclosure goals of § 102(2)(C), though certainly compatible, are not necessarily coextensive. Thus, § 102(2)(C) contemplates that in a given situation a federal agency might have to include environmental considerations in its decisionmaking process, yet withhold public disclosure of any NEPA documents, in whole or in part, under the authority of an FOIA exemption. That the decisionmaking and disclosure requirements of NEPA are not coextensive has been recognized by the Department of Defense's regulations, both at the time the West Loch facility was constructed and today.

In an apparent attempt to balance what it considered to be the disclosure requirements of NEPA with national security interests, the Court of Appeals concluded that petitioners could prepare and disclose an EIS that would assess the impact of the storage of nuclear weapons at West Loch without revealing specific information regarding the number and type of nuclear weapons to be stored at the facility. 643 F.2d at 572. The EIS could hypothesize, but not concede, that the facility will be used for the purpose for which it has been made capable. *Ibid.* But in inventing the "Hypothetical Environmental Impact Statement," the Court of Appeals departed from the express intent of Congress manifested by the explicit language in § 102(2)(C). That language provides that public disclosure of the EIS shall be governed by FOIA. As we concluded in *EPA v. Mink*, 410 U.S. 73, 80 (1973), FOIA was intended by Congress to balance the public's need for access to official information with the Government's need for confidentiality. Of the nine exemptions in Subsection (b) of FOIA, we think two are relevant in determining whether the Navy must release an EIS. Exemption 3, 5 U.S.C. § 552(b)(3), which authorizes the withholding of documents "specifically exempted from disclosure by statute," arguably exempts the publication of an EIS under the Atomic Energy Act. But we find it unnecessary to decide this question, because to us it is clear that Exemption 1, 5 U.S.C. § 552(b)(1), is applicable.

Exemption 1 exempts from disclosure matters that are "(A) specifically authorized under criteria established by an Executive order to be kept secret in the interest of national defense or foreign policy and (B) are in fact properly classified pursuant to such Executive order." * * *

Virtually all information relating to the storage of nuclear weapons is classified. Thus, any material properly classified pursuant to Executive Order No. 12065 is exempt from disclosure under Exemption 1, and therefore is exempt from the public disclosure requirements of NEPA.

Congress has thus effected a balance between the needs of the public for access to documents prepared by a federal agency and the necessity of nondisclosure or secrecy. The Court of Appeals in this case should have accepted the balance struck by Congress, rather than engrafting onto the statutory language unique concepts of its own making. By requiring the Navy to prepare a "hypothetical" EIS, the Court of Appeals required the production of a document that would not exist save for what that court thought to be NEPA's public disclosure requirements. But NEPA's public disclosure requirements are expressly governed by FOIA. In *NLRB v. Sears, Roebuck & Co.*, 421 U.S. 132, 161-62 (1975), we held that FOIA "does not compel agencies to write opinions in cases in which they would not otherwise be required to do so. It only requires disclosure of certain documents which the law requires the agency to prepare or which the agency has decided for its own reasons to create." It follows that if the Navy would not be required by FOIA to release an EIS were one already prepared, it is obviously not required to prepare a "hypothetical" EIS nowhere mentioned in NEPA.

Since the public disclosure requirements of NEPA are governed by FOIA, it is clear that Congress intended that the public's interest in ensuring that federal agencies comply with NEPA must give way to the Government's need to preserve military secrets. In the instant case, an EIS concerning a proposal to store nuclear weapons at West Loch need not be disclosed. As we indicated earlier, whether or not nuclear weapons are stored at West Loch is classified information exempt from disclosure to the public under Exemption 1.

If the Navy proposes to store nuclear weapons at West Loch, the Department of Defense's regulations can fairly be read to require that an EIS be prepared solely for internal purposes, even though such a document cannot be disclosed to the public. The Navy must consider environmental consequences in its decisionmaking process, even if it is unable to meet NEPA's public disclosure goals by virtue of FOIA Exemption 1.

It does not follow, however, that the Navy is required to prepare an EIS in this case. The Navy is not required to prepare an EIS regarding the hazards of storing nuclear weapons at West Loch simply because the facility is "nuclear capable." As we held in *Kleppe v. Sierra Club*, 427 U.S. 390, 405-06 (1976), an EIS need not be prepared simply because a project is contemplated, but only when the project is proposed. To say that the West Loch facility is "nuclear capable" is to say little more than that the Navy has contemplated the possibility that nuclear weapons, of whatever variety, may at some time be stored here. It is the proposal to store nuclear weapons at West Loch that triggers the Navy's obligation to prepare an EIS. Due to national security reasons, however, the Navy can neither admit nor deny that it proposes to store nuclear weapons at West Loch. In this case, therefore, it has not been and cannot be established that the Navy has proposed the only action that would require the preparation of an EIS dealing with the environmental consequences of nuclear weapons storage at West Loch.

Ultimately, whether or not the Navy has complied with NEPA "to the fullest extent possible" is beyond judicial scrutiny in this case. In other circumstances, we have held that "public policy forbids the maintenance of any suit in a court of justice, the trial of which would inevitably lead to the disclosure of matters which the law itself regards as confidential, and respecting which it will not allow the confidence to be violated." *Totten v. United States*, 92 U.S. 105, 107 (1876). See *United States v. Reynolds*, 345 U.S. 1 (1953). We confront a similar situation in the instant case.

The decision of the Court of Appeals for the Ninth Circuit is reversed, and the case is remanded with instructions to reinstate the judgment of dismissal entered by the District Court. *It is so ordered.*

Justice BLACKMUN, with whom Justice BRENNAN joins, concurring in the judgment.

The law to be applied in this case is relatively simple and straightforward. If the Navy proposes to engage in a major action that will have a significant environmental effect, it must prepare an environmental impact statement (EIS) addressing the consequences of the proposed activity. If disclosing the contents, or even the existence, of the EIS will reveal properly classified materials, the Navy need not publish the document. If nonclassified data is segregable and properly disclosable under Executive Order No. 12065, it must be released to the public. I write separately because I believe that the Court understates the first and third of these points, and overstates the second.

The Court states rather obliquely that if the Navy proposes to store nuclear weapons, "the Department of Defense's regulations can fairly be read to require that an EIS be prepared solely for internal [Navy] purposes." In fact, the Defense Department regulations explicitly declare that "[t]he fact that a proposed action is of a classified nature does not relieve the proponent of the action from complying with the NEPA," although in such a circumstance the required EIS "shall be prepared, safeguarded and disseminated in accordance with the requirements applicable to classified information." * * *

It seems to me that this follows necessarily from the function of the EIS. One of its purposes—if not its principal purpose—is to guarantee that "environmental concerns are . . . interwoven into the fabric of agency planning." * * * This is no less true when the public is unaware of the agency's proposals. Indeed, the public's inability to participate in military decisionmaking makes it particularly important that, in cases such as the one before us, the EIS "serve practically as an important contribution to the decisionmaking process." § 1502.5.

The Court obviously is quite correct in holding that properly classified materials need not be disclosed under NEPA; even information concerning the existence of an EIS may be withheld when publication would divulge sensitive military information. It remains true, however, that the statute is in part intended to inform the public, and this informational purpose does not entirely lose its vitality when classified documents are involved. Again, the Defense regulations specifically direct that "[w]hen feasible, [EIS's] shall be organized in such a manner that classified portions are included as annexes so that the unclassified portions can be made available to the public," * * * . In a given case, then, the military must determine whether the information at issue, consistent with the dictates of the relevant Executive Orders, can be released. That principle is applicable in this and in every other case involving classified military material; I must assume that the Court does not hold differently.

* * *

Accordingly, I concur in the judgment of the Court.

NOTES

1. The Court of Appeals for the Ninth Circuit held that the Navy should prepare a "hypothetical EIS" to address the possible storage of nuclear weapons at the West Loch facility. Not surprisingly, Justice Rehnquist rejected this holding on the grounds that it is not required by NEPA. How might the Ninth Circuit have used NEPA's requirement for an analysis of all reasonable alternatives so as to better ground its holding in the requirements of law?

2.   What is the relationship between the Freedom of Information Act (FOIA) and NEPA? Note that Exemption 1 of FOIA applies only to documents that are properly classified. Can a party request, and the Court order, an *in camera* inspection of documents to insure that they were properly classified? *See* 5 U.S.C. § 552(a)(4)(B).

3.   Agencies often withhold site specific information on endangered species to prevent poaching or harassment. For instance, BAs and EISs that discuss the effects of logging on endangered northern spotted owls often do not divulge locations of nest trees any more precisely than the section (a square mile of land) location. The ESA contains no provisions providing for the confidentiality of endangered species information. In contrast, the Archeological Resources Protection Act of 1979 explicitly exempts from FOIA disclosure information that would create a risk of harm to archeological resources. 16 U.S.C. § 470hh. What are the limits, if any, of the public's right to examine all of the environmental information, including endangered species surveys, contained in agency records? *See Audubon Soc'y v. U.S. Forest Serv.*, 104 F.3d 1201 (10th Cir. 1997).

4.   The majority finds that "whether or not the Navy has complied with NEPA 'to the fullest extent possible' is beyond judicial scrutiny in this case." Is this statement true? If the Court has the authority to order *in camera* inspection of documents to insure FOIA compliance, does it have the same authority to insure NEPA compliance?

5.   Professor Stephen Dycus discusses the *Catholic Action* case and the tensions between public disclosure and national security in *NEPA Secrets*, 2 N.Y.U. ENVTL. L.J. 300 (1993).

6.   Even assuming that a plaintiff can demonstrate that a defense agency has failed to comply with NEPA, it may be difficult to obtain an adequate remedy. In *Concerned About Trident v. Rumsfeld*, 555 F.2d 817 (D.C. Cir. 1976), the plaintiffs challenged the adequacy of the Navy's EIS for the proposed Trident submarine base at Bangor, Maine. Although the court acknowledged NEPA's application to strategic military decisions, and although it found that the EIS was defective, it nonetheless refused to enjoin the action pending correction of the defects because of its concern about the nation's defense posture. *See also Wisconsin v. Weinberger*, 745 F.2d 412 (7th Cir. 1984), *infra* Chapter 9.

RIVERSIDE IRRIGATION DISTRICT V. ANDREWS
758 F.2d 508 (10th Cir. 1985)

McKay, Circuit Judge.

The issue in this case is whether the Corps of Engineers exceeded its authority when it denied plaintiffs a nationwide permit for deposit of dredge material for construction of Wildcat Dam and Reservoir. The Corps based its decision on the potential downstream impact on an endangered species due to the resulting increased consumptive use of water.

Plaintiffs seek to build a dam and reservoir on Wildcat Creek, a tributary of the South Platte River. Because construction of the dam involves depositing dredge and fill material in a navigable waterway, the plaintiffs are required to obtain a permit from the Corps of Engineers under Section 404 of the Clean Water Act, 33 U.S.C. § 1344. The regulations under the Clean Water Act create categories of nationwide permits that provide automatic authority to place fill material if certain conditions are met. 33 C.F.R. § 330.4. If the conditions are not met, the party must seek an individual permit through a public notice and hearing process. The Corps determined that the proposed deposit did not meet the required conditions because the increased use of water that the resulting reservoir would facilitate would deplete the stream flow and endanger a critical habitat of the whooping crane, an endangered species. The Corps therefore informed the plaintiffs that they would be required to obtain an individual permit before the project could proceed.

Plaintiffs filed this suit seeking declaratory and injunctive relief and review of the agency action, claiming that the project is entitled to proceed under a nationwide permit and that the Corps exceeded its authority when it considered the effect of depletions caused by consumptive use of the water to be stored in the reservoir. * * * On remand, the district court held that the engineer had acted within his authority and that he was required, under the Clean Water Act and the Endangered Species Act, to deny the nationwide permit. Plaintiffs appeal.

A nationwide permit is one covering a category of activities occurring throughout the country that involve discharges of dredge or fill material that will cause only minimal adverse effects on the environment when performed separately and that will have only minimal cumulative effects. See 33 U.S.C. § 1344(e)(1). Such a permit is automatic in that if one qualifies, no application is needed before beginning the discharge activity. The Corps has the authority and duty, however, to ensure that parties seeking to proceed under a nationwide permit meet the requirements for such action. One condition of a nationwide permit is that the discharge not destroy a threatened or endangered species as identified under the Endangered Species Act, or destroy or adversely modify the critical habitat of such species. 33 C.F.R. § 330.4(b)(2). [Current provision at § 330.5(b)(3).] The regulations thus are consistent with the Corps' obligation, under the Endangered Species Act, to ensure that "any action authorized, funded, or carried out by such agency . . . is not likely to jeopardize the continued existence of any endangered species or threatened species or result in the destruction or adverse modification of habitat of such species which is determined by the Secretary . . . to be critical."

No one claims that the fill itself will endanger or destroy the habitat of an endangered species or adversely affect the aquatic environment. However, the fill that the Corps is authorizing is required to build the earthen dam. The dam will result in the impoundment of water in a reservoir, facilitating the use of the water in Wildcat Creek. The increased consumptive use will allegedly deplete the stream flow, and it is this depletion that the Corps found would adversely affect the habitat of the whooping crane.

The Endangered Species Act does not, by its terms, enlarge the jurisdiction of the Corps of Engineers under the Clean Water Act. However, it imposes on agencies a mandatory obligation to consider the environmental impacts of the projects that they authorize or fund. As the Supreme Court stated in *TVA v. Hill*, 437 U.S. 153, 173 (1978):

> One would be hard pressed to find a statutory provision whose terms were any plainer than those of § 7 of the Endangered Species Act. Its very words affirmatively command all federal agencies "to *insure* that actions *authorized, funded or carried out* by them do not jeopardize the continued existence" of an endangered species or "result in the destruction or adverse modification of habitat of such species." 16 U.S.C. § 1536. This language admits of no exception.

(emphasis in original). The question in this case is how broadly the Corps is authorized to look under the Clean Water Act in determining the environmental impact of the discharge that it is authorizing.

Plaintiffs claim that the Corps is authorized to consider only the direct, on-site effects of the discharge, particularly the effects on water quality, and that the Corps exceeded its authority by considering downstream effects of changes in water quantity. However, both the statute and the regulations authorize the Corps to consider downstream effects of changes in water quantity as well as on-site changes in water quality in determining whether a proposed discharge qualifies for a nationwide permit. The statute explicitly requires that a permit be obtained for any discharge "incidental to any activity having as its purpose bringing an area of navigable waters into a use to which it was not previously subject, where the flow or circulation of navigable waters may be impaired or the reach of such waters reduced." The guidelines for determining compliance with section 404(b)(1), developed by the Secretary of the Army and the Environmental Protection Agency, require the permitting authority to consider factors related to water quantity, including the effects of the discharge on water velocity, current patterns, water circulation, and normal water fluctuations. 40 C.F.R. §§ 230.23, 230.24. Thus, the statute focuses not merely on water quality, but rather on all of the effects on the "aquatic environment" caused by replacing water with fill material. 33 U.S.C. § 1344(f)(1)(E).

Plaintiffs argue that, even if the Corps can consider effects of changes in water quantity, it can do so only when the change is a direct effect of the discharge. In the present case, the depletion of water is an indirect effect of the discharge, in that it results from the increased consumptive use of water facilitated by the discharge. However, the Corps is required, under both the Clean Water Act and the Endangered Species Act, to consider the environmental impact of the discharge that it is authorizing. To require it to ignore the indirect effects that result from its actions would be to require it to wear blinders that Congress has not chosen to impose. The fact that the reduction in water does not result "from direct federal action does not lessen the appellee's duty under § 7 [of the Endangered Species Act]." The relevant consideration is the total impact of the discharge on the crane. In *National Wildlife Federation* [*v. Coleman,* 529 F.2d 359 (5th Cir. 1976)], the Fifth Circuit held that the federal agency was required to consider both the direct and the indirect impacts of proposed highway construction, including the residential and commercial development that would develop around the highway interchanges. Similarly, in this case, the Corps was required to consider all effects, direct and indirect, of the discharge for which authorization was sought.

The cases cited by the plaintiffs to the contrary are not controlling. Each involves the National Environmental Protection Act (NEPA), which authorizes the government to look at environmental concerns only when there is "major federal action." Thus, in each, the question is whether the project is sufficiently federal to require an environmental impact statement at all. The Clean Water Act does not require major federal action before the Corps must consider environmental impacts. Rather, the Corps must consider the environmental impact of each act that it authorizes, both major and minor. In creating categories of nationwide permits, the Corps has "acted" to authorize discharges. Thus, simply allowing a party to proceed under the nationwide permit is an action by the Corps triggering its obligation to consider environmental impacts.

There is no authority for the proposition that, once it is required to consider the environmental impact of the discharge that it is authorizing, the Corps is limited to consideration of the direct effects of the discharge. The reduction of water flows resulting from the increased consumptive use is an effect, albeit indirect, of the discharge to be authorized by the Corps. The discharge thus may "destroy or adversely modify" the critical habitat of an endangered species, and the Corps correctly found that the proposed project did not meet the requirements for a nationwide permit.

Plaintiffs claim that the Corps cannot deny them a nationwide permit because the denial impairs the state's right to allocate water within its jurisdiction, in violation of section 101(g) of the Act (the "Wallop Amendment"). Even if denial of a nationwide permit is considered an impairment of the state's authority to allocate water, a question that we do not decide, the Corps acted within its authority. As discussed above, the statute and regulations expressly require the Corps to consider changes in water quantity in granting nationwide permits. Section 101(g), which is only a general policy statement, "cannot nullify a clear and specific grant of jurisdiction, even if the particular grant seems inconsistent with the broadly stated purpose." *Connecticut Light and Power Co. v. Federal Power Commission*, 324 U.S. 515, 527 (1945). Thus, the Corps did not exceed its authority in denying a nationwide permit based on its determination that the depletion in water flow resulting from increased consumptive use of water would adversely affect the critical habitat of the whooping crane.

The Wallop Amendment does, however, indicate "that Congress did not want to interfere any more than necessary with state water management." *National Wildlife Federation v. Gorsuch*, 693 F.2d 156, 178 (D.C. Cir. 1982). A fair reading of the statute as a whole makes clear that, where both the state's interest in allocating water and the federal government's interest in protecting the environment are implicated, Congress intended an accommodation. Such accommodations are best reached in the individual permit process.

We need not reach the question raised by plaintiffs of whether Congress can unilaterally abrogate an interstate compact. The action by the Corps has not denied Colorado its right to water use under the South Platte River Compact. All that has been done is to deny them the ability to proceed under a nationwide permit and to require them to apply for an individual permit under public notice and hearing procedures. As plaintiffs may receive an individual permit and be able to proceed with the project, a decision on the question of the impact of the interstate compact would be premature.

We also need not decide whether the project will, in fact, have an adverse impact on the habitat of the whooping crane. Plaintiffs are entitled to proceed under a nationwide permit only if they can show that they meet the conditions for such a permit. Thus, plaintiffs must show "that the discharge will not destroy a threatened or endangered species as identified in the Endangered Species Act or destroy or adversely modify the critical habitat of such species." 33 C.F.R. § 330.4(b)(2). The record supports the Corps' finding that the discharge may adversely modify the critical habitat of the whooping crane. Thus, plaintiffs did not meet their burden of showing, as a matter of fact, that the discharge will not have such an adverse impact. The Corps acted within its authority in requiring the plaintiffs to proceed under the individual permit procedure.

AFFIRMED.

NOTES

1. Section 101(g) of the Clean Water Act (the Wallop Amendment) states:

It is the policy of Congress that the authority of each State to allocate quantities of water within its jurisdiction shall not be superseded, abrogated or otherwise impaired by this chapter. It is the further policy of Congress that nothing in this chapter shall be construed to supersede or abrogate rights to quantities of water which have been established by any State. Federal agencies shall co-operate with State and local agencies to develop comprehensive solutions to prevent, reduce and eliminate pollution in concert with programs for managing water resources.

33 U.S.C. § 1251(g). Suppose the Corps decides to deny Riverside an individual permit on environmental grounds unrelated to the possible harm to any endangered or threatened species. Suppose, for example, that the Corps finds that the permit should be denied because the environmental costs associated with the proposed project, including the loss of wetlands, far exceed any possible benefits associated with the project. Does the denial of a permit on these grounds violate § 101(g)?

2.   Suppose that the Corps were to deny Riverside an individual permit on the grounds that any further diversions out of the South Platte River system would jeopardize the endangered whooping crane. Suppose further that the effect of this decision is to prevent Colorado from taking its full allocation under the South Platte River Compact (an interstate agreement enacted into law by Congress). Which law takes precedence—the Endangered Species Act or the South Platte River Compact?

3.   Assume that the U.S. Fish and Wildlife Service issues a jeopardy opinion on Riverside's proposed "dredge and fill" permit, concluding that any additional consumptive uses of water rights along the South Platte River in Colorado will adversely impact critical whooping crane habitat in Nebraska. Does this decision amount to a taking of private property for a public use in violation of the Fifth Amendment to the U.S. Constitution? Is *Riverside Irrigation* consistent with the Ninth Circuit's decision in *Sylvester v. U.S. Army Corps of Engineers,* 871 F.2d 817 (9th Cir. 1989)? *See supra* at Chapter 7.B. *See Lucas v. South Carolina Coastal Council,* 505 U.S. 1003 (1992), *supra* Chapter 2.

4.   In *American Forest and Paper Ass'n v. U.S. EPA,* 28 Envtl. L. Rep. 21122 (Envtl. L. Inst.) (5th Cir. 1998), the court found that the EPA exceeded its authority when it conditioned delegation of the Clean Water Act's pollutant discharge elimination system permit program to Louisiana. The condition required the state to consult with the Service before issuing permits to ensure that the state's action, authorized by the EPA under the CWA, would not violate the ESA. The court found that CWA § 402(b), 33 U.S.C. § 1342(b), which requires the EPA to approve submitted delegation programs unless they fail to meet one of nine listed requirements, limits the EPA's ability to condition its approval of delegated discharge permit programs. None of the nine requirements addresses endangered species. The court wrote that:

> * * * EPA argues that ESA § 7(a)(2) * * * compels EPA to do everything reasonably within its power to protect endangered species. The flaw in this argument is that if EPA lacks the power to add additional criteria to CWA § 402(b), nothing in the ESA grants the agency the authority to do so. Section 7 of the ESA merely requires EPA to consult with FWS or NMFS before undertaking agency action; it confers no substantive powers.

Is this holding consistent with *Riverside Irrigation District*? *Compare American Forest and Paper Ass'n with American Iron & Steel Inst. v. EPA,* 115 F.3d 979 (D.C. Cir. 1997) (upholding the EPA's water quality guidance for the Great Lakes, which included provisions to require states to protect endangered species).

Note that the *American Forest and Paper Ass'n* court did not address the EPA obligation under the ESA to consult with the Service before approving a state water program delegation. Assuming that approval of a state program is an action authorized, funded and/or carried out under ESA § 7(a)(2), then conceivably the Service could issue a jeopardy opinion if the state program did not contain provisions to ensure the survival of listed species. Would the EPA be able to disapprove a state program that is the subject of a jeopardy opinion? Would the EPA be in a position where it would have to violate either the ESA or the Clean Water Act?

9 REMEDIES

As the materials thus far considered amply illustrate, environmental cases often follow a predictable pattern. First, a government agency proposes to take an action that is opposed by a conservation group, a state or local government, a developer, or a private individual. The opposing party then brings an action seeking to enjoin the agency from going forward. In many cases, administrative remedies are available, and generally these must be exhausted before a party can obtain judicial review. The type of administrative review that is available varies greatly among agencies. In some agencies the process is quite formal and may involve more than one level of review. In other cases, it may consist of nothing more than a simple letter of protest. Often, representation by an attorney is unnecessary at this stage, though it may be advisable, particularly if the complaining party anticipates further legal action. Indeed, if judicial review may be limited to the record generated during the initial administrative process, the complaining party must be certain that the development of the record at this stage is thorough.

Review from an adverse decision of an agency appellate body generally is available in federal district court, although for certain actions under some statutes, such as the promulgation of national rules under the Clean Air Act, the first level of judicial review is in the appropriate Court of Appeals. *See* 42 U.S.C. § 7607(b). If the agency proceedings established a sufficient process for developing an administrative record of the decision, judicial review usually will be limited to the administrative record. Often in NEPA and ESA cases, however, the dispute focuses on the adequacy of the environmental analysis, and unless the agency proceedings afford plaintiffs an adequate opportunity to demonstrate the inadequacy of the EIS (through expert testimony or some equivalent form of evidence), a trial may be necessary.

Where review is limited to the record, the parties typically will file cross-motions for summary judgment with supporting memoranda. If the plaintiffs seek expedited relief, as they often do in environmental disputes, a motion for a preliminary injunction (or, in some cases, a temporary restraining order) will be heard by the court soon after the challenged agency decision has been made. It is common for courts to consolidate the hearing on the preliminary injunction with the hearing on the merits, thus making necessary the full presentation of the case in a very short span of time.

If a court issues a preliminary injunction, the defendant may request that the plaintiff post a bond in accordance with Rule 65(c) of the Federal Rules of Civil Procedure. In most cases involving issues relating to the public interest, however, courts will impose only a nominal bond, or no bond at all. *See, e.g., California v. Tahoe Regional Planning Agency*, 766 F.2d 1319 (9th Cir. 1985); *Natural Resources Defense Council v. Morton*, 337 F. Supp. 167 (D.D.C. 1971), *aff'd on other grounds*, 458 F.2d 827 (D.C. Cir. 1972).

MASSACHUSETTS V. WATT
716 F.2d 946 (1st Cir. 1983)

BREYER, Circuit Judge.

The government asks us to set aside a preliminary injunction stopping it from auctioning rights to drill for oil on 488 tracts near Georges Bank, a fishing area in the North Atlantic off the New England Coast. The district court acting at the request of the Commonwealth of Massachusetts and the Conservation Law Foundation, issued the injunction (after a brief hearing) on March 28, 1983—sixteen days after the Commonwealth and the Conservation Law Foundation asked for a preliminary injunction and one day before the scheduled oil lease sale was to take place. * * *

I

NEPA requires that the Department of the Interior, before auctioning its oil leases, prepare a statement that describes "the environmental impact of the proposed action, . . . any adverse environmental effects which cannot be avoided . . ., [and] alternatives to the proposed action . . . ." 42 U.S.C. § 4332(C). Further regulations, binding throughout the Executive Branch, *Andrus v. Sierra Club*, 442 U.S. 347, 358 (1979), require the Department to prepare a supplement to this Environmental Impact Statement (EIS) if there are "significant new circumstances or information relevant to environmental concerns and bearing on the proposed action or its impacts." 40 C.F.R. § 1502.9(c). In this case, after the Department prepared its Final Environmental Impact Statement (FEIS), it radically revised its estimates of oil likely to be found on the tracts it intended to lease. It lowered its mean estimate from 1.73 *billion* barrels to 55.7 *million* barrels—a 97% reduction. The NEPA issue is whether the fact that the Department now believes there is only 1/31 as much oil to be found off Georges Bank is a "significant new circumstance" sufficient to require an EIS supplement.

We judge the lawfulness of the Department's decision not to supplement the EIS by asking whether that decision was reasonable under the circumstances. Having read the approximately five-hundred-page FEIS and the various decision documents placed before the Secretary, we conclude that the Department of Interior's decision not to supplement was not reasonable. Without a supplement, the FEIS did not describe the likely environmental harms well enough to allow the Secretary to make an informed decision.

* * *

II

The government argues that, regardless of any NEPA violation, the district court erred in issuing a preliminary injunction because the plaintiffs will suffer no "irreparable harm." The government correctly states that the propriety of a preliminary injunction depends upon consideration of the plaintiffs' likelihood of success on the merits, of "irreparable harm," of an appropriate "balance" of the harms to the plaintiffs and defendants, and of the effect upon the public interest. The government is wrong, however, in arguing that there is no "irreparable injury" here.

The government points out that the lease sale does not necessarily entitle the lease buyers to drill for oil. There are several further steps that must be taken, and further governmental permission must be obtained before oil exploration can begin. This fact, in the government's view, shows that the lease sale alone cannot hurt the environment. The government concludes that the district court should have allowed the sale to proceed while the court made a more thorough determination of its lawfulness. If the court were to find the lease sale unlawful, it could always set it aside after the event.

The government's argument, however, ignores an important feature of NEPA. NEPA is not designed to prevent all possible harm to the environment; it foresees that decisionmakers may choose to inflict such harm, for perfectly good reasons. Rather, NEPA is designed to influence the decisionmaking process; its aim is to make government officials notice environmental considerations and take them into account. Thus, when a decision to which NEPA obligations attach is made without the informed environmental consideration that NEPA requires, the harm that NEPA intends to prevent has been suffered. NEPA in this sense differs from substantive environmental statutes, such as the Federal Water Pollution Control Act. The Federal Water Pollution Control Act focuses upon the "integrity of the Nation's Waters, not the permit process," *Weinberger v. Romero-Barcelo*, 456 U.S. at 314. NEPA does the converse. Moreover, to set aside the agency's action at a later date will not necessarily undo the harm. The agency as well as private parties may well have become committed to the previously chosen course of action, and new information—a new EIS—may bring about a *new* decision, but it is that much less likely to bring about a *different* one. It is far easier to influence an initial choice than to change a mind already made up. *See Alaska v. Andrus*, 580 F.2d at 485; *Jones v. District of Columbia Redevelopment Land Agency*, 499 F.2d at 512-13 ("So long as the *status quo* is maintained, so long as the environmental impact statement is not merely a justification for a *fait accompli*, there is a possibility that the statement will lead the agency to change its plans . . . .").

It is appropriate for the courts to recognize this type of injury in a NEPA case, for it reflects the very theory upon which NEPA is based—a theory aimed at presenting governmental decision-makers with relevant environmental data before they commit themselves to a course of action. This is not to say that a likely NEPA violation automatically calls for an injunction; the *balance* of harms may point the other way. It is simply to say that a plaintiff seeking an injunction cannot be stopped at the *threshold* by pointing to additional steps between the governmental decision and environmental harm.

In the present case plaintiffs would suffer harm if they were denied an injunction, if the lease sale then took place, and if the court *then* held that a supplemental EIS was required. In that event, the successful oil companies would have committed time and effort to planning the development of the blocks they had leased, and the Department of the Interior and the relevant state agencies would have begun to make plans based upon the leased tracts. Each of these events represents a link in a chain of bureaucratic commitment that will become progressively harder to undo the longer it continues. Once large bureaucracies are committed to a course of action, it is difficult to change that course—even if new, or more thorough, NEPA statements are prepared and the agency is told to "redecide." It is this type of harm that plaintiffs seek to avoid, and it is the presence of this type of harm that courts have said can merit an injunction in an appropriate case.

The more difficult question here involves balancing the harm caused plaintiffs without the injunction against the harm the injunction will cause defendants. We have already expressed our view that the agency action—the lease sale—will probably be found unlawful on NEPA grounds, and we have just described plaintiffs' harm. We believe that the countervailing factor—the harm the injunction will cause defendants—is fairly small. For one thing, defendants do not argue that the Georges Bank oil is needed immediately. Nor, given the apparent recent "oil glut," do we see how they could make such an argument. For another thing, the government does not claim that the oil could make a significant difference to the national defense, or to any economic decisions that it might make. Finally, the government has already—in the SID and EA—begun to gather the information necessary to supplement the FEIS. At oral argument, government counsel said she believed that a supplement could be prepared within 120 days.

Thus, weighing the NEPA-type harm to plaintiffs against the fairly short delay, in light of the likelihood of unlawfulness, we conclude that the district court's decision as to the "irreparable harm" and its balancing of the relevant harms was reasonable and adequate to support on appeal the issuance of this preliminary injunction. The district court's weighing of the public interest and its conclusions thereon were likewise well within its sound discretion.

* * *

The decision of the district court here under review is AFFIRMED.

NOTES

1. What factors must a court consider in deciding whether to issue a preliminary injunction? *See Alpine Lakes Protection Society v. Schlapfer*, 518 F.2d 1089, 1090 (9th Cir. 1975) (three-part test: "(1) Are the moving parties likely to prevail on the merits? (2) does the balance of irreparable damage favor the issuance of the injunction? and (3) does the public interest support granting the injunction?"); *Colorado River Indian Tribes v. Marsh*, 605 F. Supp. 1425, 1429 (C.D. Cal. 1985) (four-part test: "(1) a strong likelihood of success on the merits, (2) the possibility of irreparable injury to the plaintiff if the preliminary relief is not granted, (3) a balance of hardships favoring the plaintiff, and (4) advancement of the public interest"). *See also Washington Metropolitan Area Transit Commission v. Holiday Tours, Inc.*, 559 F.2d 841, 843 (D.C. Cir. 1977) (applying a four-factor test). How would you assess *Massachusetts v. Watt* according to these tests?

2. Suppose the decision to go forward with the lease sale was made in the context of an "energy crisis" of limited fuel supplies and dramatically rising fuel costs. How might such facts affect the court's analysis? In *Alaska v. Andrus*, 580 F.2d 465 (D.C. Cir.), *vacated and remanded sub nom., Western Oil & Gas Assoc. v. Alaska*, 439 U.S. 922 (1978), plaintiffs challenged the environmental impact statement prepared by the Department of Interior in connection with its sale of over one million acres of oil and gas leases in the Gulf of Alaska. The court ruled that the impact statement improperly failed to evaluate alternative operating orders specifying safety and environmental standards for Outer Continental Shelf drilling activities or to consider the inclusion in the leases of termination clauses for lease cancellation if unforeseen environmental hazards were later discovered. Plaintiffs asked the court to set aside the lease sale as invalid and enjoin any further drilling in the Gulf of Alaska until Interior had complied with NEPA. Although the court said that, in cases of NEPA non-compliance, there was a "presumption" in favor of injunctive relief, here it found such relief inappropriate. Neither of the alternatives which Interior had failed to consider—inclusion of termination clauses or conducting the lease sale pursuant to more rigorous operating orders—was an alternative to the *holding* of the lease sale. The government could insert protective operating orders in the leases at a later time, and it retained authority to use eminent domain if sufficiently serious hazards developed. In the interim, the risk was simply too small, and the public interest (at that time) in obtaining new domestic sources of petroleum was too great, to merit an injunction.

3. Recall that one of NEPA's chief purposes is to prevent agencies from making "irreversible and irretrievable commitments of resources" until the appropriate environmental analysis is completed and considered. *See, e.g.,* 40 C.F.R. § 1502.16. Did the decision to go forward with the lease sale irretrievably commit the government to developing the leases? The Supreme Court has held that Outer Continental Shelf Lands Act leases, such as those involved in the *Massachusetts* case, did not irretrievably commit the government to development. *Secretary of the Interior v. California*, 464 U.S. 312 (1984). Do you think the Court of Appeals for the First Circuit would have decided *Massachusetts v. Watt* differently after 1984?

4. Note that the factors considered by courts in deciding whether to grant a preliminary injunction are essentially the same as those considered for a permanent injunction. *See, e.g.*, *Sierra Club v. Hennessy*, 695 F.2d 643 (2d Cir. 1982), *aff'd in part, rev'd in part sub nom. Sierra Club v. U.S. Army Corps of Engineers*, 701 F.2d 1011 (2d Cir. 1983). Indeed, a hearing on a preliminary injunction is often consolidated with a hearing on the merits, since the outcome is likely to be the same. Consolidation may occur at the request of a party or on the court's own motion. FED. R. CIV. P. 65(a)(2). By requesting preliminary relief, moreover, a plaintiff may be able to expedite the final result in a case, and thereby considerably reduce costs and expenses associated with the case. Even if the hearing on the preliminary injunction is not consolidated with the hearing on the merits, the urgency suggested by the request for preliminary relief often promotes a prompt final decree. *See* John Leshy, *Interlocutory Injunctive Relief in Environmental Cases: A Primer for the Practitioner,* 6 ECOLOGY L.Q. 639 (1977).

5. Claims by plaintiffs of irreparable harm are, not surprisingly, commonplace in NEPA and ESA litigation. If an agency goes forward with a proposed action without fully considering the impact on a roadless area or a listed species, the resource may be lost before courts can review a challenge on its merits. In *Amoco Production Co. v. Village of Gambrell*, 480 U.S. 531, 545 (1987), the Supreme Court held that:

> Environmental injury, by its nature, can seldom be remedied by damages. If such injury is sufficiently likely, therefore, the balance of harms will usually favor the issuance of an injunction.

Moreover, the Court of Appeals for the Ninth Circuit has held that "[i]rreparable damage is presumed when an agency fails to evaluate thoroughly the environmental impact of a proposed action." *Save Our Ecosystems v. Clark,* 747 F.2d 1240, 1250 (9th Cir. 1984) (citing *Friends of the Earth v. Coleman*, 518 F.2d 323, 330 (9th Cir. 1975)). According to the Ninth Circuit, "[o]nly in a rare circumstance may a court refuse to issue an injunction when it finds a NEPA violation." 747 F.2d at 1250. *See also* Zygmunt Plater, *Statutory Violations and Equitable Discretion,* 70 CAL. L. REV. 524, 575 (1982). One such "rare" instance came in *American Motorcycles Association v. Watt*, 714 F.2d 962 (9th Cir. 1983) [*AMA*] (challenging BLM's decision to curtail motorcycle races and other recreational vehicle use of the California desert). In *AMA*, the court found a "strong likelihood" that the BLM had violated NEPA. Nonetheless, the court denied the requested injunction because doing so would cause less environmental damage than granting it. Should the *AMA* standard be applied to deny a requested injunction where a court finds the FWS to have violated NEPA by failing to prepare an EA or EIS before designating critical habitat? *See, e.g., Catron County Bd. of Commissioners v. U.S. Fish & Wildlife Serv.*, 75 F.3d 1429 (10th Cir. 1996). Compare the result in *AMA* with the decision in the following case.

Wisconsin v. Weinberger
745 F.2d 412 (7th Cir. 1984)

Harlington Wood, Jr., Circuit Judge.

Plaintiff-appellee State of Wisconsin and intervening plaintiff-appellee County of Marquette, Michigan, sued federal appellants seeking the preparation of a supplemental environmental impact statement (SEIS) in connection with Project ELF, an extremely low frequency submarine communications system developed by the Navy, which the Navy undertook to reactivate and expand in 1981.[4] Plaintiffs contended that the Navy's original 1977 environmental impact statement prepared at the time the project first originated should have been supplemented because of new information regarding the biological effects of extremely low frequency electromagnetic radiation. After a trial on the merits, the district court agreed with this contention and enjoined the Navy from proceeding with any additional work on Project ELF in Wisconsin or Michigan and from installing receivers in submarines until a supplementary environmental impact statement had been prepared. This expedited appeal followed.

* * *

We hold that there was no violation of NEPA by the Navy. That being so, the injunction must necessarily be vacated, as we have already done by order, without further consideration. Nevertheless, we proceed to consider the merits of the injunction separately since this panel, although not in unanimous agreement about the underlying NEPA violation, is in unanimous agreement that the injunction was unwarranted.

IV.

The panel is in agreement that even if there had been a NEPA violation, the district court abused its discretion in not undertaking a balancing of the relative harms to the parties before entering the injunction prohibiting the Navy from continuing with Project ELF until a SEIS was filed. The district court, in denying the Navy's motion for reconsideration of the injunction, concluded that no balancing was to be undertaken because the point of NEPA is to assure that federal agencies assess the environmental impact of their proposals *before* deciding to proceed with an action. The district court found this case analogous to *TVA v. Hill*, 437 U.S. 153 (1978), the snail darter case, in which the Supreme Court held that the Endangered Species Act mandated injunctive relief despite countervailing equities. Because in the district court's view allowing the ELF proposal to proceed without first reconsidering its impact, except in certain unusual circumstances, would frustrate the purposes of the Act, the district court reasoned that there was a presumption that injunctive relief be imposed for a NEPA violation. It ruled that unless the Navy rebutted the presumption by showing that an injunction would not serve the purposes of the Act, the court did not have to undertake a balancing of the relative harms.

Although the district court's view is not without some support from *TVA v. Hill*, we disagree with its conclusions in these particular circumstances. We consider *Hill* and this case to be distinguishable. There is no presumption mandating an injunction in this type of case. NEPA cannot be construed to elevate automatically its procedural requirements above all other

---

[4] With an ELF communications system, a submarine is able to receive messages from land while maintaining operational speeds at depths at which it is practically immune from detection. Other land-based submarine communications systems require the submarine to surface completely or rise to a point near the surface at slow speeds and drag an antenna to receive messages, thereby jeopardizing the safety of the crew and vessel.

national considerations. Although there is no national defense exception to NEPA, and the Navy does not claim one, the national well-being and security as determined by the Congress and the President demand consideration before an injunction should issue for a NEPA violation.

We begin our analysis of the appropriateness of the injunction here with the Supreme Court's pronouncement in *Weinberger v. Romero-Barcelo*, 456 U.S. 305 (1982), that an injunction "'is not a remedy which issues as of course . . . .'" *Id.* at 311.

* * *

In exercising their sound discretion, courts of equity should pay particular regard for the public consequences in employing the extraordinary remedy of injunction. . . . The grant of jurisdiction to ensure compliance with a statute hardly suggests an absolute duty to do so under any and all circumstances, and a federal judge sitting as a chancellor is not mechanically obligated to grant an injunction for every violation of law.

Romero-Barcelo, 456 U.S. at 312-13. Although the Court recognized that Congress occasionally may act to foreclose the exercise of the usual discretion possessed by a court of equity, such occasions will be rare. The Court explained its decision in *TVA v. Hill* by pointing to the content of the particular statute involved there and the particular facts presented. In *Hill*, the competing interests—the proposed dam and the snail darter habitat—were clearly defined. The actual balancing of these interests, however, was already prescribed by the specific terms of the relevant statute. The Endangered Species Act contained an unequivocal ban on the destruction of critical habitats for endangered species. Because the proposed dam in *Hill* would have eliminated such a critical habitat, refusal to enjoin the construction of the dam would have ignored the explicit provisions of the Act. "Congress, it appeared to us, had chosen the snail darter over the dam. The purpose and language of the statute limited the remedies available to the District Court; only an injunction could vindicate the objectives of the Act." *Romero-Barcelo*, 456 U.S. at 314.

We believe, however, that neither the specific terms of NEPA nor the particular interests involved compel the issuance of the prohibitory injunction here. We find nothing in NEPA that explicitly or "by a necessary and inescapable inference, restrict[s] the court's jurisdiction in equity." *Id.* at 313. Although the goal of NEPA is to force agencies to consider the environmental consequences of major federal actions, *see Kleppe*, 427 U.S. at 410 n. 21, that goal is not to be achieved at the expense of a total disregard for countervailing public interests. NEPA itself is procedural in nature, *see Vermont Yankee*, 435 U.S. at 558, and the statute recognizes that agencies may decide to subordinate environmental values to other social values with which they sometimes compete. Thus, although the judicial role is to insure that this weighing of competing interests takes place, we must fulfill this role in accordance with a consideration of other social costs, as recognized by the statute itself. That, after all, is the traditional way of applying equitable principles.

The recent trend of the majority of courts is to evaluate competing public interests in fashioning permanent injunctive relief for NEPA violations.

When a court has found that a party is in violation of NEPA, the remedy should be shaped so as to fulfill the objectives of the statute as closely as possible, consistent with the broader public interest. . . . The court should tailor its relief to fit each particular case, balancing the environmental concerns of NEPA against the larger interests of society that might be adversely affected by an overly broad injunction.

Environmental Defense Fund v. Marsh, 651 F.2d 983, 1005-06 (5th Cir. 1981). * * *

The only irreparable injury under NEPA if the Navy were permitted to proceed with Project ELF, as perceived by the district court, was that it would later lead to biased decision-making by the Navy. It posited that because NEPA establishes a policy requiring decision-makers to take account of environmental values, that policy will not be fully achieved if decision-makers are predisposed to favor a particular outcome because of an agency's investment in the project. Such a predisposition can result once a commitment of resources to a project is undertaken, thus possibly upsetting objective decision-making. *See Massachusetts v. Watt,* 716 F.2d 946, 952-53 (1st Cir. 1983).

This concern is valid, and in an appropriate case this kind of possible effect may merit an injunction. The Navy points out, however, that this interest will be only marginally served by the injunction in an ongoing project such as this one. The new commitment to ELF began in 1981, when the project was reactivated, and reaffirmed the already existing commitment. This commitment, largely in terms of research and development dollars, was well established by the time plaintiffs got around to filing their lawsuit in mid-1983. By contrast, the commitment entailed by the remaining construction effort in Wisconsin and Michigan is relatively small, and thus the injunction's service to NEPA in preserving unbiased decision-making would be slight. Even if the Navy subsequently makes the mistake of being influenced by its prior resource commitment, the President and the Congress are not without power to bring the Navy back into line, and so may we if the Navy's actions are arbitrary or capricious. The risk the district court found from resource commitment, the only designated basis for the injunction, is wholly inadequate to enjoin this project.

In addition, the Navy argues that no other NEPA purpose would be served by the injunction. It notes that it has already adopted the recommendations of the National Academy of Sciences to minimize the electromagnetic fields generated by the project, and has committed itself to monitoring the potential adverse biological effects of such fields and to terminate the project should such effects become manifest. Finally, the Navy observes that whatever benefits might accrue to the public from another opportunity to comment on the content of the SEIS would not stem from the injunction enjoining the construction activities.

We find these arguments compelling. In addition, we note that even if we had found a NEPA violation here, it could not have been characterized as a blatant violation, and the injunction consequently could not have been justified on the ground that it was needed to prevent future violations. The Navy in this project has fully complied with NEPA in the past, and has publicly committed itself to a continuing monitoring of the physical and biological environmental consequences of Project ELF. The Navy has acted responsibly and not in an arbitrary or capricious manner.

More important, however, is the district court's failure to balance the weight of the alleged NEPA violation against the harm the injunction would cause the Navy and to this country's defense. The Navy has emphasized that an ELF submarine communications system is of the highest priority for national defense. The system will allow our strategic submarine fleet to operate with a greatly reduced chance for exposure and minimize the possibility of detection, thus strengthening the most survivable element of this nation's nuclear deterrent. President Reagan's directive to deploy Project ELF ordered that it achieve initial operating capability in fiscal year 1985. The Secretary of the Navy also stated in an affidavit that the latest evaluation of Project ELF is that it is essential to the national defense and that any delay in its construction is contrary to national defense interests. We have no basis to ignore those executive representations. At oral argument, counsel for the Navy informed us that preparation of a SEIS, which had already begun, could not be completed before April of 1985. Therefore, the delay occasioned by the issuance of an injunction could bring about serious consequences for our national defense. The Soviet Union allegedly is already advanced in this low frequency submarine communications technique. The district court gave no consideration to these serious circumstances.

An order requiring the preparation of a SEIS, of course, may always be appropriate to vindicate the purposes of NEPA should a violation of the CEQ regulations occur. Whether an injunction should also be entered preventing a project from continuing, however, is plainly an additional issue. We disagree with the district court that NEPA presumes that such injunctions should issue. That presumption is unrealistic in these circumstances. We conclude, therefore, that even if there had been a NEPA violation, the district court abused its discretion by failing to consider the degree to which the NEPA interest would, in fact, be served by an injunction, the efficacy of other forms of relief, and the harm to national defense interests that would result. Based on the record already before us, any traditional equitable weighing of interest could only lead to a denial of the issuance of the injunction that we have now vacated.

* * *

REVERSED.

CUDAHY, Circuit Judge, concurring in part and dissenting in part.

In my view, the district court correctly determined that the Navy abused its discretion and violated NEPA by failing to monitor new information concerning the potential environmental effects of Project ELF, and the court properly ordered the Navy to prepare a supplemental EIS. However, I agree that the district court erred when it refused to consider the countervailing equities in deciding to enjoin work on Project ELF. In light of those equities, an injunction is not warranted in this case; I therefore concur in the portion of the judgment reversing the injunction.

* * *

However, the majority overstates the case. NEPA does indeed presume that an injunction should issue in an ordinary NEPA violation case. When NEPA is violated, the fundamental harm is that the decision process has been tainted by the failure to consider fully the relevant environmental facts. The most effective way to remedy the harm is to freeze the situation until the agency reconsiders properly. If that "purification" of the decisionmaking process is to be at all effective, the court must ordinarily prevent the agency in the meantime from committing even more resources to the path previously chosen. As Judge Breyer pointed out in *Massachusetts v. Watt, supra*:

> The agency as well as private parties may well have become committed to the previously chosen course of action, and new information—a new EIS—may bring about a *new* decision, but it is that much less likely to bring about a *different* one. It is far easier to influence an initial choice than to change a mind already made up.

716 F.2d at 952 (emphasis in original). Even an injunction may, as a practical matter, be inadequate when the agency is already far down the road. However, less stringent remedies will, in most cases, not be adequate to correct the NEPA violation. Courts therefore ordinarily issue injunctions in NEPA cases as a matter of course.

Nevertheless, when an agency raises powerful countervailing equities, NEPA does not prevent the district court from weighing those factors in deciding whether to issue an injunction. Courts must recognize, though, that in doing so there is a clear risk that NEPA's goals may be too easily diluted and subverted. NEPA protects intangible values, and competing equities may often be immediate and tangible, and too difficult to analyze critically. Only in the unusual case should competing equities prevent an injunction.

The majority has properly identified most of the factors which make this such an unusual case. First, the degree of additional commitment to the project, in terms of both time and money, during the time needed to prepare a supplemental EIS would be quite marginal here when compared with the whole project. And a substantial portion of the Navy's additional commitments to Project ELF can, in a sense, be laid at the plaintiffs' doorsteps because they did not file this lawsuit until nineteen months after the Navy reactivated the project. Second, the new information here is at best equivocal—it is, as a practical matter, highly unlikely to affect the Navy's decision at this time. The information demands further study, as I have argued above, but it is too thin a reed to support an injunction closing down the project for over a year. Third, the underlying environmental threat here would not result directly from the construction of Project ELF. The only alleged environmental harms are those that might result from the eventual, long-term operation of the ELF system. An injunction here would serve only to delay the project while the Navy considered information which is at best indeterminate and equivocal concerning the possibility of environmental harm years or decades away.

The majority relies primarily, however, on the alleged harms the injunction might cause to the national defense. The national defense is without question a very important consideration and in some circumstances it could be decisive. Here, however, I do not believe it is necessary for the majority to accept the defendants' representations on this subject at face value to reach the proper result on this issue. It is quite clear that NEPA does not provide a "national security" exception, yet the majority's apparently uncritical acceptance of the Navy's claims might be an invitation in some circumstances for the government to escape NEPA's normally stiff remedies merely by asserting that an injunction might harm national security. After all, courts are simply not equipped to question such assertions. But the national security does not normally require such unquestioning solicitude from the courts in NEPA cases. Where national security concerns are truly paramount, Congress may, in most instances, simply exempt a project from NEPA's requirements. It has done so in the past and will presumably do so again in the future. It is also possible that some future case would require us to weigh national defense needs unequivocally in the equitable balance, and we might then need to base our decision on the government's representations in this respect. However, to the greatest extent possible, we in the federal courts should best leave such judgments to the political branches of government for resolution through political processes, rather than merely accept assertions which we are not in a position to challenge.

We need not entangle ourselves in speculation about the urgency of Project ELF; a far stronger basis for reversing the injunction here is that this case involves new information and an ongoing project. Although injunctions should ordinarily issue to remedy NEPA violations, special remedial problems arise with respect to new information affecting ongoing projects. The central purpose of NEPA is to ensure that agencies in fact give due consideration to environmental factors, and, as I have argued above, NEPA also imposes a duty on an agency to monitor and consider new information relevant to an ongoing project. If a project must be shut down pending preparation of a supplemental EIS, agencies will have, as a practical matter, strong incentives to subvert NEPA by merely creating a paper trail and by viewing any new information as too insignificant to require a supplemental EIS.

In cases involving new information and ongoing projects, the NEPA ideal of careful environmental planning *prior* to action is simply not achievable. The achievable goal is that agencies will indeed give their decisions fresh, hard looks in light of new information. The courts should not undermine NEPA by demanding more, by enjoining further work while the agency considers new information. Otherwise, the temptation to soft-pedal relevant information and to comply with NEPA only on paper will simply be too strong.

For similar reasons, courts should be far less concerned with the form of an agency's review of new information than with the substance. Whether the agency undertakes a full scale supplemental EIS process is less important than whether the agency gives the information *any* significant consideration. And as noted above, when the new information consists of a steady trickle of new scientific studies, it will often be impossible to determine when the information has become significant enough to require a supplemental EIS. The court should permit an agency to be flexible in considering new information relevant to ongoing projects so long as the agency shows that it has in fact given the information a hard look. As Judge Kennedy explained in his concurring opinion in *Warm Springs Dam*, courts should be satisfied with "other and less cumbersome ways for an agency to evaluate new information . . .." 621 F.2d at 1027. Of course, when an agency has failed to consider new information, the supplemental EIS remedy will often be appropriate, as I think it was here. But if we demand more of agencies under threat of injunction in the first instance, we may, as a practical matter, achieve much less.

NOTES

1. In its majority decision denying the injunction, the court cites what is perhaps the most important decision on the question of a court's authority to deny a injunction where a violation of a statute has been found. *Weinberger v. Romero-Barcelo*, 456 U.S. 305 (1982), involved the release of ordnance from U.S. Navy aircraft and ships during weapon training exercises off the coast of Puerto Rico. The Court accepted the trial court's finding that the release of ordnance was a discharge subject to the § 402 permitting program under the Clean Water Act. 33 U.S.C. § 1342. It was undisputed, however, that the EPA had promulgated no effluent limitations for such discharges and that the discharges were causing no appreciable harm to the environment. Thus, while a permit was "technically" required, it would not likely require any change in the manner in which the releases were occurring. The Court found that the purposes of the Clean Water Act were served by ordering the Navy to obtain a permit, but that since the issuance of the permit would not change the Navy's practice, an injunction was unnecessary. The Court distinguished its earlier decision in *TVA v. Hill*, 437 U.S. 153 (1978), *supra* Chapter 5, on the grounds that the purposes of the Endangered Species Act could be vindicated only by issuing an injunction. On which side of the line does the Navy's action fall in the *Wisconsin* case: *TVA v. Hill*, or *Weinberger v. Romero-Barcelo*? Are NEPA's purposes served by the court's decision? In making this determination, does *Romero-Barcelo* permit the court to consider "countervailing public interests" which are outside the scope of the statute that has been violated? Note that the majority in *Wisconsin* attempts to distinguish *TVA v. Hill*. Is its argument convincing?

2. Contrast the approach taken by the Court of Appeals for the Seventh Circuit with that of the Court of Appeals for the Ninth Circuit. *See Bob Marshall Alliance v. Hodel*, 852 F.2d 1223, 1230 (9th Cir. 1988), *cert. denied*, 489 U.S. 1066 (1989). ("The proper remedy for substantial procedural violations of NEPA and the ESA is an injunction.") (citing *Thomas v. Peterson*, 753 F.2d 754, 764 (9th Cir. 1985), *supra* Chapter 7).

3. Why does Judge Cudahy write separately? Are you persuaded by his reasons for denying the injunction?

4. In addition to national defense, the conduct of foreign affairs is another area in which courts are inclined to deny injunctive relief. In *Adams v. Vance*, 570 F.2d 950 (D.C. Cir. 1977), the court overturned a district court injunction ordering the Secretary of State to exercise a treaty right of objection to a rule promulgated by the International Whaling Commission (IWC) that would eliminate subsistence hunting of bowhead whales by Eskimos. The plaintiffs argued that the Secretary failed to comply with NEPA and that the exercise of the objection, which must be made within 90 days of the IWC announcement, would keep the United States' option open to later change its mind and withdraw its veto of the new IWC rule. The court found the injunction to be an "unwarranted intrusion on executive discretion." *Id.* at 952. The court found that an injunction in a situation involving "diplomatic interaction and negotiation" requires "an extraordinarily strong showing to succeed." *Id.* at 955.

5. Are commitments made in EISs enforceable? Somewhat disturbingly, a line of cases has developed in which plaintiffs have been denied remedies when projects have been constructed in disregard of statements made in EISs and supporting documents.

In *Ogunquit Village Corp. v. Davis*, 533 F.2d 243 (1st Cir. 1977), the village of Ogunquit, Maine, asked the federal Soil Conversation Service for its help in restoring its cherished mile-long white sand dune that had long protected the village from the sea and attracted tourists. The dunes had been lost to erosion. The Service was happy to oblige (for a fee). After preparing an EIS that gave no indication that the dune was to be restored with anything other than sand compatible with the original, the Service reconstructed the dune in the shape of a rigidly geometric, trapezoidal dike that was composed in large measure of coarse yellow sand and gravel brought from an inland source. The Service had been unable to locate an adequate amount of the fine white quartz sand that was native to the Ogunquit dune. As stated by the court, "In place of the famous white Ogunquit dune, the villagers found what to many was an ugly yellow bunker." 533 F.2d at 244. In responding to the villagers' invocation of NEPA as grounds for remedying this desecration of their dune, the court found that the EIS was plainly defective in failing to suggest that any inland fill material would be used on the project that would be different in color or texture from the white beach sand. Indeed, the court found that the plaintiffs might have been affirmatively misled by the Service's statements, that they could not have discovered that the dune was to be reconstructed of noncompatible fill until the project was almost complete, and that they filed suit as soon as could reasonably be expected. Nevertheless, both the district court and the First Circuit held that neither damages nor equitable relief could be granted once the project was completed. Although the First Circuit said that it was "deeply troubled" by the "prospect that a violation of NEPA is insulated from remedy once the project is completed," the court was more disturbed by the implications of requiring changes to federal projects that have been completed or "on which work has progressed so far that meaningful future federal decisionmaking has been foreclosed"—despite the fact that the Ogunquit dune project had been finished with nearly half of the budgeted funds remaining unused. The First Circuit said that it knew of "no set of workable principles that would not open up a vast number of completed projects to a flood of belated litigation." 553 F.2d at 245.

What message did the First Circuit convey to federal agencies with this decision? A cynic might say that agencies could get the message that if they are able to pacify potential opposition with an impressive EIS, they might then carry out a project as they see fit—if they do so in a hurry. Perhaps it is reasonable to hold that an affirmative injunction to undo a project is improper if the only defect is in the EIS. But was that the real problem in *Ogunquit*? Was there really no tenable basis for relief?

A similar situation, with a similar outcome, occurred in *City of Blue Ash v. McLucas*, 596 F.2d 709 (6th Cir. 1979). There the EIS, which the Federal Aviation Administration prepared in connection with expansion of the Cincinnati-Blue Ash Airport, recited an agreement between Cincinnati and the regional airport authority whereby jet aircraft would be prohibited from using the airport. However, after the federal grant was made and the airport improvements were completed, the FAA's published limitations on use of the airport merely specified that the airport was closed to jets not meeting certain noise levels. The City of Blue Ash sought an injunction to require the FAA to close the airport to all jets. The Sixth Circuit rejected the City's claim that the FAA was bound by the commitments that were incorporated within its EIS and further held that the FAA was not liable for enforcement of the "third party" agreement.

Is it arbitrary and capricious for an agency to suggest mitigation measures to justify a decision and then fail to implement or enforce those measures? Do the cases mean that a successful applicant for a federal permit may disregard mitigation measures and other commitments to protect the environment included in an EIS requisite to obtaining a permit? Clearly not if the measures are treated as conditions of the permit; then the issuing agency may redress any breach of such commitments by revoking or suspending its permission. *See Cabinet Mountains Wilderness/Scotchman's Peak Grizzly Bears v. Peterson*, 685 F.2d 678 (D.C. Cir. 1982).

6. Suppose the predictions regarding the environmental impacts from a proposed action included in an EIS turn out to be grossly in error. Is any remedy available to a party seeking to mitigate some of the unexpected adverse impacts? Unless it can be shown that the agency's original analysis was made in bad faith, the answer seems likely to be no. Indeed, one of NEPA's most obvious shortcomings is its failure to require any form of post-implementation monitoring to assess actual impacts, and mitigate those impacts to the extent necessary or desirable. Furthermore, the CEQ rules offer nothing to address this obvious shortcoming in the statute. Some other countries have recognized the importance of post-implementation monitoring. For example, Australia's Environmental Protection (Impact of Proposals) Act, No. 164, 1974 Austl. Acts 1843 (1974), expressly provides for the review and assessment of "the effectiveness of any safeguards or standards for the protection of the environment adopted or applied in respect of the proposed action and the accuracy of any forecasts of the environmental effects of the proposed action." *Id.* at § 10.1.1; *see also, id.* at §§ 10.1.2, 10.1.3.

7. *Citizen Suits.* Citizen suits are expressly authorized under many federal environmental statutes, including the ESA. ESA, § 11(g); 16 U.S.C. § 1540(g). They are not, however, authorized under NEPA and that is why most NEPA cases must be filed under the APA and the general federal jurisdictional statutes. One advantage of a citizen suit provision is that it generally authorizes recovery of costs and expenses, including legal fees, to plaintiffs who prevail in such litigation. Many plaintiffs can recover some or all of these expenses, however, even where no citizen suit provision applies, under the Equal Access to Justice Act (EAJA), 28 U.S.C. § 2412. EAJA establishes some limits on fee recovery, however, that do not apply to citizen suits. Under most citizen suit provisions, including the provision in the ESA, 60-days prior notice must be given to the relevant federal agency before commencing an action, thus giving the agency the opportunity to address the problem before litigation is filed. § 11(g)(2). Citizen suits can generally be filed against an agency for failing to perform non-discretionary duties under the Act, or directly against any person in violation of the Act. § 11(g)(1).

10 TAKINGS UNDER THE ENDANGERED SPECIES ACT

Thus far, the materials in this book have focused upon the common threads between NEPA and the ESA. Because NEPA's substantive mandate has been construed narrowly, this focus has primarily concerned the administrative processes for environmental decisionmaking. The prohibition against "takings" in § 9 of the ESA has no counterpart in NEPA. As you work through these materials, consider whether strict prohibitions like those contained in § 9 of the ESA are an appropriate and/or effective means of achieving environmental goals.

BABBITT V. SWEET HOME CHAPTER OF COMMUNITIES FOR A GREAT OREGON
515 U.S. 687 (1995)

JUSTICE STEVENS delivered the opinion of the Court.

The Endangered Species Act of 1973, 87 Stat. 884, 16 U.S.C. § 1531 (ESA or Act), contains a variety of protections designed to save from extinction species that the Secretary of the Interior designates as endangered or threatened. Section 9 of the Act makes it unlawful for any person to "take" any endangered or threatened species. The Secretary has promulgated a regulation that defines the statute's prohibition on takings to include "significant habitat modification or degradation where it actually kills or injures wildlife." This case presents the question whether the Secretary exceeded his authority under the Act by promulgating that regulation.

I

* * *

Respondents in this action are small landowners, logging companies, and families dependent on the forest products industries in the Pacific Northwest and in the Southeast, and organizations that represent their interests. They brought this declaratory judgment action against petitioners, the Secretary of the Interior and the Director of the Fish and Wildlife Service, in the United States District Court for the District of Columbia to challenge the statutory validity of the Secretary's regulation defining "harm," particularly the inclusion of habitat modification and degradation in the definition. Respondents challenged the regulation on its face. Their complaint alleged that application of the "harm" regulation to the red-cockaded woodpecker, an endangered species, and the northern spotted owl, a threatened species, had injured them economically.

Respondents advanced three arguments to support their submission that Congress did not intend the word "take" in § 9 to include habitat modification, as the Secretary's "harm" regulation provides. First, they correctly noted that language in the Senate's original version of the ESA would have defined "take" to include "destruction, modification, or curtailment of [the] habitat or range" of fish or wildlife, but the Senate deleted that language from the bill before enacting it. Second, respondents argued that Congress intended the Act's express authorization for the Federal Government to buy private land in order to prevent habitat degradation in § 5 to be the exclusive check against habitat modification on private property. Third, because the Senate added the term "harm" to the definition of "take" in a floor amendment without debate, respondents argued that the court should not interpret the term so expansively as to include habitat modification.

* * *

II

Because this case was decided on motions for summary judgment, we may appropriately make certain factual assumptions in order to frame the legal issue. First, we assume respondents have no desire to harm either the red-cockaded woodpecker or the spotted owl; they merely wish to continue logging activities that would be entirely proper if not prohibited by the ESA. On the other hand, we must assume arguendo that those activities will have the effect, even though unintended, of detrimentally changing the natural habitat of both listed species and that, as a consequence, members of those species will be killed or injured. Under respondents' view of the law, the Secretary's only means of forestalling that grave result—even when the actor knows it is certain to occur—is to use his § 5 authority to purchase the lands on which the survival of the species depends. The Secretary, on the other hand, submits that the § 9 prohibition on takings, which Congress defined to include "harm," places on respondents a duty to avoid harm that habitat alteration will cause the birds unless respondents first obtain a permit pursuant to § 10.

The text of the Act provides three reasons for concluding that the Secretary's interpretation is reasonable. First, an ordinary understanding of the word "harm" supports it. The dictionary definition of the verb form of "harm" is "to cause hurt or damage to: injure." WEBSTER'S THIRD NEW INTERNATIONAL DICTIONARY 1034 (1966). In the context of the ESA, that definition naturally encompasses habitat modification that results in actual injury or death to members of an endangered or threatened species.

Respondents argue that the Secretary should have limited the purview of "harm" to direct applications of force against protected species, but the dictionary definition does not include the word "directly" or suggest in any way that only direct or willful action that leads to injury constitutes "harm." Moreover, unless the statutory term "harm" encompasses indirect as well as direct injuries, the word has no meaning that does not duplicate the meaning of other words that § 3 uses to define "take." A reluctance to treat statutory terms as surplusage supports the reasonableness of the Secretary's interpretation.

Second, the broad purpose of the ESA supports the Secretary's decision to extend protection against activities that cause the precise harms Congress enacted the statute to avoid. In *TVA v. Hill*, 437 U.S. 153 (1978), we described the Act as "the most comprehensive legislation for the preservation of endangered species ever enacted by any nation." *Id.* at 180. Whereas predecessor statutes enacted in 1966 and 1969 had not contained any sweeping prohibition against the taking of endangered species except on federal lands, *see id.* at 175, the 1973 Act applied to all land in the United States and to the Nation's territorial seas. As stated in § 2 of the Act, among its central purposes is "to provide a means whereby the ecosystems upon which endangered species and threatened species depend may be conserved . . . ."

In *Hill*, we construed § 7 as precluding the completion of the Tellico Dam because of its predicted impact on the survival of the snail darter. *See* 437 U. S. at 193. Both our holding and the language in our opinion stressed the importance of the statutory policy. "The plain intent of Congress in enacting this statute," we recognized, "was to halt and reverse the trend toward species extinction, whatever the cost. This is reflected not only in the stated policies of the Act, but in literally every section of the statute." *Id.* at 184. Although the § 9 "take" prohibition was not at issue in *Hill*, we took note of that prohibition, placing particular emphasis on the Secretary's inclusion of habitat modification in his definition of "harm." In light of that provision for habitat protection, we could "not understand how TVA intends to operate Tellico Dam without 'harming' the snail darter." *Id.* at 184, n.30. Congress' intent to provide comprehensive protection for endangered and threatened species supports the permissibility of the Secretary's "harm" regulation.

* * *

Third, the fact that Congress in 1982 authorized the Secretary to issue permits for takings that § 9(a)(1)(B) would otherwise prohibit, "if such taking is incidental to, and not the purpose of, the carrying out of an otherwise lawful activity," strongly suggests that Congress understood § 9(a)(1)(B) to prohibit indirect as well as deliberate takings. The permit process requires the applicant to prepare a "conservation plan" that specifies how he intends to "minimize and mitigate" the "impact" of his activity on endangered and threatened species, § 9(a)(2)(A), making clear that Congress had in mind foreseeable rather than merely accidental effects on listed species. No one could seriously request an "incidental" take permit to avert § 9 liability for direct, deliberate action against a member of an endangered or threatened species, but respondents would read "harm" so narrowly that the permit procedure would have little more than that absurd purpose. "When Congress acts to amend a statute, we presume it intends its amendment to have real and substantial effect." *Stone v. INS*, 514 U.S. 386, 387 (1995). Congress' addition of the § 10 permit provision supports the Secretary's conclusion that activities not intended to harm an endangered species, such as habitat modification, may constitute unlawful takings under the ESA unless the Secretary permits them.

The Court of Appeals made three errors in asserting that "harm" must refer to a direct application of force because the words around it do. First, the court's premise was flawed. Several of the words that accompany "harm" in the § 3 definition of "take," especially "harass," "pursue," "wound," and "kill," refer to actions or effects that do not require direct applications of force. Second, to the extent the court read a requirement of intent or purpose into the words used to define "take," it ignored § 9's express provision that a "knowing" action is enough to violate the Act. Third, the court employed *noscitur a sociis* to give "harm" essentially the same function as other words in the definition, thereby denying it independent meaning. The canon, to the contrary, counsels that a word "gathers meaning from the words around it." *Jarecki v. G.D. Searle & Co.*, 367 U.S. 303, 307 (1961). The statutory context of "harm" suggests that Congress meant that term to serve a particular function in the ESA, consistent with but distinct from the functions of the other verbs used to define "take." The Secretary's interpretation of "harm" to include indirectly injuring endangered animals through habitat modification permissibly interprets "harm" to have "a character of its own not to be submerged by its association." *Russell Motor Car Co. v. United States*, 261 U.S. 514, 519 (1923).

* * *

We need not decide whether the statutory definition of "take" compels the Secretary's interpretation of "harm," because our conclusions that Congress did not unambiguously manifest its intent to adopt respondents' view and that the Secretary's interpretation is reasonable suffice to decide this case. *See generally Chevron U.S.A. Inc. v. Natural Resources Defense Council, Inc.*, 467 U.S. 837 (1984). The latitude the ESA gives the Secretary in enforcing the statute, together with the degree of regulatory expertise necessary to its enforcement, establishes that we owe some degree of deference to the Secretary's reasonable interpretation. *See* Breyer, *Judicial Review of Questions of Law and Policy*, 38 ADMIN. L. REV. 363, 373 (1986).

III

Our conclusion that the Secretary's definition of "harm" rests on a permissible construction of the ESA gains further support from the legislative history of the statute. The Committee Reports accompanying the bills that became the ESA do not specifically discuss the meaning of "harm," but they make clear that Congress intended "take" to apply broadly to cover indirect as well as purposeful actions. The Senate Report stressed that "'[t]ake' is defined . . . in the broadest possible manner to include every conceivable way in which a person can 'take' or attempt to 'take' any fish or wildlife." S. Rep. No. 93-307, p. 7 (1973). The House Report stated that "the broadest possible terms" were used to define restrictions on takings. H.R. Rep. No. 93-412, p. 15 (1973). The House Report underscored the breadth of the "take" definition by noting that it included "harassment, *whether intentional or not.*" *Id.* at 11 (emphasis added). The Report explained that the definition "would allow, for example, the Secretary to regulate or prohibit the activities of birdwatchers where the effect of those activities might disturb the birds and make it difficult for them to hatch or raise their young." *Ibid.* These comments, ignored in the dissent's welcome but selective foray into legislative history, support the Secretary's interpretation that the term "take" in § 9 reached far more than the deliberate actions of hunters and trappers.

* * *

The history of the 1982 amendment that gave the Secretary authority to grant permits for "incidental" takings provides further support for his reading of the Act. The House Report expressly states that "[b]y use of the word 'incidental' the Committee intends to cover situations in which it is known that a taking will occur if the other activity is engaged in but such taking is incidental to, and not the purpose of, the activity." H.R. Rep. No. 97-567, p. 31 (1982). This reference to the foreseeability of incidental takings undermines respondents' argument that the 1982 amendment covered only accidental killings of endangered and threatened animals that might occur in the course of hunting or trapping other animals. Indeed, Congress had habitat modification directly in mind: both the Senate Report and the House Conference Report identified as the model for the permit process a cooperative state-federal response to a case in California where a development project threatened incidental harm to a species of endangered butterfly by modification of its habitat. *See* S. Rep. No. 97-418, p. 10 (1982); H.R. Conf. Rep. No. 97-835, pp. 30-32 (1982). Thus, Congress in 1982 focused squarely on the aspect of the "harm" regulation at issue in this litigation. Congress' implementation of a permit program is consistent with the Secretary's interpretation of the term "harm."

* * *

The judgment of the Court of Appeals is reversed.
It is so ordered.

JUSTICE O'CONNOR, concurring.

My agreement with the Court is founded on two understandings. First, the challenged regulation is limited to significant habitat modification that causes actual, as opposed to hypothetical or speculative, death or injury to identifiable protected animals. Second, even setting aside difficult questions of scienter, the regulation's application is limited by ordinary principles of proximate causation, which introduce notions of foreseeability. These limitations, in my view, call into question *Palila v. Hawaii Dept. of Land and Natural Resources*, 852 F.2d 1106 (9th Cir. 1988) (*Palila II*), and with it, many of the applications derided by the dissent. Because there is no need to strike a regulation on a facial challenge out of concern that it is susceptible of erroneous application, however, and because there are many habitat-related circumstances in which the regulation might validly apply, I join the opinion of the Court.

In my view, the regulation is limited by its terms to actions that actually kill or injure individual animals. JUSTICE SCALIA disagrees, arguing that the harm regulation "encompasses injury inflicted, not only upon individual animals, but upon populations of the protected species." At one level, I could not reasonably quarrel with this observation; death to an individual animal always reduces the size of the population in which it lives, and in that sense, "injures" that population. But by its insight, the dissent means something else. Building upon the regulation's use of the word "breeding," JUSTICE SCALIA suggests that the regulation facially bars significant habitat modification that actually kills or injures hypothetical animals (or, perhaps more aptly, causes potential additions to the population not to come into being). Because "[i]mpairment of breeding does not 'injure' living creatures," JUSTICE SCALIA reasons, the regulation must contemplate application to "a population of animals which would otherwise have maintained or increased its numbers."

I disagree. As an initial matter, I do not find it as easy as JUSTICE SCALIA does to dismiss the notion that significant impairment of breeding injures living creatures. To raze the last remaining ground on which the piping plover currently breeds, thereby making it impossible for any piping plovers to reproduce, would obviously injure the population (causing the species' extinction in a generation). But by completely preventing breeding, it would also injure the individual living bird, in the same way that sterilizing the creature injures the individual living bird.

* * *

By the dissent's reckoning, the regulation at issue here, in conjunction with 16 U.S.C. § 1540(1), imposes liability for any habitat-modifying conduct that ultimately results in the death of a protected animal, "regardless of whether that result is intended or even foreseeable, and no matter how long the chain of causality between modification and injury." Even if § 1540(1) does create a strict liability regime (a question we need not decide at this juncture), I see no indication that Congress, in enacting that section, intended to dispense with ordinary principles of proximate causation.

* * *

Proximate causation is not a concept susceptible of precise definition. It is easy enough, of course, to identify the extremes. The farmer whose fertilizer is lifted by tornado from tilled fields and deposited miles away in a wildlife refuge cannot, by any stretch of the term, be considered the proximate cause of death or injury to protected species occasioned thereby. At the same time, the landowner who drains a pond on his property, killing endangered fish in the process, would likely satisfy any formulation of the principle. We have recently said that proximate causation "normally eliminates the bizarre," *Jerome B. Grubart, Inc. v. Great Lakes Dredge & Dock Co.*, 513 U.S. 527, 536 (1995).

* * *

Proximate causation depends to a great extent on considerations of the fairness of imposing liability for remote consequences. The task of determining whether proximate causation exists in the limitless fact patterns sure to arise is best left to lower courts. But I note, at the least, that proximate cause principles inject a foreseeability element into the statute, and hence, the regulation, that would appear to alleviate some of the problems noted by the dissent. * * *

In my view, then, the "harm" regulation applies where significant habitat modification, by impairing essential behaviors, proximately (foreseeably) causes actual death or injury to identifiable animals that are protected under the Endangered Species Act. Pursuant to my interpretation, *Palila II*—under which the Court of Appeals held that a state agency committed a "taking" by permitting feral sheep to eat mamane-naio seedlings that, when full-grown, might have fed and sheltered endangered palila—was wrongly decided according to the regulation's own terms. Destruction of the seedlings did not proximately cause actual death or injury to identifiable birds; it merely prevented the regeneration of forest land not currently inhabited by actual birds.

This case, of course, comes to us as a facial challenge. We are charged with deciding whether the regulation on its face exceeds the agency's statutory mandate. I have identified at least one application of the regulation (*Palila II*) that is, in my view, inconsistent with the regulation's own limitations. That misapplication does not, however, call into question the validity of the regulation itself. One can doubtless imagine questionable applications of the regulation that test the limits of the agency's authority. However, it seems to me clear that the regulation does not on its terms exceed the agency's mandate, and that the regulation has innumerable valid habitat-related applications. Congress may, of course, see fit to revisit this issue. And nothing the Court says today prevents the agency itself from narrowing the scope of its regulation at a later date.

With this understanding, I join the Court's opinion.

JUSTICE SCALIA, with whom THE CHIEF JUSTICE and JUSTICE THOMAS join, dissenting.

I think it unmistakably clear that the legislation at issue here (1) forbade the hunting and killing of endangered animals, and (2) provided federal lands and federal funds for the acquisition of private lands, to preserve the habitat of endangered animals. The Court's holding that the hunting and killing prohibition incidentally preserves habitat on private lands imposes unfairness to the point of financial ruin—not just upon the rich, but upon the simplest farmer who finds his land conscripted to national zoological use. I respectfully dissent.

I

* * *

The regulation has three features which, for reasons I shall discuss at length below, do not comport with the statute. First, it interprets the statute to prohibit habitat modification that is no more than the cause-in-fact of death or injury to wildlife. Any "significant habitat modification" that in fact produces that result by "impairing essential behavioral patterns" is made unlawful, regardless of whether that result is intended or even foreseeable, and no matter how long the chain of causality between modification and injury.

* * *

Second, the regulation does not require an "act": the Secretary's officially stated position is that an omission will do.

* * *

The third and most important unlawful feature of the regulation is that it encompasses injury inflicted, not only upon individual animals, but upon populations of the protected species.

* * *

None of these three features of the regulation can be found in the statutory provisions supposed to authorize it. The term "harm" in § 1532(19) has no legal force of its own. An indictment or civil complaint that charged the defendant with "harming" an animal protected under the Act would be dismissed as defective, for the only operative term in the statute is to "take." If "take" were not elsewhere defined in the Act, none could dispute what it means, for the term is as old as the law itself. To "take," when applied to wild animals, means to reduce those animals, by killing or capturing, to human control.

* * *

The Act's definition of "take" does expand the word slightly (and not unusually), so as to make clear that it includes not just a completed taking, but the process of taking, and all of the acts that are customarily identified with or accompany that process ("to harass, harm, pursue, hunt, shoot, wound, kill, trap, capture, or collect"); and so as to include attempts. § 1532(19). The tempting fallacy—which the Court commits with abandon—is to assume that once defined, "take" loses any significance, and it is only the definition that matters. The Court treats the statute as though Congress had directly enacted the § 1532(19) definition as a self-executing prohibition, and had not enacted § 1538(a)(1)(B) at all. But § 1538(a)(1)(B) is there, and if the terms contained in the definitional section are susceptible of two readings, one of which comports with the standard meaning of "take" as used in application to wildlife, and one of which does not, an agency regulation that adopts the latter reading is necessarily unreasonable, for it reads the defined term "take"—the only operative term—out of the statute altogether.

That is what has occurred here. The verb "harm" has a range of meaning: "to cause injury" at its broadest, "to do hurt or damage" in a narrower and more direct sense. * * *

To define "harm" as an act or omission that, however remotely, "actually kills or injures" a population of wildlife through habitat modification, is to choose a meaning that makes nonsense of the word that "harm" defines—requiring us to accept that a farmer who tills his field and causes erosion that makes silt run into a nearby river which depletes oxygen and thereby "impairs [the] breeding" of protected fish, has "taken" or "attempted to take" the fish. It should take the strongest evidence to make us believe that Congress has defined a term in a manner repugnant to its ordinary and traditional sense.

Here the evidence shows the opposite. "Harm" is merely one of 10 prohibitory words in § 1532(19), and the other 9 fit the ordinary meaning of "take" perfectly. * * *

What the nine other words in § 1532(19) have in common—and share with the narrower meaning of "harm" described above, but not with the Secretary's ruthless dilation of the word— is the sense of affirmative conduct intentionally directed against a particular animal or animals.

I am not the first to notice this fact, or to draw the conclusion that it compels. In 1981 the Solicitor of the Fish and Wildlife Service delivered a legal opinion on § 1532(19) that is in complete agreement with my reading:

> "The Act's definition of 'take' contains a list of actions that illustrate the intended scope of the term . . . . With the possible exception of 'harm,' these terms all represent forms of conduct that are directed against and likely to injure or kill *individual* wildlife. Under the principle of statutory construction, *ejusdem generis*, . . . the term 'harm' should be interpreted to include only those actions that are directed against, and likely to injure or kill, individual wildlife." Memorandum of April 17, 1981, reprinted in 46 Fed. Reg. 29490, 29491 (emphasis in original).

I would call it *noscitur a sociis*, but the principle is much the same: the fact that "several items in a list share an attribute counsels in favor of interpreting the other items as possessing that attribute as well," *Beecham v. United States*, 511 U.S. 368 (1994). The Court contends that the canon cannot be applied to deprive a word of all its "independent meaning," *ante*, at 2415. That proposition is questionable to begin with, especially as applied to long lawyers' listings such as this. If it were true, we ought to give the word "trap" in the definition its rare meaning of "to clothe" (whence "trappings")—since otherwise it adds nothing to the word "capture." *See Moskal v. United States*, 498 U.S. 103, 120 (1990) (SCALIA, J., dissenting). In any event, the Court's contention that "harm" in the narrow sense adds nothing to the other words underestimates the ingenuity of our own species in a way that Congress did not. To feed an animal poison, to spray it with mace, to chop down the very tree in which it is nesting, or even to destroy its entire habitat in order to take it (as by draining a pond to get at a turtle), might neither wound nor kill, but would directly and intentionally harm.

The penalty provisions of the Act counsel this interpretation as well. Any person who "knowingly" violates § 1538(a)(1)(B) is subject to criminal penalties under § 1540(b)(1) and civil penalties under § 1540(a)(1); moreover, under the latter section, any person "who otherwise violates" the taking prohibition (*i.e.*, violates it *un*knowingly) may be assessed a civil penalty of $500 for each violation, with the stricture that "[e]ach such violation shall be a separate offense." This last provision should be clear warning that the regulation is in error, for when combined with the regulation it produces a result that no legislature could reasonably be thought to have intended: A large number of routine private activities—farming, for example, ranching, road-building, construction and logging—are subjected to strict-liability penalties when they fortuitously injure protected wildlife, no matter how remote the chain of causation and no matter how difficult to foresee (or to disprove) the "injury" may be (*e.g.*, an "impairment" of breeding). The Court says that "[the strict-liability provision] is potentially sweeping, but it would be so with or without the Secretary's 'harm' regulation." *Ante*, at 2412, n.9. That is not correct. Without the regulation, the routine "habitat modifying" activities that people conduct to make a daily living would not carry exposure to strict penalties; only acts directed at animals, like those described by the other words in § 1532(19), would risk liability.

* * *

III

In response to the points made in this dissent, the Court's opinion stresses two points, neither of which is supported by the regulation, and so cannot validly be used to uphold it. First, the Court and the concurrence suggest that the regulation should be read to contain a requirement of proximate causation or foreseeability, principally because the statute does—and "[n]othing in the regulation purports to weaken those requirements [of the statute]." I quite agree that the statute contains such a limitation, because the verbs of purpose in § 1538(a)(1)(B) denote action directed at animals. But the Court has rejected that reading. The critical premise on which it has upheld the regulation is that, despite the weight of the other words in § 1538(a)(1)(B), "the statutory term 'harm' encompasses indirect as well as direct injuries." * * * Consequently, unless there is some strange category of causation that is indirect and yet also proximate, the Court has already rejected its own basis for finding a proximate-cause limitation in the regulation. In fact "proximate" causation simply *means* "direct" causation. *See, e.g.*, BLACK'S LAW DICTIONARY 1103 (5th ed. 1979) (defining "[p]roximate" as "Immediate; nearest; *direct*") (emphasis added); WEBSTER'S NEW INTERNATIONAL DICTIONARY OF THE ENGLISH LANGUAGE 1995 (2d ed. 1949) ("proximate cause. A cause which *directly*, or with no mediate agency, produces an effect") (emphasis added).

* * *

The regulation says (it is worth repeating) that "harm" means (1) an act which (2) actually kills or injures wildlife. If that does not dispense with a proximate-cause requirement, I do not know what language would. And changing the regulation by judicial invention, even to achieve compliance with the statute, is not permissible.

* * *

The second point the Court stresses in its response seems to me a belated mending of its hold. It apparently concedes that the statute requires injury to particular animals rather than merely to populations of animals. The Court then rejects my contention that the regulation ignores this requirement, since, it says, "every term in the regulation's definition of 'harm' is subservient to the phrase 'an act which actually kills or injures wildlife.'" As I have pointed out, this reading is incompatible with the regulation's specification of impairment of "breeding" as one of the modes of "kill[ing] or injur[ing] wildlife."

But since the Court is reading the regulation and the statute incorrectly in other respects, it may as well introduce this novelty as well—law a la carte. As I understand the regulation that the Court has created and held consistent with the statute that it has also created, habitat modification can constitute a "taking," but only if it results in the killing or harming of individual animals, and only if that consequence is the direct result of the modification. This means that the destruction of privately owned habitat that is essential, not for the feeding or nesting, but for the breeding, of butterflies, would not violate the Act, since it would not harm or kill any living butterfly. I, too, think it would not violate the Act—not for the utterly unsupported reason that habitat modifications fall outside the regulation if they happen not to kill or injure a living animal, but for the textual reason that only action directed at living animals constitutes a "take."

The Endangered Species Act is a carefully considered piece of legislation that forbids all persons to hunt or harm endangered animals, but places upon the public at large, rather than upon fortuitously accountable individual landowners, the cost of preserving the habitat of endangered species. There is neither textual support for, nor even evidence of congressional consideration of, the radically different disposition contained in the regulation that the Court sustains. For these reasons, I respectfully dissent.

NOTES

1.   In its second major interpretation of the ESA, the Supreme Court in *Sweet Home* relies, in part, on the language from *T.V.A. v. Hill* that stresses the purpose of the law to recover species whatever the cost. What accounts for the consistent, expansive support by the Court of the ESA's goals, in contrast to the much more limited interpretation of NEPA's mandates?

2.   In *Palila v. Hawaii Dep't of Land and Natural Resources* (*Palila II*), 852 F.2d 1106 (9th Cir. 1988), the court found that the moufton sheep—a species that had been brought to Hawaii for sport hunting purposes—was harming the mamane ecosystem, which the palila bird depended upon for its survival. Citing § 9, the court required the state to remove the sheep from palila habitat. Mamane are a tree species native to Hawaii, and the preferred habitat of the palila. Why does Justice O'Connor object to the *Palila* decision?

3.   Does *Palila* survive *Sweet Home*? Justice O'Connor clearly would limit the application of the harm regulation to situations where significant habitat modification, by impairing essential behaviors, *proximately (foreseeably)* causes actual death or injury to *identifiable* animals. On this basis, Justice O'Connor questions the Ninth Circuit's interpretation of harm. Do you agree with Justice O'Connor's analysis of the hypothetical taking liability for razing the last remaining breeding habitat for the piping plover, making reproduction impossible? How would you analyze this situation using the different interpretations of harm from:

    a.   the *Sweet Home* majority opinion;
    b.   Justice O'Connor's concurrence in *Sweet Home*;
    c.   Justice Scalia's dissent in *Sweet Home*; and
    d.   the *Palila* opinion?

4. For its part, the Ninth Circuit has stated that the majority opinion in *Sweet Home* supports continued use of the *Palila* precedent. *Seattle Audubon Society v. Moseley*, 80 F.3d 1401, 1405 (9th Cir. 1996). In *Marbled Murrelet v. Babbitt*, 83 F.3d 1060 (9th Cir. 1996), *cert. denied*, 519 U.S. 1108 (1997), the court granted an injunction based on a showing of a reasonably certain threat of imminent harm to a listed species. The court found that *Sweet Home* does not require a showing of actual past harm to sustain an injunction against logging in an old-growth forest. The First Circuit seems to share the Ninth Circuit's approach to proximate causation. In *Strahan v. Coxe*, 127 F.3d 155 (1st Cir. 1997), the court found a taking of northern right whales by the State of Massachusetts for licensing fishing gear that became entangled with the endangered whales. The court relied on an uncontested affidavit that three whales had become entangled in fishing gear deployed in Massachusetts waters, and accepted the lower court's inference that the gear was licensed by the state.

For a case more in line with Justice O'Connor's view, *see Morill v. Lujan*, 802 F. Supp. 424 (S.D. Ala. 1992), where the court denied a preliminary injunction against the construction of a lounge/restaurant/hotel on a barrier beach inhabited by an endangered species of mouse because the relationship between habitat modification and injury to the species was too tenuous.

5. How does § 9 apply to listed plant species? In the *Palila* case, suppose instead of the palila, it had been the mamane tree that was endangered. Would the court still have found a taking? *See* ESA § 9(a)(2). Would it matter whether the mamane tree were located on federal rather than state or private lands? *See* § 9(a)(2)(B).

6. Unlike *Palila*, but like *Hodel v. Virginia Surface Mining & Reclamation Ass'n*, *supra* Chapter 2, *Sweet Home* is a facial challenge. How does this procedural aspect of the case favor the government? What is the significance of the *Chevron* principle of deference to agency interpretation of statutes? Does the FWS regulation reflect the *best* interpretation of the term "harm"?

7. Does the ESA explicitly prohibit "harm" in § 9? Under what circumstances should the Court resort to the dictionary in parsing the text of a statute? In recent years, the Court has increasingly referred to dictionaries. *See* Note, *Looking It Up: Dictionaries and Statutory Interpretation*, 107 HARV. L. REV. 1437 (1994). How do Justices Stevens and Scalia differ in their interpretive use of the words surrounding "harm" in the definition of "take"? Are canons of statutory construction helpful in this context?

8. Since 1918, the Migratory Bird Treaty Act (MBTA), 16 U.S.C. § 703, has made it illegal to "pursue, hunt, take, capture, [or] kill" certain listed bird species. The MBTA, however, neither explicitly prohibits "harm" nor defines the term "take." Most courts, therefore, have found no liability for unintentional, incidental bird deaths under the MBTA. *See, e.g., Sierra Club v. Martin*, 110 F.3d 1551 (11th Cir. 1997); *Mahler v. U.S. Forest Service*, 927 F. Supp. 1559 (S.D. Ind. 1996).

PROBLEM #7: TAKINGS AND JEOPARDY

The National Aeronautics and Space Administration (NASA) shares the Kennedy Space Center in Florida with the Merritt Island National Wildlife Refuge. The two agencies coexist in the same area with shared responsibilities. The refuge is home to 17 federally listed species that occur in almost every habitat type associated with the facility. NASA continually receives criticism from environmental groups for announcing plans at the last minute for projects of the "highest priority" that must go forward without delay. Even though there are over 100,000 acres of land at the refuge, NASA insists that it cannot insure any area will not be subject to possible development. NASA claims that it must keep all of its options open for the advancement of science and national security. Environmentalists claim that NASA is worried about losing administrative control over the refuge if it admits it does not need all of the land.

You are counsel to the Vice President, who is scheduled to lay the first brick in a ground breaking ceremony in three weeks for the new space station facility. The new facility will be used to assemble both civilian and top-secret military satellites. You receive a call from NASA explaining that it "just discovered" endangered scrub jays on the development site for the new facility. NASA has been planning this facility since 1985. In 1986, NASA prepared an EA on the facility. The scrub jay was not listed at the time.

You do not want the Vice President to be embarrassed by blessing a facility that violates NEPA or the ESA. On the other hand, the V.P. is a big supporter of space exploration and needs to shore up his Florida political base. What will you recommend that the Vice President and NASA do?

HABITAT CONSERVATION PLANNING: ADDRESSING THE
ACHILLES HEEL OF THE ENDANGERED SPECIES ACT
Karin P. Sheldon
6 N.Y.U. ENVTL. L.J. 279 (1998)[*]

INTRODUCTION

There is no more controversial aspect of the Endangered Species Act (ESA) than its application to development activities on privately owned lands. Newspapers carry tales of federal zealots seizing farm equipment from unwitting farmers,[2] homeowners barred from saving their property from wildfire because of brush clearing restrictions, and businesses losing decades of investment—all because of endangered species. A typical news article attacking the ESA begins: "Would you spend $2.6 million on a cockroach? The federal government does." This opening salvo is followed by a scathing review of the "tremendous economic damage" being done to citizens on behalf of a rat, mouse, mole, tortoise, or other lowly and contemptible creature whose earthly purpose cannot be fathomed, especially when measured against economic progress and individual freedom. Even United States Supreme Court Justices chime in. Justice Scalia accused the majority of the Court in *Babbitt v. Sweet Home Chapter of Communities for a Greater Oregon* of interpreting the ESA so as to "impose unfairness to the point of financial ruin . . . upon the simplest farmer who finds his land conscripted to national zoological use."

Whatever the truth of these horror stories,[8] they have captured the imagination of some

---

[2]   In February 1994, some twenty-five federal and state wildlife officials seized the tractor of an immigrant farmer and charged him with disturbing the habitat of the Tipton kangaroo rat and other endangered species. Although the farmer had received warnings that protected species were on his land, his case became a rallying cry for property rights activists, who pointed to the incident as an example of the excesses of the ESA. The case was publicized by conservative radio commentators G. Gordon Liddy and Rush Limbaugh and discussed on the editorial page of the *Wall Street Journal*. *See* Gideon Kanner, *Rule of Law: California Rat Killer Gets Off*, WALL ST. J., May 24, 1995, at A15. Todd Woody, *Taking on the Endangered Species: The Rat, the Farmer, and the Feds*, LEGAL TIMES, July 24, 1995, at 8.

[8]   *See* Oliver Houck, *Reflections on the Endangered Species Act*, 25 ENVT. L. 689, 691-92 (1995). As Professor Houck aptly stated:

> Stories surrounded the ESA like those found at dockside in the days of sailing ships-stories of sea monsters that wrecked ships on the reefs with fatal songs and then attacked their crews. Problematically, few sailors could be found who actually witnessed these events. The stories of those who claimed to be witnesses turned out to be something less on closer examination. So it is with the ESA. *Id.* Data from the Fish and Wildlife Service (FWS) indicates that the Endangered Species Act rarely halts economic development activities. From 1987 to 1994, for example, the FWS carried out nearly 100,000 formal and informal consultations with other federal agencies on projects and activities that potentially jeopardized the continued existence of endangered or threatened species under Section 7 of the ESA. 16 U.S.C. § 1538. Of these, almost 95,000 were conducted informally and resulted in no project delays or modifications. Of the 2,719 formal consultations, 2,367 resulted in "no jeopardy" findings, allowing the projects to proceed as planned. For the 352 jeopardy opinions, 126 related to two groups of activities: timber sales and pesticide applications. Only 54 projects were actually stopped. Thus, 100,000 consultations resulted in jeopardy findings 0.054 percent of the time. *See* World Wildlife Fund, *For Conserving Listed Species, Talk is Cheaper than We Think: The Consultation Process Under the Endangered Species Act* (1994). The World Wildlife Fund's data is corroborated by the U.S. General Accounting Office, Endangered Species Act: Types and Number of Implementing Actions (1992). Professor Houck reports that the FWS does not collate or retain information on the results of consultations. He speculates that this failure to keep records "assist[s] in perpetuating what appears to be a myth—that the ESA is frustrating the development of America." Oliver Houck, *The Endangered Species Act and its*

members of Congress and have become the impetus for a growing effort to significantly amend ESA to relieve private property owners of the alleged burdens they bear in protecting endangered and threatened species.

The Department of the Interior appears to be feeling the heat of anti-ESA sentiment as well. Secretary Bruce Babbitt and the Fish and Wildlife Service (FWS) are scrambling to promote the "flexibility" of the ESA and to create policy approaches that will lessen the likelihood of drastic legislative surgery on the Act. New Interior Department programs, including "No Surprises" and "Safe Harbors," are designed to improve the acceptability of the ESA to private property owners and to decrease the temptation to "shoot, shovel, and shut up" or to destroy habitat in order to eliminate the obligation to comply with the statute. In its rush to mollify economic interests, however, the Interior Department has angered a significant portion of the environmental community which sees some of the new policies as an illegal sell-out of imperilled wildlife.

The purpose of the Endangered Species Act is to conserve plants and animals threatened with extinction, and the ecosystems upon which they depend. Congress recognized that endangered and threatened "species of fish, wildlife, and plants are of esthetic, ecological, educational, historical, recreational, and scientific value to the Nation and its people." It also acknowledged that extinctions of species are "a consequence of economic growth and development untempered by adequate concern and conservation."

After twenty-five years, the ESA's goals of ecosystem conservation remain unrealized substantially because its provisions fail to adequately protect wildlife habitat. The number of species requiring the safeguards of the Act is increasing, while the habitat available to them shrinks. The success stories of species brought back from the brink confirm the necessity of the Act and the efforts carried out pursuant to it. The enormity of the current extinction crisis illustrates the imperative of a renewed commitment in the next twenty-five years. That commitment must in major measure preserve and restore habitat on private lands.

* * *

I

THE PLIGHT OF ENDANGERED AND THREATENED SPECIES ON PRIVATE LANDS

The loss of habitat from human development activities is far and away the greatest cause of the decline and disappearance of wildlife and plant species. This loss is the principle basis for the endangerment of more than eighty percent of the species currently listed or proposed for listing under the Endangered Species Act. Federal lands alone cannot provide adequate endangered species habitat. Many protected species are migratory or have very large home ranges and cannot be confined to federally owned parks, wildlife refuges, or wilderness areas. More than fifty percent of all the species subject to the ESA have at least eighty-one percent of their habitat on privately owned lands. Between a third and a half of protected species do not live on federal land at all. Furthermore, the distribution of endangered and threatened species in the United States does not match the distribution of public land. Some states with high numbers of listed species have relatively little federal land within their borders. For example, the greatest numbers of endangered and threatened species in the United States occur in Hawaii, southern California, the southeastern coastal states, and southern Appalachia. The number of species in these areas exceeds the availability of federally owned habitat. Hawaii is home to 225 listed species, but only sixteen percent of its lands are managed by the federal government. Texas has seventy listed species within its borders, while only one percent of its land is federal.

Implementation by the U.S. Departments of the Interior and Commerce, 64 U. COLO. L. REV. 277, 318 n. 264 (1993) [*hereinafter* Houck, *The Endangered Species Act and its Implementation*].

Florida has ninety-three listed species, and nine percent federal land. By contrast, some states have considerable federal lands, but few listed species. Alaska, for example, is more than sixty-eight percent federal land, but has only five listed species.

The geographic distribution data for threatened and endangered species suggest that, although there are "hot spots" of threatened biodiversity in the United States, the amount of land that needs to be managed to protect currently listed species is a relatively small proportion of the nation's land mass. Dobson recently wrote, "[i]f conservation efforts and funds can be expanded in a few key areas, it should be possible to conserve endangered species with great efficiency."

Unfortunately, this conservation is not happening. Information compiled by the FWS and the General Accounting Office (GAO) shows that endangered species on private lands are in much worse condition than those on federal land. Of the listed plants and animals found entirely on federal land, approximately eighteen percent are judged to be improving; and the ratio of declining species to improving species is approximately 1.5 to 1. In contrast, of the species found entirely on private lands (excluding property owned by conservation groups like the Nature Conservancy) only three percent are improving, and the ratio of declining species to improving species is 9 to 1. These figures fail to paint the complete picture, however, because the FWS does not know the status of over half of the species found exclusively on private land.

* * *

II
THE LIMITATIONS OF THE ESA FOR HABITAT PROTECTION

Although the expressed purpose of the Endangered Species Act of 1973 includes the conservation of the ecosystems upon which threatened and endangered species depend, the statute is "remarkably ignorant of ecological reality." Virtually all of the regulatory mechanisms Congress chose to accomplish the Act's goals focus on the species themselves. Very few deal with the protection of habitat, and none with active beneficial management of habitat on private land. * * * [E]xcept for Section 4, which calls for the designation of critical habitat, and Section 5, which authorizes federal agencies to acquire lands for conservation programs, the ESA as enacted in 1973 had no mechanisms for habitat protection. Nor did it provide measures to control the effects of habitat altering activities or to promote beneficial management procedures on privately owned lands. Congress left ecosystem conservation as a goal without a means of achievement.

* * *

A. The Application of Section 9 on Private Property

Much of the current conflict between species protection efforts and private land development activities reflects the Endangered Species Act's species-specific approach. The protections afforded to listed species, including the prohibition on their taking or damage to their habitat, extend to private lands and affect the kinds of economic activities that may be undertaken by private property owners.

Section 9 of the ESA of 1973 makes it "unlawful for any person subject to the jurisdiction of the United States to take any [endangered] species." The prohibition applies to everyone, not just public officials. It protects species wherever they travel or live, on privately owned as well as state or federal lands. Violations of the taking prohibition may result in civil or criminal penalties. Civil penalties may be assessed regardless of whether the take was intentional.

* * *

IV

THE 1982 AMENDMENTS: HABITAT CONSERVATION PLANNING

The 1982 amendments to the ESA offer an exception for private landowners from the prohibition against the taking of endangered and threatened species. The exception was added "to give the Secretary [of the Interior] more flexibility in regulating the incidental taking of endangered and threatened species," and "to address the concerns of private landowners who are faced with having otherwise lawful actions not requiring federal permits prevented by Section 9 prohibitions against taking."

Section 10(a) of the ESA authorizes the Secretary of the Interior to allow a private property owner to engage in development or land use activities that may result in a taking of some members of a threatened or endangered species, so long as the taking is "incidental to, and not the purpose of, the carrying out of an otherwise lawful activity." The Secretary's approval is set forth in an "incidental take permit."

In order to qualify for this exception, a private landowner must submit a "conservation plan" designed to "minimize and mitigate" the impact of development activities on protected species. Such a plan has come to be known as a Habitat Conservation Plan (HCP). In addition to identifying the steps the landowner will take to "minimize and mitigate" the impacts of the development activities, an HCP must include a discussion of the potential impact of the taking, alternatives to the taking the landowner considered and the reasons for not choosing them, and other measures the Secretary may require.

The Secretary may issue an incidental taking permit, after public review and comment, if he finds that: (1) "the taking will be incidental;" (2) "the applicant will, to the maximum extent practicable, minimize and mitigate the impacts of such taking;" (3) the applicant will ensure that "adequate funding" will be provided for the plan; and (4) other required measures will be met.

Section 10(a) also directs the Secretary to determine that the proposed incidental take "will not appreciably reduce the likelihood of the survival and recovery of the species in the wild." This standard is a restatement of the regulatory definition of the "jeopardize the continued existence" standard of Section 7(a)(2).

Congress intended HCPs to be broad in scope. They are to include unlisted, as well as listed species, along with "assurances" to landowners that the terms of the plan will be adhered to and that further mitigation requirements will only be imposed in accordance with the terms of the plan. In the event an unlisted species addressed in an approved HCP is subsequently listed, no further mitigation requirements will be imposed, provided that the HCP addressed the conservation of that species. Congress did recognize that "unforeseen circumstances" might require changes in an HCP. Accordingly, each plan must include a procedure by which the parties will respond to such circumstances.

* * *

V

INITIAL EXPERIENCE WITH HCPs

Although Congress enthusiastically endorsed HCPs in 1982 * * *, the first ten years of experience with HCPs have been characterized as a "decade of disappointment." The numbers bear out this assessment: a total of fourteen HCPs were approved between 1982 and 1992; by the end of 1994, only thirty-nine HCPs had been approved.

* * *

A. Small Size/Piecemeal Approach

The first generation of HCPs covered small areas. Only five of the fourteen HCPs approved between 1982 and 1992 encompassed more than a thousand acres; thirty-one of the thirty-nine

HCPs approved by the end of 1994 involved less than a thousand acres. The resulting HCPs were parcel-specific and tailored to the needs of species at particular sites. Plans were developed in isolation with inconsistent mitigation and no evaluation of the cumulative effects of habitat fragmentation. The habitat was cut into smaller and smaller pieces incapable of supporting species. As one writer commented, the areas protected by many HCPs "amount to little more than small habitat 'postage stamps,' eventually surrounded by urban development and intense human activities."

Since 1994, the number, size, and complexity of HCPs have increased considerably. As of June 30, 1997, 225 plans had been issued by the FWS, with 200 more under development. Twenty-five of the HCPs being prepared as of August, 1996 exceeded 100,000 acres, and eighteen exceed 500,000 acres. This suggests, and it is the FWS's expressed hope, that HCPs are evolving from a process used to address the impacts of individual development to a broad-based, landscape level planning tool.

In addition to small size and piecemeal approach, other reasons given for the dearth of HCPs in the first fifteen years are: the long and cumbersome planning process; inadequate guidance from the FWS; lax enforcement of the ESA; the use of the more streamlined Section 7 process when a federal nexus was present; biological uncertainty; and the bogging down of negotiations over regional HCPs. Several of these factors are clearly interrelated and acted to hobble the HCP process.

B. Lengthy Planning Process

The duration of the planning process has been identified as a major reason for the delay in implementation of HCPs and the disinterest of landowners in the HCP process. Three factors appear to be the principal causes of delay: insufficient biological data, public controversy, and the "democratic nature of the process."

* * *

VI
NEW HCP POLICIES

Since 1994, the Department of the Interior has been working on a package of reforms to respond to the criticisms of the HCP process. The Department has instituted significant new policies to shorten and streamline the planning process; improve FWS guidance to landowners and other parties in the process; promote greater landowner trust and confidence in HCPs; and offer incentives to encourage voluntary species protection efforts. Clearly, the agency has learned some of the lessons from the first fifteen years of experience with HCPs.

On June 14, 1994, Secretary of the Interior Bruce Babbitt instructed the FWS to provide landowners more timely information on the impact of species' listing on development and land use activities, to streamline the HCP process and to give affected parties a greater role in the preparation of plans. The Secretary also directed the agency to prepare multiple listings and recovery plans for species sharing common habitat and to cooperate more fully with state and local governments in enforcing the ESA.

Secretary Babbitt recognized the need to move away from the piecemeal HCPs that characterized the first generation of conservation planning. According to the Secretary, although large scale HCPs will not be developed quickly, the resulting plans offer advantages to all types of landowners. The financial burden of biological studies can be shared by all owners, or borne by a large developer who can pass the costs on to future buyers. Mitigation requirements can be shared as well. Most importantly, large scale HCPs move in the direction of ecosystem management by assessing the needs of a number of species over a significant portion of habitat.

A. No Surprises

On August 11, 1994, the Secretary of the Interior announced the "No Surprises" policy. "No Surprises" is perhaps the most significant of the policy changes in the HCP process. Under the "No Surprises" policy, landowners who enter into an HCP for the listed species on their property will not be required to pay more or provide additional land for mitigation, regardless of whether the needs of the species change over time. Except under "extraordinary circumstances," compliance with the terms and conditions of an HCP guarantees a property owner that development or land use activities can proceed, even if unlisted species covered by the plan are subsequently listed as threatened or endangered.

* * *

The "No Surprises" policy provides certainty for private landowners in ESA Habitat Conservation Planning through the following assurances:

> In negotiating "unforeseen circumstances" provisions for HCPs, the Fish and Wildlife Service and National Marine Fisheries Service shall not require the commitment of additional land or financial compensation beyond the level of mitigation which was otherwise adequately provided for a species under the terms of a properly functioning HCP. Moreover, FWS and NMFS shall not seek any other form of additional mitigation from an HCP permittee except under extraordinary circumstances.

As the Secretary put it, the "No Surprises" policy promises that "a deal is a deal." "The key issue for non-federal landowners is certainty. They want to know that if they make a good faith effort to plan ahead for species conservation, and do so in cooperation with the relevant agencies, then their plan won't be ripped out from under them many years down the road."

. . . [T]he "No Surprises" policy only applies to species that are adequately covered by an HCP. Species should not be included in an HCP if there is insufficient information about them to design conservation or mitigation measures.

The "No Surprises" policy applies to unlisted, as well as listed species, as long as the unlisted species is addressed in an HCP as if it were listed pursuant to Section 4 of the ESA, and the HCP includes conditions for that species that would satisfy the permit issuance criteria of Section 10(a)(2)(B). The inclusion of unlisted species in an HCP is a voluntary decision of the landowner. The primary reasons to address unlisted species are greater planning certainty for the landowner and increased biological value of the HCP through comprehensive multi-species or ecosystem planning.

If an unlisted species not addressed in an HCP is subsequently listed, the landowner is subject to the take prohibitions of Section 9 or 4(d) of the ESA, regardless of the fact that an incidental take permit is held for other listed species. The landowner must either avoid a take of the newly listed species or revise the existing HCP and obtain a permit amendment.

* * *

Under the "No Surprises" policy, if the condition of a species addressed in an HCP worsens, and additional mitigation measures are deemed necessary, the primary obligation for implementing such measures will be borne by the government, private conservation organizations, or private landowners who have not yet developed HCPs. Once an incidental take permit is issued and an HCP is being implemented, the permittee "may remain secure regarding the agreed upon cost of mitigation, because no additional mitigation land, funding, or land use restrictions will be requested by the Services." The "No Surprises" policy also "protects" a permittee from other forms of additional mitigation, except in "extraordinary circumstances."

In the event the FWS concludes that "extraordinary circumstances" warrant additional mitigation from an HCP permittee, the mitigation measures must be consistent with the original terms of the HCP, to the maximum extent possible. Unless the landowner consents, changes must be limited to modifications within areas designated for habitat protection or other conservation uses in the plan or to the plan's conservation programs for the affected species. The landowner will not be expected to pay the cost of these additional measures or to apply them on parcels of land committed to development under the original terms of the HCP.

The FWS has the burden of demonstrating that extraordinary circumstances do, in fact, exist, based upon "the best scientific and commercial data available." Its findings must be clearly documented and reflect reliable technical information regarding the status and habitat requirements of the affected species. The focus of the inquiry is the "level of biological peril" to the species in question, and the degree to which the welfare of the species is tied to the particular HCP. * * *

The nature of an HCP determines whether additional mitigation will be required even when "extraordinary circumstances" cause the condition of a species to deteriorate. The Service will not demand additional mitigation if an HCP was designed to provide an overall net benefit to the species and contains measurable criteria for biological success which have been, or are being, met. This means that "the Services will not impose additional mitigation measures of any type where an HCP was intentionally designed to have a net positive impact upon a species."

The "No Surprises" policy distorts the implementation of HCPs that offer net benefits to impacted species. These benefits will be treated as a development margin. The condition of wildlife subject to such HCPs may deteriorate, using up the benefit margin, without any additional mitigation measures, to the point where the plans prevent jeopardy, nothing more.

As discussed below, the FWS has decided that an HCP need not provide a net benefit to endangered or threatened species, despite Congress's intent that enhancement of species' survival be a "basic element" of HCPs. The FWS also disregards the statutory direction of Section 10(a) that the Secretary permit incidental take only where it will not appreciably reduce the likelihood of survival and recovery of affected species, as well as the overriding conservation mandate of the ESA.

Conservation biologists have expressed concerns that the "No Surprises" policy does not reflect ecological reality. It is extremely unlikely that biological conditions will remain static throughout the life of an HCP, particularly one with a term of fifty years or more. Indeed, "uncertainty, dynamics, and flux" are "the best descriptors of ecological systems."

Biological uncertainty is magnified in HCPs that include multiple species, many of which have not been listed. Scientists have not even begun to assess what is required for their survival and recovery. Thus, it may not be possible to identify measures that will minimize and mitigate the impacts of the proposed incidental take, much less have confidence that no additional mitigation will be necessary. The potential for species loss implicit in the "No Surprises" policy is enormous.

B. Ten Points of Light

The "No Surprises" policy was followed by the March 1995 release of a set of strategies, dubbed the "Ten Points of Light," designed to give federal agencies greater flexibility to minimize the economic impact of the ESA on private landowners. The Ten Points of Light include an exemption from some of the restrictions of the ESA for small residential landowners, greater use of the "4(d) rule" for threatened species, and a new approach to encourage landowners to preserve wildlife habitat called "Safe Harbors."

C. Safe Harbors

The "Safe Harbors" concept was created by the Environmental Defense Fund, which has argued for some time that landowners need incentives, not regulatory hammers, to protect wildlife. It was adopted by the FWS "to reduce the disincentives (*e.g.*, fear of regulatory restrictions) that often cause landowners to avoid or prevent land use practices that would otherwise benefit endangered species." * * * "Safe Harbors" offers assurances to private landowners that their development and land-use activities will not be restricted if they undertake voluntary, proactive conservation efforts. In other words, landowners who improve habitat conditions for threatened and endangered species can return to baseline conditions without penalty.

* * *

On June 12, 1997, FWS published for comment a draft Safe Harbor policy and proposed rules for its implementation. The explanation accompanying the policy and the rules shed quite a different light on Safe Harbors. If implemented as described, the Safe Harbor policy fills a notable gap in the ESA. It provides a tool to promote active, beneficial management for listed species on private lands—management not mandated or required by the ESA—that may enhance the opportunity for species recovery in ways that cannot otherwise be accomplished under the Act.

Michael Bean has stated, "[t]he Achilles heel of the Endangered Species Act is the private landowner problem." He points out that Section 7 of the Act provides the government with tools to ensure that active management takes place on federal lands, but there are no comparable tools in Section 9 or elsewhere in the statute for non-federal land management. "In nearly a quarter century, there hasn't yet been a single example of Section 9 compelling a non-federal landowner to restore fire or manage to mimic its effects. In the same period, there has been only one example, the palila, of a species for which Section 9 has been employed to force a non-federal landowner to remove a non-indigenous species threatening it." For Bean, "The power of the safe harbor idea is that it not only provides habitat where otherwise there would be none, but it makes landowners willing partners in the endangered species conservation effort."

FWS bases the "Safe Harbors" policy on Section 10(a)(1)(A) of the ESA, which states: the "Secretary may permit . . . any act otherwise prohibited by section 1538 . . . to enhance the propagation or survival of the affected species." The permits to be issued under the "Safe Harbors" policy are called "enhancement of survival permits."

The goal of the "Safe Harbors" policy is to encourage private property owners to "restore, enhance, or maintain" habitats for listed species by undertaking a variety of proactive species conservation efforts on their lands. Examples of such beneficial management include prescribed burning to mimic natural fire regimes, removal of invasive, non-indigenous species, or restoration of hydrologic conditions. Priority for Safe Harbors will be given to "Agreements that provide the greatest contribution to the recovery of multiple listed species."

To qualify for a Safe Harbor Agreement a private property owner must be willing to undertake or forego land-use activities in order to provide a "net conservation benefit" to listed species present on her property. Net conservation benefits may include reduction of habitat fragmentation, the maintenance, restoration, or enhancement of habitat, the establishment of buffer zones for protected areas, and the reduction of the effects of catastrophic events. FWS must make a written finding that all protected species subject to the Safe Harbor Agreement will receive the net conservation benefit. Although a Safe Harbor does not have to offer permanent protection to covered species, it must be of "sufficient design and duration" to give net conservation benefits to all covered species. These "benefits must contribute to the recovery of the covered species."

In exchange for a commitment to carry out beneficial management of their lands, property owners are given assurances that additional land-use or resource-use restrictions will not be imposed. If a property owner meets all the conditions of a Safe Harbor Agreement, FWS will authorize the incidental take of covered species to enable the property owner to return the enrolled property to its "baseline conditions" in the future.

This does not mean protect now in order to destroy later. The Safe Harbor policy requires that "[r]eturning the habitat or population numbers to the baseline conditions must be possible without negating the net conservation benefit provided by the Agreement." The property owner has the burden of showing that the agreed upon baseline conditions were maintained and the activities identified in the Safe Harbor Agreement as necessary to achieve net conservation benefits were carried out for the duration of the Agreement. If the property owner has fulfilled her obligations under the Agreement, FWS will authorize the use of the property in a manner that returns it to its baseline.

If a property owner's efforts attract listed species to the property or increase the numbers or distribution of species already present, the Safe Harbor Agreement may be amended. The government assurances in the Agreement may not be extended to a non-covered species, if such species were excluded from the original Agreement at the property owner's request or their presence are not directly attributable to the property owner's activities. Beneficial management actions tailored specifically to the non-covered species must be developed and baseline conditions determined to provide net conservation benefits.

Safe Harbor Agreements run with the land. The rights and obligations of the Agreement transfer with property ownership. A property owner must notify FWS of a proposed transfer so that the agency may explain the Agreement and determine whether the new owner wishes to continue the old Agreement or enter into a new one.

FWS acknowledges that Safe Harbors are not appropriate in all circumstances. The policy states that they should not be used when landowners seek immediate take authorization or when net conservation benefits cannot be achieved, after considering the return to baseline conditions. Safe Harbors should not be used if the Agreement only redistributes the existing population of a listed species, or attracts species away from a habitat that enjoys long-term protection.

Safe Harbors are not a permanent fix, and, as yet, there is no established track record of success with the concept. Safe Harbors do, however, represent a useful and creative approach to the resolution of the central problem with the ESA. They may offer significant short-term and mid-term conservation benefits that would not otherwise be available. They may also improve the willingness of private property owners to cooperate with the government in the protection of species. Both are important accomplishments.

D. Small Landowners/Low Impact Exemption

On July 20, 1995, the FWS published a proposed rule to implement the small landowner/ low impact exemption policies previously announced as Points of Light. The rule seeks to amend the FWS's general regulations for threatened species by adding a new kind of incidental take exemption for certain small landowners and low impact activities that are "presumed" by the agency to have little or no lasting impact, individually or cumulatively, on the survival and recovery of the threatened species. The proposed rule would establish a general exemption for activities carried out pursuant to a state habitat conservation planning program for threatened species if the FWS determines that the program properly evaluates the potential impacts to the species and promotes their survival and recovery.

The proposed rule derives from the FWS's regulatory authority to issue a "special rule" under Section 4(d) of the ESA, when the general prohibitions applicable to threatened species are inappropriate or inadequate. (This option is not available for endangered species.) A special rule may contain different conditions and prohibitions "tailor made" for the wildlife in question.

The FWS determined that, in some cases, the existing prohibitions on threatened species are unnecessarily restrictive and discourage landowners from conserving them. Consequently, the agency concluded that it was "no longer necessary, appropriate, or advisable" to maintain a regulatory presumption that isolated takings of threatened species must be forbidden. Routine residential yard maintenance and small construction projects are the examples given in the explanation of the proposed rule. The FWS states that the habitat value of residential property is generally limited, and maintenance and construction activities are not apt to adversely affect threatened species in a significant way.

The proposed rule would add subsection (d) to 50 C.F.R. § 17.31. This subsection would allow the incidental take of threatened species, in the course of otherwise lawful activities that the FWS has identified as having negligible wildlife impacts. Three examples are included. The first involves activities that take place around a single private residence on a parcel of land of five acres or less. The second example deals with activities that cumulatively disturb over time no more than five contiguous acres within a larger parcel. The third covers all other activities identified by the FWS as having a negligible impact on a particular threatened species.

* * *

The FWS notes in its explanation of the rule that, while five acres represents the maximum permitted disturbance under the general exemption, the agency will consider special exceptions for larger areas on a case by case basis, if such disturbance is "biologically defensible."

In fact, the FWS preceded the release of the small landowner/low impact rule by applying it to an area significantly larger than five acres. In February 1995, the Department of the Interior created "the first small landowner exemption ever under the ESA." The FWS proposed a special rule to ease the regulatory burden of the ESA on timber cutting on tribal, privately owned, and other non-federal lands in Washington and California. The agency justified the exemption as biologically defensible because of the comprehensive Northwest Forest Plan adopted to provide comprehensive protection and management for the Northern Spotted Owl.

The rule exempts landowners in Washington and California with less than eighty acres of forestland from the incidental take provisions of the ESA. It lifts the prohibition against incidental take of spotted owls during timber cutting and related activities on 5.3 million acres of specified non-federal lands in Washington and California. Landowners are required to maintain only the closest seventy acres of suitable habitat around an owl site center. The rule retains incidental take restrictions on six key "Special Emphasis Areas" in the State of Washington where non-federal lands still play an essential role in the conservation and recovery of spotted owls. It offers an expedited and streamlined process for resolving spotted owl conservation conflicts for landowners of up to 5,000 acres within Special Emphasis Areas in Washington State. It calls for a cooperative planning process with the State of California for four areas where special measures are needed to conserve spotted owls. The rule offers the opportunity for additional "incidental take" relief to be granted through California's Natural Communities Conservation Planning Act. The rule "launches a new voluntary and innovative owl habitat enhancement program" designed to provide incentives for private forestland owners to undertake conservation activities for spotted owls. This program shields landowners who enter into cooperative agreements with the FWS from any future incidental take restrictions for the spotted owl. Finally, the rule offers a Safe Harbor for landowners who retain at least forty percent of suitable owl habitat within the home range of the owl after timber cutting. According to the Department of the Interior, "under no circumstances would they be liable for the 'incidental take' of an owl should it nevertheless occur despite their best efforts to avoid harm."

The preceding example illustrates that the small landowner/low impact rule can be used as a Trojan horse for a much larger exemption from the FWS's ban on taking threatened species. Few would dispute that, in most circumstances, yard maintenance on five acres or less will have little impact on a threatened wildlife species (although it might well kill individual members of that species), but timber cutting and related activities on thousands of acres is quite another matter. The Northwest Forest Plan, by which the FWS justifies much of the special rule for private forestland owners, is not an HCP or a blanket exemption from the Endangered Species Act. It cannot substitute for the protections of the ESA.

The special rule also illustrates the consequences of using threatened status as a political compromise. Although a species is listed under the ESA "solely on the basis of the best scientific and commercial data" available to the Secretary, its designation as endangered or threatened may be a political decision. Threatened status gives the Secretary greater flexibility to manage a species and to balance its needs against economic and social interests. It may not, however, accurately portray the biological condition of the species.

For years, the FWS refused to list the Northern spotted owl, despite a preliminary finding that "substantial data were available to indicate that the petitioned action may be warranted." It based its refusal, in large part, on the various plans and activities of other federal agencies to protect the owl. When owl populations plummeted, the FWS was forced to act, but chose the "threatened" as opposed to the "endangered" designation, in the face of pressure from the timber industry. Now the designation is being used to permit continuing destruction of owl habitat under HCPs and special rules.

E. Candidate Conservation Agreements

Although the legislative history of Section 10(a) indicates that Congress intended HCPs to be broad in scope and to include unlisted as well as listed species, FWS had no explicit program to target unlisted species in the HCP process. On June 12, 1997, * * * FWS and NMFS announced a joint Draft Policy for Candidate Conservation Agreements. The policy, which is similar to "Safe Harbors," is designed to offer "incentives for private and other non-Federal property owners, and State and local land managing agencies, to restore, enhance, or maintain habitats for proposed, candidate and certain other unlisted species."

The basic idea of the policy is to encourage landowners and management agencies to take actions that will eliminate the need to list species by preventing them from becoming threatened or endangered in the first place. * * *

The policy is described as a "collaborative stewardship process" to achieve early conservation efforts for both proposed and candidate species, and species likely to become either proposed or candidate in the near future. The emphasis is on the involvement and cooperation of "critical stakeholders in the conservation of these species," including private property owners, state fish and wildlife agencies, and tribal governments.

A Candidate Conservation Agreement sets forth the specific beneficial management actions a private or non-Federal landowner or manager is willing to take to conserve species or protect or restore habitat. The Agreement defines and limits the obligations of the property owner or agency to a covered species. If a covered species is subsequently listed, the property owner will not be required to do more than the actions agreed to in the Agreement. Incidental take authorization will be provided to allow the property owner to implement management activities that might result in take of individual members of listed species or modification of habitat.

Before entering into a Candidate Conservation Agreement, FWS must make a written finding that species included will receive "a sufficient conservation benefit" from activities conducted under the Agreement. The benefit must be such that, if it were provided by other similarly situated property owners or land management agencies, it would be "cumulatively significant enough to remove the need to list the covered species." The Agreement must include an estimate of the expected conservation benefits and the conditions the property owner or manager commits to maintain. The Agreement must also identify the existing population levels of the covered species and the existing habitat characteristics.

Candidate Conservation Agreements represent a promising means to forestall what for some species may be an inexorable slide toward extinction. The ESA, as enacted, protects only listed species. There is considerable merit in the effort to solicit help for those species that are likely to require the statute's protections if action is not taken.

F. The Habitat Conservation Planning Handbook

All of the new policies for implementing Section 10(a) of the ESA, except for Candidate Conservation Agreements, are brought together in the Endangered Species Habitat Conservation Planning Handbook, issued jointly by the Fish and Wildlife Service and the National Marine Fisheries Service in December 1996. The Handbook sets forth policy and procedural guidance to FWS and NMFS employees processing incidental take permits and participating in associated habitat conservation planning efforts. It is also intended for public evaluation and use. The purposes of the Handbook are to ensure that the goals and intent of the ESA's conservation planning process are realized; to establish clear standards for consistent implementation of the Section 10(a) program nationwide; and to ensure that FWS and NMFS offices retain the flexibility needed to respond to specific local and regional conditions and a wide array of circumstances.

The Handbook * * * describes two "alternative HCPs" that appear to have considerable potential to address the fundamental dilemma created by the species-specific approach of Section 10(a). The first of these is a habitat-based HCP that focuses on specific types of habitat in order to reach a broader range of species than would be targeted by a conventional HCP. The second is a Programmatic HCP, a plan that can be used to address a group of actions, rather than deal with them one at a time in separate HCPs.

1. Habitat-Based HCPs

In the habitat-based approach, a particular habitat type within the area to be covered by an HCP is selected and addressed in the plan, based on criteria agreed to by the applicant and the FWS. Management indicator species are generally used to establish management parameters for the habitat covered by the HCP. The HCP must ensure that the needs of all endemic and sensitive species associated with the habitat type, whether listed or not, are adequately met.

* * *

2. Programmatic HCPs

Programmatic HCPs may be used to address a group of actions occurring in the same place or a single related action occurring in many places. They allow the participation of numerous entities through "Certificates of Inclusion" or "Participation Certificates," which authorize incidental take.

The multi-species, state-wide HCP approved by the Secretary of the Interior on January 30, 1997, is an example of the potential for a programmatic HCP. The seventy year agreement among the FWS, the NMFS, and the Washington State Department of Natural Resources covers 1.6 million acres of state-managed forest lands, making it the largest HCP ever prepared. It is designed to protect more than 285 species of fish and wildlife, including numbers of threatened and endangered species. Similar agreements have been reached among the federal agencies and four large timber companies, placing more than two million total acres under HCP management.

The Secretary's announcement does not describe all the trade-offs included in these HCPs to make them acceptable to State and private interests. Part of the Washington State HCP replaces spotted owl "protection circles" on Washington State lands with "a more flexible approach to protect the owl." The spotted owl protection circles affected timber cutting activities on 600,000 acres of state lands. The strategy in the HCP is to conserve spotted owl populations in areas designated by scientists as the most important to owls, "based on proximity to federal reserves."

Whether the programmatic HCP strategy will really benefit the spotted owl and other species subject to the agreement remains to be seen.

CONCLUSION: STILL THE ONLY GAME IN TOWN

* * *

The best start toward healing the Achilles heel of the ESA would seem to be full and effective implementation of Section 10(a), coupled with a new, strong habitat protection program within the statute. Such a program should focus on areas of high biological diversity and strive to affirmatively protect large, contiguous habitat areas. A combination of methods and techniques will be useful, from economic incentives to regulatory restrictions. A key purpose should be to get ahead of the extinction curve, that is, to support species before they require listing as threatened or endangered. This is a test of political will and ethical values. After twenty-five years, the Endangered Species Act's goal of protecting endangered and threatened species, and the ecosystems upon which they depend, deserves to become a reality.

NOTES

1. Final rules implementing the "no surprises" policy were promulgated on February 23, 1998. 63 Fed. Reg. 8,859 (1998) (*to be codified at* 50 C.F.R. pt. 17). The rules followed from a settlement agreement in a lawsuit between a coalition of environmental groups and the Interior Department challenging the agency's decision not to promulgate the policy as a rule. *Spirit of the Sage Council v. Babbitt,* Civ. No. 1: 96CV02503 (D.D.C.). The same coalition of groups has now challenged the final rule on the grounds that it violates the ESA. *Spirit of the Sage Council v. Babbitt,* Civ. No. 1: 98CV01873 (D.D.C.). Who should prevail?

2. Proposed rules for the "safe harbor" policy and the "candidate conservation agreements" were published in the Federal Register on June 12, 1997. 62 Fed. Reg. 32,189 (*to be codified at* 50 C.F.R. pts. 13 and 17). They had not been published in final form as of the time of this writing in December, 1998. Assuming that these rules are also challenged, how are they likely to fare in the courts?

3. In *Loggerhead Turtle v. County Council of Volusia, Florida,* 148 F.3d 1231 (11th Cir. 1998), the Court of Appeals for the Eleventh Circuit found that the County's incidental take permit issued under § 10 of the ESA did not expressly or implicitly authorize the County to "take" sea turtles incidentally through its maintenance of artificial beachfront lighting. The plaintiffs had claimed that artificial beachfront lighting caused a "taking" of turtles by, in some cases, fatally disorienting and misorienting hatchling turtles. The plaintiffs also claimed that "takings" occurred when nesting female turtles aborted nesting attempts in highly lighted areas. Is the court's decision on both the hatchling and nesting female turtles consistent with *Sweet Home*? With Justice O'Connor's opinion in *Sweet Home*?

4. The incidental take permit provision is not the only species management tool in ESA § 10 that allows the Services flexibility in implementing the prohibition on takings.

The experimental population management provision of § 10(j) is another controversial program subject to recent litigation. As you read the following case, consider why it was important to the FWS to designate the wolves reintroduced to the Greater Yellowstone Ecosystem under § 10(j).

WYOMING FARM BUREAU FEDERATION V. BABBITT
987 F. Supp. 1349 (D. Wyo. 1997)

DOWNES, District Judge.

The above-captioned matter comes before the Court on Plaintiffs' appeal of Defendants' decision to introduce an "experimental population" of gray wolves in Yellowstone National Park and central Idaho. The Court, having carefully reviewed the administrative record and the various parties' memoranda, having heard oral argument of counsel and being fully advised in the premises, FINDS and ORDERS as follows:

BACKGROUND

The gray wolf (canus lupus) was extirpated from the western portion of the United States in the early 1900's. In 1973, pursuant to the Endangered Species Act (hereinafter "ESA"), the Secretary of the Interior listed the Northern Rocky Mountain Wolf (canis lupus irremotus) as an endangered species. In 1978, the Secretary listed the entire species of canus lupus as an endangered species in the lower 48 states, except in Minnesota where it was listed as a threatened species.

Between approximately 1940 and 1986, no wolf reproduction was detected in the Rocky Mountain states. However, a wolf den was discovered in Glacier National Park in 1986. This colony has since grown to approximately seventy wolves. Defendants acknowledge that, as the number of wolves in Montana increases, wolves will naturally recolonize areas of Idaho and Yellowstone. In recent years, lone wolves have been confirmed to exist south of this area within the Yellowstone and central Idaho experimental population areas.

In accordance with § 1533(f) [§ 4(f)] of the ESA, the Department of the Interior established a team to develop a recovery plan for the Northern Rocky Mountain Wolf. The Northern Rocky Mountain Wolf Recovery Plan was completed in 1980 and was "intended to provide direction and coordination for efforts toward the recovery of at least two viable [Northern Rocky Mountain Wolf] populations in the lower 48 states." The plan was updated in 1987. The 1987 Northern Rocky Mountain Recovery Plan concluded that a population of about 300 wolves was required in order for the species to recover in areas of the western United States from which it had been eliminated. The 1987 Plan recommended that the introduced population consist of at least ten breeding pairs for three consecutive years in each of three recovery areas (northwestern Montana, central Idaho and Yellowstone National Park). Natural recovery was recommended in the Idaho and Montana areas, while the establishment of a nonessential experimental population was recommended for Yellowstone National Park.

In cooperation with the National Park Service and the United States Department of Agriculture Forest Service, the Fish and Wildlife Service ("FWS") began preparing an Environmental Impact Statement ("EIS") in April of 1992. The EIS proceeded through three stages: (1) scoping (to identify issues and alternatives); (2) the draft EIS; and (3) the final EIS (FEIS). After receiving extensive oral and written comments on the draft EIS, the FEIS was issued in May of 1994. The FEIS analyzes the environmental effects of five wolf recovery alternatives. Ultimately, the FWS proposed to establish two nonessential experimental population areas (central Idaho and Yellowstone areas) under section 10(j) of the ESA ("Proposed Action Alternative"). The FWS recommended that 15 wolves would be reintroduced annually to both Yellowstone National Park and central Idaho beginning in 1994.

On June 15, 1994, Defendant Bruce Babbitt, Secretary of the Interior, signed a Record of Decision and Statement of Findings on the Environmental Impact Statement for the Reintroduction of Gray Wolves to Yellowstone National Park and Central Idaho ("ROD") essentially adopting the Proposed Action Alternative. However, the decision to implement the Proposed Action Alternative was subject to certain conditions intended to "minimize or avoid the environmental impacts and public concerns identified during the environmental review process," including the preparation of nonessential experimental population rules under section 10(j) of the ESA to implement a wolf management program. The preparation of such rules was subject to all regulatory requirements. The FWS published proposed rules for the designation of nonessential experimental populations of gray wolves to be introduced into the Yellowstone and central Idaho areas. Comments regarding the proposed rules were to be submitted by October 17, 1994. The final rules were published on November 22, 1994. The Plan and rules involve the release of 90-150 wolves from Canada into the Yellowstone and central Idaho areas over a three to five year period. 59 Fed. Reg. 60252 (1994) ("Final Rules").

* * *

III. ENDANGERED SPECIES ACT § 10(J)

Section 10(j) was added to the ESA in 1982 in an effort to grant flexibility in the treatment of populations of endangered or threatened species that are introduced into areas outside their current range. H. Rep. No. 97-567, 97th Cong., 2d Sess. § 5.

The Farm Bureaus and Urbigkits allege that Defendants have violated § 10(j)(2)(A) by introducing a population of an endangered species within that species' current range. In making this allegation, both parties, relying on reported sightings of wolves in the Yellowstone and central Idaho areas, assert that the designated "experimental population areas" are within the current range of naturally occurring gray wolves. Additionally, the Farm Bureau Plaintiffs assert that the designated areas are within the current range of the naturally occurring Montana wolf populations. These Plaintiffs further allege that Defendants cannot maintain an "experimental population" in the designated areas because the "experimental population" is not "wholly separate geographically from nonexperimental populations of the same species." In support of this argument, Plaintiffs once again rely upon the reported sightings of wolves in the Yellowstone and central Idaho areas. The Farm Bureaus further assert that the "experimental population" is not wholly separate geographically from the naturally occurring wolves in Montana because there is no geographic separation; i.e., natural or manmade barriers, that would prevent the naturally occurring wolves from overlapping with the "experimental population."

In response to such arguments, Defendants contend that the FWS' determination that the experimental population areas are outside the current range of the gray wolf is rationally based and supported in the record. Specifically, Defendants assert that such a determination was based on the conclusion that there were no known "populations," as defined by Defendants for purposes of the reintroduction plan, in either of the experimental population areas prior to the introduction. Defendants further assert that the "wholly separate geographic" requirement applies only to "populations" and not individual animals. Moreover, Defendants argue, to the extent any ambiguity exists in what constitutes a "population," Defendants are entitled to substantial deference to their interpretation.

Two questions are presented when a court reviews an agency's construction of a statute which it administers. *Chevron, U.S.A. v. Natural Resources Defense Council, Inc.*, 467 U.S.

837, 842-43 (1984). The court must first determine whether Congress has directly spoken to the precise question at issue. If so, no further questions must be asked for both the court and agency must give effect to Congress' unambiguously expressed intent. *Id.*

The Defendants' arguments are focused upon the FWS' definition of "population" formulated for purposes of determining whether a nonexperimental population of wolves existed in the experimental population areas. The FWS' definition provides: "A wolf population is at least 2 breeding pairs of wild wolves successfully raising at least 2 young each (until December 31 of the year of their birth), for 2 consecutive years in an experimental area." In accordance with *Chevron,* the Court must first determine whether Congress has spoken to the precise question of what constitutes a "population" for purposes of § 10(j).

Defendants correctly point out that the term "population" is not defined anywhere in the ESA. Neither does the legislative history provide guidance on this precise issue. Thus, the Court must determine whether the FWS' definition of "population" is based on a permissible construction of the statute. While careful review is always required, deference to an agency's judgment is especially appropriate where the challenged decision implicates special agency expertise. *National Cattlemen's Ass'n v. United Stated Environmental Protection Agency,* 773 F.2d 268, 271 (10th Cir. 1985); *Mount Graham Red Squirrel v. Espy,* 986 F.2d 1568, 1571 (9th Cir. 1993).

Applying this principle, the Court finds that the FWS' definition of "population" is based on a permissible construction of the ESA § 10(j) which seeks to secure the recovery of listed species. H. Rep. No. 97-567, 97th Cong., 2d Sess. § 5. Defendants assert that the FWS' definition is based on two core concepts of reproduction and sustainability which are soundly based in relevant scientific literature. Defendants also assert that such concepts are further supported by the opinions of numerous scientists with knowledge and expertise specific to wolf biology. Defendants contend that the FWS' definition promotes the recovery objective of the ESA, and specifically § 10(j). Given Congress' expressed objective, the Court finds that the FWS' definition is not "arbitrary, capricious, or manifestly contrary to the statute." *See Chevron,* 467 U.S. at 844.

While the Court must defer to the FWS' definition of "population," a more thorough analysis of the reintroduction plan's compliance with the requirements of § 10(j) is necessary. First, § 10(j)(1) only allows an "experimental population" to be maintained "when, and at such time as, the [experimental] population is *wholly separate geographically* from nonexperimental populations of the same species." (Emphasis added.) In analyzing what Congress meant by the phrase "wholly separate geographically," it is helpful to review the legislative history to determine the Congressional intent behind the enactment of § 10(j). In adding this section, Congress sought to reduce public opposition associated with the release of experimental populations of predators such as wolves. H. Rep. No. 97-567, 97th Cong., 2d Sess. § 5. Congress intended § 10(j) to allow the Secretary, under limited circumstances, to relax certain restrictions, such as taking of an endangered species, that would otherwise be applicable to listed species. *Id.* The legislative history makes it clear that by enacting § 10(j), Congress did not intend to allow reduction of ESA protections to existing natural populations in whole or in part. This is evidenced by the following comments made by the Merchant Marine and Fisheries Committee's House Report:

> To qualify for the special treatment afforded "experimental populations," a population must have been authorized by the secretary for release outside the current range of the species. Populations resulting from releases not authorized by the secretary are not considered "experimental populations" entitled to the special provisions of this subsection.

The Committee carefully considered how to treat introduced populations that overlap, in whole or in part, [with] natural populations of the same species. To protect natural populations and to avoid potentially complicated problems of law enforcement, the definition [of "experimental population"] is limited to those introduced populations that are wholly separate geographically from nonexperimental populations of the same species. Thus, for example, in the case of the introduction of individuals of a listed fish species into a portion of a stream where the same species already occurs, the introduced specimens would not be treated as an "experimental population" separate from the non-introduced specimens. . . . If an introduced population overlaps with natural populations of the same species during a portion of the year, but is wholly separate at other times, the introduced population is to be treated as an experimental population at such times as it is wholly separate. *The Committee intends, however, that such a population be treated as experimental only when the times of geographic separation are reasonably predictable and not when separation occurs as a result of random and unpredictable events.*

H. Rep. No. 97-567, 97th Cong., 2d Sess. § 5 (Merchant Marine and Fisheries Committee) (1982) U.S. Code Cong. & Admin. News 1982 p. 2833 (emphasis added). Based upon the foregoing comments, it is clear that Congress, in enacting § 10(j), did not intend to lessen the protections afforded to naturally occurring, or non-introduced, individual members of the same species. In order to give effect to this intent, Congress limited the definition of "experimental population" to such times as when the experimental populations are wholly separate geographically from nonexperimental populations of the same species. In the event that an experimental population overlaps, in whole or in part, with natural populations of the same species, the introduced specimens can no longer be treated as an "experimental population" separate from the non-introduced specimens and, therefore, full ESA protections must be afforded to all members of the species in the area of overlap.

Defendants argue that the geographic separation provision applies only to "population" overlap and not to overlap with "lone dispersers" or individual members of the species. However, the Congressional history does not support such an argument. As set forth above, the Committee's discussion of this issue specifically refers to the overlap of "individuals" and "specimens" of a particular species as well as populations. Hence, it is clear that Congress did not intend to allow an "experimental population" to exist where it was not wholly separate geographically from any natural population, unless the times of geographic separation are "reasonably predictable and not . . . a result of random and unpredictable events."

Erroneously focusing only on the definition of "population," Defendants argue that no geographic overlap exists, given their conclusion that no "populations" of wolves exist in the experimental areas. However, Defendants' own statements contained in the administrative record establish that members (or "part") of the natural wolf populations in Montana and/or Canada exist, and will continue to exist, in the experimental population areas. Further, the mere fact that Defendants have drawn a line which purports to ensure "no geographic overlap" between the existing wolf population in Montana and either of the proposed experimental population areas is insufficient and contrary to law. The legislative history and Defendants' own regulations require that an experimental population may be maintained only when the times of geographic separation from nonexperimental (non-introduced) specimens are reasonably predictable as a result of fixed migration patterns or natural or man-made barriers. H. Rep. No. 97-567, 97th Cong., 2d Sess. § 5; 50 C.F.R. § 17.80(a). This interpretation is consistent with the expressed concerns regarding law enforcement problems created by mixing naturally occurring and introduced specimens of the same species. Obviously, where non-introduced specimens intermingle with introduced specimens of the same species it would be impossible for law enforcement to effectively identify and treat the specimens separately.

Defendants resolve this problem by treating all wolves found within the boundaries of the designated experimental population areas as nonessential experimental animals. 50 C.F.R. § 17.84(i)(7)(iii). However, such treatment is contrary to law as provided in the Defendants' own regulations:

> The term "experimental population" means an introduced and/or designated population (including any offspring arising solely therefrom) that has been so designated in accordance with the procedures of this subpart but only when, and at such times as the population is wholly separate geographically from nonexperimental populations of the same species. Where part of an experimental population overlaps with natural populations of the same species on a particular occasion, but is wholly separate at other times, *specimens of the experimental population will not be recognized as such while in the area of overlap*. That is, experimental status will only be recognized outside the areas of overlap. Thus, such a population shall be treated as experimental only when the times of geographic separation are reasonably predictable; e.g., fixed migration patterns, natural or man-made barriers. A population is not treated as experimental if total separation will occur solely as a result of random and unpredictable events.

50 C.F.R. § 17.80(a) (emphasis added). Thus, where artificially introduced and naturally occurring wolves overlap, all of the overlapping animals (both introduced and non-introduced) must be accorded the full protections due them as members of an endangered species. The foregoing passage evidences an intent to ensure that ESA protections afforded an endangered animal not be diminished as a result of its presence in the same area as an experimental population. Any other interpretation would fly in the face of the statutory language and legislative history which forms the foundation of species preservation. * * *

The same problems exist with Defendants' arguments concerning the Farm Bureaus' and Urbigkits' claims that the experimental population areas are not outside the current range of the gray wolf. In attempting to refute such claims, Defendants ignore the plain language of the statute and attempt to turn the "current range of such species" into the current range or "territory" of naturally occurring "packs" or "populations" of such species. Because they contend that no "pack" or "populations" of wolves presently exist in the experimental population areas, Defendants argue that their determination that the experimental population areas are outside the current range of the gray wolf is rationally based and supported in the record. However, the plain language of § 10(j)(2)(A) speaks to the range of the "species" without specific reference to a "population."

Such an interpretation is consistent with the Court's previous analysis regarding the "wholly separate" requirement. To further prevent the occurrence of overlap between experimental and nonexperimental populations, Congress required that an experimental population could only be introduced to the extent it was "outside the current range of such species." As evidenced by the legislative history set forth and discussed supra, Congress clearly intended to guard against the overlap of introduced and non-introduced "individuals" or "specimens" of a particular species. The requirement that an experimental population only be authorized if it is "outside the current range of the species" is a reflection of that intent. Given Congress' intent, and the Defendants' acknowledgment that naturally occurring wolves exist in and will likely migrate to the experimental population areas, Defendants' determination that the designated areas are outside the current range of the species is arbitrary and capricious.

The National Audubon Plaintiffs contend that the central Idaho reintroduction plan illegally withdraws and denies full ESA protections from wolves naturally migrating to central Idaho in violation of the ESA § 4, 16 U.S.C.A. § 1533. In support of this argument, these Plaintiffs assert that the experimental population rules operate as a de facto "delisting" of the naturally occurring wolves. In response, Defendants point out that their action taken under § 10(j) was not based upon any petition for revision of the wolf's listing. While Defendants argue that § 10(j) provides the authority and criteria for the treatment of an experimental population, § 10(j) only allows the reduction of ESA protections afforded members of the "experimental population" (including any offspring arising solely therefrom). As set forth above, Congress has stated the "experimental population" cannot include naturally occurring wolves. To avoid a conflict in the application of § 10(j) and § 4, the introduction of an experimental population cannot operate as a de facto "delisting" of naturally occurring wolves. Accordingly, to reduce the ESA protections afforded to naturally occurring wolves, or any offspring not arising solely from an experimental population, the procedure set forth under § 4 must be followed. Therefore, Defendants' blanket treatment of all wolves found within the designated experimental population areas as experimental animals is contrary to law.

CONCLUSION

Mindful of the dedication, talents and money which have been expended in the development and implementation of the wolf recovery program, the Court reaches this decision with the utmost reluctance. The Court is especially mindful of the concerted efforts of the Government and wolf-recovery advocates to accommodate the interests of stockgrowers and others who may be adversely affected by the wolf recovery program. The fact that the program has been responsibly implemented, however, cannot obviate the limitations Congress has imposed upon the application of § 10(j).[43] The laudable ends aspired to by the wolf recovery plan cannot justify the Secretary's impermissible means.

Given the importance of the issues presented and the ramifications of this Order, this Court, *sua sponte*, imposes a stay upon this Order pending appeal.

THEREFORE, it is

ORDERED that Defendants' Final Rules establishing a nonessential experimental population of gray wolves in Yellowstone National Park in Wyoming, Idaho, Montana, central Idaho and southwestern Montana are hereby found unlawful and set aside pursuant to 5 U.S.C. § 706; it is further,

ORDERED that by virtue of the plan being set aside, Defendants must remove reintroduced non-native wolves and their offspring from the Yellowstone and central Idaho experimental population areas; it is further,

ORDERED, *sua sponte*, that the judgment entered hereby is stayed pending appeal.

---

[43] It is ironic that as a result of the inability to implement an experimental population in these areas, no flexibility in ESA protections will be available to those individuals economically effected by natural wolf recovery. As the adage goes, "Be careful what you wish for, you might just get it."

NOTES

1.   At the time of this writing, an appeal of this decision was pending in the Court of Appeals for the Tenth Circuit. Interestingly, the National Audubon Society moved to realign itself as a party defendant. How should the court rule on appeal?

2.   Note the court's warning to the plaintiffs—in particular the Wyoming Farm Bureau Federation—in note 43. What does the Farm Bureau ultimately get with this victory? How do their interests diverge with the National Audubon Society.

3.   From a biological perspective, the reintroduction of wolves into the Greater Yellowstone Ecosystem has been a resounding success. *See* Michael Mistein, *Wolves are Thriving,* BOSTON GLOBE, November 30, 1998, at C; *The Wolf Finds a Home*, LOS ANGELES TIMES, July 4, 1998 at B7.

CHRISTY V. HODEL
857 F.2d 1324 (9th Cir. 1988), *cert. denied,* 490 U.S. 1114 (1989)

ALARCON, Circuit Judge:

Plaintiffs-Appellants Richard P. Christy (Christy), Thomas B. Guthrie (Guthrie), and Ira Perkins (Perkins) appeal from the district court's grant of summary judgment in favor of Defendants-Appellees Donald P. Hodel, Secretary of the Interior (Secretary) and the United States Department of Interior (Department). The district court rejected plaintiffs' claim that the Endangered Species Act (ESA) and certain regulations promulgated thereunder are unconstitutional as applied because they prevent plaintiffs from defending their sheep by killing grizzly bears. The court also rejected plaintiffs' claims that the ESA unlawfully delegated legislative authority to the Secretary and that the Secretary exceeded his lawful authority in promulgating the regulations at issue. We affirm.

I. FACTS

Christy owned 1700 head of sheep. On or about June 1, 1982, he began grazing the sheep on land he had leased from the Blackfeet Indian Tribe. The land was located adjacent to Glacier National Park in Glacier County, Montana.

Beginning about July 1, 1982, bears attacked the herd on a nightly basis. The herder employed by Christy frightened the bears away with limited success by building fires and shooting a gun into the air. Christy sought assistance from Kenneth Wheeler, a trapper employed by the United States Fish and Wildlife Service. Wheeler set snares in an attempt to capture the bears.

By July 9, 1982, the bears had killed approximately twenty sheep, worth at least $1200. That evening, while Christy and Wheeler were on the leased land together, Christy observed two grizzly bears emerge from the forest. One of the bears quickly retreated to the trees. The other bear moved toward the herd. When the animal was 60-100 yards away, Christy picked up his rifle and fired one shot, which hit the bear. It ran a short distance, then fell to the ground. Christy approached the bear and fired a second shot into its carcass to ensure that it was dead.

Wheeler's subsequent efforts to capture any bears were unsuccessful. On July 22, 1982, the Tribe agreed to terminate the lease and to refund Christy's money. On July 24, 1982, Christy removed his sheep from the leased land, having lost a total of 84 sheep to the bears during the lease term.

Pursuant to authority conferred by the ESA, the Secretary has listed the grizzly bear (*Ursus arctos horribilis*) as a threatened species throughout the 48 contiguous states. 50 C.F.R. § 17.11(h) (1987). Regulations promulgated by the Department forbid the "taking" of grizzly bears, except in certain specified circumstances. *See id.* § 17.40(b).

The Department assessed a civil penalty of $3,000 against Christy for killing a grizzly bear in violation of the ESA and the regulations. On August 13, 1984, at Christy's request, the Department held an administrative hearing. At the hearing, Christy admitted that he had killed the bear knowing it to be a grizzly, but contended that he did so in the exercise of his right to defend his sheep. The administrative law judge (ALJ) upheld the imposition of a penalty but lowered the amount to $2,500.

Christy filed an administrative appeal, arguing that the imposition of a penalty violated his alleged constitutional right to defend his sheep. The appeal was denied on the ground that the Department had no jurisdiction to determine the constitutionality of federal laws or regulations.

* * *

On May 4, 1987, the district court issued a Memorandum and Order granting the defendants' motion for summary judgment. The court found that "[t]he material facts preceding and arising from this lawsuit are not in dispute." The court ruled that the defendants were entitled to judgment as a matter of law. The court rejected plaintiffs' argument that there is a fundamental right to possess and protect property. Accordingly, the court evaluated the ESA and the grizzly bear regulations under the "rational basis" test and found that they satisfied that test. The court next rejected plaintiffs' contention that the loss of their sheep constituted a taking of their property by the federal government without just compensation. The court held that damage to private property by protected wildlife does not constitute a taking.

The court further concluded that "the ESA is a valid delegation of legislative authority," and that "the regulations at issue are a rational reflection of Congressional will, properly promulgated under the authority vested in the Secretary of the Interior." Finally, the court affirmed the penalty assessed against Christy by the ALJ, finding that it was supported by substantial evidence contained in the administrative record. Plaintiffs now appeal from the judgment entered against them.

* * *

II. Discussion

* * *

A. Do the ESA and the Regulations, as Applied, Deprive Plaintiffs of Property Without Due Process?

Plaintiffs contend that application of the ESA and the regulations so as to prevent them from defending their sheep against destruction by grizzly bears deprives them of property without due process, in violation of the fifth amendment. The first step in our analysis is to determine the standard to be applied in reviewing the challenged legislation.

Strict judicial scrutiny of legislation that allegedly violates the due process clause is reserved for those enactments that "impinge upon constitutionally protected rights." *San Antonio Indep. School Dist. v. Rodriguez,* 411 U.S. 1, 40 (1973). * * *

On the other hand, when the legislative enactment infringes on no fundamental right, "the law need only rationally relate to any legitimate end of government." 2 ROTUNDA § 15.4, at 59. The law will be upheld if the court can hypothesize any possible basis on which the legislature might have acted.

The right claimed by the plaintiffs in this action is the right "to protect their property from immediate destruction from federally protected wildlife." In their opening brief, plaintiffs characterize this as a "natural and fundamental constitutional right." In their reply brief, plaintiffs backtrack somewhat, arguing that the right "should be deemed fundamental."

Certain state courts have construed their own constitutions to protect the sort of right claimed by the plaintiffs in this case. *See, e.g., Cross v. State,* 370 P.2d 371, 376-77 (Wyo. 1962) (due process clause in state constitution construed to guarantee "the inherent and inalienable right to protect property"); *State v. Rathbone,* 100 P.2d 86, 90 (1940) (state constitution expressly guaranteed the right "of acquiring, possessing, and protecting property"). No court, however, has construed the United States Constitution to protect such a right. *See Mountain States Legal Found v. Hodel,* 799 F.2d 1423, 1428 n.8 (10th Cir. 1986) (en banc) (noting the absence of authority on the question), *cert. denied,* 480 U.S. 951 (1987).

The ESA expressly provides that no civil penalty shall be imposed on a defendant who proves that, in killing a member of a threatened species, the defendant was acting in self-defense or in defense of others. 16 U.S.C. § 1540(a)(3) (1982); *see* 50 C.F.R. § 17.40(b)(1)(i)(B) (1987) ("Grizzly bears may be taken in self-defense, or in defense of others. . . ."). The defendant may raise the same defense in criminal prosecutions under the ESA. 16 U.S.C. § 1540(b)(3) (1982). The ESA makes no mention, however, of a right to kill a member of a threatened species in defense of property.[4] One circuit court has opined that this omission evinces a congressional view that no such right exists under the United States Constitution. *See Mountain States,* 799 F.2d at 1428 n.8.

The U.S. Constitution does not explicitly recognize a right to kill federally protected wildlife in defense of property. Plaintiffs, nevertheless, urge that we infer such a right, in much the same way that the Supreme Court has inferred a constitutional right to privacy despite the absence of language expressly recognizing such a right. *See Griswold v. Connecticut,* 381 U.S. 479, 484-85 (1965) (state law forbidding married couples from using contraceptives violated constitutional right to privacy).

The Supreme Court has recently expressed reluctance "to discover new fundamental rights imbedded in the Due Process Clause." *Bowers v. Hardwick,* 478 U.S. 186, 194 (1986). The Court explained:

> There should be . . . great resistance to expand the substantive reach of [the due process clauses of the fifth and fourteenth amendments], particularly if it requires redefining the category of rights deemed to be fundamental. Otherwise, the Judiciary necessarily takes to itself further authority to govern the country without express constitutional authority.

Id. at 195. The Court in *Bowers* refused to recognize a fundamental constitutional right of homosexuals to engage in sodomy, rejecting the argument that the constitutional right to privacy extended to protect such conduct. * * *

* * *

In light of the Supreme Court's admonition that we exercise restraint in creating new definitions of substantive due process, we decline plaintiffs' invitation to construe the fifth

---

[4]   On the other hand, neither the ESA nor the regulations appear to forbid a property owner from attempting to fence out grizzly bears or to drive them away by nonharmful means. Indeed, in the present case, Christy's herder enjoyed limited success in driving bears away by building fires and shooting a gun into the air. Thus, it is inaccurate to say that the laws prevent an owner from defending his property against grizzly bears. The laws merely operate to bar certain means of defending property from grizzly bears.

amendment as guaranteeing the right to kill federally protected wildlife in defense of property. In so doing, we do not minimize the seriousness of the problem faced by livestock owners such as plaintiffs nor do we suggest that defense of property is an unimportant value. We simply hold that the right to kill federally protected wildlife in defense of property is not "implicit in the concept of ordered liberty" nor so "deeply rooted in this Nation's history and tradition" that it can be recognized by us as a fundamental right guaranteed by the fifth amendment.

* * *

B. Do the ESA and the Regulations, as Applied, Deny Plaintiffs Equal Protection of the Laws?

Plaintiffs also argue that the ESA and the grizzly bear regulations, as applied to prevent them from killing grizzly bears to protect their sheep against imminent destruction, deny them equal protection of the laws.

The due process clause of the fifth amendment has been construed to require the federal government to accord every person within its jurisdiction equal protection of the laws. *See Jimenez v. Weinberger,* 417 U.S. 628, 637 (1974) (referring to "the equal protection of the laws guaranteed by the due process provision of the Fifth Amendment"); *Bolling v. Sharpe,* 347 U.S. 497, 499 (1954) (invalidating racial segregation of public schools under the fifth amendment); *Eskra v. Morton,* 524 F.2d 9, 13 (7th Cir. 1975) ("The United States, as well as each of the several States, must accord every person within its jurisdiction the equal protection of the laws.").

"[I]n order to subject a law to any form of review under the equal protection guarantee, one must be able to demonstrate that the law classifies persons in some manner." 2 ROTUNDA § 18.4, at 343-44. A classification may be demonstrated in one of three ways: by showing that the law, on its face, employs a classification; by showing that the law is applied in a discriminatory fashion; or by showing that the law is "in reality . . . a device designed to impose different burdens on different classes of persons." *Id.* at 344.

Once a legislative classification has been demonstrated, it will be subjected to strict judicial scrutiny if it employs a "suspect" class or if it classifies in such a way as to impair the exercise of a fundamental right. 2 ROTUNDA § 15.4, at 60. On the other hand, "where the law classifies persons on a non-suspect basis for the exercise of liberties which are not fundamental constitutional rights," the law will be upheld if it rationally relates to a legitimate governmental objective. 2 ROTUNDA § 15.4, at 60.

Plaintiffs argue that the ESA and the grizzly bear regulations classify persons along two lines. "The first classification," they contend, "is between a group of persons who, like Plaintiffs, are raising livestock near grizzly bear habitat and all remaining citizens and taxpayers of the U.S." Plaintiffs have made no showing, however, that the ESA or the grizzly bear regulations employ such a classification. This is certainly not a classification that appears on the face of the challenged enactments. Nor have the plaintiffs proffered any evidence to suggest that the prohibition on the killing of grizzly bears is applied with greater severity against persons raising livestock near grizzly bear habitat. Finally, plaintiffs do not contend that the enactments constitute a device for imposing excessive burdens on such persons. In short, the first so-called classification identified by plaintiff—persons raising livestock near grizzly bear habitat—is simply not a classification made by the ESA or by the grizzly bear regulations.

The second classification identified by plaintiffs "is that which allows a certain group of people to hunt and kill grizzly bears under certain conditions for sport while withholding this same authority to livestock owners like Plaintiffs, even in immediate defense of their stock."
* * *

Plaintiffs do not contend that the foregoing classification is "suspect," and no case so holds. Nor does this classification impair the exercise of any fundamental constitutional right. *See* Part III(A) *supra*. Accordingly, the classification should be upheld if it satisfies the "rational basis" test, *i.e.*, if any state of facts can be conceived to justify it.

Plaintiffs argue that no rational basis supports the provision for sport hunting of grizzly bears: "Not only is the hunting of a threatened species *unrelated* to the goals of the Act, it is *in complete derogation* of its purposes, *i.e.*, the preservation of threatened species. . . . Indeed, given the threatened nature of their existence, allowing hunters to take even one [grizzly bear] arguably would be in direct conflict with the Act. Since this classification is in complete contradiction of the purposes of the Act, it can in no way have even a rational relationship to the purposes of the Act, as a matter of law."

Plaintiffs' argument is premised on the unsupported assumption that a program of carefully controlled killings of bears in limited geographic regions cannot promote "conservation" and, therefore, necessarily conflicts with the purpose of the ESA. On the contrary, Congress expressly contemplated that "in the extraordinary case where population pressures within a given ecosystem cannot be otherwise relieved," conservation may require "regulated taking." 16 U.S.C. § 1532(3) (1982). Further, although it expressly prohibited the killing of endangered species, Congress delegated to the Secretary the task of determining whether the killing of threatened species should also be prohibited. *Compare id.* § 1538(a)(1)(B) (imposing general prohibition on killing of endangered species) *with id.* § 1533(d) (Secretary "shall issue such regulations as he deems necessary and advisable to provide for the conservation of" threatened species). Congress authorized, but did not require, the Secretary to forbid the killing of threatened species. *Id.* § 1533(d). This legislative scheme reflects Congress's conclusion that certain killings of a threatened species could be consistent with the goal of conserving that species.

The Secretary had a rational basis for authorizing "regulated taking" of grizzly bears, by means of sport hunting, in those regions specified in the regulations. The basis is set forth in Amendment Listing the Grizzly Bear of the 48 Coterminous States as a Threatened Species, 40 Fed. Reg. 31,734-35 (1975) [hereinafter Amendment]. Briefly, relying on investigations by Fish and Wildlife Service biologists, data submitted by the Governors of Colorado, Idaho, Montana, Washington, and Wyoming, and comments filed by interested members of the public, the Director of the Fish and Wildlife Service, on behalf of the Secretary, determined that "grizzly bear population pressures definitely exist in the Bob Marshall Ecosystem." *Id.* at 31,735. The Director considered easing such pressures through live-trapping and transplantation of the animals but rejected that approach as "too dangerous and too expensive to be used with sufficient frequency to relieve the . . . population pressures." *Id.* The Director concluded that "[a] limited amount of regulated taking is necessary." *Id.*

The Director then considered whether such regulated "taking" should be accomplished through the isolated killing of nuisance bears or through seasonal sport hunting. The Director concluded that isolated killings, while necessary, were "not sufficient to prevent numerous depredations and threats to human safety. This is because the occasional killing of one bear does not create a fear of man among the grizzly bear population in general." *Id.* A carefully controlled seasonal hunt, on the other hand, would both relieve the population pressures and condition the bears "to avoid all areas where humans are encountered," thus minimizing human-bear contact and the resultant risks to both. *Id.* Accordingly, the Director ruled that the best system of relieving the population pressures in the Bob Marshall Ecosystem would be "to combine limited taking of specific nuisance bears with a closely regulated sport hunt." *Id.* The promulgated regulations strictly controlled the total number of bears killed each year by mandating the cessation of hunting in any year "where the total number of bears killed for whatever reason . . . reaches 25 bears for that year." *Id.*

In light of the foregoing, the regulations authorizing a carefully controlled and limited sport hunt of grizzly bears in designated geographic regions had a rational basis. Plaintiffs have proffered no evidence to suggest otherwise. The classification employed by the regulations, therefore, does not deny plaintiffs equal protection of the laws.

C. Do the ESA and the Regulations Effect a "Taking" of Plaintiffs' Property Without Just Compensation, in Violation of the Fifth Amendment?

The fifth amendment provides that private property shall not "be taken for public use, without just compensation." U.S. Const. amend. V. This prohibition applies only to takings by the federal government. Plaintiffs contend that by protecting grizzly bears, the Department has transformed the bears into "governmental agents" who have physically taken plaintiffs' property.

The defendants analyze this case under the principles applicable to regulatory takings. Plaintiffs, on the other hand, insist that their property has been physically taken, because their sheep have been "destroyed, killed, and rendered absolutely useless by the bear's act."

The defendants properly focus on the regulations, promulgation of which constituted governmental action. The regulations themselves, however, do not purport to take, or even to regulate the use of, plaintiffs' property. The regulations leave the plaintiffs in full possession of the complete "bundle" of property rights to their sheep. Perhaps because plaintiffs recognize this fact, they choose to focus on the conduct of the bears. Undoubtedly, the bears have physically taken plaintiffs' property, but plaintiffs err in attributing such takings to the government.

Numerous cases have considered, and rejected, the argument that destruction of private property by protected wildlife constitutes a governmental taking. The pertinent cases were recently summarized by the Tenth Circuit: "Of the courts that have considered whether damage to private property by protected wildlife constitutes a 'taking,' a clear majority have held that it does not and that the government thus does not owe compensation." *Mountain States Legal Found. v. Hodel,* 799 F.2d 1423, 1428-29 (10th Cir. 1986). * * *

Plaintiffs do not challenge the constitutional power of Congress to enact legislation to protect threatened species. Yet plaintiffs would, in effect, require that the government insure its citizens against property damage inflicted by such species. The federal government does not "own" the wild animals it protects, nor does the government control the conduct of such animals. Plaintiffs assume that the conduct of the grizzly bears is attributable to the government but offer no explanation or authority to support their assumption.

Plaintiffs cite the following language from a recent Supreme Court opinion in support of their argument that the government should compensate them for the killing of their sheep by grizzly bears: "It is axiomatic that the Fifth Amendment's just compensation provision is 'designed to bar Government from forcing some people alone to bear public burdens which, in all fairness and justice, should be borne by the public as a whole.'" *First English Evangelical Lutheran Church v. County of Los Angeles,* 482 U.S. 304, 318-19 (1987). The foregoing principle is inapplicable to the present case, because neither the ESA nor the grizzly bear regulations "force" plaintiffs to bear any burden. The losses sustained by the plaintiffs are the incidental, and by no means inevitable, result of reasonable regulation in the public interest.
* * *

For the foregoing reasons, we hold that the ESA and the grizzly bear regulations do not effect a taking of plaintiffs' property by the government so as to trigger the just compensation clause of the fifth amendment, and that the government is not answerable for the conduct of the bears in taking plaintiffs' property.

* * *

IV. CONCLUSION

For the reasons set forth herein, we AFFIRM the district court's entry of summary judgment in favor of defendants.

NOTES

1. In a dissent to the Court's denial of the defendants' petition for a writ of *certiorari*, Justice White wrote that Christy's claimed right to defend his property "has long been recognized at common law and is deeply-rooted in the legal traditions of this country" and may be entitled to protection under the due process clause. 490 U.S. at 1115. Even more compelling for Court review, according to Justice White, were the defendants' taking claims. Justice White speculated that:

> perhaps a government edict barring one from resisting the loss of one's property is the constitutional equivalent of an edict taking such property in the first place. Thus, if the government decided (in lieu of the food stamp program) to enact a law barring grocery store owners from "harassing, harming, or pursuing" people who wish to take food off grocery shelves without paying for it, such a law might well be suspect under the Fifth Amendment.

490 U.S. at 1115-16.

2. Are the wolves reintroduced in the Greater Yellowstone Ecosystem "instrumentalities of the government" for takings purposes? Robert Keiter and Peter Froelicher, in *Bison, Brucellosis, and Law in the Greater Yellowstone Ecosystem,* 28 LAND & WATER L. REV. 1 (1993), discuss cases concerning governmental liability for damage to domestic cattle that contract disease from wildlife.

3. Putting aside the constitutional authority of Congress to impose the § 9 prohibitions, is it fair to impose the costs of grizzly bear conservation on people who coexist in its habitat? Defenders of Wildlife has financed a program to compensate Montana ranchers for livestock lost to depredating wolves. Minnesota has a state-run compensation program for ranchers affected by its wolf population. Jeffrey P. Cohn, *Endangered Wolf Population Increases,* 40 BIOSCIENCE 628, 631 (1990). Should the government voluntarily finance a compensation program for sheep lost to grizzly bear depredation?

4. Do you agree with Judge Alarcon's conclusion in footnote 4 that the ESA does not prevent a sheep owner from "defending his property against grizzly bears"? How realistic are Judge Alarcon's suggestions for sheep protection? Can grizzly bears be fenced out? Might Christy risk § 9 liability for harassing the bears if he effectively scared them off with loud gunshots?

5. Under what provision of the ESA does the FWS have authority to allow a sport hunt of a listed species? How does the ESA moderate the strict takings prohibition for threatened species?

In *Sierra Club v. Clark*, 755 F.2d 608 (8th Cir. 1985), environmentalists successfully challenged FWS regulations allowing the trapping of threatened gray wolves in Minnesota under certain circumstances where wolves were believed to be preying on livestock. The court rejected the Secretary's contention that § 9(a)(1)(G) granted him broad discretion to determine the conditions under which the takings prohibition will apply to a threatened species. Section 4(d) of the ESA requires the FWS to issue regulations for threatened species that are "necessary and advisable to provide for the[ir] conservation." The ESA provides for conservation measures to include regulated taking "in the extraordinary case where population pressures within a given ecosystem cannot be otherwise relieved." § 3(3). The court ruled that the Secretary could promulgate a rule allowing takings of wolves only under the relatively narrow circumstances where population pressures could not be otherwise relieved. The Secretary had made no such findings in issuing the wolf trapping regulations. The court rejected the Secretary's argument that applying the § 3(3) restrictions to threatened species would eliminate the distinction between endangered and threatened species. 755 F.2d at 614.

Judge Ross dissented from *Sierra Club v. Clark*, arguing that the § 3(3) definition of conservation allowed for any measures that would promote recovery. Judge Ross, however, would still have remanded the trapping rule to the Secretary for an explanation of the conservation purpose it served. The dissent includes a troubling hypothetical:

> Several members of a pack of wolves became afflicted with a disease which is highly contagious between members of the species and which leaves visible signs of its presence. The Secretary seeks to utilize a regulated taking of the diseased animals to prevent the spread of the disease. However, a regulated taking of diseased animals which might infect an entire threatened species is not expressly set forth as a method of conservation in [§ 3(3)]. Nor would such a circumstance constitute a "case where population pressures cannot be otherwise relieved."

Id. at 621. Would *Sierra Club v. Clark* prohibit the Secretary from taking diseased wolves as suggested by this scenario?

6.   Proponents of hunting and trapping of threatened species often argue that these activities provide an outlet for local farmers and ranchers to kill the animals that they would otherwise take illegally. Would this be a legitimate basis for a regulated take? Should it be? In *Fund for Animals v. Turner*, No. 91-2201, 1991 WL 206232 (D.D.C. Sept. 27, 1991), the court granted environmentalists a preliminary injunction against the FWS rule authorizing a sport hunt of threatened grizzly bears in northwestern Montana. After scrutinizing the FWS administrative record in much more detail than the *Christy* court, the *Fund for Animals* court rejected the FWS argument that increased conflict between bears and humans living in the same area constitutes "population pressures" under § 3(3). The court held that "population pressures" refers only to a situation where the actual number of animals exceeds the carrying capacity of the ecosystem. Should the carrying capacity of an area incorporate human encroachments? If the number of bears in northwestern Montana remains the same but the carrying capacity of the ecosystem diminishes because of increased logging, drilling, and ranching, could the FWS begin to allow hunting?

The FWS also argued in *Fund for Animals* "that a limited hunt of the grizzly bear creates a wariness of humans, which protects the bears by confining them to their range and reducing bear-human conflicts, and which, in the long run, promotes the conservation and recovery of the species." *Id.* at *7. The court relied on *Sierra Club v. Clark* in holding that this is not a legitimate justification for a hunt under the ESA. This is similar to the conclusion reached by the district court in *Sierra Club v. Clark*, when it rejected the Secretary's argument that sport trapping of wolves would enhance the value of wolves in the minds of the local farmers and reduce illegal kills. 577 F. Supp. 783, 790 (D. Minn. 1984), *aff'd and rev'd*, 755 F.2d 608 (8th Cir. 1985).

7. The FWS has promulgated a blanket rule extending coverage of all the ESA § 9 prohibitions to threatened animal species unless otherwise indicated by regulation. 50 C.F.R. § 17.31(a). Therefore, whenever the FWS wants to allow for some taking of a threatened species, it must affirmatively promulgate a special rule.

In order to promote a comprehensive, area-wide planning effort in California, the FWS has issued a special rule under § 4(d) for the coastal California gnatcatcher. 50 C.F.R. § 17.41(6). Under the rule, landowners who participate in state-sponsored Natural Community Conservation Planning for the coastal sage scrub habitat will not be subject to liability for incidental takes of the threatened bird.

8. ESA § 4(f) requires the FWS to develop recovery plans containing site-specific management actions; objective, measurable criteria for monitoring progress; and an estimate of the time and cost required to achieve recovery. In *Sierra Club v. Lujan*, 36 Env't Rep. Cas. (BNA) 1533 (W.D. Tex. 1993), the court ordered the FWS to develop and implement recovery plans for endangered species dependent on natural spring discharges from the 3,600-square-mile Edwards Aquifer in central Texas. Over a million people pump water from the aquifer for drinking, agriculture, and industry. These withdrawals disrupt the natural discharges of the springs that support the endangered species. The court found that disruptions in the spring flows had resulted in takings. *Id.* at 1543. The court rejected the agency's defense that budget constraints prevented it from developing and implementing recovery plans for the Edwards Aquifer. *Id.* at 1542. The regional water districts will develop their own aquifer management plans using minimum spring-flows specified by the FWS as necessary to prevent takings. Protection of the springs dependent on the Edwards Aquifer continues to be controversial. In 1998, the Fifth Circuit Court of Appeals found the U.S. Department of Agriculture to have violated the ESA § 7(a)(1) Conservation Mandate because it had not consulted with the FWS to develop a species conservation program for its activities involving farmers who pump irrigation water from the Edwards Aquifer. *Sierra Club v. Glickman*, 156 F.3d 606 (5th Cir. 1998).

Does the ESA provide any guidance for the FWS to set recovery priorities within its limited budget? Are recovery plans likely to be useful tools for comprehensive management of ecosystems? *See* Timothy H. Tear *et al.*, *Recovery Plans and the Endangered Species Act: Are Criticisms Supported by Data?*, 9 CONSERVATION BIOLOGY 182 (1995). How would you design ecosystem protection legislation, and what problems would you foresee with its implementation? Julie B. Bloch, *Preserving Biological Diversity in the United States: The Case for Moving to an Ecosystems Approach to Protect the Nation's Biological Wealth*, 10 PACE ENVTL. L. REV. 175 (1992).

Recent scholarship has focused on the recovery concept as the key to prioritizing endangered species conservation and integrating ecosystem management. *See* Federico Cheever, *The Road to Recovery: A New Way of Thinking About the Endangered Species Act*, 23 ECOLOGY L.Q. 1 (1996).

9. Recovery plans are required to include "objective, measurable criteria which, when met, would result in a determination, in accordance with the provision of this section, that the species be removed from the list * * * ." ESA § 4(f)(1)(B)(ii); 16 U.S.C. § 1633(f)(1)(B)(ii). In *Fund for Animals v. Babbitt*, 903 F. Supp. 96, 111 (D.D.C. 1995), the court held that these objective criteria must address each of the five criteria for listing or delisting a species at § 4(a)(1) of the ESA. *Fund for Animals* rejected the grizzly bear recovery plan because it failed to design criteria to address each of these factors.

10. The ESA imposes both civil and criminal penalties for violations of the takings provisions. *See* ESA §§ 11(a), 11(b); 16 U.S.C. §§ 1540(a), 1540(b). In addition, the statute authorizes citizen suits against the government or private persons who are alleged to be in violation of the law. If successful, plaintiffs may recover their litigation costs (including attorney and expert witness fees) against the losing party. ESA § 11(g).

PROBLEM #8: HABITAT CONSERVATION PLANNING

This problem is designed to explore issues related to ESA §§ 9 and 10. It is based on material contained in MICHAEL J. BEAN, SARAH G. FITZGERALD, AND MICHAEL A. O'CONNELL, RECONCILING CONFLICTS UNDER THE ENDANGERED SPECIES ACT: THE HABITAT CONSERVATION EXPERIENCE 90-100 (World Wildlife Fund 1991). We suggest students divide up into interest groups and simulate an HCP negotiation.

THE RIVERSIDE COUNTY-STEPHEN'S KANGAROO RAT HABITAT RECOVERY PLAN
MICHAEL BEAN ET AL. at 90

Southern California is by far the fastest growing area in the United States. Astounding economic statistics point out that nearly 10 percent of all development growth (in value) in the nation over the last decade occurred in three counties—Riverside, San Bernardino, and San Diego—converting nearly 50 square miles of wildlife habitat each year. The Southern California housing industry alone is valued at $19 billion annually. * * *

[For many years, approval for construction in Southern California was a simple process involving local zoning commissions in coordination with comprehensive land use plans. All that changed when the FWS listed the Stephen's kangaroo rat (SKR) as endangered.]

Historically, the SKR occupied a range of more than 300,000 acres in Riverside, San Diego, and San Bernardino counties. First agricultural then residential and then commercial development in the latter part of this century eliminated two-thirds of the species' habitat and severely fragmented the remainder. Much remaining habitat exists in parcels of less than four acres, rendering the species vulnerable to demographic and dynamic extinction factors such as predation, catastrophe, and genetic problems.

Researchers speculate that the SKR exists as a metapopulation. These are characterized by a group of local populations tied together by dispersal. Local populations arise, flourish, and decline over time without affecting the health of the species. The most important impact of habitat conversion and fragmentation, then, has been elimination of dispersal pathways between existing peripheral populations, isolating them and making them susceptible to extinction. Habitat loss has also obliterated most potential new colonization sites.

Now that the SKR has been listed, county officials, concerned about § 9 liability, are interested in working with local developers, environmentalists, and the FWS to create an HCP. What should the proposed SKR HCP contain? In addressing this question you may wish to consider the following possible issues:

1. funding for land acquisition and management
2. habitat improvement
3. research needs
4. restraints on construction design and practices
5. mitigation
6. area of HCP coverage
7. use of permits
8. monitoring and evaluation
9. enforcement

GLOSSARY OF ABBREVIATIONS

APA: Administrative Procedure Act (5 U.S.C. §§ 551 *et seq.*)

BA: Biological Assessment (ESA § 7(c); 50 C.F.R. § 402.12)

BO: Biological Opinion (ESA § 7(b); 50 C.F.R. § 402.12(h))

CEQ: Council on Environmental Quality (NEPA §§ 201-209)

CWA: Clean Water Act (33 U.S.C. §§ 1251 *et seq.*)

DEIS: Draft Environmental Impact Statement (40 C.F.R. § 1502.9)

EA: Environmental Assessment (40 C.F.R. § 1508.9)

EIS: Environmental Impact Statement (40 C.F.R. Part 1502)

EPA: U.S. Environmental Protection Agency

ESA: Endangered Species Act (16 U.S.C. §§ 1531 *et seq.*)

FEIS: Final Environmental Impact Statement (40 C.F.R. § 1502.9)

FONSI: Finding of No Significant Impact (40 C.F.R. § 1508.13)

FWS: U.S. (Department of the Interior) Fish and Wildlife Service

HCP: Habitat Conservation Plan (ESA § 10(a))

NEPA: National Environmental Policy Act (42 U.S.C. §§ 4321 *et seq.*)

NHPA: National Historic Preservation Act

NMFS: National Marine Fisheries Service (U.S. Department of Commerce)

SEIS: Supplemental Environmental Impact Statement (40 C.F.R. § 1502.9)

SHPO: State Historic Preservation Office

SIR: Supplemental Information Report

INDEX